Organizational
Issues
In
Industrial
Society

Prentice-Hall Sociology Series
Neil J. Smelser, Editor

Organizational Issues In Industrial Society

Edited by

Jon M. Shepard

University of Kentucky

Prentice-Hall, Inc.

Englewood Cliffs, New Jersey

Library of Congress Catalog Card Number: 75–163395

Printed in the United States of America
ISBN: P 0–13–640995–4
       C 0–13–641001–4
10 9 8 7 6 5 4 3 2 1

PRENTICE-HALL INTERNATIONAL, INC., *London*
PRENTICE-HALL OF AUSTRALIA, PTY. LTD., *Sydney*
PRENTICE-HALL OF CANADA, LTD., *Toronto*
PRENTICE-HALL OF INDIA PRIVATE LIMITED., *New Delhi*
PRENTICE-HALL OF JAPAN, INC., *Tokyo*

To my son, Jon

Contents

2 / Occupational Mobility: A Cross-National Similarity in Pattern? 62

3 / Bureaucracy: Is There An Alternative? 98

Preface

This reader presents for study eight controversial areas of research in the field of organizational behavior. Each chapter is specifically devoted to one of these areas; chapter headings present each issue in question form. Within each chapter are included several selections reflecting two or more aspects of each controversy. Starting at the larger societal level, the issues dealt with proceed to more microscopic levels of analysis, ending with the social-psychological question of whether workers really desire job enlargement.

This format has a number of advantages. First, the study of organizational behavior involves a number of unsettled controversies. Much of the literature is more accumulative than cumulative; various contributions on a research question do not add up to one conclusion. One of the primary purposes of this reader is to assemble writings on issues and problems which expose the gaps in our present knowledge; another is to make apparent differences in perspective, levels of analysis, variables, samples, and so forth.

Secondly, a primary aim of learning, in or out of the classroom, is intellectual growth, especially the development of critical judgment and self-determination. Instructors often spend a great deal of time on the presentation of facts but neglect the multifaceted nature of problems and the possibly contradictory evidence surrounding them. Because of this neglect, one aim of this volume is to promote the development of critical judgment and balanced thought, as well as to expose students to literature in selected areas of study, the traditional aim of textbooks and collections of readings. Although the information itself is important, the intellectual benefit is derived more from students evaluating and judging for themselves. As John Holt writes, "The subject matter of a course is frequently little more than merely a vehicle for the achievement of... (certain) educational goals (abstraction, curiosity, appreciation)—yet, all too often, the subject matter becomes an end in itself."*

Present and future generations face a society changing at such a swift pace that the answers of one generation are of questionable utility to the next. A society of this nature requires people who can meet new situations with the intellectual flexibility necessary for creative adaptation to a changing environment. It is therefore essential that our educational system turn a portion of the learning process over to the students, who must be able to grapple with conflicting and inconsistent information, sifting these data until they reach a new synthesis. If this ability is not developed, the optimum benefits of education will not have been realized. The format of this book subscribes to Holt's definition of intelligence: "...a style of life, a way of behaving in various situations, and particularly in new, strange, and perplexing situations. The true test of intelligence is not how much we know how to do, but how we behave when we don't know what to do."** Or as John Dewey believed, we must not mistake education as preparation for life; it is life.

A professed goal of all teachers is to help their students learn to think. Any good teacher loves to see a mind "opening up." In many ways the textbook, lecture, and testing format conflicts with this process. Perhaps too often, in his zeal and excitement over ideas, the instructor forgets that students are more than passive recipients of information. And even though an important function of the teacher is to provide conclusions and offer generalizations based on his or her professional evaluation of the literature, factual knowledge often comes into existence only to be modified or abandoned in a short time. Students may leave the academic setting with knowledge that is frequently impermanent, sometimes even irrelevant to the demands of life. For this reason, they ultimately must have acquired the

---

* John Holt, *How Children Fail* (New York: Dell, 1967), p. 13.
** *Ibid.*, p. 205.

capability to do for themselves what their teachers have done for them all along—judge, evaluate, think logically.

The format of this reader permits students to see that problems of organizational behavior are multidimensional. It is designed to stimulate discussion; class participation and intellectual involvement can be important results. It may be that this reader's approach to issues and questions runs the risk of students concluding that even the experts don't know much about these topics. To the extent that this reaction occurs, we have a reflection of the kind of educational system which conditions students to accept final, or at least current answers, and to believe whatever their books and teachers serve up as the truth.

Several of my professional colleagues have offered helpful advice. I wish to acknowledge my appreciation to Henry Barlow, Ieva Berzins, William Faunce, William Form, Henry Landsberger, Mike Miller, John Stephenson, George Strauss and Alan Weinstein for their suggestions and support. I also wish to acknowledge the *Industrial and Labor Relations Review* and the *Academy of Management Journal* for their permission to include some of my own previously published work. And my thanks and gratitude to Carolyn Anderson, Susan Fields, Jean Greenwell, and especially Linda Holt for their contributions to the typing, editing, and myriad other tasks necessary to the production of this volume.

1 / The Impact of Industrialization: Are Industrial Societies Becoming Alike?

Are the structural and cultural characteristics of economically developing countries becoming similar? If so, can the alleged homogeneity be attributed to the industrialization process? These questions have received several conflicting answers. One position views industrialization as a neutral process which can have no definite recurring set of impacts. Another describes the "logic of industrialism." According to yet another viewpoint the question is irrelevant, since industrializing societies are a mixture of tradition and modernity.

The first selection in this chapter, "Industrialism and World Society" by Clark Kerr, John Dunlop, Frederick Harbison, and Charles Myers, espouses the "convergence" position. This theory predicts the development of similarity in the social organization and social relationships of industrializing countries. Kerr and his associates discuss the powerful unifying forces which they contend will ultimately override the sources of diversity. The decline in competing ideologies and the corresponding trend toward consensus regarding the successful models of industrialization are factors promoting uniformity. It is not difficult to determine the most productive technology. As societies adopt the newest technological arrangements they develop commonalities, because a particular technology carries in its wake a particular occupational structure, which in turn exercises similar wide-ranging effects on different social structures and social relationships. The necessity of an industrializing society to develop an educated populace is another unifying force. Other sources of uniformity include the inevitable large role of government, the accelerated growth of large-scale organizations, and the desire for progress and participation among industrial men.

Herbert Blumer, in "Industrialization and the Laboring Class," pronounces as myth the contention that early industrialization is intrinsically so foreign and repelling to new industrial recruits that it produces in them deep-seated alienation and subsequent radicalism. Analyzing the factors which he believes mold the character of early industrial workers, Blumer portrays industrialization as a neutral framework having no definite predictable social consequences. We must, according to Blumer, look to idiosyncratic social and cultural forces and to factors accompanying rapid social change to explain the emergence of new social patterns in industrializing societies.

In contrast to Blumer, William Form ("The Accommodation of Rural and Urban Workers to Industrial Discipline and Urban Living: A Four Nation Study") finds similar patterns of adjustment to certain aspects of industrial work and the urban community among both urban workers and industrial workers from nonindustrial, nonurban backgrounds. Form's study of automobile workers of various skill levels from four countries at varying levels of economic development supports the "industrial man," or convergence, hypothesis.

Joseph Gusfield ("Tradition and Modernity: Misplaced Polarities in the Study of Social Change") questions the validity of classifying "tradition" and "modernity" as polar opposites. He challenges the view that traditional values and institutions impede innovation and modernization. Instead, he argues, traditional social patterns interact with the new, creating variations in social structures and social relationships that are obscured in uni-linear models of evolution. Using information on modern India as well as on other developing countries, Gusfield outlines and challenges several assumptions of the linear theory of social change. Attributing rigidity, normative consistency, or structural homogeneity to traditional societies contradicts reality. On meeting new cultural forms and patterns, traditional elements do not necessarily vanish; they blend with the new. Traditional and modern forms are not necessarily incompatible or mutually exclusive. Gusfield's position on the question of convergence or divergence is contained in his closing sentence: "We need to recognize that there is a variety of events on the wrestling program and that the outcomes, unlike many wrestling matches, are quite in doubt."

Yet another perspective is added by Neil Smelser in "Structural Changes Associated with Development." National variations in pre-industrial conditions, in impetus to development, in path toward modernization, in advanced stages of modernization, and in content and timing of dramatic events are forces that preclude the prediction of a general pattern of social structural development for modernizing societies. In the ideal-typical mode Smelser discusses three structural changes that occur in the process of social and economic development: structural differentiation, integration, and social disturbances. These three "universal aspects of development" retain their universality in spite of the unique forms they may assume as a result of the factors producing national variation.

1 / Industrialism and World Society

Clark Kerr, John T. Dunlop,
Frederick Harbison, Charles A. Myers

IF WE WATCH the way the world is industrializing day by day, we are likely to get a confusing and bewildering picture. There seems to be little consistency in the multitude of patterns followed by various nations, except that the underdeveloped ones are trying to catch up, and the developed ones are trying to stay ahead. Long-range predictions about the future of industrial man seem impossible.

But if we stand back from the day-to-day news picture and take a broader, more historical perspective, we find that there *is* a pattern to all the apparent chaos. From Southeast Asia to Western Europe and from Chile to the Congo, the forces making for uniformity—especially uniformity in the all-important relations between labor, management, and government —tend surely to become stronger than the forces perpetuating diversity. The imperatives of industrialization cause the controlling elites to overcome certain constraints and to achieve objectives *which are the same in all societies undergoing transformation....*

The Road to Similarity

We have seen that the natural, historical tendency of each of the five types of elite is to change—sometimes completely. Will these changes keep on occurring in the future as in the past and, if so, in what direction? This brings us to some important—and unconventional—conclusions about the strength of pressures for uniformity.

It will help us to appreciate these forces [for uniformity] all the more if we keep in mind that the sources of diversity are great, too, and are all the time working in the world, even if with not quite so much effect. Thus:

(1) *The differing elites each want to organize the process of industrialization in a different fashion.* Once structured, the institutions and the ways of doing things tend to develop a life and a persistency of their own, provided the ruling elites are reasonably successful in handling industrialization and other problems of the nation. There are, after all, several possible

Reprinted by permission of the authors and publisher from "Industrialism and World Society," *Harvard Business Review,* Vol. 39, No. 1 (January–February 1961) pp. 113, 122–25. © 1961 by the President and Fellows of Harvard College; all rights reserved.

ways of organizing an industrial society. Furthermore, the slogans, the heroes, the vested interests that collect around an ideology and a strategy for organizing society give any system considerable tenacity and are a great source of diversity in an industrializing world.

(2) *The culture of a nation and the degree of its continual adherence to that culture also create world-wide diversity.* The family and the class carry on, particularly under the dynastic elite. Education often adapts quite slowly from its traditional forms, again particularly under the dynastic elite. But other national traits carry on as well. Take, for instance, the discipline and energy of the Germans, the individualism of the French, and the easy-going approach of the Indonesians.

(3) *The stage of development makes for variation.* Early industrialization, regardless of the overall strategy, has its own special problems, its own special attitudes, its own special approaches. Mature industrialization, with its well-developed institutions and web of rules, its full complement of industries and services and trades, its settled labor force, its greater consensus, is a different phenomenon regardless of the organizing forces. Degree of development, of course, relates both to the date of the start and rate of the change.[1]

(4) *The special character of the basic resources and the central industries causes variations from one country to another.* Plantation agriculture, crude oil production, heavy industry, light industry, and so on, each give a tone to their society. Some industries are more prone to industrial unrest than others; some are more likely to engage in paternalistic practices; some are occupationally more highly stratified; some are more subject to a system of norms; some have more large-scale enterprises. Each industry has its own character—the waterfront, coal mining, banking—and these cast their reflections on the surrounding society. A small or a newly industrialized economy is more likely to reflect the special character of one or a few industries than is a large and mature economy. Thus oil gives a special flavor to Iraq, much as textiles and coal mining once did to England.

(5) *The demographic aspects of a nation impart to its industrialization continuing characteristics.* A relatively empty country, like Australia, has quite a different course of development than a heavily populated one, like India. Wages tend to be higher, recruitment more difficult, a significant increase in the standard of living more possible, a high evaluation of the worth of the individual worker and the attention he deserves more likely, and so forth.

But time moves along and, as it does, many a battle is joined between the forces perpetuating diversity and those promoting uniformity. Many of these battles are the impersonal clashes of old ways and new facts, and in any case they are fought under many banners and in a myriad of places. But the more we look at these battles collectively, in some kind of time

---

[1] See W. W. Rostow, "Economics for the Nuclear Age," HBR January–February 1960, p. 41—*The Editors* [of the Harvard Business Review].

and intercontinental perspective, the more impressed we become with the power of the forces for uniformity. What are the most striking ones?

History and Homogeneity

The passage of history itself is a force. Each industrializing nation moves farther from its introduction into the industrial world, from its pre-existing forms, from its original leadership. The early elites bring in new recruits from other strata. The elite group grows in size and becomes less identifiable, merging into each successively lower level in the new hierarchy. The second, third, and fourth generations of leaders and the led alike are different from the first.

The age of ideology fades. When man first entered the irreversible journey into industrialization, there were innumerable views about the best way to organize society. Some of them have largely disappeared from the scene: anarchism, syndicalism, communalism, cooperativism. Others of them have been blunted and revised from their original form, particularly capitalism and socialism. The age of utopias is past. An age of realism has taken its place—an age in which there is little expectation of either utter perfection or of complete doom. One of the results of the past century is the accumulation of experience about the realistic alternatives.

Thus the conflict of ideologies is blunted and fades between societies. Consensus develops wherever industrialization is successful. The labor force becomes committed to and settled into industrial life. It accepts the pace of work, the web of rules, the surrounding structure. The sense of protest subsides. The business managers, left to their own devices, push less hard. Society provides more of the amenities of life. Men learn from experience how better to do things, and the rough edges are evened off. Industrialization is accepted.

Finally, as the elites become less differentiated and the ideological controversies become more barren, the cultural patterns of the world intermingle and merge. These changes are in evidence although the majority of nations in the world have been in the active throes of industrialization only two generations or less.

Technology and Society

Technology is also a unifying force. At one moment of time there may be several best economic combinations or social arrangements, but only one best technology. The technology can be up-to-date or antiquated, but there is no question which is which, and the modern is constantly replacing the ancient. The same technology calls for much the same occupational structure around the world—in steel, in textiles, in air transport. The occupational role of a man gives him a place in society and affects his behavior in many ways. Also, there comes to be a growing diversity of occupations and of levels of management, and no really clear-cut dividing lines visible to all. The occupation takes the place of the class.

The technology is dynamic and it calls for change. Men change their locations and their occupations. A labor market must be created with substantial mobility within it. A fully paternalistic system at the plant level becomes less possible. Mobility calls at least for the semi-independent rather than the dependent worker.

The skill level rises. Men are given responsibility for more expensive equipment, more essential processes. Their consent becomes more important. The need for their consent gives them influence. It may even give them organized power, for there is a tendency to organize around the occupation. True, only scientists may be given this right at first, but the pressure will always exist to spread professional and occupational organization.

Push of Progress

The thrust of progress also serves the cause of uniformity. The industry mix, country by country, becomes more balanced and thus more like that elsewhere. There is insistent pressure to obtain a rough balance of supply and demand in the labor market.

The development of consumer-goods industries and service trades requires the creation of markets—in spite of the addiction to plans (the market mentality and the planning mentality are quite different). The rising standard of living and increasing leisure create the capacity to read and travel and compare. They also encourage an aggressive materialism on the part of people. Progress brings the great metropolitan center and the city as the natural habitat of man. The city has been the home of variety and of freedom throughout the centuries.

Education and Equality

An industrial society must educate its people. There are at least two imperatives: (1) The vast bulk of the population must be literate in order to receive instructions, follow directions, and keep records. (2) Managers, engineers, and civil servants must be trained to operate the new productive system. Beyond that are the needs for doctors, lawyers, scientists, and university professors. Education becomes a leading industry.

Out of education come several results. Education is intended to reduce the scarcity of skilled persons, and this after a time reduces the wage and salary differentials they receive. It also pulls people out of the least skilled and most disagreeable occupations and raises wage levels there. It conduces to a new equality which has nothing to do with ideology; in fact, it may come faster and more fully in a middle-class society than in a society under the revolutionary intellectuals who proclaim equality as a primary goal. This equality is at first economic, but it also affects class status and political outlook.

Out of education may also come a new call for freedom. This call will be most insistent at the highest levels in the educational pyramid, for knowledge knows no geographical boundaries; but it may spread down through many of the ranks of society. Education and personal independence have usually walked the road together. With an educated labor force, jobs tend to change or be changed. On the average, more responsibility adheres to them; they are made more interesting; and their incumbents are treated more individually and humanely.

Government and Business

The state, everywhere, becomes an important instrument in society. It becomes responsible for the general rate of growth, the level of economic activity, the distribution of power in society, the settlement of conflicts, and the prevention of economic or other sabotage of the economy by special interest groups. It may, of course, do much more. But at least it must set the many basic rules for the economy, *and it inevitably becomes a partner, if not the sole partner, in labor–management relations.*

At the same time, the productive enterprise, whether public or private, becomes a large-scale organization in many industries. It comes to be run by professional managers, recruited and trained through the educational system, separated from ownership and protected from power politics. These enterprise managers must be placed under the constraints of the market or planning budgets to assure their suitable performance, and the structuring of these pressures and controls is an essential task in society. The professional administrator has great power, but it is power subject to checks and balances in all developed industrial societies.

The managers are basically responsible for the web of rules in the plant and industry which relate them to the managed, although they share this responsibility with the state and the organized workers. Basically, this web of rules must spell out the authority of the managers and how far they may go, for economic enterprise is always essentially authoritarian under the necessity of getting things done, and the limits to executive authority must be specified.

Compulsion of Comparisons

Man everywhere wants progress and participation. The two are sub-stitutes for each other, and often progress will be accepted for a time in lieu of participation; but in the end industrial man wants both and will keep pressing for both. Progress means a higher standard of education, better health, more consumer goods and services; participation means choice of jobs, choice of consumer goods, a chance to influence the web of rules, and even an opportunity to influence those who guide society itself. These same pressures develop regardless of culture and ideology.

The pressures for progress and participation are enhanced by the world-wide character of industrialization, by international trade, by travel, and by the exchange of ideas. Generally the impact will be to bring greater uniformity in the nature of the societal product which people widely judge to be the best. People may not be willing to settle for much less in their own systems than the standards and performance of competing systems.

Pluralistic Industrialism

Men attempt to peer ahead, to understand the structure of history, and to alter the process of history, if possible, in accord with their preferences. The future they appear to be choosing and pressing for is what might be called *pluralistic industrialism*. We use this term to refer to a society which is governed neither by one all-powerful elite (e.g., the monistic model) nor by the impersonal interaction of innumerable small groups with relatively equal power (e.g., the atomistic model in economic theory). The complexity of the fully developed industrial society requires, in the name of efficiency and initiative, a degree of decentralization of control, particularly in the consumer-goods and service-trades industries; but it also requires a large measure of central control by the state and conduct of many operations by large scale organizations.

As the skill level rises and jobs become more responsible, any regime must be more interested in consent, in drawing forth relatively full cooperation. For the sake of real efficiency, this must be freely given. The discipline of the labor gang no longer suffices. With skill and responsibility goes the need for consent, and with consent goes influence and even authority. Occupational and professional groups, of necessity, achieve some prestige and authority as against both the central organs of society and the individual members of the occupation or profession.

Education brings in its wake a new economic equality and a new community of political outlook. This, in turn, along with many other developments, helps bring consensus to society. The harsh use of power by the state is no longer so necessary to hold society together at the seams. Education also opens the mind to curiosity and to inquiry, and the individual seeks more freedom to think and to act. It brings a demand for liberty, and can help create conditions in which liberty can safely be granted. It leads to comparisons among nations with respect to progress and participation.

Industrialism is so complex and subject to such contrary internal pressures that it never can assume a single, uniform, unchanging structure; but it *can* vary around a general central theme, and that theme is pluralism. While it will take generations before this theme will become universal in societies around the world, the direction of the movement already seems sufficiently clear. . . .

2 / Early Industrialization and the Laboring Class

Herbert Blumer

THE DEVELOPMENT OF the industrially retarded regions of the world has reawakened interest in the social consequences of early industrialization. The thinking of present-day scholars concerned with this problem is permeated by two major themes. The first is that the main social effect of early industrialization is the emergence of a class of industrial workers. The second is that this working class undergoes a typical and common development that is set by the intrinsic nature of the industrializing process. I am not going to concern myself in this brief paper with the first of these themes even though I think it is wrong. Instead I intend to consider the second theme. Tersely put, this latter theme or view holds that industrial life introduces a working environment which is strange, harsh, and unbearable for the newly recruited workers, with the consequence that they become disaffected and rebellious. This view has been derived chiefly from a picture of the industrial revolution in Great Britain; it is strongly tinctured by Marxian class analysis; and it draws support from anthropological theory on cultural contact and from psychological theory on frustration and aggression. In my judgment the view is basically false and misleading. Its critical inspection is timely.

Let me spell out briefly the point of view. It presumes that the new industrial workers are wrenched loose from rural, village, or tribal communities, in which they have satisfactory status positions, supporting social ties, a familiar and acceptable authority system, and personalized work rhythms to which they are habituated. They are thrust into a strange and forbidding industrial setting, centered in the factory and the job. In this setting they have no status, little sense of personal dignity, no property or tools, no independence, and no customary work rights. They are forced to adjust to unfamiliar and onerous work rhythms and to bow to an alien and harsh system of discipline. They suffer, also, from inadequate communal or socialized relations with their fellow workers. In the face of these new and alienating conditions of work the workers are said to become insecure, discontented, and disaffected. "They hate the factory," as one prominent scholar puts it. Thus, unrest and feelings of protest germinate and grow among them. The feelings of protest are believed to express themselves in different ways: mildly, in curtailment of production, absenteeism, and the quitting of jobs; more vigorously, in sabotage, the destruction of industrial

Reprinted by permission of the author and publisher from "Early Industrialization and the Laboring Class," *Sociological Quarterly,* Vol. I, No. 1 (January 1960), pp. 5–14.

property, strikes, and riots; compensatorily, in personal and social disorganization or in orgiastic religious cults; and, above all, more lastingly in "radicalism," in militant labor movements or in revolutionary political movements.

The view rests on three tenets, each of which I wish to challenge: (1) that the background environment of the new industrial workers is in some significant way superior to that of the new industrial establishments; (2) that the workers find the new working environment to be alien and repelling, and thus that they become disaffected and discontented; and (3) that such feelings of disaffection lead the workers to "radicalism" and to "protest activity."

(1) The belief that the tribal, rural, or village situation from which the new workers come is for them superior to the factory system into which they enter is not true in a large number of instances. On the economic side this belief is essentially self-contradictory. Workers usually migrate to factories because they prefer industrial employment to their current economic lot. Frequently, new industrial workers are impoverished rural tenants, poorly paid rural workers, small land owners eking out a precarious existence, poor village dwellers without steady employment, displaced artisans and moneyless tribesmen. On the social side the original background of the new workers may be as impoverished as their economic background. Frequently they have no property and they suffer corresponding social disadvantages. Frequently they are enmeshed in the lower levels of a highly personalized or padronal system, with little independence and with little opportunity for improving their social lot. Admittedly there is no uniformity to the economic and social conditions of the localities from which the new workers come. However, the evidence is more than sufficient to challenge the idea that for the workers these background conditions typically represent superior economic or social advantage to those encountered in industrial establishments.

(2) The second tenet, that the industrial setting is indigenously alien, repelling, and intolerable to the new workers, does not seem to me to have solid grounds. It is argued that the factory milieu—with its fixed working hours, mandatory work assignments, steady pace of work, and presumed monotonous tasks—clashes with the cultural background of the workers. The workers are said to be repelled by the new routines and to have great difficulty in adjusting to them. There is a large amount of evidence to controvert this allegedly typical picture. As repeated instances show, new workers may adjust quickly and satisfactorily to such routines. Especially when thoughtful and serious attention is given to programs of training—as is happening more frequently these days in newly industrializing regions— it is found that inexperienced workers fit readily and effectively into the industrial routines. Empirical evidence compels us, I think, to reject the idea that factory work, *ipso facto,* constitutes for the new workers a kind of cultural alienation or shock which they have great difficulty in resolving.

Similarly, I find flimsy evidence for the contention that the new workers naturally find factory authority and discipline to be unpalatable. Factory authority under early industrialization is in no sense a constant but runs the gamut from being ruthless and arbitrary to being enlightened and hemmed in by legislation. Even when harsh, factory authority, frequently, is no worse than paternal or padronal authority in the field or the village. And further, even when it is unusually severe it is frequently taken to be a natural part of the new working situation which one has to live by.

It is also alleged by some students that relations with fellow workers at the work stations are barren of social and communal feelings and hence are found to be seriously wanting. The evidence seems to me to indicate clearly that this sort of condition is relatively rare. Usually fellow workers become acquainted with one another and weave into their work relations play, humor, banter, gossip, and interest in common topics of discourse.

In short, I find little evidence to support—and much evidence to contradict—the contention that for the workers the new industrial environment is intrinsically unnatural, menacing, and harsh. Today in the industrialization of underdeveloped countries one finds marked variation in conditions of employment, managerial practices, and work relations. Managers may have a free hand in setting hours, wages, and work assignments and be unrestricted in the exercise of disciplinary authority; or, as happens not infrequently, they may be subject to legislation which sets minimum wages and maximum hours, provides protection against unrestricted managerial authority, prohibits child labor, and accords a variety of worker privileges. Management may follow harsh or enlightened labor practices. Training programs may be available to the workers, or they may be left to struggle for themselves. Free opportunities may exist for promotion, or, instead castelike barriers and ceilings may be imposed on upward progression. In short, as a result of such factors as differing managerial policies, the presence or absence of controlling legislation, the interest or lack of interest in following standards of the advanced industrial countries, and the relaxations or pressures that are set by the state of the market, the social setting in industrial establishments may vary greatly.

Given this varied picture, it is a mistake to assume that the characteristic response of the new industrial workers is one of frustration, shock, resentment, and discontent. Such responses do occur. However, the instances are many indeed in which workers prize industrial employment as a source of unaccustomed cash income, as an opportunity for a better standard of living, as a ladder to social advancement, and as an escape from a depressing local life. In view of the range of difference in the new industrial setting and in the background expectations of the workers entering into it, it is clearly hazardous to declare that the natural response of the workers to the new industrial setting is one of disaffection.

(3) On the basis of what has been said one must reject the remaining tenet that the new industrial workers are naturally led to "radicalism" and "protest behavior." As stated, they need not hate or reject their work situation. Even granting instances in which the workers resent and dislike their working situation they still need not engage in protest behavior. They may be fatalistic about their situation and, as human beings commonly

do, accept it as in the order of existence. They may see no way of doing anything about their plight and turn their backs to protest activity. Any psychology which assumes that feelings such as discontent move relentlessly forward to overt expression is basically false. Feelings may be suppressed, held in abeyance, tempered, and transformed.

This ends my discussion of the three tenets. Enough has been said to show the fallacies of the view that early industrialization, by nature, alienates and disaffects workers, makes them radical, and propels them to protest behavior. The view should be discarded as a myth.

If we are to be realistic in our analysis we have to go even further than this. I think that the evidence points clearly to the conclusion that industrialization, by its very make-up, can have no definite social effect. It is neutral and indifferent to what follows socially in its wake. To attribute specific social effects to it is to misread its character; to seek in it the causes of specific social happenings is to embark on a false journey. While it lays down the lines along which new social forms may emerge, it does not explain the new forms that come into existence. It merely provides a neutral framework for the operation of other factors which produce and shape what comes into being. This view is so opposite to our deeply entrenched beliefs, so contrary to what students from Marx to the present have taken for granted, that it is necessary to defend and exemplify it as clearly as limited space permits. I shall confine my discussion to early industrialization and the laboring class, even though the thesis of the neutrality of industrialization holds true for all areas of its operation.

In providing new forms of work, new occupations and jobs, and new sets of social relations, industrialization obviously brings a working class into existence. Yet it does not explain the make-up of that class nor the experience to which its members are subject nor the behavior which they develop. The nature of the early class of industrial workers may be said to depend on four factors: the composition of the class; the milieu encountered in industrial establishments; the conditions of life to which workers are subject outside of industrial establishments; and the schemes or definitions which the workers use to interpret their experience. It is my position that early industrialization is indifferent and neutral to each of these four basic conditions. Let me discuss each of them briefly.

Composition. The make-up of the working class depends on the kind of people who are recruited to it and on the differentiation which develops among them.

It should be obvious that industrialization is indifferent to the kinds of people who are recruited to fill its work positions. As mentioned earlier, the recruits may and do vary a great deal. They may be tribesmen, dispossessed land owners, members of a rural proletariat, villagers, city dwellers, or imported aliens. They may differ greatly in the conditions which lead them to seek industrial employment. Also, they may enter employment with widely different expectations, hopes, and demands. Industrialization, as such, is neutral with regard to these features of recruitment and exercises no control over them.

This condition of neutrality extends to the variety of conditions differentiating the workers from one another. Whether the working class is to be homogeneous or heterogeneous, whether marked by unity or by inner antagonisms, are matters for which industrialization is not responsible. To be true, a part of the differentiation of the working class is set by the character of the occupational structure and the wage structure: the occupations may be very varied or they may be similar, and the wage structure may show a wide range of differentials or a lumping of wages within narrow limits. However, a large measure of such occupational and work differentiation is not due to the intrinsic nature of industrialization; more important, industrialization does not account for the ways in which workers define the occupational and wage differences between them. The more significant forms of differentiation inside of the new industrial classes come from the types of social discrimination which the workers apply to one another. All kinds of social discriminations may flow into the ranks of the workers—discriminations of geographical origin, ethnic make-up, caste membership, and religious affiliation. Anyone who runs his eyes over past and current instances of early industrialization must be acutely aware of the extent to which such established discrimination shapes the make-up of the class of workers.

What I wish to assert is that early industrialization is indifferent to, and has no responsibility for, the composition of the new working class, either in terms of who enter into it or in terms of how its members come to develop differentiation among themselves.

Nature of the Industrial Milieu. This same condition of neutrality is to be seen, oddly enough, in the case of the milieu to which the workers are subjected in their working establishments. Most students of early industrialization regard this milieu as the primary factor in moulding workers into a homogeneous and typical class. Yet the evidence shows great differences in working environments under early industrialization. As suggested in earlier remarks, the milieu in industrial establishments is subject to impressive variation. Working hours may be long and unregulated or moderate and state controlled. Working conditions may accord to the workers many rights and privileges or be barren of them. There may be open promotion or castelike barriers to upward progression. Management may be enlightened or be callous and indifferent to the workers. Inner discipline may be harsh, with no devices for worker protection, or be fair and provide some type of grievance procedure. Workers may be alien to each other or be members of a community group. It should be painfully clear that many alternate possibilities exist in the case of each element of the industrial situation. Now, the crucial point is that industrialization as a system of production does not determine the particular alternatives which, so to speak, are selected. Instead, the selections are a result of other factors such as managerial policies, governmental laws and regulations, the state of the market, traditional attitudes toward labor in the community, community prejudices, and local social movements. This is what I mean by saying that industrialization provides a neutral framework but that other factors provide the filling.

Conditions of Life outside of Working Establishments. If we consider, next, the life of industrial workers outside of working establishments we find the same picture of the neutrality of industrialization. In the interest of conserving space, let me take a single but highly important line of illustration—the crowding of new industrial workers into cities. While industrialization may lead to the assembling of workers in cities it does not account for their living conditions. It is not responsible for the congestion, the inadequate housing, the poor sanitation, the faulty school and social service facilities, or the social disorganization which frequently attend such urban residence. Instead, such conditions are due to non-industrial factors such as the presence of physically deteriorated dwellings, the unavailability of land, the high cost of building materials, deficient means of transportation, high rentals, deficient municipal revenue, and archaic municipal policies with regard to the provision of facilities. Industrialization is neutral to the presence and to the play of such factors.

Definitions Used to Interpret Experience. The neutrality of industrialization is to be noted, also, in the interpretations which workers make of their experiences. The role of interpretation, of course, is crucial, for it represents how people judge their situations and organize themselves for action. As implied in my earlier remarks, workers under early industrialization may differ greatly in the schemes which they use to evaluate their work experiences. They may view their work situation as novel and exciting, as providing a source of much needed money, as offering possibilities for personal and family advancement, as being onerous but to be endured for other purposes, or as being exploitative, as being marked by unfair discrimination, and as denying opportunities for improving one's lot. Such schemes do not come from the "objective" nature of the work situation; anyone with wide familiarity with working situations under early industrialization must be acutely aware of the fact that the same kind of objective work condition may lead to discontent for one set of workers but may not do so for other sets of workers. The schemes of evaluation come from other sources such as traditional ideas that antedate industrial employment, a comparison with previous work experiences, a comparison with the lot of other types of workers, ideas from the outside world, and particularly agitation on behalf of local social movements. Industrialization is not responsible for the divergent schemes used by workers to judge their experience.

To sum up, we need to note that early industrialization is neutral with regard to each of the four basic conditions which set the character of the classes of early industrial workers. Industrialization does not account for the differences in the composition of these classes, it does not account for the differences in the industrial mileux, it does not account for the differences in outside conditions of life, and it does not account for the definitions used to interpret experience and to organize action. We have to look elsewhere for explanations of the make-up, the experiences, and the conduct of the working classes that come into existence. In my judgment students—theorists and research workers alike—who seek to use early industrialization to account for the character of the new working class are operating with a false scheme.

I have one final observation to make. One may grant the thesis that industrialization is a neutral process, as I hold to be true, yet ask why there is such a high frequency of labor discontent and protest under early industrialization. The answer, I believe firmly, is that early industrialization coincides frequently with situations of intense social change in which strong disruptive forces may be thrown into play. Let me mention a few of such forces: rapid urbanization, setting grievous problems of community and family living, and bringing together a host of unemployed and underemployed people; modernization, introducing new ideas of how to live and new conceptions of rights and privileges which challenge traditional codes and views; the play of interest groups, both vested and new, which seek to exploit the new social setting to their advantage; unenlightened policies and acts by existing governments which are frequently held in distrust because of administrative corruption; and, of particular importance today, vigorous radical and nationalistic movements. Such forces are potent in engendering restlessness and discontent and in promoting protest among both industrially employed and nonindustrially employed people.

It is a grave error in analysis to regard industrialization as responsible for such forces. Early industrialization can take place and does take place without them. In turn, they can take place and do take place without industrialization. It is questionable scholarship to take their coincidence—when they coincide—as grounds for saying or implying that early industrialization causes labor discontent and protest. Sociologists and other students will do well to re-examine their naive assumption that the industrializing process has definite social results.

3 / The Accommodation of Rural and Urban Workers to Industrial Discipline and Urban Living: A Four Nation Study[*]

William H. Form

Some Persistent Questions

SOCIOLOGISTS INTERESTED IN industrialization and urbanization have long speculated about the problems rural migrants face when they move to the city. Unfortunately, available knowledge on this subject has not been systematically organized (Beijer 1963). Two contradictory positions focus on the accommodation of rural migrants to urban and industrial situations. The more widely accepted position hypothesizes that rural people reluctantly leave home to seek work in the city. Unsocialized to grapple with impersonality, they find urban and factory life restrictive, bureaucratized, and alienating. Therefore, they tend to avoid social contacts with their fellow workers and are frequently absent from work[1] (Mayo 1945). Lack of socialization to urban organizational life is reflected in lower attendance at union meetings, lower rates of community participation (Freedman and Freedman 1956), and lower rates of voting (Wright and Hyman 1958).

Reprinted by permission of the author and publisher from William H. Form, "The Accommodation of Rural and Urban Workers to Industrial Discipline and Urban Living: A Four Nation Study," *Rural Sociology,* (December 1971).

[*] We are grateful to the following agencies for supporting the research: The Social Science Research Council, The National Science Foundation, and The American Fulbright Commission. At Michigan State University support was provided by International Programs (Ford Foundation), The School of Labor and Industrial Relations, and the All-University Research Fund. We wish to thank William A. Faunce and Alex Inkeles for a critical reading of the original manuscript and Noreen Channels and Camille Legendre for their assistance in data preparation.

[1] There is a curious contradiction in the literature. Whyte (1955: 42) found that rural workers in industry avoid interacting with urbanites, but that ruralites have low absenteeism and are rate busters. Feldman and Moore (1960: 41–54) suggest that rural workers in less developed societies have low commitment to factory life and have high absenteeism rates.

Their nostalgia is reflected by frequent visits to the home community and returning to it to retire and die (Beegle 1970).

Supporters of the second position assert that rural people, when given the opportunity, eagerly leave the rural scene to work in industry. The massive shifts of rural people to urban areas all over the world suggest that income and economic well-being are more important than preserving a traditional way of life (Touraine and Ragazzi 1961; Kerr *et al.* 1960: 181–85). Consequently, adaptation to industrial discipline is not difficult because work autonomy is not a salient value (Lambert 1963). Recent farm migrants become tractable employees and, since they hold no preconceived attitudes toward labor unions, they assimilate the dominant orientations of their workmates. Where the union is strong and where participation in it is high, the migrant accepts the union and attends its meetings. He quickly adopts the style of life of the neighborhood and community which is characteristic of urbanites of his class level (Touraine *et al.* 1961).

Although there are different views regarding the accommodation of urban workers to industry, there is widespread agreement that for them work is not a central life interest. They tend to be more concerned with family, social, and leisure activities (Dubin 1956). Urban workers find satisfaction from social contacts wherever they occur: in the factory, neighborhood, organizations, and in informal activities (Blauner 1964; Form and Dansereau 1957; Wilensky 1961). Although participation is low and episodic in the union, neighborhood, and community (Spinrad 1960), the urban worker adapts with little strain to the urban-industrial way of life (Wyatt and Marriott 1956).

Most research dealing with the urban-industrial adaptation of farm and city workers has been done in the highly industrialized countries of the West. Perhaps the patterns of accommodation differ for workers in countries at different levels of industrialization. There is no consensus on this point, but two major orientations exist. First, the industrial man hypothesis emphasizes that, irrespective of the level of industrialization of a country, workers, whatever their backgrounds, make quick and effective adjustments to industrial demands (Inkeles 1960; Reynolds and Gregory 1965). The second and more popular development hypothesis holds that since rural workers are more traditionally oriented than urban workers, they experience more stress in industrial and urban situations. The lower the level of industrialization, the more stress rural workers experience (Kerr *et al.* 1960). The reverse idea is also held; that rural workers, especially in impoverished countries, feel so fortunate to have secure industrial jobs that they experience no stress and become overcommitted to them (Chaplin 1967; Feldman and Moore 1960; Lambert 1963; Reynolds 1965).

Contradictory findings result in part from the fact that comparative studies use different research designs. Typically, employees in certain occupations and industries in one country have been compared to workers in different occupations and industries in other countries (Faunce and Smucker 1966; Smith and Inkeles 1966). The present research attempts to reduce the confounding variables by studying workers only in one industry (automobile) in four countries at different levels of industrialization: India, Argentina, Italy, and the United States.[2] Moreover, stratified representative samples of the skill composition of the factories were drawn: skilled craftsmen, machine operators, and assembly line workers.[3] Also, the industries were all located in metropolitan areas. In short, the workers in the four countries had worked in similar industries, occupations, and work organizations for at least one year and were residing in metropolitan areas.

This study is guided by the industrial man perspective. Two major hypotheses are considered. First, no differences in adaptation are expected between workers from rural and urban backgrounds irrespective of the degree of industrialization of the country. Second, no adaptation differences are expected between the countries. These hypotheses are stated negatively not to present null-hypotheses, but to stress the theoretical position which posits the primacy of occupations in the lives of industrial workers everywhere (Durkheim 1947) and the primacy of technology in the organizational milieu of industrial cities (Cottrell 1955; Kerr *et al.* 1960; Ellul 1967). We hold that wherever automobile industries may be located, there exists a mature industrial sector of the economy, and participation in this sector imposes a uniform discipline on its workers regardless of their rural or urban origins and the level of economic development of the broader society (Inkeles 1969; Karsh and Cole 1968). Moreover, the discipline workers experience in the factory will affect their adaptation in other social systems such as the family, labor union, neighborhood, community and nation (Inkeles 1969). While more variability in adaptation may appear in social systems increasingly distant from the factory, all systems tend to articulate in a similar direction.

Rural–Urban Backgrounds

Four variables were employed to reflect the rural–urban background of the respondents: father's occupation, community of birth, community of socialization, and main sector of work experience prior to present employment. The probabilities of the chi-square tests of association among these variables were all below the five per cent level. Moreover, the variables were moderately inter-correlated as measured by the coefficient of contingency. Each

[2] No completely satisfactory index of industrialization is available. Farace (1966), who used 54 variables to place 109 countries along a development continuum, ordered the countries as follows: United States, 1; Italy, 23; Argentina, 27; and India, 96.

[3] For a fuller description of the sampling procedures and the samples, see Form (1969).

of the variables was run against all of the data presented in this study and they provided almost identical results. Father's occupation was the most sensitive independent variable, so for parsimony it was selected to represent community background.[4] For this study, sons of farmers are defined as rural and the others are defined as urban.

Despite differences in the degree of industrialization in the four countries, sons of farmers were similarly represented in the four factories (see Table 1). About one-third of all workers were sons of farmers except for the Argentine factory, where the ratio was one-fifth. Understandably, rural origins were more similar going back two generations. Almost all workers of rural origins had grandfathers who were farmers; in contrast, half of the non-rural had grandfathers who were farmers.[5] As anticipated, the overwhelming majority of rural-origin workers were reared in small rural-like communities, but a fifth to a half of the others were also reared in small communities. Rural background also affected the choice of community of present residence for, except in India, more rural-origin workers than others presently lived outside the central city.[6]

Despite the fact that one-quarter to two-thirds of all workers were reared in small towns or rural areas, fewer than a fifth had worked primarily in agriculture prior to locating a job in the industrial sector. Three-tenths of the Indians and five-tenths of the Italians whose fathers were farmers also worked in agriculture, but one-tenth or less of the Americans and Argentinians had done so. With the exception of rural-born Italians, the great majority of both urban and rural workers became employed in the urban sector soon after leaving school. Only in Argentina did as many persons of rural origin work in the service sector as in the industrial sector prior to their present employment. Unless the situation for automobile workers is unique, these results cast some doubt on the belief that rural migrants in recently industrializing society typically move from the agricultural sector into the service sector prior to locating in industry (Moore 1966). However, the two-step migration process from service to industrial employment does seem to be most widespread among rural origin workers in the less industrialized societies (Ammassari 1968).

What effect does rural or urban origin have on occupational experiences? The data in Table 2 reveal that sons of farmers experienced more intra- and intergenerational upward occupational mobility than urban workers.[7] This is partly but not entirely a function of classifying all farmers as

4 Community of socialization and community of birth were almost as sensitive as father's occupation and sector background was somewhat less sensitive. The relevance of length of time rural migrants were employed in non-rural situations is discussed in the conclusion of this paper.

5 The Indian case is a deviation, and the statistic is less reliable because one-fifth of the respondents did not know their grandfather's occupation.

6 Greater Bombay is a conglomerate of sub-communities, making it difficult to define the boundaries of the central city.

7 Occupational mobility was measured as the algebraic sum of all job moves along an eight point occupational ladder.

Table 1. Occupational Derivation, Community Backgrounds, and Sector Experiences of Automobile Workers in Four Countries, According to Fathers' Occupations, in Percentages

Variables	U.S.A. Oldsmobile		Italy Fiat		Argentina IKA		India PAL	
	FATHERS' OCCUPATIONS							
	Farmer	Other	Farmer	Other	Farmer	Other	Farmer	Other
Grandfathers' occupation—farmer	87*	54	95*	48	87*	56	96*	36
Fathers' occup.—farmer, total sample	(37)		(34)		(21)		(34)	
Community of birth—state or province	73*	48	53*	32	54*	19	48*	37
Community of socialization—rural or small town	91*	45	89*	48	46*	17	78*	37
Community of residence—outside central city	72*	51	40*	22	25*	17	8	11
Number of communities resided—two or more	52*	52	52*	30	68*	41	73	62
Main sector of previous work experience								
Agriculture	12*	2	47*	5	8*	—	31*	5
Manuf. and artisan	88	90	44	81	44	72	44	65
Business and service	—	8	10	14	47	27	25	30
Number of cases	86	143	101	195	57	213	89	168

* Probabilities of the χ^2 test at or below the .05 level. The tests of significance are based on the original tables where the "other" was comprised of three independent categories: sons of fathers in manufacturing, white collar, and skilled trades.

unskilled workers. This procedure has the effect of exaggerating the amount of generational upward mobility which farmers' sons experience, but it does not necessarily produce a similar effect on their career mobility rates.[8]

Those who are most upwardly mobile do not necessarily occupy the highest skilled jobs. The data in Table 2 demonstrate this point. Thus, there were no statistically significant differences in the skill level of United States and Argentine workers according to rural–urban origins, but in Italy and India urban workers were more highly skilled. However, in all countries a somewhat higher percentage of urban than rural workers were skilled. Why isn't the relationship of origin to skill level unambiguously clear for all countries?

Job tenure, age, and education are related to skill level in complex ways. In all four factories the rural-born tended to be older, had longer tenure (except for Italy), but had less education than the urban workers. There were no consistent or significant differences between the two categories on other characteristics such as marital status, number of children, age at first job, number of jobs held, and duration of unemployment. Apparently, special situations in each of the plants accounted for the skill distribution. Thus, in the United States, some older rural workers with long tenure and low education were promoted to skilled jobs during periods when skilled labor was scarce. In India, the oldest workers were the plant's original employees when it only assembled automobiles, but later, as the plant added other operations, these workers increased their skills. In Italy and Argentina, where workers were quite young,[9] the companies hired better educated urban applicants at higher skill levels and less educated applicants from rural areas for unskilled and semi-skilled jobs.

In conclusion, the only consistent differences between workers of rural and urban origin in all four countries were the greater upward occupational mobility of the rural and the higher educational level of the urban. The employment experiences of both origin groups in each country were quite similar and did not directly determine their skill placement.

Adaptation to Work Organizations

Does rural or urban background of the worker affect his adaptation to industrial discipline and the social organization of the city? An important objective of the research was to ascertain how industrial workers in different countries adapted to a widening set of relationships: work group, family, labor union, neighborhood, community, and the nation. According to the industrial man hypothesis, workers should accommodate rapidly to the work situation and the social systems in the city irrespective of their community origins and level of industrialization of their society.

[8] Thus there was no statistically significant difference in the career mobility of rural and urban workers in India.

[9] The mean ages of workers were: Oldsmobile, 42; Fiat, 35; IKA, 30; and PAL, 32.

Table 2. Demographic and Occupational Characteristics of Automobile Workers in Four Countries According to Fathers' Occupations

	U.S.A. Oldsmobile		Italy Fiat		Argentina IKA		India PAL	
	FATHERS' OCCUPATIONS							
Variable	*Farmer*	*Other*	*Farmer*	*Other*	*Farmer*	*Other*	*Farmer*	*Other*
Age—mean	44.6	39.7	36.5	35.2	33.4*	29.5	35.2	32.0
Married—per cent	95	93	80	73	79	69	90*	77
Number of children—mean	2.7	2.7	1.0	.7	1.7	1.5	2.4	2.1
Education—mean years	8.9*	10.2	3.8*	5.7	4.7*	7.1	5.5*	6.9
Age at first job—mean	17.3	17.4	13.4	14.0	15.5	15.2	17.6	17.5
Unemployed—mean number of months	5.6*	3.8	2.4	3.8	2.7	3.7	4.8	5.2
Jobs—mean	3.9	3.8	3.6	3.3	3.9	3.6	4.0	3.9
Job tenure—mean number of years	14.0	12.4	7.6*	9.7	5.8	4.9	8.3	8.3
Occupational skill—per cent								
Unskilled	31	26	44*	24	63*	44	48	31
Semi-skilled	56	52	49	52	32	37	29	43
Skilled	13	22	7	24	5	19	23	26
Upward career mobility—per cent	58*	47	59*	43	53*	40	65	51
Intergenerational mobility—per cent above father	69*	26	58*	26	51*	21	79*	16
Number of cases	86	143	101	195	57	213	89	168

* Probabilities of differences statistically significant by chi-square test at the .05 level. The tests were based on the original tables and not the classes reported in this table.

The first set of adaptations we examined centered around work: adaptations to the industrial situs, occupation, job routines, work group, and the labor union. Respondents were asked to evaluate six conditions of work in the agricultural, industrial, and the office sectors. The first question was: "With the same hourly pay would you prefer to work on a farm machine, an office machine, or on a machine in a factory?" Data in Section 1 of Table 3 reveal that six-tenths of the Indian and American workers preferred to work in a rural environment, while the Italians and especially the Argentinians preferred an industrial environment. The office sector was preferred least by workers in all countries. A curvilinear trend characterized the relationship between the sector preference and the level of industrialization; workers in the least and the most industrialized nations, the Indians and Americans, most preferred the agricultural sector while those in the rapidly industrializing nations, the Italians and Argentinians, preferred the industrial sector (Gale 1968).

As a supplement to the question on sector preference, workers were asked to evaluate five dimensions of work in each of three sectors (small independent farmer, skilled factory worker, office worker). They were asked which occupation was the most desirable, respected, necessary, satisfying, and monotonous. An index of industrial sector preference was constructed by determining the number of times the skilled factory worker was selected first (see Table 3). The same curvilinear relationship among the countries appeared as in the earlier question on sector choice; i.e., the United States and Indian workers least preferred the industrial sector and the Italians and Argentinians most preferred it. However, in no instance were there statistically significant differences between the choices of sons of farmers and sons of other workers. Similar indexes were also constructed for the agricultural and office sectors. Rural migrants in the United States and Italy, in contrast to urban workers, more strongly preferred the agricultural sector, but the differences were much weaker among the Argentine and the Indian respondents. The former tended to devaluate the agricultural sector while the latter esteemed it more highly (see Table 3).

Whatever his sector preference, each worker must respond to situations he daily confronts in the industrial environment. Respondents were asked about their occupations, physical conditions in the shop, specific job routines, sources of work satisfaction and dissatisfaction, occupational aspirations for themselves and their children, how friends, family, and fellow workers evaluated their occupations, and related questions. The findings were generally consistent: when the responses of the sons of farmers were compared to sons of industrial, white-collar, and skilled workers, very few statistically significant differences appeared.[10]

Section 2 of Table 3 summarizes some of the data on occupational adaptation. One striking finding is that, while the Argentinians appeared

---

[10] Of the 96 chi-square tests of significance, ten had probabilities at or beyond the .05 level.

Table 3. Sector and Occupational Adaptation of Automobile Workers in Four Countries, According to Occupation of Father, in Percentages

Variable	FATHERS' OCCUPATIONS							
	U.S.A. *Oldsmobile*		*Italy* *Fiat*		*Argentina* *IKA*		*India* *PAL*	
	Farmer	*Other*	*Farmer*	*Other*	*Farmer*	*Other*	*Farmer*	*Other*
1. Sector preferred								
Farm machines	58*	32	34	16	4	8	62	48
Factory machines	36	56	52	54	77	69	30	42
Office machines	6	11	14	30	19	23	8	10
Total	100	99	100	100	100	100	100	100
Sector preference indexes (medians)								
Agricultural (0–5)	3.12*	2.25	1.68*	1.09	1.71	1.74	3.61	3.00
Industrial (0–5)	1.65	1.78	2.38	2.67	3.29	3.57	1.89	2.37
Office (0–5)	1.49	1.71	1.88	2.14	1.67	1.63	1.52	1.70
2. Occupational adaptation items**								
Occupational evaluation—good	62	70	50*	52	89	89	54	61
Occupational satisfaction—high	77	78	73	72	91	87	62*	65
Job routines—satisfied	81	83	76	77	83*	87	65	70
Reference group occup. evaluation index (0–5); high (5)	60	62	87	80	91	85	84	86
Thought of having different job?—no	42	80	50	44	56	53	n.a.	n.a.
Planning a job change?—no	87	83	87	81	77	69	n.a.	n.a.
Index of overall work satisfaction (0–6); high (5, 6)	34	36	38	35	42	47	21	10

* Probability of the χ^2 test at or below the five per cent level. The χ^2 tests for the sector preferences indexes were computed for the original tables.

** Each item in this section is selected from a table to provide the reader a feel for the data; it cannot there more represent the entire table.

to be most adapted and the Indians least adapted to industrial work, the responses of workers in all four nations were quite similar. Half or more evaluated their occupations as good and a somewhat larger percentage evidenced high occupational satisfaction. Two-thirds or more indicated high satisfaction with the specific routines associated with their jobs, although those from rural backgrounds were slightly less satisfied. Again, as reflected in a reference group job satisfaction index, about two-thirds or more of all respondents felt that their families, friends, and co-workers positively evaluated their occupations. Further evidence of high work adaptation is reflected by the fact that less than three-tenths of the workers were planning to change their jobs. Fewer workers from rural than urban backgrounds had considered or had planned to change jobs.

Differences in the level of occupational adaptation of rural and non-rural workers were by and large not statistically significant. Since employees with rural backgrounds tended to concentrate in lesser skilled jobs, one might have expected them to evaluate their jobs lower than more highly skilled workers. The absence of such a relationship may reflect the fact that rural origin workers had experienced relatively more upward occupational mobility; they had relatively well paid jobs, and therefore were not ready to risk a job change. While their own job aspirations were low, their occupational aspirations for their children were almost as high as those of urban reared workers.[11]

Social Interaction at Work

Sociologists commonly assert that the modern industrial worker finds little satisfaction in his job but considerable satisfaction from contacts with fellow workers (Goldthorpe and Lockwood 1968; Wyatt and Marriott 1956). Our data reveal a high level of satisfaction of workers with their workmates and no differences between workers from rural and urban backgrounds. We attempted to measure the amount of social contact workers had with their mates both at work and outside the factory. There were no differences between rural and urban respondents in the number of work-mates they they talked to while working[12] (see Table 4).

Since this finding could reflect uniform constraints to interaction imposed by the technology and ecology of work organization, a ratio was computed of the number of people with whom the respondent *actually* talked compared to the number of people in his work space to whom he could talk. The application of this ratio showed considerable variation in the opportunity for interaction, but still no differences appeared between the origin groups on the ratio. Finally, two indexes were constructed—one which measured

11 Over half of the sons of farmers expected their children to become white-collar workers. Although the comparable percentage for other workers is somewhat higher, the differences between the two categories are not significant.

12 In three of the four plants rural workers had slightly lower percentages among those who interacted with eleven or more co-workers.

Table 4. Interaction and Participation of Automobile Workers in Various Social Systems According to Fathers' Occupations, in Percentages

Variable	FATHERS' OCCUPATIONS							
	U.S.A. Oldsmobile		Italy Fiat		Argentina IKA		India PAL	
	Farmer	Other	Farmer	Other	Farmer	Other	Farmer	Other
Workmate contacts—satisfied	96	90	91	84	91	94	75	74
High workplant interaction—talks to 11 or more workers	34	36	28	40	14	9	25	38
Index of quality of workmate interaction (0–6); high (3–6)	57	59	49	47	47	54	66	67
Potential of workplace interaction realized (0–1.0); high (1.0)	60	53	38	32	62	76	37	40
Union participation (0–2); high (2)	31	36	20	24	65	58	44	33
Union evaluation (0–3); high (3)	49	59	26*	39	32	38	63	61
Conservative and radical index (0–3); liberal and radical (2–3)**	24	27	61	70	25	32	39*	48
Family interaction (0–3); high (2, 3)	41	42	61	69	51	42	26*	40
Neighborhood involvement (0–6); high (5, 6)	42	40	28	25	25	30	28	35
Community involvement (0–3); high (3)	23	29	16	24	33	25	40	45
National involvement (0–3); high (3)	27	36	10*	23	28	36	45	54
Index of total social interaction (0–5); high (5–6)	28	31	17	22	11	19	28	43
Anomie (normlessness) index (0–5); means	2.6	2.5	3.2	3.2	1.8	1.7	3.1	3.4

* Probability of the χ² test at or below the .05 level.
** There were no radicals in Oldsmobile; liberals had a score of 2.

the total amount of interaction with fellow workers outside the plant and the other which measured the intimacy or quality of that interaction.[13] No statistically significant differences were found between the two origin categories within the plants and no pattern was evident among the countries.

Next we examined involvement in the labor union. A commonly held belief is that rural-born workers participate less in labor union activities than urban workers because ruralites tend to mistrust organizations devoted to conflict (Whyte 1944, 1955). Moreover, in most countries labor unions tend to favor one political party over another, thereby pressing their members to endorse a particular political or ideological stance. While there is some disagreement in the literature on the ideological leanings of rural migrants in industry, most studies conclude that they tend to be either conservative or apathetic (Lipset 1960: 101–14).

The researchers extensively probed the attitudes of workers toward the labor union, their amount of participation in its activities, and their political inclinations. No statistically significant differences appeared between the origin categories for interest in labor unions, amount of participation in them, or judgment of them either as collective bargaining or political instruments (see Table 4). There was a slight tendency for rural workers to participate less in the union, but this probably reflected their lower occupational and educational backgrounds. Although there was also a slight tendency for sons of farmers to be less enthusiastic about labor unions than the sons of urban workers, in all countries the preponderance of both groups accepted and supported the union. In responses to five item indexes of conservatism–radicalism in politics (adapted to the conditions peculiar to each country), there were no sharp differences between the rural origin and other workers. However, those with farm backgrounds had slightly higher conservatism scores than the others except for the rural Indians who were more politically polarized than their urban fellow workers (see Table 4).

Social Interaction in Non-plant Social Systems

To complete the profiles of social interaction, the researchers constructed indexes which measured the extent to which auto workers were involved in family, neighborhood, community, and broader societal activities. Traditional theory led us to expect that workers with rural backgrounds would be more heavily involved in family and local neighborhood activities while workers reared in cities would be more heavily involved in activities of the city and the nation (Toennies 1957). The index of family involvement

[13] This index was made up of items which probed satisfaction with daily contacts with fellow workers, ability to talk to workmates about important personal problems, number of good friends in workgroup, visiting workmates outside of work, getting into political discussion with workmates, and valuing opinions of workmates above all others.

was constructed by ascertaining whether any of a number of activities (visiting, vacationing, going to a bar, discussing politics) was done with a family member or a relative. Only in the case of India was there a significant difference in the extent of kin involvement of workers from rural and non-rural areas; in this instance, those with urban background were more heavily involved than those from rural areas. In the arena of neighborhood activities, no significant or consistent differences were found within or among the nations (see Table 4).

Rural–urban differences did appear in the extent of worker involvement in community and national activities. A higher percentage of workers from urban backgrounds were heavily involved in organizations and issues of a city-wide or national character. However, only in one instance (Italy, for national involvement) were these differences statistically significant (see Table 4).

Finally, two summary measures were constructed—the first, an index which summarized the totality of social interactions in all social systems[11] and the second, a Guttman scale of normlessness anomie (see Table 4). There were no statistically significant differences between workers from urban and rural backgrounds in their total interaction scores, but in all four nations rural workers had slightly lower scores. Six item Guttman anomie scales were constructed especially for this study.[15] Their coefficients of reproducibility were all over 85 per cent. Applications of the scales showed no statistically significant differences between workers from rural and urban areas, but the anomie scores were higher for the Italians and Indians than for Americans and Argentinians. There was no evidence that the summary rates of social interaction bore any relationship to the anomie scores.

Discussion

The major findings of this study are clear. Very few differences appeared between workers from rural and urban backgrounds in the four factories. Sons of farmers were less educated and more upwardly mobile than sons of urban workers, but in only two countries were they in occupationally inferior positions. Workers in countries at the extreme ends of economic development, United States and India, tended to be more rural oriented than workers in the other countries. Irrespective of their backgrounds, all workers except the Indians tended to be satisfied with industrial work. In various participational arenas (factory, union, family, neighborhood, community, and nation), very few differences could be accounted for by rural or urban background. When the social characteristics and behavior of the workers in the four countries were compared, no pattern emerged. In

14 A cumulative index of interactions in social systems both inside and outside of the plant. For the best analysis of rural–urban differences in different types of social systems by type of community, see Key (1968).

15 Available on request.

short, the developmental model was not supported and the industrial man model was generally supported.

Recent American studies have found increasingly fewer differences between workers from rural and urban backgrounds (Blau and Duncan 1967: 277–92). The explanation offered is that urban-industrial culture has permeated the open country, wiping away its traditional characteristics (Fuller 1970). The data from this study suggest that a similar mechanism may be at work in countries at lower levels of economic development which presumably have stronger rural traditions. Probably even there the urban-industrial way of life has penetrated urban hinterlands, making it quite possible for those reared on farms to accommodate to industrial discipline and urban social organization about as well as the workers reared in the cities. It may well be that dual societies which accompany the dual economies in poorer countries (Boeke 1942; Higgins 1956) are poorly articulated. Either the workers recruited into industry are selectively socialized to a new way of life or the alleged barriers to their urban and industrial assimilation do not exist. Since most of the rural workers in this study migrated from nearby regions, we are inclined to the latter interpretation.

Since a few differences were found between workers of rural and urban origin, we were tempted to undertake an extensive multivariate analysis to ascertain whether these differences would persist when other variables such as age, education, and tenure in industry are controlled. This decision was abandoned because other data indeed strongly suggest that socioeconomic status, education, and skill level are the most important determinants of industrial and urban adaptation (Form, undated).

Yet it is possible that our comparison of workers of farm origins with the separate urban occupational origin categories (factory, white-collar, artisan, and service) might have hidden some rural–urban differences. It is also possible that workers from farm areas eventually become socialized to urban-industrial life, but that they experience greater adaptation difficulties in the early years of their industrial employment. For the Indian workers, adaptation difficulties could be compounded by caste. For them, the two traditional factors of caste and recency of rural origin might affect their urban-industrial adaptation. These possible effects were explored.

Since urban and rural were defined in terms of occupation of the father of the respondent, an attempt was made to ascertain which occupational origin category in the urban sector (factory, white-collar, artisan, or service) was most similar or dissimilar to the rural origin workers. This was done by comparing the responses of all origin categories on all the items included in this study. In every instance but one, the sons in an urban origin category responded almost identically to the sons of farmers. The one exception was situs preferences where the sons of farmers desired to be farmers far more so than the sons in other categories. There was a slight tendency for sons of farmers to respond more like the sons of factory workers in Italy and more like the sons of craft workers in Argentina, but in the United States and India, no pattern appeared. We then sought to discover which occupational origin category differed most in its responses from the sons of farmers. No pattern became apparent for Italy and India, but for the United States, sons of craft workers differed the most and for Argentina, the sons of white-collar workers.

The largest differences in all countries between sons of farmers and the others were for interaction rates in the factory, situs preference, union evaluation, and community involvement. However, the direction of these differences and occupational categories involved in the comparisons differed in all the four countries, pointing to random or unpatterned results. Thus, as far as we could ascertain, although some rural–urban differences were evident in the four nations, they did not represent a consistent pattern among occupational origin groups.

Last, we decided to compare the responses of the sons of farmers with those of all other occupational categories combined; i.e., a direct farm–non-farm comparison. The primary effects of this operation were to emphasize the background differences between the two categories; they differed more in grandfathers' occupation, community of socialization, number of communities of residence, present community of residence, sector occupational experiences, and age. Also, the two categories differed more clearly in skill and education, the farmers being relatively less skilled and less educated. However, all of the eleven other shifts[16] resulting from treating the non-urban occupational categories as a single entity were random. When statistically significant differences appeared where none were evident in the earlier rural–urban classification, they appeared only for one country and were not in the critical areas of occupational adaptation and patterns of interaction inside and outside of the factory. In conclusion, the same results of little or no difference in adaptation patterns appeared regardless which classification we used to designate the non-rural workers.

The number of years spent in the plant—or tenure—may affect the adaptation of all workers, but those from farm origins may experience more shock in the first years. We found no consistent relationship between origins and tenure in the four plants. However, tenure was related to the standard demographic and career background variables: age, education, marital status, number of children, skill level, and occupational mobility. With the exception of India, tenure was positively related to occupational, job, work, and reference group satisfaction, but not to sector preference. The fewest number of differences by tenure were found in the interactional areas. Although higher tenured workers interacted somewhat more with their mates at work and participated more in the union, there were no differences by tenure for family, neighborhood, community, and national involvement and no differences in quality of interaction with workers, political ideologies, or anomie scores. Apparently interaction patterns of workers became quickly or randomly established.

[16] A shift is defined as a change in the probability of the chi-square from a significant (.05) to a non-significant level or vice versa.

The critical question then is whether rural–urban origins differentially affect workers according to their length of service in industry. Our analyses proved the reverse of our expectations; that for the lower developed countries, Argentina and India, the seniority of rural and urban workers was not related to their demographic and career attributes, nor to adaptation in the social systems in or outside of the plant. For the more highly developed countries, a few differences appeared but they tended to be small quantitatively. In Italy, the high tenured urban workers tended to be older than the rural, less educated, spent more time in the manufacturing sector, were better adapted to their work, job, occupation, and situs, were more involved in the social system of work, family, community, and nation, but less involved with the labor union and had higher anomie scores. They approximated the classic model of the urban proletariat.

In the United States, the low tenured urban workers followed the Italian pattern with few exceptions. They had spent relatively more time in industry, were more adapted to their occupations and jobs, engaged in more interaction at work, were more heavily involved in the work, family, neighborhood, and national social systems, but were more liberal politically, and had lower anomie scores.

Finally, caste in India was not associated strongly with rural–urban background. Although the higher caste workers were younger and better educated than those in the lower castes, the latter had higher seniority and were disproportionately more concentrated in the higher skills according to the company's classification. No statistically significant differences among the castes were noted in work, occupation, job, and sector adaptation. Neither were there important or consistent differences in caste involvement in the various social systems in which the workers interacted inside or outside of the factory.

In conclusion, our attempts to ascertain whether the mode of classifying our respondents into urban and rural affected the results of the study turned out to be largely negative. The exploration of the possible differential impact of time spent in the plant by rural and urban origin also was negative for the two countries at the lower levels of development and inconsistent for the other two countries. No pretense is made that the general negative results of this study have universal application. It may be that the rural origin workers in automobile plants are highly selected in terms of their education and socioeconomic status, making them more urban-industrially oriented prior to migration. A second more persuasive explanation is offered by Inkeles (1969). In a study of individual modernization attitudes, he demonstrated that the factory functions as a later socialization school for modernization (1969: 212–16), almost as effective as formal education. In this study, all of the workers had at least one year tenure, and the lowest mean for rural migrants was about five years for the Argentinian factory. Thus, sufficient time had elapsed for considerable training in modernization to have occurred. This interpretation explains other findings in the literature of both highly developed and less highly developed societies. Thus, in a study of Flint, Michigan, Zimmer

(1955: 223) demonstrated that the rates for social and political participation of rural migrants was especially low during the first five years of residence, but they increased rapidly after that time. Touraine and Ragazzi (1961) found that French automobile workers from rural background seemed to adapt quickly to industrial situations, although they did not become fully integrated into the industrial way of life. And Signorini (1970) found that Italian industrial workers of rural background experienced some adaptation difficulties during the first year, but soon became adapted. Both the French and the Italian studies support the findings that rural migrants who are economically motivated to migrate experience little difficulty in urban-industrial adaptation.

Results from this research and hints from other studies provide increasing evidence that the same processes of modernization are occurring about at the same rates in countries at different levels of industrialization. The factory and the city seem to exert the same type of influence on rural migrants at about the same rates everywhere. Such evidence tends to support an industrial man or convergence hypothesis.

References

Ammassari, P. The italian blue-collar worker. *International Journal of Comparative Sociology,* 1968, 10, 3–21.

Beegle, J. A. Patterns of dispersion for burials as a reflection of migration flow. Unpublished manuscript, 1970.

Beijer, G. *Rural migrants in urban setting.* The Hague: Martinus Nijhoff, 1963.

Blau, P. M. and O. D. Duncan. *The american occupational structure.* New York: Wiley, 1967.

Blauner, R. *Alienation and freedom: the factory worker and his industry.* Chicago: University of Chicago Press, 1964.

Boecke, J. H. *The structure of the netherlands indian economy.* New York: Institute of Pacific Relations, 1942.

Chaplin, D. *The peruvian industrial labor force.* Princeton, New Jersey; Princeton University Press, 1967.

Cottrell, F. *Energy and society.* New York: McGraw-Hill, 1955.

Dubin, Robert. Industrial workers' worlds: a study of "central life interests" of industrial workers. *Social Problems,* 1956, 3, 131–42.

Durkheim, E. *The division of labor in society,* G. Simpson (trans.). Glencoe, Illinois: The Free Press, 1947.

Elull, J. *The technological society,* J. Wilkinson (trans.). New York: Vintage Books, 1967.

Farace, R. V. A study of mass communication and national development. *Journalism Quarterly,* 1966, 43, 305–13.

Faunce, W. A. and M. J. Smucker. Industrialization and community status structure. *American Sociological Review,* 1966, 31, 390–99.

Feldman, A. S. and W. E. Moore (eds.), *Labor commitment and social change in developing areas.* New York: Social Science Research Council, 1960.

Form, W. H. Occupational and social integration of automobile workers in four countries, a comparative study. *International Journal of Comparative Sociology,* 1969, 10, 95–116.

Form, W. H. and H. K. Dansereau. Union member orientations and patterns of social integration. *Industrial and Labor Relations Review,* 1957, 11, 3–12.

Form, W. H. A comparative study of work and social structure. Monograph in preparation.

Freedman, R. and D. Freedman. Farm-reared elements in the non-farm population. *Rural Sociology,* 1956, 21, 50–61.

Fuller, V. *Rural worker adjustment to urban life.* Ann Arbor: University of Michigan–Wayne State University and National Manpower Policy Taskforce, 1970.

Gale, R. P. *Industrial man in argentina and the united states: a comparative study of automobile workers.* Ph.D. dissertation. East Lansing: Michigan State University, 1968.

Higgins, B. The dualistic theory of underdeveloped areas. *Economic Development and Cultural Change,* 1956, 4, 99–115.

Inkeles, A. Industrial man: the relation of status to experience, perception and value. *American Journal of Sociology,* 1960, 66, 1–31.

Inkeles, A. Making man modern: on the causes and consequences of individual change in six developing countries. *American Journal of Sociology,* 1969, 75, 208–25.

Karsh, B. and R. E. Cole. Industrialization and the convergence hypothesis: some aspects of contemporary japan. *Journal of Social Issues,* 1968, 24, 45–64.

Kerr, C., J. T. Dunlop, F. H. Harbison, and C. A. Myers. *Industrialism and industrial man.* Cambridge, Massachusetts: Harvard University Press, 1968, 305–12, 1960.

Key, W. H. Rural–urban social participation, in S. F. Fava (ed.), *Urbanism in world perspective.* New York: Crowell, 1968, 305–12.

Lambert, R. D. *Workers, factories and social change in india.* Princeton, Press, 1963.

Lipset, S. M. *Political man.* New York: Doubleday, 1960.

Mayo, E. *The social problems of an industrial civilization.* Boston: Graduate School of Business Administration, Harvard University, 1945.

Moore, W. E. Changes in occupational structure, in N. J. Smelser and S. M. Lipset (eds.), *Social structure and mobility in economic development.* Chicago: Aldine Press, 1966, 194–212.

Reynolds, L. G. and P. Gregory. *Wages, productivity and industrialization in Puerto Rico.* Homewood, Illinois: R. D. Irwin, 1965.

Signorini, M. Aspetti e fasi dell integrazione del contadino nella società urbana. *Rassegna Italiana di Sociologia,* 1970, 11, 121–41.

Smith, D. H. and A. Inkeles. The o m scale: a comparative socio-psychological measure of individual modernity. *Sociometry,* 1966, 29, 353–77.

Spinrad, W. Correlates of trade union participation: a summary of the literature. *American Sociological Review,* 1960, 25, 237–44.

Toennies, F. *Community and society,* trans. and edited by C. P. Loomis. East Lansing: Michigan State University Press, 1957.

Touraine, A. *et al.* Ourvièrs et syndicats d'amerique latine. *Sociologie du Travail,* 1961.

Touraine, A. and O. Raggazzi. *Ouvrièrs d'origine agricole.* (No place). Aux Editions du Seuil, 1961.

Whyte, W. F. *Money and motivation.* New York: Harper and Brothers, 1955.

Whyte, W. F. Who goes union and why. *Personnel Journal,* 1944, 23, 215–30.

Wilensky, H. L. Orderly careers and social participation: the impact of work history on social integration in the middle mass. *American Sociological Review,* 1961, 26, 521–39.

Wright, C. R. and H. H. Hyman. Voluntary association memberships of american adults: evidence from national sample survey. *American Sociological Review,* 1958, 23, 284–94.

Wyatt, S. and R. Marriott. *A study of attitudes to factory work.* London: Her Majesty's Stationery Office, 1956.

Zimmer, B. G. Participation of migrants in urban structure. *American Sociological Review,* 1955, 20, 218–24.

4 / Tradition and Modernity: Misplaced Polarities in the Study of Social Change[1]

Joseph R. Gusfield

WHILE RIDING THE Kodama express from Tokyo to Kyoto several years ago, I saw what might be taken as a symbolic expression of transitional development. The Japanese passenger in the seat across from mine had made himself comfortable during his nap by unlacing his shoes and pulling his socks partly off. Half in and half out of both shoes and socks, he seemed to make a partial commitment to the Western world which his clothing implied. One could only wonder about his future direction either back into his shoes and socks or out of them and into sandals and bare feet.

This particular example has been chosen because it accentuates the idea of change in contemporary new nations and economically growing societies as one which entails a linear movement from a traditional past toward a modernized future.[2] A significant assumption in this model of change is that existing institutions and values, the content of tradition, are impediments to changes and are obstacles to modernization. It is with this assumption that our paper is concerned. We wish to call attention to the manifold variations in the relation between traditional forms and new institutions and values, variations whose possibilities are either denied or hidden by the polarity of the traditional–modern model of social change. We want, further, to explore the uses of tradition and modernity as explicit ideologies operating in the context of politics in new nations. Our materials

---

[1] Presented at the annual meeting of the American Sociological Association, Chicago, September 2, 1965.

[2] There is a wide literature analyzing concepts of tradition and modernity or development. Leading efforts to conceptualize these societal types are W. W. Rostov, *The Stages of Economic Growth* (Cambridge: Cambridge University Press, 1960); Gabriel Almond and James Coleman, *The Politics of Developing Areas* (Princeton, N.J.: Princeton University Press, 1960), chap. i; Daniel Lerner, *The Passing of Traditional Society* (Glencoe, Ill.: Free Press, 1958), chaps. ii, iii.

are largely drawn from modern India, although we shall refer to other Asian and African countries as well.

The concepts of economic development and of economic modernization have now been generalized to many areas of national life by social scientists. There is now a discussion of communication development, educational development, and, most widely used, of political development.[3] While these are sometimes used to relate specific institutions to economic growth and development as possible correlative influences or effects, they are also utilized as independent concepts. Some writers have viewed political modernization as implying the necessary framework within which nation-hood can be achieved and operate. Others have seen certain institutions and political values as inherently valuable and legitimate perspectives toward change.[4]

At the same time that the concept of development has become gener-alized, a large number of specific studies of new nations (many to be discussed here) have made us aware of the wide variety of outcomes and possibilities for change and continuity. These have led to a more critical appreciation of the many possible interrelations between new and old aspects of social, economic, and political life. The view that tradition and innovation are necessarily in conflict has begun to seem overly abstract and unreal.

In the study of economic growth we have come to be aware that Weber's conception of traditional versus rational economic behavior is a great distortion of the realities of many concrete situations. In the study of political alternatives and possibilities we have become sensitive to the reifying effect of unilinear theories. They make Anglo-American political forms either inevitable or necessarily superior outcomes of political processes in new nations. Functional theories of political and economic development now seem less viable.[5] An emphasis on what Shils calls the issue of consensus

[3] See the various volumes published by Princeton University Press under the series title "Studies in Political Development." Also see A. F. K. Organski, *The Stages of Political Development* (New York: Alfred A. Knopf, Inc., 1965).

[4] We can distinguish several different uses of the concept "political development." Sometimes it is used as functional to economic development. Here the writer seeks to determine the political conditions essential to support effective economic change. For one example, see Wilfred Malenbaum, "Economic Factors and Political Development," *Annals,* CCCLVIII (March, 1965), 41–51; in the same volume, Lucien Pye uses the concept as independent of economic forms but gives it a substantive content (see Pye, "The Concept of Political Development," *Annals,* CCCLVIII [March, 1965]). Shils gives the concept of "modernity" a meaning closer to that of a goal toward which political elites aspire. This makes concern for a given state of society a perspective rather than an empirical theory and is thus doser to the use we make of it in the last section of this paper. "Our central concern will be with the vicissitudes of the aspiration toward the establishment of a political society" (Edward Shils, "On the Comparative Study of the New States," in C. Geertz [ed.], *Old Societies and New States* [New York: Free Press, 1963], pp. 1–26, at p. 6).

[5] Moore has suggested that we now know that a variety of political forms are capable of both congruence and conflict with economic development (Wilbert Moore, *Social Change* [Englewood Cliffs, N.J.: Prentice-Hall, Inc., 1963], p. 112).

at the macrosociological level leads to a concern for how pre-existing values and structures can provide bases for identification with and commitment to larger social frameworks than those of segmental groups and primordial loyalties.[6] Here traditional symbols and leadership forms can be vital parts of the value bases supporting modernizing frameworks.

In exploring the concepts of tradition and modernity we shall discuss the assumptions of conflict between them. These assumptions are inconsistent with recent studies which will reveal a wide range of possible alternatives and show that "tradition" is a more specific and ambiguous phenomenon than usually realized.

Fallacies in the Assumptions of the Traditional–Modern Polarity

In assuming that new economic and political processes face an unchanging and uniform body of institutional procedures and cultural values, the linear theory of change greatly distorts the history and variety of civilizations. In this section we will examine seven assumptions of this theory and indicate the difficulties in its use.

Fallacy 1: Developing Societies Have Been Static Societies

It is fallacious to assume that a traditional society has always existed in its present form or that the recent past represents an unchanged situation. What is seen today and labeled as the "traditional society" is often itself a product of change. The conquests of foreign powers and the growth of social and cultural movements deeply influenced the character of family life, religious belief and practice, and social structure in India over many centuries.[7] Islamic civilization provided vital alternatives to caste and to political groupings. The impact of British culture and institutions has been immense.[8] Even India's caste system has by no means been a fixed and invariant system.[9]

The conception of India as a non-industrial and agricultural society, only now opened to industrialism, also needs revision. The decline of native Indian industries in the late eighteenth and early nineteenth centuries was a consequence of the protection of British textile manufacturers, then

6 This is a major problem discussed in Clifford Geertz (ed.), *op. cit.* See especially papers by Shils, Geertz, D. Apter, and M. Marriott.

7 For a critical analysis and refinement of those views of India based on Hindu scriptures, as were those of Max Weber, see M. N. Srinivas, *Caste in Modern India* (Bombay: Asia Publishing House, 1962), especially Introduction and chaps. i and xii. A similar point is made in Harold Gould, "The West's Real Debt to the East," *Quest* (January–March, 1962), pp. 31–39.

8 Percival Spears, India (Ann Arbor: University of Michigan Press, 1960); Charles Heimsath, *Indian Nationalism and Hindu Social Reform* (Princeton, N.J.: Princeton University Press, 1964), chap. i; Srinivas, *op. cit.,* chap. v; Gould, *op. cit.*

9 Srinivas, *op. cit.*; Bernard Cohn, "Power, Land and Social Relations in 19th Century Banaras" (Paper presented at meeting of the American Asian Studies Society, Washington, D.C., 1964).

spearheading the Industrial Revolution in England. The shift of both rural and urban artisans to the land was an important ingredient in the buildup of an agricultural surplus population. Even the system of land tenure in existence just before independence was the product of fairly recent changes.[10] To speak of the traditional feudal structure of India is to confuse recent history with past history. Tradition has been open to change before its present encounters with the West and with purposeful, planned change.

Fallacy 2: Traditional Culture is a Consistent Body of Norms and Values

In elaborating the distinction and interaction between the "great tradition" of urban centers and the "little tradition" of village communities, anthropologists have called our attention to the diversity and the existence of alternatives in what has been supposed to be a uniform body of rules and values. We must avoid accepting the written and intellectualized versions of a culture as only the literate form of a common set of beliefs and behavior patterns. The distinction between "popular" religion and the religion of the literati elite has long been a recognition of this difficulty in characterizing the "religion" of a society.[11]

Even within the literate forms of a tradition, inconsistency and opposition are marked; the Sermon on the Mount and *The Wealth of Nations* are both part of Western culture, Catholicism and Protestantism are Christian religions, and even within the single Church of Peter, diverse monastic orders have expressed a catholicity of values. Hindu philosophical and religious teaching is consistent with a number of diverse orientations to life. The doctrine of the four *ashramas,* for example, conceives of the good life as one in which men pursue different values at different stages in the life cycle.[12]

The importance of this diversity is that it provides legitimizing princi-

---

[10] R. C. Dutt, *Economic History of India* (London: Routledge & Kegan Paul, 1908), pp. 32, 261; S. Bhattacharya, *East India Company and the Economy of Bengal* (London: Luzac, 1954), pp. 158–59; Vikas Misra, *Hinduism and Economic Growth* (London: Oxford University Press, 1962), chap. iii; Milton Singer, "Changing Craft Traditions in India," in W. Moore and A. Feldman (eds.), *Labor Commitment and Social Change in Development Areas* (New York: SSRC, 1960), pp. 258–76; Neil Smelser, *Social Change in the Industrial Revolution* (Chicago: University of Chicago Press, 1959), pp. 109–16; Robert Frykenburg, "Traditional Processes of Power: Land Control in Andrha" (Paper presented to the meeting of the Association for Asian Studies Society, Washington, D.C., 1964); Daniel Thorner, *The Agrarian Prospect in India* (Delhi: University Press, 1956).

[11] In a study of religious behavior among low-caste sweepers, Pauline Kolenda has recently presented a vivid picture of the differences in the Hinduism of higher and of lower social levels ("Religious Anxiety and Hindu Fate," *Journal of Asian Studies,* XXIII [June, 1964], 71–82).

[12] For a description of the doctrine of Ashramas, see K. M. Sen, *Hinduism* (London: Penguin Books, 1961), chap. iii.

ples for a wide set of alternative forms of behavior. This point has been rather convincingly made in the recent discussion of economic development and cultural values in India.[13] Neither the behavior of popular religion nor teachings of the scriptures are devoid of moral bases for materialistic motivations or for disciplined and rational pursuit of wealth. Everyone need not be a *sadhu* (holy man) at all times.

Fallacy 3: Traditional Society is a Homogeneous Social Structure

Like other societies, Indian society has institutionalized different styles of life in different groups, both within and without the caste system. Such divisions of labor make it possible for specific communal and status groups to be the bearers of traditions which differ from the dominant streams yet enable valued social functions to be performed. While Weber referred to "the Protestant ethic," the specific sects who carried the ethic were by no means typical of all Protestant groups.[14] The role of foreign and pariah peoples has often been commented upon as a source of economic growth, innovation, and entrepreneurial behavior.[15] The Jews in Europe, the Muslims in West Africa, the Chinese in Indonesia, and the East Indians in East Africa are examples of groups whose marginality has rendered them able to engage in the impersonality of market behavior and to remain aloof from the status consumption demands of the indigenous population. In India, the Parsees and the Jains have been potent carriers of economic innovation and the development of large-scale industrial production.

Generalizations about the anti-economic character of the Hindu traditions lose sight of the provision for specific groups which are ethically capable of carrying a logic of economic growth and change. Within the caste system of Hinduism, the untouchables have been able to perform tabooed occupations necessary to the economy. Other castes have developed traditions of business and commerce which, although dishonored in Hindu "tradition," are permissible and even obligatory for the Marwari, the Chettiar, and the Baniya. It is their very legitimation within existing structure that permits their acceptance and implementation of innovating economic behavior.

[13] Milton Singer, "Cultural Values in India's Economic Development," *Annals,* CCCV (May, 1956), 81–91. See the clash of viewpoints among Goheen, Singer, and Srinivas in the discussion of "India's Cultural Values and Economic Development," *Economic Development and Cultural Change,* VIII (October, 1958), 1–13. Vikas Misra (*op. cit.*), similarly to Singer and Srinivas, does not see the cultural elements of Hinduism as an impediment to economic growth.

[14] For an account of the atypicality of Quaker economic rationality among American colonials, see F. B. Tolles, *Meeting House and Counting House; The Quaker Merchants of Colonial Philadelphia, 1682–1763* (Chapel Hill: University of North Carolina Press, 1948).

[15] Sheldon Stryker, "Social Structure and Prejudice," *Social Problems,* VI (1959), 340–54; Bert Hoselitz, "Main Concepts in the Analysis of the Social Implications of Technical Change," in Hoselitz and Moore, *Industrialization and Society* (New York: UNESCO, 1963), pp. 11–29, especially pp. 24–28.

Fallacy 4: Old Traditions Are Displaced by New Changes

The capacity of old and new cultures and structures to exist without conflict and even with mutual adaptations is a frequent phenomenon of social change; the old is not necessarily *replaced* by the new. The acceptance of a new product, a new religion, a new mode of decision-making does not necessarily lead to the disappearance of the older form. New forms may only increase the range of alternatives. Both magic and medicine can exist side by side, used alternatively by the same people.

The syncretism of inconsistent elements has long been noted in the acceptance of religious usages and beliefs. Paganism and Catholicism have often achieved a mutual tolerance into a new form of ritualism drawn from each in Spanish-speaking countries.[16] The "great tradition" of the urban world in India has by no means pushed aside the "little tradition" of the village as they made contact. Interaction has led to a fusion and mutual penetration.[17] We have become increasingly aware that the outcome of modernizing processes and traditional forms is often an admixture in which each derives a degree of support from the other, rather than a clash of opposites.

Fallacy 5: Traditional and Modern Forms Are Always in Conflict

The abstraction of a "traditional society" as a type separate from a specific historical and cultural setting ignores the diversity of content in specific traditions which influence the acceptance, rejection, or fusion of modernist forms. Japan is unlike the Western societies in the ways in which "feudalism" and industrial development have been fused to promote economic growth.[18] Commitment to emperor and to family, a collectivistic orientation, and a high degree of vertical immobility have been factors supporting social and economic change in the Japanese context while they appear to have been factors producing resistance in the individualistic culture of the West. In this context the hardened commitment of labor to a specific

16 For one account of such syncretisms, see Robert Redfield, *The Folk Culture of Yucatan* (Chicago: University of Chicago Press, 1941), chap. ix.

17 "While elements of the great tradition have become parts of local festivals, they do not appear to have entered village festival custom 'at the expense of' much that is or was the little tradition. Instead we see evidence of accretion in a transmutation form without apparent replacement and without rationalization of the accumulated and transformed elements" (McKim Marriott, "Little Communities in an Indigenous Civilization," in M. Marriott [ed.] *Village India* [Chicago: University of Chicago Press, 1955], p. 196).

18 For some analyses of this phenomenon in Japan, see Reinhard Bendix, *Nation-Building and Citizenship* (New York: John Wiley & Sons, 1965) chap. vi; Robert Scalapino, "Ideology and Modernization: The Japanese Case," in D. Apter (ed.) *Ideology and Discontent* (New York: Free Press, 1965), pp. 93–127; Everett Hagen, *On the Theory of Social Change* (Homewood, Ill.: Dorsey Press, 1962), chap. xiv.

employer operated to promote economic growth while the same process appeared an impediment in the West.[19]

Traditional structures can supply skills, and traditional values can supply sources of legitimation which are capable of being utilized in pursuit of new goals and with new processes. In one Indonesian town, Geertz found the sources of economic expansion largely among the *prijaji*, the Muslim group representing new forces in religion as well as in business. In another town, the source of economic innovation and business expansion was in the traditional nobility. The *prijaji* could build on, but were also hampered by, the characteristics of the bazaar modes of trading and the closed social networks of a pariah group. The traditional nobility, however, was well equipped to form a business class through the wide social networks and the strength of their authority, which rested on a traditional base.[20]

Anthropologists have made the same point in connection with problems of selective culture change. One traditional culture may possess values more clearly congruent with modernization than another; another may cling more tenaciously to its old ways than another. Ottenberg's study of tribes in West Africa found them able to accept and utilize the British culture in Nigeria to a much greater extent than was true of the other major Nigerian tribes. The Ibo's system of voluntary associations, coupled with their values of individualism and achievement, adapted them well to the kinds of opportunities and demands which British colonialism brought. In contrast, the Masai in East Africa are a notorious case of resistance to culture change, fiercely upholding existing ways with very little accommodation.[21]

Fallacy 6: Tradition and Modernity Are Mutually Exclusive Systems

A given institution or cultural system contains several aspects or dimensions. Each dimension does not function in the same way in response to new influences on a society. Tradition and modernity are frequently mutually reinforcing, rather than systems in conflict.

[19] For a description and analysis of labor commitment in Japan, see James Abegglen, *The Japanese Factory* (Glencoe, Ill.: Free Press, 1958); Solomon B. Levine, *Industrial Relations in Postwar Japan* (Urbana: University of Illinois Press, 1958), chap. ii. Richard Lambert describes a similar process operating in western India but sees it as a possible impediment to economic growth (Lambert, *Workers, Factories and Social Change in India* [Princeton, N.J.: Princeton University University Press, 1963], especially chap. iii and pp. 214–21).

[20] Clifford Geertz, "Social Change and Economic Modernization in Two Indonesian Towns," in Hagen, *op. cit.*, chap. xvi.

[21] Simon Ottenberg, "Ibo Receptivity to Change," in M. Herskovits and W. Bascom, *Continuity and Change in African Culture* (Chicago: University of Chicago Press, 1959), pp. 130–43; Harold Schneider, "Pakot Resistance to Change," *ibid.*, pp. 144–67. Also see the description and analysis of labor commitment in East Africa in A. Elkin and L. Fallers, "The Mobility of Labor," in W. Moore and A. Feldman, *op. cit.*, pp. 238–54.

Earlier theories of economic growth viewed extended family systems and caste structure as impediments to economic growth.[22] We now recognize, however, that such relations are complex and can vary from one context to another. Caste as an unalloyed impediment to economic growth has been much exaggerated through failing to balance its role in the division of labor and in caste mobility (one dimension) against its tendencies toward status demands as limitations on desire to accumulate capital (a second dimension).[23] Efforts on the part of castes to become mobile, to attempt improvements in their material as well as their ritual position are by no means new to Indian life. The expanded scope of regional castes, the development of caste associations, and the importance of castes in politics are not impediments to economic growth.[24] They enable credit facility, occupational sponsorship and training, and political influence to be made available on a basis of segmental, traditional loyalties. This brings an element of trust and obligation into an economic context where suspicion and distrust are otherwise frequently the rule between persons unconnected by other ties than the "purely" economic.

Studies of the impact of industrialization on family life in preindustrial and primitive societies similarly indicate the compatibility of extended family forms with industrialism.[25] In the context of Indian economic growth, the large extended families of the Tatas, Birlas, and Dalmias are among the most striking instances of major industrial organizations growing out of and supported by traditional family units. Berna's study of entrepreneurship in Madras provides additional information, among small businesses, of the extended family as a major source of savings and capital accumulation.[26]

The role of traditional values in the form of segmental loyalties and principles of legitimate authority are of great importance in understanding the possibilities for the occurrence of unified and stable polities at a national

[22] For a generalized statement of this view, stressing an open system of social mobility as a prerequisite for economic growth, see Kingsley Davis, "The Role of Class Mobility in Economic Development," *Population Review,* VI (July, 1962), 67–73.

[23] This is a major conclusion of V. Misra, *op. cit.*

[24] Caste associations and caste loyalties appear to be important sources of social support in urban India and are growing in size and number (see Srinivas, *op. cit.*; M. Weiner, *The Politics of Scarcity* (Bombay: Asia Publishing House, 1962), chap. iii; Bernard Cohn, "Changing Traditions of a Low Caste," *Journal of American Folklore,* LXXI (July–September, 1958), 413–21; Lloyd and Suzanne Rudolph, "The Political Role of India's Caste Associations," *Pacific Affairs,* XXXIII (March, 1960), 5–22.

[25] William Goode, "Industrialization and Family Change," in B. Hoselitz and W. Moore, *op. cit.,* chap. xii; Jean Comhaire, "Economic Change and the Extended Family," *Annals,* CCCV (May, 1956), 45–52; Manning Nash, *Machine Age Maya* (Glencoe, Ill.: Free Press, 1958).

[26] James Berna, "Patterns of Entrepreneurship in South India," *Economic Development and Cultural Change,* VII (April, 1959), 343–62.

level. The contemporary Indian political process utilizes caste, village, and religious community as basic segmental groups through which the individual and the family are drawn into modern political institutions. Primary ties of kinship and clan are in process of fusion to centralized structures of national, participative politics.[27]

The "stuff" of much modern politics in India is itself drawn from the pre-existing struggles between caste, religion, region, and economic groupings. We have become aware that much of what appears to be ideological and economic conflict in Indian politics is actuated and bolstered by struggles for social and economic position among the various caste groups.[28]

The setting of traditional and pre-existing conflicts in the context of new institutions is crucial to understanding Indian educational change. Critics of Indian education often point to the intensive desire for humanistic curriculums among both educators and students, contrasting this with the presumed necessities of technical and agricultural skills in economic development. They fail to see that the politics of egalitarianism revolves around the quest for status in traditional terms. Groups that have not been part of the educational structure in the past now utilize it to gain status increases as well as jobs. This is of great importance in a nation attempting to draw formerly isolated groups into a national identity.[29]

Fallacy 7: Modernizing Processes Weaken Traditions

This discussion of Indian education suggests that new institutions and values may, and often do, fuse and interpenetrate the old. In his influential paper on caste mobility, M. N. Srinivas has shown that, while higher social levels appear to be "westernizing" their life styles, when lower and middle levels seek mobility they do so by becoming more devotedly Hinduistic, following more Brahminical styles, and otherwise Sanskritizing their behavior.[30] The fluidity introduced by political competition under independence and democracy becomes harnessed to a more traditional orientation.

[27] This is a dominant theme in contemporary discussion of Indian politics (Joseph Gusfield, "Political Community and Group Interests in Modern India," *Pacific Affairs*, XXXVI [Summer, 1965], 123–41, and the literature cited there).

[28] "The 'revolution of rising expectations' is in reality an explosion of social competition...not aimed at American, British or Russian living standards, but are demands by one group for improvement...vis-à-vis another group within India" (Weiner, *op. cit.*, p. 71).

[29] The social composition of university students in India shows a very high preponderance of high castes in the student bodies, although leveling processes are at work. This situation, and its significance is described in my forthcoming "Equality and Education in India," in Joseph Fisher [ed.], *Social Science and the Comparative Study of Educational Systems* (Scranton, Pa.: International Textbook Publishers, 1967). For a general analysis of Indian higher education, see Allen Grimshaw, "National Goals, Planned Social Change and Higher Education: The Indian Case," in R. Feldmesser and B. Z. Sobel, *Education and Social Change* (New York: John Wiley & Sons, in press).

[30] "Sanskritization and Westernization," in Srinivas, *op. cit.*

The technological consequences of increased transportation, communication, literacy, and horizontal mobility, in furthering the spread of ideas, also intensifies the spread and influence of the "great tradition" into more and more communities and across various social levels.[31] Pilgrimages to distant shrines become easier and enable the conception of a unified, national religion to take firmer root. Caste groups can now be formed on regional and even national lines, buttressed by associational life and written journals. The spread of community development and of educational facilities brings in its wake new, semiurban personnel who carry the Sanskritic traditions fully as much, if not more so, than they do the westernizing influences.[32] The communities of the "little tradition" are, in fact, more open to such traditional winds of change than to wholly new movements. The holy men and the wandering players who carry religious messages and dramas drawn from the Hindu great traditions are more likely to effect attention than the movies.[33]

Tradition, Ideology, and Nationhood

Tradition is not something waiting out there, always over one's shoulder. It is rather plucked, created, and shaped to present needs and aspirations in a given historical situation. Men refer to aspects of the past as tradition in grounding their present actions in some legitimating principle. In this fashion, tradition becomes an ideology, a program of action in which it functions as a goal or a justificatory base. The concern for tradition as an explicit policy is not an automatic response to change but is itself a movement capable of analysis.

In similar fashion, to be "modern" appears in many new nations as an aspiration toward which certain groups seek to move the society. "Modern" becomes a perceived state of things functioning as a criterion against which to judge specific actions and a program of actions to guide policy. In Scalapino's apt phrase, intellectuals in new nations utilize "teleological insight"—the assumed ability to read the future of their own society by projecting it in accordance with the experience and trends of "advanced" nations.[34] Such insight operates as a crucial determinant in developing goals, but it too is a creation of choice among possibilities, not a fixed and self-evident set of propositions.

The desire to be modern and the desire to preserve tradition operate as significant movements in the new nations and developing economies.

[31] McKim Marriott, "Changing Channels of Cultural Transmission in Indian Civilization," in L. P. Vidyarthi (ed.), *Aspects of Religion in Indian Society* (Meerut: Kedar Nath Ram Nath, 1961), pp. 13–25.

[32] The schoolteacher, in these decades of expanding primary education, is a source of Sanskritic as well as Western influences. See David Mandelbaum's account in "The World and the World View of the Koda," in M. Marriott (ed.), *Village India,* pp. 223–54, especially pp. 239 ff.

[33] John Gumperz, "Religion as a Form of Communication in North India," *Journal of Asian Studies,* XXIII (June, 1964), 89–98.

[34] Scalapino, *op. cit.,* p. 106.

It is our basic point here that these desires, functioning as ideologies, are not always in conflict; that the quest for modernity depends upon and often finds support in the ideological upsurge of traditionalism. In this process, tradition may be changed, stretched, and modified, but a unified and nationalized society makes great use of the traditional in its search for a consensual base to political authority and economic development.

Tradition and National Unification

Writing about African intellectuals in the formerly French colonies, Immanuel Wallerstein remarks that these parts of Africa are the chief centers for the ideological development of "Negritude"—the preservation and development of a uniquely indigenous African culture.[35] Here, where the intellectuals were trained in the French language and where they fully accepted the French culture, it is necessary to identify and discover a national cultural tradition and to self-consciously aid its development. In a similar fashion, an Indian colleague of mine once remarked that "Indians are obsessed with Indianness."

Many observers have noted the phenomenon of the revival of indigenous tradition as a phase of nationalistic and independence movements, especially where intellectuals had come to look to some other country as a basic source of new values.[36] Such reactions have set in among Russian intellectuals against France in the nineteenth century, among the Indonesians against the Dutch, among the Japanese against Europe; and against the British among the Indians both during and after the struggle for independence. The Indian intellectuals, westernized and European in cultural orientation, underwent a renaissance of traditional Hinduism as one aspect of the struggle against colonial dominion.[37] Despite their general commitment to modernization (often against the British post–Sepoy rebellion policy of maintaining native custom), a recrudescence of Indian national identity was partially fostered by explicit adoption of customs and styles which were both traditional and closer to popular behavior. It was this ideology which Gandhi gave to the movement, even as he sought the abolition of many features of that tradition.

The issue of the nationalist movement is not abated in its victory. For the new elites of newly independent nations, the issue is not so much that of overcoming tradition but of finding ways of synthesizing and blending tradition and modernity. While it is now possible for the urbanized and

[35] Immanuel Wallerstein, *Africa—the Politics of Independence* (New York: Vintage Books, 1961), pp. 75–76.

[36] *Ibid.,* chap. vii; John Kautsky, *Political Change in Underdeveloped Areas* (New York: John Wiley & Sons, 1962), pp. 53–54; Heimsath, *op. cit.,* chap. xii; Mary Mattosian, "Ideologies of Delayed Industrialization," *Economic Development and Cultural Change* (April, 1958), pp. 217–28.

[37] This "revivalist" stream was only one of the major themes in Indian nationalism, but it had a great impact throughout the movement (Heimsath, *op. cit.*; A. R. Desai, *Social Background of Indian Nationalism* [Bombay: Popular Book Depot, 1959], chaps. xiii, xviii).

intellectual elite to wear Saville Row and avoid the clothes of Chowri Bazaar without being a traitor, the issues of personal integrity and of political functions still remain.

Those who depict the elites in India as cut off from roots in an indigenous civilization ignore the ways in which Hinduism and Indian family life exert strong pulls as continuing aspects of Indian life, even where highly westernized. Almost always the Indian intellectual speaks a regional language as his mother tongue, is steeped in classic Sanskrit literature, and is deeply tied to an extended family. Parental arrangement is still the very dominant mode of marital selection, and he is often married to a highly traditional wife.[38]

Independence, even within the westernized circles, has given continuing support to a movement toward the recapturing of Hindu folklore and the furtherance of tradition as a source of national unity in a common culture. What Indian book or journal does not have its section that links modern thought or institutions to analogues in Hindu scripture? How often is the romanticization of the village and the rejection of the city not found among vigorous exponents of political democracy and economic change? This ideological construction of Indian tradition is offered as a "great tradition," and this Indian populism is found among intellectual and urbanized elites as it is in the provincial and peasant villages.

Nationalism is deeply committed to both horns of the dilemma of tradition and modernity. The effort to define a national heritage in the form of a set of continuing traditions is also a way of coping with the wide gap that separates elite and mass, city and village, region and region in the Indian context. It is a complement to the modernizing processes which are involved in the aspiration toward a unified nation. A common culture that cuts across the segmental and primordial loyalties is a basis for national identity and consensus. Without it, the modernization based on nationhood lacks a foundation for legitimating central authority.

In describing these movements we are not referring to efforts to pit tradition against modernity. This is certainly to be discovered in populist and aristocratic movements which call for the rejection of economic growth and the resistance or abolition of imported institutions and values. In India this can be seen in the xenophobic and militant Hinduism which characterized the RSS and still is a potent political force in the Hindu Mahasabha and, to a lesser degree, in the Jan Sangh party.[39] This appeal

---

[38] Shils has made this point in his study of Indian intellectuals (Edward Shils, *The Intellectual between Tradition and Modernity* [The Hague: Mouton & Co., 1961], especially pp. 60–67).

[39] See Richard Lambert, "Hindu Communal Groups in Indian Politics," in R. Park and I. Tinker (eds.), *Leadership and Political Institutions in India* (Madras: Oxford University Press, 1960), pp. 211–24). Even in the Swatantra Party, a movement led by an antitraditionalist set of ideologies, its anti-Congress character has drawn to it strong forces of antimodernism (see Howard Erdman, "India's Swatantra Party," *Pacific Affairs* [Winter, 1963–64], pp. 394–410).

to an undisturbed society avoids the dilemma fully as much as does the ideology based on a linear theory of change.

The synthesis of tradition and modernity is evident in Gandhian influence. Was Gandhi a traditionalist or a modernizer? Asking the question poses the immense difficulty in separating the various streams in reform and social change blowing over the Indian subcontinent. Certainly his genius lay in uniting disparities, in utilizing the traditional authority of the holy man for social reforms and for political union. His leadership of the independence movement gave India a common experience which has been one of the crucial legacies of the independence movement to its present national existence and to the authority of the Congress Party.

The Gandhianism of the neo-Gandhians, such as Vinoba Bhave and Jayaprakash Narayan, represents an important ideological development in the search for political institutions which will cope with the problems of nationhood within indigenous cultural forms.[40] But Gandhian Socialism represents only one form in which this drive toward a synthesis is manifest. The recent movement toward the development of local autonomy and participation in India rests both on the growing political power of village communities and the ideological force which has recreated a tradition of Indian village democracy. In the various proposals for a system of Panchayati Raj (movement toward greater local power in economic decisions at the village level), Indian government and politics are wrestling with the problem of creating a consensus for developmental policies which will have the legitimating support in tradition, even if the tradition is newly discovered.[41]

The Mediating Elites

Elsewhere we have analyzed the growing political power of new, less westernized, and more localistic political elites and sub-elites in India.[42] Such people, with sources of power in state and region, mediate between the westernized elites and the mass of the Indian society in ways which bring a greater degree of traditional commitments and styles, of caste and other primordial ties, into the political and cultural arena.

The very process of political egalitarianism and modernization contains the seeds of new ideologies of tradition. Literacy in India not only stimulates a common cultural content but has also led to ideologies of regionalism,

[40] This quest for an indigenous form of political democracy is marked in Narayan's writings, as well as in conversation (see Jaya Prakash Narayan, *The Dual Revolution* [Tanjore: Sarvodaya Prachuralaya, 1959]; *Swaraj for the People* [Varanasi: Ahkhih Bharat Sarva Seva Sangh, 1961]).

[41] See the analysis of the Panchayats in my paper on Indian political community, cited above (n. 27); and in Reinhard Bendix, "Public Authority in a Developing Political Community: The Case of India," *Archives Europeennes de Sociologie*, IV (1963), 39–85, especially 61 ff.

[42] Gusfield, "Political Community and Group Interests in Modern India," *op. cit.*

extolling the virtues of regional languages and cultures.[43] While such movements impede the development of an all-India cultural consensus, they are neither antimodern nor specifically anti-India. They do, however, presage the decline of that form of national elite that has been associated with colonial cultural influences. India appears to be approaching and entering a phase in which modernization will be directed and implemented by persons whose loyalties and ideologies are considerably more traditionalized than has been true in the past decades.

The Ambiguities of Modernity

Just as "tradition" is renewed, created, and discovered, so too "modernity" as a goal toward which men aspire appears in some specific historical guise. The post-colonial elites owed much to the cultures of the colonial powers in India. Through travel, through language and literature, through colonial educational institutions, they had absorbed a picture of modernity as it was practiced in one country at one time. It is not a random selection that led the Indian elites to conceive of politics in the British mode or led Nehru's political pronouncements and judgments of the 1950's to echo the liberalism of Harold Laski in the 1920's.

But being modern is far more ambiguous than being British. The disappearance of the postcolonial elites carries with it an increase in the range of alternatives ideologically open to the new, more traditionalized political groups. The possible routes to economic wealth and political nationhood are considerable, as we have shown in the earlier section of this paper. As countries come onto the scene of self-conscious aspiration toward the modern, they are presented with more and more successful models of the process. England, Germany, the United States, Japan, the Soviet Union are highly diverse in political institutions and histories. In the sense of having achieved high standards of living and egalitarian societies, they are all reasonably "developed."

The Cultural Framework of Modernity

We cannot easily separate modernity and tradition from some *specific* tradition and some *specific* modernity, some version which functions ideologically as a directive. The modern comes to the traditional society as a particular culture with its own traditions. In this respect it has been impossible to divorce modernization from some process of westernization. McKim Marriott has made this point most vividly in analyzing the reasons for villagers' rejection of Western and westernized doctors. The role of the doctor, as a technical expert, grants him authority in modern culture

---

[43] Witness the rise of self-conscious rediscovery of Hindi literary tradition. The linguistic and cultural renaissances in many parts of India are postindependence phenomena [see Selig Harrison, *India: The Most Dangerous Decade* (Princeton, N.J.: Princeton University Press, 1960].

but not in the Indian village where technical and commercial skills have a low approval. Efficiency and thrift, those two great Western virtues, are not such in the eyes of the peasant in Utter Pradesh.[44]

The social scientist's designation of specific institutional forms as modern may also function as ideology and as aspiration, specifying what it is in a particular culture which is emulative. The concept of political development is far more difficult and culture-bound than is that of economic development. Even with the latter, we clearly recognize a diversity of institutional routes to industrialization and higher incomes. To label, apart from a specific context, either a capitalistic, socialistic, or communistic approach to economic growth as antithetical to economic growth would certainly seem fallacious to the economist. Similarly, the industrialized and egalitarian societies of the West have by no means demonstrated either a uniform or an unchanging form of polity. The Soviet Union, France, Germany, and the United States (and we might well include Japan) are hardly a single form of political structure, and each of these has in turn undergone many changes during its history. They are all national polities, to be sure, and all ones in which the population is mobilized, to a degree, to political participation and loyalty. These facts, however, state problems in a wider fashion, without specific institutional directives.

To conclude, the all too common practice of pitting tradition and modernity against each other as paired opposites tends to overlook the mixtures and blends which reality displays. Above all, it becomes an ideology of antitraditionalism, denying the necessary and usable ways in which the past serves as support, especially in the sphere of values and political legitimation, to the present and the future. We need a perspective toward change which does not deny the specific and contextual character of events.

I do not know much about the total style of life of that passenger on the Kodama express. To think of him as fixed on a continuum between tradition and modernity (as well as between Kyoto and Tokyo) hides the immense variations and possibilities, the capacity for blending opposites, which human beings and nations possess. In the concepts of the traditional and the modern, we are certainly wrestling with a feature of social change. We need to recognize that there is a variety of events on the wrestling program and that the outcomes, unlike many wrestling matches, are quite in doubt.

---

44 "It is important to note that a distinction can be made between 'Western' and 'scientific' medicine. Westerners conceive of a Western medicine as a system of curing based on 'rational' techniques and 'scientific' concepts of cause and effect. But this characteristic...only partly determines the total range of practices involved in treatment and cure. Treatment is bedded in a social as well as a scientific matrix, and many practices of the Western doctor are based on cultural values and ideas of personal relationships that are peculiar to Western society" (McKim Marriott, "Western Medicine in a Village of Northern India," in S. N. Eisenstadt [ed.], *Comparative Social Problems* [New York: Free Press, 1964], pp. 47–60, at p. 59).

5 / Structural Changes Associated with Development

Neil J. Smelser

Variability in the Process of Development

LET US NOW assume that the vicious circle of poverty has been broken—by what exact mechanism it does not matter for now—and that economic growth has begun. What happens to the social structure under such circumstances?

No simple answer to this question is available, because national differences make for a variety of patterns of development. Processes of economic development may differ in the following ways:

1. Variations in the *pre-industrial conditions* of the country. A society's value-system may be congenial or antipathetic to industrial values. The society may be tightly or loosely integrated. Its level of wealth may be low or high. This wealth may be evenly or unevenly distributed. From the standpoint of population, the society may be "young and empty" (e.g., Australia) or "old and crowded" (e.g., India). The society may be politically dependent, recently independent, or altogether autonomous. Such pre-existing conditions shape the impact of the forces of economic development and make for great differences in national experiences with development.

2. Variations in the *impetus* to development. The pressures to develop may stem from the internal implications of a value-system (as in Weber's theory of ascetic Protestantism), from a desire for national security and prestige, from a desire for material prosperity, or from a combination of these. Political coercion may be used to form a labor force. Or these pressures may be economic, as in the case of population pressure on the land, or loss of handicraft markets to cheap imported products. Or economic and political pressures combine, as in the case of a tax on peasants payable only in money. Or the pressures may be social, as in the case of the desire to escape burdensome aspects of the old order. Such differences influence the adjustment to modernization greatly.

3. Variations in the *path* toward modernization. The development sequence may begin with light consumer industries. Or there may be an attempt to introduce heavy, capital-intensive industries first. The government may take an active or passive role in shaping the pattern of investment. The tempo of industrialization may be fast or slow. All these affect the nature of structural change and the degree of discomfort created by this change.

Reprinted from *The Sociology of Economic Life,* © 1963, pp. 105–15. Reprinted by permission of the author and Prentice-Hall, Inc., Englewood Cliffs, New Jersey.

4. Variations in the *advanced stages* of modernization. Societies may vary in the emergent distribution of industries in their developed economics. They may vary in the emergent relations between state and economy, state and religion, and so on. While all advanced industrialized societies have their "industrialization" in common, unique national differences remain. For instance, social class differs in its social significance in the United States and Great Britain, even though both are highly developed countries.

5. Variations in the *content and timing of dramatic events* during development. Wars, revolutions, rapid migrations, and natural catastrophes may influence the course of economic and social development.

Because of these sources of variation, it is virtually impossible to discover hard and fast empirical generalizations concerning the evolution of social structures during economic and social development. Our purpose, therefore, in this chapter, is not to search for such generalizations, but to outline certain very general, ideal-type structural changes associated with development. These changes are three: structural differentiation, integration, and social disturbances. On the basis of these changes we may classify, describe and analyze varying national experiences. Variations such as those just described determine in part the distinctive national response to these universal aspects of development, but this in no way detracts from their "universality."

Structural Differentiation in Periods of Development

The concept of structural differentiation can be employed to encompass many of the structural changes that accompany the movement from pre-industrial to industrial society. Simply defined, differentiation refers to the evolution from a multi-functional role structure to several more specialized structures. The following are typical examples: (1) In the transition from domestic to factory industry, the division of labor increases, and the economic activities previously lodged in the family move to the factory. (2) With the rise of a formal educational system, the training functions previously performed in large part by the family and church are established in a more specialized unit, the school. (3) The modern political party has a more complex structure than tribal factions, and is less likely to be fettered with kinship loyalties, competition for religious leadership, etc. Formally defined, then, structural differentiation is a process whereby "*one* social role or organization...differentiates into *two or more* roles or organizations which function more effectively in the new historical circumstances. The new social units are structurally distinct from each other, but taken together are functionally equivalent to the original unit."[1]

Differentiation concerns only changes in role-structure. We should not confuse the concept with two closely related notions. The first of these is the cause or motivation for entering the differentiated role. Wage-labor, for instance, may result from a desire for economic improvement, from

---

[1] Neil J. Smelser, *Social Change in the Industrial Revolution* (Chicago: University of Chicago Press, 1959), p. 2.

political coercion, or even from a desire to fulfill traditional obligations (e.g., to use wages to supply a dowry). These "reasons" should be kept conceptually distinct from differentiation itself. The second notion concerns the integration of differentiated roles. As differentiated wage-labor begins to appear, for instance, there also appear legal norms, labor exchanges, trade unions, and so on, which regulate—with varying degrees of success— the relations between labor and management. Such readjustments, even though they sometimes produce a new social unit, should be considered separately from role-specialization in other functions.

Let us now inquire into the process of differentiation in several different social realms.

Differentiation of Economic Activities

Typically in underdeveloped countries production is located in kinship units. Subsistence farming predominates; other industry is supplementary but still attached to family and village. In some cases occupational position is determined largely by an extended group such as the caste. Similarly, exchange and consumption are embedded deeply in family and village. In subsistence agriculture there is a limited amount of independent exchange outside the family; this means that production and consumption occur in the same social context. Exchange systems proper are lodged in kinship and community (e.g., reciprocal exchange) in stratification systems (e.g., redistribution according to caste membership) and in political systems (e.g., taxes, tributes, payments in kind, forced labor). Under such conditions market systems are underdeveloped, and the independent power of money to command the movement of goods and services is minimal.

As the economy develops, several kinds of economic activity are removed from this family-community complex. In agriculture, the introduction of money-crops marks a differentiation between the social contexts of production and consumption. Agricultural wage-labor sometimes undermines the family production unit. In industry it is possible to identify several levels of differentiation. Household industry, the simplest form, parallels subsistence agriculture in that it supplies "the worker's own needs, unconnected with trade." "Handicraft production" splits production and consumption, though frequently consumption takes place in the local community. "Cottage industry," on the other hand, frequently involves a differentiation between consumption and community, since production is "for the market, for an unknown consumer, sold to a wholesaler who accumulates a stock."[2] Finally, manufacturing and factory systems segregate the worker from his capital and frequently from his family.

---

2 These "levels," which represent points on the continuum from structural fusion to structural differentiation, are taken from J. H. Boeke, *The Structure of the Netherlands Indian Economy* (New York: Institute of Pacific Relations, 1942), p. 90.

Similar differentiations appear simultaneously in the exchange system. Goods and services, previously exchanged on a non-economic basis, are pulled more and more into the market. Money now commands the movement of more and more goods and services, and thus begins to supplant— and sometimes undermine—the religious, political, familial or caste sanctions which previously had governed economic activity.

Empirically we may classify underdeveloped or semi-developed economies according to how far they they have moved along this line of differentiation. Migratory labor, for instance, may be a kind of compromise between full membership in a wage-labor force and attachment to an old community life; cottage industry introduces extended markets but retains the family-production fusion; the hiring of families in factories maintains a version of family production; the expenditure of wages on traditional items such as dowries also shows this half-way entry into the more differentiated industrial-urban structure. The reasons for these partial cases of differentiation include resistances on the part of the populace to give up traditional ways of life, the economics of demand for handmade products, and systems of racial discrimination against native labor. In any case, the concept of structural differentiation provides a yardstick to indicate the distance which the economic structure has evolved.

Differentiation of Family Activities

One implication of the removal of economic activities from the kinship nexus is that the family loses some of its previous functions, becoming a more specialized agency. The family ceases to be an economic unit of production; one or more members now leave the household to seek employment in the labor market. The family's activities become more concentrated on emotional gratification and socialization. While many compromise arrangements such as family hiring and migratory systems persist, the tendency is toward the segregation of family functions and economic functions.

Several related processes accompany this differentiation of the family from its other involvements: (a) Apprenticeship within the family declines. (b) Pressures develop against the intervention of family favoritism in the recruitment of labor and management. These pressures often lie in the demands of economic rationality. The intervention often persists, however, especially at the managerial levels, and in some cases (e.g., Japan) family ties continue as a major basis for labor recruitment. (c) The direct control of elders and collateral kinsmen over the nuclear family weakens. This marks, in structural terms, the differentiation of the nuclear family from the extended family. (d) One aspect of this loss of control is the growth of personal choice, love, and related criteria as the basis for courtship and marriage. Correspondingly, marriage arranged by elders and extended kinsmen declines in importance. (e) One result of this complex of processes is the changing status of women, who become generally less subordinated economically, politically, and socially to their husbands than under earlier conditions. Frequently these developments are accompanied by feminist movements.

In such ways structural differentiation undermines the old modes of integration in society. The control of extended family and village begin to dissolve in the enlarged and complicated social setting which differentiation involves. New problems are posed by this growing obsolescence of old integrative forms. We shall inquire presently into the emergence of new forms of integration.

Differentiation of Religious Systems

. . . Religious and nationalistic belief-systems vary in their effects on economic development. They may constitute a stimulus or an obstacle.[3] The logic of differentiation permits us to account for these contrasting effects. In the early phases of development, for instance, many traditional loyalties may have to be broken in order to set up more differentiated social structures. Because these established commitments and methods of integration are deeply rooted in the organization of traditional society, a very generalized and powerful value commitment is often required to "pry" individuals from these attachments. The values of ascetic and this-worldly religious beliefs, xenophobic national aspirations, and political ideologies such as socialism provide such a lever. All three have an "ultimacy" of commitment in the name of which a wide range of sacrifices can be demanded and procured.

The very success of these value-systems, however, breeds the conditions for their own weakening. In a perceptive statement, Weber noted that by the beginning of the twentieth century, when the capitalistic system was already highly developed, it no longer needed the impetus of ascetic Protestantism.[4] Capitalism had, by virtue of its conquest of much of Western society, solidly established an institutional base and a secular value-system of its own—"economic rationality." These secular economic values no longer needed the "ultimate" justification required in the newer, unsteadier days of economic revolution.

The development of autonomous values such as economic rationality constitute the secularization of religious values. In this process, other institutional spheres—economic, political, scientific, etc.—come to be established on an independent basis. The values governing these spheres are no longer sanctioned directly by religious beliefs, but by autonomous rationalities. Insofar as such rationalities replace religous sanctions in these spheres, secularization occurs.

Similarly, nationalistic and related value-systems undergo a process of secularization as differentiation proceeds. As a society moves toward more and more complex social organization, diffuse nationalism gives way to

[3] Above, pp. 41–42.

[4] *The Protestant Ethic and the Spirit of Capitalism* (London: Allen & Unwin, 1948), pp. 181–82.

more autonomous systems of rationality. The Soviet Union, for instance, as its social structure grows more differentiated, seems to be introducing more "independent" market mechanisms, "freer" social scientific investigation in some spheres, and so on. These measures are not, moreover, directly sanctioned by an appeal to nationalistic or communistic values.

Thus the paradoxical element in the role of religious or nationalistic values: Insofar as they encourage the breakup of old patterns, they may stimulate economic development; insofar as they resist their own subsequent secularization, however, the very same values may becomes a drag on economic advance and structural change.

Differentiation of Systems of Stratification

In discussing stratification, . . . we noted the importance of ascription-achievement in classifying ranking systems. We also asserted that collective forms of mobility (as opposed to individual mobility) are typically associated with ascribed systems of stratification.[5]

Many underdeveloped societies are characterized by ascribed systems of stratification and correspondingly by collective forms of mobility. Under conditions of economic development, moreover, structural differentiation involves a change in both these characteristics:

1. Other evaluative standards intrude on ascribed memberships. For instance, McKim Marriott has noted that in the village of Paril in India,

> . . . Personal wealth, influence, and morality have surpassed the tradi tional caste-and-order alignment of kind groups as the effective bases of ranking. Since such new bases of ranking can no longer be clearly tied to any inclusive system of large solidary groupings, judgments must be made according to the characteristics of individual or family units. This individualization of judgments leads to greater dissensus (*sic*).[6]

Castes, ethnic groups, and traditional religious groupings do not necessarily decline in importance in every respect during periods of development. As we shall see presently, they may even increase in salience as political interest groups or reference groups for diffuse loyalty. As the sole bases of ranking, however, ascriptive standards become more differentiated from economic, political, and other standards.

2. Individual mobility through the occupational hierarchies increases. This signifies the differentiation of the adult's functional position from his point of origin. In addition, individual mobility is frequently substituted for collective mobility. Individuals, not whole castes or tribes, compete for higher standing in society. This phenomenon of increasing individual mobility seems to be one of the universal consequences of industrializa-

---

5 Above, pp. 65–67.
6 "Social Change in an Indian Village," *Economic Development and Cultural Change* (1952–1953), I: 153.

tion.[7] Patterns of class symbolization and class ideology, however, may continue to differ among industrialized countries.

The Integration of Differentiated Activities

One of Durkheim's insights concerned the role of integrative mechanisms under conditions of growing social heterogeneity. One of the concomitants of a growing division of labor (differentiation), he argued, is an *increase* in mechanisms to coordinate and solidify the interaction among individuals with increasingly diversified interests.[8] Durkheim located this integration mainly in the legal structure, but one can locate similar kinds of integrative forces elsewhere in society.

Differentiation alone, therefore, is not sufficient for modernization. Development proceeds as a contrapuntal interplay between differentiation (which is divisive of established society) and integration (which unites differentiated structures on a new basis). Paradoxically, however, the process of integration itself produces more differentiated structures—e.g., trade unions, associations, political parties, and a mushrooming state apparatus. Let us illustrate this complex process of integration in several institutional spheres.

Economy and Family

Under a simple kind of economic organization—subsistence agriculture or household industry—there is little differentiation between economic roles and family roles. All reside in the kinship structure. The *integration* of these diverse but unspecialized activities also rests in the local family and community structures, and in the religious traditions which fortify both of these.

Under conditions of differentiation, the social setting for production is separated from that for consumption, and productive roles of family members are isolated geographically, temporally, and structurally from their distinctively familial roles. Such differentiation immediately creates integrative problems. How is information concerning employment opportunities to be conveyed to workpeople? How are the interests of familes to be integrated with the interests of firms? How are families to be protected from market fluctuations? Whereas such integrative exigencies were faced by kinsmen, neighbors, and local largesse in pre-modern settings, development gives birth to dozens of institutions and organizations geared to these new integrative problems—labor recruitment agencies and exchanges, labor unions, government regulation of labor allocation, welfare and relief arrangements, cooperative societies, and savings institutions. All these involve agencies which specialize in integration.

[7] Above, p. 67.
[8] Above, pp. 14–15.

Community

If industrialization occurs only in villages, or if villages are built around paternalistic industrial enterprises, many ties of community and kinship can be maintained under industrial conditions. Urbanization, however, frequently creates more anonymity. As a result of this anonymity we find in expanding cities a compensating growth of voluntary associations—churches and chapels, unions, schools, halls, athletic clubs, bars, shops, mutual aid groups, etc. In some cases this growth of integrative groupings may be retarded because of the back-and-forth movement of migratory workers, who "come to the city for their differentiation" and "return to the village for their integration." In cities themselves the original criterion for associating may be common tribe, caste, or village; this criterion may persist or give way gradually to more "functional" groupings based on economic or political interest.

Political Structure

In the typical pre-modern setting political integration is closely fused with kinship position, tribal membership, control of the land, or control of the unknown. Political forms include chieftanships, kingships, councils of elders, powerful landlords, powerful magicians and oracles, etc.

As social systems grow more complex, political systems are modified accordingly. Meyer Fortes and E. E. Evans-Pritchard have specified three types of African political systems, which can be listed according to their degree of differentiation from kinship lineages: (a) small societies in which the largest political unit embraces only those united by kinship; thus political authority is coterminous with kinship relations; (b) societies in which the political framework is the integrative core for a number of kinship lineages; (c) societies with an "administrative organization" of a more formal nature. Such systems move toward greater differentiation as population grows and economic and cultural heterogeneity increases.[9] In colonial and recently freed African societies, political systems have evolved much further, with the appearance of parties, congresses, pressure groups, and even parliamentary systems. Sometimes this wider political integration, like community integration, is based on an extension and modification of an old integrative principle. Selig Harrison has argued, for instance, that modern developments in India have changed the significance of caste from the "traditional village extension of the joint family" to "regional alliances of kindred local units." This modification has led to the formation of "new caste lobbies" which constitute some of the strongest and most explosive political forces in modern India.[10] We shall mention some of the possible political consequences of this persistence of old integrative forms later.

[9] *African Political Systems* (London: Oxford University Press, 1940), pp. 1–25.
[10] *India: The Most Dangerous Decades* (Princeton University Press, 1960), pp. 100 ff.

Those examples illustrate how differentiation in society impinges on the integrative sphere. The resulting integrative structures coordinate and solidify—with varying success—the social structure which the forces of differentiation threaten to fragment. In many cases the integrative associations and parties display tremendous instability—labor unions turn into political or nationalistic parties; religious sects become political clubs; football clubs become religious sects, and so on.[11] The resultant fluidity points up the extremely pressing needs for re-integration under conditions of rapid, irregular, and disruptive processes of differentiation. The initial response is often a kind of trial-and-error floundering for many kinds of integration at once.

We have sketched some structural consequences of technological advance, agricultural commercialization, urbanization, and industrialization. We have analyzed these consequences in terms of differentiation and integration. The structural changes are not, it should be remembered, a simple function of "industrialization" alone. Some of the most far-reaching structural changes have occurred in countries which have scarcely experienced the beginnings of industrialization. For instance, colonialism—or related forms of economic dominance—creates not only an extensive differentiation of cash products and wage labor but also a vulnerability to world price fluctuations in commodities. Hence many of the structural changes described above—and many of the resulting social disturbances to be described presently—characterize soceties which are still technically "pre-industrial."

Discontinuities in Differentiation and Integration: Social Disturbances

The structural changes associated with economic development are likely to be disruptive to the social order for the following reasons:

1. Differentiation demands the creation of new activities, norms, and sanctions—money, political position, prestige based on occupation, and so on. These often conflict with old modes of social action, which are frequently dominated by traditional religious, tribal, and kinship systems. These traditional standards are among the most intransigent of obstacles to modernization, and when they are threatened, serious dissatisfaction and opposition arise.

2. Structural change is, above all, *uneven* in periods of development. In colonial societies, for instance, the European powers frequently revolutionized the economic, political, and educational frameworks, but simultaneously encouraged or imposed a conservatism in traditional religious, class, and family systems.

> ...The basic problem in these [colonial] societies was the expectation that the native population would accept certain broad, modern institutional

[11] Thomas Hodgkin, *Nationalism in Colonial Africa* (New York: New York University Press, 1957), pp. 85 ff.

settings...and would perform within them various roles—especially economic and administrative roles—while at the same time, they were denied some of the basic rewards inherent in these settings.... They were expected to act on the basis of a motivational system derived from a different social structure which the colonial powers and indigenous rulers tried to maintain.[12]

Under non-colonial conditions of development similar discontinuities appear. Within the economy itself, rapid industrialization, no matter how coordinated, bites unevenly into the established social and economic structure. And throughout the society, the differentiation occasioned by agricultural, industrial, and urban changes always proceeds in a see-saw relationship with integration; the two sets of forces continuously breed lags and bottlenecks. The faster the tempo of modernization, the more severe are the discontinuities.

3. Dissatisfactions arising from these discontinuities sometimes are aggravated by attempts to overcome them. Some discontinuities may be relieved in part by integrative devices such as unions, associations, clubs, and government regulations. Such innovations are often opposed, however, by traditional vested interests because the new forms of integration compete with the older, undifferentiated systems of solidarity. The result is a three-way tug-of-war among the forces of tradition, the forces of differentiation, and the new forces of integration. Such conditions create virtually unlimited potentialities for the formation of conflicting groups.

Three classic responses to these discontinuities are anxiety, hostility, and fantasy. These responses, if and when they become collective, crystallize into a variety of social movements—peaceful agitation, political violence, millenarianism, nationalism, revolution, underground subversion, etc. There is plausible—though not entirely convincing—evidence that those drawn most readily into such movements are those suffering most severely the pains of displacements created by structural change. For example,

> [Nationalism appeared] as a permanent force in Southeast Asia at the moment when the peasants were forced to give up subsistence farming for the cultivation of cash crops or when (as in colonized Java) subsistence farming ceased to yield a subsistence. The introduction of a money economy and the withering away of the village as the unit of life accompanied this development and finally established the period of economic dependence.[13]

Other theoretical and empirical evidence suggests that social movements appeal most to those who have been dislodged from old social ties by differentiation but who have not been integrated into the new social order.[14]

---

[12] S. N. Eisenstadt, "Sociological Aspects of Political Development in Underdeveloped Countries," *Economic Development and Cultural Change* (1956–1957), V: 298.

[13] Erich H. Jacoby, *Agrarian Unrest in Southeast Asia* (New York: Columbia University Press, 1949), p. 246.

[14] William Kornhauser, *The Politics of Mass Society* (Glencoe, Ill.: The Free Press, 1959), Parts II and III; Seymour Martin Lipset, *Political Man* (Garden City, N.Y.: Doubleday, 1960), Chapter II.

Many belief-systems associated with these movements envision the grand and almost instantaneous integration of society. In many cases the beliefs are highly emotional and unconcerned with realistic policies. In nationalistic colonial movements, for instance, "the political symbols were intended to develop new, ultimate, common values and basic loyalties, rather than relate to current policy issues within the colonial society."[15] Furthermore, such belief-systems reflect the ambivalence resulting from the conflict between traditionalism and modernization. Nationalists alternate between xenophobia and xenophilia; they predict that they will "out-modernize" the West in the future and simultaneously "restore" the true values of the ancient civilization; they argue for egalitarian and hierarchical principles of social organization at the same time.[16] Nationalistic and related ideologies unite these contradictory tendencies in a society under one large symbol; then, if these ideologies are successful, they are often used as a vehicle for further economic development.

Not all cases of development produce violent nationalistic or other social movements. When such movements do arise, furthermore, they take many different forms. The following factors seem to be most decisive in the genesis and molding of social disturbances:

1. The scope and intensity of the social dislocation created by structural changes. "The greater the tempo of these changes...the greater the problems of acute malintegration the society has to face."[17]

2. The structural complexity of the society at the time when development begins. In the least developed societies, where "the language of politics is at the same time the language of religion," protest movements more or less immediately take on a religious cast. In Africa, for instance, utopian religious movements seem to have relatively greater appeal in the less developed regions, whereas the more secular types of political protest such as trade union movements and party agitations have tended to cluster in the more developed areas.[18] The secularization of protest increases as development and differentiation proceed.

3. The access of disturbed groups to channels of influencing social policy. If dislocated groups have access to those responsible for introducing reforms, agitation tends to be relatively peaceful and orderly. If this access is blocked, either because of the isolation of the groups or the intransigence of the ruling authorities, demands for reform tend to take more violent, utopian, and bizarre forms. Hence the tendency for fantasy and unorganized violence to cluster among the disinherited, the colonized, and the socially isolated migrants.

---

15 Eisenstadt, "Sociological Aspects of Political Development in Underdeveloped Countries," *op. cit.,* p. 294.

16 Mary Matossian, "Ideologies of Delayed Industrialization," *Economic Development and Cultural Change* (1957–1958), VI: 217–28.

17 Eisentadt, "Sociological Aspects of Political Development in Underdeveloped Countries," *op. cit.,* p. 294.

18 Hodgkin, *op. cit.,* pp. 95–150.

4. The overlap of interests and lines of cleavage. As we discovered above, those societies in which economic, political, and ethnic cleavages coincide are likely to produce more diffuse kinds of conflicts and social movements than societies in which these cleavages crisscross.[19]

5. The kind and extent of foreign infiltration and intervention on behalf of protest groups. Here we have tried to sketch, in ideal type terms, the ways in which economic and social development is related to social structure. We have centered the discussion around three major concepts—differentiation, which characterizes a social structure moving toward greater complexity; integration, which in certain respects balances the divisive character of differentiation; and social disturbances, which result from the discontinuities between differentiation and integration. . . .

---

[19] *African Political Systems* (London: Oxford University Press, 1940), pp. 1–25.

2 / Occupational Mobility: A Cross-National Similarity in Pattern?

Cross-cultural analysis has grown more important and useful to social scientists in recent years. In addition to broad societal analysis, there have been studies of particular social structures and institutions which have been guided by the hypothesis of similarity among industrialized nations. This chapter examines comparative rates of intergenerational mobility among industrialized nations.

Unlike Western European countries, American society is popularly said to have a fluid stratification structure, in which sons can advance beyond their fathers' occupational status. Seymour Lipset and Hans Zetterberg, in "Social Mobility in Industrial Society," challenge this contention. Using intergenerational occupational mobility data from several countries, they conclude that the total amount of social mobility in all Western societies appears to be relatively high and very similar. They cannot attribute this finding to the rate of economic expansion, since the countries involved showed differential rates. They offer the tentative explanation that rates of intergenerational mobility reach a high level in countries which have achieved a certain level of industrialization.

Blau and Duncan, in "Opportunity and Democracy," present data that confirm the Lipset–Zetterberg conclusion regarding the relatively uniform effect of industrialization on total intergenerational occupational mobility across the manual–nonmanual line. It is the corollary—that the chance for upward mobility is therefore no greater in the United States than in other industrial countries—which Blau and Duncan challenge. Blau and Duncan question the reliability of some of the data used by Lipset and Zetterberg. But a more important point is that Lipset and Zetterberg deal only with movement across the manual–nonmanual occupational line, failing to examine national differential opportunities for mobility from the lower strata to the top. Using national samples from ten countries, Blau and Duncan assemble evidence supporting the conclusion that the sons of manual workers in the United States have substantially greater opportunities for mobility into the elite stratum than do their counterparts in other industrialized countries; some credence is given the Horatio Alger myth. Blau and Duncan attribute the fluidity from the bottom to the top of the occupational structure to the high level of industrialization and education in the United States and to the informality regarding distinctions based on social status.

The Lipset–Zetterberg thesis has recently been challenged by F. Lancaster Jones, whose reanalysis of their data was prompted by his belief that the issue had been closed without conclusive evidence. In "Social Mobility and Industrial Society: A Thesis Re-Examined," Jones questions the method of analysis employed by Lipset and Zetterberg and the validity of their empirical data. Jones's interest is in conducting a broader test of the Lipset–Zetterberg thesis using their own data, specifically examining international differences in upward and downward intergenerational mobility and including the non-farm segment of the labor force. A reanalysis of the data convinces Jones that social mobility can be said to be similar in these industrialized Western countries only if the direction of mobility is ignored and if farm occupations are excluded. However, even that concession is withdrawn in the second part of the paper, in which Jones concludes that sampling biases invalidate any conclusion based on the Lipset–Zetterberg data.

6 / Social Mobility in Industrial Societies

Seymour Martin Lipset
Hans L. Zetterberg

WIDESPREAD SOCIAL MOBILITY has been a concomitant of industrialization and a basic characteristic of modern industrial society. In every industrial country, a large proportion of the population have had to find occupations considerably different from those of their parents. During the nineteenth century, the proportion of the labor force in urban occupations increased rapidly, while the proportion in agriculture decreased.

In the twentieth century the West has been characterized by a rapid growth of trade and of service industries, as well as of bureaucracy in industry and government; more people have become employed in white-collar work, and the comparative size of the rural population has declined even more rapidly than before.[1] These changes in the distribution of occupations from generation to generation mean that no industrial society can be viewed as closed or static.

This apparently simple statement runs counter to widely held impressions concerning the different social structures of American and Western European societies. According to these impressions, America has an "open society" with considerable social mobility, but the countries of Western Europe (specifically England, France, Italy, Germany, the Low Countries, and the Scandinavian nations) have societies that are "closed," in the sense that the children of workers are forced to remain in the social position of their parents. This judgment reflects earlier European beliefs. In the age of the French Revolution, America appeared to be a land free from traditional institutions and historical legacies: the country of the future, Hegel called it, where each man was master of his fate just as American democracy itself was the product of human reason. This notion has been reiterated in many analyses, all contrasting American and European societies.

For the most part these discussions deal with the differences between democratic and autocratic institutions; but they also express assumptions about contrasting patterns of social mobility. Sometimes the political and social aspects of the contrast between America and Europe have been linked

---

[1] See Colin Clark, *The Conditions of Economic Progress,* 3d ed. (London: Macmillan, 1957), pp. 490–520.

Reprinted from Seymour Martin Lipset and Reinhard Bendix, *Social Mobility in Industrial Society* (Berkeley and Los Angeles: University of California Press, 1964), pp. 11–28. Originally published by the University of California Press; reprinted by permission of the authors and the Regents of the University of California.

as cause and effect: differences in political institutions and values have cited as evidence for the assertion that the society of America is "open," those of Europe "closed"; and the supposedly greater rate of social mobility in American society has been viewed as a major reason for the success of American democracy. For example, some fifty years ago Werner Sombart referred to the opportunities abundant in America as the major reason why American workers rejected the Marxist view that there is little opportunity under capitalism, while European workers accepted it because their opportunities were more restricted.[2] Such judgments as Sombart's were, however, no more than inferences based on the general contrast between the American tradition which proclaimed the goal of opportunity for all and the European emphasis upon social stability and class differences.[3] For as a matter of fact, it is not really clear whether the different political orientation of the American and European worker reflects different opportunities for social mobility or only a difference in their ethos!

The questions implicit in these alternative interpretations can be answered today with somewhat more assurance than was possible even two decades ago because of recent research in social mobility. In this chapter we attempt to summarize the findings available for a number of countries. Since our object is to assemble a large amount of empirical evidence, it will be useful to state at the outset that *the overall pattern of social mobility appears to be much the same in the industrial societies of various Western countries.*[4] This is startling—even if we discount the mistaken efforts to

[2] Werner Sombart, *Warum gibt es in den Vereinigten Staaten keinen Sozialismus?* (Tuebingen: J. C. B. Mohr, 1906), p. 135.

[3] It may be noted, however, that Sombart also emphasized the subjective factor: "Consideration should also be given to the mere awareness of the worker that he could become an independent farmer at any time. This consciousness was bound to give the American worker a feeling of security and peace of mind which the European worker did not know. One can tolerate any coercive situation much more easily if one has at least the illusion that one could escape that situation if worse came to worst." *Ibid.,* p. 140. Such an awareness was, in Sombart's opinion, relatively independent of the actual number of workers who availed themselves of opportunities for upward mobility, though he did not develop this point further.

[4] See S. M. Lipset and Natalie Rogoff, "Class and Opportunity in Europe and America," *Commentary,* 18 (1954), 562–68; and David V. Glass, ed., *Social Mobility in Britain* (London: Routledge and Kegan Paul, 1954), pp. 321–38, 344–49; P. Sorokin, *Social Mobility* (New York: Harper, 1927), pp. 414–80; S. M. Lipset and Hans L. Zetterberg, "A Theory of Social Mobility," in *Transactions of the Third World Congress of Sociology,* Vol. III (London: International Sociological Association, 1956) pp. 155–77; Sigeki Nishira, "Cross-National Comparative Study on Social Stratification and Social Mobility," *Annals of the Institute of Statistical Mathematics,* 3(1957): 181–91; Colin Clark, *The Conditions of Economic Progress,* pp. 545–64; and Robert J. Havighurst, "Educação Mobilidade Sociale Mudança Social em Quatro Sociedades—Estudo Comparativo," *Educação e Ciencias Sociais,* 2 (1957): 103–31. For an annotated bibliography of articles on social mobility which appeared in the major American sociological journals between 1924 and 1953, see Raymond W. Mack, Lanton Freeman, and Seymour Yellin, *Social Mobility: Thirty Years of Research and Theory* (Syracuse: Syracuse University Press, 1957).

explain differences in political institutions by reference to different degrees of social mobility in the United States and in Western Europe. Further, although it is clear that social mobility is related in many ways to the economic expansion of industrial societies, it is at least doubtful that the rates of mobility and of expansion are correlated. Since a number of the countries for which we have data have had different rates of economic expansion but show comparable rates of social mobility, our tentative interpretation is that the social mobility of societies becomes relatively high once their industrialization, and hence their economic expansion, reaches a certain level.

Occupational Mobility

Before World War II, studies of social mobility were usually limited to investigations of the social origins of different occupational groups, employees of single factories, or inhabitants of single communities. Since World War II there have been at least fifteen different national surveys in eleven countries which have secured from representative samples of the population information that relates the occupations of the respondents to the occupations of their fathers. In addition, there have been a number of studies conducted in different cities of various countries. Taken together, these investigations permit the comparison of current variations in occupational mobility, as well as some estimate of differences during the past half century.

To make such comparisions and estimates is difficult. Few of the studies were made with the intention of facilitating the comparison of findings in different countries. Many of them employ systems of classifying occupations which cannot be compared with each other and the questions concerning the occupations of respondents and fathers are seldom similar. In order to use the results for a comparative analysis, we have reduced the occupational categories for most countries to the closest approximation of manual, nonmanual, and farm occupations. In presenting these materials, we make the assumption that a move from manual to nonmanual employment constitutes upward mobility among *males*. This assumption may be defended on the following grounds:

1. Most male nonmanual occupations have more prestige than most manual occupations, even skilled ones.[5]

5 See National Opinion Research Center, "Jobs and Occupations: A Popular Evaluation," *Opinion News,* 9 (1947): 3–13. A comparison of occupational-prestige studies in six countries has shown a high level of agreement among these studies in the rankings of occupations. See Alex Inkeles and Peter Rossi, "National Comparisons of Occupational Prestige," *American Journal of Sociology,* 61(1956): 329–39. Surveys in two additional industrial countries reveal the same prestige pattern. See Ronald Taft, "The Social Grading of Occupations in Australia," *British Journal of Sociology,* 4(1953): 181–88, and F. van Heek, *et al., Sociale stijging en daling in Nederland,* Vol. I (Leyden: H. E. Stenfert Kroese N.V., 1958), pp. 25–26. Two studies in relatively underdeveloped countries, Brazil and the Philippines, show that in both, occupational evaluations agree closely with those of industrial nations.

2. Among males, white-collar positions generally lead to higher incomes than manual employment.[6]

3. Nonmanual positions, in general, require more education than manual positions.[7]

4. Holders of nonmanual positions, even low-paid white-collar jobs,

---

See Bertram Hutchinson, "The Social Grading of Occupations in Brazil," *British Journal of Sociology,* 8(1957): 176–89; and Edward A. Tiryakian, "The Prestige Evaluation of Occupations in an Underdeveloped Country: The Philippines," *American Journal of Sociology,* 63(1958): 390–99.

A recent report on a study of occupational prestige in Poland reports that even under Communism, "passage of the better paid skilled manual worker to the position of the slightly lower paid white collar workers...in the majority of cases is looked on as a promotion...[although] from the point of view of the new criteria of prestige, this should not be considered a promotion." S. Ossowski, "Social Mobility Brought About by Social Revolutions," (Working Paper Eleven submitted to the Fourth Working Conference on Social Stratification and Social Mobility, International Sociological Association, December, 1957), p. 3.

Similar findings are reported in a 1952 German study which attempted to find out whether a high-income manual job had more prestige than a low-income non-manual position, by asking the following question: "Who do you think receives more prestige from the population in general: A bookkeeper, who earns 300 marks a month, or a foundry worker, who brings home 450 marks a month?" The results (in percentages) were as follows:

Answer	Total sample	Manual worker respondents only
The bookkeeper	58	56
The foundry-worker	24	28
Don't know	18	16

From Erich Peter Neumann and Elizabeth Noelle, *Antworten, Politik im Kraftfeld der öffentlichen Meinung* (Allensbach am Bodensee: Verlag für Demoskopie, 1954), p. 107.

6 The evidence on the relationship between income and occupation in a number of countries shows that the income of white-collar workers has traditionally been higher than that of skilled workers. In periods of prolonged prosperity and inflation, the gap tends to narrow considerably. However, in the United States in 1951, "in each age group beyond 35, nonfarm occupational groups could be ranked by average income in the following order: professional workers; managerial workers; clerical and sale workers; craftsmen; operatives; service workers; and laborers." Herman P. Miller, *Income of the American People* (New York: Wiley, 1955), p. 54. Similar results are reported for Germany in the data gathered in a sample survey study of the German population by the UNESCO Institute in Cologne in 1953.

7 The median schooling reported for American males in the 1950 census for clerical and sales workers was slightly over 12 years; that of craftsmen and foremen was 9.3 years. See Lawrence Thomas, *The Occupational Structure and Education* (New York: Prentice-Hall, 1956), p. 39. The German study cited above indicates that in Germany, about 30 percent of lower white-collar workers have more than an elementary education, compared to only 2 percent of the skilled workers.

are more likely than manual workers to think of themselves as members of the middle class and to act out middle-class roles in their consumption patterns.[8]

5. Low-level nonmanual workers are more likely to have political attitudes which resemble those of the upper middle class than those of the manual working class.[9]

It is true, of course, that many white-collar positions are lower in income and prestige than the higher levels of skilled manual work; however, most of these poorly paid white-collar positions are held by women, and male white-collar workers are often able to secure higher-level supervisory posts.[10]

[8] See Richard Centers, *The Psychology of Social Classes* (Princeton University Press, 1949), p. 86; Natalie Rogoff, "Social Stratification in France and in the United States," in R. Bendix and S. M. Lipset, eds., *Class, Status and Power* (Glencoe: The Free Press, 1953), p. 585; Marcel Bresard, "La mobilité sociale: Le choix d'une échelle sociologique," in *Transactions of the Second World Congress of Sociology,* Vol. II, p. 399. Bresard indicates that white-collar workers and lower civil servants in France were much more likely to own property than manual workers, and that a somewhat higher proportion had automobiles and telephones. The tendency for white-collar workers to consume more like the middle class than the working class may be inferred from data on the employment of wives in Sweden. C. Arnold Anderson reports that white-collar workers are about twice as likely to have working wives as are manual workers, and that the majority of the working wives are concentrated in the lower-income groups of white-collar workers. The employment of wives of manual workers is more evenly distributed among income groups. It seems that when the income of a white-collar worker goes below that required to maintain a middle-class consumption style, his wife goes to work to regain it. See "Employment, Occupation, and Socio-Economic Status of Swedish Wives in Relation to Occupation and Status of Husbands," *Statistisk Tidskrift,* 6 (1957): 3–15. See also W. H. Form and Gregory P. Stone, *The Social Significance of Clothing in Occupational Life,* Technical Bulletin 247 (East Lansing: Michigan State University, 1955). There is evidence from a number of countries which demonstrates that white-collar and manual workers have different styles of life, as indicated by divergent consumption patterns. "Comparable data for these occupational classes are available for Belgium, Czechoslovakia, Finland, Bulgaria, Norway, Germany, Sweden, the Netherlands, Japan, Denmark and Switzerland... *Within the same income group,* manual workers spend more of their income for food than white-collar employees and officials [civil servants]." W. S. Woytinsky and E. S. Woytinsky, *World Population and Production Trends and Outlook* (New York: The Twentieth Century Fund, 1953), p. 276.

[9] Findings bearing out this statement have been reported for Great Britain, the United States, Germany, Norway, Canada, and Australia. For a summary of data on voting behavior and occupation, see S. M. Lipset, *et al.,* "The Psychology of Voting: An Analysis of Political Behavior," *in* Gardner Lindzey, ed., *Handbook of Social Psychology,* Vol. II (Cambridge: Addison Wesley, 1954), pp. 1124–75.

[10] Gallup Poll data analyzed and kindly supplied by Dr. John Bonham show that over one-third of the British male white-collar workers held upper-level white-collar jobs in 1950–1951, as contrasted with 12 percent of the female white-collar workers. In the U.S., 56 percent of the male white-collar workers earned more than $3,000 per year in 1949, as contrasted with 15 percent of women employees. See L. Thomas, *The Occupational Structure . . . ,* p. 137. In countries for which we have data, low-level male white-collar workers are considerably younger on the

Consequently, we believe that using the break between manual and nonmanual occupations as an indicator of low and high occupational status is justified whenever a dichotomous division of males in urban occupations is used. It is important to remember, however, that like all single-item indicators of complex phenomena this one will necessarily result in some errors; that is, some nonmanual positions which have lower status than some manual occupations will be classified in the high group though they should be in the low.[11]

Postwar National Samples

Figure 1 presents the inter-generational shifts between manual and nonmanual occupations for adult males in six countries. The data indicate that a large minority of the sons of the industrial labor force achieve nonmanual positions. In France this group comprises 35 percent of the sons, in Germany 26 to 30 percent, in Switzerland 44 percent, in Sweden 29 percent, in Japan 33 percent, and in the United States 31 to 35 percent. A smaller minority in each country declines from nonmanual to manual positions, the percentages ranging from a low of 13 percent to a high of 38 percent.[12]

An obvious drawback of the studies from which these data are derived

---

average than male manual workers. Thomas suggests that one explanation of this fact is that, "the clerical and sales occupations may be stepping stones for considerable numbers of young men seeking eventual positions as proprietors or managers." *Ibid.*, p. 40.

In Germany in the mid-twenties, a study of white-collar workers revealed that 20 percent of the males and only 2.5 percent of the females held upper-level white-collar jobs (responsible work), while 71 percent of the females and 32 percent of the males held lower-stratum white-collar positions. See Hans Speier, *The Salaried Employees in German Society* (New York: Works Progress Administration and Department of Social Science, Columbia University, 1939), p. 120. Speier suggested in this study that with the growth in magnitude of white-collar positions, "the chances of the male employees to exercise some authority in virtue of his position and sex becomes more intense [greater]...the ratio between male and female employees has shifted quantitatively in favor of women and qualitatively in favor of men. The difference in stratification between both sexes has been widened. Subordinate positions are being filled still more with young and cheap female forces." *Ibid.*, pp. 121–23.

11 See Peter M. Blau, "Occupational Bias and Mobility," *American Sociological Review*, 22 (1957): 392–99. In a secondary analysis of the NORC data on occupational prestige, Blau found that the break between manual and nonmanual occupations was the most relevant in explaining varying amounts of bias in occupational prestige ratings. His analysis is congruent with the assumption that the boundary between manual and nonmanual work is the most significant point in dichotomizing the stratification hierarchy if one is concerned with accounting for differential behavior.

12 An analysis of mobility patterns among a sample of Russian émigrés after World War II shows a pattern similar to that reported for Western Europe and America, as the following table shows.

is that they depend upon a "common-sense" evaluation of occupational prestige: we have sought to correct for this deficiency by elaborating in detail the distinction between manual and nonmanual occupations. However, several recent studies have attempted to give a firmer empirical foundation to the status of occupations by ascertaining first the esteem in which various occupations are held by a cross-section of the public; then, rates of social mobility were established with reference to these *known* prestige rankings, in which, for example, routine clerical jobs, are categorized as "low" even though they are nonmanual positions. The first such study was made by Professor David Glass of the London School of Economics.[13]

Social Mobility among Russian Emigrés
(Percentages)

SON'S OCCUPATION	FATHER'S OCCUPATION		
	Nonmanual	*Manual*	*Farm*
Nonmanual	90	28	20
Manual	10	69	36
Farm	..	3	44
Number in sample	265	376	541

From R. A. Feldmesser, "Observations on Trends in Social Mobility in the Soviet Union and Their Implications," *in* A. Kassof, *et al., Stratification and Mobility in The Soviet Union: A Study of Social Class Cleavages in the U.S.S.R.* (Cambridge: Harvard Russian Research Center, n.d.; mimeographed).

Substantiating evidence for the high rate of social mobility in the U.S.S.R. found by Feldmesser is given in Alex Inkeles, "Social Stratification and Social Mobility in the Soviet Union: 1940–1950," *American Sociological Review,* 15(1950): 465–79.

A study of the 1957 Norwegian elections received from the Oslo Institute for Social Research after this book had gone to the publisher indicates that 22 percent of the sons of Norwegian manual and farm workers moved up into nonmanual occupations, and that 31 percent moved down from nonmanual to manual and farm-labor jobs. These figures are not precisely comparable with the others since the Norway survey listed farm owners separately and combined farm and manual workers.

Social Mobility in Norway, 1957
(Percentages)

SON'S OCCUPATION	FATHER'S OCCUPATION		
	Nonmanual	*Manual**	*Farm owner***
Nonmanual	63	22	26
Manual*	31	70	44
Farm Owner**	5	8	30
Number in sample	153	369	253

* Includes farm workers.
** Includes self-employed in fish and lumber industries.

13 David Glass, ed., *Social Mobility in Britain.*

Its sophisticated methodology has inspired researchers in Denmark,[14] Japan,[15] and Sweden[16] to proceed along similar lines. When completed, this series of studies will yield much detailed information about mobility rates. At present we can show two comparable summaries from Denmark and Great Britain, and a reasonably comparable study from Italy (see figure 2). We find here evidence of considerable upward mobility from the occupational categories of manual workers, farm workers, and routine nonmanual employees into farm-ownership and high-level nonmanual positions. In Denmark 22 percent of them rise in this way; in Great Britain, 20 percent; and in Italy, 8 percent. Downward mobility between these categories appears to be greater: 44 percent in Denmark, 49 percent in Great Britain, and 34 percent in Italy. The actual decline is probably not as great as shown by these figures. The classification employed in these studies, which grouped together positions of comparable prestige regardless of whether these were in the farm or nonfarm sectors of the economy, is, whatever its merits on other grounds, likely to exaggerate the rate of downward mobility, since sons of farmers who come from the rural middle class and go to the city are more likely to become manual workers than young men from the urban middle class.[17] This consideration does *not* apply as much to Great Britain, which has a very small proportion of its population engaged in farming, but it does apply to agricultural countries like Denmark and Italy. A method of mobility analysis that is quite adequate for the former country might, therefore, be misleading in the latter countries.[18]

[14] Studies in progress by Professor Kaare Svalastoga, University of Copenhagen.

[15] Research Committee, Japanese Sociological Society, *Social Mobility in Japan: An Interim Report on the 1955 Survey of Social Stratification and Social Mobility in Japan,* (1957; mimeographed). Two additional sources of data on Japanese mobility, received after the present manuscript had gone to press, describe changes in occupational structure as a consequence of industrialization and the influences on mobility of education. These data appear congruent with the earlier findings above. See Kunio Odaka, ed., *Shokugyô to Kaisô* (Occupation and Stratification) (Tokyo: Mainichi Shimbunsha, 1958); Japanese Sociological Society, *Nihon Shakai no Kaisô teki Kozô* (The Stratification System in Japanese Society), (Tokyo: Yuhikaku, 1958).

[16] Studies in progress by Professor Gösta Carlson, Sociological Institute, Lund University.

[17] For documentation see chapter viii.

[18] The Japanese researchers computed so-called indices of association which measure the relationship between fathers' and sons' occupational status by calculating "the ratio of actual to the expected number of sons who, having category 1 fathers, arrive in category 1." See D. Glass, ed., *Social Mobility in Britain,* pp. 194–95. The British researchers also used this index, which is arrived at by calculating the expected number on the assumption that sons are distributed on a random basis among occupational categories. It should be noted that the Japanese indices of association show a slightly greater tendency for Japanese to remain in the father's occupational prestige class than for the British. See Research Committee, Japanese Sociological Society, *Social Mobility in Japan,* p. 10, and Glass, *Social Mobility in Britain,* p. 199. See also p. 27, n. 24.

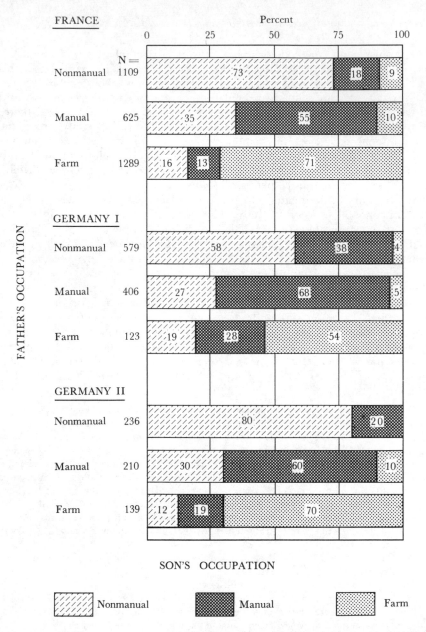

Fig. 1. *Mobility between manual and nonmanual occupations and between agriculture and nonagriculture. Details do not always add to 100 percent because of rounding. Source.—France: M. Bresard, "Mobilité sociale et dimension de la famille," Population, 5 (1950): 553–66. Germany: (I) From data supplied by Dr. Erich Reigratski, Cologne, Germany, from his study* Soziale Verflechtungen in der Bundesrepublik *(Tubingen: Mohr-Siebeck, 1956); (II) From data supplied by Institut für Demoskopie, Allensbach, Germany* (Figure continued on next page.)

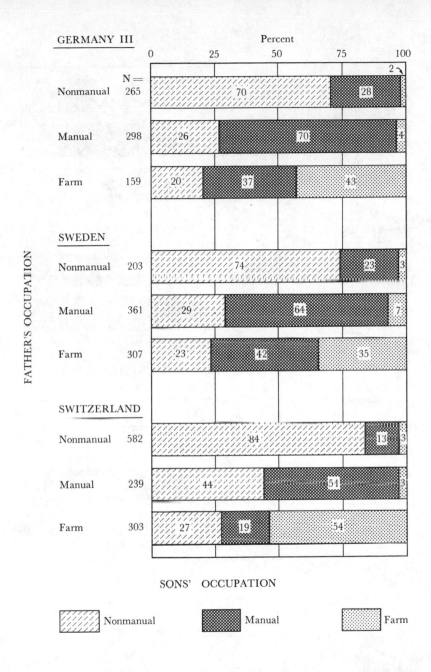

Fig. 1. *(continued)*. Source.—*Germany (III): From data supplied by DIVO, Frankfurt A.M. Sweden: From data collected by H. L. Zetterberg, partly reported in "Sveriges fem rangrullor," Vecko-Journalen, 48 (1957): 40. Switzerland: Recalculated from information supplied by Professor Roger Girod.*

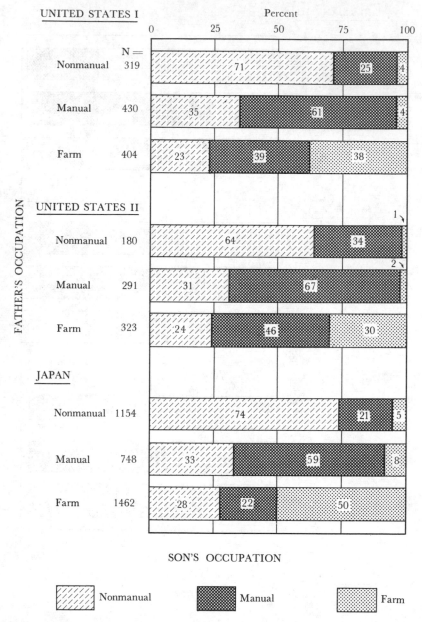

Fig. 1. *(continued)*. Source.—*United States: (I) Derived by Dr. Natalie Rogoff from data published by the National Opinion Research Center in "Jobs and Occupations,"* Opinion News, *September 1, 1947, pp. 3–33; (II) From data supplied by the Survey Research Center of the University of Michigan from their study of the 1952 presidential election. Japan: Research Committee on Stratification and Social Mobility of The Japanese Sociological Association,* Social Stratification and Mobility *(Tokyo: 1956; mimeographed), p. 13.*

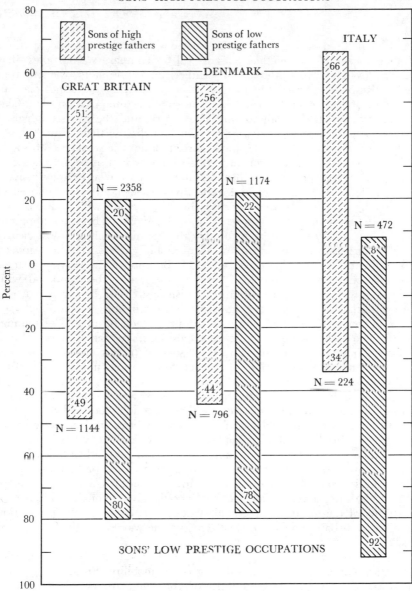

Fig. 2. *Mobility between occupations of high and low prestige. Occupations of high prestige are high levels of nonmanual occupations and farm owners, except in the high-prestige data for Italy, which include all nonmanual occupations and well-to-do peasants. Occupations of low prestige include routine nonmanual occupations, manual occupations, and farm occupations, except the low-prestige data for Italy, which include only manual occupations (including farm workers) and poor peasants. Source.—Great Britain: Calculated from David Glass,* Social Mobility in Britain. *Denmark: Computed from data furnished by Professor K. Svalastoga, Copenhagen, Denmark. Italy: L. Livi, "Sur la mesure de la mobilité sociale,"* Population, *5 (1950): 65–76.*

A third method of determining the relationship between the occupations of fathers and sons—the method least useful for comparative purposes—has been employed in two Scandinavian studies, one in Finland, the other in Sweden. Respondents were themselves asked to identify the social class to which they and their fathers belonged. Since the meaning of class identification varies considerably from country to country, and the two studies used very different social-class categories, we will not discuss them here.[19]

The lack of comparable classifications in nationwide surveys of social mobility makes it difficult to conclude this summary with more than general impressions. Moreover, we must bear in mind that we deal here exclusively with a single index to complex and quite diverse societies, so that inferences can carry us only part of the way and should be made with caution. Yet, the value of a comparative approach to social mobility becomes apparent when we set side by side for each country the figures which are most clearly indicative of upward, downward, and total mobility across the line between the middle and the working class (table 1). Because of the varying systems of occupational classification the Italian figures cannot be compared with any of the others, and the British and Danish figures can be compared only with each other. The remainder, however, are reasonably comparable.

The figures in the first column give the proportion of all sons of manual workers who now occupy middle-class positions. In the second column the figures indicate the proportion of all sons of middle-class fathers who are now in manual occupations. In order to get some index of the total mobility in society, the figures in the third column were computed: out of all the sons of fathers in urban occupations who are themselves in urban occupations, those who were mobile in either direction were added together, and this figure was expressed as a percentage of the total. For example, of those persons in the nonfarm population of the United States who were sons of fathers in nonfarm occupations, 30 percent had either fallen into a manual position from their fathers' nonmanual position, or had risen from their fathers' working-class occupation into a middle-class one. Though this is, to be sure, a very crude index, it should give a rough indication of the fluidity of the urban occupational structure. It expresses the proportion of the native urban population which has, in one way or another, "changed class."

The first impression one gains from table 1 is that all the countries studied are characterized by a high degree of mobility. From one generation to another, a quarter to a third of the non-farm population moves from working class to middle class or vice versa. Second, there is among the first six countries a high degree of similarity in this total mobility rate. The total range is between 23 and 31 percent, and five of the six countries (United States, Germany, Sweden, Japan, France) range between 27 and 31 percent. Such narrow differences lead quickly to one interpretation: total mobility rates in these countries are practically the same.[20]

---

19 For a presentation of the results of these studies see Lipset and Zetterberg, "A Theory of Social Mobility," p. 165.

20 Data from Morris Janowitz' study of social mobility based on a survey con-

Table 1.   Comparative Indices of Upward and Downward Mobility
(Percentages)

NONFARM POPULATIONS

Country	Upward mobility (Nonmanual sons of manual fathers)	Downward mobility (Manual sons of nonmanual fathers)	Total vertical mobility (Nonfarm population mobile across the line between working and middle class)
United States[a]	33	26	30
Germany[b]	29	32	31
Sweden	31	24	29
Japan	36	22	27
France	39	20	27
Switzerland	45	13	23

POPULATIONS WITH RURAL AND URBAN OCCUPATIONS CLASSIFIED TOGETHER

Country	High prestige occupation sons of fathers in low prestige occupations	Low prestige occupation sons of fathers in high prestige occupations	Proportion mobile across high and low occupation prestige lines
Denmark	22	44	31
Great Britain	20	49	29
Italy	8	34	16

Sources: See figures 1 and 2.
a Average of three studies: two cited in figure 1, and the third computed from data in R. Centers, "Occupational Mobility of Urban Occupational Strata," *American Sociological Review*, 13 (1948):203.
b Average of three studies cited in figure 1.

This similarity does not hold, of course, if the relationship between parental occupations and sons' occupations are compared in terms either

ducted by DIVO in 1955 in Western Germany indicate lesser opportunities for personal social mobility in Germany as compared to the United States, than are shown by the three German studies we have cited in figure 1. However, Janowitz included both men and women in his sample. Since quite recent data supplied by DIVO from a 1957 survey indicate that German women have a much lower rate of social mobility than men, this factor could account for these apparently contradictory findings. Morris Janowitz, "Social Stratification and Mobility in Western Germany," *American Journal of Sociology*, 64(1958): 6–24. The considerably greater upward mobility of German men as compared to women is also reflected in sharply different levels of aspiration. A study of Hesse youth aged 14 to 21 found that 64 percent of the males were striving "for a higher social position than your father's" as compared with 34 percent of the females. See "Intensität des Aufstiegsstrebens," *Offene Welt*, 54 (1958): 102.

of upward or of downward mobility, rather than the total amount of mobility. Then it appears that there is considerable variation among countries in the degree to which a father's occupation is an asset or a handicap. Thus, we see that the sons of middle-class fathers are more likely to fall in status in the United States and Germany than they are in Japan, France, or Switzerland. There is less variation in the degree to which a working-class family background handicaps a man in securing a nonmanual position; only Switzerland stands out as permitting higher rates of upward movement than the other countries.[21] Given the variations in the methods of collecting data, it would be premature to place much reliance on these differences.

Information about career patterns might yield results different from those cited above. The length of the step up or down the ladder of occupations might well be substantially greater in one country than in another, although in each the same proportion of the population could obtain better positions than their fathers when we compare them solely in terms of movement across the manual–nonmanual line. Studies of intra-generational mobility have been made in the Netherlands[22] and Sweden.[23] The Dutch study shows that intra-generational mobility has increased over the past few decades; the Swedish study, that advancement from general and industrial labor was slower in the depression years 1930–1935 than in the war year 1940–1945. Both studies support the proposition that intra-generational mobility increases with industrial expansion.

Finally, it should be mentioned that the fact that one country contains a greater percentage of mobile individuals than another, does *not* mean that country approximates a model of equal opportunity more closely. There may be *more mobility* in one country than in another, and yet *less equality* of opportunity. For example, if a country is 90 percent peasant, even with completely equal opportunity most children of peasants must remain peasants. Even if every nonpeasant position should be filled by a peasant's son, only about 11 percent of the sons of peasants could change occupation; an upward mobility rate of 9 percent would indicate complete equality of opportunity. On the other hand, if a country undergoes rapid economic transformation and the proportion of nonmanual positions increases to, say, one-half of all positions, then anything less than a 50 percent upward mobility rate would indicate inequality.[24]

---

[21] For a detailed discussion of the high rates of social mobility in Switzerland, see Roger Girod, "Mobilité sociale en Suisse: changements de milieu d'une généra-tion à l'autre," *Revue de l'institut de sociologie*, 1957, No. 1, pp. 19–32.

[22] J. J. M. van Tulder, "Occupational Mobility in the Netherlands from 1919 to 1954," in *Transactions of the Third World Congress of Sociology*, Vol. III (London: International Sociological Association, 1956), pp. 209–18. An earlier Dutch refer-ence is F. van Heek, *Stijging en daling op de maatschappelijke ladder* (Leiden: E. J. Brill, 1945).

[23] C. Arnold Anderson, "Lifetime Inter-Occupational Mobility Patterns in Swe-den," *Acta Sociologica*, 1 (1955): 168–202.

[24] For statistical techniques developed to handle this problem, see Rodolfo Benini, *Principii di Demografia* (Florence: G. Babèra, 1901), pp. 129–38; Emily Perrin,

Our major finding in this section is that the countries involved are comparable in their high amounts of total vertical mobility. The reservations and cautions which are in order do not invalidate this finding, which a number of other researchers in this area, such as Pitirim Sorokin, Robert Havighurst, Natalie Rogoff, David Glass, and Colin Clark, also agree is warranted by the extant statistical data. In this connection, it is worth reporting that the Australian-British economist, Colin Clark, "found [it] *rather surprising,* [that] of the sons of French urban manual and clerical workers, a higher proportion succeeded in securing 'social promotion' than in the U.S.A."[25]

"On the Contingency between Occupation in the Case of Fathers and Sons," *Biometrika,* 3 (1904): 407–09, Donald Marvin, "Occupational Propinquity as a Factor in Marriage Selection, *Publications of the American Statistical Association,* 16 (1918): 131–50; Natalie Rogoff, *Recent Trends in Occupational Mobility* (Glencoe: The Free Press, 1953), pp. 29–33; David V. Glass, ed., *Social Mobility in Britain,* pp. 218–59; see also Frederico Chessa, *La Transmissione Ereditaria delle Professioni* (Torino: Fratelli Bocca, 1921), for an early presentation of the logic of this approach. Several critical papers on this technique appear in *Population Studies,* 9 (1955). An important recent critique may be found in Edward Gross, *Work and Society* (New York: Thomas Y. Crowell, 1958), pp. 150–54.

25 Colin Clark, *The Conditions of Economic Progress,* 3d ed., p. 554. Clark also found British mobility patterns somewhat similar to those of the United States, and that "Italy is a society of much greater hereditary stratification than any of the other countries examined."

In "Class and Opportunity in Europe and America," Natalie Rogoff has pointed out that the French mobility survey that she has previously cited as suggesting higher rates of mobility in the United States than in France actually does not do so. (See "Social Stratification in France and the United States.") The French study used fewer occupational classes than the N O R C, one with which it was compared— e.g., the American analysis counted movement among unskilled, semiskilled and skilled as social mobility, while the French used only one category, *ouvrier,* for all three—and since there were fewer classes in France there was less mobility. It is obvious that one can increase or decrease the proportion who are "mobile" by increasing or decreasing the number of classes among which movement may take place.

It is interesting to note, moreover, that not only can the same data yield different statistical conclusions depending on whether or not comparable classifications are used, but the same statistical results may yield widely divergent interpretations, even in the same book. Citing the first Rogoff comparison which suggested greater mobility in the United States than in France, Jessie Bernard writes: "The relative mobility which prevails in a society is, however, apparently more closely related to its technology than to its historic tradition. Thus, for example, one study which compared occupational mobility in the United States and France found that although mobility was greater in the first—67.5 percent as compared with 48.3 percent—both showed a great deal of mobility in spite of the feudal tradition in one and the frontier tradition in the other." Jessie Bernard, "The United States," *in* Arnold M. Rose, ed., *The Institutions of Advanced Societies,* (Minneapolis: University of Minnesota Press, 1958), p. 610. In the same book François Bourricaud, in the chapter dealing with France, cites these data from the early Rogoff study to argue that "the mobility of the French workers is absolutely and relatively low." *Ibid,* p. 487.

To this note on the varying interpretations of data one must add that the comment of Colin Clark, quoted in the text, that French workers have greater opportunities for advancement than Americans is also based on a comparison of American data with the results of the same French mobility survey cited by Rogoff, Bernard, and Bourricaud. The French data which have been the subject of so many varying interpretations are those reported in Figure 1 above, and also form the basis for our conclusions about the relative amount of social mobility in France.

7 / Opportunity and Democracy

Peter M. Blau, Otis Dudley Duncan

LIPSET AND BENDIX found in their secondary analysis of mobility surveys from nine different countries that the rates of occupational mobility in all those industrial societies are high, with surprisingly little difference between them.[1] Contrary to the belief that America is a land of superior opportunities, the comparison revealed that the rates of upward mobility in several countries are higher than those in the United States, and so are the combined rates of upward and downward mobility. The authors' conclusion that generic conditions in industrialized societies—not any distinguishing features of the United States—are responsible for the high rates of occupational mobility observerable conforms to the conclusion we have reached. Nevertheless the specific point that opportunities for upward mobility in the United States are not as good as those in several European countries or in Japan (the only other non-European country included) may be questioned on several grounds. The prevailing impression that chances of social mobility are superior in the United States should not be dismissed out of hand, particularly in view of the doubtful reliability of some of the data with which Lipset and Bendix had to work. The outstandingly high degree of industrialization and level of education in American society as well as the less pronounced and less formalized distinctions in social status here compared to Europe or Japan would lead one to expect more social mobility in this country. Last but not least, whereas

---

[1] Seymour M. Lipset and Reinhard Bendix, *Social Mobility in Industrial Society,* Berkeley: Univer. of California Press, 1960, pp. 17–28.

Lipset and Bendix only examine movements from the blue-collar into the white-collar class and vice versa, a meaningful study of national differences in opportunities must take into account differential chances of achieving elite status in one of the top strata. Industrialization may have the result that many sons of craftsmen become clerks, but such movements would hardly constitute evidence of great opportunities.[2]

As far as mobility between the blue-collar and the white-collar class is concerned, the conclusion of Lipset and Bendix is essentially confirmed by the OCG data, which are more reliable than the American data that were available to them. The combined rate of mobility in either direction between the manual and the nonmanual class is 34 percent for the OCG sample, slightly higher than that reported for any other country, the second-highest rate being Germany's 31 percent. With respect to upward mobility of working-class sons into white-collar occupations, the rate in the United States, 37 percent according to the OCG sample, is exceeded by that in two of the nine countries, France's 39 percent and Switzerland's 45 percent. It should be noted, however, that the Swiss data, which are not based on a representative sample, were judged to be unreliable by Miller.[3] To sum up, there is indeed little difference among various industrialized nations in the rate of occupational mobility between the blue-collar and the white-collar class, though the United States has higher rates than most countries, corresponding to its advanced level of industrialization and education.

To investigate national differences in opportunities for upward mobility into a top stratum, the comparative data assembled by Miller are used.[4] Miller's own secondary analysis of these data centers on the proportion of sons from a given social class who move up into the top stratum. But since both the occupational composition and the proportionate size of the elite strata in different countries vary widely, the direct comparison of the proportion of men moving into the elite, ignoring differences in its size and composition, may easily be misleading. For this reason we have decided to use, in addition to the proportions, the mobility ratios that standardize for size, despite the reservations we have about employing mobility ratios in comparative analysis.... The data presented in Table 1 are derived from the raw frequencies in Miller's tables, except that the orginal source was used for Sweden because Miller does not present this table, and that

2 See Lewis A. Coser, Letter to the Editor, *Commentary*, 19(1955), 86–87. Although Lipset and Bendix do point out that mobility into the professions is probably higher in the United States than elsewhere (*op. cit.*, p. 38), their theoretical analysis tends to ignore this point and centers on the lack of differences in opportunity for mobility between the United States and other countries.

3 S. M. Miller, "Comparative Social Mobility," *Current Sociology*, 9(1960), 37. It should also be noted that if the OCG data are compared with those of other countries presented by Miller (p. 30) instead of with those presented by Lipset and Bendix, the proportion of American working-class sons who move up into white-collar strata is greater than that in any other country. These differences show that all such international comparisons must be interpreted with a great deal of caution.

4 *Ibid.*, pp. 1–89.

Lopreato's recent study of mobility in Italy has been substituted for the one used by Miller, which he considered to be of questionable reliability.[5] Only countries for which national samples are available are included, and the OCG data are substituted for the American ones used by Miller. The broader of his two criteria for elite (Elite I and II) is employed, and the two professional strata in the United States are considered to comprise the American elite. (The considerable gap in social distance between the two professional groups and all other occupational strata makes their designation as elite not entirely unjustified.) Following Miller's procedure, we examine movement into the elite from the working class (blue-collar), from the manual class (blue-collar and farm laborers, who could not always be separated from other manual workers), and from the middle class (white-collar excluding the elite).

Upward mobility from the working class into the top occupational stratum of the society is higher in the United States than in other countries. The proportion of American sons originating in the working class who move into the elite is exceeded only by that in Puerto Rico (column 2), and when differences in the size of the elite, which includes business owners as well as professionals for Puerto Rico, are taken into account, the mobility ratio for the United States is higher than that for any other country (column 3). Farm laborers must be combined with the various blue-collar workers into a manual class to permit comparisons with all countries. The chances of manual sons to experience upward mobility into the elite

Table 1. Outflow from Specified Origins into Elite[a] Destinations: International Comparisons

PER CENT OF ALL MEN IN ELITE		WORKING CLASS INTO ELITE		MANUAL CLASS INTO ELITE		MIDDLE-CLASS INTO ELITE	
		Mobility		*Mobility*		*Mobility*	
Country		*Per Cent*	*Ratio*	*Per Cent*	*Ratio*	*Per Cent*	*Ratio*
	(1)	*(2)*	*(3)*	*(4)*	*(5)*	*(6)*	*(7)*
Denmark	3.30	...	...	1.07	.32	4.58	1.39
France I (Bresard)	8.53	4.16	.49	3.52	.41	12.50	1.46
France II (Desabie)	6.12	1.99	.33	1.56	.25	10.48	1.71
Great Britain	7.49	...	...	2.23	.30	8.64	1.15
Italy	2.77	.48	.17	.35	.13	5.76	2.08
Japan	11.74	...	...	6.95	.59	15.12	1.29
Netherlands	11.08	...	...	6.61	.60	11.55	1.04
Puerto Rico	13.79	11.42	.83	8.60	.62	23.17	1.68
Sweden	6.66	4.43	.67	3.50	.53	18.09	2.72
USA (OCG)	11.60	10.41	.90	9.91	.85	20.90	1.80
West Germany	4.58	1.55	.34	1.46	.32	8.28	1.81

Source: S. M. Miller, *op. cit.*, pp. 69–80, except for Sweden (Carlsson, *op. cit.*, p. 93), Italy (Lopreato, *op. cit.*, p. 314), and the U.S.A. (OCG).
a "Elite" here is equivalent to Miller's "Elite I and II" for data from Miller and Carlsson, to Lopreato's "Ruling Class" for Italy, and to "Professional, Technical and Kindred" for the United States.

5 Carlsson, *op. cit.*, p. 93; and Joseph Lopreato, "Social Mobility in Italy," *American Journal of Sociology,* 71(1965), 311–14.

are greater in the United States than in any other country, whether raw proportions (column 4) or mobility ratios (column 5) are considered. The countries with the next best chances of mobility from manual origins into top-ranking positions are Puerto Rico, Japan, and the Netherlands. The likelihood that the middle class, consisting of the white-collar strata below the elite, sees its sons moving up into the elite is greater in the United States than in most countries, though not in all. The proportion of American men originating in the middle class who move into the elite is only exceeded by that in Puerto Rico (column 6), but when the size of the elite is taken into account, the mobility ratio reveals Sweden to be in the first place, with Italy, West Germany, and the United States following in that order (column 7). It should be noted that the mobility ratio for the middle class is not entirely independent of that for the manual class in the same country, so that a high manual ratio tends to depress the middle-class ratio. What is of special significance for an understanding of the oppor tunities of the poor is the relative size of the mobility ratio for manual sons.

The relative opportunities of underprivileged Americans with manual origins to move up into the top stratum are particularly good compared to those in other societies. Nearly 10 percent of manual sons achieve elite status in the United States, a higher proportion than in any other country. Lest it be suspected that this result is misleading because it only reflects the large size of the American elite—close to 12 percent of the population— the mobility ratios have been compared, despite the reservation we have about this measure. Doing so merely accentuates the earlier result. The proportion of manual sons who achieve elite status is six-sevenths of that of all men occupying such status in the United States (.85), whereas this proportion is in no other country as great as two-thirds of that of the total (Puerto Rico being in second place with .62). In respect to mobility from the middle class into the elite, however, the ratio for the United States, though high, is not outstanding. It is the underprivileged class of manual sons that has exceptional chances for mobility into the elite in this country. There is a grain of truth in the Horatio Alger myth. The high level of popular education in the United States, perhaps reinforced by the lesser emphasis on formal distinctions of social status, has provided the disadvantaged lower strata with outstanding opportunities for long-distance upward mobility.[6]

[6] Correlations between father's and son's occupational status, however, do not reveal a similar superiority of American opportunity. Thus, Kaare Svalastoga ("Social Mobility: The Western European Model," *Acta Sociologica*, 9, 1965, 176) concludes his regression analysis of data from nine European nations by stating "that it would not be very far off the mark in any industrialized European country to predict a father-son mobility equal to $r = .4$," which is the same correlation exhibited by the OCG data for the United States. The apparent contradiction may well be a result of the fact that the amount of mobility, even when presumably standardized, is not the sames thing as the degree to which son's status depends on father's. The exceptionally large amount of occupational mobility in the United States, a result of the structural changes that have occurred with rapid industrialization, has inclined people to ignore the degree to which social origins influence occupational achievements here as well as in other societies.

8 / Social Mobility and Industrial Society: A Thesis Re-Examined

F. Lancaster Jones

It is a lasting tribute to the clarity and force with which Lipset and Bendix (1959:12–28) developed their argument concerning the basic similarity in rates of social mobility in different industrial societies that their generalization has been so widely accepted. Thus we find Melvin Tumin (1967:92) citing Lipset and Bendix's research and concluding that:

> The net impact of these findings suggests that America is no more the land of opportunity than older European industrialized societies. Rather, opportunities for mobility seem to be roughly the same in the major industrial countries.

Similarly, T. B. Bottomore (1968:295) in a recent review of Blau and Duncan's study of the American occupational structure, writes that:

> They begin by questioning the Lipset–Bendix thesis that, *since rates of mobility are not significantly higher in the U.S.A. than in other countries,* it is the American ideology of equality and opportunity which makes class and status distinctions less important and prevents the formation of antagonistic classes. (my italics)

While the relationship between ideology and social structure should not be overlooked both Bottomore and to some extent Blau and Duncan (1967:432–41) tend to accept the general proposition that rates of social mobility across the nonmanual–manual line are not significantly higher in the United States than in other countries.

This is not to suggest that the Lipset–Bendix thesis has won universal acceptance. Indeed S. M. Miller, in what remains the most thorough-going survey of comparative social mobility, distinguished four groups of countries (admittedly not all highly industrialized or "western") with differing patterns of mobility. He concluded this section of his analysis thus:

> The four patterns of mobility outlined here strongly suggest that rather than omnibus statements on gross similarities or differences in some overall rate of mobility, we need to develop explanations of *each* of these four different patterns in terms of their causes, processes and consequences (Miller 1960:35, 31–33).

Reprinted by permission of the author and publisher from "Social Mobility and Industrial Society: A Thesis Re-Examined," *The Sociological Quarterly*, Vol. 10, No. 3 (Summer 1969), pp. 292–305.

Yet it is clear from even the most cursory review of sociological literature on social stratification and social mobility that Lipset and Bendix's analysis continues to exert a greater influence than Miller's work, perhaps because their analysis attempted to link their empirical findings directly with ideology, cultural values, social structure and social change. This link also leads to speculation about possible convergence in the social structures of industrial development which may in effect tend to "standardize" initially divergent social structures.

To discuss the merits of this last hypothesis is beyond the scope of this paper, which has the much more limited aim of examining the empirical support for Lipset and Bendix's original argument. How firmly can we rely on their empirical generalization that the overall pattern of social mobility appears to be much the same in industrial societies? To answer this requires a reanalysis of their data. Although a complete assessment of this generalization would require the examination of all the available material, I have made here no attempt to incorporate more recent findings than they consider. Needless to say, this review is not meant to be negative but, rather, reopens an issue which may have been prematurely closed. Indeed it may even be that readers of Lipset and Bendix have imbued their findings with greater finality than was indicated, since in their original monograph they stress the tentative nature of their interpretation. As an interpretation their study remains masterful, and this critique should be seen in this context. One final qualification is that since the chapter in which this analysis appears was in fact written by Lipset and Zetterberg, it may be more proper to refer to this thesis as the Lipset–Zetterberg thesis.

The Thesis Propounded

A question to which the Lipset–Zetterberg analysis incidentally addressed itself was the assumption that America, by contrast with the older countries of Western Europe, has (or had) a relatively "open" society and is (or was) characterized by relatively high rates of social mobility. The data available to them led them to question the validity of that assumption. Indeed, they believed their findings to be at such variance with this accepted dogma that they prefaced their analysis with the global conclusion (1959:13) that *"the overall pattern of social mobility appears to be much the same in the industrial societies of various Western countries"* (italics in original). Although they accepted in principle that there must be a relationship between rates of social mobility and rates of economic expansion, they found nothing in their data to suggest that the rate of economic growth is systematically correlated with rates of social mobility. Their tentative interpretation (1959:13) was that "the social mobility of societies becomes relatively high once their industrialization, and hence their economic expansion, reaches a certain level." In other words, the absence of marked differences in mobility rates among the countries considered can be taken as evidence that these countries have reached that "certain level" where social mobility between the generations becomes uniformly high.

As I have already indicated, the object of this paper is not to examine to what extent the social structures of different countries tend to converge under the process of industrialization. It is rather to examine the evidence which gave rise to Lipset and Zetterberg's specific interpretation of comparative rates of social mobility. This examination resolves itself into two parts: (1) given the evidence available to them, was their conclusion a reasonable one; and (2) how valid was the evidence on which their conclusion was based.

The Thesis Re-examined

For the purpose of an empirical test, the Lipset–Zetterberg thesis can be stated as a generic proposition: *the overall pattern of social mobility is the same in Western industrial countries.*

In operational terms, social mobility is indicated by movements between occupational strata, in this (the generational) case by movements between the occupational stratum occupied by a son and that occupied by his father. Formulated in this way this proposition gives rise to three hypotheses, as follows:

1. the percentage of sons remaining immobile in their fathers' occupational stratum does not differ significantly among Western industrial countries;
2. conversely, the rates of outflow mobility from specific strata of origin to specific strata of destination do not differ significantly among Western industrial countries; and
3. the overall patterns of immobility and mobility for specific strata of origin and destination do not differ significantly among Western industrial countries.

A test of these hypotheses calls for national data on the occupations of sons relative to those of their fathers. Lipset and Zetterberg present data from twelve postwar national sample surveys for nine countries. However, only nine of these twelve surveys use an occupational classification that can be regrouped in terms of nonmanual, manual and farm jobs. Figures for Great Britain, Denmark and Italy cannot be regrouped in this way and are therefore excluded from this test. Data from urban samples must also be excluded as they are inappropriate for testing hypotheses about nations.

It is unlikely that these exclusions unfairly prejudice our reanalysis against Lipset and Zetterberg's original interpretation. Lopreato (1965: 311–14) reports that the Italian figures did not confirm their generalization, and doubts also can be raised about the legitimacy of comparing mobility rates for countries with different proportions of their workforce engaged in farming, *if* farm and non-farm occupations are not distinguished (Lipset and Bendix, 1959:23). This paper considers, therefore, only the results of national surveys in France, Germany (three surveys), Sweden, Switzerland, the United States (two surveys), and Japan (Lipset and Bendix, 1959:19–21). Following Lipset and Zetterberg, we shall count Japan among the industrial nations of the West.

There is unfortunately an immediate difficulty in making this empirical test of the Lipset–Zetterberg thesis. Their analysis makes it clear that their general conclusion about the similarity of social mobility rates in industrial societies is not based on a consideration of detailed patterns of occupational mobility, but only on the *total* rate of mobility, upward *and* downward, across the nonmanual/manual line among the non-farm population. Indeed, they readily admit that there are differences in rates of upward and downward mobility (Lipset and Bendix, 1959:26). However, their concentration on the *total* mobility rate in the *non-farm* population is doubly favorable to their contention, since they thereby eliminate two major sources of international variation—the direction of mobility, and differential rates of mobility between farm and non-farm occupations. Nonetheless it seems essential to include both these factors in any test of propositions relating to social mobility in industrial societies.

The inclusion of farm occupations in this reanalysis involves a significant departure from Lipset–Zetterberg's definition of social mobility. The justification for this departure is that any generalization about countries as wholes can only be tested with evidence for countries as wholes, and not with evidence simply for the non-farm population. While the logic of their decision to count as social mobility only occupational movements across the nonmanual/manual line must be recognized, it can also be questioned. Clearly many movements between farm and non-farm jobs also indicate social mobility. How many is a question that may have to be answered differently at different times and for different countries. For the present we, like Lipset and Zetterberg, give no firm answer to this question. Unlike them, however, we do include this dimension of the occupational structure for mobility analysis, with full awareness of the conceptual difficulty involved. There is room for disagreement with this strategy, and ideally differentiation of prestige levels within the farm population is required. Nonetheless, the inclusion of farm occupations in this reanalysis does at least encourage recognition of this problem and of the magnitude of differences in the rates of farm/non-farm mobility. The very difficulty of equating social mobility with movements between non-farm and farm occupations suggests that more detailed occupational categories are required for comparative analysis. (For one recent study in which movements from farm to non-farm occupations are treated as social mobility, see Allingham [1967].)

Table 1 presents data relevant to testing the first hypothesis: that the degree of stratum immobility does not differ significantly among the countries considered. Details concerning the source and reliability of these figures can be found in Lipset and Bendix (1959:18–23) and also in Miller (1960:23–24). For the moment we adopt the simplifying assumption that all are equally reliable (in relation to their respective sample size) and that they can be accepted at face value.

For the first hypothesis to be supported we should expect to find relatively few significant differences among these percentages. Yet even a casual inspection reveals several marked differences, particularly in the farm

Table 1. Percent Immobile from Father's to Son's Occupational
Stratum in Nine National Surveys

PERCENT IMMOBILE

COUNTRY	*Nonmanual*	*Manual*	*Farm*
France	73	55	71
Germany I	58	68	54
Germany II	80	60	70
Germany III	70	70	43
Sweden	74	64	35
Switzerland	84	54	54
United States I	71	61	38
United States II	64	67	30
Japan	74	59	50

Source: Lipset and Bendix, 1959:19–21.

stratum. For example, the percentage immobile in farm occupations in the
United State (second survey) is less than half the figure for France. In the
nonmanual stratum, equally sharp contrasts can be noted, the maximum
difference being 26 percentage points. The range of values in the manual
stratum appears, however, to be less extreme.

A more exact impression of the importance of these differences can be
obtained by conventional techniques of statistical analysis. How many of
the percentages shown in Table 1, for example, are statistically significantly
different one from the other? Is it reasonable to attribute differences of
these magnitudes to sampling error alone? To answer this question, the t
statistic was computed for each possible pair of proportions shown in the
three columns of Table 1. For each column there are $N(N-1)/2$ such
comparisons, where N is the number of surveys. Only differences exceeding
the one percent level of probability (two-tailed test) have been reported.
A relatively conservative level of significance was selected partly because
national survey samples tend to be areally clustered samples, not simple
probability samples.

Of the 36 possible comparisons between the percentages remaining
immobile in nonmanual occupations, 16 (about one-half) are significantly
different. The figure for France, for example, is significantly higher than
that for Germany I, and significantly lower than all except the United
States II figure. That for Switzerland is significantly higher than all except
Germany II. If the low Germany I and high Switzerland figures are excluded, the number of significantly different comparisons is reduced from
just under half the possible total to under one-third. However, it seems
unreasonable to reject dissonant findings simply because they are dissonant,
or to average them if surveys of the same country are at variance.

For respondents immobile in the manual stratum, the ratio of significant
to non-significant comparisons is lower: only nine of the thirty-six are
statistically significant at the one percent level. This confirms the visual
impression that the relative spread of values is less marked among immobile
manual respondents. However, fully two-thirds (24/36) of the comparisons

for immobile farm respondents are significantly different, reflecting the very diverse range of values in the third column of Table 1.

Thus, a statistical analysis suggests that the evidence presented in Table 1 is inconclusive and a verdict of "Not proven" must be entered against the first hypothesis. Even at a conservative level of statistical significance (conservative in the sense that it tends to favor acceptance of the hypothesis even when it should be rejected), only in the second column of Table 1 are the similarities between the percentages immobile more marked than the differences. The evidence from the first column is evenly divided, that from the third predominantly against the acceptance of Hypothesis 1. Of all 108 tests made on the percentages shown in Table 1, 49 (45 percent) indicate significant differences between respective pairs of percentages.

It may at this point be fairly objected that statistical tests of this type tell us nothing about the intrinsic meaningfulness of observed differences, only that with probability samples of stated sizes the observed differences cannot reasonably be attributed to sampling error alone. With very large samples even quite small differences in proportions may be statistically significant. This comment does have a general force. Yet few of the samples cited are in fact very large samples: they range in size from 3,364 respondents (Japan) to 585 respondents (Germany II). Their average size is just over 1,400. There is, moreover, no sound reason to dismiss these differences as being sociologically trivial. A demographer presented with national fertility differentials of equal magnitude might well consider a classification into high, medium and low fertility countries. One can likewise consider distinguishing societies with differing levels of social mobility, if the data justify such distinctions. To dismiss as unimportant relative differences of 25 to 50 percent—even greater if we consider the farm stratum—would inhibit much of the discussion in which social scientists rightly engage.

Table 2 presents data relevant to testing the second and third hypotheses. Again comparisons are made column by column for each possible pair of percentages.

Table 2. Percentages of Occupational Mobility from Father's to Son's Occupational Stratum in Nine National Surveys

	NONMANUAL TO:		MANUAL TO:		FARM TO:	
COUNTRY	Manual	Farm	Nonmanual	Farm	Nonmanual	Manual
France	18	9	35	10	16	13
Germany I	38	4	27	5	19	28
Germany II	20	0	30	10	12	19
Germany III	28	2	26	4	20	37
Sweden	23	3	29	7	23	42
Switzerland	13	3	44	3	27	19
United States I	25	4	35	4	23	39
United States II	34	1	31	2	24	46
Japan	21	5	33	8	28	22

Sources: See Table 1.

Considering the first two columns of Table 2, and ignoring at this point the substantial inconsistencies between the German and (to a lesser degree) the American surveys, we find variations in rates of generational mobility from the nonmanual stratum. The rates for mobility into manual jobs range from a high of 38 percent (Germany I) to a low of 13 percent (Switzerland), and other differences of lesser, but still considerable, magnitude can be observed. Similarly the rates for movement into the farm stratum, while absolutely low, indicate some marked relative differences.

As before, tests of significance were computed for all possible pairs of values in each column. For the first column 19 of the 36 tests indicate statistically significant differences. In the second 22 out of 36 are significant. Thus, the rates of outflow mobility from the nonmanual stratum lend at best negative support to the second hypothesis: they do not show it to be false.

The range of variation in the rates of mobility from manual to nonmanual and farm occupations is relatively narrow. Only one in four tests between the percentages in the third column yielded significant results (9 out of 36 tests), as against one in three (12 out of 36 tests) for the percentages in the fourth. Overall the empirical evidence on outflow mobility from manual to nonmanual and farm jobs tends to support the second hypothesis: only 21 of 72 tests, or 29 percent, reveal differences that are statistically significant at the one percent level.

The evidence from columns 5 and 6 of Table 2 is again evenly divided. The movement from farm to nonmanual occupations varies from 12 percent for Germany II to 28 percent for Japan. Mostly, however, the figures range from one sixth to one quarter. Ten of the 36 comparisons on this column are statistically significant. For column 6, there are twice as many significant results—21 out of 36. Considerable variation exists in the rates of mobility from farm to manual occupations, a finding which supports the earlier contention that movements between farm and non-farm occupations cannot reasonably be ignored in international comparisons of mobility differentials. The rate at which men of farm origins move into manual, and nonmanual, jobs is presumably related to the rate at which men of manual origins move into the nonmanual stratum, and vice versa.

We are now able to test the third hypothesis, that the overall patterns of immobility and mobility for specific strata do not differ significantly among Western industrial countries. For the nonmanual stratum of origin, 54 of the 108 comparisons between the immobility and mobility rates are statistically significant: there are as many differences as similarities between these observed rates. For the manual stratum of origin, only 30 (28 percent) of the tests are significant, and the pattern of movement from this stratum yields partial, but not overwhelming, support for the third hypothesis. For the farm stratum of origin, 55 (51 percent) of the tests are significant, a ratio of significant to non-significant findings that cannot be taken as support, or denial, of the third hypothesis.

Thus, a statistical examination of these data suggests that the generalization that "overall pattern of social mobility appears to be much the same in the industrial societies of various Western countries" lacks a firm empirical base. It is supported by the evidence only if the direction of mobility and the category of farm occupations are ignored, and if it is interpreted in the limited sense that "total mobility rates in these countries are practically the same" (Lipset and Bendix, 1959:26). However, even this can be doubted, as an examination of the reliability of the data available to Lipset and Zetterberg indicates.

The Reliability of the Data

Many studies of social mobility have tended to concentrate on rates of outflow mobility from stratum of origin to stratum of destination. The data presented above represent a standard outflow analysis. An inflow perspective—that is, an examination of the social origins of men currently occupying the same occupational stratum—not only complements outflow analysis: it permits a direct assessment of the reliability of the basic data. Table 3 re-expresses the raw data of Tables 1 and 2 as inflow proportions of the occupational strata occupied by sons at time of interview. These figures have been recalculated from the marginals of Figure 2.1 in Lipset and Bendix, and some rounding errors have undoubtedly occurred. They are nonetheless sufficiently exact for my present purposes.

By re-expressing the data in this form we can form some impression of the representativeness of these national surveys. Since they are typically probability samples of the adult male work-force, it is a reasonable expectation that the distribution of respondents (in this case "sons") should represent a relatively close fit with that of the male work-force as a whole. The degree of fit may be slightly variable. Although most mobility studies are based on samples of the male work-force, the precise range of ages included in the sampling frame sometimes differs from one survey to another, a difference ignored in most comparisons despite its influence on mobility findings.

An inspection of Table 3 indicates what appear to be substantial biases towards the over-representation of nonmanual at the expense of manual and farm respondents. According to the 1950 Census of the United States, 30 percent of the male labor force had nonmanual occupations. Yet all nine surveys report nonmanual percentages considerably in excess of this figure. The figures for Switzerland indicate a severely biased sample: as late as 1960 only 26 percent of the Swiss male work-force held nonmanual jobs. Miller (1960:27) rejected these Swiss data in his 1960 survey, mainly because "the high mobility of the manual class in Switzerland as computed by L-B-Z...seemed unreasonable to some who knew Switzerland closely— Kurt Mayer was moved to comment on this in a personal communication." But an examination of labor force statistics for other countries indicates that several surveys utilized by Lipset and Zetterberg are not much more reliable. So much do the surveys cited differ in their apparent reliability that any observed "similarity" between the rates of total mobility in the

Table 3. Mobility Profiles for Six Countries: Inflow Percentages to Son's Occupation from Father's Occupation

SON'S OCCUPATION BY FATHER'S OCCUPATION

COUNTRY	Nonmanual				Manual				Farm				N (100%)
	NM	M	F	Total	NM	M	F	Total	NM	M	F	Total	
France	27	7	7	41	7	11	6	24	3	2	30	35	3,023
Germany I	30	10	2	42	20	25	3	48	2	2	6	10	1,108
Germany II	32	11	3	46	8	22	4	34	0	4	16	20	585
Germany III	26	11	4	41	10	29	8	47	1	2	9	12	722
Sweden	17	12	8	37	5	27	15	47	1	3	12	16	871
Switzerland	44	9	7	60	7	11	5	23	2	1	15	18	1,124
United States I	20	13	8	41	7	23	14	44	1	1	13	15	1,153
United States II	15	11	10	36	8	25	19	52	0	1	12	13	794
Japan	25	7	12	44	7	13	10	30	2	2	22	26	3,364

six countries might be more reasonably attributed not to the convergence of mobility rates under conditions of industrial expansion, but to a convergence of sample biases of differing severity.

It is not proposed to discuss Table 3 in detail. The patterns it reveals do, to be sure, raise a number of issues. Its main purpose, however, is to provide a means of exploring the possible effects of sample bias on the observed patterns of outflow mobility. In some other studies it has simply been assumed that a bias of this type can be ignored. Thus Jackson and Crockett (1964:11) noted that the 1945 and 1947 studies analysed in their trend comparison of occupational mobility in the United States over-represented persons from higher social strata. They assumed that "the effect of this bias is not so great nor so focused as to distort any overall mobility trend." Of course, it should be pointed out that the biases in the sample discussed by Jackson and Crockett are less substantial than in some of the samples discussed here.

To illustrate the possible effects of sample bias we can take the figures for France as an example. Although occupational figures are not available for France in 1948, the date of the Bresard study utilized by Lipset and Zetterberg, we can estimate the proportionate distribution of the male work-force as 25 percent nonmanual, 42 percent manual, and 33 percent farm (U.N., 1956:373). This manual figure may be a slight underestimate (the farm percentage can be accurately estimated from the industry results for the 1946 census). On these figures the Bresard study appears to have almost twice as many nonmanual, and almost half as many manual, respondents as expected. On the optimistic assumption that only the totals in the nonmanual, manual and farm strata are in error, the internal cells of Table 3 can be scaled to conform to a more representative occupational distribution. Thus, if nonmanual sons in the French workforce as a whole did originate from nonmanual, manual and farm fathers in the ratio of 27:7:7, then for a "true" percentage of 25 percent (not 41 percent as observed) currently in nonmanual jobs the distribution by stratum of origin must be approximately 16, 5, and 4 percent respectively. We can similarly adjust the inflow percentages for manual and farm respondents. Once the inflow percentages have been adjusted, they can be re-expressed as outflow percentages from stratum of origin.

Table 4 presents a series of such re-calculated outflow mobility rates, obtained by adjusting the internal cells of Table 3 to the following occupational distributions. To the extent that many mobility studies exclude the youngest and oldest cohorts of workers, the nonmanual figure may be

COUNTRY AND YEAR	NONMANUAL	MANUAL	FARM
France, 1946	25	42	33
West Germany, 1955	25	59	16
Sweden, 1955	23	56	21
Switzerland, 1955	23	59	18
U.S.A., 1950	30	54	16
Japan, 1955	28	40	32

a slight, but only slight, underestimate. The figures for the United States are from the 1950 census. The remainder are interpolations from occupational data (Germany, Sweden, Switzerland and Japan) and industrial data (France). Sources used were U.N., (1956:344–418) and I.L.O., (1960:136–239). The analysis by Blau and Duncan (1967:102–3) uses a similar technique of adjustment.

The results of these adjustments demonstrate the sensitivity of out-flow mobility rates to changes in the relative size of the nonmanual, manual, and farm strata. A comparison of Table 4 with Tables 1 and 2 reveal very marked discrepancies between the observed and the adjusted values. The adjusted figures for Switzerland are vastly different from those reported by Lipset and Zetterberg: the mean deviation between the two sets of percentages is 20 percent. In fact, only for the American and Swedish surveys is the fit between the two series moderately close. Although it is not suggested that these adjusted rates are accurate estimates of the "true" rates of generational mobility in these countries at the time the various surveys were conducted, it is interesting to note that the adjusted rate of upward mobility from manual into nonmanual occupations is considerably higher for the United States than for the other countries. Thus, the conclusion that "America is no more the land of opportunity than older European industrialized societies" (Tumin, 1967:92) may be not only premature but positively wrong. In any case, it is a generalization that requires careful scrutiny and more reliable evidence than has so far been presented. (For a partial re-examination, see Blau and Duncan [1967:432–41].)

Conclusions

A statistical evaluation of the empirical basis for the generalization that the pattern of social mobility is similar in Western industrial societies suggests that the data actually cited neither support nor refute that generalization. It can be said to receive support only if it is interpreted in a quite limited sense, to refer to movements across the nonmanual/manual line, without reference to their direction or to movements involving farm occupations. However, the comparative analysis of national mobility rates requires the consideration of farm as well as non-farm occupations, particularly in view of the historical importance of changes in labor force distribution between the primary, secondary and tertiary sectors of industrializing societies. The relative, and in some countries absolute, decline in the rural labor force has consequences for social mobility which ramify throughout the occupational structure. Movements between nonmanual and manual strata are closely related to and partly dependent upon movements out of farm occupations.

More than this, we have tried to show that the overall quality of these data is so suspect that they are incapable of supporting any sound generalization. Apart from the United States II survey, the ratio of nonmanual to manual workers is much higher than expected from labor force statistics,

Table 4. Hypothetical Outflow Mobility Rates for Nine National Surveys, after Adjustment for Possible Sample Bias

FATHER'S OCCUPATION BY SON'S OCCUPATION

COUNTRY	Nonmanual				Manual				Farm			
	NM	M	F	Total	NM	M	F	Total	NM	M	F	Total
France	52	39	9	100	19	73	8	100	9	21	70	100
Germany I	39	54	7	100	15	78	7	100	7	21	72	100
Germany II	55	45	0	100	13	83	4	100	9	32	59	100
Germany III	53	43	4	100	15	78	7	100	8	40	52	100
Sweden	61	33	6	100	16	75	9	100	13	46	41	100
Switzerland	46	49	5	100	9	88	3	100	10	38	52	100
United States I	60	36	4	100	25	72	2	99	14	47	39	100
United States II	62	38	0	100	26	72	3	101	19	47	34	100
Japan	59	33	8	100	17	75	8	100	16	27	57	100

Note: The rates shown above are illustrative only of the effect of varying the marginal totals of nonmanual, manual, and farm respondents. They are not assumed to be reliable estimates of the actual rates. See text.

95

in some cases very much higher. The effects of such biases on the observed rates of outflow mobility cannot be ignored. Indeed they seem sufficient to vitiate any conclusions that might be drawn from them. Clearly the sensitivity of outflow rates to different degrees of sample bias is of critical importance in comparative analysis. The need for re-evaluation and new comparisons that do not minimize these problems is obvious.

Despite deficiencies in available data, nonetheless Lipset and Zetterberg have introduced a challenging hypothesis. It promises much as an organizing principle and interpretative framework. But textbook assurances apart, there is no reliable evidence that rates of mobility defined as occupational movement between the generations in Western industrial societies are, or are not, similar. It is equally questionable that the vision of America as a land of social opportunity is, or was, mistaken. Materials adequate for an analytic task of this subtlety are not as readily available as some have believed. There are now relatively reliable national surveys for several countries. But reliability is only one of many requirements for comparability. Some surveys do not differentiate farm from non-farm occupations; some are based on samples of household heads, others on the adult work-force; some exclude young and old workers, while others include them; some are now separated by half a generation in a period of rapid social change and economic growth. And there are numerous methodological and conceptual problems not discussed here, such as marginal-free measures of mobility and long-distance social mobility (Blau and Duncan, 1967:Ch. 3; Svalastoga, 1965:118–26; Duncan, 1966). Challenging as the Lipset–Zetterberg thesis is, its validity as an interpretation of social mobility rates in industrial societies remains to be demonstrated.

References

Allingham, J. D.
  1967 "Class regression: An aspect of the social stratification process." American Sociological Review 32 (June): 442–49.
Blau, Peter M. and Otis Dudley Duncan
  1967 The American Occupational Structure. New York: John Wiley and Sons.
Bottomore, T. B.
  1968 "Review symposium." American Sociological Review 33 (April): 294–6.
Duncan, Otis Dudley
  1966 "Methodological issues in the analysis of social mobility." Pp. 51–97 in Neil J. Smelser and Seymour Martin Lipset, Social Structure and Mobility in Economic Development. Chicago: Aldine Publishing Co.

International Labour Office
  1966 Yearbook of Labour Statistics
Jackson, E. F. and H. J. Crockett, Jr.
  1964 "Occupational mobility in the United States: a point estimate and trend comparison." American Sociological Review 29 (February): 5–15.
Lipset, Seymour Martin and Reinhard Bendix
  1959 Social Mobility in Industrial Society. Berkeley and Los Angeles: University of California Press.
Lopreato, J.
  1965 "Social mobility in Italy." American Journal of Sociology 71 (November): 311–14.
Miller, S. M.
  1960 "Comparative social mobility." Current Sociology 9:1–89.
Svalastoga, Kaare

1965 Social Differentiation. New York: D. McKay Co.

Tumin, Melvin M.
1967 Social Stratification: The Forms and Functions of Inequality. Englewood Cliffs: Prentice-Hall.

United Nations
1956 Demographic Yearbook.

3 / Bureaucracy:
Is There
An Alternative?*

The term *bureaucracy* has become a stone to be hurled against any institution that represents the "establishment." There are more legitimate and useful grounds for criticizing the bureaucratic organizational form. Even Max Weber, the German sociologist responsible for the early formulation of the bureaucratic model as an ideal type, expressed the fear that bureaucracy would breed excessive organizational conservatism.

The first reading in this chapter, "Bureaucracy: Its Nature and Superiority," was written by Weber. He outlines the central characteristics of bureaucracy, then makes a case for the technical superiority of bureaucracy over other organizational forms.

* Though written initially for the present volume, this introduction was first published as part of a paper entitled "Participative Management and Voluntary Turnover: Concepts, Theories and Implications for Management," in *National Study of Social Welfare and Rehabilitation Workers, Work, and Organizational Contexts: Working Papers #1* (Washington, D. C.: Social and Rehabilitation Service, United States Department of Health, Education, and Welfare, 1971).

More recently, dissident voices have been heard among scholars in many disciplines. In "The Decline of Bureaucracy and Organizations of the Future," Warren Bennis, one of the most vocal contemporary critics of bureaucracy, contends that the bureaucratic organizational form was well suited to the social and economic conditions under which it was developed and adopted. Those social and economic conditions have changed, however, and organizational models and managerial practices adapted to contemporary realities are emerging. According to Bennis, two factors will successfully overcome bureaucracy: the increasing demand for a balance between individual goals and organizational objectives, and the rapid environmental changes wrought by scientific and technological advancements. "Organic-adaptive" structures, or "temporary systems," will be the model for structuring future organizations. Skill and professional training will supplant rank as the principle of differentiation. Organizations will be staffed by a variety of specialists in temporary systems assembled to meet the problem at hand. Management's job will be to coordinate and link the various changing task forces within the organization.

Though less extreme than that of Bennis, an earlier and kindred conception is advanced by Burns and Stalker in "Mechanistic and Organic Systems." They introduced the "organic" and "mechanistic" organizational models alluded to by Bennis. According to Burns and Stalker, a mechanistic management system based essentially on the bureaucratic model is suited for organizations operating in a stable internal and external environment. Under constantly changing conditions, where the emergence of new problems and the adoption of unpredictable courses of action are commonplace, the organic management system is needed for goal attainment.

Victor A. Thompson ("Bureaucracy and Innovation") elaborates on the frequent observation that monocratic (bureaucratic) organizations breed conservatism and parochialism and thereby stifle the generation and implementation of new ideas. Bureaucratic structural principles like centralized control from the top, use of extrinsic rewards (money, power, and status) to assure compliance, and emphasis on accountability at all organizational levels create a psychological and social climate inappropriate for individual and organizational creativity. Thompson offers some general requirements and structural changes requisite to the creation of an innovative organization. He also discusses some necessary alterations in administrative practice that must be undertaken.

In "Models of Bureaucracy Which Permit Conflict," Eugene Litwak outlines three models of organization: Weberian (emphasis on impersonal relations and rules and regulations), "human relations" (stress on primary relations and organizational objectives), and "professional" (including both the Weberian and human relations emphases). Organizations dealing with uniform events and emphasizing reliance on traditional knowledge are best served by the Weberian model. The human relations model is most efficient for organizations facing nonuniform events and needing effective interpersonal relations. However, the majority of contemporary organizations face a dilemma: part of the organization requires a Weberian approach while another segment needs the human relations approach. The professional model contains the central features of both of those organizational types. Since the operating principles of the Weberian and human relations models conflict, "mechanisms of segregation" must be evolved to permit the coexistence of these incompatible social arrangements without organizational inefficiency or destruction.

Richard Hall's article, "Intraorganizational Structural Variation: Application of the Bureaucratic Model," illustrates the recognition of Litwak's model, at least in practice, by management. According to Hall's data, internal structural segments of organizations differ in the degree to which they are bureaucratized. In lieu of studying the three organizational models outlined by Litwak, Hall sets up a continuum of bureaucratization. Using attitude questions on six dimensions of bureaucracy, Hall presents measures of the degree of bureaucratization as perceived by organization members. He finds partial verification for the general proposition that organizational units engaging in nonuniform and nonroutine tasks will be less bureaucratically structured than segments performing uniform and routine tasks.

9 / Bureaucracy: Its Nature and Superiority

Max Weber

Characteristics of Bureaucracy

MODERN OFFICIALDOM FUNCTIONS in the following specific manner:

I. There is the principle of fixed and official jurisdictional areas, which are generally ordered by rules, that is, by laws or administrative regulations.

1. The regular activities required for the purposes of the bureaucratically governed structure are distributed in a fixed way as official duties.
2. The authority to give the commands required for the discharge of these duties is distributed in a stable way and is strictly delimited by rules concerning the coercive means, physical, sacerdotal, or otherwise, which may be placed at the disposal of officials.
3. Methodical provision is made for the regular and continuous fulfillment of these duties and for the execution of the corresponding rights; only persons who have the generally regulated qualifications to serve are employed.

In public and lawful government these three elements constitute 'bureaucratic authority.' In private economic domination, they constitute bureaucratic 'management.' Bureaucracy, thus understood, is fully developed in political and ecclesiastical communities only in the modern state, and, in the private economy, only in the most advanced institutions of capitalism. Permanent and public office authority, with fixed jurisdiction, is not the historical rule but rather the exception. This is so even in large political structures such as those of the ancient Orient, the Germanic and Mongolian empires of conquest, or of many feudal structures of state. In all these cases, the ruler executes the most important measures through personal trustees, table-companions, or court-servants. Their commissions and authority are not precisely delimited and are temporarily called into being for each case.

II. The principles of office hierarchy and of levels of graded authority mean a firmly ordered system of super- and subordination in which there

Reprinted by permission of the publisher from H. H. Gerth and C. Wright Mills, translators and editors, *From Max Weber: Essays in Sociology* (New York: Oxford University Press, 1958), pp. 196–98, 214–16.

is a supervision of the lower offices by the higher ones. Such a system offers the governed the possibility of appealing the decision of a lower office to its higher authority, in a definitely regulated manner. With the full development of the bureaucratic type, the office hierarchy is monocratically organized. The principle of hierarchical office authority is found in all bureaucratic structures: in state and ecclesiastical structures as well as in large party organizations and private enterprises. It does not matter for the character of bureaucracy whether its authority is called 'private' or 'public.'

When the principle of jurisdictional 'competency' is fully carried through, hierarchical subordination—at least in public office—does not mean that the 'higher' authority is simply authorized to take over the business of the 'lower.' Indeed, the opposite is the rule. Once established and having fulfilled its task, an office tends to continue in existence and be held by another incumbent.

III. The management of the modern office is based upon written documents ('the files'), which are preserved in their original or draught form. There is, therefore, a staff of subaltern officials and scribes of all sorts. The body of officials actively engaged in a 'public' office, along with the respective apparatus of material implements and the files, make up a 'bureau.' In private enterprise, 'the bureau' is often called 'the office.'

In principle, the modern organization of the civil service separates the bureau from the private domicile of the official, and, in general, bureaucracy segregates official activity as something distinct from the sphere of private life. Public monies and equipment are divorced from the private property of the official. This condition is everywhere the product of a long development. Nowadays, it is found in public as well as in private enterprises; in the latter, the principle extends even to the leading entrepreneur. In principle, the executive office is separated from the household, business from private correspondence, and business assets from private fortunes. The more consistently the modern type of business management has been carried through the more are these separations the case. The beginnings of this process are to be found as early as the Middle Ages.

It is the peculiarity of the modern entrepreneur that he conducts himself as the 'first official' of his enterprise, in the very same way in which the ruler of a specifically modern bureaucratic state spoke of himself as 'the first servant' of the state.[1] The idea that the bureau activities of the state are intrinsically different in character from the management of private economic offices is a continental European notion and, by way of contrast, is totally foreign to the American way.

IV. Office management, at least all specialized office management—and such management is distinctly modern—usually presupposes thorough and expert training. This increasingly holds for the modern executive and employee of private enterprises, in the same manner as it holds for the state official.

[1] Frederick II of Prussia.

V. When the office is fully developed, official activity demands the full working capacity of the official, irrespective of the fact that his obligatory time in the bureau may be firmly delimited. In the normal case, this is only the product of a long development, in the public as well as in the private office. Formerly, in all cases, the normal state of affairs was reversed: official business was discharged as a secondary activity.

VI. The management of the office follows general rules, which are more or less stable, more or less exhaustive, and which can be learned. Knowledge of these rules represents a special technical learning which the officials possess. It involves jurisprudence, or administrative or business management.

The reduction of modern office management to rules is deeply embedded in its very nature. The theory of modern public administration, for instance, assumes that the authority to order certain matters by decree—which has been legally granted to public authorities—does not entitle the bureau to regulate the matter by commands given for each case, but only to regulate the matter abstractly. This stands in extreme contrast to the regulation of all relationships through individual privileges and bestowals of favor, which is absolutely dominant in patrimonialism, at least in so far as such relationships are not fixed by sacred tradition. . . .

Technical Advantages of Bureaucratic Organization

The decisive reason for the advance of bureaucratic organization has always been its purely technical superiority over any other form of organization. The fully developed bureaucratic mechanism compares with other organizations exactly as does the machine with the nonmechanical modes of production.

Precision, speed, unambiguity, knowledge of the files, continuity, discretion, unity, strict subordination, reduction of friction and of material and personal costs—these are raised to the optimum point in the strictly bureaucratic administration, and especially in its monocratic form. As compared with all collegiate, honorific, and avocational forms of administration, trained bureaucracy is superior on all these points. And as far as complicated tasks are concerned, paid bureaucratic work is not only more precise but, in the last analysis, it is often cheaper than even formally unremunerated honorific service.

Honorific arrangements make administrative work an avocation and, for this reason alone, honorific service normally functions more slowly; being less bound to schemata and being more formless. Hence it is less precise and less unified than bureaucratic work because it is less dependent upon superiors and because the establishment and exploitation of the apparatus of subordinate officials and filing services are almost unavoidably less economical. Honorific service is less continuous than bureaucratic and frequently quite expensive. This is especially the case if one thinks not only of the money costs to the public treasury—costs which bureaucratic administration, in comparison with administration by notables, usually substantially increases—but also of the frequent economic losses of the governed caused by delays and lack of precision. The possibility of administration by notables normally and permanently exists only where official management can be satisfactorily discharged as an avocation. With the qualitative increase of tasks the administration has to face, administration by notables reaches its limits—today, even in England. Work organized by collegiate bodies causes friction and delay and requires compromises between colliding interests and views. The administration, therefore, runs less precisely and is more independent of superiors; hence, it is less unified and slower. All advances of the Prussian administrative organization have been and will in the future be advances of the bureaucratic, and especially of the monocratic principle.

Today, it is primarily the capitalist market economy which demands that the official business of the administration be discharged precisely, unambiguously, continuously, and with as much speed as possible. Normally, the very large, modern capitalist enterprises are themselves unequalled models of strict bureaucratic organization. Business management throughout rests on increasing precision, steadiness, and, above all, the speed of operations. This, in turn, is determined by the peculiar nature of the modern means of communication, including, among other things, the news service of the press. The extraordinary increase in the speed by which public announcements, as well as economic and political facts, are transmitted exerts a steady and sharp pressure in the direction of speeding up the tempo of administrative reaction towards various situations. The optimum of such reaction time is normally attained only by a strictly bureaucratic organization.[2]

Bureaucratization offers above all the optimum possibility for carrying through the principle of specializing administrative functions according to purely objective considerations. Individual performances are allocated to functionaries who have specialized training and who by constant practice learn more and more. The 'objective' discharge of business primarily means a discharge of business according to *calculable rules* and 'without regard for persons.'

'Without regard for persons' is also the watchword of the 'market' and, in general, of all pursuits of naked economic interests. A consistent execution of bureaucratic domination means the leveling of status 'honor.' Hence, if the principle of the free-market is not at the same time restricted, it means the universal domination of the 'class situation.' That this consequence of bureaucratic domination has not set in everywhere, parallel to the extent of bureaucratization, is due to the differences among possible principles by which polities may meet their demands.

The second element mentioned, 'calculable rules,' also is of paramount importance for modern bureaucracy. The peculiarity of modern culture, and specifically of its technical and economic basis, demands this very

---

2 Here we cannot discuss in detail how the bureaucratic apparatus may, and actually does, produce definite obstacles to the discharge of business in a manner suitable for the single case.

'calculability' of results. When fully developed, bureaucracy also stands, in a specific sense, under the principle of *sine ira ac studio*. Its specific nature, which is welcomed by capitalism, develops the more perfectly the more the bureaucracy is 'dehumanized,' the more completely it succeeds in eliminating from official business love, hatred, and all purely personal, irrational, and emotional elements which escape calculation. This is the specific nature of bureaucracy and it is appraised as its special virtue.

The more complicated and specialized modern culture becomes, the more its external supporting apparatus demands the personally detached and strictly 'objective' *expert,* in lieu of the master of older social structures, who was moved by personal sympathy and favor, by grace and gratitude. Bureaucracy offers the attitudes demanded by the external apparatus of modern culture in the most favorable combination. As a rule, only bureaucracy has established the foundation for the administration of a rational law conceptually systematized on the basis of such enactments as the latter Roman imperial period first created with a high degree of technical perfection. During the Middle Ages, this law was received along with the bureaucratization of legal administration, that is to say, with the displacement of the old trial procedure which was bound to tradition or to irrational presuppositions, by the rationally trained and specialized expert....

10 / The Decline of Bureaucracy and Organizations of the Future*

Warren G. Bennis

MOST OF US spend all of our working day and a great deal of our nonworking day in a unique and extremely durable social arrangement called "bureaucracy." I use the term "bureaucracy" descriptively, not as an epithet about "those guys in Washington" or as a metaphor *à la* Kafka's *Castle,* which conjures up an image of red tape, faceless masses standing in endless lines, and despair. Bureaucracy, as I shall use the term here, is a social invention, perfected during the Industrial Revolution to organize and direct the activities of the firm. To paraphrase Churchill's ironic remark about democracy, we can say of bureaucracy that it is the worst possible theory of organization—apart from all the others that have so far been tried.

The burden of this book rests upon the premise that this form of organization is becoming less and less effective, that it is hopelessly out of joint with contemporary realities, and that new shapes, patterns, and models—currently recessive—are emerging which promise drastic changes in the conduct of the corporation and in managerial practices in general. So within the next twenty-five to fifty years, we should all be witness to, and participate in, the end of bureaucracy and the rise of new social systems better able to cope with twentieth-century demands.†

---

* Adapted from an Invited Address presented to the Division of Industrial and Business Psychology at the American Psychological Association meeting. Los Angeles, Calif., Sept. 5, 1964. Reprinted by permission from *Transaction,* where it was originally published in July, 1965.

† The number of years necessary for this transition is, of course estimated from forecasts for the prospects of industrialization. Sociological evolutionists are substantially agreed that within a twenty-five- to fifty-year period, most of the people in the world will be living in industrialized societies. And it is this type of society that concerns me here, not the so-called underadvanced, semiadvanced, or partially advanced societies.

From Warren G. Bennis, *Changing Organizations* (New York: McGraw-Hill Book Company, 1966), pp. 3–15.
Reprinted by permission of TRANS-action, Inc., the original publisher of the article and the author.

The argument will be presented in the following sequence:

1. A quick look at bureaucracy: what it is and what its problems are;
2. A brief survey of how behavioral scientists and practitioners have attempted to modify and alter the bureaucratic mechanism so that it would respond more appropriately to changing times (in this section I shall show how these emergency remedies have been only stopgap measures and how more basic changes are required);
3. A general forecast of how most organizations of the future will operate.

Bureaucracy and its Discontents

Corsica, according to Gibbon, is much easier to deplore than to describe. The same holds true for bureaucracy. Basically, though, it is simple: bureaucracy is a social invention which relies exclusively on the power to influence through reason and law. Max Weber, the German sociologist who conceptualized the idea of bureaucracy around the turn of the century, once likened the bureaucratic mechanism to a judge qua computer: "Bureaucracy is like a modern judge who is a vending machine into which the pleadings are inserted together with the fee and which then disgorges the judgment together with its reasons mechanically derived from the code."[1]

The bureaucratic "machine model" Weber outlined was developed as a reaction against the personal subjugation, nepotism, cruelty, emotional vicissitudes, and subjective judgment which passed for managerial practices in the early days of the Industrial Revolution. Man's true hope, it was thought, was his ability to rationalize and calculate—to use his head as well as his hands and heart. Thus in this system roles are institutionalized and reinforced by legal tradition rather than by the "cult of personality"; rationality and predictability were sought for in order to eliminate chaos and unanticipated consequences; technical competence rather than arbitrary or "iron" whims was emphasized. These are oversimplifications, to be sure, but contemporary students of organizations would tend to agree with them. In fact, there is a general consensus that bureaucracy can be dimensionalized in the following way:

1. A division of labor based on functional specialization
2. A well-defined hierarchy of authority
3. A system of rules covering the rights and duties of employees
4. A system of procedures for dealing with work situations
5. Impersonality of interpersonal relations
6. Promotion and selection based on technical competence[2]

These six dimensions describe the basic underpinnings of bureaucracy, the pyramidal organization which dominates so much of our thinking and planning related to organizational behavior.

It does not take a great critical imagination to detect the flaws and problems in the bureaucratic model. We have all *experienced* them: bosses without technical competence and underlings with it; arbitrary and zany rules; an underworld (or informal) organization which subverts or even replaces the formal apparatus; confusion and conflict among roles; and cruel treatment of subordinates, based not upon rational or legal grounds, but upon inhumane grounds. Unanticipated consequences abound and provide a mine of material for those comics, like Chaplin or Tati, who can capture with a smile or a shrug the absurdity of authority systems based on pseudologic and inappropriate rules.

Almost everybody, including many students of organizational behavior, approaches bureaucracy with a chip on his shoulder. It has been criticized for its theoretical confusion and contradictions, for moral and ethical reasons, on practical grounds such as its inefficiency, for its methodological weaknesses, and for containing too many implicit values or for containing too few. I have recently cataloged the criticisms of bureaucracy, and they outnumber and outdo the Ninety-five Theses tacked on the church door at Wittenberg in attacking another bureaucracy.[3] For example:

1. Bureaucracy does not adequately allow for personal growth and the development of mature personalities.
2. It develops conformity and "group-think."
3. It does not take into account the "informal organization" and the emergent and unanticipated problems.
4. Its systems of control and authority are hopelessly outdated.
5. It has no adequate juridical process.
6. It does not possess adequate means for resolving differences and conflicts among ranks and, most particularly, among functional groups.
7. Communication (and innovative ideas) are thwarted or distorted because of hierarchical divisions.
8. The full human resources of bureaucracy are not being utilized because of mistrust, fear of reprisals, etc.
9. It cannot assimilate the influx of new technology or scientists entering the organization.
10. It will modify the personality structure such that man will become and reflect the dull, gray, conditioned "organization man."

Max Weber himself, the developer of the theory of bureaucracy, came around to condemning the apparatus he helped immortalize. While he felt that bureaucracy was inescapable, he also thought it might strangle the spirit of capitalism or the enterprenuerial attitude, a theme which Schumpeter later on developed. And in a debate on bureaucracy he once said, more in sorrow than in anger:

> It is horrible to think that the world could one day be filled with nothing but those little cogs, little men clinging to little jobs and striving towards bigger ones—a state of affairs which is to be seen once more, as in the Egyptian records, playing an ever-increasing part in the spirit of our present administrative system, and especially of its offspring, the students.

This passion for bureaucracy...is enough to drive one to despair. It is as if in politics...we were deliberately to become men who need "order" and nothing but order, who become nervous and cowardly if for one moment this order wavers, and helpless if they are torn away from their total incorporation in it. That the world should know no men but these: it is such an evolution that we are already caught up in, and the great question is therefore not how we can promote and hasten it, but what can we oppose to this machinery in order to keep a portion of mankind free from this parcelling-out of the soul from this supreme mastery of the bureaucratic way of life.[4]

I think it would be fair to say that a good deal of the work on organizational behavior over the past two decades has been a footnote to the bureaucratic "backlash" which aroused Weber's passion: saving mankind's soul "from the supreme mastery of the bureaucratic way of life." At least, very few of us have been indifferent to the fact that the bureaucratic mechanism is a social instrument in the service of repression; that it treats man's ego and social needs as a constant, or as nonexistent or inert; that these confined and constricted needs insinuate themselves into the social processes of organizations in strange, unintended ways; and that those very matters which Weber claimed escaped calculation—love, power, hate—not only are calculable and powerful in their effects but must be reckoned with.

Modifications of Bureaucracy

In what ways has the system of bureaucracy been modified in order that it may cope more successfully with the problems that beset it? Before answering that, we have to say something about the nature of organizations, *all* organizations, from mass-production leviathans all the way to service industries such as the university or hospital. Organizations are primarily complex goal-seeking units. In order to survive, they must also accomplish the secondary tasks of (1) maintaining the internal system and coordinating the "human side of enterprise"—a process of mutual compliance here called "reciprocity"—and (2) adapting to and shaping the external environment—here called "adaptability." These two organizational dilemmas can help us organize the pivotal ways the bureaucratic mechanism has been altered—and found wanting.

Resolutions of the Reciprocity Dilemma

Reciprocity has to do primarily with the processes which can mediate conflict between the goals of management and the individual goals of the workers. Over the past several decades, a number of interesting theoretical and practical resolutions have been made which truly allow for conflict and mediation of interest. They revise, if not transform, the very nature of the bureaucratic mechanism by explicit recognition of the inescapable tension between individual and organizational goals. These theories can be called, variously, "exchange," "group," "value," "structural," or "situational," depending on what variable of the situation one wishes to modify.

The exchange theories postulate that wages, incomes, and services are given to the individual for an equal payment to the organization in work. If the inducements are not adequate, the individual may withdraw and work elsewhere.[5] This concept may be elaborated by increasing the payments to include motivational units. That is to say, the organization provides a psychological anchor in times of rapid social change and a hedge against personal loss, as well as position, growth and mastery, success experience, and so forth, in exchange for energy, work, and commitment.[6]

I shall discuss this idea of payment in motivational units further, as it is a rather recent one to gain acceptance. Management tends to interpret motivation by economic theory. Man is logical; man acts in the manner which serves his self-interest; man is competitive. Elton Mayo and his associates were among the first to see human affiliation as a motivating force, to consider industrial organization a social system as well as an economic-technical system. They judge a manager in terms of his ability to sustain cooperation.[7] In fact, once a cohesive, primary work group is seen as a motivating force, a managerial elite may become obsolete, and the work group itself become the decision maker. This allows decisions to be made at the most relevant point of the organizational social space, where the data are most available.[8]

Before this is possible, some believe that the impersonal value system of bureaucracy must be modified.[9] In this case the manager plays an important role as the instrument of change, as an interpersonal specialist. He must instill values which permit and reinforce expression of feeling, experimentalism and norms of individuality, trust, and concern. Management, according to Blake,[10] is successful as it maximizes "concern for people"—along with "concern for production."

Others[11,12] believe that a new conception of the structure of bureaucracy will create more relevant attitudes toward the function of management than formal role specifications do. If the systems are seen as organic rather than mechanistic, as adapting spontaneously to the needs of the system, then decisions will be made at the critical point, and roles and jobs will devolve to the "natural" incumbent. The shift would probably be from the individual to cooperative group effort, from delegated to shared responsibility, from centralized to decentralized authority, from obedience to confidence, and from antagonistic arbitration to problem solving.[13] Management which is centered around problem solving, which assumes or relaxes authority according to task demands, has most concerned some theorists. They are as concerned with organizational success and productivity as with the social system.[14,15,16,17]

However, on all sides we find a growing belief that the effectiveness of bureaucracy should be evaluated on human as well as economic criteria. Social satisfaction and personal growth of employees must be considered, as well as the productivity and profit of the organization.

The criticisms and revisions of the *status quo* tend to concentrate on the internal system and its human components. But although it appears on the surface that the case against bureaucracy has to do with its ethical-moral posture and the social fabric, the real *coup de grâce* has come from the environment. While various proponents of "good human relations" have been fighting bureaucracy on humanistic grounds and for Christian values, bureaucracy seems most likely to founder on its inability to adapt to rapid change in the environment.

The Problem of Adaptability

Bureaucracy thrives in a highly competitive, undifferentiated, and stable environment, such as the climate of its youth, the Industrial Revolution. A pyramidal structure of authority, with power concentrated in the hands of few with the knowledge and resources to control an entire enterprise was, and is, an eminently suitable social arrangement for routinized tasks.

However, the environment has changed in just those ways which make the mechanism most problematical. Stability has vanished. As Ellis Johnson said: "...the once-reliable constants have now become 'galloping' variables...."[18] One factor accelerating change is the growth of science, research and development activities, and intellectual technology. Another is the increase of transactions with social institutions and the importance of the latter in conducting the enterprise—including government, distributors and consumers, shareholders, competitors, raw-material and power suppliers, sources of employees (particularly managers), trade unions, and groups within the firms.[19] There is, as well, more interdependence between the economic and other facets of society, resulting in complications of legislation and public regulation. Thirdly, and significantly, competition between firms diminishes as their fates intertwine and become positively correlated.[20]

My argument so far, to summarize quickly, is that the first assault on bureaucracy arose from its incapacity to manage the tension between individual and management goals. However, this conflict is somewhat mediated by the growth of an ethic of productivity which includes personal growth and/or satisfaction. The second and more major shock to bureaucracy has been caused by the scientific and technological revolution. It is the requirement of adaptability to the environment which leads to the predicted demise of bureaucracy and to the collapse of management as we know it now.

A Forecast for the Future

A forecast falls somewhere between a prediction and a prophecy. It lacks the divine guidance of the latter and the empirical foundation of the former. On thin empirical ice, I want to set forth some of the conditions that will dictate organizational life in the next twenty-five to fifty years.

1 *The environment* Those factors already mentioned will continue in force and will increase. That is, rapid technological change and diversification will lead to interpenetration of the government and legal and economic

policies in business. Partnerships between industry and government (like Telstar) will be typical, and because of the immensity and expense of the projects, there will be fewer identical units competing for the same buyers and sellers. Or, in reverse, imperfect competition leads to an oligopolistic and government-business-controlled economy. The three main features of the environment will be interdependence rather than competition, turbulence rather than stability, and large rather than small enterprises.

2 *Aggregate population characteristics* We are living in what Peter Drucker calls the "educated society," and I think this is the most distinctive characteristic of our times. Within fifteen years, two-thirds of our population (living in metropolitan areas) will attend college. Adult education programs, especially the management development courses of such universities as M.I.T., Harvard, and Stanford, are expanding and adding intellectual breadth. All this, of course, is not just "nice," but necessary. As Secretary of Labor Wirtz recently pointed out, computers can do the work of most high school graduates—more cheaply and effectively. Fifty years ago, education was called "nonwork," and intellectuals on the payroll (and many staff) were considered "overhead." Today, the survival of the firm depends, more than ever before, on the proper exploitation of brainpower.

One other characteristic of the population which will aid our understanding of organizations of the future is increasing job mobility. The lowered expense and ease of transportation, coupled with the real needs of a dynamic environment, will change drastically the idea of "owning" a job—and of "having roots," for that matter. Participants will be shifted from job to job even from employer to employer with much less fuss than we are accustomed to.

3 *Work-relevant values* The increased level of education and mobility will change the values we hold vis-à-vis work. People will be more intellectually committed to their jobs and will probably require more involvement, participation, and autonomy in their work. [This turn of events is due to a composite of the following factors: (1) There is a positive correlation between education and need for autonomy; (2) job mobility places workers in a position of greater influence in the system; and (3) job requirements call for more responsibility and discretion.]

Also, people will tend to be more "other-directed" in their dealings with others. McClelland's data suggest that as industrialization increases, other-directedness increases;[21] so we will tend to rely more heavily than we do even now on temporary social arrangements, on our immediate and constantly changing colleagues.

4 *Tasks and goals of the firm* The tasks of the firm will be more technical, complicated, and unprogrammed. They will rely more on intellect than on muscles. And they will be too complicated for one person to handle or for individual supervision. Essentially, they will call for the collaboration of specialists in a project form of organization.

Similarly there will be a complication of goals. "Increased profits" and "raised productivity" will sound like oversimplifications and clichés. Business will concern itself with its adaptive or innovative-creative capacity. In addition, *meta*-goals will have to be articulated and developed; that is, supra-goals which shape and provide the foundation for the goal structure. For example, one *meta*-goal might be a system for detecting new and changing goals; another could be a system for deciding priorities among goals.

Finally, there will be more conflict, more contradiction among effectiveness criteria, just as in hospitals and universities today there is conflict between teaching and research. The reason for this is the number of professionals involved, who tend to identify as much with the supra-goals of their profession as with those of their immediate employer. University professors are a case in point. More and more of their income comes from outside sources, such as private or public foundations and consultant work. They tend not to make good "company men" because they are divided in their loyalty to professional values and organizational demands. Role conflict and ambiguity are both causes and consequences of goal conflict.

5 *Organizational structure* The social structure in organizations of the future will have some unique characteristics. The key word will be "temporary"; there will be adaptive, rapidly changing *temporary systems*.[22] These will be organized around *problems-to-be-solved*. The problems will be solved by groups of relative *strangers* who represent a set of diverse professional skills. The groups will be conducted on *organic* rather than mechanical models; they will evolve in response to the problem rather than programmed role expectations. The function of the "executive" thus becomes *coordinator,* or "linking pin" between various project groups. He must be a man who can speak the diverse languages of research and who can relay information and mediate among the groups. *People will be differentiated not vertically according to rank and role but flexibly according to skill and professional training.*

Adaptive, temporary systems of diverse specialists, solving problems, linked together by coordinating and task-evaluative specialists, in organic flux, will gradually replace bureaucracy as we know it. As no catchy phrase comes to mind, let us call this an "organic-adaptive" structure.

As an aside, what will happen to the rest of society, to the manual laborers, to the less educated, to those who desire to work in conditions of high authority, and so forth? Many such jobs will disappear; automatic jobs will be automated. However, there will be a corresponding growth in the service-type of occupation, such as the "War on Poverty" and the Peace Corps programs. In times of change, where there is a discrepancy between cultures, industrialization, and especially urbanization, society becomes the client for skill in human interaction. Let us hypothesize that approximately 40 percent of the population would be involved in jobs of this nature and 40 percent in technological jobs, making an *organic-adaptive* majority, with, say, a 20 percent bureaucratic minority.

6 *Motivation in organic-adaptive structures* The section of this chapter on reciprocity stated the shortcomings of bureaucracy in maximizing employee effectiveness. The organic-adaptive structure should increase

motivation and thereby effectiveness because of the satisfactions intrinsic to the task. There is a congruence between the educated individual's need for meaningful, satisfactory, and creative tasks and flexible structure or autonomy.

Of course, where the reciprocity issue is ameliorated, there are corresponding stresses between professional identification and high task involvement. Professionals are notoriously disloyal to organizational demands. For example, during the Oppenheimer hearing, Boris Pash of the FBI reported: "It is believed that the only undivided loyalty that he [Oppenheimer] can give is to science and it is strongly felt that if in his position the Soviet government could offer more for the advancement of scientific cause he would select that government as the one to which he would express his loyalty."[23]

There will be, as well, reduced commitment to work groups. These groups, as I have already mentioned, will be transient and changing. While skills in human interaction will become more important because of the necessity of collaboration in complex tasks, there will be a concomitant reduction in group cohesiveness. I would predict that in the organic-adaptive system, people will have to learn to develop quick and intense relationships on the job and to endure their loss.

In general I do not agree with the emphasis of Kerr et al.[24] on the "new bohemianism," whereby leisure—not work—becomes the emotional-creative sphere of life, or with Leavitt,[25] who holds similar views. They assume a technological slowdown and leveling off and a stabilizing of social mobility. This may be a society of the future, but long before then we will have the challenge of creating that pushbutton society and a corresponding need for service-type organizations with the organic-adaptive structure.

Jobs in the next century should become *more*, rather than less, involving; man is a problem-solving animal, and the tasks of the future guarantee a full agenda of problems. In addition, the adaptive process itself may become captivating to many. At the same time, I think the future I describe is far from a utopian or a necessarily "happy" one. Coping with rapid change, living in temporary systems, and setting up (in quickstep time) meaningful relations—and then breaking them—all augur strains and tensions. Learning how to live with ambiguity and to be self-directing will be the task of education and the goal of maturity.

New Structures of Freedom

In these new organizations, participants will be called on to use their minds more than at any other time in history. Fantasy and imagination will be legitimized in ways that today seem strange. Social structures will no longer be instruments of repression (see Marcuse,[26] who says that the necessity of repression and the suffering derived from it decreases with the maturity of the civilization) but will exist to promote play and freedom on behalf of curiosity and thought.

Not only will the problem of adaptability be overcome through the organic-adaptive structure, but the problem we started with, reciprocity, will be resolved. Bureaucracy, with its "surplus repression," was a monumental discovery for harnessing muscle power via guilt and instinctual renunciation. In today's world, it is a prosthetic device, no longer useful. For we now require organic-adaptive systems as structures of freedom to permit the expression of play and imagination and to exploit the new pleasure of work.

References

1. Bendix, R., *Max Weber: An Intellectual Portrait*, Doubleday & Company, Inc., Garden City, N.Y., 1960. p. 421.
2. Hall, R. H., "The Concept of Bureaucracy: An Empirical Assessment," *The American Journal of Sociology*, vol. 69, p. 33, 1963.
3. Bennis, W. G., "Theory and Method in Applying Behavioral Science to Planned Organizational Change," MIT Paper presented at the International Operational Research Conference, Cambridge University, Cambridge, Sept. 14, 1964.
4. Bendix, *op. cit.*, pp. 455–56.
5. March, J. G., and H. A. Simon, *Organizations*, John Wiley & Sons, Inc., New York, 1958.
6. Levinson, H., "Reciprocation: The Relationship between Man and Organization," Invited Address presented to the Division of Industrial and Business Psychology, Washington, D.C., Sept. 3, 1963.
7. Mayo, E., *The Social Problems of an Industrial Civilization*, Harvard University Press, Cambridge, Mass., 1945, p. 122.
8. Likert, R., *New Patterns of Management*, McGraw-Hill Book Company, New York, 1961.
9. Argyris, C., *Interpersonal Competence and Organizational Effectiveness*, Dorsey Press, Homewood, Ill., 1962.
10. Blake, R. R., and J. S. Mouton, *The Managerial Grid*, Gulf Publishing Company, Houston, 1964.
11. Shepard, H. A., "Changing Interpersonal and Intergroup Relationships in Organizations," in J. March (ed.), *Handbook of Organization*, Rand McNally & Company, Chicago, 1965.
12. Burns, T., and G. M. Stalker, *The Management of Innovation*, Quadrangle, Chicago, 1961.
13. Shepard, *op. cit.*
14. McGregor, D., *The Human Side of Enterprise*, McGraw-Hill Book Company, New York, 1960.
15. Leavitt, H. J., "Unhuman Organizations," in H. J. Leavitt and L. Pondy (eds.), *Readings in Managerial Psychology*, The University of Chicago Press, Chicago, 1964, pp. 542–56.
16. Leavitt, H. J., and T. L. Whisler, "Management in the 1980's," in Leavitt and Pondy, *ibid*.
17. Thompson, J. D., and A. Tuden, "Strategies, and Processes of Organizational Decision," in J. D. Thompson, P. B. Hammond, R. W. Hawkes, B. H. Junker, and A. Tuden (eds.), *Comparative Studies in Administration*, The University of Pittsburgh Press, Pittsbugh, Pa., 1959, pp. 195 216.
18. Johnson, E. A., "Introduction," in McClosky and Trefethen (eds.), *Operations Research for Management*, The Johns Hopkins Press, Baltimore, 1954, p. xii.
19. Wilson, A. T. M., "The Manager and His World," *Industrial Management Review*, Fall, 1961.
20. Emery, F. E., and E. L. Trist, "The Causal Texture of Organization Environments," Paper read at the International Congress of Psychology, Washington, September, 1963.
21. McClelland, D., *The Achieving Society*, D. Van Nostrand Company, Inc., Princeton, N.J., 1961.
22. Miles, M. B., "On Temporary Systems," in M. B. Miles (ed.), *Innovation in Education*, Bureau of

Publications, Teachers College, Columbia University, New York, 1964, pp. 437–90.

23. Jungk, R., *Brighter than a Thousand Suns,* Grove Press, Inc., New York, 1958, p. 147.

24. Kerr, C., J. T. Dunlop, F. Harbison,

and C. Myers, *Industrialism and Industrial Man,* Harvard University Press, Cambridge, Mass., 1960.

25. Leavitt, *op. cit.*

26. Marcuse, H., *Eros and Civilization,* Beacon Press, Boston, 1955.

11 / Mechanistic and Organic Systems

Tom Burns, G. M. Stalker

...[WE WISH TO] set down the outline of the two management systems which represent for us the two polar extremities of the forms which such systems can take when they are adapted to a specific rate of technical and commercial change. The case we have tried to establish from the literature, as from our research experience,... is that the different forms assumed by a working organization do exist objectively and are not merely interpretations offered by observers of different schools.

Both types represent a 'rational' form of organization, in that they may both, in our experience, be explicitly and deliberately created and maintained to exploit the human resources of a concern in the most efficient manner feasible in the circumstances of the concern. Not surprisingly, however, each exhibits characteristics which have been hitherto associated with different kinds of interpretation. For it is our contention that empirical findings have usually been classified according to sociological ideology rather than according to the functional specificity of the working organization to its task and the conditions confronting it.

We have tried to argue that these are two formally contrasted forms of management system. These we shall call the mechanistic and organic forms.

A *mechanistic* management system is appropriate to stable conditions. It is characterized by:

(*a*)   the specialized differentiation of functional tasks into which the problems and tasks facing the concern as a whole are broken down;

Reprinted by permission of the authors and publisher from *The Management of Innovation* (London: Tavistock Publications, 1961).

(*b*)   the abstract nature of each individual task, which is pursued with techniques and purposes more or less distinct from those of the concern as a whole; i.e., the functionaries tend to pursue the technical improvement of means, rather than the accomplishment of the ends of the concern;

(*c*)   the reconciliation, for each level in the hierarchy, of these distinct performances by the immediate superiors, who are also, in turn, responsible for seeing that each is relevant in his own special part of the main task.

(*d*)   the precise definition of rights and obligations and technical methods attached to each functional role;

(*e*)   the translation of rights and obligations and methods into the responsibilities of a functional position;

(*f*)   hierarchic structure of control, authority and communication;

(*g*)   a reinforcement of the hierarchic structure by the location of knowledge of actualities exclusively at the top of the hierarchy, where the final reconciliation of distinct tasks and assessment of relevance is made.[1]

(*h*)   a tendency for interaction between members of the concern to be vertical, i.e., between superior and subordinate;

(*i*)   a tendency for operations and working behaviour to be governed by the instructions and decisions issued by superiors;

(*j*)   insistence on loyalty to the concern and obedience to superiors as a condition of membership;

(*k*)   a greater importance and prestige attaching to internal (local) than to general (cosmopolitan) knowledge, experience, and skill.

The *organic* form is appropriate to changing conditions, which give rise constantly to fresh problems and unforeseen requirements for action which cannot be broken down or distributed automatically arising from the functional roles defined within a hierarchic structure. It is characterized by:

(*a*)   the contributive nature of special knowledge and experience to the common task of the concern;

---

[1] This functional attribute of the head of a concern often takes on a clearly expressive aspect. It is common enough for concerns to instruct all people with whom they deal to address correspondence to the firm (i.e., to its formal head) and for all outgoing letters and orders to be signed by the head of the concern. Similarly, the printed letter heading used by Government departments carries instructions for the replies to be addressed to the Secretary, etc. These instructions are not always taken seriously, either by members of the organization or their correspondents, but in one company this practice was insisted upon and was taken to somewhat unusual lengths; *all* correspondence was delivered to the managing director, who would thereafter distribute excerpts to members of the staff, synthesizing their replies into the letter of reply which he eventually sent. Telephone communication was also controlled by limiting the numbers of extensions, and by monitoring incoming and outgoing calls.

(b)   the 'realistic' nature of the individual task, which is seen as set by the total situation of the concern;

(c)   the adjustment and continual re-definition of individual tasks through interaction with others;

(d)   the shedding of 'responsibility' as a limited field of rights, obligations and methods. (Problems may not be posted upwards, downwards or sideways as being someone's else's responsibility);

(e)   the spread of commitment to the concern beyond any technical definition;

(f)   a network structure of control, authority, and communication. The sanctions which apply to the individual's conduct in his working role derive more from presumed community of interest with the rest of the working organization in the survival and growth of the firm, and less from a contractual relationship between himself and a non-personal corporation, represented for him by an immediate superior;

(g)   omniscience no longer imputed to the head of the concern; knowledge about the technical or commercial nature of the here and now task may be located anywhere in the network; this location becoming the *ad hoc* centre of control authority and communication;

(h)   a lateral rather than a vertical direction of communication through the organization, communication between people of different rank, also, resembling consultation rather than command;

(i)   a content of communication which consists of information and advice rather than instructions and decisions;

(j)   commitment to the concern's tasks and to the 'technological ethos' of material progress and expansion is more highly valued than loyalty and obedience;

(k)   importance and prestige attach to affiliations and expertise valid in the industrial and technical and commercial milieux external to the firm.

One important corollary to be attached to this account is that while organic systems are not hierarchic in the same sense as are mechanistic, they remain stratified. Positions are differentiated according to seniority—i.e., greater expertise. The lead in joint decisions is frequently taken by seniors, but it is an essential presumption of the organic system that the lead, i.e. 'authority', is taken by whoever shows himself most informed and capable, i.e., the 'best authority'. The location of authority is settled by consensus.

A second observation is that the area of commitment to the concern— the extent to which the individual yields himself as a resource to be used by the working organization—is far more extensive in organic than in mechanistic systems. Commitment, in fact, is expected to approach that of the professional scientist to his work, and frequently does. One further consequence of this is that it becomes far less feasible to distinguish 'informal' from 'formal' organization.

Thirdly, the emptying out of significance from the hierarchic command system, by which co-operation is ensured and which serves to monitor the working organization under a mechanistic system, is countered by the development of shared beliefs about the values and goals of the concern. The growth and accretion of institutionalized values, beliefs, and conduct, in the form of commitments, ideology, and manners, around an image of the concern in its industrial and commercial setting make good the loss of formal structure.

Finally, the two forms of system represent a polarity, not a dichotomy; there are, as we have tried to show, intermediate stages between the extremities empirically known to us. Also, the relation of one form to the other is elastic, so that a concern oscillating between relative stability and relative change may also oscillate between the two forms. A concern may (and frequently does) operate with a management system which includes both types. . . .

We have endeavoured to stress the appropriateness of each system to its own specific set of conditions. Equally, we desire to avoid the suggestion that either system is superior under all circumstances to the other. In particular, nothing in our experience justifies the assumption that mechanistic systems should be superseded by organic in conditions of stability.[2] The beginning of administrative wisdom is the awareness that there is no one optimum type of management system.

[2] A recent instance of this assumption is contained in H. A. Shepard's paper addressed to the Symposium on the Direction of Research Establishments, 1956. 'There is much evidence to suggest that the optimal use of human resources in industrial organizations requires a different set of conditions, assumptions, and skills from those traditionally present in industry. Over the past twenty-five years, some new orientations have emerged from organizational experiments, observations and inventions. The new orientations depart radically from doctrines associated with "Scientific Management" and traditional bureaucratic patterns.

'The central emphases in this development are as follows:

1. Wide participation in decision-making, rather than centralized decision-making.
2. The face-to-face group, rather than the individual, as the basic unit of organization.
3. Mutual confidence, rather than authority, as the integrative force in organization.
4. The supervisor as the agent for maintaining intragroup and intergroup communication, rather than as the agent of higher authority.
5. Growth of members of the organization to greater responsibility, rather than external control of the member's performance or their tasks.'

12 / Bureaucracy and Innovation

Victor A. Thompson

It has become a commonplace among behavioral scientists that the bureaucratic form of organization is characterized by high productive efficiency but low innovative capacity. There is a growing feeling that modern organizations, and particularly the large, bureaucratic business and government organizations, need to increase their capacity to innovate. This feeling stems in part from the obvious fact of the increased rate of change, especially technological change, but also from a rejection of the older process of innovation through the birth of new organizations and the death or failure of old ones. It seems difficult to contemplate the extinction of existing and well-known organizational giants, for too many interests become vested in their continued existence. Consequently, many behavioral scientists feel that innovation must increasingly occur within the bureaucratic organizations. Also technical innovation is becoming costlier, and financing it may be easier through healthy, existing, organizations than through newly created ones.

This paper considers the obstacles to innovation within the modern bureaucratic organization and makes some suggestions for changes that would facilitate innovation. No attempt is made to answer the question as to whether innovation is desirable or not. By innovation is meant the generation, acceptance, and implementation of new ideas, processes, products or services. Innovation therefore implies the capacity to change or adapt. An adaptive organization may not be innovative (because it does not generate many new ideas), but an innovative organization will be adaptive (because it is able to implement many new ideas).

For a group of people to act as an entity, an ideology is required. This ideology explains what the group is doing, what it ought to do, and legitimizes the coercion of the individual by the group. For the modern bureaucratic organization, this body of doctrine could be called a production ideology. The organization is conceived as having an owner who has a goal to be maximized by means of the organization.[1] The organization is a tool (or weapon) for reaching this objective. The various participants are given money in return for the use of their time and effort as means of achieving the owner's goal. As Henry Ford said, "All that we ask of the men is that they do the work which is set before them." Management consists

---

[1] See Richard M. Cyert and James G. March, *A Behavioral Theory of the Firm* (Englewood Cliffs, N. J.: Prentice-Hall, 1963), pp. 27–28.

of functions and processes for perfecting the tool for this purpose, that is controlling intraorganizational behaviors so that they become completely reliable and predictable, like any good tool. From the standpoint of this production ideology, innovative behavior would only be interpreted as unreliability.

The production ideology leads to rapid and detailed specification and commitment of resources. Of especial interest is the detailed specification of human resources. Adam Smith's advice to reduce the job of pin making to that of making a part of the pin has been generally followed. This response will be termed the "Smith's pins" effect. It has been said that the detailed specification of human resources reduces investment costs per unit of program execution.[2] The production ideology results in jobs which typically require only a small part of the worker's training or knowledge. Consequently, this detailed specification of resources will be called "overspecification" of resources, somewhat argumentatively, no doubt.

Monocratic Social Structure and Innovation

Large, modern bureaucratic organizations dominated by production ideology are framed around a powerful organization stereotype, which following Max Weber, will be called the monocratic organization. This stereotype reflects conditions prevalent in the past, two being important because they no longer hold: (*1*) great inequality among organization members in social standing and abilities and a corresponding inequality in contributions and rewards; and (*2*) a technology simple enough to be within the grasp of an individual.

In this stereotype, the organization is a great hierarchy of superior–subordinate relations in which the person at the top, assumed to be omniscient, gives the general order that initiates all activity. His immediate subordinates make the order more specific for their subordinates; the latter do the same for theirs, etc., until specific individuals are carrying out specific commands. All authority and initiation are cascaded down in this way by successive delegations. There is complete discipline enforced from the top down to assure that these commands are faithfully obeyed. Responsibility is owed from the bottom up. To assure predictability and accountability, each position is narrowly defined as to duties and jurisdiction, without overlapping or duplication. Problems that fall outside the narrow limits of the job are referred upward until they come to a person with sufficient authority to make a decision. Each person is to receive orders from and be responsible to only one other person—his superior.

Such a system is monocratic because there is only *one* point or source of legitimacy. Conflict cannot be legitimate (although it may occur because of the weakness and immorality of human beings). Therefore, the organization does not need formal, legitimate, bargaining devices. Thus, although

---

2 James G. March and Herbert A. Simon, *Organizations* (New York: John Wiley, 1958), p. 158; and Herbert A. Simon, *The New Science of Management Decision* (New York: Harper and Row, 1960), p. 7.

it might be considered empirically more fruitful to conceive of the organization as a coalition,[3] according to the monocratic stereotype, the organization as a moral or normative entity is the tool of an owner, not a coalition. Coalitional and other conflict-settling activities, therefore, take place in a penumbra of illegitimacy.

The inability to legitimize conflict depresses creativity. Conflict generates problems and uncertainties and diffuses ideas. Conflict implies pluralism and forces coping and search for solutions, whereas concentrated authority can simply ignore obstacles and objections. Conflict, therefore, encourages innovations. Other things being equal, the less bureaucratized (monocratic) the organization, the more conflict and uncertainty and the more innovation.[4]

The monocratic stereotype dictates centralized control over all resources. It can control only through extrinsic rewards such as money, power, and status, because it demands the undifferentiated time of its members in the interests of the owner's goals. Even as the organization is a tool, so are all of its participants. There can be no right to "joy in work." To admit such a right would be to admit an interest other than the owner's and to lose some control over the participants.

The necessity of relying upon such extrinsic rewards forces the organization to make its hierarchical positions rewards for compliance. Such a reward system depends upon the organization's ability to find enough people who are willing to exchange their time for a chance at a small group of status positions. It is doubtful that this would have been possible without help from other social institutions, including religious ones. The general belief that work is not supposed to be enjoyable has helped, as has the social definition of success as moving up a managerial hierarchy. The further belief that the good man is the successful one has closed the system.

With education as a criterion of social class, the blue-collar group and a large part of the lower white-collar group have been eliminated from the competition for these scarce, status prizes. Furthermore, highly educated people are increasingly seeking basic need satisfaction outside of the organization—in hobbies, community activities, their families.[5] Consequently, organizations have become sorely pressed to find rewards sufficient to induce the needed docility. Although the use of money alone has raised the price of goods, it does not seem to have been very successful in promoting production interests.[6]

[3] Cyert and March, *op. cit.*

[4] See Tom Burns and G. M. Stalker, *The Management of Innovation* (London: Tavistock, 1959); and Gerald Gordon and Selwyn Becker, "Changes in Medical Practice Bring Shifts in the Patterns of Power," *The Modern Hospital,* 102 (Feb., 1964), 89.

[5] See Robert V. Presthus, *The Organizational Society* (New York: Knopf, 1962).

[6] Recent investigations of work motivation indicate quite strongly that a poorly administered wage and salary system can make for dissatisfaction, but that a well-administered one has little power to motivate to high performance. See Frederick Herzberg, Bernard Mausner, and Barbara Snyderman, *The Motivation to Work*

With the enormous expansion of knowledge flooding the organization with specialists of all kinds and with the organization increasingly dependent upon them, this reward system is facing a crisis. With all his pre-entry training, the specialist finds that he can "succeed" only by giving up work for which he is trained and entering management—work for which he has had no training.[7]

The extrinsic reward system, administered by the hierarchy of authority, stimulates conformity rather than innovation. Creativity is promoted by an internal commitment, by intrinsic rewards for the most part. The extrinsic rewards of esteem by colleagues, and the benevolent competition through which it is distributed, are largely foreign to the monocratic, production-oriented organization. Hierarchical competition is highly individualistic and malevolent. It does not contribute to co-operation and group problem solving.

For those committed to this concept of success, the normal psychological state is one of more or less anxiety. This kind of success is dispensed by hierarchical superiors. Furthermore, the more success one attains, the higher he goes, the more vague and subjective become the standards by which he is judged. Eventually, the only safe posture is conformity. Innovation is not likely under these conditions. To gain the independence, freedom and security required for creativity, the normal individual has to reject this concept of success. But even those who have adopted a different life pattern and measure their personal worth in terms of professional growth and the esteem of professional peers must feel a great deal of insecurity within these monocratic structures, because the opportunity for growth is under the control of the organization, and especially the work they are asked to perform.

One further aspect of monocratic structure needs to be briefly described before we proceed to assess the implications of these structural variables for innovation within the organization. The hierarchy of authority is a procedure whereby organizationally directed proposals from within are affirmed or vetoed. It is a procedure which gives advantage to the veto, because monocratic systems do not provide for appeals. An appeal implies conflicting rights which must be adjudicated, but the superior's veto of a subordinate's proposal legitimately rejects the proposal. An approval must usually go higher, where it is again subject to a veto. Thus, even if the monocratic organization allows new ideas to be generated, it is very apt to veto them.

(New York: John Wiley, 1959), and M. Scott Meyers' unpublished report on recent motivation research at the Texas Instrument Company, "The Management of Motivation to Work."

7 See Lewis C. Mainzer, "The Scientist as Public Administrator," *Western Political Quarterly,* 16 (1963), 814–29. Of the Federal executives in grades GS–14 and above, only about one in forty-five has had college training in public administration (derived from Table 42B, p. 361, in W. Lloyd Warner, Paul P. Van Riper, Norman H. Martin, and Orvis F. Collins, *The American Federal Executive* [New Haven, Conn.: Yale University, 1963]).

Because production interests lead to overspecification of human resources, organizations in the past were composed largely of unskilled or semiskilled employees who carried out more or less simple procedures devised within the particular organization without previous special preparation. The white-collar unskilled or semiskilled have been conveniently labeled the "desk classes."[8] The work of the desk classes, as distinguished from scientific and technical workers, is determined by the organization rather than by extensive pre-entry preparation. Deprived of intrinsic rewards related to the work or the rewards of growing esteem of professional peers, they become largely dependent upon the extrinsic rewards distributed by the hierarchy of authority, thereby greatly reinforcing that institution. Their dependence upon organizational programs and procedures for whatever function they acquire induces a conservative attitude with regard to these programs and procedures.

Except for the successful few, the morale of the desk classes is one of chronic, though not necessarily acute, dissatisfaction.[9] Over-specification plus dependence upon extrinsic rewards of promotion result in vast over-requirement of qualifications. The individual often becomes qualified for the minor incremental increase in difficulty of the next higher job years before it becomes available. The resulting, easily recognized, mental and emotional condition has been called the bureaucratic orientation.[10]

The bureaucratic orientation is conservative. Novel solutions, using resources in a new way, are likely to appear threatening. Those having a bureaucratic orientation are more concerned with the internal distribution of power and status than with organizational goal accomplishment. This converts the organization into a political system concerned with the distribution of these extrinsic rewards.[11] The first reaction to new ideas and suggested changes is most likely to be, "How does it affect us?" Some observations of the decision-making process in business organizations suggest that search in these organizations is largely an attempt by the groupings in this political system to find answers to that question—"how does it affect us?" They also suggest that the expectations of consequences upon which these organizations base their decisions are heavily biased by these same political interests.[12]

---

8 Nigel Walker, *Morale in the Civil Service: A Study of the Desk Worker* (Edinburgh: Edinburgh University, 1960).

9 *Ibid.*

10 The contrast between the professional and the bureaucratic orientation has been studied and discussed by many people. A few references are: Alvin W. Gouldner, "Cosmopolitans and Locals," *Administrative Science Quarterly*, 2 (1957–1958), 281–306, and 444–80; Leonard Reissman, "A Study of Role Conceptions in a Bureaucracy," *Social Forces*, 27 (1949), 305–10; and Harold L. Wilensky, *Intellectuals in Labor Unions* (Glencoe, Ill.: Free Press, 1956), pp. 129–44.

11 Burns and Stalker, *op. cit.*, and Melville Dalton, "Conflict between Line and Staff Managerial Officers," *American Sociological Review*, 15(1950), 342–51.

12 See R. M. Cyert, W. R. Dill, and F. G. March, "The Role of Expectations in Business Decision-Making," *Administrative Science Quarterly*, 3 (1958), 307–40; and Cyert and March, *op. cit.*, ch. iv.

If new activities cannot be blocked entirely they can at least be segregated and eventually blocked from the communication system if necessary. Typically, the introduction of technical innovative activities into modern organizations is by means of segregated units, often called research and development units. Segregating such activities prevents them from affecting the *status quo* to any great extent. The organization does not have to change.[13]

We should add that it is not only the organizational political system which causes the segregation of new problems. There is often no place in the existing structure into which they can be fitted. When a new problem appears, the monocratic production-oriented organization is likely to find that the resources of authority, skills, and material needed to cope with it have already been fully specified and committed to other organization units. Since no existing unit has the uncommitted resources to deal with the new problem, a new organization unit is established.

An organization runs into a great deal of trouble trying to stimulate innovativeness within these segregated units. Since it cannot use the extrinsic reward system upon which the political system is based, it must fumble toward a reward system alien to the monocratic organization. It must establish conditions entirely foreign to the conditions of production upon which the monocratic organization is based. Two milieus, two sets of conditions, two systems of rewards, must be established, the one for innovation, the other for the rest of the organization's activities. This duality is divisive and upsetting to the existing distribution of satisfactions.

Beyond the political interests in the distribution of extrinsic rewards, there are other factors which strengthen tendencies toward parochialism. The organization seems to factor its activities into narrow, single-purpose, exclusive categories and to assign these to subunits composed of a superior and subordinates. Very often strong subunit and subgoal identifications arise from this pattern so that members of any unit know and care little about what other units are doing.[14] The organization tends to become a collection of small entities with boundaries and frontiers. When work is completed in one entity, it is handed over to another, and interest in it is dropped. Interest tends to be in protecting the records and protocols of the hand-over transaction so that blame can always be placed on another unit. Although the narrow-mission assignments are justified as needed "to pinpoint responsibility," they actually encourage irresponsibility as far as new problems are concerned because they facilitate dodging responsibility for them.[15]

The production-oriented overspecification and commitment of resources

[13] Burns and Stalker, *op. cit.*

[14] See Eliot O. Chapple and Leonard R. Sayles, *The Measure of Management* (New York: Macmillan, 1961), pp. 18–40; March and Simon, *op. cit.*, pp. 150–54; Victor A. Thompson, *The Regulatory Process in OPA Rationing* (New York: King's Crown Press, 1950), Pt. II; and James R. Bright, ed., *Technological Planning on the Corporate Level* (Boston: Harvard University Graduate School of Business Administration, 1962), *passim*.

[15] Burns and Stalker, *op. cit.*

prevent the accumulation of free resources needed for innovative projects, including time, and deprives participants of the diversity of input so important in the generation of new ideas. Thus, even when people are hired to *innovate* they may be treated as though they were hired to *produce* and kept tied to their work. Diversity of input is also lost because of the tendency to assign each activity to a separate unit, which concentrates whatever diversity of input there is at one or a few local points. Thus, there may be stimulating ideas and information discussed within a planning unit or a research unit, but it does not extend to the rest of the organization. The research unit may be very creative, but the organization cannot innovate.

In monocratic responsibility, praise and blame attach to jurisdictions. People are to be punished for mistakes as well as wrong-doing, and they are to be punished for failures which occur within their jurisdictions whether due to their activities or not. ("He should have prevented it. It was his responsibility.") [16] Although this theory is not strictly applied any more, it is still feared. Thus, an individual may hesitate to advise an organization to take a particular action even though he has good reason to believe that the probabilities for a satisfactory outcome are good. Should the project fail in this instance, he may be a personal failure. It is difficult to apply the concept of probability to personal failure. One feels, rightly or wrongly, that he can only fail once. Therefore, what would be rational from the standpoint of the organization's goal may appear irrational from the standpoint of the individual's personal goals. [17]

New ideas are speculative and hence particularly dangerous to personal goals and especially the goals of power and status. Consequently, the monocratic organization, structured around such extrinsic goals and explicitly committed to this stringent theory of responsibility, is not likely to be highly innovative.

A monocratic variant which is highly innovative should be mentioned. New organizations are sometimes begun by highly creative individuals who attract like-minded people, maintain an atmosphere conductive to innovation, build up a powerful *esprit de corps* and achieve a very high level of organizational creativity. Often these are small engineering or research organizations started by an engineer or scientist assisted by a small group of able and personally loyal peers. The organization is new and small and not yet bureaucratized. Many able young people may be attracted to it because of the opportunity provided for professional growth. As these organizations grow larger and particularly after the charismatic originator is no longer there, the monocratic stereotype reasserts itself and they become bureaucratized. This phenomenon is an old one, discussed by Weber as the "institutionalization of charisma." It is seen in one form in the post-revolutionary bureaucratization of successful revolutionary organizations.

---

[16] See Victor A. Thompson, *Modern Organization* (New York: Knopf, 1961), pp. 129–37.

[17] Derived from Kurt W. Back's discussion of nonrational choice. See "Decisions under Uncertainty," *American Behavioral Scientist,* 4(1961), 14–19.

The Innovative Organization

In summarizing the scattered suggestions for an organization with a high capacity to innovate, first the qualities and conditions needed will be discussed, then the structures or structural changes that will facilitate or create the required qualities and conditions.

General Requirements

First are needed resources for innovation—uncommitted money, time, skills, and good will. In human resources this means upgraded work and workers, optimally a person who has developed himself thoroughly in some area, about to the limits of his capacities, so that he has that richness of experience and self-confidence upon which creativity thrives—a professional. Complex technology requires the administration of "technical generalists," or professionals. A technology is incorporated into an organization through individuals. To incorporate it through overspecification or task specialization requires enormous co-ordination. Furthermore, co-ordinating the elements of a technology is part of the technology itself, as the current technical emphasis on systems design, systems engineering, etc., testify. The technology deals not only with simple relationships, but with the relationships between relationships as well. Hence, co-ordination is not a different, non-technical process, such as management, but part of the complex technology itself. Although production interests may be well served by employing a few technical professionals to co-ordinate the many overspecified workers, the innovative potential of the technology can hardly be realized in this way.

The innovative organization will allow that diversity of inputs needed for the creative generation of ideas. Long periods of pre-entry, professional training, and wide diffusion of ideas within the organization, including a wide diffusion of problems and suggested solutions, will provide the variety and richness of experience required. Included should be a wide diffusion of uncertainty so that the whole organization is stimulated to search, rather than just a few professional researchers. Involving larger parts of the organization in the search process also increases chances of acceptance and implementation. This wide diffusion, in turn, will depend upon ease and freedom of communication and a low level of parochialism.

Complete commitment to the organization will not promote innovation, as we have seen; neither will complete alienation from the organization. The relationship between personal and organizational goals, ideally, would seem to be where individuals perceive the organization as an avenue for professional growth. The interest in professional growth provides the rising aspiration level needed to stimulate search beyond the first-found satisfactory solution, and the perception of the organization as a vehicle for professional growth harnesses this powerful motivation to the interests of the organization in a partial fusion of goals, personal and organizational.[18]

Instead of the usual extrinsic organizational rewards of income, power,

[18] See Peter M. Blau and W. Richard Scott, *Formal Organizations* (San Francisco: Chandler, 1962), pp. 60–74.

and status, satisfactions come from the search process, professional growth, and the esteem of knowledgeable peers—rewards most conducive to innovation. Benevolent intellectual competition rather than malevolent status and power competition is needed. For these reasons, creative work, the process of search and discovery, needs to be highly visible to respected peers. Dedication to creative work cannot be expected if positional status continues to be defined as the principal sign of personal worth. But reduction of status-striving is also important because it is inescapably associated with personal insecurity,[19] which is hardly compatible with creativity. What is needed is a certain level of problem insecurity and challenge, but a high level of personal security.

The creative atmosphere should be free from external pressure. A person is not likely to be creative if too much hangs on a successful outcome of his search activities, for he will have a strong tendency to accept the first satisfactory solution whether or not it seems novel or the best possible. Thus, he needs indulgence in time and resources, and particularly in organizational evaluations of his activities. He needs freedom to innovate. He also needs considerable, but not complete, autonomy and self-direction and a large voice in deciding at what he will work.[20]

In summary, the innovative organization will be much more professional than most existing ones. Work will be much less determined by production-oriented planners on the Smith's pins model and more determined by the extended periods of pre-entry training. The desk classes will decline in number and importance relative to professional, scientific, and technical workers. There will be a great increase in interorganizational mobility and a corresponding decline in organizational chauvinism. The concept of organizations as organic entities with some claim to survive will tend to be replaced by the concept of organizations as opportunities for professional growth. In the innovative organization, professional orientations and loyalties will be stronger relative to organizational or bureaucratic ones. Esteem striving will tend to replace status striving. There will be less control by superiors and more by self and peers. Power and influence will be much more broadly dispersed.

The dispersal of power is important because concentrated power often prevents imaginative solutions of problems. When power meets power, problem solving is necessarily called into play. The power of unions has undoubtedly stimulated managerial innovations.[21] Dispersed power, paradoxically, can make resources more readily available to support innovative

[19] Rollo May, *The Meaning of Anxiety* (New York: Ronald, 1950), especially pp. 181–89.

[20] A good part of the literature on individual creativity is summarized in Morris I. Stein and Shirley J. Heinze, *Creativity and the Individual* (Glencoe, Ill.: Free Press, 1960).

[21] See Eric Hoffer, *The Ordeal of Change* (New York: Harper and Row, 1964), pp. 81–82; and Seymour Melman, *Decision-making and Productivity* (Oxford: Oxford University, 1958).

projects because it makes possible a larger number and variety of subcoalitions. It expands the number and kinds of possible supporters and sponsors.

Structural Requirements

The innovative organization will be characterized by structural looseness generally, with less emphasis on narrow, nonduplicating, nonoverlapping definitions of duties and responsibilities. Job descriptions will be of the professional type rather than the duties type. Communications will be freer and legitimate in all directions. Assignment and resource decisions will be much more decentralized than is customary.

The innovative organization will not be as highly stratified as existing ones. This is implied in the freedom of communication, but the decline in the importance of the extrinsic rewards of positional status and the growth of interest in professional esteem would bring this about anyway. Salary scales will be adjusted accordingly and no longer reflect chiefly awesome status differences.

Group processes will be more, and more openly, used than at present. The freer communication system, the broader work assignments, the lack of preoccupation with overlap and duplication, the lessened emphasis upon authority will all work in the direction of a greater amount of interpersonal communication and multiple group membership. Multiple group membership will facilitate innovation by increasing the amount and diversity of input of ideas and stimulation, and by acting as a discipline of the hierarchical veto. When a new idea is known and supported by groupings beyond the authority grouping, it is not easy to veto it. Multiple-group membership helps to overcome the absence of a formal appeal by providing an informal appeal to a free constituency of peers.

In an atmosphere which encourages and legitimizes multiple-group membership, the malignant peer competition of the authority grouping (of fellow subordinates) will no longer exercise the powerful constraints against "showing-up" with new ideas.[22] The greater ease of acquiring group memberships and the greater legitimacy of groups will reduce the risk of innovation to the individual. Responsibility for new ideas can be shared as can the onus of promoting them. Wide participation in the generation process will greatly facilitate acceptance and implementation.

Present methods of departmentalization encourage parochialism with its great resistance to new ideas from outside. Often it is not goals that are assigned, actually, but jurisdictions. (For example, although ninety-eight percent of the farms are electrified, the Rural Electrification Administration has not been abolished.) It is not a group of interdependent skills brought together to carry out some project, but a conference of sovereignty. At the simple unit level (superior and subordinates), it is often, but not always, an aggregative grouping—a number of people with the same skills doing the same thing. Lacking the stimulation of different skills, views, and

22 See William H. Whyte, Jr., *The Organization Man* (Garden City, N. Y.: Doubleday, 1957), chs. x and xvi.

perspectives, and the rewards of project completion and success, such groupings are likely to seek extrinsic rewards and to seek them through the organizational political system.

Other simple units, even though not composed of aggregations of people doing the same thing, are very often composed of overspecified desk classes carrying out some continuing program—getting out the house organ, or managing the budget, or recruiting, or keeping stores. In such an integrative grouping there may be more interpersonal stimulation, but overspecification —the sheer subprofessional simplicity of the jobs—prevents the diversity and richness required for anything but very minor innovations.

The aggregative grouping has neither interdependence nor goal. Group innovation is therefore impossible. Individual innovation in the interest of the organization is hardly likely, unless the organization offers rewards for it. Sometimes organizations reward individual innovative suggestions through suggestion-box systems. Such systems are rarely successful. As far as aggregative units are concerned, the lack of input diversity prevents any important innovative insights. For integrative units, suggestion boxes are frequently disruptive because the true authorship of the suggestion is likely to be in dispute, and the group will often feel that the idea should have been presented to the group rather than individually presented for an award.[23]

In the innovative organization, departmentalization must be arranged so as to keep parochialism to a minimum. Some overlapping and duplication, some vagueness about jurisdictions, make a good deal of communication necessary. People have to define and redefine their responsibilities continually, case after case. They have to probe and seek for help. New problems can not with certainty be rejected as *ultra vires*.[24]

The simple unit should be an integrative grouping of various professionals and subprofessionals engaged upon an integrative task requiring a high degree of technical interdependence and group problem solving. Or else the simple unit should be merely a housekeeping unit. Project teams could be drawn from such housekeeping units. Ideally, individuals would have project rather than continuing assignments. If project organization is not feasible, individuals should be rotated occasionally. Even if continuing

[23] See Norman J. Powell, *Personnel Administration in Government* (Englewood Cliffs, N. J.: Prentice-Hall, 1956), pp. 438–44. Powell believes that suggestion-box systems are better than no communication with the rank and file at all. Because of disputed authorship of suggestions, the TVA decided to give only group (noncash) awards.

[24] Burns and Stalker, *op. cit.* See also B. Klein, "A Radical Proposal for R and D," *Fortune,* 57(May, 1958), 112; B. Klein and W. Meckling, "Application of Operations Research to Development Decisions," *Operations Research,* 6(1958), 352–63; Albert O. Hirshman, *The Strategy of Economic Development* (New Haven, Conn.: Yale University, 1958); Albert O. Hirshman and Charles E. Lindblom, "Economic Development, Research and Development, Policy Making: Some Converging Views," *Behavioral Science,* 7(1962), 211–22; and David Braybrooke and Charles E. Lindblom, *A Strategy of Decision* (New York: Free Press, 1963).

assignments, or jurisdictions, seem to be technically necessary, organization units can probably convert a large part of their activities into successive projects, or have a number of projects going on at the same time, so that individuals can be constantly renewing themselves in new and challenging problems and experiencing a maximum input of diverse stimulation and ideas. It might even be possible for individual and unit jurisdictions and responsibilities to be exchanged occasionally.

If formal structures could be sufficiently loosened, it might be possible for organizations and units to restructure themselves continually in the light of the problem at hand. Thus, for generating ideas, for planning and problem solving, the organization or unit would "unstructure" itself into a freely communicating body of equals. When it came time for implementation, requiring a higher degree of co-ordination of action (as opposed to stimulation of novel or correct ideas), the organization could then restructure itself into the more usual hierarchical form, tightening up its lines somewhat.

Empirical evidence that different kinds of structure are optimal for different kinds of problems is compelling.[25] Almost equally compelling is the evidence that leadership role assignments need to be changed as the situation changes.[26] Bureacratic rigidity makes such rational structural alterations almost impossible. It is hard to escape the conclusion that current organization structures are *not* the most rational adaptations for *some* kinds of problem solving. Although experimental groups have been successfully restructured from bureaucratic to collegial by means of verbal redefinitions of roles along lines perceived to be more appropriate to the task at hand,[27] such restructuring is probably impossible in real-life "traditionated" organizations as presently constituted.

The abandonment of the use of hierarchical positions as prizes or rewards, however, and the decline in the importance of extrinsic rewards generally, would render organizational structure much more amenable to manipulation. The personal appropriation of administrative resources (such as position and authority), almost universal in modern bureaucratic organizations and reminiscent of primitive agrarian cultures, could decline considerably.[28] If it should prove impossible for organizations to become flexible enough to allow restructuring themselves in the light of the problem at hand, it would be preferable to retain a loose structure in the interest of generating new ideas and suffer from some fumbling in the attempt to co-ordinate action for the purpose of carrying them out. After all, thought

25 Some of this evidence is reviewed in Blau and Scott, *op. cit.,* ch. v.

26 The evidence is reviewed in Cecil A. Gibb, "Leadership," in Gardner Lindzey, ed., *Handbook of Social Psychology* (Reading, Mass.: Addison-Wesley, 1954), Vol. II, pp. 877–917.

27 André L. Delbecq, *Leadership in Business Decision Conferences* (unpublished Ph.D. dissertation, Indiana University, 1963).

28 See Victor A. Thompson, "Bureaucracy in a Democracy," in Roscoe Martin, ed., *Public Administration and Democracy* (Syracuse, N. Y.: Syracuse University, forthcoming).

and action cannot be sharply distinguished, and a good deal of problem solving occurs during implementation. The thinking is then tested and completed.

Integrative departmentalization, combined with freedom of communication, interunit projects, and lessened subunit chauvinism, will create extra-departmental professional ties and interests, resulting in an increase in the diversity and richness of inputs and in their diffusion, thereby stimulating creativity. Intellectual competition is more likely to be provided by this broader milieu. It is more likely to be the generating area than the smaller authority grouping or the larger organization.

We need to think in terms of innovative areas rather than formal departments, in terms of the conditions for generating new and good ideas rather than of jurisdiction. In the innovative organization, innovation will not be assigned to an isolated or segregated jurisdiction such as research and development. The innovative contributions of everyone, including the man at the machine, are needed. Characteristically, the innovative area will be larger than the formal unit and smaller than the organization. Resource control should be sufficiently decentralized so that appropriate resource accumulation through subcoalition would be possible within the innovative area. In effect, the formal distribution of jurisdictions should be just a skeleton to be used when an arbitrary decision was required.

In the physical aspect of organizations, the architecture and furnishings of today's bureaucratic organizations seem to be departing further and further from the needs of the innovative organization. The majestic, quiet halls and closed, windowless office doors are not designed to encourage communication. They fill a potential communicator with fear. "Will I be disturbing him?" he wonders. It is doubtful that deep blue rugs have anything to do with discovery and invention. We all remember where the first atomic chain reaction took place. Modern bureaucratic architecture and furnishings seem to reflect an increased concern with the extrinsic reward system. We seem to be in the midst of a new primitivism; the means of administration seem to be increasingly appropriated by the officials. This may reflect an attempt by the monocratic organization to attract innovative technical and scientific talent. With success available to only a few and the organization increasingly dependent upon large numbers of highly trained professionals and subprofessionals, it is hoped that richness of surroundings will do what an inappropriate reward system cannot do.

The purchase of motivation with extrinsic rewards is becoming more and more costly, and innovation cannot be purchased in this way at all. What is needed is both much less expensive and much more costly—the devaluation of authority and positional status and the recognized, official sharing of power and influence.

Implications for Administrative Practice

Associated with all of these structural changes there will need to be many changes in administrative practices. Only a few of the most obvious ones will be mentioned. The present common practice of annual performance ratings by superiors would probably have to be dropped. Many believe that this practice is hostile even to production interests. It is clearly inconsistent with increasing professionalism, since professional standing is not determined by a hierarchical superior. Rather than a single system of ranks, with corresponding salaries, there will be a multiple ranking system and multiple salary scales. The managerial or hierarchical ranking system will be only one among many. Presumably, it will not carry the highest ranks. The American public has for a long time ranked several occupations above management.[29]

Job descriptions and classifications will have to accommodate an increasing proportion of professionals. The duties and responsibilities approach to job descriptions was designed for a desk class age. It does not accommodate professional work easily.

Peer evaluations will become more important in recruitment and placement, and it is possible that a kind of election process will be used to fill authority positions. At any rate, the wishes of subordinates will probably be considered a good deal more than is present practice. One would expect considerable modification in procedures relating to secrecy and loyalty. The innovative organization will be more indulgent with regard to patents, publications, and so on. The relationship between visibility and professional growth will require this, and increased interorganizational mobility will enforce it. Present fringe benefit devices that tend to restrict mobility will have to be altered.

Administrative innovation requires the same conditions and structures as technical innovation. Professionalization in this area also requires the elimination of overspecified resources. The unskilled administrative worker should go along with his blue-collar counterpart. Many administrative technologies are poorly accredited and some are perhaps spurious—pseudo skills in handling some more or less complex procedure. If the procedure is changed, these "skills" will no longer be needed. It is doubtful that the rapid expansion of administrative overhead in recent years has contributed to productivity, suggesting that some of this expansion may not have been technically justified and that it represents organizational slack made possible by increased productivity resulting from other causes.[30]

Administrative activities should be dispersed and decentralized down to the level of the innovative area, allowing administrative personnel to become part of integrative problem-solving groups rather than resentful onlookers sharpshooting from the outside. The innovative organization is innovative throughout and the innovative insights of the engineer, the

[29] Alex Inkeles and Peter H. Rossi, "National Comparisons of Occupational Prestige," in Seymour Martin Lipset and Neil J. Smelser, eds., *Sociology: The Progress of a Decade* (Englewood Cliffs, N. J.: Prentice-Hall, 1961), pp. 506–16.

[30] See Seymour Melman, "The Rise of Administrative Overhead in the Manufacturing Industries of the United States, 1899–1947," *Oxford Economic Papers*, 3(1951), 62–93, and *Dynamic Factors in Industrial Productivity* (New York: John Wiley, 1956).

research scientist, the machine tender, the administrative expert are all needed. If responsibilities and jurisdictions are occasionally exchanged, as suggested above, administrative responsibilities should be included in such exchanges. To paraphrase a famous expression, administrative work is too important to be left entirely to administrators.

Resistance to suggestions of this kind will be especially strong in the monocratic organization oriented to production and control. The re-evaluation of the relative importance of managerial and nonmanagerial activities and the declining emphasis on extrinsic rewards, both implied in increasing professionalization of organizations, will reduce this resistance. The "need to control" is an almost inevitable psychological product of the structured field which the modern bureaucratic organization constitutes. Altering the field alters the product.

The emphasis on the need for free resources, time, indulgence with regard to controls, decentralization, and many more, all suggest on the surface that the innovative organization will be a costly one. Perhaps a high level of innovation is too costly, but the available knowledge is not adequate to reach a conclusion. We do not know the value of the novel ideas, processes, and products, which might be produced by the innovative organization, and we do not know that our present methods of costing and control are the best approach to achieving low-cost production. Likert's arguments that present methods of cost reduction are superficial and actually increase costs in the long run by impairing the health of the social organism are impressive.[31] It would seem that the overspecification of work would automatically create the need for a costly administrative overhead apparatus to plan, schedule, co-ordinate and control so that all the overspecified parts are kept fully meshed and fully occupied. The problem is like that of keeping inventory costs down when a very large number of items must be kept on inventory. We cannot say that the organizational structure outlined will be either more or less costly, more or less beneficial to society, but it will be more innovative. We also suspect that it may be a fair projection of the organization of the future.

---

[31] Rensis Likert and Stanley E. Seashore, "Making Cost Control Work," *Harvard Business Review*, 41(Nov.–Dec., 1963), 96–108.

13 / Models of Bureaucracy Which Permit Conflict*

Eugene Litwak

IN THE PRESENT paper an attempt will be made to suggest some conditions for polar models[1] of bureaucracy. This will in turn permit some specifications of an intermediate model of bureaucracy which may more clearly fit contemporary urban society.

The two models of bureaucracy to be contrasted are that which stresses secondary relations and organizational rules (i.e., as Weber's), and that which stresses primary-group relations and organizational goals[2] (as in the "human-relations" approach). Weber's model is most efficient when the organization deals primarily with uniform events and with occupations stressing traditional areas of knowledge rather than social skills. The human-relations model will be most efficient for dealing with events which are not uniform (research, medical treatment, graduate training, designing) and with occupations emphasizing social skills as technical aspects of the job (as that of psychiatric social worker, salesman if there is little differentiation in the products, and politician).

However, for most organizations in our society a theoretical model of bureaucratic organization must be developed that combines the central and conflicting features from both types. Since they are conflicting, what characterizes this third model and distinguishes it from the other two is a need for mechanisms of segregation." These permit mutually antagonistic social forms to exist side by side in the same organization without ruinous friction.

The Uniform and the Non-Uniform

Weber's model of bureaucracy[3] can be characterized by: impersonal social relations, appointment and promotion on the basis of merit, authority and

---

* Thanks are owed to Peter Blau, Rosemary Conzemius, and Robert Vinter for their helpful suggestions.

1 The term "model" is not being used in a rigorous sense: all that is meant is that a given organization may have unique dimensions, no rules being specified to predict the interrelations between the dimensions.

2 *From Max Weber: Essays in Sociology*, trans. and ed., H. H. Gerth and C. Wright Mills (New York: Oxford University Press, 1946), pp. 196–203. Similarly, James G. March and Herbert A. Simon differentiate between process and purpose theories of organization (*Organizations* [New York: John Wiley & Sons, 1958], p. 29).

3 These do not exactly duplicate Weber's statement, but they are sufficiently close to do no violence to it (see Weber, *op. cit.,* pp. 196 ff.).

obligations which are specified a priori and adhere to the job rather than the individual (i.e., separation of work from private life), authority organized on a hierarchical basis, separation of policy and administrative positions, the members of the bureaucracy being concerned with administrative decisions, general rules for governing all behavior not specified by the above, and, finally, specialization. If the organization is large and structured by these ideal conditions, it will be more efficient[4] than any other kind of organization. Weber's theoretical model assumes that the organization will be dealing with uniform situations.

By "uniform" two things are meant: The task to be dealt with is recurrent (in time as well as among many people) and important, exemplified in such occupations as that of: research scientist or developmental engineer, as opposed to supervisor of an assembly line; doctor or surgeon providing treatment in areas of medicine where little is known (neurosurgeon), as opposed to one dealing with standardized problems; soldier in combat, as opposed to in peacetime; administrator of a large organization producing a rapidly changing product (e.g., chemicals, electronic apparatus, pharmaceuticals, or missiles), as opposed to one dealing with standardized procedures, such as a public utility or a large governmental agency administering well-established regulations.

The importance of distinguishing between the uniform and the non-uniform as well as noting Weber's assumption of uniformity can best be seen if the criticisms of his model are reviewed.[5] The critics point out that the larger the organization, the more likely is it to encompass diverse social situations and people. If a general rule is developed for each situation, the rules would be so numerous as to defy learning. If rules are not developed, then either the administrator will apply rules which are not appropriate or substitute for them his private system of values. In all cases there is likely to be a drop in efficiency when general rules are used and the task is not uniform.

The same point can be made with regard to the hierarchy of authority and delimitation of duties and privileges of the office, for both are only special cases of general rules. Thus, for maximum efficiency, a hierarchy or delimitation of jobs should be based on merit. Setting up a hierarchy based on merit is a relatively simple matter when dealing with one uniform event.

[4] The terms "efficiency" and "productivity" are deliberately left undefined since many well-known problems of value would require extensive consideration if a formal definition were attempted. But it is here assumed that efficiency is defined in terms of some central set of liberal social values which have dominated our society within the last two hundred years; and that when the value problems revolving around the definition of efficiency are more fully solved they will not be inconsistent with this usage.

[5] Julian Franklin, *Man in Society* (New York: Columbia University Press, 1955), I, 941–42; Peter M. Blau, *Bureacracy in Modern Society* (New York: Random House, 1956), pp. 58, 62; Robert K. Merton, "Bureaucratic Structure and Personality," in *Reader in Bureaucracy,* ed. R. K. Merton, A. P. Gray, B. Hockey, and H. C. Selvin (Glencoe, Ill.: Free Press, 1952), p. 364; Philip Selznick, "A Theory of Organizational Commitment," in *Reader in Bureaucracy,* pp. 194–202.

However, if the event is relatively unique, it is difficult for any one hierarchy to suffice for all tasks in the organization. Yet this is the assumption which must be made in all cases where Weber's specifications are applied to organizations dealing with the non-uniform. Since this is too heroic, the individuals concerned might do better to internalize the values of the organization and reach *ad hoc* rather than a priori decisions as to job hierarchy and boundaries.

In his pioneering work, Pelz investigated a large industrial concern whose parts were classified into several groups: those dealing with non-uniform events (i.e., scientists and engineers) and those working with relatively uniform events (central staff and manufacturing).[6] He found that among those in the occupations dealing with non-uniform tasks there was a higher correlation between their motivation to work and productivity when they were free to make their own decisions. In contrast, among those working on uniform tasks there was a higher correlation between motivation and productivity when they were restricted in making decisions. Permitting each individual to control decisions on the job indicates a trend toward a colleague rather than a hierarchical relationship. Pelz's study supports the point of view advocated here, that is, there are differential efficiencies in organizational structure depending on whether the task is uniform or not.

Somewhat the same analysis holds with regard to specialization, which is efficient where there are relatively constant problems. Where there are many problem areas and where they change rapidly, the demand for specialization may lead to premature organizational closure and great inflexibility in deciding, as in the armed forces where a rapidly changing technology has made traditional specialties obsolete. Many argue that the clinging to the traditional specialties has led to a dangerous lag in military preparedness as well as wasteful conflict between specialties.[7]

Weber's demand for impersonality also assumes uniform events. Individuals faced with non-uniform events which are not clearly covered by rules are insecure. In such situations, they must be able to call on colleagues in whom they put great trust[8] if they are to perform efficiently. In other words, in the ambiguous situation brought about by non-uniform events,

6 D. C. Pelz, "Conditional Effects in the Relationship of Autonomy and Motivation to Performance," (August, 1960) (mimeographed). The development of colleague relations among scientists and members of graduate departments of universities would also provide evidence on the point.

7 It is frequently said that, because of their commitment to a specialty, members of the armed services tend to overlook the general problem of defense in favor of their own immediate tasks, with a consequent loss for the basic goals of defense (see H. L. Wilensky and C. N. Lebeaux, *Industrial Society and Social Welfare* [New York: Russell Sage Foundation, 1958], pp. 235–65).

8 Blau, *op. cit.*, pp. 63–64. This point is buttressed by the studies of combat troops or miners engaged in dangerous operations, both cases involving great uncertainty and severe risk where, apparently, strong primary group relations are effective (see E. A. Shils and M. Janowitz, "Cohesion and Disintegration in the *Wehrmacht* in World War II," in *Public Opinion and Propaganda* [New York: Dryden Press, 1954], pp. 91–108).

frequently personal primary group relations conduce to more efficiency than would impersonal ones.

Finally, it can be argued that the separation of policy and administrative decisions is inefficient when the organization is confronted with non-uniform situations. Such separation implies that general rules can be laid down a priori to guide administrative decisions along common lines of policy. As suggested above, such general rules become impossibly complex when the organization faces non-uniform situations. Internalizing organizational policy and localizing discretion (combining administrative and policy decisions) would then be more efficient.

In short, where organizations deal with non-uniform events, a model of bureaucracy may be more efficient which differs in degree from Weber's in at least six characteristics: horizontal patterns of authority, minimal specialization, mixture of decisions on policy and on administration, little a priori limitation of duty and privileges to a given office, personal rather than impersonal relations, and a minimum of general rules. This form of organization generally characterizes the "human-relations" model described as ideal by many contemporary industrial psychologists.

Social and Traditional Job Skills

Weber also implicitly assumes in his discussion of bureaucracy that occupations stressing traditional areas of knowledge (as compared to social skills) dominate the organization. By traditional areas of knowledge is meant, say, knowledge of engineering, of chemistry, of economics, of the law, of company rules, and the like. By social skills or abilities is meant the actual capacity to communicate with others, to motivate them to work, to co-operate with others, and to internalize the values of the organization.

Granted Weber's assumptions about traditional areas of knowledge, his model of bureaucracy does not necessarily lead to efficiency when the job requirements stress social skills.

Personal and impersonal.—Weber's strictures concerning the importance of impersonal social relations are far from self-evident when social abilities rather than traditional knowledge are at issue. The capacity to motivate others to work, to co-operate and to communicate with others, to internalize the norms of the organization, might well increase, not decrease, as a consequence of positive emotional involvement. Thus, studies of psychiatric wards, involving professions whose chief technical tools are social, suggest that greatest efficiency requires some positive emotional involvement.[9] Weber's analysis tends to overlook the virtues of close personal relations,

---

[9] D. A. Hamburg, "Therapeutic Aspects of Communication and Administrative Policy in the Psychiatric Section of a General Hospital," in *The Patient and the Mental Hospital,* ed. M. Greenblatt, D. S. Levinson, and R. H. Williams (Glencoe, Ill.: Free Press, 1959), pp. 91–107, and P. Barrabee, "The Community, the Mental Hospital and the Aged Psychotic," *ibid.,* pp. 530–35. For a general statement relating primary group relations to communication, see E. Katz and P. F. Lazarsfeld, *Personal Influence* (Glencoe, Ill.: Free Press, 1955), pp. 15–30.

concentrating on negative features. Since in an advanced bureaucratic society these latter are minimized,[10] many of Weber's objections to close personal relations are not so important.

Strict delimitation of obligation and duties to the office.—Weber's view that in an efficient organization there should be a strict delimitation of obligations and duties to a specified office assumes that the work can be shut off from private life (e.g., the family). This assumption has considerable validity when one is dealing with the traditional areas of knowledge. However, it is questionable when the chief technical demand of the job is for social skills. This is so because family and friends are major sources for the development of social skills. Therefore, experience in primary groups is likely to enter into one's life at work.[11] More generally, where it is difficult to separate work from other situations, such as family life, the organization must seek to control the latter for the sake of efficiency. The development in large organizations, such as the DuPont Corporation, of family counseling services can be understood in this light.

Separation of policy and administrative decisions.—The inability to isolate work from other situations also makes it difficult, if not impossible, to keep decisions on policy and administration separate. To do so would require that administrative decisions have a code of ethics of their own. Thus an engineer working on a bomb, a dam, or an automobile can say how good an engineer he is in terms of common engineering standards and somewhat independently of organizational policy. By contrast, the psychiatric social worker, because her major technical tool is social skills, finds such distinctions hard to maintain: is participation of the client or the avoidance of physical punishment an administrative technic or the agency's policy? When such distinctions are hard to make, it is more efficient to inculcate policy and give the professional discretion with regard to "administrative" decisions.

Specialization and generalization.—In part, Weber's assumptions regarding efficiency of specialization would not hold where social skills are the technique required for the job. The ability to communicate with others is general in every area of work and is the same for the engineering administrator, the accounting administrator, and every other administrator. The need to train "generalists" for administration is seen in the systematic efforts to move promising executives to a variety of departments in the company.[12] It can also be noted that the most recent recommendation concerning the curriculum in schools of social work (dealing with occupa-

10 E. Litwak, "The Use of Extended Family Groups in the Achievement of Social Goals," *Social Problems,* VII (Winter, 1959–60), 184–85.

11 This point is clearly illustrated in Jules Henry's analysis of an institution for child treatment which provides twenty-four-hour care on the assumption that successful treatment concerns every aspect of life. He notes how much the therapist's own life becomes involved with that of the patient ("Types of Institutional Structures," *The Patient and the Mental Hospital,* pp. 73–91).

12 M. Janowitz, *The Professional Soldier* (Glencoe, Ill.: Free Press, 1960), pp. 166–71.

tions whose chief technical tool is social abilities) was to drop the specialties and train all students in the basic social skills.[13]

Thus, in some technical fields there has been increasing specialization, while in the fields characterized by administration and by the demand for social skills there has been increasing generalization; and the total picture may indeed suggest the growth of both specialization and generalization.

Hierarchical and horizontal relations.—Hierarchical relations may well lead to efficiency when the job is defined by traditional areas of knowledge. However, there is some evidence that participation in making decisions is crucial where it is necessary to motivate people to identify themselves with organizational goals, to co-operate in their social relations, and to communicate.[14] Since these involve social skills, participation in making decisions is important where jobs are chiefly defined by those abilities. Put differently, jobs characterized by social skills might be carried out most efficiently under a horizontal structure of authority, that permits all individuals to participate equally in decisions.[15]

Specifications for a Third Model of Bureaucracy

To point out the weaknesses of Weber's model is not to suggest its elimination. Quite the contrary; this paper argues that there are several models of organization with differential efficiencies depending on the nature of the work and the types of tasks to be performed. In this regard, at least three types have been suggested: Weber's, that found in "human relations," and what may be called the "professional bureaucracy."[16] The third model, not discussed as yet, is characterized by the degree to which the organization must deal with events both uniform and not uniform, or by the need to have jobs requiring great social skills as well as jobs requiring traditional areas of knowledge. Perhaps the outstanding illustrations of the third type would be a large hospital, a graduate school, or a research organization. To more systematically highlight the difference between the three models, Table 1 has been presented.

It can be seen from Table 1 that the chief distinguishing characteristic of the professional model is its inclusion of contradictory forms of social relations. This model is particularly relevant to contemporary society where

13 The stress toward generalization can also be noted among ward personnel in psychiatric wards (R. A. Cohen, "Some Relations between Staff Tensions and the Psychotherapeutic Process," *The Patient and the Mental Hospital*, pp. 307–8).

14 For a review of the literature see March and Simon, *op. cit.,* p. 81.

15 Hamburg (*op. cit.,* pp. 95–96) points out that where nurses, ward attendants, and patients are permitted to participate in decision-making—among other things—the efficiency of the ward goes up, there is a smaller labor turnover, fewer aggressive actions of the patients, etc. This is not to rule out the importance of vertical relations but only to suggest that they are least likely to lead to efficiency in bureaucratic organizations where jobs require social skills.

16 See Robert Vinter, "Notes on Professions and Bureaucracy" (unpublished manuscript, September, 1960).

most large-scale organizations have to deal with uniform and non-uniform tasks[17] or with occupations that demand traditional knowledge as well as social skills.[18]

Granted this assertion, one of the key theoretical and empirical problems facing the student of complex organizations is the study of "Mechanisms of Segregation"—the procedures by which potentially contradictory social relations are co-ordinated in some common organizational goals.[19] That this central issue might be clearly seen as well as to suggest possible paths of inquiry, four mechanisms of segregation will be discussed in greater detail.

1. *Role separation as a mechanism of segregation.*—One way of co-ordinating contradictory forms of behavior is to restrict primary group behavior to one set of individuals and formal relations to another.[20] This is a well-known procedure, in part recognized in Parsons' analysis of current occupational structure.[21] One particularly relevant illustration of role segregation comes from Blau's analysis of bureaucracy.[22] Using the analogy of the civil service, he suggests that all hiring and firing functions

[17] One assumption which should be made explicit is that non-uniform events will constitute a major factor in organizational analysis in the foreseeable future. This assumption rests on the following considerations: (*a*) scientific advance not only reduces prior areas of ignorance to known uniformities but reveals new areas; (*b*) as Talcott Parsons suggests (*The Social Systems* [Glencoe, Ill.: Free Press, 1951], pp. 44–45), the processes of socialization are inevitably imperfect, and as a consequence one must always assume the idiosyncratic to be part of any model of human behavior; and (*c*) a society committed to technological advance must be prepared for constant social change, and for dealing with phenomena for which it has no prior uniform modes of interaction.

[18] The assumption is made that jobs calling for social abilities will constitute a significant proportion of all jobs in the foreseeable future. This assumption is based on investigations such as were made by Nelson N. Foote and Paul K. Hatt who in their paper, "Social Mobility and Economic Advancement" (*American Economic Review,* XLIII [May, 1953], 364–67), suggest a shift from the primary extractive and secondary manufacturing industries to the tertiary, quaternary, and quinary industries consisting largely of human services. It also rests on analyses such as made by Reinhard Bendix (*Work and Authority in Industry* [New York: John Wiley & Sons, 1956], pp. 216 ff.), who points out that as the organization becomes larger, personal relations become important as technical features of the job.

[19] To stress mechanisms which permit the coordination of potentially conflicting relations is not to deny that there are certain relations which can never be reconciled. Thus, one important aspect of organizational analysis (the resolution of conflict rather than its co-ordination), not included in this discussion, would have involved an analysis of physical violence, strikes, arbitration, propaganda, etc.

[20] Robert K. Merton, in "The Role-Set: Problems in Sociological Theory" (*British Journal of Sociology,* VIII [June, 1957], 106–20), suggests by analogy several additional mechanisms of segregation which will not be discussed here.

[21] Parsons points out the need to keep the family separated from the occupational life, one of the major devices being to keep the family physically isolated by a division of labor by sex ("The Social Structure of the Family," *The Family: Its Function and Destiny,* ed. Ruth N. Anshen [New York: Harper & Bros., 1949]).

[22] Blau, *op. cit.,* pp. 64–66.

Table 1.   Characteristics of Three Models of Bureaucracy

CHARACTERISTIC	WEBER'S MODEL[a]	HUMAN RELATIONS[b]	PROFESSIONAL MODEL[c]
Impersonal relations	Extensive	Minimal	One part extensive One part minimal
Appointment on merit	Extensive	Extensive	Extensive
A priori specification of job authority	Extensive	Minimal	One part extensive One part minimal
Hierarchical authority	Extensive	Minimal	One part extensive One part minimal
Separation of policy and administrative decisions	Extensive	Minimal	One part extensive One part minimal
General rules to govern relations not specified by above dimensions	Extensive	Minimal	One part extensive One part minimal
Specialization	Extensive	Minimal	One part extensive One part minimal

a This model would be most efficient where tasks are uniform and involve traditional areas of knowledge, such as: governmental agencies given little discretion by law—police force, enforcing traffic and criminal law, the army during peacetime, processing most income tax returns; and private concerns with constant products and technologies—public utilities such as gas, water, and electricity.

b This model would be most efficient where tasks are relatively not uniform or involve social skills; to illustrate: situations which are so non-uniform that government cannot lay down highly specified laws but rather sets up commissions with broad discretionary powers—National Institutes of Mental Health, National Labor Relations Board, etc.; and situations involving the selling of undifferentiated products—large advertising firms.

c This model would be most efficient where the job requires dealing with both uniform and non-uniform events or with social skills as well as traditional areas of knowledge; e.g., situations requiring standardized administrative tasks and great professional autonomy—large hospitals, large graduate schools, large research organizations—and situations requiring both knowledge of administrative details as well as high interpersonal skills—large social work agencies or psychiatric hospitals.

be handled by a special group which has no responsibilities for production or administration. In this way, the potential contradiction between positive affect and objectivity can be minimized, while the virtues are maximized.

Another principle of segregation by role is illustrated by Melman in his study of a large auto concern organized into several large gangs, with each being given a production goal.[23] The management paid individuals on the basis of their gang's endeavor. Within the gang the management made little effort to deal with the non-uniform everyday problems of man-to-man supervision. This was left to the gang, with its own mechanisms of supervision.

However, the setting-up of gangs and the over-all policy of expansion and contraction of goals of production (relatively uniform problems dealing with traditional areas of knowledge) were based on a hierarchy of authority. Thus, within the same organization there were two kinds of decision sys-

[23] Seymour Melman, *Decision Making and Productivity* (Oxford: Basil Blackwell, 1958), pp. 92–135; also see Blau, *op. cit.*, p. 66, and Ralph J. Cordiner, *New Frontiers for Professional Managers* (New York: McGraw-Hill Book Co., 1956), pp. 40–80.

tems. On the one hand, there was a centralized hierarchy of authority and, on the other hand, local discretion. There was little conflict between the two systems because management and workers had agreed in advance that interaction between one set of roles was to be handled by local discretion, but between another set of roles by centralized authority. Since the roles were clearly differentiated, it was possible to do this with minimal friction.

2. *Physical distance as a mechanism of segregation.*—A mechanism of segregation suitable only in limited cases is physical separation. Perhaps the most dramatic use of this procedure is illustrated by recent developments in research departments in business concerns.[24] The purer the research, that is, the more non-uniform the event, the more likely will physical distance be put between the departments of research and production. The Bell Laboratories, a subsidiary of American Telegraph and Telephone Company, which is a case in point, tends to fit the "human-relations" model of bureaucracy,[25] while the part of it dealing with the production of telephones and the installation of telephones is, comparatively speaking, more likely to follow Weber's model. Conflict between the two systems is minimized by their being kept physically apart.

Though the mechanism of physical separation permits a solution, it is inadequate because, as studies of larger organizations indicate, there are within the same job or closely interrelated jobs both uniform and non-uniform events, or there is within the same job the demand both for knowledge and for social skills. In such cases, mechanisms of physical separation are, by definition, inappropriate.

3. *Transferral occupations as mechanisms of segregation.*—Where the organization is based on technological innovation, such as the modern industrial concern, the advances of science might transform an event from non-uniform to uniform, or vice versa. This means that there must be certain occupations whose major function is to switch areas of work from one set of social relations to another without contaminating the atmospheres

---

[24] Between 1953 and 1956 there was an estimated 67 per cent increase in the total amount of money spent for research in America ($5.4 billion to $9 billion). Business concerns whose major purpose was not research increased their expenditures almost 50 per cent (from $3.7 billion to $6.5 billion) (see *Reviews of Data on Research and Development* [National Science Foundation, No. 10, NSF–58–10, May, 1958], pp. 1–2). There seem to be no estimates of business expenditures or research which go past 1953; however, estimates of federal expenditures for research, which might be correlated with business expenditures, are that between 1940 and 1958 the federal government expanded its research budget almost three times (*Proceedings of a Conference on Research and Development and Its Impact on the Economy* [National Science Foundation, NSF–58–36, 1958]).

[25] The Bell Laboratories will frequently hire scientists with the explicit provision that they are free to work on the problems they like and in the manner, within reason, they choose, with the restriction that any resulting product belongs to the company. As a consequence, social relations within the laboratory may be like a university's colleague relationship—non-hierarchical, personal, informal, face to face, with few a priori rules on duties and obligations.

of either. For instance, the engineer must frequently be in a position to take the pure scientist's work and put it on the production line. This means that he must move between the world of science, with its colleague relationships, to the world of production, with its formal hierarchical relations, without permitting the attitudes to mix.[26]

Transferral occupations have unique problems and become central when the assumption is made that organizations consist of potentially conflicting modes of behavior working harmoniously toward some over-all goal. As such, transferral occupations deserve considerable attention on the part of those interested in elaborating bureaucratic theory.

4. *Evaluation procedures as mechanisms of segregation.*—Highly related to the transferral occupations are the procedures of evaluation. If the organization contains contradictory social relations and, at the same time, is subject to constant changes, then there must be some procedure for determining points at which one kind of social relations should be replaced by another. Melman indicates that management has set up occupations for evaluating all new machines for eventual incorporation into the organization.[27] In an analogous manner, the organizations containing conflicting social relations will operate more efficiently if they have procedures for deciding at what point there should be a shift from one form of social relation to another. This is in contrast to the common assumption that the structure is permanent. Focusing on evaluation will be a major concern of future research if the model of bureaucracy geared to organizational change suggested here is to be effected.

This now sums up consideration of some possible mechanisms of segregation. It also indicates why a key area for advancing the theory of complex organizations is the study of ways by which contradictory forms of organizational structure exist side by side without ruinous friction.

---

26 The same phenomena can be seen in the mass media if the analysis of Katz and Lazarsfeld and Inkeles can be taken as a given. These men see two elements in the mass media: (*a*) the formal organization which broadcasts messages, and (*b*) the small primary groups which receive and interpret them. Katz and Lazarsfeld suggest that these two diverse and somewhat antithetical worlds are breached by the opinion leader, and Inkeles argues (to a lesser extent) that they are breached by the agitator. Like the engineer, the opinion leader and the agitator move between the two worlds without contaminating either (see Elihu Katz and Paul F. Lazarsfeld, *Personal Influence* [Glencoe, Ill.: Free Press, 1955], pp. 162–208; Alex Inkeles, *Public Opinion in Soviet Russia* [Cambridge, Mass.: Harvard University Press, 1951], pp. 38–135).

27 Melman, *op. cit.*

14 / Intraorganizational Structural Variation: Application of the Bureaucratic Model

Richard H. Hall

MODERN ORGANIZATIONS ARE composed, according to Victor Thompson, of a highly elaborated hierarchy of authority superimposed upon a highly elaborated division of labor.[1] This well-established definition has served as the basis for characterizing such organizations as bureaucracies. While this characterization in general has not been seriously questioned, attention has recently been focused on the probability of important variations in the hierarchical and horizontal segments within the complex whole.

In a theoretical discussion of such intraorganizational variations, Litwak has suggested that certain internal segments of organizations (departments or divisions) may have a structure that is divergent from, or even incompatible with, the structure of the bureaucratized remainder of the organization.[2] He suggests that in some organizational segments a bureaucratized structure would be dysfunctional for the achievement of the segmental task.

In this study[3] ten organizations are examined in order to determine whether variations in structure did occur among organizational segments engaged in divergent activities. Structural variations between hierarchical levels were also considered in order to determine whether such variations would have any significant influence on the over-all organizational structure.

The Problem

In labeling the complex modern organization a bureaucracy, organizational theorists have demonstrated uncommon agreement about the nature of

---

[1] Victor A. Thompson, *Modern Organization* (New York, 1961), pp. 3–4.

[2] Eugene Litwak, "Models of Organization Which Permit Conflict," *American Journal of Sociology,* 67(1961), 177–84.

[3] This research was supported by the United States Air Force under Contract No. AF49(638)–447 monitored by the Air Force Office of Scientific Research of the Office of Aerospace Research while the author was affiliated with the Department of Sociology and the Personnel Research Board of the Ohio State University. This article is a revised version of paper read at the annual meeting of the Ohio Valley Sociological Society, May 4, 1962.

bureaucracy. This agreement has had as a common basis the formulations of Weber,[4] who may be looked upon as the progenitor of subsequent discussions of bureaucracy. Such men as Merton, Friedrich, Udy, Heady, Parsons, Berger, and Litwak have substantially agreed on the characteristics of bureaucracy.[5] Table 1 indicates the extent of this agreement.

While pointing to the high level of agreement on the abstract concept of bureaucracy, it should also be noted that these authors have suggested and used other approaches in their more specific formulations. Nevertheless, the agreement has allowed students of the field to use the bureaucratic model as a major theoretical orientation. This bureaucratic orientation is most commonly stated in terms of a series of attributes or dimensions of bureaucracy. Organizations considered bureaucratic are thought to have these dimensions present to a high degree; nonbureaucratic organizations, in these terms do not show these dimensions. The dimensions used by the various writers in their formulations are summarized in Table 1.

Six of the dimensions cited in Table 1 were selected as the basis for the present study. They are: (1) a well-defined hierarchy of authority, (2) a division of labor based upon functional specialization, (3) a system of rules covering the rights and duties of positional incumbents, (4) a system of procedures for dealing with work situations, (5) impersonality of interpersonal relationships, and (6) selection for employment and promotion based upon technical competence.

In discussing the dimensions of bureaucracy, an assumption implicit in the notion of "dimension" itself should be made explicit. The concept of a dimension assumes that the phenomenon under study exists in the form of a continuum along the dimension. This has been overlooked at times by researchers who have taken the dimensions cited as "given" in their study. Alvin Gouldner has suggested that the bureaucratic concept be used in this dimensional manner,[6] and Udy's study of bureaucratization among nonindustrial societies also suggests such an approach.[7] In this study each of the dimensions is approached as a continuum, along which any organization can be located. This approach will allow maximal use of the dimensional model suggested, as well as allowing organizations to be located

---

[4] Max Weber, *The Theory of Economic and Social Organization,* trans. A. M. Henderson and Talcott Parsons (New York, 1947), esp. pp. 330–34.

[5] Robert K. Merton, *Social Theory and Social Structure* (Glencoe, 1949), pp. 151–52; Karl J. Friedrich, "Some Observations on Weber's Analysis of Bureaucracy," in R. K. Merton *et al.,* eds., *Reader in Bureaucracy* (Glencoe, 1952), p. 29; Stanley H. Udy, Jr., " 'Bureaucracy' and 'Rationality' in Weber's Organization Theory: An Empirical Study," *American Sociological Review,* 24 (1959), 791–95; Ferrel Heady, Bureaucratic Theory and Comparative Administration, *Administrative Science Quarterly,* 3 (1959), 516; Talcott Parsons, *The Structure of Social Action* (New York, 1937), p. 506; Morroe Berger, *Bureaucracy and Society in Modern Egypt* (Princeton, 1957), p. 48; and Litwak, *op. cit.*

[6] *Studies in Leadership* (New York, 1950), pp. 53–54.

[7] *Op. cit.* It should be noted that Udy uses the dimensions in a present–absent dichotomy rather than as continua.

Table 1. Characteristics of Bureaucracy as Listed by Major Authors.

DIMENSIONS OF BUREAUCRACY	WEBER	LITWAK	FRIEDRICH	MERTON	UDY	HEADY	PARSONS	BERGER
Hierarchy of authority	*	*	*	*	*	*	*	*
Division of labor	*		*	*	*	*	*	*
Technically competent participants	*	*	*	*	*		*	*
Procedural devices for work situations	*	*	*	*		*		
Rules governing behavior of members	*	*	*	*				
Limited authority of office	*			*		*	*	
Differential rewards by office					*			
Impersonality of personal contact	*	*		*				
Administration separate from ownership	*	*						
Emphasis on written communication	*							
National discipline	*							

along the dimensions in terms of the degree to which they are bureaucratized.

Although organizations as a whole can be characterized as being bureaucratic to some degree, variations in structure within a particular organization must be recognized in order to have a complete structural picture. The historically predominant approach to internal variations has been through the study of the evolved, informal, or unofficial work arrangements which are at variance with the officially prescribed structure.[8] These studies of the unofficial structures of organizations typically focus on structural variations within a particular work group.

An alternative approach to intraorganizational variations is to determine whether there are significant structural differences among the officially prescribed organizational segments. Litwak has suggested that various departments or divisions within any one organization may perform functions that demand different forms of behavior on the part of the participants.[9] In his theoretical development he divides organizational segments into two basic categories. The first category contains those departments dealing with uniform events and traditional skills, as, for example, assembly-line work, standardized administrative tasks, clerical tasks, and so on. These uniform, easily routinized tasks, classified as *Type I* tasks for the purposes of this study, are realistically analyzed from the perspective of the classical Weberian bureaucratic model. Litwak suggests that this model is both applicable and organizationally rational for organizations and organizational segments specializing in these tasks.[10]

On the other hand, Litwak suggests that some organizations and some component parts of organizations may engage in tasks that are nonuniform and difficult to routinize. Tasks which require social or creative skills, such as research, sales, design, advertising, and so forth, are not as appropriately analyzed by the bureaucratic model. According to Litwak, such tasks, here classified as *Type II* tasks, are more accurately approached through the human-relations model.[11] This model is characterized by having the various bureaucratic components present to a minimal degree.

For the purposes of studying organizations that encompass divisions specializing in both Type I and Type II tasks, Litwak suggests a third organizational model—the "professional model." This model would be applicable to such organizations in that it includes the essential elements of both the bureaucratic and human-relations models. In short, this model suggests that the various bureaucratic components may be present both extensively and minimally in a single organization.[12]

Although relatively little attention has been paid to the horizontal

---

8 For example, see F. J. Roethlisberger and William J. Dickson, *Management and the Worker* (Cambridge, Mass., 1939); Charles H. Page, Bureaucracy's Other Face, *Social Forces*, 25 (Oct., 1946), 88–94; and K. H. Turner, The Navy Disbursing Officer as a Bureaucrat, *American Sociological Review*, 12 (1947), 342–48.

9 *Op. cit.*, p. 181.

10 *Ibid.*, pp. 178–81.

11 *Ibid.*, p. 181.

12 *Ibid.*, p. 182, Table I.

differentiations noted, even less has been paid to the factor of vertical or hierarchical structural variations. This lack of attention appears unwarranted since it is readily observed that executives and workers behave differently. Different types of behavior and interpersonal relationships are expected at different hierarchical levels and these differences would appear to influence the structure. There is not as great a division of labor among executives as among nonexecutives, nor are procedures followed as rigidly. In general, Litwak's distinction between the uniform and the nonuniform tasks appears to be applicable in these hierarchical distinctions as well as in segmental distinctions.

An alternative to the use of the three distinct organizational models suggested for studying organizational structural variations is the application of one model, the bureaucratic model, to organizations having such variations. Organizational segments that are characterized by a need for social skills (Type II) would exhibit the various bureaucratic dimensions to a lesser degree, while those which demand traditional skills (Type I) would exhibit such dimensions to a higher degree. With this single model, analyses can be made of the varying degrees of bureaucratization exhibited by organizations, either as wholes or as segments.

The use of this model assumes that each of the bureaucratic dimensions discussed does in fact exist along a continuum and that these are measurable continua. If this assumption is correct, then organizations can be more accurately studied with the bureaucratic model, with allowances for variations from the model. In order to test the applicability of the model suggested here, the following specific hypotheses were developed:

1. Organizational divisions or departments that specialize in tasks that are nonuniform or difficult to routinize (Type II) will be significantly less bureaucratic in all dimensions than those departments specializing in more uniform or routinizable tasks (Type I).

2. Those hierarchical levels (typically the executive levels) whose tasks are less uniform and routinizable will be significantly less bureaucratic in all dimensions than the hierarchical levels (typically the nonexecutive) in which the tasks are uniform and easily routinized.

Method

In order to utilize the bureaucratic model proposed here, it was necessary to develop a technique for the measurement of each dimension. After weighing possible alternatives, we decided to develop Likert internal-consistency scales for the measurement of each dimension. These scales consisted of a series of statements related to each dimension. The scales were designed for administration to organizational employees, each of whom was to indicate how accurately each statement described his own organization.[13] Each scale was demonstrated to be reliable and all were judged valid.

[13] A complete description of the methods of scale development is included in Richard H. Hall, "An Empirical Study of Bureaucratic Dimensions and Their Relation to Other Organizational Characteristics" (unpublished Ph.D. dissertation, Ohio State University, 1961).

The measurement technique used here was obviously designed to reflect the participants' own perceptions of their organization. Although an outsider's observations based upon some absolute standard of degree of bureaucratization might be more valid, no such absolute standard exists at present. The method utilized here appears to be an appropriate alternative to such a procedure.

The six scales were administered to a random sample of the personnel of ten organizations; five of these organizations were profit-making organizations and five were governmental organizations. Studies of bureaucracy have typically been conducted in one organization or one type of organization such as hospitals or employment agencies. In order to be able to generalize at all, it appeared preferable to extend the organizational sample to include as many types of organizations as possible. Valid generalizations about the nature of bureaucracy cannot logically be made from the study of one organization or one organizational type.

The random sample of personnel within each organization was asked to complete a brief questionnaire giving background information as well as the scales themselves. This background information included data about their departmental affiliation and their hierarchical level and served as the basis for departmental and hierarchical categorization.

Interdepartmental Differences

In order to test the first hypothesis, dealing with interdepartmental differences, each of the ten organizations' departments were divided into categories of nonuniform or social tasks (Type II), and uniform or traditional tasks (Type I). Only three organizations were found to have departments in the Type II category. Despite this small number of organizations, analysis was possible through the comparison of the Type I departments with Type II departments of the same three organizations. A total of sixteen departments were thus analyzed. Departmental scores were determined by using the mean scores of the respondents from each of the sixteen departments. Table 2 gives the results of the analysis, which was accomplished by means of the nonparametric U-test.[14]

As Table 2 indicates, the first hypothesis was partially upheld. On three dimensions, hierarchy of authority, division of labor, and presence of external procedural specifications, the Type II departments were significantly less bureaucratic. These findings, which substantiate Litwak's contentions, demonstrate that such departments, because of the nature of their tasks, are not and perhaps cannot be as bureaucratized as other departments within the same organization. Procedures are doubtlessly followed, but, since the personnel of such departments deal primarily with people and not paperwork, the procedures are probably much less specific

[14] The U-test is designed to compare two at least ordinally measured groups of phenomena in order to determine whether significant differences do exist between the groups. A lower U-value indicates a greater difference between groups than a higher value.

Table 2. Differences Between Type I Departments and
Type II Departments.

DIMENSION	($N = 16$ DEPARTMENTS)	U-VALUE
Hierarchy of authority		0[a]
Division of labor		3[a]
Rules		13
Procedures		1[a]
Impersonality		12
Technical qualifications		11[b]

[a] Difference significant at .05 level, other differences not statistically significant.
[b] The direction of the relationship that did exist was reversed on this dimension.

and serve as general outlines for action rather than exacting specifications for work flow and step-by-step work patterns.

Correspondingly, although there would be division of labor in Type II departments, it would not be as highly specific as in the Type I departments, since the social skills demand a broader range of behavior for successful job performance. Although each member of the department may have a specific job to do, each job itself allows a behavioral spectrum which may overlap with other job specifications. The outcome is a less specific division of labor in the Type II departments.

The lower degree of hierarchical emphasis among Type II departments is less easily explained. Litwak proposes that this difference is due to the necessity for Type II department employees to identify themselves with organizational goals through participation in decision making.[15] Although there are no data available here to contradict Litwak's contention, it appears that such involvement with organizational goals might be equally vital in the Type I departments in order to keep personnel in routinized jobs interested in the welfare of the organization. An alternative explanation of this finding may be that differences in the skills of the personnel in the Type II departments are less clearly evident. The sales manager of a sales department may even admittedly be little better as a salesman than his subordinate salesmen. In order to resolve this "source of conflict" (in Thompson's terms[16]), the emphasis on hierarchical differences may be minimized. In the more traditional skill-oriented departments, such skill differences may be more highly correlated with hierarchical differences.

The lack of a significant difference in regard to the importance of rules is not unexpected. Such rules are often company-wide rather than departmental. Although it was expected that there would be less emphasis on the rules in the Type II departments, perhaps in the organizations studied the rules were enforced uniformly across departmental lines. The organizations themselves varied in the extensiveness of their rules, but such a variation was not evident internally.

[15] *Op. cit.*, p. 181.
[16] *Op. cit.*, p. 109.

The finding in regard to impersonality was somewhat of a surprise. Litwak strongly suggested that there would be more personal involvement with clients or customers in the Type II departments.[17] This was not the case in this study. Perhaps the particular departments studied here were atypical in being able to maintain impersonality. A more defensible alternative explanation is that the organizations as a whole may be characterized by varying degrees of emphasis on impersonality. There may be more stress on an over-all approach to internal relationships, and customers and clients. At best, additional data should be analyzed before serious generalizations are proposed on this point.

The technical qualifications dimensions also yielded no significant difference between the two types of departments. Litwak's outline of the important differences between the departmental types also suggests that there is no such difference. Although different skills are undoubtedly called for, there is probably an organization-wide emphasis on hiring and promoting on the basis of merit. The degree of such organizational emphasis can vary, but apparently not intraorganizationally. This would be especially true in large organizations which have central personnel divisions in charge of all personnel policies.

Hierarchical Differences

In testing the second hypothesis a different procedure was followed. The respondents were first classified into executive and nonexecutive categories. This dichotomization was based on the respondents' own listing of their hierarchical position. Although more hierarchical levels were present in most of the organizations, insufficient respondents in several possible categories led to grouping the respondents into these two categories. The executives from all ten organizations were combined into one category and the nonexecutives into another. Since the organizations were common for both categories, such a combination should not weaken or strengthen any possible relationships. The responses of each group were also categorized. The median of all scores on each dimension was used to divide both the executive and nonexecutive groups into those who perceived a high degree of bureaucratization in their organization and those who perceived a low degree. The chi-square technique was used to analyze these data. In Table 3 the six two-by-two tables used for the chi-square analysis comparing the degree of bureaucratization between the hierarchical levels are summarized.

As Table 3 indicates, the second hypothesis was upheld on four of the six dimensions. The executive levels operate in a less bureaucratic fashion in terms of the emphasis on hierarchy, division of labor, procedures, and impersonality. Since the executive is responsible for the behavior of his subordinates,[18] the functional areas of work which he manages cover a wider range than the range of work of his subordinates. Similarly, since the

17 *Op. cit.,* p. 180.
18 Thompson, *op. cit.,* p. 136.

Table 3. Differences Between Executives and Nonexecutives
in Degree of Bureaucratization.

| | | | DEGREE OF BUREAUCRATIZATION | | | |
| | | | Executives (N 116) | | Nonexecutives (N 187) | |
Dimension	$\chi^2 d.f.\ 1$	Level of signifi- cance	High	Low	High	Low
Hierarchy of authority	8.69	.01	15.2	23.1	35.0	26.7
Division of labor	8.69	.01	15.2	23.1	35.0	26.7
Rules	0.002	—	19.1	19.1	31.0	30.9
Procedures	5.14	.05	16.2	22.1	34.3	27.4
Impersonality	5.14	.05	16.2	22.1	34.3	27.1
Technical qualifications	12.24	.001	24.1	14.2	26.1	35.6

executive is closer to the top of the hierarchy, such restrictions on decision making and rights to proceed without additional authorization as face the subordinates are not restrictive for the executive.

Procedural restrictions are similarly not as relevant for the executive. The nature of his work, involving decision making, delegation of authority, and guidance of subordinates, would make any emphasis on procedural minutiae both dysfunctional and meaningless. Procedures are doubtlessly followed, but in a much more general and broader context. The lessened impersonality at the executive levels is probably a function of the need for greater interpersonal contacts, or at least the occurrence of a greater frequency of such contacts whether they are needed or not.[19] The executives also will tend to have common social backgrounds and interests and thus may consider themselves as part of an executive group, although this factor is certainly not absent among the nonexecutives. False personalization may also be a factor if the executive engages in superficial joviality and good fellowship.[20]

The lack of difference on the rules dimension may be due to the pervasiveness of the rules throughout the organizations. It may also result from the fact that the executives are the rule enforcers, and therefore may have internalized the rules and may seek to act as good examples for their subordinates.

The finding on the technical qualifications dimension is a reversal of the predicted direction. Executives placed more emphasis on merit-based hiring and promotion than nonexecutives. Two explanations may be offered for this phenomenon. The first of these is that the executives have

[19] *Ibid.,* p. 87; and William H. Whyte, Jr., *The Organization Man* (New York, 1957), p. 145.

[20] David Reisman, Nathan Glazer, and Reuel Denney, *The Lonely Crowd* (New York, 1956), p. 302.

observed that those who have been promoted, including themselves, do in fact have training and capabilities superior to those not promoted. If the organizations are operating rationally, this could be the explanation. On the other hand, the executives may be stating what they prefer to believe—they are better qualified than the nonexecutives and have attained their position solely on the basis of merit, when other factors not related to merit may have been involved. Neither of these arguments can be validated on the basis of the evidence, but both may be operative.

Conclusion

This study has demonstrated that there are significant differences in the degree of bureaucratization among internal structural segments of organizations. These differences, both departmental and hierarchical, are variations within the over-all organizational structure. It has been argued that through the study of the varying degrees of bureaucratization of internal organizational segments a simpler alternative than Litwak's three-model approach can be used, which will yield comparable results. It has also been proposed that such segmental differences have important consequences for both the understanding of organizational structure itself and for more complete understanding of the behavior of the participants within the organization.

Organizations may be meaningfully studied as totalities. When the bureaucratic model is used, it can be demonstrated that the organizations studied are more or less bureaucratic. Varying degrees of bureaucratization would certainly have concomitant effects on other organizational phenomena such as participants' behavior, effectiveness of goal-attaining endeavors, and relations with the external environment both in terms of individuals and other organizations.

More detailed study of an organization should, however, take the differences among segments into consideration. The sum of such segments constitutes the organization as a whole, but such a total is less relevant for organizational analysis than an understanding of the structural variations of the parts. These variations in pattern from the whole, with their concomitant effects on other organizational phenomena, are an important intermediate point between the officially prescribed organizational structure and the small informal work groups that emerge. Both the formal structure and the informal work groups have received scientific attention. This "bridging" aspect of intraorganizational structural differentiation may also yield important contributions to the understanding of organizations if it too is given such attention.

If additional research is carried out on these internal variations, new categories for separating the internal segments should be developed where applicable. Those used in this study are suggestive of one approach to such variations. Both the horizontal distribution of departments and the vertical hierarchical arrangements could be reclassified for more intensive analysis.

4 / Informal Organization in Industry: Functional or Dysfunctional?

One research area growing out of experiments at the Hawthorne Western Electric plant is concerned with the impact of informal organization on the formal organization. Early studies, starting with the Bank Wiring Room experiment, suggested that restriction of output—behavior counter-productive to organizational objectives—resulted from the formation of cohesive work groups. Since the "discovery" by the Hawthorne researchers in the 1930s of the relevancy of interpersonal relations to the functioning of a work organization, researchers and managers have been concerned with harnessing primary group relations for the achievement of organizational goals. Later studies demonstrated the relationship between work group cohesion, morale, and productivity to be more complex than originally supposed, a fact supported by some of the selections in this chapter.

Donald Roy's "Efficiency and 'The Fix': Informal Intergroup Relations in a Piecework Machine Shop" is an example of those studies that document the subversion of professed managerial procedures and goals by a network of informal relations among workers. Unique to this study is its focus on intergroup rather than intragroup cooperation.

While some research underlines the dysfunctions of cohesive work groups for organizational performance, other researchers and theorists portray informal organization as enhancing the successful operation of an organization. A crucial assumption is that personally rewarding social relations at work improve morale, which in turn contributes to organizational efficiency. Raymond Van Zelst ("Sociometrically Selected Work Teams Increase Production") notes that while much literature has focused upon intragroup social relations and their impact on group morale and productivity, a useful technique for forming work groups—sociometric selection—has been ignored. Using the sociometric technique to establish work teams among carpenters and bricklayers, Van Zelst found an increase in workers' feelings of job satisfaction and participation, a decrease in friction and anxiety between work partners, and the creation of a friendly, cooperative atmosphere on the job—all of which promoted a reduction in turnover rates and higher levels of productivity.

Functional analysis, the implicit or explicit model on which are based most studies of the impact of informal organization on the attainment of formal organizational goals, is challenged by Bensman and Gerver in "Crime and Punishment in the Factory: The Function of Deviancy in Maintaining the Social System." Proposing an alternative perspective, and applying it to the illegal but unofficially sanctioned use of a tool in the production of airplanes, they conclude that viewing deviancy as functional or dysfunctional is an artificial creation of the functional model.

15 / Efficiency and "The Fix": Informal Intergroup Relations in a Piecework Machine Shop[1]

Donald Roy

As PART OF a broader examination and appraisal of the application of piecework incentive to the production line of an American factory this paper essays the simple but largely neglected task of exploring the network of intergroup relations in which the work activity of machine operatives is imbedded. Exploration will be restricted to a limited sector of the total web of interaction in one shop; description will center upon those relationships that provide support to the operator group in its resistance to and subversion of formally instituted managerial controls on production. It is hoped that observations reported here not only will bear upon the practical problem of industrial efficiency but will also contribute to the more general study of institutional dynamics.

This could be considered the third in a series of attempts to make more careful discriminations in an area of research that has been characteristically productive of sweeping generalizations, blanket conceptualizations, or algebraic gymnastics that tend to halt inquiry at the same time that they lay a fog over otherwise easily discerned reality. Data for all three papers were acquired in an investigation of a single work situation by a single technique of social inquiry, participant observation. The writer was employed for nearly a year as radial-drill operator in one of the machine shops of a steel-processing plant, and he kept a daily record of his observations and experiences relating to work activity and social interaction in the shop. His major interest lay in the phenomenon of restriction of output, or "systematic soldiering," the practice of which various sociological soundings have revealed in the lower depths of our industrial organization. To complete the analogy: the writer donned a diving suit and went down to see what it looked like on the bottom.

---

[1] This report is drawn from materials presented in the writer's doctoral dissertation, "Restriction of Output in a Piecework Machine Shop" (University of Chicago, 1952), under the direction of Everett C. Hughes.

One conclusion has already been set forth,[2] namely, that the usual view of output restriction is grossly undifferentiating. Different kinds of "institutionalized underworking" were practiced, each with its characteristic pattern of antecedents and consequences. The blanket term "restriction" was found to cloak all-important contrarieties of work behavior. Machine operatives not only held back effort; sometimes they worked hard. The very common failure to note such contrarieties has tended, of course, to impede the progress of research by checking consideration of the specific conditions under which differences in behavior occur.

A second finding was the discovery of complexity where simple lines of relationship had generally been assumed to exist.[3] When inconsistencies in the operator's behavior seemed to contradict the hypothesis that variations in application of economic incentive could account for the variations in work effort, a more intensive examination of response to piecework was undertaken. This disclosed that piecework incentive was not equivalent to economic incentive and that attainment of piecework "quotas" afforded machine operators a complex of rewards in which the strictly economic might or might not play a part.

The third set of observations, to be here discussed, again exhibits complication in a picture that has come to be accepted as simple in design. Here the focus of interest is the structure of "informal" intergroup connections that bear directly upon work behavior at the machine level. The material will not deny the hypothesis that the willingness of operatives to put forth effort is a function of their relationship with management or the widely held affirmation that this relationship is mediated by the organization of operatives into "informal groups." It will indicate, however, that further advances in the understanding of work behavior in the factory may involve attention to minor as well as major axes of intergroup relations. It will show that the relevant constituents of problematic production situations may include "lateral" lines of interaction between subgroups of the work force as well as "vertical" connections between managerial and worker groups.

It will be seen, in other words, that the interaction of two groups in an industrial organization takes place within and is conditioned by a larger intergroup network of reciprocal influences. Whyte has called attention to the limitations of studying groups in "isolation," without regard for the "perspectives of large institutional structures."[4] A second warning might be: The larger institutional structures form networks of interacting groups.

As a bona fide member of an informal group of machine operatives the

[2] Donald Roy, "Quota Restriction and Gold-bricking in a Machine Shop," *American Journal of Sociology,* LVII (March, 1952), 427–42.

[3] Donald F. Roy, "Work Satisfaction and Social Reward in Quota Achievement: An Analysis of Piecework Incentive," *American Sociological Review,* XVIII (October, 1953), 507–14.

[4] William F. Whyte, "Small Groups and Large Organizations," *Social Psychology at the Crossroads,* ed. John R. Rohrer and Muzafer Sherif (New York: Harper & Bros., 1951), pp. 297–312.

writer had an opportunity to observe and experience management–work group conflict in its day-to-day and blow-by-blow particulars. Also, he participated in another kind of social process, intergroup co-operation. Not only did workers on the "drill line" co-operate with each other as fellow-members of a combat team at war with management; they also received considerable aid and abetment from other groups of the shop. This inter-group co-operation was particularly evident when operators were trying to "make out," or attain "quota" production, on piecework jobs.

It has been noted in another connection that machine operators charac-teristically evinced no reluctance to put forth effort when they felt that their group-defined piecework quotas were attainable.[5] It might seem, at first glance, that the supporting of operators during intensive application to "getting the work out" would represent cooperation *with* and not *against* management. However, the truth is that operators and their "allies" joined forces in certain situations in a manner not only unmistakably at variance with the carefully prepared designs of staff experts but even in flagrant violation of strongly held managerial "moral principles" of shop behavior. In short, machine operators resorted to "cheating" to attain their quotas; and since this often involved the collusion of other shop groups, not as mere "accessories after the fact" but as deeply entangled accomplices, any mana-gerial suspicion that swindling and conniving, as well as loafing, were going on all the time was well founded. If the workers' conviction that the echelons of management were packed with men addicted to the "dirty deal" be additionally considered, it might appear that the shop was fairly overrun with crooks. Since a discussion of "contrast conceptions"[6] cannot find a place within the limited scope of this paper, it must suffice at this point merely to declare that the kind of effort made by operators and their aids to expedite production, when they did try to expedite it, was actually in many respects conflict with management.

One belief, universally accepted in the work group, may be phrased thus: "You can't 'make out' if you do things the way management wants them done." This gem of shop wisdom thus negatively put is hardly a prescription for action, but its obverse, "You've got to figure the angles," gave all hands plenty to do.

According to Al McCann (all names used are fictitious), the "Fagan" of the drill line, "They time jobs to give you just base rates. It's up to you to figure out how to fool them so you can make out. You can't make any money if you run the job the way it's timed."

We machine operators did "figure the angles"; we developed an impres-sive repertoire of angles to play and devoted ourselves to crossing the expectations of formal organization with perseverance, artistry, and orga-

---

5 Roy, "Work Satisfaction and Social Reward in Quota Achievement," *op. cit.*

6 See L. Copeland, "The Negro as a Contrast Conception," in *Race Relations and the Race Problem,* ed. E. T. Thompson (Durham: Duke University Press, 1939), and S. Kirson Weinberg, "Aspects of the Prison's Social Structure," *American Journal of Sociology,* XLVII(March, 1942), 717–26.

nizing ability of our own. For instance, job timing was a "battle all the way" between operators and time-study men. The objective of the operators was good piecework prices, and that end justified any old means that would work. One cardinal principle of operator job-timing was that cutting tools be run at lower speeds and "feeds" than the maximums possible on subsequent production, and there were various ways of encouraging the institution of adequate differentials. Also, operators deemed it essential to embellish the timing performance with movements only apparently functional in relation to the production of goods: little reachings, liftings, adjustings, dustings, and other special attentions to conscientious machine operation and good housekeeping that could be dropped instanter with the departure of the time-study man.

However, the sophistication of the time-study men usually matched the strategy employed against them. The canniest operators often gave of their best in timing duels only to get "hopeless prices" for their pains:

> Gus Schmidt was timed early in the evening on a job, and given a price of $1.00 per 100 for reaming one hole, chamfering both sides of three holes, and filing burrs on one end of one hole. All that for one cent!
> "To hell with them," said Gus.

This is not to say that the "hopeless price" was always truly hopeless. Since the maintenance of an effective control over job-timing and hence price-setting was an uncertain, often disheartening matter, operators were forced to develop skills for turning bad into good. Under the shaping hands of the "angle-applicators" surprising metamorphoses sometimes took place. Like the proverbial ugly duckling that finally feathered out into a beautiful swan, piecework jobs originally classified in operator vernacular as "stinkers" came to give off the delightful aroma of "gravy." Without going into the particulars of the various types of operation, one might say that jobs were "streamlined." This streamlining was, of course, at times "rough on the tools" and adverse in its effects on the quality of output. The jettisoning of quality called, necessarily, for a corresponding attention to ways and means of shielding supervisors and inspectors from discovering the sacrifices and consequently brought into further play the social graces of equivocation, subterfuge, and prestidigitation.

Still, the adroitness of the machine operators, inventing, scheming, and conniving unto themselves to make quotas attainable, was not enough. Many "stinkers" would not yield before the whitest heat of intelligence or the most cavalier disregard for company property. An appreciable incidence of failure should not be surprising when it is kept in mind that the black arts of "making out" were not only responses to challenge from management but also stimulations, in circular interaction, to the development of more effective countermagic in the timing process. It would be hard to overestimate the wizardry of the time-study men with pencil and paper in computing "angle-tight" piecework prices. During the latter months of his employment, months that marked the peak of his machine performance, the writer was able to achieve quota earnings approximately half the time that piecework jobs were offered. If this experience is roughly representative of the fortunes of the drill-line group, the battle with the stopwatch men was nip and tuck.

It is to be expected that a group of resourceful operatives, working with persistent intent to "make out" at quota levels, and relying heavily upon illegal practices, would be alert to possibilities of assistance from groups that were able and willing to give it and would not hesitate at further flouting the rules and regulations in cultivating it. It is also to be expected that the upholders of a managerial rational and moral order would attempt to prevent corruptive connections and would take action to stamp out whatever subversive organization did develop. During the eleven-month study, machine operators, including the drill-line men, were enjoying the co-operation of several other shop groups in an illegal facilitation of the "make-out" process. This intergroup network effectively modified certain formally established shop routines, a too close attachment to which would handicap the operators. The "syndicate" also proved adequate in circumventing each of a series of "new rules" and "new systems" introduced by management to expurgate all modifications and improvisations and force a strict adherence to the rules.

The shop groups that conspired with the operators were, namely, the inspectors, the tool-crib men, the time-checkers, the stockmen, and the setup men. With a single exception, these "service" groups stemmed from lines of authority distinct from the one for which the operators formed the base. The one exception was the setup group; it was subordinate to the same set of officials in the "production" line of authority that controlled the operators. A brief description of the duties of each of these service groups and a rough tracing of the sequences of interaction involved in the prescribed work routine of the drill men will indicate the formal pattern of intergroup relations within which informally instituted variations were woven.

The Setup Men

A chief function of the setup men was to asist machine operators in the "setting-up" of jigs and fixtures preparatory to operation of machines in the processing of materials. It included the giving of preliminary aid and advice at the beginning of the production process, at which time the setup men would customarily "run the first piece" to show operators how to do it and to indicate that the setup was adequate to meet work specifications. The duties of the setup men also included "trouble-shooting" on occasions when operators encountered difficulties that effected a lowering of the quality of output below inspection standards or a reduction of the rate of output unsatisfactory to operators or supervisors.

The Inspectors

The chief function of the inspectors was to pass judgment on the quality of the output of the machine operators, either accepting or rejecting work turned out, according to blueprint specifications. Their appraisals came at the beginning of operations, when especially thorough examinations of the first pieces processed were made, and subsequently at varying intervals during the course of a job.

The Tool-Crib Men

The tool-crib attendants served the operators as dispensers of jigs, fixtures, cutting tools, blueprints, gauges, and miscellaneous items of equipment needed to supplement basic machinery and operator-owned hand tools in the processing of materials. They worked inside a special inclosure conveniently located along one of the main arterials of shop traffic and did most of their dispensing across the wide sill of a "window," an aperture which served, incidentally, as locus of various and sundry transactions and communications not immediately relevant to tool-dispensing. There were two other openings into the crib, a door, two steps from the window, and a wide gate, farther down the corridor.

The Stockmen

The stockmen were responsible for conducting a steady flow of materials to the machines for processing. Their work called for the removal of finished work as well as the moving-up of fresh stock and involved a division of labor into two specializations "stock-chasing" and "trucking." The chief duties of the stock-chasers were to "locate" unprocessed materials in the various storage areas, when operators called for stock, and to direct the activities of the truckers, who attended to the physical transportation.

The Time-Checkers

The time-checkers worked in another special inclosure, a small "time cage," from which they distributed to the operators the work orders "lined up" by the schedulemen of the Planning Department and within which they registered the starting and completion times of each job. There were four time-registering operations for every work order. First, upon presenting an operator with a work-order slip, the checker would "punch" him "on setup" by stamping a separate order card with a clocking mechanism that registered the hours in tenths. Later, when the operator would call at the cage window to announce completion of all preparatory arrangements for the actual processing of materials, the checker would punch him "off setup" and "on production." Finally, following another operator announcement, the checker would clock the termination of the machining process with a fourth punch. At the time of his terminal punch the operator would report the number of "pieces" completed on the job just concluded and would receive a new work order to start the cycle over again. And, since the terminal punch on the completed job would be registered at the same time as the initial punch on the new one, hours on shift would be completely accounted for.

Operator Interaction with Service Groups

The machine operator's performance of each individual job or order assigned to him involved formal relationships with service groups in well-defined sequences or routines.

First, the operator would receive his work order from the time-checker. Next, he would present the work order to a tool-crib attendant at the crib window as a requisite to receiving blueprints, jigs, cutting tools, and gauges. At the same time, that is, immediately before or after approaching the crib attendant, sometimes while waiting for crib service, the operator would show his work order to a stock-chaser as a requisite to receiving materials to work on. The stock-chaser, after perusing the order slip, occasionally with additional reference to the blueprint, would hail a trucker to bring the necessary stock to the operator's machine. If there were no delay in contacting a stock-chaser or in locating and moving up the stock, a load of materials would await the operator upon his arrival at his machine with equipment from the tool crib.

Upon returning to his machine, the operator would proceed with the work of "setting up" the job, usually with the assistance of a setup man, who would stay with him until a piece was turned out whose quality of workmanship would satisfy an inspector. In appraising a finished piece, the inspector would consult the blueprint brought from the crib for work specifications and then perform operations of measurement with rules, gauges, micrometers, or more elaborate equipment. The inspector might or might not "accept" the first piece presented for his judgment. At any rate, his approval was requisite to the next step in the operator's formal interactional routine, namely, contacting the time-checker to punch "off setup" and "on production."

The operator would ordinarily have further "business" contact with a setup man during the course of production. Even if the job did not "go sour" and require the services of a "trouble-shooter," the setup man would drop around of his own accord to see how the work was progressing. Likewise, the operator would have further formal contact during the course of his job with inspectors and tool-crib attendants. Each inspector would make periodic "quality checks" at the machines on his "line"; and the operator might have to make trips to the tool crib to get tools ground or to pick up additional tools or gauges. He might also have to contact a stock-chaser or truckers for additional materials.

Upon completion of the last piece of his order the operator would tear down his setup, return his tools to the tool crib, and make a final report to the time-checker. Should the job be uncompleted at the close of a shift, the operator would merely report the number of pieces finished to a checker, and the latter would register a final punch-out. The setup would be left intact for the use of the operator coming in to work the next shift.

Major Job Categories

Certain variations in types of jobs assigned to operators are pertinent to a discussion of intergroup collusion to modify formal work routines. These variations could be classified into four categories: (1) piecework; (2) time study; (3) rework; and (4) setup.

Each piecework job carried a price per 100 pieces, determined by the timing operations mentioned earlier. Time-study and rework jobs carried no prices. The time-study category included (*a*) new jobs that had not yet been timed and (*b*) jobs that had once carried a piecework price. As the label indicates, rework jobs involved the refinishing of pieces rejected either by inspectors or in the assembly process but considered salvageable by reprocessing.

Since time-study and rework jobs carried no piecework prices, operators engaged in these two types of work were paid "day rate," that is, according to an hourly base rate determined in collective bargaining. The base rates represented minimal wage guaranties that not only applied to "day work" but also covered piecework as well. If an operator on piecework failed to exceed his base rate in average hourly earnings on a particular job on a particular day, he would be paid his base rate. Failure to produce at base rate or above on the first day of a piecework job did not penalize an operator in his efforts to earn premium pay on the second day; nor did failure to attain base rate on one piecework job on a given day reduce premiums earned on a second job performed that day.

Not a fourth type of job, but measured separately in time and payment units, were the setup operations. Piecework jobs always carried piecework setups; failure to equal or exceed base rate on setup did not jeopardize chances to earn premium on "production," and vice versa. Time-study jobs frequently carried piecework setups; rework never.

Obviously, these formal work routines may easily be modified to fit the perceived needs of machine operators. Possibilities for the development of "make-out angles" should be immediately apparent in a work situation characterized by job repertoires that included piecework and day-work operations; minimum-wage guaranties uniform for all work done; and separate payment computations by jobs and days worked. If, for instance, time formally clocked as day work could be used to gain a "head start" on subsequent piecework operations, such a transferral might mean the difference between earning and not earning premiums on doubtful piecework jobs. Similarly, time on "hopeless" piecework jobs might be applied to more promising operations; and the otherwise "free time" gained on "gravy" jobs might be consumed in productive anticipation of the formal receipt of ordinarily unrewarding piecework. Especially lush "gravy" jobs might even contribute extra time enough to convert "stinkers" into temporary "money-makers." Realization of such possibilities in any given case would necessarily involve obtaining, without a work order, the following: (1) identification of future operations as listed in sequence on the schedule board inside the time cage; (2) jigs, blueprints, and cutting tools appropriate to the work contemplated; (3) stock to work on; (4) setup help and advice; (5) inspection service; and (6) "trouble-shooting" assistance as needed. Obviously, this sequence of accomplishments would call for the support of one or more service groups at each step. That the required assistance was actually provided with such regularity that it came to be taken for granted, the writer discovered by observation and personal experience.

The following diary recording of interaction between the writer and a time-checker may be indicative of the extent to which service-group collaboration with the operators in perverting the formal system of work routine had become systematized:

> When I came to punch off the rework, the time-cage girl said, "You don't want to punch off rework yet, do you?"—suggesting that I should get a start on the next job before punching off rework.

Even line foremen, who, in regard to intergroup collusion preferred the role of silent "accessory after the fact," became upset to the point of actual attempted interference with formal rules and regulations when the naïve neophyte failed to meet the expectations of his own informal system.

> Art [foreman] was at the time cage when I punched off the day work of rereaming and on to the piecework of drilling. He came around to my machine shortly after.
> "Say," he said, "when you punch off day work onto piecework, you ought to have your piecework already started. Run a few; then punch off the day work, and you'll have a good start. You've got to chisel a little around here to make money."

Acceptance of such subversive practices did not extend, however, to groups in management other than local shop supervision. The writer was solemnly and repeatedly warned that time-study men, the true hatchet men of upper management, were disposed to bring chiselers to speedy justice.

> Gus went on to say that a girl hand-mill operator had been fired a year ago when a time-study man caught her running one job while being punched in on another. The time-study man came over to the girl's machine to time a job, to find the job completed and the girl running another.

New Rules and New Systems

During the near-year that he spent in the shop the writer felt the impact of several attempts to stamp out intergroup irregularities and enforce conformity to managerial designs of procedure. He coincidentally participated in an upholding of the maxim: "Plus ça change, plus c'est la même chose."

Attempts to tighten controls came in a series of "new rules" or "new systems" promulgated by bulletin-board edicts. How far the beginning of the series antedated the writer's arrival is not known. Old-timers spoke of a "Golden Age" enjoyed before the installation of the "Booth System" of production control; then operators "kept their own time," turning in their work orders as they saw fit and building "kitties" on good jobs to tide them over rainy days on poor jobs.

The first new rule during this study went into "effect" less than two months after the writer was hired. It was designed to tighten controls in the tool-crib sector, where attendants had not only been passing out setups ahead of time but allowing operators or their setup men to enter the toolroom to make the advance pickups themselves. An aim of the new rule was also to curb the operators' practice of keeping "main setups" at the machines instead of turning them in at the completion of operations.

> A new crib ruling went into effect today. A memorandum by Bricker [superintendent] was posted on the side of the crib window. Those who check out tools and jigs must sign a slip in triplicate, keeping the pink one and turning it in with the tools in exchange for the white original, which would constitute proof that the tools had been returned. No new setups would be issued until the old ones had been turned in.

An optimistic perception of the new procedures was expressed by young Jonesy, a tool-crib attendant and otherwise willing conniver with the operators: "Tools are scattered all over the shop. This way we'll have them all in order in the crib, and the fellows can get them anytime they need them."

But multiple-drill operator Hanks, old-timer on the line, drew upon his lengthy experience with managerial efficiency measures and saw the situation differently:

> Hanks commented unfavorably on the new ruling. He and the day man [his machine partner on the other shift] had been keeping the tools for their main setups at their bench, or, rather, under it. This practice, according to Hanks, was to insure their setting up promptly without inordinate waste of time and to insure their having all the tools needed. Hanks said that on a previous occasion he was told to turn in one of his main setups, which included over a dozen drills, reamers, taps, etc., of varying sizes. He did so, but, when he needed this setup again, the crib man couldn't locate all the tools. He asked Hanks to come back in the crib and help him find them. Hanks refused. After several hours of futile search, Hanks was finally induced to "come back and find his tools." He did so on condition that it would not be on his own time. The foreman agreed to this.
>
> "The same thing is going to happen again," predicted Hanks. "And I'm not going back there to find my tools they scatter all over, on my own time."

Though the operators went through the formality of an exchange of slips when they exchanged setups, the new procedures did not modify the practice of getting setups from the crib ahead of time. Appreciable effects of the new ruling included making more paper work for crib attendants at the same time that more work at assembling setups was thrust upon them. Jonesy's happy prediction did not materialize: the tools were not "always in order." Subsequent events confirmed Hanks's gloomy forebodings:

> It took Paul [setup man] and me several hours to get set up for the sockets, as the setup given was incomplete.
>
> Some time was spent in looking for an angle plate that was specially made for the job. Both Paul and Steve [superintendent] were irritated because the crib men could not find the plate.
>
> We spent an hour setting up because we could not find the jig.

Included in the new ruling was a stipulation that blueprints and gauges be turned in by the operators at the end of each shift, though setup paraphernalia other than prints and gauges were to be left at the machines as long as jobs were in operation. Calling for prints and gauges at the beginning of the shift, waiting at the crib window in the line that naturally formed, even when these items were "located" immediately, consumed operator time.

> Owing to the new crib ruling, he [Joe Mucha, the writer's machine partner on another shift] turned in the tap gauge. I spent 20 minutes trying to get it back again. The crib man could not find it and claimed that Joe had not turned it in. Joe stayed after three o'clock to help me get it, countering the arguments of the crib with the slip that he retained as evidence. Finally the gauge was located in the crib.
>
> I started out a half-hour late on operation 55 on the pedestals, due to delay at the crib waiting to check out the print and gauge that Joe had just turned in.

Four months later the new crib ruling was modified by another that canceled the stipulation regarding the turning-in of blueprints and gauges and called for changes in the paper work of operator–crib-attendant relations. These changes were featured by a new kind of work order, duplicates of which became involved in tool-crib bookkeeping. The change reduced the waste of operator time at the start of shifts, but to the burden of the crib attendants paper-work irritations were now added.

> When I punched in on the rework and asked Walt [crib attendant] for a print, he fumed a bit as he sought a duplicate of my new-type yellow work order in a new file of his.
>
> "I haven't been able to find more than one in five duplicates so far," he said. "And there's supposed to be a duplicate for every one."
>
> Walt said tonight, when I presented him with a work-order card for tools, "That makes the twelfth card I've had and no duplicate!"
>
> The tool crib under the new system is supposed to have duplicate work orders in their file of all jobs given operators. These duplicates are to be put in the toolroom files as soon as they are put on the board; and the operators are to sign these duplicates when checking out setups.

The "new system" did operate to handicap operators in that they were not to receive new setups from the crib until they received the new yellow work orders from the time cage to check with the duplicates in the crib. However, setup men roamed at will in the toolroom, grinding tools and fixing jigs, and were able to help the operators by picking up setups ahead of time for them. Their detailed knowledge of the various setups made it possible for them to assemble the necessary tools without the use of setup cards.

> "This is a good job," I said to McCann [now setup man]. "I wish I could get it set up ahead of time, but I guess it's no use trying. I can't get the setup now from the toolroom until I get the new work order from the time girls."
>
> McCann thought a moment. "Maybe I can get the jig and tools out of the crib for you."
>
> McCann did get the jig and tools, and I got a half-hour's head start on the job.

The writer had found Ted, a stock-chaser, and his truckers, George and Louie, willing connivers in the time-chiseling process. They moved up stock ahead of time, even after the new system made presentation of the new work order to the stock-chaser a prerequisite to getting stock. Contrary to first impressions, for all practical purposes the situation was unchanged under the new system.

> I could not go ahead with the next order, also a load of connecting rods, because the new ruling makes presentation of a work order to the stock-chaser necessary before materials can be moved up. So I was stymied and could do nothing the rest of the day.
>
> About an hour before I was to punch off the connecting rods, I advised Ted that I would soon be needing another job. He immediately brought over a load of reservoir casings.

The new system also included complication of operator-inspector relations. Inspectors were now to "sign off" operators from completed jobs before new work orders could be issued at the time booth. The "signing-off" process included notation by the inspector of the time of operation completion, a double check on the time-checker's "punch out." This added, of course, to the paper work of inspectors.

Drill-man Hanks's first response to this feature of the new system was "individualistic":

> Hanks commented on the new system tonight. He thinks that its chief purpose is to keep the operators from getting ahead on an operation and starting the next job on saved time. He said that the inspector checked him off a job tonight at 4:40, and he was not due to punch in on the next one until 6:10. He changed the time recorded by the inspector on his work slip to 6:10 and went ahead as usual. If he had not done so, there would have been a "gap" of an hour and a half unaccounted for in the records.

The writer found himself "stymied" at first but soon discovered that the new obstacle could be overcome without engaging in such a hazardous practice as "forging."

> It was ten o'clock when we were ready to punch off setup, and Johnny [setup man] asked Sam [inspector] to sign me off setup earlier, so that I could make out on setup.

"Punch me off at nine o'clock," I said, not expecting Sam to check me off earlier, and purposely exaggerating Johnny's request.

Sam refused. "I can't do that! If I do that for you, I'll have to do it for everybody!"

Sam seemed somewhat agitated in making the refusal.

A few minutes later he said to Johnny, "Why did you ask me to do that when Hanks was standing there?"

Hanks had been standing by my machine, watching us set up.

"I can't take you off an hour back. Go find out when you punched in on this job in the first place."

Johnny consulted the time-cage girl as to the time I punched on the job, later talked to Sam at Sam's bench while I was working, and came to me with the announcement that it was "fixed up" so that I made out on setup and was credited with starting production at 9:30. This gave me an hour and a half of "gravy."

By the time the "new system" was a month old, Sam was not only doing this for everybody but actually taking the initiative:

When I punched off setup for the eight pieces, Sam asked me if I wanted him to take me off setup at an earlier time in order that I might make out on the setup. I refused this offer, as it wasn't worth the trouble for me to stop to figure out the time.

Instead of looking at the clock when an operator asks to be taken off setup, Sam usually asks the operator, "When do you want to be taken off?"

No sooner had the shop employees adjusted to this "new system" and settled down to normal informal routine than they were shocked by a new pronunciamento that barred admittance to the toolroom to all save superintendents and toolroom employees:

A new crib ruling struck without warning today. Typewritten bulletins signed by Faulkner [shop manager] were posted on the toolroom door, barring admittance to all save the toolroom employees and the two departmental foremen [superintendents], Bricker and Steve. Other foremen and setup men are not to be admitted without permission from Milton, toolroom supervisor.

Hanks predicts that the new ruling won't last out the week.

Stimulated by Hanks's prediction, the writer kept an eye on the toolroom door. The rule seemed to be enforced.

On one occasion tonight Paul [setup man] asked Jonesy to let him into the crib; he was in a hurry about something. But Jonesy shook his head, and Paul had to wait at the crib window with the rest of us.

Johnny, the setup man, predicted that the new ruling would be "tough on" the tool-crib employees, not on setup men.

Johnny says that the new rule is going to be tough on grinders and crib attendants, because setup men and foremen have been doing much of the grinding and have made it easier for them by coming in to help themselves to tools, jigs, etc.

Johnny says that the new rule suits him fine. Now he can just stand at the window and holler and let the toolroom employees do the work.

The line foremen seemed to take offense at the new "exclusion act" and threatened reprisals to the crib attendants.

At quitting time I noticed Gil [line foreman] talking to Walt at the crib window. Gil seemed very serious; Walt was waving his arms and otherwise gesturing in a manner indicating rejection of responsibility. I didn't catch any words but gathered that Gil was voicing disapproval or warning, and after Gil left I said to Walt, "Looks like you're behind the eight-ball now!"

I noticed that Walt's hair was mussed, and he looked a little wild. He denied that he was in any trouble whatsoever; nor was he worried about anything whatsoever.

"I'm just working here!" he exclaimed. "I just go by the cards, and beyond that I've got no responsibility!"

I was curious as to what Gil had told him and asked Johnny later, on the way home. I had noticed that Johnny was standing near by when Gil was talking to Walt. Johnny said that Gil was telling Walt that from now on the crib was going to be charged with every minute of tool delay to the operators —that, if there was any waiting for tools, Gil was going to make out allowance cards charging these delays to the crib.

Contrary to Hanks's prediction, the new rule did "last out the week," and crowds milled around the crib window.

The boys seemed very much disgusted with the slow service at the tool crib. They crowd around the window (always a crowd there) and either growl or wisecrack about the service.

It was at this time that Jonesy, erstwhile optimist and regarded by shop employees as the most efficient of the crib attendants, decided that he had "had enough." He transferred to the quiet backroom retreat of tool-grinding. But several days later, just ten days since the new rule was promulgated, the sun began to break through the dark clouds of managerial efficiency. Hanks's prediction was off by four days.

While I was waiting for tools at the crib window tonight, I noticed the jockey [turret-lathe man] dash into the tool crib through a door that was left ajar; he was followed soon after by Gil. Later, when the door was closed, Paul shook it and shouted to the attendant, "Let me in!" He was admitted.

Steve [superintendent] called out, "Hey!" when he saw the jockey go into the crib. When the jockey came out, he spoke to him, and the jockey joshed him back. Steve did not seem to be particularly put out about it.

Soon the boys were going in and out of the crib again, almost at will, and setup men were getting setups ahead of time for operators, ignored by the crib attendants.

I noticed that Johnny and others seemed to be going in and out of the crib again, almost at will.

I noticed tonight that Johnny got into the tool crib by appearing at the door and saying to the attendant, "Let me in!"

So much for Faulkner's order—until he makes a new one!

When I asked Walt for some jaws to fit the chuck I had found, he said, "We've got lots of jaws back here, but I wouldn't know what to look for. You'd better get the setup man to come back here and find you some."

Walt said to me, "I break the rules here, but not too much—just within reason to keep the boys on production."

Faulkner's order still hangs at eye level on the crib door.

"So much for Faulkner's order!" The "fix" was "on" again, and operators and their service-group allies conducted business as usual for the remaining weeks of the writer's employment.

Conclusions

This rough sketch of the operation of one shop "syndicate" has been no more than indicative of the existence of intergroup cooperation in the lower reaches of factory social structure. No attempt has been made here to account for the aid extended by service groups, though suggestion that this assistance might be part of a larger system of reciprocal obligations has been implicit. It is apparent, for instance, that tool-crib attendants benefited from their practice of admitting operators and setup men to the toolroom to seek and pick up equipment

A more complete picture of intergroup relations would include conflict, as well as co-operation, between operators and the various service groups. It could be shown, if space permitted, that changes in relationship accompanied, in cyclical fashion, changes in basic conditions of work.

Furthermore, attention has not been drawn to intragroup role and personality variations in intergroup relations. Such additional discriminations and the questions that they might raise in regard to the study of institutional dynamics must be left for future discussion.

As for their possible bearing on practical industrial administration, materials presented here seem to challenge the view held in some research circles that the "human" problem of industrial efficiency lies in faulty communication between an economically "rational" or "logical" management and "nonrational" or "nonlogical" work groups. While nothing has been offered to deny linkage between communication and efficiency, observations reported here suggest examination of the stereotypes of the two parties.[7] And questioning the fitness of the stereotypes may lead to a more fruitful conceptualization of the process that is reputedly in need of attention: communication.

Do we see, in the situation studied, an economically "rational" management and an economically "nonrational" work group? Would not a reversal of the labels, if such labels be used, find justification? Does it not appear

[7] William F. Whyte, "Semantics and Industrial Relations," *Human Organization,* VIII (Spring, 1949), 1–7.

that operatives and their allies resisted managerial "logics of efficiency" because application of those "logics" tended to produce something considerably less than "efficiency"? Did not worker groups connive to circumvent managerial ukase in order to "get the work out"? Did not Walt, for instance, break the rules "to keep the boys on production"? May not the common query of industrial workers, "What in the hell are they trying to do up there?" be not merely reflective of faulty communication but also based on real managerial inadequacy, quite apart from a failure in "explanation"? May it not be assumed that managerial inefficiency is and has been for some time a serious problem to those who labor?

If managerial directives are not the guides to efficient action that they are claimed to be, then, perhaps, "logics of efficiency" would be better designated as "sentiments of efficiency." When failure to "explain" is additionally considered, perhaps bulletin-board pronunciamentos might properly be classified with the various exorcisms, conjurations, and miscellaneous esoteric monkey-business of our primitive contemporaries.

If we conceive of "logical" behavior not as self-contained ratiocinative exercises but as intellectual operations in continuous reciprocal interplay with concrete experience, machine operators and their service-group allies would appear the real holders of "logics of efficiency." Like big-city machine politicians, they develop plans for action that, under given conditions of situational pressures, "work."

But this rejection of commonly held stereotypes cannot lead to mere reversal of invidious distinctions; the situation is far too complex for that. The group life that the writer shared was by no means devoid of "sentiments." To the contrary, operator interaction was rich in shared feelings, attitudes, and practices not only of doubtful bearing on getting the work out but often undeniably preventing production maximization. Nor can it be maintained that management, in applying its "sentiments of efficiency," was always ineffective. Perhaps solution to the human problem of industrial efficiency would best be expedited by abandoning altogether the use of contrasted caricatures handed down to us from a preindustrial social class structure. Instead of concerning ourselves with such blind-alley issues as who is "rational" and who is not, we might recognize with John Dewey that both intellectual and emotional activity are essentials of goal-directed behavior[8] and that the development of effective communication focusing on production goals is a matter of instituting interactional processes that engender ideas, sentiments, and plans for action held in common.

[8] *Art as Experience* (New York: Minton, Balch & Co., 1934), p. 55.

16 / Sociometrically Selected Work Teams Increase Production

Raymond H. Van Zelst

A GREAT DEAL of the psychological literature has been devoted to the study of intra-group relations and their effect upon group morale and productivity. However, in spite of the research findings concerned with this interesting facet of social psychology a specific application of a well-known technique has been, perhaps, most grieviously neglected. The technique referred to is, of course, the sociometric principles introduced by Moreno (3) which have been utilized so successfully by Jenkins (11) and by Jennings (2), among others, in the study of leadership and interpersonal relations.

The purpose of sociometry is, perhaps, defined most aptly by Moreno (3, p. 11) as, "A process of classification, which is calculated to bring individuals together who are capable of harmonious interpersonal relationships, and so create a social group which can function at the maximum efficiency and with a minimum of disruptive tendencies and processes."

The technique then in the light of the above statement would seem to be ideally suited for the structuring of work groups on the basis of the workers' choice of work partners.

In a previous study (5) the author tested the hypothesis that socio-metrically arranged work teams would be significantly superior in both quantity and quality of output and also maintain a higher standard of group morale. Comparisons made during a three month experimental period showed the sociometric group to decidedly outperform the matched control group in job performance and also to report a greater degree of satisfaction with their job.

It is the purpose of this research to pursue further the findings of the above cited experiment in order to determine the genuineness of the observed differences and to explore the operational function of the application of "buddy work-teams" in industry. Somewhat similar comparisons of performance were made throughout the 11 month duration of this construction project.

The Subjects and Their Occupations

The subjects used in this study were from building trades in the Chicago area. They comprised two work groups of carpenters and bricklayers

Reprinted by permission of the publisher from *Personnel Psychology*, Vol. 5, No. 3 (Autumn 1952), pp. 175–85.

composed originally of 38 and 36 members respectively. The workers had been together on the same job for an average of at least five months, and, so, were well acquainted with each other's personality and skill. The formulation of such opinions was facilitated by a considerable amount of fluctuation of work partner assignments previous to the experiment and, also, by the custom of members of the groups to meet with their specific group in an unfinished home to eat lunch and talk.

The workers were all union members and had a minimum of seven years experience in their trade. None of the subjects was employed in a supervisory capacity. The occupations in which they were engaged were of a highly skilled nature and came under a fixed wage standard rigidly maintained by both managements and union through mutual agreement. Their work was transitory in nature. The worker was seldom employed by the same company for longer than a six to nine month period.

The construction job upon which these groups were employed was a large housing project separated into two parts by a highway running through its center—one group working on each side of the thoroughfare. The homes were constructed in identical rows of eight—beginning on the highway and moving away.

Methodology

Prior to the beginning of the present experiment each worker was requested to nominate in order of preference three of his co-workers as his choice of work partner. The procedure used followed the three points of methodological significance as outlined by Young (6) for the restructuring of groups. "First, every individual is included as a center of affective response. Second, the choice of the subject is motivated by some wish or practical consideration. Third, the choice of the subject is always relative to some criterion."

The workers of the two groups were assembled on successive days prior to the beginning of the work day and were instructed as follows: "You are now working with a partner who was not chosen by you, nor were you chosen by him. You are now given the opportunity to choose the persons with whom you would most like to work. You can choose any of the individuals in your own group. Write down your first choice; then your second and third choices, in order. Look around and make up your mind. Remember that one of the persons you choose now will probably be assigned as your work partner."

In the regrouping, workers were first arranged into mutual choice teams of two. Then, in view of the occasional necessity for larger work teams for certain duties, compatible patterns for the fusion of two teams into a single group were worked out—also on the basis of co-worker choices. It was not deemed necessary in the opinion of the foremen and supervisor to go beyond this number since the jobs to be performed would not require larger groups. Twenty-two of the workers received their first choice as partners. Twenty-eight received their second and 16 their third. Eight of the workers were isolates.

In the formation of work teams isolates were paired until they could be successfully incorporated into a mutual choice group.... It was at no time necessary to cross skill lines and pair off a skilled worker with a comparatively unskilled partner in order to effect a mutually acceptable team. Perhaps skill level was one of the criteria used by the subjects in selecting their work partner.

Assignment of the newly formed teams was made two days after the collection of choices. The appointments were made by the foremen of the groups when they announced the work assignments of the day. This in no way violated previous procedures of work duty assignments. The structure put into effect was regarded as optimum by the author, supervisor and foremen.

In order to ensure the satisfactory alignment of workers into teams periodic checks of stability of choices were made. In all cases care was taken to leave undisturbed satisfactory worker groups. Instructions and methodology were identical with the above cited procedure save for a slight alteration of instructions to make them more amenable to the situation.

The checks as to stability of co-worker choices revealed only one noteworthy fluctuation which occurred in the groups assigned on the basis of third choice. In this group four incidences of voluntary change in co-worker partner choice and six changes for the incorporation of isolates and newly-hired individuals were made. The group structured on the basis of second choices had one voluntary alteration, while the first choice group had none. The former had two imposed alterations and the latter none. Such alterations as occurred voluntarily among the groups may be accounted for by the introduction of new choice possibilities in the form of the newly-hired employees, and by the possible reformulation of desirability opinions as to present work partner.

One-half of the changes made, both voluntary and imposed, occurred during the first two month period, while the remaining one-half was rather evenly distributed throughout the duration of the experiment No disrupting incidences occurred during the course of the project.

The Criteria

In order to assess the effectiveness of the sociometric procedures used, comparisons were made utilizing actual cost of construction indices, engineers' estimates of these costs (corrected for any wage or materials cost increase) made for the purpose of submitting a contractor's bid, and monthly-compiled turnover records.

Construction costs were made available from cost account records and were broken down into labor costs and materials costs, based upon a row of units basis (eight houses per row). The comparisons made were between the 11 month production record of the sociometric group and engineers estimate of cost and with the groups' production record (nine months) prior to restructuring.

No actual monetary results will be reported here because of the company's desire for anonymity of identity and of cost figures. Instead the indices of

Table 1. Critical Ratio Matrix Comparing Period Performance of
Pre-experimental Group Productivity on Labor Costs (lower half of matrix)
and Materials Costs (upper half of matrix)

LABOR COSTS PERIOD		I	II	III	IV	V	VI		MATERIALS COSTS PERIOD
I. Mean	36.50		.72	1.60	.72	.72	.43	32.70	Mean I.
S.D.	.50							.44	S.D.
II. Mean	36.50	.00		.48	.00	.00	.00	33.00	Mean II.
S.D.	.50							.71	S.D.
III. Mean	36.80	.62	−.61		−.48	−.48	−.91	33.20	Mean III.
S.D.	.83							.44	S.D.
IV. Mean	36.70	.60	−.61	−.21		.00	.00	33.00	Mean IV.
S.D.	.44							.71	S.D.
V. Mean	37.00	1.16	1.12	.36	1.02		.00	33.00	Mean V.
S.D.	.71							.71	S.D.
VI. Mean	36.50	.00	.00	−.61	−.61	−1.41		33.00	Mean VI.
S.D.	.50							.00	S.D.

labor cost and materials cost used were arrived at by taking actual expenses in dollars and dividing through by a constant to arrive at the particular index used.

To determine if possible changes in the over-all skill level of the groups brought about by the turnover of employees and the hiring of new individuals might contaminate the criterion, several preliminary comparisons were made between pre-sociometric group output. In order to facilitate the proposed comparisons the 24 rows of units completed during the nine-month pre-experimental period were divided into six periods of four rows of units each to form a matrix. Critical ratios between labor cost and between materials costs were computed between the various cells. These results are shown in Table 1.

The number of employees leaving during the periods were as follows: 2, 4, 4, 6, 6, 7. The number of workers hired were 4, 6, 2, 4, 6, 6. The fact that a difference existed in the number of employees working from one period to the next is irrelevant since the criteria used is unaffected by the size of the work force. Table 1 shows none of the critical ratios to be significant.

The only factors which could conceivably have affected the productivity of these groups and so have contaminated the criteria used are changes in management practices, and there were none, changes in group level of skill, and changes in the weather. Since none of the critical ratios computed are significant it is reasonable to conclude that over-all group productivity was unaffected by changes in the work force. Whether this result was produced by the restriction of individual output to group standards, to the tendency for deviations in ability of the newly-hired individuals to be counterbalanced and so cancelled, or to the possible increment of change being too slight to exert a difference, is not known. Such minor fluctuations as did occur are presented in Figure 1. These fluctuations are probably due to weather changes—resulting in the switching from indoor

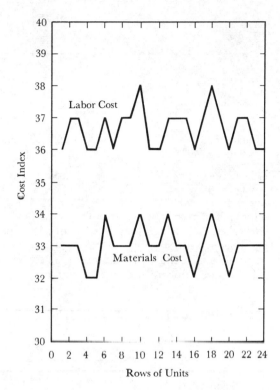

Figure 1. *Fluctuation of the Labor Costs and Materials Costs Based on Row of Units (8 Houses per Row) During the Pre-experimental Period*

to outdoor tasks, etc. However, this uncontrollable variable tends to be "averaged out" during the 20 month period of study.

The data, therefore, seem to support the conclusion that the productivity of these groups for the pre-sociometric period is a relatively stable and reliable criterion and that any changes in group level of productivity during the sociometric period can be explained on bases other than the introduction of new workers. That the engineers' estimate of costs is an accurate one is obvious since such an estimate must be precise to be used in competitive bidding for a contract.

Results and Discussion

Analysis of the sociometric groups' productivity as compared with both engineers' costs estimates and pre-experimental group productivity is presented in Table 2. Critical ratios of 27.75 on labor costs and 13.16 on

Table 2.   Comparative Criteria Performance Data of Groups and Engineers'
Estimates of Anticipated Performance

VARIABLE	MEAN	S.D.	CRITICAL RATIO
1. Turnover			3.69
a) before experimental period	3.11	1.03	
b) during experimental period	.27	.23	
2. Labor Cost—per row of units			27.75
a) engineers' estimate	37.20		
b) before experimental period	36.66	.52	
c) during experimental period	32.22	.67	
3. Materials Cost—per row of units			13.16
a) engineers' estimate	33.50		
b) before experimental period	33.00	.57	
c) during experimental period	31.00	.56	

materials costs between the restructured group's productivity and the pre-
sociometric output criteria clearly indicate a definitely superior level of
group output traceable only to the successful application of sociometric
procedures and their effect in the work situation. Furthermore, Figure 2
and 3 show that at no time during the experiment did actual costs even

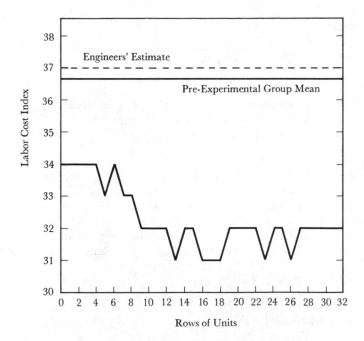

Figure 2.   *Labor Costs of Sociometric Group as Compared with
Mean Pre-experimental Group and Engineers' Estimate of
Labor Costs*

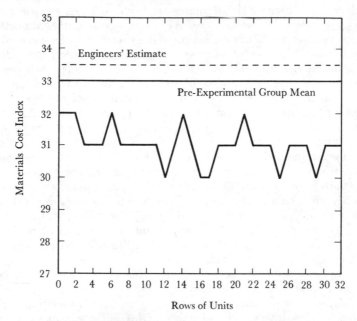

Figure 3. *Materials Costs of Sociometric Group as Compared with Mean Pre-experimental Group and Engineers' Estimate of Materials Costs*

approximate previous costs. The continued decline in production costs is in all likelihood due to the success of improved techniques for the incorporation of isolates and of newly-hired workers into the work force. Also of interest is the significant drop in turnover between the two periods. Such a decrease probably indicates a greater sense of satisfaction on the part of the worker with his job and with the work situation.

Just what happened is best summed up by one of the men when he stated, "Seems as though everything flows a lot smoother. It makes you feel more comfortable working—and I don't waste any time bickering about who's going to do what and how. We just seem to go ahead and do it. The work's a lot more interesting too when you've got your buddy working with you. You certainly like it a lot better anyway."

It must be noted, however, that the building trades with their "buddy-work-teams" are especially suited for a sociometric regrouping. The main drawback to a universal adoption of such techniques is the shifting of workers to different jobs while avoiding any change in job duties which would affect job performance, necessitate re-training the worker, etc. Among these building trades workers such a limitation was not a hindrance, for these workers do not operate according to assembly line procedures and so must be more or less equally adept at all phases of construction.

Further suppositions which must be met lie on management's side of the ledger. It is necessary that management have a democratic approach to the government of workers as well as recognizing the importance of group relations and manifesting an interest in worker preferences. Moreno's approach must allow social situations to define themselves and allow the participants in the situation to define the nature of their own needs and problems. An adequate handling of such procedures as used here should be based upon objective study and a recognition of the social stimuli impinging upon the worker, his attitudes and his expectations. As Newcomb (4) declares, the nature of the group influence is in large part determined by the person to person relations within the group.

Sociometric methods, as is true of other methods, cannot be applied in a situation devoid of mutual trust and confidence. The methods of sociometry permit the worker to ventilate his needs and interests and allow him to his advantage to determine in part the social structure of the group in which he operates. Attitudes and values prevailing in the group are reflected by these measurements and the interpersonal relationships established are realistic and have meaning. The utilization of such data extends democracy into the work situation.

Looking back upon the results of both this study and its predecessor it would seem that a careful employment of "interpersonal relations" procedures increases the worker's sense of satisfaction and participation through an increase in his interest in and liking of his job, the removal of anxiety due to friction between work partners and the creation of a friendly, cooperative atmosphere.

The end result in this study has been a happier, more productive worker, who has given management a *5% savings in total production cost.*

References

1. Jenkins, J. G. *The Nominating Technique: Its Uses and Limitations.* Paper delivered Eastern Psychological Association annual meeting, Atlantic City: April, 1947.
2. Jennings, H. H. *Leadership and Isolation.* New York: Longmans Green, 1947.
3. Moreno, J. L. *Who Shall Survive?* Washington, D.C.: Nervous and Mental Disease Publishing Company, 1937.
4. Newcomb, T. M. Studying social behavior. In T. E. Andrews (Ed.), *Methods of Psychology.* New York: Wiley and Sons, 1948, 372.
5. Van Zelst, R. H. Validation of a sociometric regrouping. *J. abnor. soc. Psychol.* (to be published).
6. Young, P. T. Motivation, feeling and emotion. In T. E. Andrews (Ed.), *Methods of Psychology.* New York: Wiley and Sons, 1948, 688.

17 / Crime and Punishment in the Factory: The Function of Deviancy in Maintaining the Social System*

Joseph Bensman, Israel Gerver

FUNCTIONAL AND STRUCTURAL-FUNCTIONALIST theories represent attempts to describe on-going social systems as operating units. Instead of describing factors, parts of systems or "single causes," the theorist attempts to describe the total system. The social system is a complex system of reciprocal actions and social relationships involving a plurality of individuals. In short, it is the abstracted actions of a "group."

Functional theory requires the following: (a) specification of system, the actors and actions involved, including some clear notion of the boundaries of the system; (b) specification of parts of the system (the structural elements); and (c) specification of the interrelation (function) of the parts of the system to each other and thus, to the system as a whole.[1]

The concept of function includes (though not exclusively) concepts of motivation, "ends" or purposes.[2] Even though they are not often called "ends," ends are attributed to the system as a whole. These usually include the end of maintaining the system as an on-going social system, itself. These system-maintaining ends are sometimes called the functional prerequisites of the social system or of group life.

Thus, the structural units are evaluated for their contribution to

---

* Revised version of a paper originally presented at the annual meetings of the American Sociological Association, Washington, D.C., September 1955. A somewhat shorter and different version of this paper appears in Gouldner & Gouldner, *Modern Sociology*, New York: Harcourt Brace, 1963.

[1] Any one of the whole host of books and articles can be used to illustrate systematic attempts to state the methods of functional analysis. Typical attempts are to be found in R. K. Merton, *Social Theory and Social Structure*, Glencoe: Free Press, 1957 and in Talcott Parsons, *The Social System*, Glencoe: The Free Press, 1951. A fairly complete bibliography on functionalism is provided by Harold Fallding, "Functional Analysis in Sociology," *American Sociological Review*, 28 (February, 1963), p. 5.

[2] Merton, *op. cit.*, p. 19. Emile Durkheim, *The Rules of Sociological Method*, Chicago: University of Chicago Press, 1938, p. 95.

Reprinted by permission of the publisher from "Crime and Punishment in the Factory: The Function of Deviancy in Maintaining the Social System," *American Sociological Review*, Vol. 28, No. 4 (August 1963), pp. 588–98.

maintenance of the systems as an operative unit. *Functions,* then, are more than interrelationships of structural elements; they define and describe, how a particular structural unit contributes to the maintenance of the system. Dysfunctions are defined as actions and interrelationships that operate against the maintenance of the on-going social system.[3]

The problem of *ends* in functional and structural-functional theory remains one of the most difficult problems in the theory. If *ends* (especially the end of maintaining itself) are attributed (no matter how indirectly) to the system as a whole than there are relatively few problems. By and large the problem becomes one of selecting, defining and analyzing the ends of the system. If this is done the system has the attributes of a person, it has ends of its own, provides goals for its members, means for achieving such goals and rewards for successful achievement of goals by the use of approved means. It distributes these goals, means and rewards throughout its structural units and its membership. If it performs these functions efficiently and intelligently, it will be a closely integrated, tightly functioning system. It does not do so if it provides competing goals or insufficient means for attaining socially valued rewards; it creates anomie. Dysfunctional elements develop.

If one takes the opposite tack, that "systems" do not have ends, that only people do, and that the collective behavior of persons in a stable group or organization represents an accommodation of differing individual (but socially developed) ends and interests, in which "cooperation" is an implicit transaction, containing elements of coercion, sanctions, genuine cooperation, and altruism, then the entire problem becomes a different one.[4]

There is no requirement for the system as a whole to have "ends"; functions are only the "deal," the transaction, which brings people together. "Dysfunctions" represent either the attempt "to make a new deal" or the dissatisfactions of some individuals with the deal they are forced to make, short of withdrawing from the system.

With this alternative set of assumptions, it is not necessary to attribute a

---

[3] Harry C. Bredemeier, "The Methodology of Functionalism," *American Sociological Review,* 20 (April, 1955), pp. 173–79; and Kingsley Davis, "The Myth of Functional Analysis," *American Sociological Review,* 24 (December, 1959), pp. 765–66.

[4] This "alternative" approach represents nothing new or novel, but is rather the standard method of such approaches to sociology as Verstehen sociology, symbolic interactionism or almost all "non-functional" sociologies. The approach is explicit in Weber's *Wirtschaft and Gesellschaft,* as translated in *The Theory of Social and Economic Organization,* New York: Oxford University Press, 1947, p. 118. Similarly it is implicit in all work stemming from G. H. Mead's *Mind, Self and Society,* Chicago: University of Chicago Press, 1934. This approach is made explicit by John R. Commons, "A Sociological View of Sovereignty," *American Journal of Sociology,* V (1899–1900), and presented in text book form by E. T. Hiller, *Social Relations and Structures,* New York: Harper, 1947, and R. M. MacIver, *Society: Its Structure and Changes,* New York: Ray Long and Richard R. Smith, Inc., 1932.

functional pre-requisite of the system for maintaining itself, nor is it necessary to attribute to "functions" the requirement of contribution to the maintenance of the system.

Norms, under such a model, are not the "norms" of a system but rather the rules which determine the nature of socially permissible actions and transactions. They are established either in the past or in the present by the participants themselves and by those who achieve or have achieved authority, under whatever system or power or authority that prevails at a given historical moment.

"Deviancy" is thus simply the acceptance or non-acceptance of these rules in terms of implicit or explicit estimates of consequences of conforming to or rejecting the norms of others, especially the norms of those who have authority. Since social life involves acceptance and rejection of proffered norms or expectancies, "deviancy," i.e. deviant actions, are the expectable actions of individuals who have divergent ends, and of individuals who do not comply exclusively to others or those in authority but who sometimes comply to their self-expectancies.

Deviant actions thus are not a separate category of actions, defiant of the central ends of a total system, but are simply part of the totality of actions that make up the hundreds of individual transactions in an organization. With such a conception of "social systems" it is unnecessary to have a "clear definition" of the system or its parts. It is only necessary to describe the actions and interrelations of persons with respect to a common enterprise. Analytical description thus results in a different type of functionalism.

This paper is a case study in the internal law of one organization. The social functions of the violation of one "law" are treated in detail, in order to ascertain which of the two conceptions of function are operative in an "actual social system." The violation of "law" is specifically a rule of workmanship. For the sake of simplicity, the rules and their violations relevant to one instrument—the tap—are the subject of study. This is because the study of the tap summarizes an entire area of rules of workmanship and their violations. One could also have selected other violations of workmanship rules such as counter-sinking dimples, rolling of edges in fairing, stretching of metal skins, or greasing and waxing screw threads. The tap was selected as a major example because of its frequent usage, and because it is the most serious violation of rules of workmanship.

While suggesting the engineering complexity of the data, our theoretical interest is in the social function of crime, particularly violations of private organizational law.

The research was carried out in an airplane factory employing 26,000 people in the New York metropolitan area. One of the authors was a participant observer from September 1953 through September 1954. He gathered his data in the daily course of work while working as an assembler on the aileron crew of the final wing line. No special research instruments were used; the ordinary activities of workers along the line were observed and noted as they occurred, and recorded daily. All aspects involved in the use of the tap were discussed in the context of the work situation when they were relevant and salient to the personnel involved, and without their realizing that they were objects of study.

The Tap and Its Functions

The tap is a tool, an extremely hard steel screw, whose threads are slotted to allow for the disposal of the waste metal which it cuts away. It is sufficiently hard so that when it is inserted into a nut it can cut new threads over the original threads of the nut.

In wing assembly work bolts or screws must be inserted in recessed nuts which are anchored to the wing in earlier processes of assembly. The bolt or screw must pass through a wing plate before reaching the nut. In the nature of the mass production process alignments between nuts and plate-openings become distorted. Original allowable tolerances become magnified in later stages of assembly as the number of alignments which must be coordinated with each other increase with the increasing complexity of the assemblage. When the nut is not aligned with the hole, the tap can be used to cut, at a new angle, new threads in the nut for the purpose of bringing the nut and bolt into a new but not true alignment. If the tap is not used and the bolt is forced, the wing plate itself may be bent. Such new alignments, however, deviate from the specifications of the blueprint which is based upon true alignments at every stage of the assembly process. On the basis of engineering standards true alignments are necessary at every stage in order to achieve maximum strength and a proper equilibrium of strains and stresses.

The use of the tap is the most serious crime of workmanship conceivable in the plant. A worker can be summarily fired for merely possessing a tap. Nevertheless, at least one-half of the work force in a position to use a tap owns at least one. Every well-equipped senior mechanic owns four or five of different sizes and every mechanic has access to and, if need be, uses them. In fact, the mass use of the tap represents a widespread violation of this most serious rule of workmanship.

The tap is defined as a criminal instrument, primarily because it destroys the effectiveness of stop nuts. Aviation nuts are specifically designed, so that, once tightened, a screw or bolt cannot back out of the nut under the impact of vibration in flight. Once a nut is tapped, however, it loses its holding power and at any time, after sufficient vibration, the screw or bolt can fall out and weaken the part it holds to the wing and the wing itself.

In addition, the use of a tap is an illegal method of concealing a structural defect. If the holes, for example, were properly drilled and the nuts were properly installed, the use of the tap would be unnecessary, since specifications calling for alignment would be fulfilled. Whenever a tap is used, there are indications of deviations from standards. Furthermore, such deviations make subsequent maintenance of the airplane difficult since maintenance mechanics have no records of such illegal deviations from specifications.

Taps can be used in certain cases by special mechanics when such usage is authorized by engineers and when proper paper work supports such use. But such authorization usually requires one to three days for approval.

The tap, then, is an illegal tool, the use or possession of which carries extreme sanctions in private organizational law, but which is simultaneously widely possessed and used despite its illegal status. The problem of such a pattern for the meaning of private organizational law is to account for the wide acceptance of a crime as a means of fulfilling work requirements within a private organization, the aircraft plant.

The Socialization of the Worker

To most workers entering an aircraft plant the tap is an unknown instrument. Dies which thread bolts, i.e., the process opposite to tapping, are relatively well known and are standard equipment of the plumbing trade. The new worker does not come into this contact with the tap until he finds it impossible to align the holes in two skins. In desperation and somewhat guiltily as if he had made a mistake, he turns to his partner (a more experienced worker) and states his problem. The experienced worker will try every legitimate technique of lining up the holes, but if these do not succeed, he resorts to the tap. He taps the new thread himself, not permitting the novice to use the tap. While tapping it he gives the novice a lecture on the dangers of getting caught and of breaking a tap in the hole, thereby leaving telltale evidence of its use.

For several weeks the older worker will not permit his inexperienced partner to use a tap when its use is required. He leaves his own work in order to do the required tapping and finishes the job before returning to his own work. If the novice demonstrates sufficient ability and care in other aspects of his work he will be allowed to tap the hole under the supervision of a veteran worker. When the veteran partner is absent, and the now initiated worker can use the tap at his own discretion he feels a sense of pride. In order to enjoy his new found facility, he frequently uses the tap when it is not necessary. He may be careless in properly aligning perfectly good components and then compensate for his own carelessness by using the tap.

He may forego the easier illegal methods (which are also viewed as less serious crimes) of greasing and waxing bolts or enlarging the misaligned holes and indulge himself in the more pleasurable, challenging and dangerous use of the tap. Sooner or later he inevitably runs into difficulties which he is technically unprepared to cope with. When his partner and mentor is not available, he is forced to call upon the assistant foreman. If the situation requires it, the foreman will recommend the tap. If he has doubts about the worker's abilities, he may even tap the hole himself. In doing this, he risks censure of the union, because as a foreman he is not permitted to handle tools.

At the time the research was conducted, there were four levels of foremen. These were: assistant foreman (one star); foreman (two stars); assistant general foreman (three stars); and general foreman (four stars). The stars are on the foremen's badges and are their insignia of rank. The assistant foreman is the immediate supervisor of a work crew. The four star is the shop supervisor. The two and three star foremen have authority over increasingly larger sections of the assembly line. In the following discussion the foreman refers to the one star, assistant foreman, unless otherwise noted.

While the foreman taps the hole, he also lectures on the proper and technically workmanlike ways of using the tap: "The tap is turned only at quarter turns. . .never force the tap. . .it has to go in easy or it's likely to snap. . .if it snaps, your ass is in a sling and I won't be able to get you out of it."

The foreman warns the worker to make sure "not to get caught, to see that the coast is clear, to keep the tap well hidden when not in use, and to watch out for inspectors while using it." He always ends by cautioning the worker, "It's your own ass if you're caught."

When the worker feels that he is experienced and can use the tap with complete confidence, he usually buys his own, frequently displaying it to other workers and magnanimously lending it to those in need of it. He feels himself fully arrived when a two star foreman or, even higher, an assistant general foreman borrows his tap or asks him to perform the tapping. The worker has now established his identity and is known as an individual by the higher ups.

Once the right to use the tap is thus established, the indiscriminate use of it is frowned upon. A worker who uses a tap too often is considered to be a careless "botcher." A worker who can get his work done without frequently using a tap is a "mechanic," but one who doesn't use the tap when it is necessary does not get his own work done on time. Proper use of the tap requires judgement and etiquette. The tap addict is likely to become the object of jokes and to get a bad work reputation among workers, foremen and inspectors.

Agencies of Law Enforcement

The enforcement of the plant rules of workmanship devolves upon three groups: foremen, plant quality control and Air Force quality control. The ultimate and supreme authority resides in the latter group. The Air Force not only sets the blue print specifications, but also and more importantly, can reject a finished airplane as not meeting specifications.

Furthermore, the Air Force inspectors reinspect installations which have been previously "bought" by plant quality control. If these installations do not meet Air Force standards they are "crabbed," i.e., rejected. When this happens, the plant inspectors who bought the installations are subject to "being written up," i.e., disciplinary action for unintentional negligence which may lead to suspensions, demotions or in extreme cases loss of jobs. The Air Force inspector has the absolute right to demand that any man be fired for violating work rules.

There were only two Air Force inspectors to a shop at the time of these observations, so that it was almost impossible for Air Force inspectors to police an entire shop of over 2,000 men. As an Air Force inspector walks up the line, it is standard procedure for workers to nudge other workers to inform them of the approach of the "Gestapo." When tapping is essential and when it is known that Air Force inspectors are too near, guards of workers are posted to convey advance notice of this approach to any one who is actively tapping. This is especially true when there are plant drives against the use of the tap.

In all instances, when the Air Force inspector is in the vicinity, workers who have a reputation for open or promiscuous use of the tap are instructed by the assistant foreman to "disappear." Such types can return to work when the "coast is clear."

Despite the Air Force inspectors' high authority and the severity of their standards, they are not sufficiently numerous to be considered the major policing agency for detecting and apprehending violators of the rules of workmanship. Plant quality control is the actual law enforcement agency in terms of the daily operations of surveillance. There are approximately 150 plant inspectors to a 2,000 man shop. They work along the assembly line along with the workers. In some cases a panel of inspectors is assigned to inspect the work done by a number of crews who are supervised by a two star foreman. In this system a call book which guarantees the equal rotation of inspections is kept. When a worker has completed a job and requests an inspection, he enters his wing number and the requested inspection in the call book. The inspector, after completing an inspection, marks the job as completed and takes the next open inspection as indicated in the call book.

A result of either type of inspection setup is the free and intimate intermingling of inspectors, and workers. In off moments, inspectors and workers gather together to "shoot the breeze and kill time." Inspectors, unlike workers, may have long waiting periods before their next assignment. During such periods out of boredom and monotony they tend to fraternize with workers. This causes conflict between the role of "good egg" and the role of policeman. A cause of leniency on the part of inspectors is intrinsic to the relationship between mechanics and themselves in circumstances not involving the tap. There is a sufficient amount of mechanical work which is not easily and immediately accessible to inspectors. This is particularly true if the inspector does not want to spend several hours on a fairly simple inspection. In order for the inspector to complete his work and make sure that the work he "buys" will be acceptable to later inspectors, he must rely on the workmanship of the mechanic. In brief he must have faith not only in the mechanic's workmanship but also in his willingness not to "louse him up." If the inspector gets the reputation of being a "bastard," the mechanic is under no obligation to do a good job and thus protect the inspector. Since the penalties for the use of the tap are so severe, no inspector feels comfortable about reporting a violation. A number of subterfuges are resorted to in an effort to diminish the potential conflict.

There is a general understanding that workers are not supposed to use a tap in the presence of plant inspectors. At various times this understanding is made explicit. The inspector frequently tells the workers of his crew:

"Now fellas, there's a big drive now on taps. The Air Force just issued a special memo. For God's sakes, don't use a tap when I'm around. If somebody sees it while I'm in the area, it'll be my ass. Look around first. Make sure I'm gone."

At other times the verbalization comes from the worker. If a worker has to use a tap and the inspector is present, he will usually wait until the inspector leaves. If the inspector shows no signs of leaving, the worker will tell him to "Get the hell outa here. I got work to do and can't do it while you're around."

If the worker knows the inspector he may take out the tap, permitting the inspector to see it. The wise inspector responds to the gesture by leaving. Of course, a worker has already "sized up" the inspector and knows whether or not he can rely upon him to respond as desired.

When there is an Air Force–inspired drive against the tap, the inspectors will make the rounds and "lay the law down": "I want no more tapping around here. The next guy caught gets turned in. I can't cover you guys any more. I'm not kidding you bastards. If you can't do a decent job, don't do it at all. If that s.o.b. foreman of yours insists on you doing it, tell him to do it himself. He can't make you do it. If you're caught, it's your ass not his. When the chips are down, he's got to cover himself and he'll leave you holding the bag!"

For about three or four days thereafter, taps disappear from public view. The work slows down, and ultimately the inspectors forget to be zealous. A state of normal haphazard equilibrium is restored.

Other types of social relations and situations between workers and inspectors help maintain this state of equilibrium. An inspector will often see a tap in the top of a worker's tool box. He will pick it up and drop it into the bottom of the box where it cannot be seen easily. Perhaps he will tell the worker that he is a "damned fool for being so careless." The inspector thus hopes to establish his dependability for the worker, and creates a supply of good will credit, which the worker must repay in the form of protecting the inspector.

Another typical worker–inspector situation occurs when a mechanic is caught in the act of tapping, and the inspector does not look away. The inspector severely reprimands the mechanic, "throws the fear of God into him," holds him in suspense as to whether he will turn him in, and then lets him go with a warning. This, generally, only happens to new workers. Occasionally when a worker has a new inspector and no previously established trust relationship, the same situation may arise. In both cases they are an integal part of the socialization of the worker to the plant or, rather, to a specific phase of its operation.

The Role of the Foreman

Another type of cermonial escape from law enforcement through pseudo-law enforcement involves the foreman. In rare cases an inspector will catch a worker using the tap, reprimand him and turn him over to his foreman. The foreman then is forced to go through the procedure of reprimanding the errant worker. The foreman becomes serious and indignant, primarily because the worker let himself get caught. He gives the worker a genuine tongue lashing, and he reminds him once again that he, as foreman, has to go to bat to save the worker's neck. He stresses that it is only because of *his* intervention that the worker will not lose his job. He states, "Next time be careful. I won't stick my neck out for you again. For God's sakes don't use a tap, *unless it's absolutely necessary.*"

The worker is obliged to accept the reprimand and to assume the countenence of true penitent, even to the extent of promising that it won't happen again. He will say, "Awright, awright. So I got caught this time. Next time I won't get caught." Both the foreman and worker play these roles even though the worker tapped the hole at the specific request of the foreman. The most blatant violation of the mores in such a situation is when the worker grins and treats the whole thing as a comic interlude. When this happens, the foreman becomes truly enraged, "That's the trouble with you. You don't take your job seriously. You don't give a damn about nothing. How long do I have to put up with your not giving a damn!"

The public ritual therefore conceals an entirely different dimension of social functions involved in the use of the tap. It is inconceivable that the tap could be used without the active or passive collusion of the foreman. As noted, the foreman instructs the worker in its use, indicates when he wants it used, assists the worker in evading the plant rules, and when the worker is caught, goes through the ritual of punishment. These role contradictions are intrinsic to the position of the foreman. His major responsibility is to keep production going. At the same time he is a representative of supervision, and is supposed to encourage respect for company law. He is not primarily responsible for quality since this is the province of plant quality control, i.e., inspection. He resolves the various conflicts in terms of the strongest and most persistent forms of pressures and rewards.

The work requirements of a particular foreman and his crew are determined by the Production Analysis Section, another staff organization. Workers call it Time Study although this is only one part of its function. Production Analysis determines, on the basis of time studies, the amount of men to be assigned to a specific crew, the locations of crews on the line, and the cutting-off points for work controlled by a particular foreman. Having done this, they determine the work load required of a foreman and keep production charts on completed work. These charts are the report cards of the foreman. At a moment's glance, top supervision can single out foremen who are not pulling their weight. In aviation assembly, since the work cycle for a particular team is relatively long (four to eight hours) and since a foreman has relatively few teams (usually three) all doing the same job, any slow-down which delays one team damages the foreman's production record in the immediate perceivable terms of the report card. Moreover, delay caused by the inability of one crew to complete its task prevents other crews from working on that wing. The foremen of these crews will complain to the two or three star foremen that they are being held up and that their production records will suffer because of another foreman's incompetence.

As a result of these considerations, the pressures "to get work out" are paramount for the foreman. There is a relatively high turnover among foremen, even at the two star level. In the last analysis, production records are the major consideration in supervisory mobility. All other considerations—e.g., sociability, work knowledge, personality, etc.—are assumed to be measured by the production chart.

In this context the foreman, vis à vis the ticklish question of the tap, is compelled to violate some of the most important laws of the company and the Air Force. Crucial instances occur at times when the Air Force institutes stringent anti-tap enforcement measures. When key holes do not line up it may be necessary, as an alternative to using the tap, to disassemble previous installations. The disassembling and reassembling may take a full eight hours before the previously reached work stage is again reached. The production chart for that eight-hour period will indicate that no work has been done. In such a situation the worker may refuse to tap a hole since he risks endangering his job. The foreman also may be reluctant to request directly that the worker tap a hole. To get the work done he therefore employs a whole rhetoric of veiled requests such as "Hell, that's easy...you know what to do...you've done it before." "Maybe you can clean out the threads," or "Well, see what you can do."

If the worker is adamant, the foreman will practically beg him to do the *right* thing. He will remind him of past favors, he will complain about his chart rating and of how "top brass doesn't give a damn about anything but what's on the chart." He usually ends his plea with: "Once you get this done, you can take it easy. You know I don't work you guys too hard most of the time."

If the veiled requests and pitiful pleadings don't produce results, the foreman may take the ultimate step of tapping the hole himself. He compounds the felony, because he not only violates the rules of workmanship but also violates union rules which specifically state that no foreman can use a tool. To add insult to injury, the foreman furthermore has to borrow the tap in the midst of an anti-tap drive when taps are scarce.

From the viewpoint of production the use of the tap is imperative to the functioning of the production organization, even though it is one of the most serious work crimes. This is recognized even at official levels, although only in indirect ways.

Taps, being made of hard steel, have the disadvantage of being brittle. If not handled carefully, they may break within the nut. This not only makes further work impossible, but makes for easier detection of the crime. To cope with such a problem, the tool crib is well equipped with a supply of tap extractors. Any worker can draw an appropriately sized tap extractor from the tool crib. All these are official company property. He can do this even amidst the most severe anti-tap drives without fear or the danger of punishment.

Crime and the Social System

Deviancy, in the sense that it implies a rejection of the norms of a social system or behavior outside of a system, is not a useful concept for analyzing this type of crime. Rather, the use of the tap is literally a major crime which is intrinsic to the system. The conception of a social system as a tightly knit series of interlocking functions, mutually supporting each other and contributing to the support and continuance of the system, is not at all applicable to an understanding of this case.

Crime as defined by the use of the tap (and the other crimes of workmanship subsumed under our discussion of the tap) supports in its own way the continuance of the system, just as the avoidance of the use of the tap contributes to the perfection of the system. The notion of deviancy or of "patterned deviancy" as a residue of systemic analysis—i.e., action not conforming to the demands of the system, or resulting in dysfunctions of the system—does not adequately describe the system. One reason for this inadequacy is that deviance as thus understood derives from a prior postulation of some primary but not specifically located end, which the analyst himself attributes to the system. The "deviant" action may be as central to the system as is the norm it allegedly deviates from.

On the other hand, if one considers the actions called "deviant behavior" as intrinsic to the system, deviant behavior contributes to and supports the system just as does conformity, simply because the system is composed of its interrelated parts. From the standpoint of the past, any change is dysfunctional; that is, it represents a disruption of the system as it was. From the standpoint of the present, those same changes, when adopted, can be viewed as functions, since they become for the moment intrinsic parts of the system.

In terms of the above analysis, the conceptualization of deviancy as functional or dysfunctional reduces to a semantic problem. Attributions of function and dysfunction are artifacts of the mode of analysis, and are based upon the analyst's assumptions of ends for a system, rather than upon attributes of the actual collective behavior. The resolution of problems concerning the interrelations of specific social phenomena can best be performed by dealing with substantive data rather than at the level of the verbal pyrotechnics of formal model and deductive theory building. The real problems lie in relating data and concepts and not in the preoccupation with how concepts are related to each other.

Verbal play, however, is a less important concern than the problem of the assumption of ends. A system is imputed to have ends and the functions of its structural elements contribute to these ends and the maintenance of this system. The problem for research is to *locate* and *specify* these ends. It is in principle, though not necessarily in practice, fairly easy to locate and specify the ends of specific individuals as related to their social actions, but the ends of social systems and collectivities are much more difficult to locate. There is a prevalent tendency to succumb to an ever present danger of selecting some one set of social ends as primary, and then to attribute them to the system as a whole. In such cases, the "objective world" becomes a projection of the personal values of the analyst, or the values of some group or individuals in the system, to which the analyst is consciously or unconsciously linked.

If these considerations are applied to our analysis of the tap, a whole new level of analysis is brought into focus.

Obviously profit-making through production is the major end of the company, i.e., its stock-holders, board of directors, officers, and supervisory staff. Even here, though, there is a complex problem related to conflicts of ends, e.g., between reinvestment and distribution of profits, expansion and profit taking. These are considerations which probably complicate the picture, but they are not treated here.

For the Air Force the major end is a high rate of production of high quality planes at low cost. Reducing costs and maintaining quality are secondary ends, or if one wishes to so describe it, means to the primary end of producing efficient aircraft. For the individual foreman, maintaining his job, gaining a promotion or staying out of trouble may be his primary private ends. The maintaining or exceeding of his production quota, while a major end for the "company" as a whole and as defined by the executives, is the means of attaining the private goals of the foreman.

Similarly the primary ends of plant inspectors are to get along with workers, to avoid buying jobs which will be rejected in later inspection, and in some cases to achieve a supervisory position. Again, the actions of inspectors in developing a mutual trust situation, and in protecting themselves and workers in the tap situation, represents a compromise between different private ends. Similarly the ends of workers are to get their work done with a minimum of effort, to get along at least minimally with foremen and inspectors, to stay out of trouble and to avoid being fired. The semi-secret use of the tap, then, represents a compromise between these complexes of ends.

Taking these means-ends situations together, we find that what are means for one group are ends for another. In all cases, means and ends can be defined as either public or private attributes. Public ends are means to private ends, and private ends are in some cases limited by "public," i.e., organizationally sanctioned, ends and means. In brief the empirical situation is extremely complex, and not analyzable in *a priori* terms. The complex of public and private means and ends constitutes a specific research problem insofar as it accounts for an overall operation of the organization.

In terms of the specific problem of the tap as an instrument, and its relationship to means-and-ends relationships within the organization, we find that use of the tap is a private means to publicly stated ends. But those ends to which the use of the tap is oriented are, from both the standpoint of that abstraction "the company" and from the standpoint of its members, only one of a number of possible ends. It is the plurality of ends that accounts for "deviant behavior" rather than the conflict between means and ends. Production is a major end, and quality is a necessary condition for the attainment of that end. Moreover, as individuals are distributed at different levels and in different lines of the status hierarchy, different ends become more salient to individuals occupying different positions. The relationship of means to ends at both the public and private levels is different (in fact is some times reversed) for individuals in different positions in the organization. The statement of "public ends" attached to the organization or the social system describes the ends of a limited number of particular and publicly accessible or visable positions in the system.

Thus any theoretical model which accepts as an initial postulate the dominance of an ultimate end, and which conceptualizes disorganization as a conflict between means and ends, overlooks the possibility that conflicting means and ends are actually conflicts between the means to one end with the means to another end.

Moreover, in any complex organization where plural ends are distributed in different ways among office holders, the conflict of ends and the conflicts between means and ends, are institutionalized as conflicts between various departments of segments in the organization. Thus from the point of view of production supervision, quality control is a major obstacle to the achievement of its ends. From the standpoint of quality control, sloppy workmanship is a major crime which may result in sanctions to the inspector. The tolerance of the tap is a means by which workers, inspectors and production supervisors attempt to achieve their respective ends in a mutually tolerable manner in a situation where they are forced to work together according to directives, which if closely followed would result in mutual frustration. For the worker, the inspector and the foreman, the development of a satisfactory social environment, the minimization of conflict, and the development of tolerable social relations become a major end. Crime, and the toleration of crime within the limits of avoiding extreme sanctions, becomes a means to these social ends, as well as means to the publicly recognized ends of the organization.

In sum, a large part of behavior, visible to an insider or to a sophisticated observer, is "criminal," i.e., it violates publicly stated norms. But since such behavior is accepted—in fact often stimulated, aided and abetted by the effective on-the-spot authorities—the criminality of such behavior has limited consequences.

Conclusion

The resolution of the "means–end conflict" results in crime. But such crime often becomes fairly acceptable behavior and is stabilized as a permanent aspect of the organization. Crime becomes one of the major operational devices of the organization. As such it is hard to consider it as a form of *anomie*. The use of the tap is neither an innovation, a form of rebellion, ritualism nor retreatism. It is more aptly described as a permanent unofficial aspect of the organization. It is not an innovation since, for almost all of the personnel in the plant, the use of the tap in the plant precedes their knowledge of it. It is not rebellion since it is a means to a company end, quantity production. It is neither a ritual nor a retreat since it is in some sense functional to all concerned. It is a crime only in that there is an official ruling against its use, and that there are a wide range of ceremonial forms of law-enforcement and punishment. With respect to the Air Force, use of the tap still remains a serious crime. But in this area the wide range of cooperative behavior between workers, foremen, and plant inspectors combines to reduce the importance of Air Force law-enforcement as a significant factor in this situation.

The ceremonial aspects of law enforcement are, however, of importance. These include secrecy in the use of the tap to avoid embarrassing the inspector, the reporting of tap violations by the inspector to the foreman who initially requested the use of the tap, the rhetoric used by the foreman in requesting the use of the tap, the mock severity of the foreman in reprimanding the reported violator, and the penitence of the apprehended criminal before his judge, the foreman.

All of these are serious social accompaniments to the use of the tap. They enable the personnel involved to maintain the public values, while performing those actions necessary to attain the public or private ends appropriate to their evaluations of their positions. Thus a form of institutional schizophrenia is the major result of the conflict of ends and the conflict of means and ends. Individuals act and think on at least two planes, the plane of the public ideology and the plane of action. They shift from plane to plane, as required by their positions, their situations, and their means–ends estimations. In a sense, it is a form of double-think, and double-think is the major result of means–ends conflict.

From the point of view of the actors involved, and in the light of the double-think mechanism, the major definition of "deviancy" takes on another dimension. The major crime for the actors involved, is the lack of respect for the social ceremonialism surrounding the tap. The worker who allows an inspector to see him possessing or using a tap, threatens the defenses of the inspector, and is likely to be reprimanded for not being careful. He is likely to find it harder to "sell" his work to that inspector. He gets a bad reputation and is thought of as a "character." Similarly in talking to an inspector, the worker who casually mentions illegal workmanship is told by this inspector not to mention it. Finally, a worker who grins while being reprimanded for the use of the tap, is likely to be bawled out for lack of awareness of the seriousness of his act and his flippant attitude. The foreman is likely to threaten him with a withdrawal from the circle of protection given by the foreman to apprehended criminals.

Thus, lack of seriousness in adhering to the ceremonial forms of law violation is defined as a case of inappropriateness of affect and lack of reality orientation to which serious forms of informal social control are addressed. The major crime, then, is the violation of the *rules* of criminal behavior.

The fact that tapping is a crime, a violation of an inoperative public ideology, does not mean that it is uncontrolled anomalous behavior. On the contrary, the very pervasiveness of the use of the tap and its functional indispensibility result in a relatively close control of tapping by supervisory authority.

The worker is taught the proper techniques of tapping, and he is taught the situations for which use of the tap is appropriate. Misuse of the tap (using the tap as a substitute for lining up holes and for careless workmanship) is frowned upon by supervisors. Using the tap as a substitute for less severely defined illegal techniques of workmanship is also frowned upon.

The worker who uses the tap promiscuously is subject to a wide variety of informal controls. He is kidded and teased by other workers. Inspectors become sensitive to his action and when he is caught, he is reported and bawled out, primarily because of his reputation and not so much for the use of the tap in a specific situation. The foreman rides him unmercifully and tends to become more sensitive to all his faults of workmanship. If he persists in abusing the use of the tap, he ultimately gets transferred to another foreman who is short of men. The floating worker is presumed to be a botcher by the very fact of his being transferred.

In no case, however, are formal actions, which involve the possibility of dismissal, taken against the worker. This is because, in writing up a worker for abusing the tap, the foreman would risk the danger of bringing into the open and into official and public channels the whole issue of the use of the tap. In punishing promiscuous tappers by official means, the foreman might risk losing opportunities to have the tap used in situations which are advantageous to him. Moreover, in bringing serious charges against the deviant tapper, the foreman might find that workers necessarily would be hesitant to use the tap in situations the foreman regards as necessary.

For these reasons, foremen and inspectors do not use the formal channels of law enforcement, but rely instead on informal controls. The informal controls tend to limit the use of the tap to necessary situations. In addition, the use of such controls results in a new definition of crime and its function at the behavioral level. A "crime" is not a crime so long as its commission is controlled and directed by those in authority towards goals which they define as socially constructive. A violation of law is treated as a crime when it is not directed and controlled by those in authority or when it is used for exclusively personal ends.

The kind, type and frequency of crime are functions of the system of authority. The ranges of "socially permissible crime" and the degree and severity of punishment are determined by the ends and interests of those who are responsible for law enforcement. Severe law enforcement limits the freedom of leadership groups in attainment of their own ends. Loosening the fabric of law enforcement enables these groups to have greater freedom of action in the attainment of their ends, but also permits a greater amount of crime at lower levels.

5 / Union
Organization:
Can
Labor Unions
Be Democratic?

Until relatively recently the question of whether business organizations are democratic was not raised, simply because in theory they are not purported to be. On the other hand, union organization is founded on the principle of democracy. Claims that union organization, as a countervailing power, has helped to maintain a pluralistic society and that unions have protected workers against the sometimes arbitrary exercise of power by management (and that unions have thereby contributed respectively to societal and plant democracy), are not widely challenged. One of the most prevalent charges leveled at union organization is its alleged violation of internal democracy. Robert Michels's "Iron Law of Oligarchy,"[1] which states that power even in democratically based organizations will eventually gravitate into the hands of a small minority which manipulates organizational resources and capitalizes on membership apathy to perpetuate its position, is regularly offered as an accurate description of labor unions.

[1] Robert Michels, *Political Parties* (Glencoe, Illinois: The Free Press, 1958).

Emanuel Stein ("The Dilemma of Union Democracy") agrees that the diminution in union democracy has organizational antecedents, but of a somewhat different order from that Michels had in mind. If the unbalanced power position of union leaders vis-à-vis the rank and file is due partly to self-aggrandizing leaders and membership apathy, then market forces beyond leadership control, the growth in union organization size, and organizational goals would have produced the internal shift of power from followers to leaders anyway.

Using responsiveness of officers to the demands of the members as their standard of internal democracy, Sayles and Strauss ("Are Unions Democratic?") conclude that most local unions they studied were basically democratic, in spite of rank-and-file apathy and leadership power control. The democratic nature of local unions is particularly apparent when contrasted with unions at the international level. Sayles and Strauss also outline factors dampening union democracy and forces checking the decline in democracy. Finally, they attempt to explain why some local unions operate democratically while others develop along oligarchical lines.

Dismissing as unrealistic the theory of union democracy which envisions direct participation by members through voting and opinion expression at the national level, Philip Marcus ("Union Conventions and Executive Boards: A Formal Analysis of Organizational Structure") examines two alternative routes of membership influence. The first channel of influence, the national union convention, is shown to be limited by union size, age, and number of locals. The specification in a union's constitution that certain subgroups (which may be based on sex, geographical location, trade, and like factors) be represented on its executive board is proposed as a more viable means for the rank and file to influence national leaders. Subgroup representation on executive boards was found to be independent of union size and number of locals.

In "Size of Locals and Union Democracy," William Faunce considers both the national and local levels, analyzing the impact of local union size on the degree of democracy in locals and on democratic processes at the national level. Consistent with prior research, Faunce finds the greatest contribution to the democratic operation of the national union issuing from larger locals. At variance with expectation is his conclusion that large local union leaders are more concerned with internal democratic processes than their counterparts in small locals. Faunce has to question the more traditional measures of union democracy at the local level to reach this conclusion.

18 / The Dilemma of Union Democracy

Emanuel Stein

UNDERLYING MUCH OF the recent writing on American trade-union government are assumptions which, through insistent repetition, have come to be widely regarded as self-evident truths and as sound guides to policy. These assumptions, which are often implicit rather than articulate, run something like this: the trade union is philosophically and traditionally a democratic institution which differs from other types of association, notably the business corporation, in the degree to which it emphasizes internal democracy; it is highly desirable for both internal and external considerations that unions should be democratic; through a variety of circumstances—especially the apathy of large segments of the membership and the self-aggrandizement of power-hungry leaders—power and authority have progressively been transferred from the rank and file to the leaders; this has led to many abuses which would be eliminated by the restoration of democratic government, which, in turn, can be achieved by the institution of various structural devices, statutory proscription of certain conduct, and education of the membership.

Insofar as these assumptions individually purport to describe a fact situation, it may be conceded that they contain a large and uncomfortable amount of truth. As explanations of developments in the basic character of union government, however, they are often dubious or irrelevant. Indeed, because of their stress upon behavioral excesses, they may hinder a correct assessment of the state of union government and of the factors which condition it. Stated briefly, the theme of this paper is that the lessening of union democracy is inextricably and inevitably interwoven with the large growth of the individual union, that the prospects for the re-creation of literal democracy diminish as the size of the union is increased, and that the problems of union government, if they are to be dealt with successfully, must be approached in other ways.

If we measure democracy by the extent and vigor of member participation, it is evident that most unions are less democratic than they used to be. Even where the leadership strives to attain what it believes to be the members' objectives, members are free to exercise their civil rights within the organization even to the point of forming opposition parties, and the leaders give regular and detailed accounts of their stewardship—in short, even where there are present within a union the elements commonly regarded as essentials of democracy,[1] the plain fact is that control has increasingly devolved upon small groups of leaders and their retinues. To an ever-larger extent, government has become the business of a more-or-less full-time officialdom, with the membership occupying mainly a ceremonial or ritualistic role.

The much greater membership participation in the early days of a union is far less the product of a philosophical commitment to democratic principles than of the circumstances attending organization. Apart from personal grievances which impel them to join a union, when workers are solicited individually or in small groups in the face of employer hostility, and are thus invited in effect to become targets of retaliatory measures, it is scarcely surprising that they should assume a prominent role in the affairs of the organization. But unions are not established to illustrate the theory of democracy; their function is to advance the economic interests of the members. In the circumstances of our times, the performance of this function induces, if it does not compel, a transfer of power from the membership to the leaders. Of course, the organization will be stronger, other things being equal, if the members identify themselves with it actively and continuously. It is also true that persons interested in the self-organization of workers are likely to be much more firmly committed than the general run of the population to democratic principles. However, the link between democracy and the trade union cannot withstand the pressure exerted by the needs of the organization in its principal areas of activity.

Unions are not alone in having to face issues of democratic government. Senator Fulbright, speaking of the political community, said recently:[2]

> ...government by the people is possible but highly improbable. The difficulties of self-government are manifest throughout the world.
>
> The history of political thought in the last century and a half is largely one of qualification, modification, and outright repudiation of the heady democratic optimism of the eighteenth century....
>
> The case for government by elites is irrefutable insofar as it rests on the need for expert and specialized knowledge. The average citizen is no more qualified for the detailed administration of government than the average politician is qualified to practice medicine or to split an atom. But in the choice of basic goals, the fundamental moral judgments that shape the life of a society, the judgment of trained elites is no more valid than the judgment of an educated people. The knowledge of the navigator is essential to the conduct of a voyage, but his special skills have no relevance to the choice of whether to take the voyage and where we wish to go.
>
> The distinction of course is between means and ends. The experience of modern times shows us that when the passengers take over the navigation

[1] C. P. Magrath, "Democracy in Overalls," *Industrial and Labor Relations Review,* Vol. 12, No. 4 (July 1959), pp. 504–5.

[2] J. W. Fulbright and Others, *The Elite and the Electorate* (New York: Fund for the Republic, 1963), pp. 3–5.

of the ship it is likely to go on the rocks. This does not mean that their chosen destination is the wrong one or that an expert would have made a better choice, but only that they are unlikely to get there without the navigator's guidance.

Exigencies of Union Function

How is the distinction between means and ends to be made in a union? In contrast to the state, the union is a single- or, at most, limited-purpose institution.[3] As to the general goals—improvements in wages and conditions of work—there would certainly be no disagreement. But who is to determine whether, in a particular year, wage increases should be sought and of what size? Whether a strike should be called? How much shall be given up in wages in return for paid vacations or holidays? Whether the union shall consent to a program of automation, notwithstanding substantial reductions in employment, in exchange for enlarged benefits to those remaining at work? Of course, these and similar crucial questions are generally submitted to the membership, but such submission comes as a request for ratification of action taken by the leadership, and the consultation of the membership is mostly an empty formality. There is no basic difficulty in having the membership decide such peripheral matters as whether the union should establish a bank, a home for its "senior citizens," or scholarships for the children of its members. However, in the central area of union function—collective bargaining—the leadership must have the authority to act if it is to be effective. Successful collective bargaining today calls for a great deal of specialized knowledge and for experience in utilizing that knowledge. It is utterly unrealistic to expect that the membership will be able to pass informed judgment upon the mass of economic, actuarial, and technological considerations underlying a collective-bargaining agreement. Hence, the membership is obliged to rely upon the recommendations of the leaders; in substance, therefore, in most unions, the power to make collective-bargaining agreements has been effectively concentrated in the hands of the leaders, notwithstanding that the rituals of formal ratification by the membership have, for the most part, been scrupulously preserved.

Even if the membership possessed the expertise necessary for collective bargaining or if it were felt that, nevertheless, the membership should retain effective power to act, it is plain that the facts of economic life would still entail the transfer of power to the leadership. Given the "business unionism" characteristic of the American scene, the locus of power within a union is going to be found at the point where the collective bargaining takes place, and this in turn is determined by market considerations. If, in many unions, locals have become mere administrative subdivisions of the national, the operative factor has been the nature of the product or factor market. As the markets have widened, the area covered by the individual collective-bargaining agreement has also widened. It would be absurd to have a single

---

[3] Magrath, *loc. cit.,* pp. 506–7.

local in a multiplant company negotiate an agreement for itself on wages and conditions without regard to what sister locals in other plants were doing. It would be no less absurd for one local dealing with one employer in a competitive industry to ignore the actions of the locals dealing with the other employers. The necessities of the situation thus produce centralized bargaining which enhances the power and prestige of the bargainers and diminishes the importance of the locals for whom the bargaining is being done. It follows that the ability of the membership to participate effectively is likewise diminished. I am not suggesting that the leadership has played a wholly passive role in the process of acquiring power or that it has not sought to add to that which was dictated by market forces. However, it seems to me that the personal ambitions of leaders have been far less significant in the building of their power than the market factors over which they have no control. For, where the markets have remained local, power has not tended to gravitate to the national to any material extent. Leaders of unions have thus been in the position of having power thrust upon them, power which they could not have seized in the absence of a propitious market situation.

I have no intention of making light of labor racketeering or similar malpractices, but these are not materially different from racketeering and corruption in other segments of the community and are susceptible of control through the application of the criminal law. Moreover, we cannot equate undemocratic unions with corrupt unions; corrupt unions are almost certain to be undemocratic, but many undemocratic unions are the embodiment of financial integrity. Nor do I minimize the extent or significance of infringements upon the civil rights of members—denial of the right to speak at union meetings, or to run for office, or to be consulted on matters required to be submitted to the membership, or protection against the unwarranted imposition of discipline. While such abuses are not easily dealt with, promising efforts at control have been commenced both within the unions—for example, through the public review boards—and by statutory enactment. However, it seems to me that the most rigid emphasis upon civil rights would not produce widespread and effective participation by members as long as the size of the union and the complexity of its affairs compel the concentration of power in the hands of the leadership.

Many writers have pointed out that there tends to be more democracy at the local level than at the national. I agree that this is so and think it is to be attributed to the relatively small size of the local. Where the membership of a local is numbered in the thousands, we find the same forces operating as in the nationals to make membership participation difficult, if not impossible. Of course the membership is apathetic, as has been so often observed![4] Having so little of consequence to do, what reason is there for attending union meetings? Hence, as George Brooks has said, members

---

4 G. W. Brooks, *The Sources of Vitality in the American Labor Movement* (Ithaca: New York State School of Industrial and Labor Relations, 1960), pp. 5–6. See also George Strauss, "The Shifting Power Balance in the Plant," *Industrial Relations,* Vol. 1, No. 3 (May 1962), pp. 74–75.

exercise "their inalienable right to be indifferent" and to leave the affairs of the organization to the small number who control it.

The Corporation Analogy

The many significant differences between business corporations and trade unions argue against the validity of comparisons between them. Yet, it seems to me that the history of the government of corporations does provide insights which may be valuable for the study of union government. Despite many assertions to the contrary, the corporation is based upon assumptions of democratic government *in relation to its stockholders*. Early corporations were free associations of investors for agreed-upon purposes. Corporate functions and powers were limited by charter; stockholders elected directors as their representatives in the conduct of the enterprise, and the directors in turn appointed the officers. Power and authority vested in directors by statute were predicated upon the view that the directors were, in fact as well as in law, responsible to the stockholders for the proper performance of their duties. In the small, closely held corporation, it is true even today that stockholders have an effective voice. But, in the large, publicly held corporation, it has long been apparent that the stockholder has been substantially disfranchised. Studies made over a generation ago by Brandeis, Ripley, and Berle pointed to the separation of ownership of the corporation and its control. Then, the trends in corporate government were obscured by the emphasis placed upon malpractice, including the looting of corporations, the mulcting of stockholders, and the building of vast personal empires. As time has gone on, however, it has become increasingly apparent that malpractice has very little to do with the matter but that size has everything to do with it. As corporate assets mount into the hundreds of millions or billions of dollars and their stockholders are counted by the tens or hundreds of thousands, control of the enterprise passes securely and irrevocably from the owners to the insiders. These may be men of the most punctilious integrity with an unswerving dedication to the welfare of the business, but their ownership interest is typically minuscule.

Now, determined efforts are made to preserve some vestigial remains of stockholder democracy. The New York Stock Exchange refuses to list nonvoting common shares; the Securities and Exchange Commission requires detailed proxies; annual reports are distributed; stockholders are solicited to attend meetings; at the meetings, stockholders—the tiny number who attend—may speak freely and criticize the management, vote for directors, and pass upon a variety of proposals. However, the most exacting observance of the ritual of consulting the stockholders cannot conceal their almost total lack of power. Indeed, the wide publicity accorded the upheaval in which incumbent management is ousted is eloquent testimony to the rarity of the event.

To describe what has happened is not to pass judgment upon its desirability. Doubtless, considerable support would be forthcoming for the proposition asserted by some corporate managers that the corporation must serve, in addition to the interests of stockholders, the interests of its suppliers, its employees, its customers, and the community generally. A recent study has argued that the traditional view of the corporation as solely a money-making enterprise is no longer adequate and that "the directors of large corporate enterprises are in need of more substantial doctrine than legal and economic theory has provided as a rationale for the powers they must exercise."[5] In any event, I do not think it can be successfully disputed that the managers of our large corporations do not have quite the same philosophy and do not respond to quite the same motivations as their stockholders or the managers of small corporations and that in some instances the differences are very large. The professional managers tend, I suggest, to develop institutional and personal goals which vary, in greater or lesser degree, from those the corporation would pursue if the stockholders could participate effectively in the enterprise.

The Membership-Leadership Gap

As in the corporation, so in the union! When membership increases to the point that full-time officials are required and can be afforded, a gulf between the members and the leaders begins to appear, a gulf which widens progressively with the growth of the union. It is not only that the official's salary is greater than that of the man at the bench and that, in the case of important officials, the difference may be quite substantial, though it is plain that the living standards would almost certainly be higher. Nor is it only the fact that the official has power both within and outside the union, though this, too, has obvious significance. It is, rather, that the men at the top and those at the bottom seem to live in different spheres, to concern themselves with different problems, and to respond to different motivations. The head of a large union—for example a Reuther or a Dubinsky—may continue to live in a modest home in a working-class district; he may talk wistfully of "the old days in the shop" and may exchange social visits with former fellow workers. But there is no blinking the fact of the vast separation. In innumerable ways—some subtle, some obvious—this separation makes itself felt: in living standards, in travel, in community activities, in power vis-à-vis the employer, in political influence, in publicity. And the greater the tenure of office, the deeper and more unbridgeable the separation, so that one is tempted to ask what there is really in common between the man in the shop and the national president of his union.

One must not conclude that leaders are not sensitive to the sentiments of the rank and file concerning such matters as dues and collective-bargaining gains. Quite the contrary is true! If nothing else, a prudent regard for the security and continued enjoyment of his own position would compel a leader to strive to "bring home the bacon," in which lies ultimate immunity from successful revolt. Of course, there is more—much more. I do not for a

5 Richard Eels, *The Government of Corporations* (New York: The Free Press of Glencoe, 1962), p. 11.

moment doubt that the overwhelming majority of union leaders have a
sense of genuine loyalty to their constituents, a real desire to secure economic
gains for them, and a conviction that the cause is just. And I suspect that
a kind of "instinct of workmanship" would operate to induce a drive for
achievements which would compare favorably with those of their "opposite
numbers" in other unions. Yet, doing *for* the members is not the same as
doing *with* them. A union is not democratic because it has made impressive
gains in wages and conditions; even the most selfless dedication to his constituents does not indicate that the leader is acting democratically. J. B. S.
Hardman made the point tellingly long ago in his discussion of the stakes
of leadership, distinguishing between a "leader of labor"—a democrat in a
democratic union—and a "labor leader"—a professional skilled in the arts
of manipulation and in selling the labor power of his members at advantageous rates.[6]

The gap between the membership and the leadership is manifested at
numerous points. To the individual member, the most important considerations are income and job security; his loyalty to the union is apt to reflect
faithfully the degree to which he believes the union has "delivered the
goods." The leader, too, is interested in the wages and conditions of his
constituents, but his primary allegiance is to the union; it is the union, as
an institution, which must at all costs be preserved. Often, of course, both
sets of interests may be served simultaneously and harmoniously, but there
are times when the interests diverge. Shall a concession be made on wages
in return for a provision on union security? How much is a checkoff worth?
How much shall be given up in potential gains in order to create a public
image of a responsible and restrained union or to accommodate the wishes
of a president or governor whose good will may be viewed as important to
the union and its leaders?

It has been fashionable in some circles to criticize union leaders for not
being statesmen, for being unmindful of the public interest or long-range
economic considerations. In other words, they are taken to task for pressing
too vigorously for what are held to be excessive adjustments in the terms of
employment. Of course, the real pressure for wage increases comes from the
rank and file, and the more responsive the leader is to rank-and-file senti-
ment, the more persistent his efforts towards the so-called "unstatesmanlike
goals."

Criticism has come also from quarters friendlier to unions. This has taken
the form of assertions that "business unionism" can no longer serve as
adequate trade-union philosophy, that unions need a "new look," possibly
in the form of "social unionism" which will serve the whole community and
contribute to the realization of democratic ideals generally. Assuming that
union leaders were to set out on such a course, one wonders to what extent
the membership would approve and follow.

We cannot have it both ways! Realistically, if the membership is to

6 "XYZ Has It Out With His Younger Self," in J. B. S. Hardman (ed.),
American Labor Dynamics (New York: Harcourt, Brace and Co., 1928).

determine union policy, directly or indirectly, it follows inevitably that the policy will express primarily the traditional objectives of increased income and enhanced job security for the individual to be obtained through the traditional medium of collective bargaining. Public-policy considerations and the interests of other segments of the community, including other groups of organized workers, will play a distinctly secondary role. It is only as the leadership acquires a measure of independence from the membership that it is able to have a broader perspective. In time, the situation may change, and the rank and file may moderate its emphasis upon historic business-union objectives, but such a change is, putting it mildly, not imminent. If anything, the pressure upon leaders to win bargaining concessions is increasing. One newspaper account, entitled "Union Men's Rising Defiance Over Contracts Imperils Labor Leaders and Managements,"[7] pointing to a marked increase in members' rejection of collective-bargaining agreements negotiated by their leaders, says in part:

> ...Hampered at the bargaining table by high unemployment, the threat of greater job-cutting because of automation and a more skilled and determined management opposition, union officials are finding it harder to get the comfortable contract concessions they once won.
>
> This has aroused a certain amount of dissatisfaction among workers against their leaders. "In some cases this failure is because the leaders know they aren't strong enough to get what they'd like," says one union aide, "but it's also true that some of the chiefs have lost close touch with the wants of the Indians." Whatever the reason, the result has been that union dissidents have found it easier to mobilize opposition to their leaders' wishes. . . .
>
> To some union men, the solution to the contract rejection problem is simple: "Get more (in benefits) and the members will have less to beef about."

I think it would be generally agreed that union leaders, for whatever reasons, are far more willing to go along with the notion of noninflationary wage adjustments than their members are with the collective bargaining agreements embodying such adjustments. Further, it has often been remarked that, in recent years, unions have not, for the most part, fought technological change with anything like the intensity of earlier times; on the contrary, many leaders have expressly approved automation and have sought only to cushion its impact. One wonders whether the longshoreman who has been automated out of a job by the so-called "containerization" has quite the same attitude toward the technological change as the officers of his union. However desirable moderation in wage policy and cooperation in technological progress, to cite only two illustrations, may be from the standpoint of the public interests, it is to be doubted that unions would act as they have acted on these matters if the rank and file could exert real influence.

[7] *The Wall Street Journal,* June 3, 1963, p. 26.

Prospects

If we evaluate union government in terms of its consequences and impact upon public economic policy, we may quite properly conclude that the outlook is not at all bad, for union leaders have broader perspectives and better understanding than their predecessors and than their constituents. On their own, or under the tutelage of their economic advisers, they talk easily about gross national product, economic growth, and the requisites for sound domestic and foreign economic policies. So viewed, it becomes a matter of concern if the leaders are unable to deliver the vote—that is, unable to get their constituents to endorse a collective-bargaining agreement based upon "sound" economic ideas. And it is not utterly fantastic to suppose that, if a number of outstanding unions should, as it were, become "runaways" and insist upon maximizing the gains to their members without regard for public policy, we might witness a reimposition of public wage controls.

However, if we evaluate union government as *process,* I think we must conclude that the prospects for effective mass participation are very dim—not because of member apathy, nor because of the ambition or cupidity of the leaders, but simply because the size of the union and the complexity of its functions make such participation substantially impossible. It is regrettable, but nonetheless true, that visions of a really workable trade-union democracy are doomed to disappointment. This does not mean that the civil rights of members cannot be effectively protected or that they should be ignored. I think that unions have made encouraging progress on these civil rights and that the delinquents can be reached by legislation. Nor does it mean that corruption and racketeering cannot and should not be brought under workable control. It does mean, however, that we may have to revise our notions as to what is possible in trade-union government. We may be compelled to recognize that the preservation of the *forms* of democratic government, important as it may be for sentimental reasons as well as to safeguard the ultimate right of revolution by the members, may not be a sufficient answer to the challenges posed by union structure and function in a highly integrated economy. We may have to invent new concepts and devices which will permit a viable balancing of the competing interests in light of the realities of contemporary unionism.

19 / Are Unions Democratic?

Leonard R. Sayles, George Strauss

DEFINITIONS ARE ALWAYS a problem, particularly where the term is invested with as much emotion as is the word "democracy." A common approach to this subject stresses the union's constitutional structure. According to this view, every union is democratic if its constitution provides machinery whereby the members can change their officers and determine basic union policy. By this criterion, few unions are undemocratic!

Another approach is to look at union democracy from the point of view of participation in union politics. This approach considers questions such as: How many candidates are there in elections? How often is there a turnover in officers? Are there organized political parties? How much disagreement is there at meetings, and what is the average attendance at them? Were locals required to meet all these criteria, we would find few democratic.

Both approaches are somewhat limited. Both are concerned only with the superficial, or most easily measurable, indicators of democracy. Many people evaluate unions unconsciously in terms of the town meeting. They feel that unless everyone participates actively there is no democracy. Yet, ...in most locals the important decisions are made behind the scenes, in meetings of the executive and grievance committees, at informal discussions among the officers, and during casual contacts between the officers and rank and file in the plant. The local meeting is primarily a ceremony to ratify decisions made elsewhere.

From the point of view of our study, union democracy can best be measured in terms of the responsiveness of the officers to the demands of the members. A good way to evaluate this form of democracy is through the attitudes of the membership. How free do the workers feel to express their grievances or complaints? What is the average member's estimate of his chances of being heard by the officers and of having something done about his particular problem? How well do union policies reflect the views of the rank and file?

If we apply such a definition of democracy, we may utilize such criteria as these: the ability of member-interest groups to use internal union pressures (rather than self help techniques) to obtain favorable consideration of their grievances; the extent to which important questions of policy enter into union elections; the degree to which officers can combine the roles of administrator with those of the social leader; the vigor of the stewards; and the effectiveness of the grievance procedure as a line of communication.

From *The Local Union*, Revised Edition, by Leonard R. Sayles and George Strauss, copyright © 1953, 1967, by Harcourt Brace Jovanovich, Inc., and reprinted with their permission.

Of course, informal channels of communication can be easily blocked unless there is an ever present possibility that "poor service" will result in grievances being aired in a membership meeting or at the ballot box. In general, democracy of the sort we are speaking of functions effectively only as a corollary of lively meetings and contested elections.

Why Union Democracy Is Important

If democracy flourishes on the face-to-face level, the chances are greater that it will flourish in the nation as a whole. Roughly 25 per cent of the labor force in the United States consists of union members. For the most part, they do not have the opportunity to participate in the traditionally middle-class service organizations which bulk so important in training community leaders. Democratic unions encourage individual expression and self-development and thus train democratic citizens.

Union democracy is equally important from the standpoint of enlightened management. One reason workers join unions is to express their grievances. They want to speak with a voice which management will hear. The union is their channel of communication with management. When grievances are hidden, discontent festers and saps the morale of the workers and the strength of the productive enterprise.

Democracy is also preferable from the point of view of the union organizer who is interested solely in maximizing the effectiveness of his union. Without democracy, participation falls off. Even if the dues stream continues, identification with the organization is impaired. This may well affect worker solidarity when there is no strike.

Without democracy, there is no way of discovering good leaders within the rank and file who will donate their services and gain the confidence of their fellows. Without such leaders, the organization is crippled, for the paid officers cannot do all the work.

The Local Is More Democratic than the International

Many authors have been discouraged about the future of union democracy. They deplore the concentration of power in the hands of a few leaders who are never defeated in elections, and they deplore the paucity of discussion on basic union policy. In most cases, their conclusions are based on studies of the Internationals. Our own research has been on the local level, and here we find that conditions are better for both participation and communication.

The vitality of the local lies in its relatively simple organization; its work can be done by men off duty or on lost time. Because of the officers' daily contact with the rank and file, their effectiveness and responsiveness can be directly evaluated. This is particularly true in grievance-handling. Of course, a few industrial locals have paid business agents, but even these can be easily supervised by unpaid executive committees composed of men working in the shop.

In local elections, the informal nominating procedure and the ease of voting contribute to relatively high participation and a large number of candidates. The ever present possibility of being defeated spurs the officers to alertness.

The International bureaucracy contrasts sharply with the responsiveness of the local officers. The International requires, and can afford, a team of paid professional experts: organizers, field representatives, education directors, research economists, statisticians, and actuaries. These "porkchoppers" do not have regular contact with the rank and file and once in office are extremely hard to oust. Most utilize highly specialized skills that the rank and file can neither understand nor directly oversee.

To the unpaid union leader, his office is just another form of leisure-time activity; to the porkchopper it is a livelihood. Of course, if defeated, most porkchoppers can go back to the shops, but as A. J. Muste asks:

> How many people will one encounter in a year's travel who can bring themselves to exchange a white-collar official position for a dirty, monotonous, hot, exacting obscure wage-slave's job in a mine or mill?[1]

Not only will he fight harder to keep his office, but his means of doing so will be more effective. The local president who must manage his campaign in his spare time has little advantage over his opponent. But this advantage increases enormously once he goes on the full-time payroll as an International officer. The mere fact that he occupies a focal point of communications gives him a commanding lead over those who would clip his wings. Added to this are other sources of strength, as Reynolds enumerates:

> The methods used are those of machine politics anywhere. The union leader makes friends with as many members of the organization as he can, performs various services for them, distributes salaried positions in the right quarters, uses the union newspaper to present himself in a favorable light, stage-manages the union conventions, and makes full use of oratory and the other political arts. All this he does in perfectly good faith. He becomes convinced after a few years that he can run the union better than anyone else, and in many cases, he is right.[2]

To a much greater extent than is possible in governmental politics, the International administration personifies the union. It can "educate" the rank and file to think of the administration and the union as somehow identical. It can make them think that a vote against the administration is also a vote against the union and everything it stands for. It can extol its own activities in "building" the union and protecting the organization from its enemies and it can castigate the "destructive" activities of the opposition.

Furthermore, the average member has no standard by which to judge

[1] A. J. Muste, "Factional Fights in Trade Unions," *American Labor Dynamics,* J. B. S. Hardman, Ed. (New York: Harcourt, Brace & World, 1928), p. 341.

[2] Lloyd Reynolds, *Labor Economics and Labor Relations* (Englewood Cliffs, New Jersey: Prentice-Hall, Inc., 1949), p. 147.

whether the International president does a good job in his nation-wide activities, but he has well-informed opinions about how his grievanceman handles problems in the plant.

An informed public opinion can be better developed on the local level than on the International. Except in locals of 10,000 or more members or in polyglot locals consisting of many small shops, the interested members (and more particularly the active leaders) can rely on face-to-face contacts to maintain communications. The work of the local gets a thorough going over whether the men meet at the workplace, at the plant gate, in the plant cafeteria, or at the neighborhood bar.

With all its shortcomings, the local membership meeting is still an effective forum for group discussion. In spite of much confusion, it affords ample opportunity for the members to criticize their officers. And in times of crisis, when alternatives are clearly defined, it does make decisions.

On the International level, the ability of members to exchange opinions and place pressure on the leadership is limited:

> As in modern corporations and the government bureau, the relations between the leaders of the national union and the individual workers in the shop may become tenuous sometimes to the point of extinction.
>
> . . . There are a variety of levels of organizational authority in the typical union, and whatever influence the individual worker can exert must frequently be filtered through the complicated delegation-of-power system. . . . The worker must rely on the intelligence and honesty of persons delegated to represent him, and these delegates in turn must authorize a still smaller group (usually the national officers) to act for the union.[3]

Certainly the existence of a large number of "layers" between the rank and file and the International officers makes it more difficult for the officers to know what the rank-and-file members want and for the rank-and-file members to control the officers.

The administration of the International can mend its fences and consolidate support fifty-two weeks a year, but the opposition must wait for the few caucuses in the early days of the International convention before making its plans. Prior to that, contact must often be made by letter or mimeographed "opposition bulletin." While the administration is always able to use official publicity for its purposes, many unions prohibit the publication of opposition newspapers or the formation of opposition factions.

Consequently, even if the opposition is not driven underground, it is forced to become conspiratorial. The semihysterical attacks to which it must resort in order to gain attention are no match for the friendly handshake of the International representative or the slick-paper journal written by the professional publicity man.

In general, then, locals are more democratic than their parent Internationals. In fact, a majority of those we examined maintained an energetic political life, with lively (although often poorly directed) debate in their

[3] Frank C. Pierson, "The Government of Trade Unions," *Industrial and Labor Relations Review,* Vol. 1, No. 4 (July 1948), p. 595.

meetings and a substantial turnover of officers. Although only a small proportion of the members were active in union affairs, there was nothing to prevent others becoming more active if they wished. There were many opportunities for dissatisfied members to protest decisions—even more than those specified in the contract grievance procedure. A determined member could take his case to many different levels of the local hierarchy.

Loss of Initial Democratic Enthusiasm

Most new locals start life being democratic and then go through a period of decline in which they lose some of their youthful vigor. However, this decline goes further in some locals than in others. . . . We can outline the reasons for both this initial decline in democracy and for the eventual development of some sort of equilibrium, where forces toward and away from democracy are balanced. Finally, we will try to suggest reasons why some locals are more democratic than others.

Decline in Participation

Immediately after a new union is organized, interest is high, and this is reflected in meeting attendance, as it is in other union activities. But once the original excitement has passed and the first contract is signed, meetings become increasingly dull. Attendance picks up when the contract is being negotiated or a strike is imminent, but there is a tendency for negotiations to become less dramatic. As relations with management become more "mature," there is less to fight about.

The leaders learn that their task will be easier and they will subject to fewer pressures if they keep reasonably quiet about what happens at the bargaining table. Since they no longer rush to the membership to report and ask instructions, the rank and file loses its sense of vicarious participation in contract and grievance bargaining. Thus, meeting attendance tends to decline until it reaches a stable median (from 2 to 8 per cent in the locals we studied). Aside from a few lonely isolates and departmental representatives, the "hard core" becomes increasingly narrowed down to leaders and their followers.

Provided it does not take too much time, a large portion of the members still go through the motions of voting in officer elections. However, as the union loses its novelty, their interest and excitement decline. Increasingly, the members say, "The man who is now in is doing a good job, so why kick him out?" or "The new man will be just as bad." Although election upsets may take place, there is an observable trend toward concentration of leadership among the top-status groups.

The Leaders and the Rank and File Become Two Groups

When the union is new, its leaders are anxious to recruit people to help them. Anyone with sufficient time and energy can participate, not only in the ratification of decisions already made but in the decision-making process itself. But as it grows older a twofold change takes place. The leaders tend to restrict the number with whom they consult before making a decision; the rank and file increasingly look upon the officers as "they" rather than "we" —a group separate and distinct from themselves.

. . . [The] rank and file [harbor a] suspicion of their officers. It is natural that the officers should be aware of this feeling. In turn, they resent the passivity of the membership, their willingness to sit back and criticize while the officers do all the work.

They begin to doubt the sincerity of members who are "too greedy." They say:

> Sometimes I wonder whether this democracy is really worth the cost. They [the members] don't want leaders, they want messenger boys. No wonder some of those guys [leaders of undemocratic unions] get hard [unresponsive].

In spite of sharp differences among themselves, the leaders enter into a tacit agreement to protect each other in public. They accentuate their isolation further in order to protect themselves from "pressures" brought to bear on grievance cases.

Decline in Communication

In most instances, the new union is organized by a coalition of "natural leaders." But once in power, these natural leaders have a tendency to freeze out any young upstart who challenges them. As this clique excludes a larger and larger proportion of these leaders, it begins to lose contact with the rank and file. In theory, the shop steward should be the intermediary between the officers and the rank and file. In practice, as we have seen, his decline in prestige and authority also reduces his value as a communications link.

In this way, the communications channels within the union tend to dry up. The rank and file feel less free to bring their problems to the officers; the officers are less interested in hearing them. Members take the increasingly fatalistic attitude that voting and attending meetings are useless. Few are willing to run for office. There is little interest in other forms of union activity.

Of course, such developments are uneven. Some groups still find that participation "pays off," while others feel that they are the forgotten minority. And of those who feel left out, some resort to self-help measures, and others become apathetic.

Such, then, is the discouraging story of the way many locals lose part of their democracy. Some locals might carry this process further, say to the point where officers completely abolish elections and meetings without the rank and file objecting. But none of the locals studied went this far. In every case, there were checks which seemed to prevent any further decline of democracy—even if the officers had so desired.

Checks on Declines in Democracy

Without question, the tradition of the union movement itself is a strong force favoring democracy. The vast majority of leaders became interested in unionism precisely because of their dedication to democratic principles. In most instances, they would rather be defeated in a fair election than win an unfair one. They are proud of their union's democracy; many officers take a wry pride in the amount of opposition they receive.

But even if the officers were not committed to the democratic ethic, rank-and-file attitudes would help to keep them in line. Although the general attitude of the rank-and-file worker is "Let George do it," there is a hidden string. What he really means is "Let George do it as long as George delivers the goods." Since economic conditions are variable, George cannot deliver indefinitely. When the union faces reverses, George will have unpleasant news—for instance, that the men will have to go out on strike or that they will have to accept a pay cut.

At this point the relationship between the leaders and the membership becomes important. If the leadership has maintained its lines of communication, its explanations will be accepted and the rank and file will stand by loyally. But if the lines of communication have become clogged, then these members will be suspicious, restless, and resentful—they will lose confidence in their leaders.

What does the rank and file do when it loses confidence in its leaders? It has a number of alternatives, the most obvious being to vote for a new slate of officers at the next elections. Of course, . . . economic factors rarely enter into such elections, but when they do, the toll among incumbents is great.

This assumes that the local maintains the formal trimmings of procedural democracy. It assumes, for instance, that if a member attacks the officers in a meeting he will not be subject to retaliation, that regular elections are held, that nominations are free, that all are given a chance to vote, and that the ballots are counted fairly. Even in the small minority of locals in which the leadership met no apparent opposition, these minimal protections were provided.

Suppose, however, that the dissatisfied members are unsuccessful at the polls or that the leadership is somehow able to restrict the exercise of procedural rights. What prevents these locals from going all the way to one-man rule?

Even in dictatorial unions workers have grievances. If the officers do not react to the normal "internal" pressures previously discussed, the workers still have a final recourse: following their "informal" leaders, they can resort to wildcat strikes, work restriction, and other forms of self-help. What better way for the members to express their frustration than to go on a spontaneous strike? But this is highly dangerous for the union administration, for if the *official* leaders cannot call off the strike, management will deal with the leaders who can.

Even if resentment against the union leadership leads to neither an election battle nor self-help activities, it may result in apathy. And too great apathy is dangerous both to the union and to its leaders. A union's strength depends upon the loyalty of its rank and file and the number and ability of its active participants. Without an active group of unpaid leaders the union may fall apart—the paid full-time officials just can't do all the work. Apathy loses strikes. And when there is no union shop, it results in loss of members and the disintegration of locals. Even with a union shop an apathetic local is easy prey for any competing International with a penchant for raiding.

All these possibilities scare the average leader. Of course, he is already strongly committed to democracy as a system of values, but he learns along the way that it also builds a stronger union. Looked at from another point of view, unions with sound human-relations structures will be able to solve tougher problems than those where human relations are weak.

Situational Determinants of Democracy

As we have pointed out, some locals are more democratic than others. All unions are buffeted by the forces discussed above—yet why does their dynamic balancing sometimes result in an active, highly participating local and other times in one whose members are completely apathetic? In order to seek a further answer to this question, we will list *some* of the situational factors that influence the union's internal life. Of course, in any given instance, some of these may be exceedingly important and others of negligible significance.

Locus of Control

To the extent that the "locus of control" over collective bargaining is concentrated in the International, rank-and-file opportunity to participate is reduced. Most unions which sign multiplant agreements provide for membership votes before demands are submitted or the contract ratified, but at best this type of participation is not satisfactory. It makes a tremendous amount of difference if one of the members of the negotiating committee is a man from your shop from whom you can get the "straight dope" as to what is happening—who will even give you an eyewitness account of how the superintendent lost his temper and how the International representative made the company president eat dirt.

To the workers in one automobile plant studied, the 1950 wage agreement came as a complete surprise. A few knew that negotiations were in process, but their chief source of information was the daily paper. Consequently, there was almost no feeling of involvement in the negotiations.

In another plant, the local did its own negotiating. In this plant, the situation was entirely different. In large departments, every worker had a good picture of what happened within a few hours after each negotiation session broke up. Consequently, the officers were continually able to sound out their constituents as to the relative importance of different demands—and to prepare them for necessary concessions.

But it must be emphasized once again that contract negotiations are only part of the picture. Even where contracts are negotiated on a country-wide basis, the rank and file may exercise considerable influence over the processing of grievances.

Negotiations on the local level are not an automatic guarantee of rank-

and-file participation. In locals in service and craft industries which must bargain with many small firms, most of the negotiations are conducted by the business agents without extensive membership participation. Since the firms are highly competitive, the business agent must spend most of his time preventing "chiseling" on the standard rate for the job. Therefore, he has little opportunity to handle other types of grievances—and rank-and-file opportunities to communicate are circumscribed.

History and Organization of the Union

The formal structure of the International and the unwritten traditions which lie behind this have a definite effect upon the local, for the law and its interpretations are intricately entwined.

Although Hoxie's division of unions into functional types is far less relevant now than it was in the 1920's,[4] echoes of the past constantly reverberate in the union's present. Since all unions are basically mutual self-help associations, they all have some tradition of democracy. But the tradition is far stronger in formerly "uplift" unions like the I.L.G.W.U. than in "business" unions like the Carpenters. To be sure, apathy at the rank-and-file level is characteristic of many locals in clothing unions, but the clothing union officers observed consistently reaffirmed their belief in democracy, in striking contrast to business agents of many "business unions." In the same way, the U.A.W.'s sad experience with Homer Martin (its first president and would-be dictator) did much to cement its democratic tradition.

Even the new local inherits a wealth of tradition from the International. The auto locals we studied were located far from Detroit, yet the democracy they showed probably reflected conditions there. In one newly formed local of another C.I.O. International, the members were told again and again by the International president and the International representative, "in the C.I.O. we don't do things that way."[5]

Unions which have been organized "from the top down" by the International may show less political activity than those built "bottom up" from self-organized locals.

The role of historical accident should not be forgotten. In one situation we studied, the NLRB split the workers into two separate units: clerical and production. The stock record clerks were placed in the clerical unit, although they might easily have been placed in the production unit. Since this group was made up of the most active and able leaders in the company, it easily established control over the clerical local. As a consequence, its political life was far less turbulent than that of its sister local. Perhaps, had

[4] Robert F. Hoxie, *Trade Unionism in the United States* (New York: Appleton-Century-Crofts, 1921), pp. 44–52. Hoxie describes four "functional" types: business unions, uplift unions, revolutionary unions, predatory unions.

[5] Among the suggestions which met this treatment were: (1) that seniority demands be decided by mail referendum, (2) that shop stewards dispose of grievances by themselves, or submit them to the third stage without executive board approval, (3) that shop stewards as a body be given certain legislative powers.

the NLRB ruled otherwise, the production local would have been the inactive one.

Structure

It has already been suggested that participation declines proportionally as the size of the local increases. Any factor which increases the size of the local will make participation that much more difficult.

The size of the local is often determined by the size of the plant unit. Some International constitutions require that locals be large enough to support a business agent. Even in areas with large concentrations of members, this requirement can make the local large enough to be unwieldy. Where members are spread over a broad geographical area, it makes attendance by more than a small proportion unlikely, if not impossible.

Certainly this was the case in a Teamsters local whose jurisdiction extended from central Pennsylvania to the southern tip of New Jersey. Compare the effect on democracy of this structure with that of the International Typographers' Union, where every workplace is organized into a chapel.

Local 688, a giant Teamsters local comprising 10,000 members in the St. Louis area, has taken drastic action to cut down the effect of size. Instead of one large meeting for the entire local, at which attendance doubtless would be small, meetings are held on a "shop" or industry basis, and local-wide policy is formulated by the executive committee and a shop stewards' council.

Much of the union politicking revolves around officers' elections. The more frequent the election the greater the interest. Other things being equal, one would expect locals whose officers serve short terms to be more democratic than those with long terms.

Geography

The Western Federation of Miners and the I.W.W. were in the best rip-roaring western tradition. Small-town craft locals are very different animals from their big-city brothers. As one International representative explained:

> It's been my experience that you get more interest in small town locals than in the big city. In a big city, you have all the troubles of travel to the meeting hall, and no matter what we can offer them, they get better entertainment at the shows.

Autocratic union leaders can exist in some industries without rank-and-file support if they have the aid of the local government. In some craft unions particularly, there is evidence pointing to a close tie-in between "dictatorial" union leaders and corrupt city bosses.

Character of Work Groups

...[S]tatus, cohesiveness, and homogeneity of work groups [affect] relative participation of departments. It might be expected that these same factors would affect the over-all level of participation within local unions.

Following this reasoning, we can list some of the factors which we would expect to be favorable to democracy: whether the members work close together in one location instead of being spread out over a large area where they cannot communicate with one another; whether all have a similar ethnic background; whether they earn roughly the same pay; whether they are relatively highly skilled; and whether they comprise a stable work force. Each of these factors contributes to higher participation in the union and, other things being equal, to greater democracy.

One additional factor should be mentioned: certain industries seem to attract workers who have had more experience with democratic procedure than others. Members of white-collar locals often have considerable education. Education gives a man confidence to express himself; it makes him less frightened of the complex and frequently technical matters which daily confront the union. Lipset cites the high educational level of the Typographers as contributing to their democratic traditions and two-party system.[6]

A local of engineers we studied provided another example of this. Discussing a draft of their constitution, the members made continual references such as: "In organizations to which I belong. . ." or "In my experience. . ."

In contrast to this, pandemonium reigned in early meetings of a newly organized production local because few members knew even the rudiments of parliamentary procedures. Later, when they had learned it, they played with it like a toy, tying themselves up in endless procedural knots.

The Collective-Bargaining Relationship

The collective-bargaining relationship has its effects upon the internal life and democracy of the union, an effect which may be as important as any of those so far discussed. Much of the continuing research interest in collective bargaining has been concentrated on factors contributing to industrial peace as opposed to industrial conflict. While generally considered to be a desirable social goal, we can now ask what is the impact of such industrial peace on union democracy? Does one strengthen the other, or are they mutually exclusive alternatives between which society must choose?

Muste suggests that the union has two conflicting functions, that of an army and that of a town meeting, and one tends to interfere with the other. It would follow that, when the union is at war, political democracy should be curtailed, for criticism of the war itself, of the objectives for which it is fought, and even of the leaders and their tactics, becomes high treason.

Although victory requires unity, and perhaps even the suppression of too-violent disagreement, can we say that the reverse is true? Does democracy flourish best under peace and security? Clyde Summers would seem to think so:

> As long as a union operates under a constant fear and anticipation of having to battle the employer for economic gains, it is bound to look upon

6 Seymour Lipset, Martin Trow, and James Coleman, *Union Democracy* (New York: Doubleday & Co., Anchor Books, 1962).

any activity within the union which creates dissension or division, not merely as an exercise of democratic rights, but as a threat to its safety. The Typographical Union has been able to develop and maintain a two-party system with conventions, nominations, platforms, and free-campaigning on the issues and the candidates. It may be more than coincidence that this union was fully accepted by the employer and did not have to strike to obtain its objectives for 25 years.[7]

But much of the evidence seems to point in the opposite direction. Some of the most enthusiastically democratic unions are those which until recently have been fighting for their lives. In many instances, good relations with management have been associated with a decline in democracy.

As long as such an "armed truce" relationship continues, in which the parties believe their major objectives are in conflict,[8] the union must be kept in fighting trim. If it wishes to retain the support of the rank and file during strikes, it must respond quickly to their needs. It must develop a strong body of noncommissioned officers in the stewards. Member grievances will be pushed with extra vigor, first, because the union cannot afford to antagonize members and second, because each grievance is a weapon in the battle.

Apathetic locals cannot win long strikes, suffer from declining membership, and are fair game for rival unions. Other things being equal, we might then expect undemocratic locals to be those which are relatively sheltered from the threats of long strikes, declining membership, and competing unions. If this is true, the possibility of extensive strikes, the open shop, and the presence of rival unions are all favorable to union democracy.

On the other hand, the greatest concentration of undemocratic unions exists where they are strong enough to "stabilize" the industry. Most of these industries are highly competitive, and the employer unit is relatively small. Some of these unions enjoy unparalleled security; yet, as Lens points out:

> In craft unions with a closed shop contract, he [the member] is dependent
> to a large extent on the business agent for his jobs and for the choice of
> jobs. To oppose official policy, particularly in the face of overwhelming odds,
> is definitely to jeopardize his livelihood and possibly force himself out of the
> union entirely.[9]

The most dangerous situations of all occur in the small minority of cases in which basic disagreement is impossible because the union and the employer have apparently reached collusive agreement. Under these circumstances, there is little need for rank-and-file support; the stimulus of external danger is at a minimum.

"Working harmony" is another form of industrial peace. In contrast to

---

[7] "Disciplinary Powers of Unions," *Industrial and Labor Relations Review*, Vol. 3, No. 4 (July 1950), p. 491. Lipset, Trow, and Coleman, *op. cit.,* seem to agree.

[8] Frederick H. Harbison and John R. Coleman, *Goals and Strategy in Collective Bargaining* (New York: Harper & Row, 1951), p. 20.

[9] Sidney Lens, *Left, Right and Center* (Hinsdale, Ill.: Henry Regnery Co., 1949), p. 106.

the situations where the union is stronger than the employer, parties of roughly equal strength develop a "mature" relationship in which:

> Employer and union leaders look upon collective bargaining more as a means of working together than as a competitive struggle for power. In such cases, the union-management relationship provided machinery not merely for compromising conflicting interests, but also for advancing the common or joint interests of the parties involved.[10]

Some of the problems created for the union by this new maturity have been discussed in previous chapters. When the union places a positive value on maintaining good relations with management, the officers must take responsibility for such unpleasant tasks as preserving rank-and-file discipline (through preventing wildcat strikes and other self-help techniques), screening grievances, resolving intergroup disputes (particularly in areas like seniority and job evaluation). Under some circumstances this may lead to a decline in communication and, as a consequence, the separation of the membership into two distinct groups: officers and rank and file. The long-run consequences of this may well be a general reduction in the members' interest and participation in the union.

Conclusion

In spite of apathy (on the part of the rank and file) and concentration of power (in the hands of the officers), the vast majority of the locals studied were essentially democratic. They are a wholesome influence upon our society. The opportunity they give to their members to express themselves is an important contribution to the American way of life.

What of tomorrow? Will a more general acceptance of working harmony result in general membership apathy? Will the union become just another bureaucratic organization?

We are guardedly optimistic. Working harmony provides its own incentives for greater membership activity. The expansion of the grievance procedure and the growing influence of the union in plant affairs mean that the net effect of the local upon the lives of its members is increasing. The members have a larger stake in keeping tabs on their officers and more to lose by being inactive. Thus, along with increased dependence upon the officers, the rank and file may well develop greater interest in controlling them.

We may, then, conclude that the possibilities for democracy are less a function of the degree of industrial peace than they are of the number of problems which the rank and file can help to solve. If democratic unionism is to survive, it must constantly meet new challenges. Thus, although the development of harmonious labor-management relationships creates new problems for the union leadership, it also provides an opportunity for broadening the range of decisions in which the worker can participate, and thus it expands the concept of industrial democracy itself.

---

10 Harbison and Coleman, *op. cit.,* p. 53.

20 / Union Conventions and Executive Boards: A Formal Analysis of Organizational Structure*

Philip M. Marcus

MUCH OF OUR thinking about voluntary organizations has been shaped by the work of Michels.[1] Even in organizations whose very goal is to attain greater democracy for the membership, said Michels, oligarchical structure develops to prevent the fullest expression of members' interests and desires. The "Iron Law of Oligarchy" holds because organizations require concerted action which virtually demands the delegation of special tasks to a few leaders. The separation of leadership from the rank and file contributes to member apathy, and this tends to strengthen the leaders' powers and permit their self-perpetuation. Frequently the organization's existence becomes an end in itself for the leaders who wish to retain the rewards of their high position. The organization's original goals are often compromised and subverted as a result of these oligarchical tendencies.

Lipset has reformulated the Iron Law, specifying other social conditions that underlie the emergence of oligarchy and restrict the development of democracy.[2] For example, he hypothesized that the size and structure of the industry, as well as that of the union organization, conrtibutes to the development of oligarchical leadership in American trade unions. Management in large centralized industries prefers to negotiate with union leaders who represent the entire membership, rather than with local leaders. This tends to deprive local leaders of much of their power, concentrating the

---

* Many persons have read earlier drafts of this paper and have provided a good deal of critical assistance. The following deserve special mention: Peter M. Blau, Peter H. Rossi and Seymour M. Warkov of the University of Chicago; Joan W. Moore of the University of California at Riverside; Robert Perrucci of Purdue University; Arnold S. Tannenbaum of the University of Michigan.

1 Robert Michels, *Political Parties,* Glencoe, Ill.: The Free Press, 1958.

2 Seymour M. Lipset, "The Political Process in Trade Unions: A Theoretical Statement," in Morroe Berger, Theodore Abel, and Charles H. Page (eds.), *Freedom and Control in Modern Society,* New York: Van Nostrand, 1954, pp. 82–124.

Reprinted by permission of the author and publisher from "Union Conventions and Executive Boards: A Formal Analysis of Organizational Structure," *American Sociological Review,* Vol. 31, No. 1 (February 1966), pp. 61–70.

power at the national level. Similarly, management in large industries demands that the national union control wildcat strikes to insure continued production, once an agreement has been reached, and national union leaders are urged to punish locals that do not conform to the negotiated contract. Looking for sources of support for divergent union views, Lipset examined social contacts that are free of the organizational hierarchy. Clubs, friendships and other social activities in which workers participate permit them to develop and exchange opinions that are often opposed to those of the incumbent leaders. Internal democracy is enhanced when local leaders are relatively independent of the national union for their positions and can refuse to delegate full authority to the national officers, thus maintaining a tradition of autonomy. If the elected union leaders can return to the jobs they held before obtaining office, then, Lipset argued, they will be less inclined to use undemocratic means to retain office. Thus, a low wage scale in the industry may be a factor contributing to oligarchy.

A problem common to many such discussions of organizational structure has to do with the very nature of democracy, i.e., the channels available to the rank and file for influencing their leaders. Michels and Lipset almost equate it with a functioning two-party system, but very few unions could qualify as democratic by this criterion. Seidman suggests that "the test of democracy in unionism is the responsiveness of leaders to the desires of the rank and file members."[3] This criterion evades the question of influence channels and allows many more unions to be classified as democratic. Critics of Seidman would undoubtedly point out that it is patently naive, since modern propaganda techniques make manipulation of members' opinions all too easy.

What are some of these channels for rank and file influence? The more traditional theories of democracy would insist that *each member* of a voluntary organization have both a vote and an opportunity to express his opinions directly, at conventions. This ideal is virtually impossible to uphold because union memberships are too large and dispersed to permit direct participation.[4] Even the use of referenda has been limited to electing officers and voting on such issues as contract and strike authorizations. Because the

3 Joel I. Seidman, *Democracy in the Labor Movement*, Ithaca, N. Y.: New York State School of Industrial and Labor Relations, Bulletin No. 39 (February, 1958), p. 8.

4 Attendance, let alone participation at local meetings, tends to be very low, except on certain issues. For a review of literature on membership participation see William Spinrad, "Correlates of Trade Union Participation: A Summary of the Literature," *American Sociological Review*, 25 (April, 1960), pp. 237–44. There is also some evidence that members who can nominate their own candidates for office at the national level do not use this privilege. For example, Rothbaum reports that in the old Oil Workers Union, one-third of the locals did not return their ballots in 1942. The number of members voting in locals that did return ballots varied from 3 to 55 per cent. Melvin Rothbaum, *The Government of the Oil, Chemical and Atomic Workers Union*, New York: Wiley, 1962, p. 61.

referendum is expensive, cumbersome and frequently time-consuming, some unions do not provide for it at all.[5]

The union convention, composed of *delegates* elected by the rank and file from their respective locals, has emerged as an alternative channel for membership influence. Each delegate is enjoined, more or less, to represent the majority of his local. Some unions have tried to combine the referendum and the convention, so that, for example, convention delegates may nominate candidates for national offices and introduce legislation and constitutional amendments. Rank and file members then have the final vote, selecting both the officials and the laws that will govern them. While the democratic ideal would be more closely approximated by the use of referenda, some researchers have found that whether they are used makes little difference in the extent of actual membership influence and determination of union affairs.[6]

In this paper I shall consider two channels of membership influence on union leadership: conventions and sub-group representation on executive boards. Both variables may be considered measures of democracy. Union conventions, when held frequently, give members an opportunity to vote on crucial issues and offices in the organization. Executive boards with specific representation of sub-groups within the union, (i.e., members in a certain geographical area, a certain trade, etc.) are also a channel of membership influence because the officers are elected and are responsible to specific constituencies. Should an executive board officer fail to represent his sub-group adequately, he can be voted out of office at the next election.[7]

Members' influence on union leadership is structured by the size, age and complexity of the union. Specifically, I shall show that larger unions convene less frequently than smaller unions; size limits direct participation in union affairs as well as the use of elected delegates to represent the membership.

Another constraint on the use of conventions for membership representation may be the development of fixed expectations within the union. If certain sub-groups or their delegates know the power distribution in the union and have little hope of modifying it, they may seek other channels of influence, forming coalitions with other sub-groups or even withdrawing

[5] In their study of 194 union constitutions, Bambrick and Haas reported that 29 of the unions' constitutions required no membership vote to authorize strikes, and 98 required no vote to authorize contracts. James J. Bambrick, Jr. and George H. Haas, *Handbook of Union Government Structure and Procedures,* New York: National Industrial Conference Board, 1955, pp. 47 and 51.

[6] Bambrick and Haas, *ibid.,* p. 77.

[7] To be sure, some union executive boards are almost completely dependent on the president of the union because members' salaries are not determined by the convention. And some executive boards have specific representatives who are elected by the entire membership and are therefore not completely dependent on the constituency they represent. But in most cases, union constitutions that specify sub-group representation on the executive board also make board members responsible to the constituency.

from the union to reaffiliate with another. Fixed expectations develop through time, and we would not expect to find them in young unions. The early stages of union development are usually marked by much bargaining and compromise among sub-groups. In what follows I shall use age of union as an indicator of fixed expectations, assuming that older unions have more rigid structures; older unions convene less frequently than younger unions.

Compared with homogeneous unions, unions with many sub-groups face problems of integration and coordination. If the sub-groups are powerful enough to demand consideration in union policy formulation, then the union structure must provide for it; when the convention does not function as a channel of influence, then alternative mechanisms must be established for sub-group representation. Shister reports that sub-groups within a union are sometimes represented and integrated at the executive board level.[8] My hypothesis was that unions with many sub-groups tend to cite in their constitutions the specific groups entitled to send delegates to their executive boards.

Method and Data Collection

Union constitutions were my basic source of data. A sourcebook compiled by Bambrick and Haas of the National Industrial Conference Board (NICB) contains verbatim copies or accurate abstracts of union constitutional provisions.[9] Of the 194 unions Bambrick and Haas included, I selected 185 for this study. Those omitted were: (1) subsidiaries of larger unions, e.g., the Airline Hostesses (a subsidiary of the Airline Pilots), and the Inland-Boatmen (a subsidiary of the Seafarers), etc.; (2) unions with collective bargaining agreements in only one state, e.g., the Texas unions, the New Jersey Telephone Operators, etc.; (3) unions included by Bambrick and Haas but which merged prior to 1955, e.g., the Diamond Workers who merged with the Jewelry Workers, the Fur and Leather Workers who merged with the Meat Cutters, etc. Data on union size, number of locals, and frequency of conventions were reported by the Bureau of Labor Statistics.[10] Of the 199 unions included in the BLS *Directory*, 14 were excluded, using the same criteria. Some very small and new unions, e.g., the Authors League of America, the Seattle Professional Engineering Employee Association were also omitted because data from the NICB study were not available. Although

[8] Joseph Shister, "Trade Union Government: A Formal Analysis," *Quarterly Journal of Economics,* 60 (November, 1945), p. 86.

[9] James J. Bambrick, Jr. and George H. Haas, *Sourcebook of Union Government, Structure and Procedures,* New York: National Industrial Conference Board, 1956.

[10] U.S. Department of Labor, Bureau of Labor Statistics, *Directory of National and International Labor Unions,* Washington, D.C.: U.S. Government Printing Office, Bulletin No. 1185, 1955.

these two sets of data were gathered at approximately the same time, 1953–1954, they are not from the same study and slight discrepancies exist, though not of a magnitude sufficient to affect the overall findings.[11]

A comment on union constitutions as data for sociological analysis is worth making. Durkheim long ago pointed out that some of the basic social facts he sought to uncover are in written law. Union constitutions are considered valid documents in law courts and judges have been known to uphold the letter of their application.[12] Actual practices may not coincide perfectly with specific provisions, of course, but union constitutions cannot be violated without severe internal repercussions. Recently, Lipset, one of the few sociologists who have ventured to explore the relations between law and union structure, stated:

> ...though legislation and juridically protected guarantees may seem relatively ineffective in enhancing the prospects for real union democracy, their importance should not be underestimated. The significance of a law does not necessarily lie in the extent to which it is obeyed: one of its major functions is to set a moral code or standard which society considers proper, but whose parts can be violated within certain limits.[13]

In this paper I shall examine union age, size, and number of locals, and the two measures of democratic influence—frequency of conventions, and whether the constitution provides for sub-group representation on the executive board. In addition, an index of union homogeneity was developed from eight items which were considered potential membership restrictions the union or its affiliates could employ. The eight restrictions were coded as either absent or present, and *every effort was made to maximize the union's potential restrictiveness.* For example, if a union allowed locals to determine whether to admit a given type of worker, this was coded as a restriction because it could be imposed without violating the union constitution. In other words, unless the constitution specifically barred a given restriction, that restriction was coded as present in the constitution.

The eight items included in the scale were:

1. A competency test required prior to admission.
2. Foremen and employers barred from admission.
3. Workers with certain political affiliations barred.
4. Non-American citizens barred.
5. Female workers barred.
6. Certain specified creeds barred.
7. Certain racial groups barred.
8. Union possesses an apprenticeship program.

[11] A more thorough discussion of the adequacy of these data is in Philip M. Marcus, "Trade Union Structure: A Study in Formal Organization," University of Chicago, unpublished doctoral dissertation, 1962, pp. 31–45.

[12] Shister, *op. cit.,* p. 79.

[13] Seymour M. Lipset, "The Law and Trade Union Democracy," *Virginia Law Review,* 47 (1961), p. 35.

These items fit a Guttman scale, yielding a Coefficient of Reproducibility of 0.98. The implied single dimension was termed "restrictiveness," and the scale will be referred to henceforth as the R-scale.[14] (The above listing of items is in scale order, i.e., unions that required competency tests also tended to be restrictive with respect to certain political affiliations, certain creeds, etc.)

The distribution of unions among the scale scores was uneven, and a number of categories were combined. Of the total 164 unions that could be scaled, 47 had all of the potential restrictions, 83 had all except the competency test (a score of 7), and 34 unions were distributed among the remaining scale scores.

The scale was validated to some degree by its strong relation to the traditional classification of craft and industrial unions (see Table 1). Using

Table 1. Union R-scale Scores by Craft-Industrial Classification

		TYPE OF UNION	
R-SCALE SCORE		CRAFT	INDUSTRIAL
		%	%
High	(8)	40	15
Medium	(7)	48	53
Low	(0–6)	12	32
Total		100	100
(N)		(88)	(72)

$\chi^2=14.91$, p<.001, df=2.

criteria set forth by Bambrick and Haas, unions were coded as either craft or non-craft. The latter category contained not only industrial unions, but "mixed unions" that admit both craft and semi-skilled workers, and unions with unrestricted jurisdiction.[15] Since the R-scale is based on more than the single job-classification criterion, it is potentially a stronger classificatory device. Modern technology has blurred job distinctions, and competitive jurisdictional disputes over the past 20 years have greatly altered the composition of membership in unions. The R-scale not only constitutes a more adequate measure of potential restrictions on admissions, but, if one accepts the assumption that unions with many potential (and possibly actual) restrictions are more homogeneous than unions that admit workers with diverse backgrounds, then the R-scale is also a better measure of sub-group existence than the traditional craft–industrial classification.

14 The R-scale could also be interpreted as an indicator of another dimension of union democracy, i.e., constitutional guarantees of admission without discrimination. The consequences of admission without discrimination, however, include greater diversity of membership characteristics, or heterogeneity.

15 The Teamsters are in this category.

Findings: The Union Convention

With the possible exception of the very small unions that hold general meetings for the entire membership, conventions are one of the most direct forms of expression available to the rank and file. Here delegates assemble to formulate policies and elect officials. Amid the formal business that occupies the time of most delegates, informal communication permits delegates from different locals to recognize common problems, and, frequently, to form voting coalitions that influence the policies and practices of top officials. In many unions, horizontal communication among locals is absent or inadequate. Should the members of a local be dissatisfied with some union policy, the national is usually in a position to pacify them. Without access to a union newspaper or other channels of internal communication, the local members might conclude that their problem is unique and national officials are not responsible. At the conventions, however, their delegates may find others ready to collaborate and oppose the incumbents.[16]

The frequency of union conventions can be considered a measure of the members' ability to express themselves to officials. When conventions are less frequent, incumbents have more time to solidify their position, while the rank and file have less opportunity to communicate horizontally or to express either approval or disapproval of union policies. But conventions cost both the union and the delegates a great deal of money.[17] Some unions pay the delegates' expenses, but in others, the locals themselves cover the costs and since very small locals are frequently unable to finance their delegates, these members are not represented at the convention. (Some unions have tried to cover the expenses of these small locals when they could not afford representation.)

The data in Table 2 show that frequency of union conventions is related to union size, i.e., the larger the union, the less frequently it convenes. Table 3 indicates that the frequency of conventions is also related to the number of locals in a union.[18] Absolute size, then, limits the frequency of

[16] The 1957 convention of the autocratic Teamsters Union was able to modify the union constitution and deprive the president of many of his powers (Sam Romer, *The International Brotherhood of Teamsters: Its Government and Structure*, New York: John Wiley, 1962, pp. 19 and 53). For a thorough discussion of union convention functions, see V. L. Allen, *Power in Trade Unions*, London: Longmans, Green, 1954, pp. 108–29; William M. Leiserson, *American Trade Union Democracy*, New York: Columbia University Press, 1959, pp. 178–221.

[17] As an extreme example, the 1960 convention of the Brotherhood of Railroad Trainmen had 1,122 delegates. BRT conventions frequently ran six or seven weeks and the cost was about two and a half million dollars. Joel I. Seidman, *The Brotherhood of Railroad Trainmen: The Internal Political Life of a National Union*, New York: John Wiley, 1962, p. 161. Teamsters' conventions tend to attract approximately 2,000 delegates and almost as many alternates and guests. Romer, *op. cit.*, p. 12.

[18] Union size and number of locals are closely related. Compared with unions of equal size but with fewer locals, unions with more locals show only a slight tendency to convene less frequently.

Table 2. Union Convention Frequency by Size of Union

	UNION SIZE			
CONVENTION FREQUENCY	UNDER 6,000	6,000– 28,999	29,000– 74,999	75,000 AND OVER
	%	%	%	%
Annually or more frequently	45	24	11	15
Biannually	41	49	50	35
Triannually or less frequently	14	27	39	50
Total	100	100	100	100
(N)	(29)	(45)	(36)	(48)

$\chi^2=19.64$, p<.005, df=6.

conventions. Smaller unions are more vulnerable to management aggression as well as to raids and competition from other unions and therefore may be reluctant to alienate members by limiting their influence at the upper echelons. Larger unions face high costs for conventions and may be forced to develop alternative techniques. State bodies, newspapers, and strategically placed organizers assist in managing the union, coordinating its locals, and mediating internal grievances against the top leadership. Smaller unions have neither the funds nor the personnel for these alternative mechanisms.

Larger unions with more locals may also be more complex organizations than their smaller counterparts; a larger number of members must be coordinated and disciplined to support strikes and prohibit wildcat actions. Coordination and discipline are usually effected through the locals. Their loyalty must be secured and their actions coordinated to enhance the na-

Table 3. Union Convention Frequency by Number of Locals

	NUMBER OF LOCALS			
CONVENTION FREQUENCY	1–48	49–166	167–472	473 OR MORE
	%	%	%	%
Annually or more frequently	44	23	16	12
Biannually	39	51	46	37
Triannually or less frequently	17	26	38	51
Total	100	100	100	100
(N)	(36)	(43)	(37)	(41)

$\chi^2=15.94$, p<.05, df=6.

tional organization's flexibility and power in negotiations with employers.[19] Annual conventions may very well provide too loose and informal a structure to accomplish these objectives efficiently. The power structure may shift too rapidly and lack the stability for policies to be tested and developed. Less frequent conventions might not satisfy the democratic norms but they might meet organizational demands for stability.

The age of the union is inversely related to the frequency of union conventions: older unions convene less frequently than younger unions (Table 4). I shall explore only a few of the several possible explanations for this finding here.

Table 4.   Convention Frequency by Year Union Formed

CONVENTION FREQUENCY	YEAR UNION FORMED		
	PRE-1900	1900–1929	1930 OR LATER
	%	%	%
Annually or more frequently	15	25	32
Biannually	26	48	54
Triannually or less frequently	59	27	14
Total	100	100	100
(N)	(65)	(40)	(63)

$\chi^2 = 36.13$, $p < .001$, $df = 4$.

When a union is first formed, a number of diverse small locals combine. Usually, they are unwilling to delegate much control to the central body. With time, however, a hierarchy tends to develop as coalitions are formed, as opposition becomes somewhat stifled and subdued, as greater mutual confidence is established, and as a shared body of expectations develops among the various segments. Sub-groups that remain very dissatisfied with the distribution of power will look for other alliances and possibly even affiliate with another union.

A second explanation for the relation between age and convention frequency may be that administrative knowledge is less adequate in younger unions than in older ones. When a union is first formed, its leaders may not know how to handle collective bargaining or what to expect of management or government representatives in the negotiations. Hence, information received from the rank and file becomes valuable data in their deliberations. Frequent conventions may be a necessity when the national officers lack both technical information and knowledge of member support. But as the union matures, as past negotiations form precedents, as proven strategies and tactics become part of the union's repertoire, frequent conventions be-

---

[19] A very obvious example of this occurs in the auto industry, where the UAW has traditionally used a tactic of striking one plant or company while other locals work. This provides an inducement for the struck company to yield on some matters while funds from the employed workers maintain the union treasury.

come less necessary. Other channels of communication and influence tend to develop, though determination of goals and formulation of new policies may still involve membership influence and support.

Another explanation is that older unions tend to be larger than those more recently formed and larger unions convene less frequently. But within the same size category older unions convene less frequently than younger ones (Table 5). The strength of the association, however, is considerably

Table 5. Convention Frequency by Union Size and Year of Formation

UNION SIZE

Convention Frequency	Under 29,000			29,000 or More		
	Pre-1900	1900–1929	1930+	Pre-1900	1900–1929	1930+
	%	%	%	%	%	%
Annually or more frequently	29	25	40	9	21	17
Biannually	42	50	43	21	50	75
Triannually or less frequently	29	25	17	70	29	8
Total	100	100	100	100	100	100
(N)	(17)	(24)	(30)	(46)	(14)	(24)

$\chi^2 = 2.14$, p>.05, df=4. $\chi^2 = 24.22$, p<.001, df=4.

reduced for the smaller unions. This suggests, among other things, that fixed expectations are less likely to develop in smaller unions.

Between the years 1944 and 1955 frequency of conventions declined somewhat among these unions generally (Table 6). Only 11 per cent of the unions that had been convening triannually in 1944 changed to biannual conventions by 1955, but of those unions convening annually or more often, 41 per cent decreased convention frequency to the biannual level.

Table 6. Convention Frequency in 1955 by Convention Frequency in 1944

1944 CONVENTION FREQUENCY

1955 Convention Frequency	Annually or More Frequently	Biannually	Triannually or Less Frequently
	%	%	%
Annually or more frequently	56	0	3
Biannually	41	76	11
Triannually or less frequently	3	24	86
Total	100	100	100
(N)	(39)	(46)	(36)

There was no relation between the frequency of union conventions and the R-scale.[20]

Membership influence in unions, as measured by frequency of conventions, is thus constrained by union size, number of locals, and the age of the union. I shall now consider an alternative channel of influence, representation on the executive board.

Findings: Union Executive Boards

Originally, the union executive board was created to check the activity of the president.[21] In the small unions of the 19th century, the president was usually the only full-time officer. Many of the small locals were unwilling to delegate unlimited power to a national president who frequently came from the largest local. The majority of members, widely dispersed in many small locals, demanded some representation as a price of affiliation, and this representation took the form of union executive boards. Many of these early executive boards convened infrequently, were seldom in continuous session, and usually met in times of crisis. As the amount of administrative work increased and union affairs became more complex, full-time executive boards became necessary. Sometimes salaries for the board members were drawn from operating expenses provided for the president; in other cases, unions specified salaries at conventions. Although one might expect boards whose salaries were fixed by conventions to be less dependent on the president and consequently more critical of his actions, at present no evidence indicates that either type of financing produces a board more responsive to the membership.[22]

Executive boards vary in size and composition. Some contain only officers; others are composed of union organizers, research directors, vice-presidents, and membership representatives. Neither union size nor the number of locals is associated with the size of the executive boards.

Executive boards were classified according to whether the constitution specified certain sub-groups to be represented on the board. Sub-groups granted this kind of representation are presumably stronger; they could threaten the national with non-compliance, or withdraw and reaffiliate with another union. Strong sub-groups can demand representation when policies are formulated, and the upper echelons would have to take their

[20] The R-scale was not related to union size or to the number of locals. Older unions, however, scored higher on the R-scale than younger unions, even when the craft–industrial typology was used as a control.

[21] One of the most useful books on the development of union organization is Lloyd Ulman, *The Rise of the National Trade Union,* Cambridge, Mass.: Harvard University Press, 1955. Interestingly, empirical analysis of union executive boards is almost absent from the literature. Perhaps the most useful works, besides Ulman's historical analysis, are Joel I. Seidman and Arlyn J. Melcher, "The General Executive Board in National Union Constitutions," *Labor Law Journal,* 8 (January, 1962), pp. 71–82 and, Bambrick and Haas, *op. cit.,* 1955, pp. 82–85.

[22] Bambrick and Haas, *ibid.,* p. 85.

demands into account. Weak sub-groups are more dependent on the national organization, and more compliant, because they lack these alternative courses of action.

Some union constitutions are very explicit about which sub-groups are to be represented on the executive boards. Most of these specified sub-groups are geographical, i.e., one member is to come from the West Coast, another from Canada, etc. But other unions specify along different dimensions, e.g., one member is to be a woman or should represent some specific trade within the jurisdiction of the union. Such provisions increase sub-group influence at the higher echelons, but they may also give the national officers more control over the sub-groups because they can be reached through their own representatives. The *total amount of influence* within a union is increased by these exchanges because they bring about greater mutual influence between the national officers and the membership.[23]

Frequency of union conventions is positively related to specification of sub-group representation on executive boards (Table 7). Convention frequency is limited by structural factors, however, so that this relationship will not necessarily hold in the future if unions continue to increase in

Table 7. Executive Boards with Sub-Group Representation Specified by Convention Frequency

Sub-Group Representation on Executive Boards	CONVENTION FREQUENCY		
	Annually or More Frequently	Biannually	Triannually or Less Frequently
	%	%	%
Specified	62	43	36
Unspecified	38	57	64
Total	100	100	100
(N)	(37)	(60)	(56)

$\chi^2 = 6.36$, p<.05, df=2.

[23] Only a few social scientists have begun to consider influence or power as a non-fixed entity. Talcott Parsons does so quite explicitly in "On the Concept of Influence," *Public Opinion Quarterly*, 27 (Spring, 1963), pp. 59–62, and "On the Concept of Political Power," *Proceedings of the American Philosophical Society*, 107 (June, 1963), pp. 232–62. David Riesman implicitly makes a similar assumption in his analysis of the American power structure, "Who Has The Power?," in Reinhard Bendix and Seymour M. Lipset (eds.), *Class, Status and Power*, Glencoe, Ill.: The Free Press, 1953, pp. 154–62. Total control as a variable has been studied empirically by Tannenbaum and his associates. For example, see Arnold S. Tannenbaum and Robert L. Kahn, "Organizational Control Structure," *Human Relations*, 10 (1957), pp. 127–40. For a critique of the non-fixed theory of power, see Ralf Dahrendorf, *Class and Class Conflict in Industrial Society*, Stanford: Stanford University Press, 1959, pp. 157–240.

size. But the strength of this relationship does suggest that these two variables tap a basic dimension of membership influence.

Sub-group representation on the executive boards was not related to either the size of the union or the number of locals. Table 8 shows, how-

Table 8. Executive Boards with Sub-Group Representation
Specified by Average Size of Local

SUB-GROUP REPRESENTATION ON EXECUTIVE BOARDS	AVERAGE SIZE OF LOCALS			
	0–74	75–169	170–369	370+
	%	%	%	%
Specified	32	38	69	46
Unspecified	68	62	31	54
Total	100	100	100	100
(N)	(34)	(37)	(35)	(39)

$\chi^2=10.65$, p<.05, df=3.

ever, that the average size of the union local is related to the composition of the executive board. Unions with larger locals are more likely to specify sub-group representation on their executive boards. Although this relationship is weak, and not linear,[24] it suggests that independent sources of strength in a union affect the amount of influence sub-groups exert over policy formulation and practices. Generally, larger locals tend to be more independent;[25] they have more adequate funds for support should the national union not approve a strike, and with sufficient funds to employ their own experts they need not depend on the national for these services. When larger locals negotiate separately with management, an entire union walkout may be threatened. Some locals are so large that their withdrawal would deprive a union of a large fraction of its membership as well as its income. For example, 10 per cent of the approximately 100,000 members of the International Typographers Union belong to the New York local, and of the 630,000 members of the International Brotherhood of Electrical Workers, slightly less than 5 per cent are in Local 3. No national can afford to ignore such large locals.

Faunce found that, at UAW conventions, delegates from larger locals tended to oppose incumbent officials more frequently than did those from smaller locals. Further interviews with delegates revealed that those from larger locals were also more concerned about the interests and representa-

24 Additional analysis of these data did not produce any explanation of this curvilinear relationship.

25 Seymour M. Lipset, Martin A. Trow, and James S. Coleman, *Union Democracy,* Glencoe, Ill.: The Free Press, 1957, pp. 364–90; Joel I. Seidman, *op. cit.,* 1958, p. 33.

tion their constituents received.[26] In larger locals, officials gain more experience in handling administrative problems and more training for potential leadership positions; they therefore feel better equipped to oppose national incumbents.

The data in Table 9 indicate that unions with low R-scale scores tend to have executive boards with specified sub-group representation, that is,

Table 9.   Executive Boards with Sub-Group Representation
Specified by R-Scale

SUB-GROUP REPRESENTATION ON EXECUTIVE BOARDS	R-SCALE SCORE		
	HIGH (8)	MEDIUM (7)	LOW (0–6)
	%	%	%
Specified	48	36	71
Unspecified	52	64	29
Total	100	100	100
(N)	(46)	(80)	(34)

$\chi^2=11.40$, p<.005, df=2.

unions that had the fewest restrictions on membership admissions are most likely to specify the sub-groups to be given access to the policy-making board. Of course, the groups admitted to the union are not necessarily the same as those represented on the boards. No union could see that all diverse groups were represented. This finding does suggest, however, that smaller sub-groups—ethnic, occupational, regional, etc.—can form coalitions on the basis of shared interests and be represented at the higher level. The less restrictive unions are, presumably, relatively heterogeneous; in the more homogeneous unions, officials elected at large should be better able to represent the entire membership.[27]

Conclusions

I have explored alternative channels of influence between national union leaders and rank-and-file members. As a union grows larger, direct expres-

26 William A. Faunce, "Size of Locals and Union Democracy," *American Journal of Sociology,* 68 (November, 1962), pp. 291–98.

27 Unions with smaller locals score higher on the R-scale. Pressure for more rigid selection of members comes from these unions rather than unions with larger locals. Since a small membership means that each person has a very limited group from which he can choose his social contacts, admission criteria may be used to prevent association with people defined as undesirable. In a large local, members can admit many different types of people because each person can make friends within a sub-group; i.e., the possibilities for voluntaristic friendship choices increase in large locals. Lipset, Trow and Coleman, *op. cit.,* p. 162.

sion of membership influence tends to be increasingly constrained. Some traditional channels of influence become blocked or are even deliberately subverted by leaders who wish to remain in power. The general meeting becomes impractical, and responsibility and authority are delegated to representatives who convene at regular intervals. Mastery of the convention now becomes the arena for control of the union.[28]

Frequency of conventions is limited by the size and structure of the union. Large unions, those with many locals, and older unions tend to convene less frequently. When conventions decrease in frequency, rank-and-file influence on national leaders will also decrease if an alternative channel is not established. The union executive board is just such an alternative and it is independent of the size of the union or the number of locals. The national executive board can provide the national leadership with information from the rank and file; representatives can compensate, to some extent, for the decreased membership control at the higher levels; and the national leaders may be influenced to modify some of their policies or face the consequences of alienating rank-and-file support. National leaders who do not accurately estimate rank-and-file support, through either conventions or executive boards, may easily overestimate their strength and formulate policies that the membership will not accept.

Estimating rank-and-file support is more difficult for leaders of unions with a heterogeneous membership than it is in the relatively homogeneous unions. Unions that are relatively less restrictive on admissions, and hence may be assumed to be more heterogeneous, are more likely to have constitutions that specify sub-group representation on the executive board.

The Iron Law is essentially an evolutionary concept: voluntary organizations are viewed as developing toward oligarchical structures. In this paper, I have tried to show that although certain conditions do diminish membership control, others actually increase rank-and-file influence over leaders. Too often, as Gouldner has said, we focus on the more negative aspects of organizational structure and neglect alternative developments that promote democracy.[29]

---

[28] Bromwich feels that union presidents have almost complete control over conventions. He reports that presidents select and control committees, that delegate strength is too widely diffused for effective protection of rank-and-file interests, etc. See Leo Bromwich, *Union Constitutions,* New York: The Fund for the Republic, 1959, pp. 9–15.

[29] Alvin W. Gouldner, "Metaphysical Pathos and the Theory of Bureaucracy," in Amitai Etzioni (ed.), *Complex Organizations: A Sociological Reader,* New York: Holt, Rinehart and Winston, 1961, pp. 71–82.

21 / Size of Local and Union Democracy[1]

William A. Faunce

Introduction

THE SIZE OF an organization has an important bearing upon the nature of its control structure. Both the necessity for formal mechanisms of control and the character of authority relations within an organization are affected by its size. This paper is concerned with the relationship between local union size and the internal political structure of a trade union. Because local unions are in some measure autonomous political units, union government may be studied at either the local or the national union level. Data regarding political processes at both levels were collected in this study. The data permit analysis of the contribution of larger and smaller locals to democratic control of the national union as well as analysis of the extent of democracy within locals of varying size.

There is some agreement among students of union government that small locals tend to be more democratic internally than large locals but contribute less to democratic processes at the national union level. Large locals are seen as a force for democracy in the national union primarily because they are less dependent upon the national office and therefore in a better position to express opposition to it. Organized party conflict, which is more likely to occur in large than in small locals, may produce pressures that also result in more active opposition to policies of the national officers. It has also been suggested that members of small locals are less likely to be exposed to, and are less well informed about, opposing views on political issues at the national union level.[2]

The proposition that large locals are less democratic internally than small locals is based primarily upon their lower rate of rank-and-file participation

---

[1] I am indebted to Professors Jack Stieber and William H. Form, Michigan State University, and to Professor George Y. M. Won, University of Hawaii, who worked with me on this project.

[2] Cf. Joel Seidman, *Democracy in the Labor Movement* (Bulletin 39, February, 1958 [Ithaca, N.Y.: New York State School of Industrial and Labor Relations, Cornell University, 1958]), pp. 19–36; Seymour Martin Lipset, Martin Trow, and James Coleman, *Union Democracy* (Glencoe, Ill.: Free Press, 1956), pp. 364–90.

Reprinted by permission of the author and publisher from *The American Journal of Sociology,* Vol. 68, No. 3 (November 1962), pp. 291–98. © 1962 by the University of Chicago. All rights reserved.

in union politics and lower rate of turnover of officers.[3] According to this view, officers of large locals are more likely to use undemocratic means to stay in office because the rewards of office are much greater. Their success in subverting democratic procedures results from greater control of means of communication, a more complete monopoly of political skills, and less rank-and-file concern with union affairs. Seidman summarizes this point of view as follows:

> Conditions are most favorable for the development of local union democracy in a small organization, of several hundred at the most, all of whose members are employed in a single plant. There the members are likely to be in daily contact with each other and also with their officers. Typically, they work side by side because the organization neither needs nor can it afford the services of a full-time official. In these circumstances the union officer can have no greater income, not much more prestige, and little more power than the rank-and-file membership. The factory worker is hired by management and, assuming proper conduct on his part, his job lasts for a relatively long period of time so he enjoys a reasonable degree of economic security. As a union member he has little reason to be fearful of his union official or dependent upon him. The officer, in turn, has little reason to seek to perpetuate his stay in office by undemocratic means and little opportunity to accomplish that objective should he have the desire. The rewards of offices of this type are meagre, the annoyances many, and relatively few wish to perpetuate themselves in office. Contests for this type of office are frequent and turnover is high.[4]

The results of the study reported in this paper support the view that large locals contribute more to democracy in the national union. They cast some doubt, however, upon the assertion that small locals are more democratic than large locals and raise some questions regarding the meaning of democracy under the conditions described above by Seidman.

Research Design

Data bearing on the relationship between local size and union democracy were collected from two sources. The first was a study conducted at the Seventeenth Constitutional Convention of the United Auto Workers in 1959. A questionnaire was distributed to all delegates in attendance on the second day of this convention. Although not all the delegates were present

---

[3] Cf. Seidman, *op. cit.*; Lipset *et al., op. cit.*, pp. 14, 78; George Strauss, "Control by the Membership in Building Trades Unions," *American Journal of Sociology*, LXI (1955–56), 527 ff.; Joel Seidman, Jack London, Bernard Karsh, and Daisy L. Tagliacozzo, *The Worker Views His Union* (Chicago: University of Chicago Press, 1958), pp. 185–219; Leonard R. Sayles and George Strauss, *The Local Union* (New York: Harper & Bros., 1953), pp. 238–58; Arnold S. Tannenbaum and Robert L. Kahn, *Participation in Local Unions* (Evanston, Ill.: Row, Peterson & Co., 1958).

[4] Seidman, *op. cit.*, p. 33.

at these sessions, completed questionnaires were obtained from 1,815 delegates representing 753 UAW locals. Approximately three-fourths of all delegates who attended the convention are included in our sample. The various geographic regions of the UAW, locals of various sizes, and cities of various sizes are represented in almost exactly the same proportion among our respondents as in the total delegate population.

Questions dealing with delegate attitudes toward the convention, delegate election procedures, and general background characteristics of delegates were included in the questionnaire. The number of votes allotted each local at the convention was used as the basis for classifying locals according to size.

After the convention, an intensive followup study of delegates from locals in Lansing and Flint, Michigan, was conducted: 108 of the 112 delegates from these two cities were interviewed. The emphasis in this study was upon varying orientations to the delegate role. Information was also collected regarding the delegates' experience at the convention, their experience upon reporting back to their locals, the general level and nature of political activity within each local, and opinions regarding the extent of democratic control of the convention and of the policy-making process generally at the national and local union levels. While it cannot be assumed that the Lansing and Flint locals are representative of all locals within the UAW, there is no apparent reason to assume that differences observed between large and small locals in these two cities would not be found elsewhere. The limitations of the sample should be kept in mind, however, in interpreting findings from this study.[5]

Findings

The focus of these two studies upon a constitutional convention provided an opportunity to study the relationship between local size and local contributions to democratic policy-making processes at the national union level. In principle, at least, the convention has primary responsibility for determining UAW policies. The national officers and executive board are elected by the delegates and presumably operate within a broad policy framework established by the convention. Observation of the convention in operation and data collected from the delegates suggest that the 1959 UAW Convention functioned democratically in the sense that important issues were brought before it, were thoroughly debated with opposing views freely expressed, and were resolved in favor of the majority view. The extent to which delegates from larger and smaller locals participate in this process is one index of their respective contributions to democratic union government.

5 For reports of other findings from these studies see William A. Faunce, "Delegate Attitudes toward the Convention in the UAW," *Industrial and Labor Relations Review*, XV (1962), 463–73; George Y. M. Won, "Democratic Sentiments in Unionism: A Case Study of the UAW Convention" (unpublished doctoral dissertation, Michigan State University, 1962); and Jack Stieber, *Democracy in the UAW* (New York: John Wiley & Sons, 1962).

While there are many informal channels of communication between UAW locals and the national office, the convention is the only *formal* structure in the UAW through which local views on general policy issues are expressed. One way in which these views may be presented is in the form of resolutions submitted to the convention. Resolutions are sent to the national office at least three weeks before the convention begins and may be considered by the convention whether or not the locals submitting them are represented at the convention. Table 1 indicates that resolutions are submitted almost exclusively by the larger UAW locals.

Table 1. Percentage of Resolutions Submitted to 1959 UAW Convention and of Locals Not Sending Delegates to Convention, by Size of Locals*

SIZE OF LOCAL	NO. ($N = 1,239$)	PER CENT	PERCENTAGE OF RESOLUTIONS SUBMITTED ($N = 339$)	PERCENTAGE OF LOCALS NOT SENDING DELEGATES
149 or fewer members	443	35.7	1.5	51.7
150–1,049	535	43.2	6.8	17.9
1,050–1,549	59	4.7	1.5	5.1
1,550–4,049	145	11.7	44.2	4.1
4,050 or more	57	4.8	46.0	0.0

* Because number of votes at the convention was used as the basis for classifying locals according to size, the intervals in this table and subsequent tables reflect the formula used in the UAW for distributing votes among locals. Locals are allotted one vote for the first hundred or fewer members and an additional vote for each additional hundred members or major fraction thereof.

Whether or not they initiate policy issues, small locals may have their views represented at the convention if their delegates participate in debate on issues with which they are concerned. Data in Table 1 indicate, however, that smaller locals are less likely to even send a delegation to the convention.[6] If it can be assumed that small locals have some common interests that are different from those of large locals, at least these interests may be served to the extent that they are actively pursued by delegates from those small locals that are represented. Data from both the questionnaire and interview studies suggest, however, that the size of the local the delegate represents affects his views of the purpose for the convention, his definition of the delegate role, and, consequently, the nature of his participation in the convention proceedings.

The delegates at the convention were asked to rank various purposes for the convention in order of their importance. Table 2 indicates that delegates from large locals are significantly more likely to regard the primary function of the convention as the determination of UAW policy. Among the 125 delegates from the smallest locals in our sample, 27.7 per cent indicated that

[6] Small locals are also underrepresented at conventions of the International Typographical Union (cf. Lipset *et al., op. cit.,* p. 370).

Table 2. Function Attributed to Convention by
Delegates from Large and Small Locals

LOCAL SIZE	FUNCTION OF CONVENTION*	
	Policy-making	*All Others*
1,049 or fewer members	290	329
1,050 or more members	609	478

*$\chi^2=13.33$; P<.001.

the convention's primary purpose was "to make sure that members back home are informed about UAW policies." Only 18.6 per cent of the 501 delegates from the largest locals gave this response. The desire to simply keep the membership informed, or in fact any view of the convention that excludes policy-making as its most important function, is unlikely to serve as a motive for active participation in the business of the convention.

Data from the Flint and Lansing interviews also suggest that there is a difference between delegates from large and small locals in their conception of the delegate role. The UAW constitution specifies that convention delegates are not bound by local instructions on any issue they may vote on at the convention. There are variations, however, in the extent to which delegates feel a personal commitment to act in accord with the wishes of their constituents. Delegates from small locals are, first of all, less likely to have even received any instructions regarding local preferences on issues to be considered by the convention. Of the twenty delegates from locals having 2,300 or fewer members, almost three-fourths indicated they had not received any instructions prior to the convention while only a little over one-third of the eighty-eight delegates from larger locals indicated that this was the case. Among delegates who were instructed how to vote on any issue, half of those from the smaller locals but over two-thirds from the larger locals indicated that they felt bound by these instructions when they went to the convention. Most of this difference is accounted for by the responses of the forty-seven delegates from the two largest locals in our sample, 81.5 per cent of whom felt that they should vote as instructed. When asked how they had actually voted at the convention, 66.7 per cent of delegates from the smaller locals and 87.2 per cent of those from larger locals answered that they had voted in accord with what a majority of the local membership wanted.

A much higher proportion of delegates from large locals indicated that important issues should be decided by a referendum rather than by the convention. This may be interpreted as another indication of greater concern on the part of these delegates with rank-and-file views. In this instance, however, it may also reflect a greater willingness to oppose the administration of the national union. Use of the referendum became an issue during debate on a proposed dues increase. The International Executive Board, which favored the dues increase, argued that the issue should be decided by the convention. Almost two-thirds of the forty-seven delegates from the largest locals in our sample indicated that "important issues like the dues increase should be decided by a referendum." A considerable majority of delegates from smaller locals supported the International Executive Board's position.

There is other evidence that delegates from large locals are more willing to oppose national officers. The Flint-Lansing delegates were asked which caucuses, if any, they attended at the convention. The few delegates who reported attending an anti-administration caucus were exclusively from large locals. They were also asked whether they felt that the national officers had a right to expect them to support proposals they favored. Well over half the delegates from the largest locals indicated that the officers had no right to expect delegates to vote the way they wanted them to while only a third of the delegates from the smallest locals reported this view. When asked about the legitimacy of rank-and-file expectations, half the small local delegates indicated that their constituents had "every right" to expect them to vote for proposals they favored. This view was reported by more than three-fourths of the delegates from the largest locals. Responses to questions dealing with the kinds of pressures the national officers might use during a convention to get support for resolutions they favored suggest that delegates from large locals are more aware of the existence of such pressures but less concerned with them. Their awareness of these pressures may result from greater political sophistication while their lack of concern may reflect the greater autonomy of large locals.[7]

Delegates from small locals who are less likely to regard policy-making as the purpose of the convention, who are less concerned with representing rank-and-file views in this process, and who are more willing to simply accept the International Executive Board's program could be expected to be less active at the convention. There is some evidence that this is the case. Of delegates from Flint and Lansing locals with 2,300 or fewer members, only 16.7 per cent reported having addressed a general session of the convention while 25.8 per cent of those from larger locals reported having done so. Delegates from small locals also appear to be less active in convention politics. Over half these delegates reported that they had not attended any caucuses at the convention while two-thirds of those from large locals indicated that they had attended at least one caucus.

The findings from these two studies appear to be consistent with the position that large locals contribute more to democratic processes at the national union level. We will turn now to analysis of political processes at the local level. If we rely solely upon the customary indexes of union democracy, rates of rank-and-file participation and turnover of leadership, our data would support the hypothesis that small locals are more democratic internally than large locals. The delegates at the convention were asked to estimate the percentage of the membership of their unit or local voting in

---

[7] Difference in size of locals is likely to have a greater effect upon local autonomy in industrial unions like the UAW than in most craft unions where fewer decisions are made at the international level.

Table 3. Percentage of Membership Voting in Delegate Elections
in Locals of Varying Size

PERCENTAGE OF LOCALS*

MEMBERSHIP VOTING (PER CENT)	149 or Fewer Members (N = 143)	150–1,049 (N = 320)	1,050–1,549 (N = 51)	1,550–4,049 (N = 132)	4,050 or More Members (N = 55)
0–25	19.6	23.5	29.4	32.6	41.8
26–50	23.1	30.0	31.4	31.8	27.3
51–75	26.6	24.4	13.7	25.8	23.6
76–100	30.8	22.2	25.5	9.8	7.3
Total	100.1	100.1	100.0	100.0	100.0

* Totals may not add to 100 due to rounding.

the delegate elections for the 1959 convention. Table 3 shows a strong
relationship between local size and rank-and-file participation in the elections with the greatest participation occurring in the smallest locals.[8] Data
from the followup interviews indicate that small locals may have better
attendance at local meetings as well as a higher proportion voting in elections. Almost two-thirds of the delegates from small locals reported attending all local meetings while less than one-third of those from large locals
reported doing so. Both studies also suggest more frequent turnover of
leadership at least in the delegate role in small locals. Data from the questionnaire study indicate that 57.4 per cent of the 125 delegates from the
smallest locals and 40.2 per cent of the 501 from the largest locals were
attending their first convention.

Rank-and-file participation in union politics and turnover of leaders are
used as indexes of democracy under the assumption that they produce
leadership that is more responsive to the wishes of a majority of the members. For this assumption to hold, it is necessary that elections involve a
choice of candidates. The data in Table 4 show that there is a much higher
proportion of *uncontested* elections in small locals. In addition, if it is the
election process that is responsible for turnover in the delegate position, we
would expect that there would be delegates at the convention who had previously run for this position and lost. The relationship between this variable
and local size is clearly shown by the data in Table 4.

These findings plus the fact that delegates from small locals are less

[8] Because the questionnaires were completed independently, the extent of
agreement among the estimates of delegates from the same local provides some
indication of the accuracy of these estimates. The mean deviation among estimates
in each local and the average mean deviation in all locals were computed. Since
there is a limited range of possible estimates, the maximum possible deviation could
also be computed. The average observed deviation for all locals was less than 9 percent of this maximum.

Table 4. Locals with Uncontested Elections and Delegates Who
Had Run for Election Previously and Lost, by Size of Local

SIZE OF LOCAL	LOCALS IN WHICH ELECTIONS WERE UNCONTESTED		DELEGATES HAVING PREVIOUSLY RUN AND LOST	
	No.	*Per Cent*	*No.*	*Per Cent*
149 or fewer members	143	35.0	154	9.1
150–1,049	311	21.2	484	18.6
1,050–1,549	52	3.8	139	21.7
1,550–4,049	131	3.8	495	27.1
4,050 or more	54	3.7	500	29.0

likely to regard the convention as having a policy-making function suggest
that the delegate selection process in these locals may involve something
other than a choice among candidates advocating differing positions on
policy matters. While we do not have data bearing directly upon this interpretation of these findings, it is possible that turnover in the delegate position in some small locals simply reflects the distribution of an honorific title
(and a trip to Atlantic City) among a local elite. Turnover of leadership
may have a different meaning and greater relevance to democratic decision-
making processes in large UAW locals where there is more likely to be an
active, internal political structure with an organized party system.[9]

Differences in the internal political climate of large and small locals are
clearly in evidence in the Flint and Lansing locals. Political party systems
exist in virtually all locals with 4,000 or more members but in only one-
third of the locals with 750 or fewer members. Even where there is a
party system in smaller locals there are less likely to be separate slates of
candidates run at elections than in large locals. Delegates from small locals
also report that the opposition party is less active between elections, that the
same groups do not oppose each other at all elections, and that there are
less likely to be recognized leaders of the opposition party. These findings
suggest that whatever factionalism exists in small locals is less likely to be
institutionalized. A much higher proportion of delegates from large locals
report that there is some tie-in between their local parties and parties from
other locals or factions in the national union. These relationships may be
a source of strength for opposition parties within large locals and may also
strengthen their position should they decide to oppose some policy of the
national officers.

[9] The differences in internal political activity between large and small UAW
locals are somewhat similar to those found between large and small shops in the
ITU. See Lipset *et al.* (*op. cit.*, pp. 150–97), who also report a curvilinear relationship in which the highest level of political involvement occurs in medium-sized
shops employing between one hundred and two hundred ITU members. Our data
do not show a pattern of this sort although it is possible that it is obscured by the
greater size of political units in the UAW and by differences in the measures of
political activity used in the two studies.

Rank-and-file participation in elections and turnover of elected leaders may have no relevance at all to union democracy if elections and other formal procedures are not important aspects of the control structure of the union. If policies are formulated and leaders selected as a result of informal social relationships on the job, the formal structure of control may serve only to legitimate these decisions.[10] The number of uncontested elections and the absence of a formal party system suggest that this may be the case in small UAW locals. There is some additional evidence that supports this position more directly. The Flint-Lansing delegates were asked whether or not they would be affected in any way if a majority of their constituents were dissatisfied with decisions made at the convention. Over three-fourths of the twenty delegates from locals with twenty-three hundred or fewer members reported that they would not be affected in any way. Less than half of the eighty-eight delegates from larger locals gave this response. Among those indicating that they would be affected, there is a difference by size of local in the type of anticipated response of the membership. The delegates were asked in what ways they would be affected by unfavorable reactions to convention decisions. Their responses were classified as either formal controls, like being voted out of office, or informal controls, such as those involved in interpersonal relationships in the plant. The delegates from small locals were concerned almost exclusively with informal controls while a majority of those from large locals were concerned with the possibility of not being re-elected. There is some related evidence from the responses to a question that asked for a definition of union democracy. Delegates from large locals were much more likely to include formal structural guarantees of democracy like free elections in their definitions while small local delegates were more concerned with certain individual rights like freedom of speech. One reason for the greater concern among delegates from large locals with the election process and with formal accountability to their constituents may be the fact that they are more interested in maintaining the positions that they occupy in their locals. Almost two-thirds of the delegates from large locals and less than half of those from small locals reported that keeping the office they hold in the local is very important to them. If the election process is to contribute toward making leaders more responsive to their constituents, it would appear that their responsiveness would have to be motivated by desire for re-election. The data reported above suggest that this motive is more likely to be found in large than in small UAW locals.

Summary and Conclusions

Data collected from delegates to the 1959 Constitutional Convention of the UAW suggest that small locals contribute less than large locals to democratic policy-making processes at the national union level. Small locals are less likely to be represented at the convention, they infrequently initiate pro-

[10] For an excellent discussion of this process see Joseph Kovner and Herbert J. Lahne, "Shop Society and the Union," *Industrial and Labor Relations Review,* VII (1953), 3–14.

posals on policy matters, and their delegates are less actively involved in the convention proceedings. A possible explanation for these differences is that delegates from small locals are less likely to regard the convention as having a policy-making function, are less concerned with representing rank-and-file views at the convention, and appear to be more willing to simply accept the position of the UAW International Executive Board on policy issues.

The data regarding political processes within local unions suggest that rates of rank-and-file participation and leadership turnover may not be appropriate indexes of democracy in small political units. The small locals in our sample had a higher proportion of members voting in elections and more frequent turnover in the delegate position. These locals, however, also had fewer elections that were contested and were less likely to have an active opposition party to represent minority views on local issues. In addition delegates from small locals appeared to be less responsive to rank-and-file wishes and less concerned with accounting to their constituents for actions at the convention. In general, the data suggest that formal control structures have a different and perhaps less important function in small local unions.

These findings have a number of implications for studies of union democracy. First, definitions of democracy are often phrased in terms of formal structural characteristics. Lipset, Trow, and Coleman, for example, define union democracy as "the possibility that an official can be defeated for re-election."[11] There is a variety of structural forms that may contribute to achieving democratic objectives. Indexes of democracy that measure the existence of particular structural forms may or may not be measures of the achievement of these objectives. Further analysis is needed of the variables that determine the effectiveness of different structural arrangements in achieving and sustaining union democracy.

Our data suggest that organizational size is one of these variables. An understanding of democratic processes in large local and national unions requires analysis of formal policy-making and policy-implementing procedures. When indexes of democracy based upon these procedures are applied to small local unions, they generally indicate that small locals operate more democratically than large locals. High rates of participation in elections and at meetings in small locals may, however, be accounted for by the nature of interpersonal relations in these locals and may have little or no bearing upon the policy-making process. Turnover of elected officials may reflect only the desire of the local elite to distribute onerous duties or to share more rewarding ones like attendance at a convention. If, as Seidman and others have suggested, officials of small locals do not wish to perpetuate themselves in office, at least one motive for responsiveness to majority views is eliminated.

More frequent interaction between officers and rank-and-file members in small locals may help to keep local policies consistent with majority views.

---

11 Lipset *et al., op. cit.,* p. 404.

Frequent interaction is not in itself, however, a guaranty that this will be the case, and primary group relationships in small locals may generate coercive pressures that prevent those with minority views from voicing their opposition.

Among the primary objectives of a democratic form of government is an orderly resolution of conflict of interest in which majority views prevail but in which the right of the minority to oppose these views is protected. Analysis of the structure of informal, interpersonal relations may contribute more than formal structural analyses to our understanding of the way in which these objectives may be achieved in small local unions.

6 / Human Relations in Industry: Will Participative Management Really Work?

The human relations movement emerged as a reaction to earlier managerial philosophies which sought to secure high employee morale, compliance, and performance without making any concessions to the mature side of the human personality. According to Argyris,[1] with whom most theorists of the human relations school would concur, mature adults strive for self-determination, self-initiative, independence, responsibility, self-integrity, and self-actualization. Bureaucratic organization, based on functional specialization, strict hierarchy of authority, and close supervision, is an environment inimical to the needs of the mature human personality. Work in a bureaucratic organization permits little individual control over job activities, provides minimal outlet for creative abilities, and encourages employee passiveness, dependence, and submissiveness. And while people are being abused, the

[1] Chris Argyris, *Personality and Organization* (New York: Harper and Row, 1957), and *Integrating the Individual and the Organization* (New York: John Wiley and Sons, Inc., 1964).

organization itself suffers from employee apathy, which results in poor organizational functioning as mirrored in turnover, absenteeism, quota restriction, and malingering. However, a more suitable organizational environment can be created through employee participation, which permits the flowering of the mature personality and contributes to the achievement of organizational goals.

An early and still active proponent of participative management, Rensis Likert, summarizes a theoretical approach to employee participation in "An Integrating Principle and an Overview." According to Likert, high-producing managers employ some ideas from classical management theory, but unlike their low-producing counterparts, they fashion their work units into "highly coordinated, highly motivated, cooperative social systems." Likert enunciates the "principle of supportive relationships," the general principle which he contends high-producing managers are using. He sketches the crucial role of the work group in his theory of management in the last part of his selection.

In contrast to Likert, Robert McMurry ("The Case for Benevolent Autocracy") believes human nature is incompatible with democratic, participative, or "bottom-up" managerial philosophies. According to McMurry, democratic management is not an unworthy goal, but it simply will not work because many employees lack the desire and ability to make contributions, shun responsibility, avoid self-direction, prefer regimentation, and constantly seek safety and security. Since participative management is at odds with human nature and is impractical for other reasons as well, McMurry proposes "benevolent autocracy" as a more realistic managerial philosophy.

A counter-position is reflected in Arnold Tannenbaum's "Control in Organizations: Individual Adjustment and Organizational Performance," which summarizes some research suggesting that man prefers to exercise power at work rather than to be controlled from above. Furthermore, asserts Tannenbaum, the opportunity to exercise control on the job contributes to employee job satisfaction, ego involvement in work, and identification with and loyalty to the organization, as well as to organizational effectiveness. Tannenbaum's selection contradicts the fixed-quantity conception of power, amplifying the idea that increasing control at one organizational level does not necessarily diminish control at other levels. The total amount of control is simply increased. Therefore, the degree of control can be enlarged at the nonsupervisory employee level without decreasing the extent of influence at supervisory and managerial levels. Tannenbaum cites some empirical evidence to support this proposition.

The final selection consists of excerpts, particularly the conclusions, drawn from a much longer piece by Robert Dubin entitled "Supervision and Productivity: Empirical Findings and Theoretical Considerations." In the longer essay Dubin reviews empirical studies on the influence of supervision on productivity. Dubin's most general conclusion is that there exists no one best style of supervision. The most successful supervisory style is one adapted to a particular organization and to its internal and external environment. Supervisory style is conditioned by technology, culture, and employee capabilities.

22 / An Integrating Principle And an Overview

Rensis Likert

THE MANAGERS WHOSE performance is impressive appear to be fashioning a better system of management....[Earlier] two generalizations were stated based on the available research findings:

- The supervisors and managers in American industry and government who are achieving the highest productivity, lowest costs, least turnover and absence, and the highest levels of employee motivation and satisfaction display, on the average, a different pattern of leadership from those managers who are achieving less impressive results. The principles and practices of these high-producing managers are deviating in important ways from those called for by present-day management theories.
- The high-producing managers whose deviations from existing theory and practice are creating improved procedures have not yet integrated their deviant principles into a theory of management. Individually, they are often clearly aware of how a particular practice of theirs differs from generally accepted methods, but the magnitude, importance, and systematic nature of the differences when the total pattern is examined do not appear to be recognized.

Based upon the principles and practices of the managers who are achieving the best results, a newer theory of organization and management can be stated. An attempt will be made...to present briefly some of the over-all characteristics of such a theory and to formulate a general integrating principle which can be useful in attempts to apply it....

Research findings indicate that the general pattern of operations of the highest-producing managers tends to differ from that of the managers of mediocre and low-producing units by more often showing the following characteristics:

- A preponderance of favorable attitudes on the part of each member of the organization toward all the other members, toward superiors, toward the work, toward the organization—toward all aspects of the job. These favorable attitudes toward others reflect a high level of mutual confidence and trust throughout the organization. The favorable attitudes toward the organization and the work are not those of easy complacency, but are the attitudes of identification with the organization and its objectives and a

---

Reprinted by permission of the author and publisher from *New Patterns of Management* (New York: McGraw-Hill Book Company, Inc., 1961), pp. 97–106.

high sense of involvement in achieving them. As a consequence, the performance goals are high and dissatisfaction may occur whenever achievement falls short of the goals set.

- This highly motivated, cooperative orientation toward the organization and its objectives is achieved by harnessing effectively all the major motivational forces which can exercise significant influence in an organizational setting and which, potentially, can be accompanied by cooperative and favorable attitudes. Reliance is not placed solely or fundamentally on the economic motive of buying a man's time and using control and authority as the organizing and coordinating principle of the organization. On the contrary, the following motives are all used fully and in such a way that they function in a cumulative and reinforcing manner and yield favorable attitudes:

- • The ego motives. These are referred to . . . as the desire to achieve and maintain a sense of personal worth and importance. This desire manifests itself in many forms, depending upon the norms and values of the persons and groups involved. Thus, it is responsible for such motivational forces as the desire for growth and significant achievement in terms of one's own values and goals, i.e., self-fulfillment, as well as the desire for status, recognition, approval, acceptance, and power and the desire to undertake significant and important tasks.

- • The security motives.

- • Curiosity, creativity, and the desire for new experiences.

- • The economic motives.

    By tapping all the motives which yield favorable and cooperative attitudes, maximum motivation oriented toward realizing the organization's goals as well as the needs of each member of the organization is achieved. The substantial decrements in motivational forces which occur when powerful motives are pulling in opposite directions are thereby avoided. These conflicting forces exist, of course, when hostile and resentful attitudes are present.

- The organization consists of a tightly knit, effectively functioning social system. This social system is made up of interlocking work groups with a high degree of group loyalty among the members and favorable attitudes and trust between superiors and subordinates. Sensitivity to others and relatively high levels of skill in personal interaction and the functioning of groups are also present. These skills permit effective participation in decisions on common problems. Participation is used, for example, to establish organizational objectives which are a satisfactory integration of the needs and desires of all members of the organization and of persons functionally related to it. High levels of reciprocal influence occur, and high levels of total coordinated influence are achieved in the organization. Communication is efficient and effective. There is a flow from one part of the organization to another of all the relevant information important for each decision and action. The leadership in the organization has developed what might well be called a highly effective social system for interaction and mutual influence.

• Measurements of organizational performance are used primarily for self-guidance rather than for superimposed control. To tap the motives which bring cooperative and favorable rather than hostile attitudes, participation and involvement in decisions is a habitual part of the leadership processes. This kind of decision-making, of course, calls for the full sharing of available measurements and information. Moreover, as it becomes evident in the decision-making process that additional information or measurements are needed, steps are taken to obtain them.

In achieving operations which are more often characterized by the above pattern of highly cooperative, well-coordinated activity, the highest producing managers use all the technical resources of the classical theories of management, such as time-and-motion study, budgeting, and financial controls. They use these resources at least as completely as do the low-producing managers, but in quite different ways. This difference in use arises from the differences in the motives which the high-producing, in contrast to the low-producing, managers believe are important in influencing human behavior.

The low-producing managers, in keeping with traditional practice, feel that the way to motivate and direct behavior is to exercise control through authority. Jobs are organized, methods are prescribed, standards are set, performance goals and budgets are established. Compliance with them is sought through the use of hierarchical economic pressures.

The highest-producing managers feel, generally, that this manner of functioning does not produce the best results, that the resentment created by direct exercise of authority tends to limit its effectiveness. They have learned that better results can be achieved when a different motivational process is employed. As suggested above, they strive to use all those major motives which have the potentiality of yielding favorable and cooperative attitudes in such a way that favorable attitudes are, in fact, elicited and the motivational forces are mutually reinforcing. Motivational forces stemming from the economic motive are not then blunted by such other motivations as group goals which restrict the quantity or quality of output. The full strength of all economic, ego, and other motives is generated and put to use.

Widespread use of participation is one of the more important approaches employed by the high-producing managers in their efforts to get full benefit from the technical resources of the classical theories of management coupled with high levels of reinforcing motivation. This use of participation applies to all aspects of the job and work, as, for example, in setting work goals and budgets, controlling costs, organizing the work, etc.

In these and comparable ways, the high-producing managers make full use of the technical resources of the classical theories of management. They use these resources in such a manner, however, that favorable and cooperative attitudes are created and all members of the organization endeavor to pull concertedly toward commonly accepted goals which they have helped to establish.

This brief description of the pattern of management which is more often characteristic of the high-producing than of the low-producing managers points to what appears to be a critical difference. The high-producing managers have developed their organizations into highly coordinated, highly motivated, cooperative social systems. Under their leadership, the different motivational forces in each member of the organization have coalesced into a strong force aimed at accomplishing the mutually established objectives of the organization. This general pattern of highly motivated, cooperative members seems to be a central characteristic of the newer management system being developed by the highest-producing managers.

How do these high-producing managers build organizations which display this central characteristic? Is there any general approach or underlying principle which they rely upon in building highly motivated organizations? There seems to be, and clues as to the nature of the principle can be obtained by reexamining some of the materials...[discussed earlier]. The research findings show, for example, that those supervisors and managers whose pattern of leadership yields consistently favorable attitudes more often think of employees as "human beings rather than just as persons to get the work done." Consistently, in study after study, the data show that treating people as "human beings" rather than as "cogs in a machine" is a variable highly related to the attitudes and motivation of the subordinate at every level in the organization.

The superiors who have the most favorable and cooperative attitudes in their work groups display the following characteristics:

- The attitude and behavior of the superior toward the subordinate as a person, *as perceived by the subordinate,* is as follows:
- • He is supportive, friendly, and helpful rather than hostile. He is kind but firm, never threatening, genuinely interested in the well-being of subordinates and endeavors to treat people in a sensitive, considerate way. He is just, if not generous. He endeavors to serve the best interests of his employees as well as of the company.
- • He shows confidence in the integrity, ability, and motivations of subordinates rather than suspicion and distrust.
- • His confidence in subordinates leads him to have high expectations as to their level of performance. With confidence that he will not be disappointed, he expects much, not little. (This, again, is fundamentally a supportive rather than a critical or hostile relationship.)
- • He sees that each subordinate is well trained for his particular job. He endeavors also to help subordinates be promoted by training them for jobs at the next level. This involves giving them relevant experience and coaching whenever the opportunity offers.
- • He coaches and assists employees whose performance is below standard. In the case of a subordinate who is clearly misplaced and unable to do his job satisfactorily, he endeavors to find a position well suited to that employee's abilities and arranges to have the employee transferred to it.

- The behavior of the superior in directing the work is characterized by such activity as:
- • Planning and scheduling the work to be done, training subordinates, supplying them with material and tools, initiating work activity, etc.
- • Providing adequate technical competence, particularly in those situations where the work has not been highly standardized.
- The leader develops his subordinates into a working team with high group loyalty by using participation and the other kinds of group-leadership practices. . . .

The Integrating Principle

These results and similar data from other studies (Argyris 1957c; March & Simon 1958; Viteles 1953) show that subordinates react favorably to experiences which they feel are supportive and contribute to their sense of importance and personal worth. Similarly, persons react unfavorably to experiences which are threatening and decrease or minimize their sense of dignity and personal worth. These findings are supported also by substantial research on personality development (Argyris 1957c; Rogers 1942; Rogers 1951) and group behavior (Cartwright & Zander 1960). Each of us wants appreciation, recognition, influence, a feeling of accomplishment, and a feeling that people who are important to us believe in us and respect us. We want to feel that we have a place in the world.

This pattern of reaction appears to be universal and seems to be the basis for the general principle used by the high-producing managers in developing their highly motivated, cooperative organizations. These managers have discovered that the motivational forces acting in each member of an organization are most likely to be cumulative and reinforcing when the interactions between each individual and the others in the organization are of such a character that they convey to the individual a feeling of support and recognition for his importance and worth as a person. These managers, therefore, strive to have the interactions between the members of their organization of such a character that each member of the organization feels confident in his potentialities and believes that his abilities are being well used.

A second factor, however, is also important. . . . An individual's reaction to any situation is always a function not of the absolute character of the interaction, but of his perception of it. It is how he sees things that counts, not objective reality. Consequently, an individual member of an organization will always interpret an interaction between himself and the organization in terms of his background and culture, his experience and expectations. The pattern of supervision and the language used that might be effective with a railroad's maintenance-of-way crew, for example, would not be suitable in an office full of young women. A subordinate tends also to expect his superior to behave in ways consistent with the personality of the superior. All this means that each of us, as a subordinate or as a peer or as a superior, reacts in terms of his own particular background, experience, and expectations. In order, therefore, to have an interaction viewed as supportive, it is essential that it be of such a character that the individual himself, in the light of his experience and expectations, sees it as supportive. This provides the basis for stating the general principle which the high-producing managers seem to be using and which will be referred to as the *principle of supportive relationships.* This principle, which provides an invaluable guide in any attempt to apply the newer theory of management in a specific plant or organization, can be briefly stated: *The leadership and other processes of the organization must be such as to ensure a maximum probability that in all interactions and all relationships with the organization each member will, in the light of his background, values, and expectations, view the experience as supportive and one which builds and maintains his sense of personal worth and importance.*

The Principle of Supportive Relationships as an Organizing Concept

This general principle provides a fundamental formula for obtaining the full potential of every major motive which can be constructively harnessed in a working situation. There is impressive evidence, for example, that economic motivations will be tapped more effectively when the conditions specified by the principle of supportive relationships are met (Katz & Kahn 1951; Krulee 1955). In addition, as motives are used in the ways called for by this general principle, the attitudes accompanying the motives will be favorable and the different motivational forces will be cumulative and reinforcing. Under these circumstances, the full power from each of the available motives will be added to that from the others to yield a maximum of coordinated, enthusiastic effort.

The principle of supportive relationships points to a dimension essential for the success of every organization, namely, that the mission of the organization be seen by its members as genuinely important. To be highly motivated, each member of the organization must feel that the organization's objectives are of significance and that his own particular task contributes in an indispensable manner to the organization's achievement of its objectives. He should see his role as difficult, important, and meaningful. This is necessary if the individual is to achieve and maintain a sense of personal worth and importance. When jobs do not meet this specification they should be reorganized so that they do. This is likely to require the participation of those involved in the work in a manner suggested...[later].

The term "supportive" is used frequently...and also is a key word in the principle of supportive relationships. Experiences, relationships, etc., are considered to be supportive when the individual involved sees the experience (in terms of his values, goals, expectations, and aspirations) as contributing to or maintaining his sense of personal worth and importance.

The principle of supportive relationships contains within it an important clue to its effective use. To apply this general principle, a superior must take into consideration the experience and expectations of each of his subordinates. In determining what these expectations are, he cannot rely solely on his observations and impressions. It helps the superior to try to put himself in his subordinate's shoes and endeavor to see things as the subordinate sees them, but this is not enough. Too often, the superior's estimates are wrong. He needs direct evidence if he is to know how the subordinate views things and to estimate the kinds of behavior and interaction which will be seen by the subordinate as supportive. The superior needs accurate information as to how his behavior is actually seen by the subordinate. Does the subordinate, in fact, perceive the superior's behavior as supportive?. . .

The Central Role of the Work Group

An important theoretical derivation can be made from the principle of supportive relationships. This derivation is based directly on the desire to achieve and maintain a sense of personal worth, which is a central concept of the principle. The most important source of satisfaction for this desire is the response we get from the people we are close to, in whom we are interested, and whose approval and support we are eager to have. The face-to-face groups with whom we spend the bulk of our time are, consequently, the most important to us. Our work group is one in which we spend much of our time and one in which we are particularly eager to achieve and maintain a sense of personal worth. As a consequence, most persons are highly motivated to behave in ways consistent with the goals and values of their work group in order to obtain recognition, support, security, and favorable reactions from this group. It can be concluded, therefore, that *management will make full use of the potential capacities of its human resources only when each person in an organization is a member of one or more effectively functioning work groups that have a high degree of group loyalty, effective skills of interaction, and high performance goals.*

The full significance of this derivation becomes more evident when we examine the research findings that show how groups function when they are well knit and have effective interaction skills. Research shows, for example, that the greater the attraction and loyalty to the group, the more the individual is motivated (1) to accept the goals and decisions of the group; (2) to seek to influence the goals and decisions of the group so that they are consistent with his own experience and his own goals; (3) to communicate fully to the members of the group; (4) to welcome communication and influence attempts from the other members; (5) to behave so as to help implement the goals and decisions that are seen as most important to the group; and (6) to behave in ways calculated to receive support and favorable recognition from members of the group and especially from those who the individual feels are the more powerful and higher-status members (Cartwright & Zander 1960). Groups which display a high level of member attraction to the group and high levels of the above characteristics will be referred to...as *highly effective groups....*

As our theoretical derivation has indicated, an organization will function best when its personnel function not as individuals but as members of highly effective work groups with high performance goals. Consequently, management should deliberately endeavor to build these effective groups, linking them into an over-all organization by means of people who hold overlapping group membership (Figure 1). The superior in one group is a subordinate in the next group, and so on through the organization. If the work groups at each hierarchical level are well knit and effective, the linking process will be accomplished well. Staff as well as line should be characterized by this pattern of operation.

The dark lines in Figure 1 are intended to show that interaction occurs between individuals as well as in groups. The dark lines are omitted at the lowest level in the chart in order to avoid complexity. Interaction between individuals occurs there, of course, just as it does at higher levels in the organization.

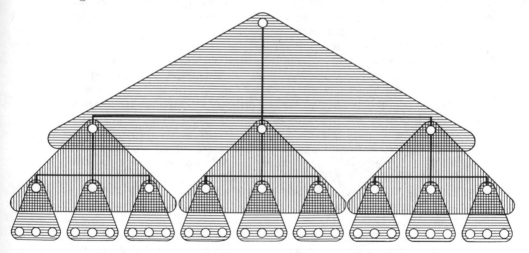

Figure 1. *The overlapping group form of organization. Work groups vary in size as circumstances require although shown here as consisting of four persons.*

In most organizations, there are also various continuing and *ad hoc* committees, committees related to staff functions, etc., which should also become highly effective groups and thereby help further to tie the many parts of the organization together. These links are in addition to the linking provided by the overlapping members in the line organization. Throughout the organization, the supervisory process should develop and strengthen group functioning. This theoretically ideal organizational structure provides the framework for the management system called for by the newer theory.

Bibliography

Argyris, C. *Personality and organization.* New York: Harper, 1957.

Cartwright, D., & Zander, A. (Eds.) *Group dynamics: research and theory* (2d ed.) Evanston, Ill.: Row, Peterson, 1960.

Katz, D., & Kahn, R. L. Human organization and worker motivation. In L. Reed Tripp (Ed.), *Industrial productivity.* Madison, Wis.: Industrial Relations Research Association, 1951. Pp. 146–71.

Krulee, G. K. The Scanlon plan: co-operation through participation. *J. Business,* Univer. of Chicago, 1955, 28(2), 100–13.

March, J. G., & Simon, H. A. *Organizations.* New York: Wiley, 1958.

Rogers, C. R. *Counseling and psychotherapy.* Boston: Houghton Mifflin, 1942.

Rogers, C. R. *Client-centered therapy.* Boston: Houghton Mifflin, 1951.

Viteles, M. S. *Motivation and morale in industry.* New York: Norton, 1953.

23 / The Case for Benevolent Autocracy

Robert N. McMurry

¶ ARE "DEMOCRATIC," "PARTICIPATIVE," "bottom-up," and similar management philosophies practical?

¶ Is it realistic to expect every company executive and supervisor, irrespective of his position in the hierarchy, to participate fully in the administrative process?

¶ To what extent do the employees in the plant actually want to accept real responsibility for the success of the enterprise?

¶ Does autocratic management—and particularly a "benevolent" autocracy—hold more promise of working? If so, how should it be put into operation?

"Humanation," according to Harold J. Ruttenberg, "is the full release of the human creativeness of the working and managing forces voluntarily cooperating with each other to apply their creative energies to their daily work through organized programs of joint participation in the production process. Its goal is to bring everyone, irrespective of his point of authority or responsibility, into full participation in the productive process."[1]

This philosophy of the roles and relationships of management and worker, and many like it—for example, the democratic-participative, consultative, and "bottom-up" schools of management, to name only a few—appear to constitute the wave of the future in the minds of many personnel experts. Everywhere the goal is becoming "groupness"; the watchword, "management must democratize."

Such a philosophy is a welcome swing of the pendulum away from the brutality of the ill-famed Pennsylvania Coal and Iron Police and the "company store." And it is a fine ideal—an ultimate goal to shoot for. But it is as one-sided as the pessimistic view of human nature it replaces. Some day it may work in many companies, but today, human nature being what it is, democratic management is practical in only a small minority of companies.

Cold Realities

I shall be candid about the reasons why I think democratic management will not work.

Not only are many employees unwilling or unable to make a positive effort to contribute to the productive process, but there is nearly always a group of workers and supervisors of indeterminate size who either dislike their work, have come without the expectation of producing (the "gold bricks"), or are chronically dissatisfied. Such employees may be actively destructive and disruptive. Typical are the employees in the automotive plants who weld pop bottles in the gasoline tanks they assemble "just for kicks"; typical also are the foremen who look the other way when such antics are taking place. To expect such persons, of whom each business has its quota, to give their creative energy and thought to the firm is downright silly.

But even if many employees are genuinely desirous of participating actively in promoting the success of the enterprise, various obstacles may keep a wholly humanistic or democratic plan of administration from working.

Inclement Climate

In the first place, democratic management cannot flourish in an unfavorable climate; its principles must be accepted throughout the organization from top to bottom, especially at the top. And the character of this climate is determined almost entirely by the management philosophies of the one or two executives who hold the actual power in the organization.

---

1 "Humanation," *Management Record,* November 1956, p. 389.

Very few members of top management are by nature sympathetic to the "bottom-up" philosophy of management. They are more likely to be hard-driving, egocentric entrepreneurs who have come up outside the business in careers where they have had to keep the power in their own hands; or they may be veterans and victors in the give-and-take, no-quarter infighting for positions of power within the business; or they may be the fortunate bureaucrats who managed to outlive and outlast their competitors for power or had sponsors on whose coattails they rode to a position of eminence in the organization.

Such men cannot ordinarily bring themselves to use any concept of management other than a purely authoritarian one. They may give lip-service to humanistic or democratic-participative philosophy of leadership, but they are never able, somehow, to implement it in their own companies. I suspect that not more than 10% of the business enterprises in the United States today have top policy-formulating managements which can accept, implement, and use a genuinely humanistic or "bottom-up" philosophy of management.

Centralized Decisions

In the second place, most commercial enterprises are very delicately balanced. One minor act—for example, a small price concession in some remote corner of the territory the company serves—can have tremendous and often costly repercussions. It can establish a chain reaction which will affect sales elsewhere. It can have implications for purchasing policies, manufacturing activities, relations with the government, public relations, and eventually profits.

It is easy to see, therefore, why so many managers feel that little true decision making may safely be delegated "down the line." Furthermore, there must be uniformity of policies and practices throughout the organization. One area cannot operate by one set of rules and another by a different set. Likewise, any deviation from policy that is permitted must be approved by those high enough in the management hierarchy to be able to see the action in proper perspective and estimate the probable consequences. This means that in practice *every* position below the one or two at the top must be almost totally structured—must be devoid of real decision-making responsibility. There may be room for some freedom of action *within* the structure, but even this is often more apparent than real.

The Bureaucratic Man

In the third place, the democratic-participative philosophy of management is completely incompatible with the bureaucratic traditions of most corporations. Business enterprises—especially large, secure, prestigeful ones— have a great attraction for those who have strong needs for security and status. Such people often make excellent subordinates. In their search for security, they do their best to meet their superiors' expectations as completely as they can, thus earning the latters' approbation and support. They are the "good soldiers," the loyal "organization men." But they cannot administer, direct, or inspire others. They belong in staff rather than in line positions.

Unfortunately, partly because management does not know how to recognize qualified candidates for leadership positions and partly because of a dearth of prospects, many of those chosen for leadership positions are taken from this pool of congenital nonleaders. Over the years, middle management comes to be composed almost exclusively of these bureaucrats who "live by the book." So strong are the pressures toward bureaucratization that any group of 100 or more employees, if not carefully controlled, will almost certainly turn into a bureaucracy within five years.

Once the organization has begun to become bureaucratized, the bureaucrats begin to perpetuate themselves. This is easy for them to do because most supervisors select their subordinates, and nearly everyone selects his subordinates in his own image. Moreover, a weak department or division head invariably tends to select as his subordinate *someone who is weaker than he* and hence no threat to him. When this selection of weaker subordinates has been repeated several times—particularly in a "tall" organization with many supervisory echelons—the low man in the hierarchy is often weak indeed. It requires only one bureaucrat in the hierarchy to insure that everyone below him will be as inadequate as he is himself, or more so.

Actual Trial

When democratic-participative management is subjected to actual trial, further weaknesses sometimes manifest themselves. While decision making stoutly refuses to remain at a low level, dissatisfaction with top management's decisions is found at every level, including the very lowest. Furthermore, to a substantial number of employees, participative or "bottom-up" management is interpreted to mean that the employees have the right to veto management's decisions. Hence, while employees have few positive contributions to make, many are not at all reluctant to demand their "rights." Others interpret democratic supervision to mean lax handling by their superiors. They become resentful of any attempt to impose discipline.

Bottom-up Resistance

When allowance is made for the fact that a great many people *prefer* regimentation, that most of those in top entrepreneurial positions tend to be autocrats, that most decision making must be centralized and structured, and that many companies drive their potential humanistic leaders out of the organization altogether (sometimes into the union), it is not surprising to find that most businesses today are autocratically administered from top to bottom, largely by bureaucrats. And the sample of companies with which I am familiar and on which I base this statement is a large one, including many firms that not only are leaders in their industries but would strenuously object to being called autocracies—even benevolent autocracies. To separate fact from fiction, here is an illustration:

One of our leading corporations is glowingly pictured in the press as a democratic-participative organization in which the president has only one vote, the same as each member of the executive committee. And although he has the right to veto, he never uses it. Journalists have considered this firm a splendid example of democracy in action.

But if you will attend the executive committee meetings, you will find that there is rarely any disagreement. This is because the president always states his position clearly in advance. In consequence, the vote is almost always unanimous. Still, management prides itself on its public image.

Even in groups where decision making is pushed far down in the organization by management fiat, it is resented—and this resentment can be kept at a low level only by the continued application of pressure from above. The minute that decision making is permitted to find its natural level, it will rise at once to the highest permissible echelon in the organization. As Harry S. Truman said of the presidency: "Only at my level did the 'buck' really stop."

Illusion of Group Decisions

The inadequacies of the democratic-participative philosophy of management in action are especially evident where group decision making is encouraged, as in many so-called "consultative" management programs. In a number of these programs, it is obligatory not only that everyone in the group participate in making the decision, but also that all of the group's decisions be unanimous.

Those who advocate group decision-making programs advance the following reasons:

(1) Several minds are usually better than one in problem solving.
(2) Having shared in its making, the members of a group will accept more readily the decision which has been reached.
(3) Participation in decision making is a stimulating, educational, and unifying experience for members of the group.
(4) Group decision making improves intragroup communication.
(5) When decisions have been made by the group, each member feels that he has the group's support in carrying them out.
(6) If the group has actual decision-making (not simply advisory) responsibility, its members' contributions will be more carefully considered, less frivolous, and hence sounder.

While the foregoing arguments in favor of group decision making are cogent, they overlook several of the more pressing reasons for questioning its merits. Chief among these are:

(1) Group decisions stimulate individual dependence on the group (which may well account for the growing popularity of this philosophy).
(2) Some members always fear to oppose the group. It is significant that in a recent study, one-fourth of a group, who had been given certain facts, were induced by the majority, which had *not* been given the

facts, to agree to a decision that these facts proved clearly to be wrong.[2]

(3)   When the group's members vary in status and power, subordinates are reluctant to disagree with their superiors.

(4)   Some members, occasionally the more brilliant and nonconformist, are so unacceptable to others in the group that their contributions are not even seriously considered; they become "isolates."

Moreover, from a purely practical point of view group decisions ordinarily require more time to make; they are ill-adapted to emergencies or to situations requiring speed of decision, for one recalcitrant can delay decision making interminably. Also, unanimous group decisions *tend* to be conservative and opposed to innovations, hence less progressive—a fact that stockholders should be interested in.

Probably the greatest weakness of group decision making, especially where the decisions must be unanimous, lies in the spuriousness of the apparent high degree of agreement reached. Those members of the group who may not be in agreement with the majority may also be reluctant for any of the reasons enumerated above to express their disagreement openly. In consequence, they voice little, or at best minor, opposition to the group's decision. Only later do they begin actively to sabotage it. The danger is that management, assuming the decision taken is representative of the group's sentiments and that its members will support the conclusions which have been reached, may make its plans accordingly—only to discover later, with a shock, that many of the members are actually in disagreement and that the plan is either being openly resisted or more subtly and insidiously sabotaged by "passive resistance."

In many organizations, especially large, bureaucratic ones, individual autocracy has tended because of the emphasis on "groupness" to be replaced by *group* autocracy. Here strategic decisions are not made by the individual leader, particularly where he is a "weak" autocrat, because he lacks the courage. Instead, he takes refuge in the principle of unanimity; he calls together a group of his subordinates and lets them decide for him. In this way, he is able to maintain a bureaucratic autocracy without leadership, imagination, or drive, functioning under the guise of democratic management.

Lights of the Future

I do not want to paint the picture of the humanistic or democratic-participative philosophy of management all black. I do not doubt, for instance, that it is superior to blind autocracy, especially when the latter leads to the development of a great inchoate and bumbling bureaucracy. Democratic leadership is obviously more productive. It stimulates and builds men; it invariably enhances morale. It has everything to recommend

[2] E. Paul Torrance, "Group Decision-Making and Disagreement," *Social Forces,* May 1957, p. 314.

it except for the one fact that only in a relatively few small, socially well-integrated, and homogeneous groups—for example, the New England town meeting, the British Foreign Office, or some types of family-run firms—can it really be made to work.

A few companies, one of the most notable of which is General Mills, are making a sincere effort to introduce the humanistic philosophy of management into their organizations. At General Mills, the program has the active support of the president, Charles H. Bell. Consequently, the climate is not only extremely favorable, but an active campaign is being waged from the top down to make everyone in management conscious of the nature and advantages of this type of supervisory leadership. It will be interesting to observe the amount of impact this campaign has over the years on the overt behavior (not statements) of those in middle management, toward whom it is primarily aimed. It will also be instructive to note what will happen to the program should the pressure from the president to support it ever be relaxed.

Leaders and Followers

If democratic management runs counter to human nature and is only rarely practical, is there any way in which conventional autocratic-bureaucratic approaches can be modified and adapted in such a manner that pressure for production can be maintained without creating low levels of morale?

The answer appears to lie in a modification of prevailing autocratic-bureaucratic practices. We must recognize their causes and limitations but endeavor to minimize their ill effects by eliminating their worst features, introducing certain "cushioning" practices, and adapting the methods utilized more specifically to the needs of the employees. We might call the result "*benevolent* autocracy."

Under such an approach we would accept the fact that top management is by nature autocratic and that much of lower and middle management is composed of insecure bureaucrats. Where natural leaders are found, they will be utilized. Moreover, since competence as a leader is far from an all-or-none matter, we will often find that much can be done to help marginal supervisors become more effective through careful job placement and job structuring. We will not assume, however, that there will be many supervisors with great potential, and we will recognize that leaders cannot be developed from scratch by training.

Autocrat at the Conference Table

Benevolent autocracy is also based upon the premise that the autocrat is not necessarily an ineffective leader or a serious source of employee ill will. This is because two types of autocrats may be distinguished, the *strong* autocrat and the *weak* one:

(1)   The strong autocrat is usually the very aggressive (often hypomanic), hard-driving, and self-reliant entrepreneur who is so preoccupied with

his other interests and problems that he forgets to give much thought to his employees. He is not a tyrant or a martinet. He does not exploit his employees or willfully mistreat them. He simply forgets at times that they are human beings with their own needs and problems. He is autocratic in his relations with others because he has learned by trial and error that this is the best way to get things done.

(2) The weak autocrat, by contrast, is the typical bureaucrat. He is often intelligent, loyal, conscientious, and technically well qualified for his position. His major weakness is his overwhelming need for *security*. He is basically a very dependent, fearful, and anxious person who is compensating for his insecurities by assuming an arbitrary, authoritarian exterior, often marked by great emphasis on his status and its symbols. He needs power. He adheres compulsively to prevailing practices, procedures, and policies. He *must* have a "book" to go by. His tyrannical manner serves as a defense mechanism to conceal his inner doubts and uncertainties; it also insures that no one will dare to question him and ask him to defend his judgments and actions. Typically, while he is a martinet to his subordinates, he is obsequious to his superiors— a veritable Uriah Heep.

It is obviously the weak autocrat who causes most of the trouble. If a system of benevolent autocracy is to be instituted, it is assumed that at least the top executives will be strong autocrats. Otherwise, little can be accomplished.

The philosophy of benevolent autocracy attempts to view the business scene realistically. In a nutshell, it assumes that most employees, regardless of their positions in the enterprise, have very real needs for security, for a well-defined structure in which to work, for opportunities to make contributions within this structure, for supervision which is permissive and supportive, and for an opportunity to feel that they have some voice in their own destinies. They must have confidence that the holder of ultimate power in top management, the "father figure" in the enterprise, while powerful and prestigeful, is also personally interested in them and in their problems. It is especially important for them to believe that he is prepared to take prompt remedial action on all valid complaints which are brought to his attention.

The benevolent autocrat structures his subordinates' activities for them; he makes the policy decisions which affect them; he keeps them in line and enforces discipline. He is like a good quarterback, who does not *ask* the line to decide what plays to attempt or what formations to use, but who *tells* them—and woe betide the hapless player who fails to follow his orders. He may encourage participation in the planning of a course of action, but much less frequently does he do so in its execution. In effect, he differs from the weak autocrat only in that he encourages participation by his subordinates prior to reaching *his* decision.

I believe that a proper utilization of these insights and a proper application of the principles which grow out of them will result in the maintenance of nearly as high a level of morale, even under continued pressure for production, as is possible where the democratic-participative type of leadership is available.

Not-Too-Great Expectations

Before any steps can be taken to institute a program of benevolent autocracy, the ineffectiveness of exposition, admonition, and threats in influencing employee attitudes and behavior (the usual tactics of the autocrat) must be recognized and accepted by management, even where they seem essential and logically defensible. It is a long-established attribute of the American value system to assume that everyone has both the desire and the capacity to overcome his weaknesses and that he is inherently ambitious, seeking tirelessly to achieve a higher position both socially and economically. Consonant with this, it is believed that all that is necessary to insure that he will institute an immediate campaign of self-improvement is to have his limitations pointed out to him—and that then he will spring into action to change himself for the better.

However, as every psychiatrist has learned, logic alone is not enough. Even when it has been possible in therapy to give an individual insight into his limitations (not a mean task in itself), it is frequently next to impossible to get the patient to translate his insights into corrective action, even though he is paying for therapy and this means relief from distressing symptoms. So, often his self-improvement campaign "withers on the vine"; for everyone is to some degree a prisoner of his past.

Even appeals to self-interest, including salaries and bonuses, are often fruitless. One of my greatest disillusionments in the course of 25 years of work for many different firms has been the discovery that at least three-fourths of those whom I have encountered in business have showed a pathetically small desire or capacity either for genuine self-improvement or for self-direction. They do not really want to improve themselves if this requires effort. They do not want responsibility. They simply want a safe, secure job and someone to tell them what to do. This conviction is one of the important reasons why I have come to look more sympathetically at the case for benevolent autocracy.

Introducing the Program

Introducing a program of benevolent autocracy does not involve management in the kinds of tortuous dilemmas that usually encumber an attempt to put a democratic-participative philosophy in action. Of course, strong leadership is required, but the steps to take can be clearly defined, and they are well suited to the practical abilities of a good top-management team.

Proclaim the Ideal

The first step in introducing the program is, paradoxically, to stress the desirability of the humanistic, democratic philosophy of management. The purpose of this first step is to create an organization-wide *climate* unfavorable to absolute autocracy and bureaucracy. Even though top executives recognize that a complete democratic philosophy is basically unworkable, they can establish at least a consciousness of the *desirability* of using more participative management methods. The impact of such a pronouncement (which should be repeated at least quarterly) will not be revolutionary, but it still will serve several worthwhile purposes:

(1) It will make everyone conscious that absolute autocracy or bureaucracy is not the *only* philosophy of management.

(2) It will convey the impression that the holders of supreme power in the company are in favor of the new avant garde philosophy of participation in management decision making—as indeed they are; only they also recognize its limitations.

(3) It will provide a new and more precise definition of the *ideal* qualities and duties of supervision; in most companies such a statement has never before existed. The supervisors can then check their own administrative practices against this standard. While they will not be able to accept it emotionally, or to practice it, they will have an intellectual awareness of the need for mature administrators.[3]

Inventory and Placement

The second step in the introduction of a program of benevolent autocracy is to take an executive and supervisory inventory. Its purpose is to evaluate the competence of the present supervisory force and particularly to determine the leadership qualifications of everyone in management. The methods to be employed have already been described in this magazine,[4] and an interesting application of them has been made at General Mills:

The General Mills supervisory appraisals take the form of periodic reports by managers, analyzing the abilities of those whose work they supervise. The field review method was selected as best for their use. A trained interviewer questions each appraiser individually concerning each man and records the appraiser's opinions. The interviewers frequently are personnel men, but some of the most successful have been operating men who were trained and used for short periods. The interviewers help overcome semantic difficulties because they can explain what is sought and can probe to find out what a man thinks on any given point and his reasons for so thinking. They ask for illustrations and examples, call attention to inconsistencies, and suggest alternatives for the appraiser's consideration. In doing this, the interviewers also train the appraisers, focus their thinking, and help them to control their prejudice and biases.[5]

---

[3] See Hrand Saxenian, "Criterion for Emotional Maturity," in this issue. p. 56.

[4] See Robert E. Shaeffer, "Merit Rating as a Management Tool," HBR November 1949, p. 693, and Robert N. McMurry, "War and Peace in Labor Relations," HBR November–December 1955, p. 48.

[5] D. E. Balch, *Executive Selection and Inventory,* American Management Association (1957), pp. 12–13.

This technique, which requires interviews of approximately one hour with each of two raters, provides a surprisingly accurate measure of each supervisor's strong and weak points without provoking an undue amount of anxiety among those appraised since they themselves are not directly tested or interviewed. It makes it possible to place supervisors in one of three categories: (1) the natural leader who is already providing effective leadership; (2) the potential leader who can be developed; and (3) those bureaucrats whose inadequacies make them marginally qualified or clearly unsuited for supervisory work.

It is this latter category which contains the "problem" supervisors. They are often quite numerous and, to make matters worse, they cannot always be replaced, immediately at least, because no replacements are available. Since few of these marginal supervisors will be amenable to training, nothing remains but to reconstitute the leadership aspects of their positions. In most instances this means providing a strong subordinate to furnish needed leadership or establishing closer supervision from above. Needless to say, such supervisors must be replaced as rapidly as substitutes can be obtained.

This kind of inventory is the crucial step of the program. If it fails, nothing will be accomplished. Therefore, it is imperative that in this respect management be vigorous and, if necessary, ruthlessly authoritarian. Supervisors *must* have their leadership responsibilities absolutely structured for them.

Job Definition

The third step in establishing a program of benevolent autocracy is to eliminate ambiguity on the job whenever and wherever it may occur. Nothing creates poor morale and anxiety in employees as much as does uncertainty with respect to company plans and prospects, their supervision, their duties, their authority, or their future with the company.

Business decisions fall into two roughly discrete classes: those which involve risk and those which do not. These two types have been defined by Drucker as "strategic" (involving risk) and "tactical" (the more routine problem-solving decisions):

> The *strategic* decisions are those which involve futurity, have simultaneous impact on many aspects of the business, or involve substantial sums or unknowns. Decisions of this risk-taking type are reserved almost exclusively to top management. *Tactical* or problem-solving decisions are made every day by everyone.
>
> The machinist who sets the speed and feed of his machine is making a problem-solving decision; the accountant who allocates a charge to a particular account is making such a decision; so is the buyer in the purchasing department who decides to give an order to a particular supplier. Even a purchasing agent in charge of an annual procurement of $450,000,000 worth of materials may operate in an almost totally structured, risk-free environment, partly because the bulk of his activities follow well-established patterns

and partly because, whenever he is faced with an unusual situation or one which involves risk, he must clear it with his superiors.

The characteristic element in all such tactical decisions is that they involve a minimum of risk; they are totally structured.[6]

Nearly all the decisions at the working level and in middle and lower management are highly structured. This is absolutely necessary in the development and maintenance of good morale. It provides the guidance and the support which most people need and insures uniformity of policies and practices throughout the organization, which is an absolute necessity for efficient operation. This rigid structuring is not inconsistent with the principles of a benevolent autocracy. It exists not because of the whim of some autocrat in management but because a majority of the people in the enterprise need and ask for it.

There is nothing to prevent the astute supervisor from giving his subordinates a reasonably high degree of latitude of action *within the structure*. The machinist may set his speeds and feeds to suit himself within a fairly wide range; the clerk may have a voice in recommending the make of calculating machine the company is to buy; and the salesman may modify his presentation to suit himself as long as he conforms to policy on price, delivery dates, and so forth.

This is the key to the use of so-called consultative, participative management principles, even in an autocracy. The employees share in the problem solving, either individually or in a group, and each is encouraged to contribute his opinions and preferences—*but always within the structure*. No one takes any real risks; the superior always has the final say.

Performance Reviews

The fourth step to insure good morale under substantial pressure for production is to make certain that everyone "knows where he stands" with his superior.

However, this should *not* be done, in my opinion, by having a superior confer periodically with a subordinate, using merit ratings or appraisal findings as a basis for his advice and judgments. In most instances the immediate superior, often a bureaucrat, is the poorest qualified person in the organization to provide counseling, at least in the conventional manner. This is partly because he usually lacks professional skill and partly because, due to his senior position, he often appears to be a threat to the employee's security.

I advocate, instead, discussions between boss and subordinate based on a statement of supervisory expectations. This statement is a composite of three elements:

(1)   A position analysis prepared on the basis of the company's formal job description which spells out the place of the incumbent in the

---

[6] See Peter F. Drucker, *The Practice of Management* (New York, Harper & Brothers, 1954), pp. 351–53.

organization as a whole, that is, the nature and scope of his duties, responsibilities, authority, to whom he reports and who reports to him, and so forth.

(2) The employee's statement of his goals and objectives for the ensuing period (usually one year or less).

(3) The superior's statement of what he expects in terms of performance and self-improvement from the employee during the period.

These three elements are then collated, reviewed by the superior, and discussed by the superior and subordinate in conference; and in the process a mutually acceptable program of objectives for the employee is developed.

The tone of the conference is neither critical nor admonitory; the mission is purely constructive. If the man is not meeting expectations, the purpose of the discussion is to discover why and to explore what he and/or the supervisor can do to improve his performance. If he is surpassing expectations, he is commended. In either event, he is helped to know how well he is doing, not in abstract, general terms, but in concrete characteristics of his job. This procedure, if properly policed, will force even an autocrat or bureaucrat to show some constructive interest in his subordinates.

Opinion Polls

The fifth and final phase in a program of benevolent autocracy is the conduct of periodic (preferably biennial) employee opinion polls. The primary purpose of such a poll is to "take the temperature" of the different employee groups, and more specifically to ascertain the state of their morale and to discern legitimate causes for such poor morale as may be evident. It enables management on its own initiative, without union pressure or prodding by employee petitions, to take or at least to consider such corrective action as may be indicated.[7] A poll does not commit the company to correct *every* condition which is causing or appears to be ground for dissatisfaction. Many dissatisfactions will be quite trivial; some will require no more than "talking out," while others will be of a nature that defies correction.

The results of the poll are then presented to the polling agency and through it to top management. The process has a sobering effect on those autocratic supervisors who are prone to become drunk with power and to tyrannize over their subordinates. While they resent bitterly this intrusion by management into the sanctity of their private, personal empires, most of them see the handwriting on the wall and will govern themselves accordingly.

The correction by management of *one* legitimate source of dissatisfaction is more valuable in building good employee morale than are a thousand speeches, bulletins, house organs, and letters to the employees' homes.

This phase of the program is of critical importance if morale is to be maintained at a high level in spite of continued pressure for production. It provides the safety valve by means of which accumulated resentments and

---

[7] For a fuller explanation, see Robert N. McMurry, op. cit., especially p. 57.

aggressions can be vented before they are channeled into such anti-employer activities as limitation of output, slowdowns, excessive absenteeism, or various acts of minor or serious sabotage. At the same time, it also permits the discovery and elimination of many of the *causes* of poor morale, few of which are directly the result of pressure for production.

Conclusion

Benevolent autocracy gets its results because it rigidly structures, routinizes, and controls the relation of the supervisor to his subordinates in such a manner that, in spite of his frequent inherent tendencies to the contrary, he will employ the sound methods which come more naturally to the humanistic or democratic leader. The typical bureaucrat is incapable of conceiving or applying sound leadership principles on his own initiative. However, if he is told precisely what to do, and if his conformity to policy is enforced by periodic employee opinion polls, he will not only be happy to follow instructions but will probably turn in a surprisingly creditable performance. After all, his security is largely dependent on how faithfully he conforms to company policies and practices.

There is little doubt that if the humanistic or "bottom-up" concept of leadership could be introduced and accepted on a company-wide basis and sponsored by the company's president, it would make possible increased productivity, even under pressure, without an adverse effect on morale. But since it cannot, benevolent autocracy is the most promising alternative. While perhaps not as effective at the person-to-person level, it aims at the same over-all objectives. It is designed to permit the employer to keep the pressure on his people for production without affecting their morale too adversely, using the supervisors that are available.

Productivity

But *can* pressure be applied without affecting morale too adversely? In studies conducted by the Institute for Social Research at the University of Michigan, as reported by Rensis Likert,[8] it was found, as might be expected, that humanistic or democratic-participative management led to increased productivity without deterioration of morale. But it was also consistently found that the greater the pressure applied to the workers (regardless of the philosophy of management used), the higher the production.

Furthermore, the differences in productivity induced by additional pressure, while not great, were nevertheless large enough to be important in any highly competitive industry. While morale did fall as a result of pressure, this did not affect production, which continued to increase. Likert states:

> On the basis of a study I did in 1937 I believed that morale and productivity were positively related; that the higher the morale, the higher the

---

[8] "Developing Patterns in Management," *Strengthening Management for the New Technology,* American Management Association (New York, 1955), pp. 10–11.

production. Substantial research findings since then have shown this relationship is much too simple. Some groups have low morale and low production. Other groups have fairly good morale and low production. Still others have fairly good production but low morale, while others have both high morale and high production.

Units with low morale and low production tend to have laissez-faire supervision. Where morale is fairly good but production is poor, the supervisors tend to try to keep people 'happy.' Such supervisors are often found in companies in which 'human relations' training programs have been introduced and emphasized. The morale of these less productive workers is essentially complacent in character. The result is a nice 'country club' atmosphere. Thus there is no clear evidence that the 'happy' employee is consistently the productive employee.[9]

Summary

Since so many members of lower, middle, and even top management in the typical large business enterprises of today are dependent, insecure, and ineffective—productive only because they are bossed by one or two hard-driving strong autocrats—the outlook for the widespread introduction of a genuine humanistic, democratic-participative philosophy of leadership in the near future looks dim indeed.

But benevolent autocracy, while it is neither idealistic nor inspiring, is practical. It accepts people as they are and recognizes particularly that most people prefer to be led. It also faces the fact that there is a dearth of leaders in industry now and in the foreseeable future. It is, in the final analysis, simply a technique for "making the best of the worst."

What benevolent autocracy offers is not a beautiful vision of a world to come. Instead, it simply accepts reality with all of its limitations. While hardly a noble philosophy of management, it does have one invaluable attribute: *where it has been tried, it works.*

[9] Ibid., p. 19.

24 / Control in Organizations: Individual Adjustment and Organizational Performance

Arnold S. Tannenbaum

MAN'S LIFE IN contemporary society can be characterized largely as one of organizational memberships. Man commits a major portion of his waking hours to participation in at least one—and more often several— social organizations. His motivation, aspirations, his general way of life, are tied inextricably to the organizations of which he is a part—and even to some of which he is not.

Organizations are of vital interest to the sociologist and the psychologist because one finds within them an important juncture between the individual and the collectivity. Out of this juncture comes much in our pattern of living that has been the subject of both eulogy and derogation. That man derives a great deal from organizational membership leaves little to be argued; that he often pays heavily for the benefits of organizational membership seems an argument equally compelling. At the heart of this exchange lies the process of control.

Characterizing an organization in terms of its patterns of control is to describe an essential and universal aspect of organization, an aspect of organizational environment which every member must face and to which he must adjust. Organization implies control. A social organization is an ordered arrangement of individual human interactions. Control processes help circumscribe idiosyncratic behaviors and keep them conformant with the rational plan of the organization. Organizations require a certain amount of conformity as well as the integration of diverse activities. It is the function of control to bring about conformance to organizational requirements and achievement of the ultimate goals of the organization. The co-ordination and order created out of the diverse interests and potentially diffuse behaviors of members is largely a function of control. It is at this point that many of the problems of organizational functioning and of individual adjustment arise.

Control is an inevitable correlate of organization. But it is more than this. It is concerned with aspects of social life that are of the utmost importance to all persons. It is concerned with the questions of choice and freedom,

Reprinted by permission of the author and publisher from "Control in Organization: Individual Adjustment and Organizational Performance," *Administrative Science Quarterly*, Vol. 7, No. 2 (September 1962), pp. 236–57. Copyright © 1962 by Cornell University.

with individual expression, with problems of the common will and the common weal. It is related not only to what goes on within the organization but also with what the organization does in its external relations. It touches on the questions of democracy and autocracy, centralization and decentralization, "flat" and "tall" organizational structures, close versus general supervision, workers' councils and joint management.

The problems of control and conformity in organizations contribute to a serious dilemma. Organization provides order—a condition necessary for man to produce abundantly and live securely. Abundance and security in turn create opportunities and choice—conditions which form the basis for human freedom. Yet social order itself requires conformity and imposes limitations. Furthermore, the responsibility for creating and sustaining order tends to be distributed unevenly within organizations. Often it is the few who decide about the kind of order to which the many must conform. But regardless of how order is created, it requires the conformity of all or nearly all to organizational norms.

The magnitude of this problem as it applies to our economic institutions has been indicated by Berle and Means:

> To the dozen or so men who are in control there is room for...
> [individual] initiative. For the tens of thousands and even hundreds of
> thousands of workers and of owners in a single enterprise, [individual] initiative
> no longer exists. Their activity is group activity on a scale so large that the
> individual, except he be in a position of control, has dropped into relative
> insignificance.[1]

And the *trend,* according to Barnard, is in the direction of greater concentration of control in the hands of fewer persons:

> There has been a greater and greater acceleration of centralization in
> this country, not merely in government, and not merely in the organization of
> great corporations, but also a great concentration on the part of labor
> unions and other organizations. There has been a social disintegration going
> along with this material development, and this formulation of organized
> activities implies payment of a price, the amount of which we are not yet
> able to assess.[2]

This, perhaps, is one of the most crucial problems of social morality which we face in the age of massive organization, although the problem is not an entirely new one. We see it in Rousseau's *Social Contract,* Freud's *Civilization and Its Discontents,* Huxley's *Brave New World,* Whyte's *Organization Man.* And social and administrative scientists have become increasingly interested in this question, as indicated by the work by F. Allport, Argyris, Likert, McGregor, and Worthy. As a result, social researchers have

[1] A. A. Berle, Jr., and G. C. Means, "The Control of the Modern Corporation," In R. Merton *et. al.,* eds., *Reader in Bureaucracy* (Glencoe, 1952).
[2] C. I. Barnard, *Organization and Management,* as quoted in *Harvard Business Review,* 29 (1951), 70.

applied themselves to the study of the problems of control, individual adjustment, and organizational performance, and a body of facts and hypotheses is growing. We would like to review some of these, drawing heavily upon the work done at the Institute for Social Research at the University of Michigan.[3]

Some Definitions

Control has been variously defined, and different terms (e.g., power, authority, influence) are sometimes used synonymously with it. Its original application in business organizations derives from the French usage meaning to check. It is now commonly used in a broader and perhaps looser sense synonymously with the notions of influence, authority, and power. We shall use it here in this broader way to refer to any process in which a person or group of persons or organization of persons determines, i.e., intentionally affects, what another person or group or organization will do.

Control, of course, may operate very specifically, as, for example, a foreman's specifying how a subordinate will do a particular job. Or it may operate more generally, as, for example, the determination of organizational policies or actions. Control may be mutual, individuals in a group each having some control over what others will do; or it may be unilateral, one individual controlling and the others controlled. We ascribe power to an individual to the extent that he is in a position to exercise control. Authority refers to the right to exercise control. If by freedom we mean the extent to which an individual determines his own behavior, being controlled can be seen in general to relate inversely to freedom. The more an individual's behavior is determined by others (i.e., is controlled), the less an individual is free to determine his own course of action.

Implications for Individual Adjustment

The elementary importance of control to people can be seen in the fact that every act of control has two implications: pragmatic and symbolic. Pragmatically, control implies something about *what* an individual must or must not do, the restriction to which he is subject, and the areas of choice or freedom which he has—whether, for example, a worker is transferred to a new machine or stays on the old, whether he is classified into a $1.75 or a $2.00 wage category, whether he is free to talk, smoke, rest, slow down, or speed up while on the job. These pragmatic implications are often of vital importance to the controlled individual as well as to the individual exercising power.

3 This article was made possible by funds granted by the Carnegie Corporation of New York. The statements made and views expressed are the responsibility of the author. I would like to thank Robert Kahn, Rensis Likert, Stanley Seashore, and Clagett Smith for their helpful suggestions.

Control also has a special psychological meaning or significance to the individuals involved. It may imply superiority, inferiority, dominance, submission, guidance, help, criticism, reprimand. It may imply (as some students of control argue) something about the manliness and virility of the individuals involved. The exercise of control, in other words, is charged emotionally.[4]

Emotional reactions to control may be explained, in part, by the predispositions which individuals develop early in life to types of authority relations. The infant's behavior is controlled by persons upon whom he is highly dependent, and the process of socialization involves the imposition of controls by parents, teachers, and other authority figures. In the development of a pattern of responses to control during this process of socialization, control takes on emotional meaning.

A great deal of research has been done regarding predisposition to varying patterns of control. Tests have been devised, for example, to measure authoritarianism, egalitarianism, need for independence, need for power. Research employing some of these measures suggests that individuals' reactions to patterns of organizational control may differ according to personality.

This is illustrated by an experiment in a large clerical organization in which about two hundred female clerks were given greater responsibility to make decisions about some of the rules that affected their work groups. They were able to make decisions affecting work assignments, vacation schedules, length of recess, overtime, and other matters. These decisions previously had been made by persons at higher levels. Most of the clerks reacted favorably to this experimental program. A small number, however, did not. Among these were a relatively high proportion of clerks whose personalities were not suited to the type of authority relations brought into play by this experimental program. These preferred to be submissive, depend on others, obey rules, and follow directions.[5] Similar results were found among male workers in an industrial service organization. Workers who received low scores on measures of authoritarianism were more likely to react favorably to supervisors who were judged to use participative methods (asking workers' advice, trying to involve them in decision making) than

[4] The criticism which labor groups have sometimes hurled at human relations research in industry is in large measure a criticism concerning the emphasis which this research has placed on the psychological or symbolic rather than the pragmatic aspect of control. The human relations approach, the argument goes, is not so much concerned with *what* decisions are made by management nor with the implications of these decisions for the welfare of the workers, but rather with *how* these decisions might be conveyed to workers so as to facilitate their acceptance. See, for example, Deep Therapy on the Assembly Line, *Ammunition*, 7 (1949), 47–51.

[5] A. S. Tannenbaum, One Man's Meat, *Adult Leadership*, 3 (1955), 22–23; A. S. Tannenbaum and F. H. Allport, Personality Structure and Group Structure: An Interpretative Study of Their Relationship through an Event-Structure Hypothesis, *Journal of Abnormal and Social Psychology*, 58 (1956), 272–80.

workers with high scores. Furthermore for workers with low scores, those who judged their supervisors to use participative methods were generally higher in productivity than those who did not judge their supervisors so.[6]

Preferences for different kinds of authority relations may develop out of early childhood experiences. They may also represent reactions to certain contemporaneous circumstances. Research on the authoritarian personality, for example, suggests that individuals who suffer anxiety because of a failure in their work may tend to prefer more structured authority relations. A study of high-producing and low-producing insurance salesmen suggests the tenability of this idea. Productivity varied widely for these agents. An agent might show high productivity during one period and low productivity during another. Those who were low producers tended to suffer some anxiety. They also indicated "a desire for interpersonal interaction where the status of a man's position was the basis for communication, where orders were to go through 'the chain of command,' where decisions 'must be made by the District Manager,' and where 'those in control' of the situation were to act 'aloof,' and/or 'be friendly but not too intimate.' "[7] The more successful, less threatened salesmen preferred more permissive, informal authority relations—no communication barriers because of status and no reporting through the chain of command.

Emotional reactions to authority relations may develop because authority, control, or power represents, as we have pointed out, an important social symbol. Power, for example, is often understood as synonymous with prestige, status, social eminence, or superiority. Indeed, it is often correlated with these criteria of success. Persons obviously are perceived and treated differently according to their power. The man with power is often looked up to and treated with respect. Equally important, individuals can be expected to evaluate themselves in this way. An individual's self-concept is very likely affected by his power in the organizations and other social situations in which he takes part. The emotional effects of authority, as they bear on the way organization members may perceive authority and nonauthority figures, is illustrated by an experiment in which Navy recruits described the physical appearances of men, some of whom wore first-class petty officer's uniforms and others of whom wore recruit uniforms. The men being judged as petty officers and those being judged as recruits were well matched in physical appearance. Differences existed, however, in their uniforms—the kind and number of stripes on their arms and whether or not they wore canvas leggings. The recruits viewed these persons through a series of lenses which distorted their appearance in varying degrees. However, a greater tendency to resist this distortion occurred in the perception of the "petty officer."

6 V. Vroom, *Some Personality Determinants of the Effects of Participation* (Englewood Cliffs, N.J., 1960).

7 L. G. Wispe and K. E. Lloyd, Some Situational and Psychological Determinants of the Desire for Structured Interpersonal Relations, *Journal of Abnormal and Social Psychology,* 51 (1955), 57–60.

Rank may create an emotional set which affects how the men holding this rank appear to those who do not.[8]

While individual differences may exist in preferences for types of authority relations, organization members generally prefer exercising influence to being powerless. Studies repeatedly show that workers and supervisors are much more likely to feel that they have too little authority in their work than too much. It is the rare individual indeed who thinks he has too much. Several thousands of workers in a large number of organizations (including one Norwegian factory) were asked to describe how much control various groups in their work places exercised and how much they *should* exercise. In all the organizations studied the "average" worker reported, as might be expected, that managerial personnel exercised more control than did the workers as a group. In response to another question, workers reported that managerial groups *should* exercise more control than the workers. However, in 98 per cent of these organizations, workers felt that the workers did not have as much control as they should [9] It is interesting to contrast these results with responses to the same questions addressed to supervisory personnel. None of the supervisory groups questioned felt that *workers* should exercise more control than they did.

For whatever reasons, power is desired. This desirability may be attributed to the gratification which individuals may derive simply by knowing that they are in control—from the psychological satisfactions which come from exercising control. Or it may derive from the pragmatic implications of power—being able to affect the work situation in ways favorable to one's personal interests, as the individual sees them.

A concern for the rewards which accompany power results in a serious oversimplification, however, unless one considers also some of the correlates of power which are sources of serious tension and frustration. Among these are the added feelings of responsibility for, commitment to, and effort on behalf of the organization. Power can be an important stimulant, pushing the individual toward a greater and greater share of the work load of the organization. Furthermore, in so far as control may imply weighty decisions, decisions affecting the welfare of people as well as the destiny of the organization itself, exercising control can be burdensome.

Individuals who are not able to exercise control are, in general, less satisfied with their work situations than those who have some power, but their dissatisfaction often has the quality of apathy and disinvolvement. For the individual in control, added dimensions of personality come into play con-

8 W. J. Wittreich and K. B. Radcliffe, Jr., Differences in the Perception of an Authority Figure and a Non-Authority Figure by Navy Recruits, *Journal of Abnormal and Social Psychology*, 53 (1956), 383–84.

9 In the Norwegian plant the question was phrased in terms of control over the setting of piece-rate standards. Not only did the workers indicate that they should exercise more control than they did, but that they should exercise more control than managerial groups.

tributing to the energies which he puts into his work and to the problems he may encounter. The man who exercises control gives more of himself to the organization. He is likely to be more identified, more loyal, more active, on behalf of the organization. A recent national survey suggests that individuals in positions of control and responsibility in industrial and business organizations are more "ego involved" in their work. Managerial personnel, for example, derive not only greater satisfactions from their jobs, but also greater frustrations.[10] The responsibility which devolves upon persons in control creates a sense of personal involvement and concern over the success or failure of the decisions made. These individuals have a personal stake in the outcome of decisions taken. This can be a satisfying, even an exhilarating experience, but it can also lead to sleepless nights.

This mixed blessing which power sometimes represents is illustrated by the experiment in the large clerical organization described in which about two hundred clerks were given greater responsibility to make decisions about their work conditions. In general, morale increased as a result of the change in control. Clerks felt more satisfied with the company, with supervision, with their work in general. They were, in large measure, favorable toward the increased control which they were able to exercise. Despite the general increase in satisfaction, however, the clerks felt less of a sense of accomplishment at the end of the work day. They were also less satisfied with their present level in the organization (see Table 1). In acquiring an increased

Table 1.   Changes in Clerk's Attitudes Following Delegation of Control to Clerks in Work Groups.

CLERK'S JOB ATTITUDES	MEAN CHANGES IN ATTITUDES*
Feeling of responsibility for getting work done on time	+.15
Feeling of self-actualization	+.14
Average satisfaction with supervisor	+.15
Satisfaction with company	+.17
Satisfaction with control	+.35
Satisfaction with accomplishment at end of work day	−.27
Clerk's satisfaction with her present level in company	−.42

* All of the differences are statistically significant at the .05 level or better.

feeling of responsibility for the work through the added control which they were able to exercise, the clerks no doubt developed standards of achievement which were harder to satisfy.

A similar result was found in a study by Mann and Hoffman comparing a newly automated electrical power plant with a less highly automated one.[11]

10 G. Gurin, J. Veroff, and Sheila Feld, *Americans View Their Mental Health: A Nationwide Interview Study* (New York, 1960).

11 F. C. Mann and L. R. Hoffman, *Automation and the Worker: A Study of Social Change in Power Plants* (New York, 1960).

Workers in the new plant exercised more control and experienced greater responsibility than those in the older plant, according to the responses of the workers in the two plants. The men in the new plant made important decisions about the work and had significant influence on their supervisors concerning their work place. They also reported greater satisfaction with their immediate supervisor, with the amount of information they received about plant operations, and with plant management in general. Despite this generally heightened state of morale, however, workers in the newly automated plant more often reported that their work made them feel "jumpy" or nervous and that they were tense and on edge when equipment was being started up or shut down. (Yet workers in the *old* plant reported slightly more danger in their work.) These may be some of the costs to the workers of their increased power and responsibility.

Certain kinds of psychosomatic ailments are known to be relatively frequent among individuals in positions of control and responsibility in organizations. Research in this country and abroad provides added documentation for this generally recognized fact. French reported a greater prevalence of psychosomatic disorders of varying kinds among supervisors than among workers in a large Midwest plant.[12] Vertin found the frequency of ulcers increases at ascending levels of the hierarchy in a large Dutch company.[13] "Uneasy lies the head that wears the crown," always seemed to make good sense. To the extent that power and responsibility are distributed widely among organization members, however, a number of heads may lie uneasy.

Control and Performance

Variations in control patterns within organizations have important—and in some cases quite predictable—effects on the reactions, satisfactions and frustrations, feelings of tension, self-actualization, or well-being of members. They also have implications for the performance of the work group and for the organization as a whole.

This can be seen in the plight of the first-line supervisor who sometimes finds himself in the anomalous position of being a leader without power. The first-line supervisor is often referred to as the man in the middle. He is often caught, as an innocent bystander, in a serious cross fire. In effect he may be a messenger transmitting orders from above. On the one hand, he must bear the brunt of resistance and expressed grievances from below and, on the other, must suffer criticism from above for the failure of his subordinates to conform to expectations. The seriousness of this situation is compounded by the fact that orders coming from above are often formed without the advantage of adequate knowledge of conditions at lower levels. The powerless supervisor lacks effective means of gaining the confidence of

12 J. R. P. French, Jr., The Effects of the Industrial Environment on Mental Health: A Theoretical Approach, (paper presented at the meetings of the American Psychological Association, 1960).

13 French, *op. cit.*

his men, of understanding their views, and of transmitting this important intelligence up the hierarchy. The orders which he is responsible for relaying, then, are often the least likely to gain full acceptance, thus making his position all the more untenable and that of his subordinates all the more difficult. The powerless leader can do little in the hierarchy on behalf of his subordinates or himself and is relatively helpless in the face of many serious problems which confront him and his work group. This is illustrated by the research of Pelz, who shows that unless the supervisor is influential with his own superiors, "good" supervisory practice on his part is not likely to make much difference to subordinates. Subordinates are more likely to react favorably to "good" and adversely to "bad" supervisory practices *if* the supervisor is influential in the company.[14]

Total Amount of Control in an Organization

Many administrators seem to face a serious problem in their understanding of supervisory-subordinate relations. They often assume that the amount of control exercised by members of a group or organization is a fixed quantity and that increasing the power of one individual automatically decreases that of others. There is good reason, however, to question this conclusion. The total amount of control exercised in a group or organization can increase, and the various participants can acquire a share of this augmented power. Conversely, the total amount of control may decrease, and all may share the loss. This is illustrated in everyday social situations—friendships, marital relations, as well as supervisory–subordinate interactions. One can easily picture the laissez-faire leader who exercises little control over his subordinates and who may at the same time be indifferent to their wishes. He neither influences nor is influenced by his men. A second supervisor interacts and communicates often, welcomes opinions, and elicits influence attempts. Suggestions which subordinates offer make a difference to him and his subordinates are responsive, in turn, to his requests. To the extent that this may contribute to effective performance—and we have reason to believe that it does if the supervisor also has influence with his manager—the group itself will be more powerful or influential. The manager under these circumstances is more likely to delegate additional areas of decision making to the group, and he, in turn, will respect and be responsive to the group's decisions. To the extent that the organizational hierarchy, from top to bottom, is characterized in these terms, we have a more highly integrated, tightly knit social system. We have, in the terms of Rensis Likert, a more substantial "interaction-influence system."[15]

The importance of the notion of "total amount of control" and of the "interaction-influence system" is illustrated in an analysis by Likert of data

14 D. C. Pelz, Influence: A Key to Effective Leadership in the First-Line Supervisor, *Personnel,* 29 (1952), 3–11.
15 R. Likert, *New Patterns of Management* (New York, 1961).

collected in thirty-one geographically separated departments of a large industrial service organization.[16] Each of the departments did essentially the same work, and careful records of department productivity were kept by the company. Nonsupervisory employees were asked the following question in a written questionnaire: "In general, how much say or influence do you feel each of the following groups has on what goes on in your department?" Answers were checked on a five-point scale from "little or no influence" to "a very great deal of influence." Employees answered this question relative to the following groups within their departments: the department manager, the supervisors, the men. Likert then divided the 31 departments into three groups according to their level of productivity. Figure 1 shows the average responses of the departments to the question for the third highest in productivity and for the third lowest in productivity.

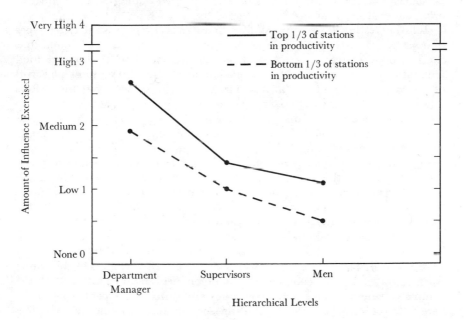

Figure 1. *Control curves of high- and low-producing departments.*

According to these employees, not only did they have more influence as a group within the high-producing departments, but so did the supervisors and managers. Likert's analysis of these departments suggests that the social

[16] R. Likert, "Influence and National Sovereignty," in J. G. Peatman and E. L. Hartley, eds., *Festschrift for Gardner Murphy* (New York, 1960).

systems differed in the high- and low-producing departments. The former was characterized by a higher total amount of control, by a greater degree of mutual influence. "The high-performing managers have actually increased the size of the 'influence pie' by means of the leadership processes which they use. They listen more to their men, are more interested in their men's ideas, and have more confidence and trust in their men."[17] There was a greater give-and-take and supportiveness by superiors, a higher level of effective communication upward, downward, and sideward. This all contributed to a greater sensitivity and receptivity on the part of each organization member to the influence of others—superiors relative to subordinates and subordinates relative to superiors. There was in all cases a higher level of mutual influence and control and a more likely integration of the interests of workers, supervisors, and managers. Under these circumstances, the high level of influence among workers was not a threat to managerial personnel. On the contrary, it was part of a process leading to more effective organizational performance.[18]

It is interesting to see that similar findings occur in several other types of organizations. In a study of four labor unions, for example, we found that the two more effective, active, and powerful unions had the highest total amount of control exercised by members and officers.[19] The most powerful of the four unions had a relatively influential membership—but the leaders (the president, executive board, and bargaining committee) were by no means uninfluential. In this union, members and leaders were relatively more active. They attended more meetings, took part in discussions at meetings, communicated informally about union affairs, and heard and considered the feelings and ideas of others. Members and leaders influenced each other and in the process created effective concerted action. This union "keeps management on its toes" as the personnel manager at the plant philosophically pointed out. In the least effective union, however, the members were relatively uninfluential in union affairs, and so were the leaders. A kind of laissez-faire atmosphere prevailed. Members were not integrated and not tied together by bonds of interaction and influence. They were not really part of an organized system. The ineffectiveness of this union was illustrated by the comments of a union field representative: "If the company wanted to take advantage, they could make the people live hard here." An old-timer of the local expressed his disillusionment: "We feel that it is not what it used to be.... Nothing happens to grievances. You can't find out what happens to them—they get lost.... The [bargaining] committee doesn't fight anymore." The differences between the most powerful and least powerful union in their distributions of control as reported

---

17 *Ibid.*

18 *Ibid.*

19 A. S. Tannenbaum and R. L. Kahn, *Participation in Union Locals* (Evanston, Ill., 1958); A. S. Tannenbaum, Control Structure and Union Functions, *American Journal of Sociology,* 61 (1956), 536–45.

by members is shown in Figure 2. Although the wording of the question in this study is somewhat different from that of the industrial service organization study discussed, the implications are very similar.[20]

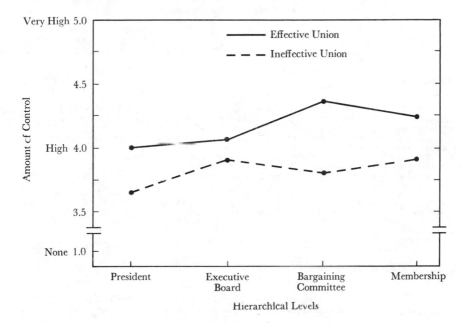

Figure 2. *Control curves of effective and ineffective unions. (From A. S. Tannenbaum and R. L. Kahn,* Participation in Union Locals *[Evanston, Ill., 1958], p. 162.)*

Mann and Hoffman applied a similar methodology in studying some of the effects of automation in a power plant. They illustrated, through a comparison of a new, highly automated plant with an older, less automated one, how changes in technology might affect the social structure of a plant, including its patterns of control, worker responsibility, and level of morale.[21] Fewer employees operated the new plant, although the ratio of nonsupervisory to supervisory personnel was about the same. The jobs in the new

[20] Question in union study: "In general, how much do you think the president [membership, plant bargaining committee, executive board] has to say about how things are decided in this local?" Responses ranged on a five-point scale from "a great deal of say" to "no say at all."

[21] Mann and Hoffman, *op. cit.*

plant required more knowledge and responsibility of the workers, and, as Table 2 illustrates, the patterns of control in the two plants differed too. According to the workers (and the supervisors were in essential agreement), the new plant was characterized by more control than the old.

Table 2. Amount of Influence Exercised by Three Levels as Perceived by the Men in Two Plants.[a]

LEVEL	OLD PLANT	NEW PLANT
Men	2.64	3.12[b]
Foremen	2.42	3.51[b]
Front office	4.56	4.48

[a] F. C. Mann and L. R. Hoffman, *Automation and the Worker: A Study of Social Change in Power Plants* (New York, 1960), p. 57; by permission of the publisher, Holt, Rinehart and Winston, Inc. The following questions were employed:
Question: In general, how much do you and the other men of your work group have to say about how things are done?"
Responses: 5—"Our foreman gives us a great deal of say in how things are done."...1—"Our foreman gives us hardly any say at all in how things are done."
Question: "In general, how much do you think the foremen have to say about how things are done in this plant?"
Responses: 5—"They have a great deal of say."...1—"They have very little or no say at all."
Question: "In general, how much say do you think the men in the front office of this plant have in how things are done in this plant?"
Responses: 5—"They have a great deal of say in how things are done in this plant."...1—"They have very little or no say at all in how things are done in this plant."
[b] Differences significant beyond the .001 level of confidence.

The difference between the plants is particularly interesting at the foreman level. In the new plant, foremen were judged to have more influence than the men; in the old, less. Nor was the more powerful supervisor considered a threat to the workers in the new plant. Despite—or should we say, because of—the greater influence of foremen together with that of the men, the men reported less often that their foreman treated them like inferiors, that he was a "driver" of men, that he was "bossy," or that he said one thing and did another. They reported more often that the foreman tried to get ideas from the work group, that he was a warm and friendly person, that he would "go to bat" for the men, and that he was a "leader" of men. When all the responses are taken into consideration, 66 per cent of the men in the new plant and 36 in the old report that they are very satisfied with their immediate supervisor. The new plant is a more tightly integrated social (as well as physical) system. Workers feel more a part of a work group and feel free to call on others in the work group for help with job problems. There is a higher degree of interdependence between foremen and men and to some extent among the men themselves. The foremen in the plant have more influence than their counterparts in the old—and so do the men.

Results from an unpublished study of forty insurance agencies show the same direction. D. Bowers and S. Seashore compared twenty insurance agencies high in sales volume with twenty agencies low in volume. In the high-producing agencies, the general agents, the district agents, and the sales agents as a group were all reported to have more influence in their agencies than were their counterparts in the low-producing agencies.

The clerical experiment discussed previously yielded similar results. The increased control which the clerks reported was not accompanied by a corresponding decrease in the control attributed to supervisory and managerial personnel. The total amount of control reported by clerks increased, accompanied by a more effective social system. Not only did morale increase in this group, but so did motivation and productivity.[22]

Interestingly, the kinds of relationships suggested by these data apply in a voluntary organization too, as indicated by research in over one hundred geographically separate local Leagues of Women Voters.[23] The effectiveness of each local league was rated by a group of judges in the national office, and a sample of the members and leaders in each was then asked several questions relating to control within their organizations. The results indicate that members in effective leagues exercised more control than did their counterparts in ineffective leagues, but leaders did not exercise less. A greater total amount of control was ascribed to effective leagues than to ineffective ones.

While these results from a variety of organizations seem to suggest an important hypothesis connecting the total amount of control and organizational performance, our research findings are not completely consistent on this point. A recent study of thirty automobile dealerships, for example, did not reveal any relationship between criteria of effectiveness (including growth in sales during the past year) and the total amount of control within the dealership as reported by salesmen. The automobile sales agency may present a somewhat different social structure in which "individual enterprise" and competitive behavior among salesmen is more at a premium. We do not know what the effect would be if agencies were structured more like the typical business organization with greater emphasis on co-ordination and co-operative effort. The total amount of control might be greater under these conditions, and this variable might prove, under these circumstances, to have important implications for effective performance.

Conclusion

American management is dollar cost conscious. Many managers are also aware of the costs of organized productive effort which cannot be calculated

---

[22] Productivity also increased in a contrasting experimental group within the company under conditions of lowering the amount of control exercised by clerks. Here, however, clerk morale, loyalty, and motivation decreased. Considerable tension was felt in this group, and it gave the appearance of high instability. There is serious doubt that this type of system could sustain itself as well as the other for an extended period under conditions which prevail in American society. See R. Likert, Measuring Organizational Performance, *Harvard Business Review*, 36 (1958), 41–50, and *New Patterns of Management* (New York, 1961), chs. v, vi.

[23] A. S. Tannenbaum, Control and Effectiveness in a Voluntary Organization, *American Journal of Sociology*, 67 (1961), 33–47.

immediately in terms of dollars and cents. These are the human costs of organization, costs paid by members and ultimately by society as a whole. Nor are they to be calculated simply in terms of the dissatisfactions which industrial man faces. They may be paid in terms of the shaping of his very personality. The evidence on this is not very clear, but we have reason to believe that adult personality may change as a result of persistent conditions in the environment. The nature of man's experiences in an organization can affect his general mentality and outlook on life. In the clerical experiment described above we saw evidence of slight changes in personality after a year's exposure of clerks to different patterns of control. These changes were in the direction of increasing the "fit" between the worker's personality and the nature of the control structure.[24] Notorious "brain washing" methods represent the ultimate in the process of institutionalized personality change, and we see illustrated in the fiction of Orwell and Huxley the psychological bludgeoning of individual personality into a perfect fit to the institutions of a "hypothetical" society of the future. As Huxley puts it, "Round pegs in square holes tend to have dangerous thoughts about the social system and to infect others with their discontent."[25] Organizations cannot often tolerate deviants, and there are pressures, sometimes subtle, on deviants to change.

Organizations in a democratic society present a seeming dilemma. As Geoffrey Vickers puts it,

> We are forever oscillating between two alternatives which seem mutually exclusive—on the one hand, collective efficiency won at the price of individual freedom; on the other, individual freedom equally frustrated by collective anarchy. Those who believe in a middle way which is more than a compromise do so in the faith that human beings are capable or can become capable of social organization which is both individually satisfying and collectively effective; and they have plenty of evidence for their faith. On the other hand, our knowledge of the laws involved is still rudimentary.[26]

Middle ways are sprouting up around the globe today. The work council systems in Yugoslavia, in Germany, France, Belgium, England, though differing radically in character and effectiveness are, within their respective cultures, experiments in the middle way. We have our Scanlon plans, profit-sharing and suggestion schemes, as well as varying degrees of participative management. However, our knowledge of the effects of these systems is, as Vickers says, rudimentary.

If the clues provided by our research so far are substantiated, the middle way will have to take into account the important facts about control: how

---

[24] A. S. Tannenbaum, Personality Change as a Result of an Experimental Change of Environmental Conditions, *Journal of Abnormal and Social Psychology,* 55 (1957), 404–6.

[25] A. Huxley, *Brave New World* (New York, 1953), p. xvi.

[26] "Control Stability and Choice," reprinted in *General Systems, Yearbook of the Society for General Systems,* 2 (1957), 1–8.

control is distributed within an organization, and how much it all amounts to. Patterns of control—as they are perceived by organization members, at least—are tied significantly to the performance of the organization and to the adjustments and satisfactions of members. If our research leads are correct, the more significant improvements in the human side of enterprise are going to come through changes in the way organizations are controlled, and particularly through changes in the size of the "influence pie." This middle way leans on the assumption that influential workers do not imply uninfluential supervisors or managers. This is a relatively novel assumption for many managers who have been weaned on the all-or-none law of power: one either leads or is led, is strong or is weak, controls or is controlled. Disraeli was no less influential a leader, however, for having questioned this when he said, "I follow the people. Am I not their leader?" And, managers who in their behavior question the all-or-none principle do not seem less influential for it.

Our middle way assumes further that the worker, or supervisor, or manager, who exercises some influence over matters of interest to him in the work situation, acquires a sense of self-respect which the powerless individual may lack. He can also elicit the respect and high regard of others. This is the key to good human relations. Supervisory training alone cannot achieve this any more than good intentions in bad organization can achieve it. The pattern of control in an organization, however, has a direct and profound effect on the organization's human relations climate. Workers who have some sense of control in the organizations we have studied, are, in general, more, not less, positively disposed toward their supervisors and managers. And their managers are more positively disposed toward them.

We assume further, with some support from research, that increasing and distributing the exercise of control more broadly in an organization helps to distribute an important sense of involvement in the organization. Members become more ego involved. Aspects of personality which ordinarily do not find expression now contribute to the motivation of the members. The organization provides members with a fuller ranger of experiences. In doing this, however, it creates its own dilemmas, similar in some respects to those described by Vickers.

A first dilemma concerns the increased control to which the influential organization members may become subject. While he controls more, he is not controlled less. The loyalty and identification which he feels for the organization lead him to accept organizational requirements and to conform to organizational norms which he might not otherwise do. We find evidence of this in the behavior of members of the effective union with high total control. Their behaviors were more uniform than were those of members in the ineffective laissez-faire union.[27] Norms and pressures toward conformity existed in the effective union which were lacking in the ineffective one. Members in the effective union pay for the increased control which they

27 Tannenbaum and Kahn, *op. cit.;* Tannenbaum, Control Structure and Union Functions.

exercise (and for the effectiveness of their organization) not only in terms of the greater effort that they put into union activities, but also by their greater sensitivity and accession to controls within the union. An analysis in the thirty-one departments of the industrial service organization described revealed a similar phenomenon. Norms, measured in terms of uniformity in the behavior of workers, were more apparent in the departments having high total control than in those having low control. In these "better" departments, influence by the men as a group was greater, morale was more favorable, productive effort was higher, and so was uniformity.[28] The exercise of control did not spare the controller from being controlled. The contrary may be true in effective organizations with high total control, where influence tends to be reciprocal.

A second dilemma arises out of the increased involvement and motivation that are likely to accompany the exercise of control. While we see greater opportunity for human satisfaction in the middle way, the result is not simple felicity. Whenever man is highly motivated he may experience the pangs of failure, as well as the joys of success. He will know some of the satisfactions which come from a challenge met and a responsibility fulfilled. He may also feel frustration from the development of goals which are not easily reached.

[28] C. G. Smith, O. Ari, and A. S. Tannenbaum, The Relationship of Patterns of Control to Norms in a Service Organization (unpublished report, 1962).

25 / Supervision and Productivity: Empirical Findings and Theoretical Considerations

Robert Dubin

THE MOST GENERAL conclusion of this...analysis is that productive supervisory practices are those appropriate to the organization in which the supervisor functions. Different kinds of supervisory behaviors are effective because they are suited to special kinds of organizations.

Reprinted by permission of the author and publisher from Robert Dubin, *et al.*, *Leadership and Productivity* (Scranton, Pennsylvania: Chandler Publishing Company, an Intext Publisher, 1965), pp. 3-4, 39-42, 46-50.

Students of industrial behavior have taken a long time to reach the pedestrian conclusion that many different styles of supervision are effective. Analyses of the management of scientists in industry make clear that the supervisory style appropriate to the direction of their work is different from foreman behavior on the automobile-assembly line.[1] From the study of coal mining has come the understanding that when the technology of mining is radically changed supervisory behaviors appropriate to the new technology differ markedly from those in established traditions.[2] Supervision that is effective with bank employees contrasts with that which is successful with sales crews.[3] Actual studies of working behaviors have sampled a fair number of work settings and have revealed significant variety in the successful supervisory practices found among them.

The growing body of evidence speaks loudly for the idea that in the supervision of industrial and commercial work highly varied practices prove successful in given work settings. Nevertheless, students of industry and industrial administrators still seek a "one best method" of supervision much as the originators of scientific management and work rationalization were captivated by the hope that individual work tasks could be standardized in a "one best method.". . .

A particularly important study in the analysis of supervisory practices was that by French and Coch,[4] in which the effects of employee participation in a decision affecting them were measured. It was concluded that those who participated in decisions regarding work changes ultimately reached somewhat higher levels of output than a comparable group of workers who were told to change their methods of work. This study has been the cornerstone of theory concluding that worker participation is desirable for efficiency reasons and improvement of output levels.

Wickert[5] studied employee turnover and feelings of ego involvement in the day-to-day operations of telephone operators and female service represen-

1 For studies of scientists in industry see William Kornhauser, *Scientists in Industry: Conflict and Accommodation* (Berkeley: University of California Press, 1962), and Simon Marcson, *The Scientist in American Industry* (Princeton: Industrial Relations Section, Princeton University, 1958). Foreman behavior on the automobile-assembly line is sketched out in Charles R. Walker, Robert H. Guest, and Arthur N. Turner, *The Foreman on the Assembly Line* (Cambridge, Mass.: Harvard University Press, 1956).

2 As well described in E. L. Trist and K. W. Bansforth, "Some Social and Psychological Consequences of the Longwall Method of Coal Getting," *Human Relations,* 4:3–38 (December 1951).

3 For a study of bank employees see: Chris Argyris, *Organization of a Bank* (New Haven: Yale Labor and Management Center, 1954), while an excellent study of supervision of sales crews is G. F. F. Lombard, *Behavior in a Selling Group: A Case Study of Interpersonal Relations in a Department Store* (Boston: Harvard Business School, Division of Research, 1955).

4 Lester Coch and John R. P. French, Jr., "Overcoming Resistance to Change," *Human Relations,* 1:512–32 (1948).

5 F. R. Wickert, "Turnover and Employee's Feelings of Ego-Involvement," *Personnel Psychology,* 4:185–97 (1951).

tatives in the Michigan Bell Telephone Company. About 700 women were studied. The principal finding was that those who stayed with the company had a greater feeling of involvement in the day-to-day operations of the company than those who left. Specifically, those who stayed tended to say (1) they had a chance to make decisions on the job, and (2) they felt they were making an important individual contribution to the success of the company. It will be noted that telephone operators and service representatives are all involved in unit production, since they each have to depend upon someone initiating a call or a service request before they go into action. Under these circumstances of technology a material degree of autonomy is probably essential in maintaining levels of output. A chance to make decisions on the job and contribute to company success are measures of participation. It might be concluded, however, that these aspects of participation in work are mediated by the need for autonomy that comes from the technology employed.

In Rice's study of the Indian weaving shed,[6] a comparison was made of production before and after a change in the organization of the work. The individual workers in the experimental weaving groups revised the production process from what had previously been a confused and relatively unstructured one. The data demonstrate that the subsequent steady state of output was markedly and significantly higher after the workers reorganized the work themselves. Furthermore, the rate of cloth damage in the weaving mill was lower than before reorganization of production.

Several comments need to be made about this study. The self-organizing productive groups increased their efficiency by about 18 per cent if we take the before-reorganization figures as the base. This improvement tends to give the impression, as Rice suggests, that the self-organization of work is one means for increasing efficiency considerably. But a disturbing feature of this situation also must be taken into account. The original structuring of the work situation, which continued to obtain in the nonexperimental groups in the same company, was one in which there were confused task and worker relationships, and no perceptible internal work-group structure. Thus the base from which change was measured in this study may be an instance of industrial "anarchy," or near anarchy, in which the designs of the production processes themselves were scarcely adequate.

Under these circumstances, any attention to the *organization* of work, whether management-initiated or worker-initiated, undoubtedly would have produced significant increases in productivity. Weaving, being a continuous-process production technology over short time spans, would require high structure for adequate performance. In the light of Fleishman's results it seems probable that structuring itself is what may have improved productivity in the Indian weaving shed, not worker participation. It may not, therefore, be desirable or warranted to draw the conclusion that high

6 A. K. Rice, "Productivity and Social Organization in an Indian Weaving Shed," *Human Relations,* 6:297–329 (1953).

autonomy and participation in decisions by the Indian weavers are what really produced higher output.

Likert, in an early paper,[7] made the point that

> Available research findings indicate, therefore, that when...the amount of participation used is less than or very much greater than expected, an unfavorable reaction is likely to be evoked. Substantially greater amounts of participation than expected appear to exceed the skill of the subordinate to cope with it and produce a negative reaction because of the threatening nature of the situation to the subordinate. The available theory and research findings suggest that the best results obtain when the amount of participation used is somewhat greater than expected by the subordinate, but still within their capacity to respond to it effectively.

Likert had made this point as early as 1952, but it is a point that is rarely given attention by those who urge participative management as the be-all and end-all of supervisory practice.

Likert clearly argued for an optimal rather than a maximal level of participation of subordinates in decision making relative to their own destinies. That is, there is a curvilinear relation between worker participation and such consequences as output. This relation recalls Fleishman's studies of initiating structure and consideration which relate in a curvilinear fashion to turnover and absenteeism. That is to say, over part of the range of consideration and initiating structure for subordinates there is no material change in their reactions, but beyond a critical point their reactions become prompt and decisive.

The general conclusion that emerges is that employee participation is probably not linearly related but rather curvilinearly related to aspects of working behavior. Likert has pointed out that his own researches have indicated that supervisory behavior in excess of normal expectations will not be favorably accepted by subordinates. This disfavor may be particularly likely if the supervisor invites participation beyond the subordinate's normal level of acceptance. This conclusion recalls Barnard's "zone of indifference," in which reactions of the subordinate become significant only if the supervisor exceeds the tolerance limits customarily adopted by the subordinate.[8]...

Conclusion

Supervision does make some difference in productivity. Supervisory practices also affect other aspects of work. The details of these conclusions depart significantly from current views, and are both unique and surprising.

1. Supervisory behavior affects the productivity of individuals by being appropriate to the work setting. One key to describing the characteristics

[7] Rensis Likert, "Effective Supervision: An Adaptive and Relative Process," *op. cit.,* p. 329.

[8] Chester I. Barnard, *The Functions of the Executive* (Cambridge, Mass.: Harvard University Press, 1938).

of work settings is to know the nature of the technologies employed. The descriptive task has just begun but the results are promising. By drawing simple distinctions between unit- and mass-production technologies, and viewing continuous production as another type of technology, supervisory styles are found appropriate to each technological type. The more a production process resembles a unit or batch technology, the greater is the probability that worker autonomy and its supervisory counterpart—general rather than close supervision—will be appropriate. The more a technology resembles a continuous-production system the more appropriate will close supervision be.

2. This first proposition leads directly to the second. There is no "one best" method of supervision. As in all human systems, there is variability in the systems of supervision of industrial and commercial work. Several styles of supervision are effective, but they are individually successful only in relation to appropriate work settings. Variety in supervisory behaviors may no longer be considered a challenge to choose the "one best" for all settings, but rather as a challenge to understand where each does or does not work.

3. As far as empirical data take us, it seems clear that the influence of supervisory behaviors on *productivity* is small. The studies are few in number, however, and not adequately designed to measure magnitude of influence of supervision on productivity.

4. Supervision of industrial and commercial work has many functions. The variety of areas in which supervisors act is the consequence of their having numerous functional contributions to make. For a given situation supervision may have relatively little to do with individual productivity, and yet supervisors, because they perform many other functions, may retain importance in work organizations. Executives must therefore constantly face the difficult problem of organizational design and the choice of operating goals for supervisors. If, for example, top management wants workers to be happy this goal may be attained by appropriate supervisory behaviors.

5. The goals of supervision and the behaviors of supervisors are independent of each other in one sense and linked in another. A variety of goals may be assigned to supervisors, and those selected do not appear to be limited or determined by any features of organizational structure or process. Thus, consideration of workers may be emphasized in unit production, in mass production, or in process production if top management chooses consideration as a goal. Supervisory practices in each technological system will be different although directed toward the same goal. It is in this sense that the goals of supervision and the behaviors of supervisors are independent of each other.

On the other hand, goals and behaviors are linked through technology since behaviors necessary to achieve a particular goal must be appropriate to the operating situation. For example, consideration of workers in unit-production technologies may exhibit itself by providing workers with maximum opportunities to pace their own work, while in continuous-production technologies the same consideration may be most appropriately expressed as detailed concern with safety or physical comfort of the worker.

6. It is now possible to take a sophisticated view of the impact of supervision on working behaviors. Most analysts up to this time have assumed that whatever the linkage, it tended to be a linear one. That is, a unit change in a particular supervisory behavior was assumed to produce a corresponding change in worker response throughout the range of supervisory action. This view is simply false. Many behaviors have thresholds above which the behavior is responded to by others, but below which the behaviors produce little or no effect. Thresholds were revealed, for example, in the relationship between supervisory consideration and worker responses in terms of grievances and absenteeism. This phenomenon was also discovered in the relation between opportunity to participate in decisions and worker responses to the opportunity.

7. A supervisory practice in the low range may have one effect on worker response, but in the high range may produce exactly the opposite effect. This disparity was exhibited in the consequence of supervisory pressure for worker morale. At least in some demonstrable instances the relationship between supervisory behavior and worker response is nonlinear and may even be parabolic. Evidence supports the contention that if a little bit of a supervisory behavior may be good, a lot may be very bad indeed. This optimization notion is sometimes overlooked in the theory and practice of personnel administration.

8. An important technological trend is making for a fundamental shift in industry from the management of people to the management of things. The detailed study of continuous-process manufacture showed the highest ratio of managers to other workers for any type of technology. It has been inferred that this high ratio reflects the need for supervisor surveillance of high-speed production processes to insure that product runs are error-free, since large numbers of defects can be produced by the time the process is halted to correct an error. As supervisors supervise machines more and people less, they will become increasingly responsible for production. Supervisory controls will not be controls on speed of output, since output will be machine- or process-paced. The supervisors will be largely concerned with controlling quality, and the operating contingencies that influence the go-no-go performance of the production process.

9. Knowledge of leadership and supervision as they affect working behavior is almost exclusively the result of studying American industrial practices. A few important English studies have been cited here, and additional studies dealing with other national economies are scattered through the literature.[9] Culture does make a difference in supervisory practices. It follows, then, that caution is necessary in applying present knowledge to cultural settings different from those in which the knowledge was gained.

[9] I cite just two studies conducted in Scandinavian countries which have been scarcely noticed by American scholars although both are significant contributions. K. Raino, *Leadership Qualities: A Theoretical Inquiry and an Experimental Study of Foremen* (Helsinki: Annales Academiae Scientiarum Fennicae, Series B, vol. 95.1, 1955); Uno Remitz, *Professional Satisfaction among Swedish Bank Employees* (Copenhagen: Munksgaard, 1960).

Generalizations may work universally, but then again they may not. We have no *a priori* reason for guessing which of these two outcomes will obtain.

10. All the studies of human relations and supervision tell little about how much productivity is affected by individual supervisory practices. Only one study attempted to tease out the answer to this question and it suggested that not more than one-fifth of the variance in productivity can be accounted for by a combination of three supervisory practices. The Western Electric and other researches showed that fellow workers influence the individual's output. Advances in technology produce steady increases in man-hour productivity. There has never been a proper analysis of variance to assay that relative importance of simultaneous factors affecting individual output. It is certainly time to turn empirical attention to just this kind of problem.

7 / Work Incentives: What Role Does Money Play in Motivation and Productivity?

Among the factors thought to motivate workers toward higher levels of productivity, financial incentive early gained a prominent place. The well-known advocate of the "economic man" concept, Frederick Taylor, was only one of many who were convinced of man's willingness to work harder if the additional exertion would be rewarded by more money. This economic conception of man was largely unchallenged until a group of Harvard researchers issued a dissenting view based on their studies of production workers at the Hawthorne plant in Chicago. Debate on the incentive issue in particular and criticism of the Hawthorne studies in general has continued since the publication of their findings at the end of the 1930s. The most recent in a long line of attacks is contained in the first selection, by Alex Carey ("The Hawthorne Studies: A Radical Criticism").

Reporting on his reexamination of the evidence from the Hawthorne studies, Carey builds a case against their scientific worth. His specific charge is that while the Hawthorne researchers concluded that financial rewards were inconsequential for worker output and morale compared to social rewards (achieved through "friendly supervision"), their own evidence supports the exactly opposite conclusion. Accusing the Hawthorne researchers of using a nonscientific approach, for example in their allegedly faulty methodological procedures and their proclivity for interpreting evidence to suit their biases, Carey judges their conclusions to be not only scientifically worthless, but detrimental if uncritically accepted by social scientists and students.

The second piece in this chapter is my own response to Carey's critique, entitled "On Alex Carey's Radical Criticism of the Hawthorne Studies." Undeniably Carey makes many telling points; however, his conclusion that the Hawthorne research is worthless needs to be challenged on the basis of some interpretive errors on his part and in light of evidence drawn from both the Hawthorne research and subsequent studies. I argue that the original and enduring contribution of the Hawthorne studies is their placement of financial incentives into a social context.

Although their essay concerns managers, Lyman Porter and Edward Lawler ("The Place of Financial Incentives in Motivation") offer a general theoretical model that attempts to specify the circumstances under which money is an effective motivator of work performance. According to their model, for which they present some empirical confirmation, pay functions as a motivator when it is important to the person receiving it, and when the person believes that his financial reward will be commensurate with his efforts to perform effectively. Porter and Lawler add to the significance of their study by locating their findings and interpretations in the context of other theories of financial incentive.

The Hawthorne research and subsequent studies focused on the conditioning effects of social factors on financial incentives. Consideration of the interaction among personal characteristics, job attributes, and financial compensation occupy Opsahl and Dunnette in their extensive review of this literature ("The Role of Financial Compensation in Industrial Motivation"). They conclude that the state of our knowledge concerning the ways in which money affects worker behavior on the job and interacts with other factors is considerably less than the voluminous literature on the topic would suggest. They call for additional research to diminish our ignorance of the effect of money on job attitudes and behavior—specifically for experimental laboratory studies and rigorously controlled field research. In keeping with their psychological orientation, they emphasize the need for research on the interplay among personal goals, motives, perception, and money.

26 / The Hawthorne Studies: A Radical Criticism

Alex Carey

THERE CAN BE few scientific disciplines or fields of research in which a single set of studies or a single researcher and writer has exercised so great an influence as was exercised for a quarter of a century by Mayo and the Hawthorne studies. Although this influence has declined in the last ten years as a result of the widespread failure of later studies to reveal any reliable relation between the social satisfactions of industrial workers and their work performance, reputable textbooks still refer almost reverentially to the Hawthorne studies as a classic in the history of social science in industry.

One might have expected therefore that the Hawthorne studies would have been subjected to the most searching and skeptical scrutiny; that before the remarkable claims of these studies, especially about the relative unimportance of financial rewards compared with purely social rewards, became so widely influential, the quality of the evidence produced and the validity of the inferences from it would have been meticulously examined and assessed. There have been broad criticisms of Mayo's approach and assumptions, many of them cogent. They include charges of pro-management bias, clinical bias, and scientific naiveté.[1] But no one has applied systematically and in detail the method of critical doubt to the claim that there is scientific worth in the original reports of the Hawthorne investigators.

Background

The Hawthorne studies comprise a long series of investigations into the importance for work behavior and attitudes of a variety of physical, economic, and social variables. The principal investigations were carried out

---

[1] For a review of these charges and criticisms see Delbert Miller and William Form, *Industrial Sociology,* New York: Harper, 1951, pp. 74–83. For a defense see Henry A. Landsberger, *Hawthorne Revisited,* New York: Cornell, 1958. Landsberger's defense is restricted to the report of the Hawthorne studies by Fritz J. Roethlisberger and William Dickson, *Management and the Worker,* Cambridge, Harvard Univ. Press, 1939. Even this report, in Landsberger's view, has "done the field of human relations in industry an amount of harm which, in retrospect, appears to be almost irreparable." Landsberger, *op. cit.,* p. 64.

Reprinted by permission of the publisher from "The Hawthorne Studies: A Radical Criticism," *American Sociological Review,* Vol. 32, No. 3 (June 1967), pp. 403–16.

between 1927 and 1932, whereafter economic depression caused their suspension. The component studies may be distinguished as five stages:

Stage   I: The Relay Assembly Test Room Study. (New incentive system and new supervision).

Stage   II: The Second Relay Assembly Group Study. (New incentive system only).

Stage III: The Mica Splitting Test Room Study. (New supervision only).

Stage IV: The Interviewing Program.

Stage   V: The Bank-Wiring Observation Room Study.

Stages I to III constitute a series of partially controlled studies which were initially intended to explore the effects on work behavior of variations in physical conditions of work, especially variations in rest pauses and in hours of work, but also in payment system, temperature, humidity, etc.

However, after the studies had been in progress for at least twelve months the investigators came to the entirely unanticipated conclusion that social satisfactions arising out of human association in work were more important determinants of work behavior in general and output in particular than were any of the physical and economic aspects of the work situation to which their attention had originally been limited.[2] This conclusion came as "the great *éclaircissement*...an illumination quite different from what they had expected from the illumination studies."[3] It is the central and distinctive finding from which the fame and influence of the Hawthorne studies derive.

This "éclaircissement" about the predominant importance of social satisfactions at work occurred during Stage I of the studies. In consequence, all the later studies are in important ways subordinate to Stage I: "It was the origin from which all the subsequent phases sprang. It was also their main focal point. It gave to these other phases their significance in relation to the whole enquiry."[4]

Stages II and III were "designed to check on" (and were taken to supplement and confirm) the Stage I conclusion "that the observed production increase was a result of a change in the *social situation*...(and) not primarily because of wage incentives, reduced fatigue or similar factors."[5] *Stage IV* was an interviewing program undertaken to explore worker attitudes. *Stage V* was a study of informal group organization in the work situation.

The two later studies (IV and V) resulted directly from conclusions

[2] George A. Pennock, "Industrial Research at Hawthorne," *Personnel Journal*, 8 (February, 1930), pp. 296–313; Mark L. Putman, "Improving Employee Relations," *Personnel Journal*, 8 (February, 1930), pp. 314–25.

[3] Fritz J. Roethlisberger, *Management and Morale*, Cambridge: Harvard University Press, 1941, p. 15.

[4] Lyndall Urwick and Edward Brech, *The Making of Scientific Management*, vol. III, London: Management Publications Trust, 1948, p. 27. See also Roethlisberger and Dickson, *op. cit.*, p. 29.

[5] Morris S. Viteles, *Motivation and Morale in Industry*, London: Staples, 1954, p. 185.

based on Stages I–III about the superior influence of social needs. Observations made in both were interpreted in the light of such prior conclusions. Hence it is clear that, as maintained by Urwick, Stage I was the key study, with Stages II and III adding more or less substantial support to it. The present paper will therefore be limited to a consideration of the evidence produced in Stages I–III for the famous Hawthorne conclusions about the superior importance for work behavior of social needs and satisfactions.

The Preferred Incentive System and Output

Stage I: Relay Assembly Test Room (new incentive and new supervision). In Stage I of the Hawthorne studies, five girls who were employed assembling telephone relays were transferred from the factory floor to a special test room. Here their output of relays was recorded for over two years during which a large number of alterations were made in their working conditions. These alterations included a much less variable assembly task,[6] shorter hours, rest pauses, freer and more friendly supervision, and a preferred incentive system.[7] These changes were introduced cumulatively and no control group was established. Nonetheless, it was originally expected that the study would yield information about the influence of one or another physical condition of work.[8]

At the end of two years, the girls' output had increased by about 30 percent.[9] By this time, the investigators were confident that the physical changes in work conditions had been of little importance, and that the observed increase was due primarily to a change in "mental attitude" of the employees resulting from changed methods of supervision.[10] This change in mental attitude was chiefly characterized by a more relaxed "relationship of confidence and friendliness...such...that practically no supervision is required."[11]

However, the standard report of the study recognizes that any of several changes introduced concurrently could, hypothetically, have caused both the observed change in mental outlook and the associated increase in output. The authors of the report list the following as providing possible "hypotheses to explain major changes" in work behavior:[12] (i) changes in the character and physical context of the work task; (ii) reduction of fatigue and monotony consequent upon introduction of rest pauses and reduced hours of work;[13] (iii) change in the payment system; and (iv)

6 Roethlisberger and Dickson, *op. cit.,* pp. 21, 26.

7 *Ibid.,* pp. 22, 30–73.

8 *Ibid.,* p. 129; Pennock, *op. cit.,* p. 299.

9 Roethlisberger and Dickson, *op. cit.,* p. 160.

10 *Ibid.,* pp. 189–90; Pennock, *op. cit.,* pp. 297–309.

11 Pennock, *op. cit.,* p. 309.

12 Roethlisberger and Dickson, *op. cit.,* pp. 86–89.

13 The investigators list fatigue and monotony as separate hypotheses. For brevity, these have been combined as one hypothesis. The same sort of critical objections are relevant to the arguments and evidence advanced by the investigators with respect to both.

changes in supervision with consequent social changes in group relations.

The remainder of this paper will critically examine the evidence and arguments from which the investigators reached conclusions favorable to the last of these alternative hypotheses.

First hypothesis: changes in work task and physical context. The investigators allow that "the fact that most of the girls in the test room had to assemble fewer types of relays could not be entirely ignored. Operator 5's performance offered a convincing example. Of all the girls in the room she had had more different types of relays to assemble and of all the girls her output rate had shown the least improvement."[14] Whitehead reports that "later (1930–31) her (Operator 5's) working conditions were in line with the rest of the group and her comparative standing in the group definitely improved."[15]

However, it was subsequently found that statistical analysis of the relevant data (i.e., the varying output of five girls who were subjected to numerous cumulatively introduced experimental changes) did not show "any *conclusive* evidence in favor of the first hypothesis." On this ground the investigators "concluded that the change from one type of relay to another familiar type did not sufficiently slow up output to explain the increased output of the relay test room assemblers as compared with the assemblers in the regular department."[16] This conclusion leads the investigators to dismiss from further consideration the possibility that changes in task and conditions played any part at all in the observed increase in output.[17]

Second hypothesis: reduced fatigue due to rest pauses and shorter hours. The investigators recognize that "the rest pauses and shorter hours (may have) provided a relief from cumulative fatigue" resulting in higher output. They acknowledge that the fact that the rate of output of all but the slowest worker declined once the girls were returned to standard hours is "rather convincing evidence in favor of this argument."[18] Yet the investigators eventually dismiss these factors on the grounds that under the new conditions of work neither work curves nor medical examinations provided evidence that fatigue effects were present. Viteles has commented bluntly in this connection: "It is interesting to note that (these grounds) are

[14] *Ibid.,* p. 87.

[15] T. North Whitehead, *The Industrial Worker,* London: Oxford Univ. Press, 1938, Vol. I, p. 65.

[16] Roethlisberger and Dickson, *op. cit.,* p. 89. (Italics added.)

[17] The scientifically illiterate procedure of dismissing non-preferred explanations on the grounds that (i) the experimenters had found no *conclusive* evidence in favor of them and/or (ii) there was no evidence that any *one* of these explanations, considered by itself, accounted for *all* the effect observed, recurs through Roethlisberger and Dickson's report of the Hawthorne studies. This procedure is never applied to preferred hypotheses, which are assumed to be well-founded provided only that the evidence *against* them is less than conclusive. See, e.g., Roethlisberger and Dickson, *op. cit.,* p. 160 and pp. 96, 108, 127.

[18] *Ibid.,* p. 87.

exactly the same used by other investigators in illustrating the effectiveness of rest pauses *by reason of reduced fatigue.*"[19]

By these arguments, the investigators eliminated the first two of the four hypotheses originally proposed as alternative explanations of the 30 percent increase in output observed in Stage I. This left two contending "explanations," the new incentive system, and the new kind of supervision and related social factors. The problem of choosing between these explanations led directly to the next two major experiments.

Stage II: Second Relay Assembly Group (new incentive system only). "The aim of (this experiment) was to reproduce the test-room situation (i.e., Stage I) only in respect to the one factor of method of payment, using another group of operators. Since method of payment was to be the only alteration from the usual situation, it was thought that any marked changes in output could be reasonably related to this factor."[20]

Five girls who were employed on the same sort of task as the girls in Stage I under normal conditions on the factory floor were given the preferred incentive system which had been used throughout Stage I. Under this system, the earnings of each girl were based on the average output of the five. Under the regular payment system, the earnings of each girl were based on the average output of the whole department (i.e., about 100 girls).

Almost at once the Stage II girls' output increased by 12.6 percent.[21] But the experiment caused so much discontent among the rest of the girls in the department, who wanted the same payment conditions,[22] that it was discontinued after only nine weeks. The output of the five girls promptly dropped by 16 percent.[23]

As Viteles comments, "the increase in output during the period when the wage incentive was in effect, followed by a production decrease with the elimination of the wage incentive, represents evidence ordinarily interpreted as indicative of the direct and favorable influence of financial incentives upon output."[24] However, the investigators reject this interpretation and, without producing supporting evidence of any substance, conclude firmly[25] that the increase was due to inter-group rivalry resulting from the setting up of this second small group.

The change in payment system alone (Stage II) produced as much increase in output in nine weeks (possibly five weeks[26]) as was produced in

[19] Morris S. Viteles, *Industrial Psychology,* New York: Norton, 1932, p. 476. Italics in original.

[20] Roethlisberger and Dickson, *op. cit.,* p. 129.

[21] *Ibid.,* pp. 131–32, 577; Pennock, *op. cit.,* p. 307.

[22] *Ibid.,* p. 133.

[23] According to an earlier report (Pennock, *op. cit.,* p. 307), the increase in output was 13.8 percent, the experiment was discontinued after five weeks, and output then fell by 19–24 percent.

[24] Viteles, Motivation ..., *op. cit.,* p. 187.

[25] Roethlisberger and Dickson, *op. cit.,* pp. 133–34, 158, 577.

[26] Pennock, *op. cit.,* p. 307.

about nine months by change in payment system together with a change to
genial supervision (Stage I).[27] Yet this comparison appears not to have
made any impression on the investigators' confidence about the superior
importance of social factors.[28]

*Stage III: Mica Splitting Test Room (new supervision but no change in
payment system).* In *Stage I,* numerous changes had been introduced,
resulting in a 30 percent increase in output. In *Stage II,* only one of these
changes (the preferred incentive system) was introduced and a rapid 12
percent increase in output resulted. In *Stage III,* "the test-room situation
was to be duplicated in all respects except for the change in pay incentive.
If...output showed a trend similar to that noted in (Stage I), it would
suggest that the wage incentive was not the dominant factor in the situation."[29] Stage III, then, sought to test the combined effect on output of
change to a separate room, change in hours, and the introduction of rest
pauses and friendly supervision. Again a selected group of five girls was
closely studied and an increase in output was recorded—15.6 percent in
fourteen months[30] or, if one follows Pennock, 20 percent in twelve
months.[31]

A comparison between Stage III and Stage I has little prospect of
scientific usefulness since in Stage III (i) the incentive system was different
from both the disliked system used at the beginning of Stage I and the
preferred system introduced shortly afterwards, (ii) the type of work was
quite different from Stage I, and (iii) the experimental changes were quite
different.[32] However, it is this comparison which has been taken by reporters
of the studies[33] and by textbook authors[34] to provide the principal experimental evidence about the relative importance of financial and social
motives as influences on output. Assuming with Roethlisberger and Dickson
that Stage I and Stage III have some minimum comparability, it is important to examine precisely how the investigators dealt with the evidence from
these stages for the purpose of the comparison.

Comparison Between Results in Stages I, II, and III. (i) Stage III
produced a claimed 15 percent increase in rate of output over fourteen
months. Thereafter the group's average rate of output declined for twelve

27 That is, by the end of Experimental Period 7 in Roethlisberger and Dickson's
output chart, *op. cit.,* p. 78.

28 Roethlisberger and Dickson, *op. cit.,* pp. 160, 577.

29 *Ibid.,* p. 129.

30 *Ibid.,* p. 148.

31 Pennock, *op. cit.,* p. 307.

32 Roethlisberger and Dickson, *op. cit.,* pp. 156, 159.

33 *Ibid.,* pp. 146–49, 159–60; Pennock, *op. cit.,* p. 307.

34 For example, "we cannot avoid being impressed by the fact that a wage
incentive alone (Stage II) increased production 12%, a change in the social situation raised output 15%, (Stage III) and a combination of the two gave an increase
of 30%. This looks surprisingly like an additive effect, with the social rewards
being somewhat more potent in influencing behaviour than the monetary reward."
Ross Stagner, *Psychology of Industrial Conflict,* New York: Wiley, 1956, pp. 131–
32. See also Milton Blum, *Industrial Psychology and Its Social Foundations,* New
York: Harper, 1949, p. 26.

months before the study was terminated due to the depression and lay-offs. The investigators attribute this decline *entirely* to anxieties induced by the depression,[35] ignoring the possibility that the preceding increase might also have been influenced by changing general economic and employment conditions. They do this despite evidence that output among a group of 5,500 Hawthorne workers rose by 7 percent in the two years preceding the experiment.[36]

(ii) In Stage III, the output rate for each girl shows continuous and marked fluctuations over the whole two years of the study.[37] To obtain the percentage increase to be attributed to each girl the investigators chose, for each girl, a "peak" output period within the study period and measured her increase as the difference between this peak and her output rate at the outset of the study.[38] These peaks occur at different dates for different girls. To secure the 15 percent increase that is claimed, the study is, in effect, terminated at different conveniently selected dates for different girls. There is *no one period* over which the group achieved the 15 percent average increase claimed.[39]

(iii) In Stage I, two measures of the workers' performance are used: total output per week,[40] and hourly rate of output by weeks.[41] It is not clear from Roethlisberger and Dickson's report of Stage I whether the increase is in *total output* or *rate of output*. It is described only as "increase in output," and "output rose... roughly 30%,"[42] which would ordinarily be taken to mean an increase in *total output*. But the investigators make it clear in passing[43] that throughout the studies they used rate of output per hour as "the most common arrangement of output data" by which to "portray the general trend in efficiency of each operator and of the group." Whitehead, who produced a two-volume statistical study of Stage I as companion volumes to Roethlisberger and Dickson's standard report, is very clear on this point: "All output will be expressed in the form of a *rate*...as so many relays per hour."[44]

However, Whitehead employs throughout his study the description *"weekly rate of output"* when he means *rate of output per hour by weeks*.[45]

[35] Viteles comments on this period of declining output: "Both 'the investigators and the operators were of the opinion that the rates on the new piece parts were not high enough in comparison with the old.' Nevertheless scant consideration is given to the possibility that...a reduced appeal to economic motives could readily account in large part for the very severe drop in output observed during this final phase of the *Mica Splitting Room experiment*." Viteles, *Motivation...*, *op. cit.*, p. 191.

[36] Whitehead, *op. cit.*, vol. II, Chart J–53.

[37] Roethlisberger and Dickson, *op. cit.*, p. 147.

[38] *Ibid.*, p. 148.

[39] *Ibid.*, pp. 146–48, 159–60.

[40] *Ibid.*, p. 78.

[41] *Ibid.*, p. 76.

[42] *Ibid.*, p. 160.

[43] *Ibid.*, pp. 55, 77.

[44] Whitehead, *op. cit.*, vol. I, p. 34.

[45] *Ibid.*, vol. II, Chart B4.

This practice, coupled with his habit of not labelling the ordinates of his charts dealing with changes in output, and added to by Roethlisberger and Dickson's use of phrases such as "increase in output" to mean both *increase in rate of output per hour* and *increase in total output,* has led to widespread misinterpretation of the Hawthorne results, and textbook accounts which are seriously in error.[46]

Several points are of present importance. For Stage I, it is not clear whether the 30 percent increase in output claimed refers to *rate of output* or *total output.* It does not matter which measure is used to calculate percent increase in output in Stage I since the total hours worked per week at the end of the study period is only 4.7 percent less than at the beginning.[47] Thus, an increase of the order of 30 percent would result from either method of calculation. In Stage III, however, it makes a great deal of difference which method is used, and hourly rate of output is the only measure used. Thus, the 15 percent "increase in output"[48] claimed for Stage III is an increase in *rate of output per hour worked,* not in *total output.* Indeed, it is only by this measure that any increase *at all* in output can be shown.

If *total output per week* is used to measure performance in Stage III, the 15 percent increase claimed for Stage III reduces to less than zero because although output per hour increased by 15 percent, the weekly hours decreased by 17 percent, from $55\frac{1}{2}$ to $46\frac{1}{6}$.[49]

From Evidence to Conclusions. By subtracting the 15 percent increase in Stage III (which is an increase in *rate* of output) from the 30 percent increase in output in Stage I (which is all, or nearly all, an increase in *total* output), the investigators conclude that 15 percent remains as "the maximum amount (of increase in output) to be attributed to the change in wage incentive" introduced in Stage I. The investigators acknowledge the wholly speculative nature of this calculation, yet go on to assert in a summary of events to date that the conclusion "seemed to be warranted from the test room studies so far...that it was impossible to consider (a wage incentive system) as a thing in itself having an independent effect on the individual."[50]

It is important to appreciate just how invalid are the inferences made.

---

[46] For example, Edwin Ghiselli and Clarence Brown, *Personnel and Industrial Psychology,* New York: McGraw Hill, 1948, pp. 435–37; and James A. C. Brown, *Social Psychology of Industry,* Harmondsworth: Penguin, 1954, pp. 71–72. These authors incorrectly report an almost continuous increase in total weekly output over the first nine months of Stage I. In fact, there was no increase except in the period of eight weeks immediately following the introduction of the preferred incentive system. There was no improvement in weekly output in either the preceding period or the four experimental periods extending over six months which followed it.

[47] Roethlisberger and Dickson, *op. cit.,* pp. 76–77.

[48] *Ibid.,* pp. 159–60.

[49] *Ibid.,* pp. 136–39.

[50] *Ibid.,* p. 160. Viteles bluntly rejects this inference as invalid, but textbook treatments of the Hawthorne studies generally accept it without demur. Viteles, *Motivation...*, *op. cit.,* p. 193.

In Stage I, friendly supervision and a change to a preferred incentive system led to an increase in total output of about 30 percent. In Stage III, friendly supervision without a change in payment system led to no increase in total output, but to a less than compensating increase in output per hour over a period during which working hours were reduced from 55½ to 46⅛. This could be interpreted to mean that when working hours exceed about 48 per week such extra working-time may bring little or no increase in total output—a finding which had been well-established many years before.[51] This interpretation would have left the way clear to attribute the 30 percent increase in Stage I entirely to the preferred incentive system. Instead, by the rather special method of analysis and argument that has been outlined, the investigators reached the conclusion that the effect of a wage incentive system is so greatly influenced by social considerations that it is impossible to consider it capable of independent effect.

A similar situation holds with regard to Stage II. As Stage II was planned, the "method of payment was to be the only alteration from the usual situation" with the express intention that "any marked changes in output" could then be "related to this factor."[52] There *was* a marked change in output—an immediate 12 percent increase. There *was* an immediate change in behavior—the other girls in the department demanded the same conditions. This would seem to require a conclusion in favor of the importance of a preferred incentive system, but no such conclusion was reached.

As a first step in the interpretation of the Stage II results, Roethlisberger and Dickson noticed, *post hoc,* that somewhere in the "daily history record" of the Stage I group was a reference to a comment by one member of that group that a "lively interest" was being taken in their output by members of the new Stage II group.[53] At this point, the investigators simply note this and hint at significance to come. Twenty-four pages later we are told that "although output had risen an average of 12% in (Stage II) it was *quite apparent* that factors other than the change in wage incentive contributed to that increase...*There was some evidence* to indicate that the operators in (Stage II) had seized upon this test as an opportunity to prove to everyone that they could do as well as the (Stage I) operators. They were out to equal the latters' record. In view of this, even the most liberal estimate would put the increase in output due to the change in payment alone at somewhat less than 12%." (Italics added). Since no additional evidence had been produced, this judgment lacks any serious foundation.

Much later (p. 577) the matter is returned to and, with no additional evidence, we are given to understand that the increase in output in Stage II

[51] Horace M. Vernon, *Industrial Fatigue and Efficiency,* London: Dutton, 1921. Ghiselli and Brown have summarized Vernon's findings as follows: "In a munitions plant, when the working week was reduced from 66 to 48.6 hours (a reduction of 26%) hourly output was increased by 68% and total output for the week by 15%. This instance could be multiplied many times." Ghiselli and Brown, *op. cit.,* p. 242.

[52] Roethlisberger and Dickson, *op. cit.,* p. 129.

[53] *Ibid.,* p. 134.

was due to certain "social consequences" of the "basic social situation." This situation is simply asserted to have been one in which "rivalry (with the Stage I group) was brought to a focus" by setting up the Stage II group whose "output rose rapidly" in consequence.

Stage II was "designed to test the effect of a (change in) wage incentive" on output.[54] The preferred incentive system was introduced and output immediately rose 12 percent. It was withdrawn and output immediately dropped 17 percent. Not encouraging results for anyone who believed that wage incentives were relatively unimportant and incapable of "independent effects." Yet these awkward results were not only explained away but converted to positive support for just such conclusions, all on the basis of a single hearsay comment by one girl.

The investigators carry the day for the hypothesis that "social factors were the major circumstances limiting output." They conclude that "none of the results (in Stages I, II and III) gave the slightest substantiation to the theory that the worker is primarily motivated by economic interest. The evidence indicated that the efficacy of a wage incentive is so dependent on its relation to other factors that it is impossible to separate it out as a thing in itself having an independent effect."[55] This conclusion is a striking contrast to the objective results obtained in Stages I, II, and III as these bear on incentive systems: (i) when a preferred wage incentive system was introduced, total weekly output per worker rose (Stage I and Stage II); (ii) when the preferred incentive system was withdrawn, output promptly dropped (Stage II); (iii) when changes in supervision, hours, etc. were introduced but with *no change in incentive system,* no increase in weekly output per worker resulted (Stage III).

Viteles, an unusually perceptive critic of the Hawthorne studies, has commented caustically on Stage III: "This increase in output, representing an average rise of 15% in the first 14 months of the experiment, would ordinarily be accepted as evidence that the introduction of rest pauses and the shortening of the work day can in themselves result in increased output, even in the absence of changes in the way of enhancing the wage incentive."[56] Yet Viteles misses the important point that there was no overall increase in total weekly output in Stage III—only a less than compensating increase in output per hour when shorter hours were worked. It is clear that he supposes the 15 percent increase to be an increase in total output.[57] Viteles' patience is great, and his criticism of the Hawthorne studies restrained. But they eventually draw from him a testy general protest about "the more 'subtle'—certainly more subjective—form of analysis and interpretation which has generally characterized interpretation of the Hawthorne data by the Harvard group."[58]

---

[54] *Ibid.,* p. 576.

[55] *Ibid.,* pp. 575–76.

[56] Viteles, *op. cit., Motivation...,* p. 190.

[57] *Ibid.,* p. 5.

[58] *Ibid.,* p. 256.

It remains to consider more closely the complementary Hawthorne claim that it was friendly supervision and social factors which were the principal influences leading to the large rise in output in Stage. I.

A Closer Look at Friendly Supervision in Action

The *whole* of the Hawthorne claim that friendly supervision and resulting work-group social relations and satisfactions are overwhelmingly important for work behavior rests on whatever evidence can be extracted from Stage I, since that is the only study in the series which exhibits even a surface association between the introduction of such factors and increased output.

Stage I began with five girls specially selected[59] for being both "thoroughly experienced" and "willing and cooperative,"[60] so there was reason to expect this group to be more than ordinarily cooperative and competent. Yet from very early in the study "the amount of talking indulged in by all the operators" had constituted a "problem," because it "involved a lack of attention to work and a preference for conversing together for considerable periods of time."[61] The first indication in the report that this might be a serious matter occurs on August 2nd, 1927, twelve weeks after the girls' installation in the test-room, when four of the five operators were brought before the foreman[62] and reprimanded for talking too much.[63] Until November, however, "no attempt had been made to do away with this privilege, although several attempts had been made by the foreman to diminish what seemed to him an excessive amount of talking." But Operators 1A and 2A in particular continued to fail to display "that 'whole-hearted cooperation' desired by the investigators." "Any effort to reprimand them would bring the reply 'We thought you wanted us to work as we feel,' "[64] since that was what the supervisors had told them at the beginning of the study.[65]

By November 17th, 1927, the situation had not improved and disciplinary rules were resorted to. All of the operators were required to call out whenever they made mistakes in assembly, and they were prevented from talking. By December, "the lack of cooperation on the part of some of the operators was seriously alarming a few of the executives concerned." Supervisors were asked to give the girls a "hint" by telling them that they

[59] Note, however, that while the five girls were "all chosen from among those with a considerable experience in the assembly of this kind of relay"..."the actual method of selection was quite informal and somewhat obscure; it appears to have been determined by the girls themselves in conjunction with their shop foreman." Whitehead, *op. cit.*, vol. I, p. 14.

[60] Roethlisberger and Dickson, *op. cit.*, p. 21.

[61] *Ibid.*, p. 53.

[62] Foremen were on a par with departmental chiefs and four ranks above operatives. *Ibid.*, p. 11.

[63] *Ibid.*, p. 38.

[64] *Ibid.*, p. 53.

[65] *Ibid.*, p. 21; Whitehead, *op. cit.*, vol. I, p. 26.

were not doing as well as expected of them and that if they didn't improve they would lose their free lunches.[66]

From now on the girls, but especially 1A and 2A, were "threatened with disciplinary action" and subjected to "continual reprimands." "Almost daily" 2A was "reproved" for her "low output and behavior" (sic).[67] The investigators decided 1A and 2A did not have "the 'right' mental attitude." 2A was called up before the test-room authorities "and told of her offenses of being moody and inattentive and not cooperative." She was called up again before the superintendent.[68] Throughout this period output for all five girls remained static or falling.[69] After eleven weeks of serious but ineffective disciplinary measures and eight months after the beginning of the study, 1A and 2A were dismissed from the test room for "gross insubordination" and declining or static output.[70] Or, as Whitehead puts it, they "were removed for a lack of cooperation, which would have otherwise necessitated greatly increased disciplinary measures."[71]

1A and 2A were replaced by two girls chosen by the foreman[72] "who were experienced relay assemblers and desirous of participating in the test." These two girls (designated Operators 1 and 2) were transferred to the test room on January 25th, 1928.[73] They *both* immediately produced an output much greater (in total and in rate per hour) than that achieved by *any* of the original five girls on their transfer to the test room and much above the performance *at any time* of the two girls they replaced.[74]

Operators 1 and 2 had been friends in the main shop. Operator 2 was

66 Whitehead, *op. cit.,* vol. I, p. 16.

67 *Ibid.,* pp. 116–18.

68 Roethlisberger and Dickson, *op. cit.,* p. 55. Superintendents controlled a branch of the works and were seven ranks above operators. *Ibid.,* p. 11.

69 *Ibid.,* p. 78. See Experimental Period 7 in Figure 7.

70 *Ibid.,* pp. 53–57.

71 Whitehead, *op. cit.,* vol. I, p. 118. In Mayo's accounts it is first said that these two operators "dropped out" (Elton Mayo, *The Human Problems of an Industrial Civilization,* Boston: Harvard Business School, 1946, p. 56) and later that they "retired." (Elton Mayo, *The Social Problems of an Industrial Civilization,* London: Routledge and Kegan Paul, 1949, p. 62.) It is also interesting to compare the above account of events in the test room and drawn from the standard reports with Mayo's picture of the test room. According to Mayo's account, success was achieved "largely because the experimental room was in charge of an interested and sympathetic chief observer. He understood clearly from the first that any hint of the 'supervisor' in his methods might be fatal to the interests of the inquiry...He helped the group to feel that its duty was to set its own conditions of work, he helped the workers to find the 'freedom' of which they so frequently speak...At no time in the (whole period of the study) did the girls feel that they were working under pressure." (Mayo, *The Human Problems...,op. cit.,* pp. 68–69).

72 Roethlisberger and Dickson, *op. cit.,* p. 60.

73 *Ibid.,* pp. 55, 56, 60.

74 *Ibid.,* Figure 6, p. 76 and Figure 7, p. 78. Compare output curves during the first seven Experimental Periods with output from the second week of Experimental Period 8.

the only Italian in the group; she was young (twenty-one) and her mother died shortly after she joined the test room;[75] after this "Operator 2 earned the larger part of the family income." "(F)rom now on the history of the test room revolves around the personality of Operator 2."[76] Operator 2 rapidly (i.e., without any delay during which she might have been affected by the new supervision) adopted and maintained a strong and effective disciplinary role with respect to the rest of the group,[77] and led the way in increased output in *every* period from her arrival till the end of the study. In this she was closely followed by the other new girl, Operator 1.[78]

At the time that Operators 1 and 2 were brought into the test room, daily hours of work were shortened by half an hour but it was decided to *pay the operators the day rate for the half hour of working time lost.* A little later, the working day was reduced by a further half hour, and again the girls were paid for the time (one hour per day) they didn't work.[79] Later still, the girls were given Saturday mornings off and again they were paid for the time not worked.[80]

Summing up experience in the test room up to *exactly* the time when the two operators were dismissed,[81] the investigators claim that "it is clear" that over this period there was "a gradual change in social interrelations among the operators themselves, which displayed itself in the form of new group loyalties and solidarities. . . (and) . . . a change in the relations between the operators and their supervisors. The test room authorities had taken steps to obtain the girls' cooperation and loyalty and to relieve them of anxieties and apprehensions. From this. . . arose. . . a change in human relations which came to be of great significance in the next stage of the experiment, when it became necessary to seek a new hypothesis to explain certain unexpected results of the inquiry."[82] In view of the evidence reviewed here this would seem to be a somewhat sanguine assessment of developments in the test room up to this point. It is, therefore, necessary to

---

[75] *Ibid.,* pp. 61 62.

[76] Whitehead, *op. cit.,* vol. I, p. 120.

[77] *Ibid.,* pp. 120–29; Roethlisberger and Dickson, *op. cit.,* pp. 63, 74, 86, 156, 167.

[78] Roethlisberger and Dickson, *op. cit.,* p. 162.

[79] Whitehead, *op. cit.,* vol. I, pp. 121–22. Roethlisberger and Dickson (*op. cit.,* pp. 60, 62) give no indication that the operators were paid for these hours not worked. Indeed, their account clearly implies that they were not so paid (*ibid.,* pp. 63–64). But Whitehead is quite explicit on this point.

[80] Roethlisberger and Dickson do report (*op. cit.,* p. 68) that the girls were paid for the half day on Saturdays which was not worked. They acknowledge that this "added a new factor to the situation which cannot be disregarded and which has to be taken into account in comparing this period with any other" (*ibid.,* p. 69). They take no further account of it, however, just as they take no further account of the unworked hours paid for on the occasions when the work day was shortened.

[81] That is, up to the end of Experimental Period 7 in Roethlisberger and Dickson's terminology.

[82] Roethlisberger and Dickson, *op. cit.,* pp. 58–59.

examine more systematically the way in which the behavior of the supervisors on the one hand and of the operators on the other (including their changing output) varied during the period under consideration.

It is already clear that whatever part satisfying social relations at work—resulting from free and friendly supervision—may have played in producing the increase in output, there were other influences likely to have been important, e.g., a period of fairly stern discipline, the dismissal of two workers, and their replacement by people of rather special personality and motivation. In order to assess these various influences on output it is necessary to consider how work performance varied during the periods when these changes were introduced. This is difficult because none of the reports of the Hawthorne studies provides actual figures covering the way in which output changed throughout Stage I. Consequently, one must work with such estimates as can be derived from the various graphs and charts of output-change that are supplied, and supplemented by occasional statements in the texts which give additional quantitative information.

An Examination of the Evidence: Variations in Supervisory Practice and Variations in Output

For present purposes, Stage I may be divided into three phases: Phase I: the first three and a half months in the test room during which supervision seems to have been fairly consistently friendly, casual, and at low pressure; Phase II: a further interval of about seven months during which supervision became increasingly stern and close. This phase culminates in the dismissal of two of the five operators and their replacement by workers of rather special character and motivation. Phase III: a final long period during which output rose rapidly and there was a return to free and friendly supervision.

Supervision during Phase I. "Besides the girls who composed the group under study there was a person in the experimental room who was immediately in charge of the test." This was the test room observer whose two-fold function was "to keep accurate records...and to create and maintain a friendly atmosphere in the test room." He "assume(d) responsibility for most of the day to day supervision" while in other matters such as accounting, rate revision, and promotion, responsibility rested with the foreman.[83]

It is quite clear from Roethlisberger and Dickson's account that during Phase I the supervisors did everything in their power to promote a free, cooperative, and noncoercive relationship.[84] At the outset of the study the girls "were asked to work along at a comfortable pace" and were assured "that no attempt would be made to force up production." They were led to expect changes in working conditions which might be "beneficial and desirable from the employees' point of view," and were told that there

[83] *Ibid.,* pp. 22, 37.
[84] *Ibid.,* pp. 32–39.

was no reason why "any (such) change resulting in greater satisfaction of employees" should not be maintained, and this "regardless of any change in production rate."[85] "The test room observer was chiefly concerned with creating a friendly relation with the operators which would ensure their cooperation. He was anxious to dispel any apprehensions they might have about the test and, in order to do this, he began to converse informally with them each day."[86] Some weeks after the study began, there was a friendly talk with the doctor about the physical examinations and ice cream was provided and a party planned. Also, the girls were "invited to the office of the superintendent who had talked to them, and in various other ways they had been made the object of considerable attention."[87] Although there had been from almost the beginning a good deal of talking among the girls, a fairly permissive attitude had been taken about this.[88]

Output during Phase I. There was "no appreciable change in output" on transfer to the test room,[89] but there was a "downward tendency" during the first five weeks thereafter,[90] despite facilities which "made the work slightly easier."[91]

At the end of five weeks, the new wage incentive system was introduced and output increased.[92] From the output chart[93] this increase may be estimated at 4 or 5 percent. However, this increase must be accepted with some caution, for the investigators report that the "change in method of payment necessitated a change in piece-rates."[94] It was apparently judged that under the new conditions of work, (which did not include all of the types of relay assembled on the shop floor, and where there was one layout operator to five assemblers instead of one to six or seven as on the shop floor) new rates were necessary. We are told that "the chief consideration in setting the new piece rates was to determine a rate for each relay type which would pay the operators the same amount of money they had received in the regular department for an equivalent amount of work."[95] But it is well-established that the unreliability of time-study ratings can be expected to yield errors of at least 5 percent between different ratings of similar tasks,[96] So no great reliance can be placed on the observed 4 or 5 percent increase in output following the introduction of the new incentive system and the associated new piece-rates. Indeed, there is perhaps some recognition of this in Roethlisberger and Dickson's introductory comment

[85] *Ibid.,* p. 33.
[86] *Ibid.,* p. 37.
[87] *Ibid.,* pp. 34, 39.
[88] *Ibid.,* p. 53.
[89] Pennock, *op. cit.,* pp. 301, 304.
[90] Roethlisberger and Dickson, *op. cit.,* p. 58.
[91] *Ibid.,* pp. 33–34, 39.
[92] *Ibid.,* p. 58.
[93] *Ibid.,* p. 56.
[94] *Ibid.,* p. 34.
[95] *Ibid.,* p. 35.
[96] Viteles, *Motivation . . . , op. cit.,* pp. 30–38.

that early in the study "a change in wage payment was introduced, a neces-sary step before the *experiment proper* could begin."[97] Phase I ends after fifteen weeks of friendly supervision with a somewhat doubtful increase of 5 percent which occurred with the introduction of a preferred incentive system.

Supervision during Phase II. "The second phase...covering an interval of approximately seven months was concerned with the effects of various kinds of rest pauses."[98] The investigators emphasize that by the *beginning* of this phase not only was supervision friendly, but the relation between workers and supervisors was "free and easy."[99] Their account of actual supervisory behavior during succeeding months supports these claims. (i) On each of the four occasions when rest pauses were varied, the girls were consulted in advance, and on all but one occasion their expressed prefer-ences were accepted. (ii) The investigators decided to pay the girls their bonuses monthly instead of weekly, but when the girls were told about this decision they objected and the plan was dropped. That the girls "felt free to express their attitudes" and that the investigators altered their plans out of regard for these attitudes is said to be "typical of the supervisory technique employed" which "proved to be a factor of utmost importance in interpreting the results of the study." (iii) Later the girls were given free lunches and were consulted about what should be served.[100]

However, the problem of excessive talking among the girls worsened. No attempt had been made to prohibit talking, although four of the girls had been "given a talk regarding their behavior."[101] Now this "lack of attention to work and preference for conversing together for considerable periods" was judged to be reaching such proportions that the "experiment was being jeopardized and something had to be done."[102] A variety of disciplinary procedures of increasing severity were applied, but with little effect. Finally, the leaders in talking (operators 1A and 2A) were dismissed from the test room "for lack of cooperation which would have otherwise necessitated greatly increased disciplinary measures."

Output during Phase II. There was no change in weekly output during this six-month period. "Total weekly output does not decline when rest pauses are introduced, but remains practically the same during all the rest period experiments."[103]

Supervision during Phase III. At the beginning of Phase III,[104] the two

97 Roethlisberger and Dickson, *op. cit.*, p. 29, italics added.
98 *Ibid.*, p. 40. This phase actually extends from Aug. 8, 1927 to January 21, 1928, a period of twenty-four weeks.
99 *Ibid.*, pp. 45–46.
100 *Ibid.*, pp. 48–9, 51.
101 *Ibid.*, p. 38.
102 *Ibid.*, pp. 53–54.
103 *Ibid.*, p. 79.
104 Actually on January 25, 1928, two days after the beginning of Phase III. Thus, the resulting sharp rise in output does not show fully on Roethlisberger and Dickson's weekly output charts (*op. cit.*, pp. 76, 78) until the second week of their Experimental Period 8.

dismissed girls were replaced by two girls chosen by the foreman. Something has already been said about the way in which these girls at once took and maintained the lead in output and about how one of them, who had a special need for more money took over the general leadership and discipline of the rest of the group. These points will bear underlining by direct quotation:

> "When Operator 2 joined the group, her home was largely dependent upon her earnings, and within a few weeks her father lost his job and became temporarily unemployed. Thus, to her natural sense of responsibility was added the factor of poverty; and Operator 2 began to urge the remainder of the group to increase their output."[105]

> "Operators 1 and 2 were very definitely the fastest workers of the group in 1928, and this was freely recognized by the others."[106]

> "On the whole, from January to November 1928, the Relay Test Group showed no very marked developments apart from a growing tendency for the discipline to pass from the hands of the supervisor to those of the group itself, largely as represented in the person of Operator 2."[107]

> "Operator 2 became recognized as the leader of the group, both by the operators themselves and by the supervisor. It is doubtful whether any operator could have secured this position unless she had been the fastest worker, but the other qualifications possessed by Operator 2 were a high sense of the importance of the work for the group and a forceful personality."[108]

> "Op. 2. 'Oh! what's the matter with those other girls. I'll kill them.' "[109] (This expostulation was provoked by the output curves showing operators 3, 4, and 5 on a downward trend.)

From then on supervision again became increasingly friendly and relaxed. This friendliness of supervision often had a very tangible character. From the arrival of the new workers in the test room, the observer "granted them (all) more and more privileges." The preferred incentive system, the rest pauses, the free lunches, and the "parties" following the regular physical examinations all continued.[110] In addition, within the next eight months the girls were first paid for half an hour per day not worked, and then for an hour a day not worked, and finally for Saturday mornings not worked. Approximately eight months after the arrival of the new girls, all these privileges except the preferred incentive system and the parties were withdrawn. The girls were warned in advance about this withdrawal of privileges and were assured that the new and heartily disliked conditions "would terminate after approximately three months." Despite this promise, the girls' work deteriorated immediately: they wasted time in various ways such as reading newspapers, eating candy, and going for drinks and the observer

---

105 Whitehead, *op. cit.*, vol. I, pp. 122–23.
106 *Ibid.*, p. 126.
107 *Ibid.*, p. 124.
108 *Ibid.*, p. 129.
109 *Ibid.*, p. 127.
110 Roethlisberger and Dickson, *op. cit.*, pp. 71, 72, 77.

shortly "discovered that the girls were attempting to keep the output rate low...so as to make sure that rest pauses would be reinstated." The observer "again tried to stop the excessive talking" by "reprimand and threat." He told the girls that "unless excessive talking ceased it might become necessary to continue the experiment without rest pauses for a longer period."[111]

At this point, the girls had been in the test room eighteen months and had achieved nearly all the eventual 30 percent increase in output. Yet it would seem that Operator 2, the incentive system, and the other privileges, as well as "reprimand and threat" played a significant part in determining the work behavior and output of the group. It is also clear from Roethlisberger and Dickson's account that for a great part of the time following the arrival of Operators 1 and 2, the girls worked very well and happily and that while they did so, supervision was relaxed and friendly and relations continued to be satisfactory. But there would seem to be good grounds for supposing that supervision became more friendly and relaxed because output increased rather than vice versa.

Output during Phase III. Output for the whole group rose markedly during the several months after the dismissal of 1A and 2A, owing chiefly to the contributions from the new operators.[112] Thereafter, the group's total output rose more slowly for a further year (with a temporary drop when the Saturday morning shift was discontinued for a time).

Summary of Evidence About Supervision and Output

(i) Apart from a doubtful 4–5 percent increase following the introduction of a preferred incentive system, there was no increase in weekly output during the first nine months in the test room, despite a great deal of preoccupation on the part of the supervisors with friendliness towards the workers, with consultation, and the provision of a variety of privileges not enjoyed on the factory floor.

(ii) From the beginning of what Roethlisberger and Dickson describe as the "experiment proper," that is, after the period in which the new incentive system was introduced, there was no increase in weekly output during the next six months. When it became apparent that free and friendly supervision was not getting results, discipline was tightened, culminating in the dismissal of two of the five girls.

(iii) The dismissed girls were replaced by two girls of a special motivation and character who *immediately* led the rest in a sustained acceleration of output. One of these girls who had a special need for extra money rapidly adopted and maintained a strong disciplinary role with respect to the rest of the group. The two new girls led the way in increased output from their arrival till the end of the study.

(iv) Total output per week showed a significant and sustained increase only after the two girls who had the lowest output[113] were dismissed and

111 *Ibid.,* pp. 70–72.
112 *Ibid.,* Figure 7, p. 78.
113 *Ibid.,* p. 162.

replaced by selected output leaders who account for the major part of the groups' increase, both in output rate and in total output, over the next seventeen months of the study.

(v) After the arrival of the new girls and the associated increase in output, *official* supervision became friendly and relaxed once more. The investigators, however, provide no evidence that output increased because supervision became more friendly rather than vice versa. In any case, friendly supervision took a very tangible turn—by paying the girls for time not worked the piece-rate was in effect increased.

Discussion and Conclusions

The critical examination attempted here by no means exhausts the gross error and the incompetence in the understanding and use of the scientific method which permeate the Hawthorne studies from beginning to end. Three further studies were conducted: the Bank Wiring Observation Room Study; the Interviewing Program; and the Counselling Program. These studies cannot be discussed here, but I believe them to be nearly as worthless scientifically as the studies which have been discussed.[114] This should not be surprising, for they arose out of "evidence" found and conclusions reached in the earlier studies and were guided by and interpreted in the light of the strongest preconceptions based on the conclusions of the earlier studies.

There are major deficiencies in Stages I, II and III which have hardly been touched on: (i) There was no attempt to establish sample groups representative of any larger population than the groups themselves. Therefore, no generalization is legitimate. (ii) There was no attempt to employ control data from the output records of the girls who were *not* put under special experimental conditions. (iii) Even if both of these points had been met, the experiments would still have been of only minor scientific value since a group of five subjects is too small to yield statistically reliable results. Waiving all these points, it is clear that the objective evidence obtained from Stages I, II, and III does not support any of the conclusions derived by the Hawthorne investigators. The results of these studies, far from supporting the various components of the "human relations approach," are surprisingly consistent with a rather old-world view about the value of monetary incentives, driving leadership, and discipline. It is only by massive and relentless reinterpretation that the evidence is made to yield contrary conclusions. To make these points is not to claim that the Hawthorne studies can provide serious support for any such old-world view. The limitations of the Hawthorne studies clearly render them incapable of yielding serious support for any sort of generalization whatever.

If the assessment of the Hawthorne studies offered here is cogent, it raises some questions of importance for university teachers, especially for teachers concerned with courses on industrial organization and management.

114 For substantiation of this judgment with respect to the Bank Wiring Observation Room Study see A. J. Sykes, "Economic Interest and the Hawthorne Researches: A Comment," *Human Relations,* 18 (August, 1965), pp. 253–63.

How is it that nearly all authors of textbooks who have drawn material from the Hawthorne studies have failed to recognize the vast discrepancy between evidence and conclusions in those studies, have frequently misdescribed the actual observations and occurrences in a way that brings the evidence into line with the conclusions, and have done this even when such authors based their whole outlook and orientation on the conclusions reached by the Hawthorne investigators? Exploration of these questions would provide salutary insight into aspects of the sociology of social scientists.

27 / On Alex Carey's Radical Criticism of the Hawthorne Studies

Jon M. Shepard

THE HAWTHORNE RESEARCH has never lacked critics. Two relatively recent articles [1, pp. 403–416; 4, pp. 253–263] have raised some issues anew. Both Sykes and Carey criticize the Hawthorne researchers for minimizing the motivational impact of economic incentive on worker behavior. It is Carey's criticism, radical by his own admission, that prompts the following comments. Is it possible that Carey's criticism of the Hawthorne studies could be elevated beyond an acceptable contribution as a critique to a questionable position of authority? This question cannot presently be answered with clear affirmative support. The writing of this note was prompted by the possibility that such a danger exists. It is felt that new generations of teachers and students deserve an exposure to Carey's errors in interpretation and logic, and that the Hawthorne studies, in the original, should continue to provide a necessary reference.

Carey argues that without any substantial evidence the Hawthorne researchers disregarded financial incentives in the explanation of work behavior and raised supervision and resulting interpersonal satisfactions to primacy. Within the research reports, Carey contends, there is evidence supporting the primary impact of financial incentive on productivity. The Hawthorne researchers, in Carey's view, groundlessly rejected this evidence.

Reprinted by permission of the publisher from *Academy of Management Journal,* Vol. 14, No. 1 (March 1971), pp. 23–32.

Some of the evidence he marshals does open the results to the interpretation that financial rewards significantly influence morale and behavior at work. Yet, Carey himself presents evidence from the original Hawthorne research supporting the position that the effects of wages are, as these investigators contended, interrelated with various social factors. Granting that some of the original evidence supports the efficacy of money in increasing productivity, this note is intended to balance the self-admitted radical critique offered by Carey. If, as Carey argues, the Hawthorne researchers overstated their case, he is vulnerable to the same charge. Pointing out the shortcomings of the Hawthorne research is a service, but categorizing this research as "worthless scientifically" is not.

General Perspective: The Role of Financial Incentives in the Hawthorne Research

Carey attributes to the Hawthorne researchers the claim of the "relative unimportance of financial rewards compared with purely social rewards." But in the writings of the original Hawthorne researchers, reference is not made to any one factor or, more particularly, to "purely social rewards." An examination of the writings of Mayo, Whitehead, and Roethlisberger and Dickson reveals that each took a balanced position. For example, this statement from *Management and the Worker* [3] indicates a more holistic approach than Carey is willing to credit them with:

> Throughout the course of the experiments matters, vitally important to management, such as hours of work, wage incentives, and methods of supervision, had been examined. The mere fact that carefully conducted experiments failed to provide conclusive findings on these subjects was in itself very illuminating. Hitherto management had tended to make many assumptions as to what would happen if a change were made in, for example, hours of work or a wage incentive. They now began to question these assumptions and saw that many of them were *oversimplified* (emphasis supplied). They began to see that such factors as hours of work and wage incentives were not things in themselves having an independent effect upon employee efficiency; rather, these factors were no more than parts of a total situation, and their effects could not be predicted *apart from the total situation*" [3, p. 185] (emphasis supplied).

This same point is made in another segment of *Management and the Worker:*

> At least two conclusions seemed to be warranted from the test room experiments so far: (1) there was absolutely no evidence in favor of the hypothesis that the continuous increase in output in the Relay Assembly Test Room during the first 2 years could be attributed to the wage incentive factor *alone* (emphasis supplied); (2) the efficacy of a wage incentive was so dependent on its relation to other factors that it was impossible to consider it as a thing in itself having an independent effect on the individual.

Only in connection with the interpersonal relations at work and the personal situations outside of work, to mention two important variables, could its effect on output be determined [3, p. 160]."

Carey quotes from this last passage, but in the process of editing gives a significantly different slant to its meaning: "the conclusion seemed to be warranted from the test room studies...that so far it was impossible to consider (a wage incentive) as a thing in itself having an independent effect on the individual" [1, p. 408–409]. By failing to note that the Hawthorne researchers saw wages as potentially important, but only as part of the mix, Carey is later able to attribute to the Hawthorne researchers the belief "that wage incentives were relatively unimportant and incapable of independent effects" [1, p. 409]. The Hawthorne researchers did state that it was impossible to consider wages as a thing in itself exerting an independent effect on the individual, but they did not conclude, as Carey states, that wages were "relatively unimportant."[1] If the above quote had not been edited, it would have shown the multiple causation approach of the Hawthorne researchers. But instead, Carey chose to make his central point without qualification.

Carey attributes to the Hawthorne researchers the "claim that friendly supervision and the resulting work group social relations and satisfactions are overwhelmingly important for work behavior" [1, p. 410]. In fact, a reading of Carey leaves the impression that supervision was considered by the Hawthorne researchers to be the cure-all for industrial relations. Over one-half of his article is devoted to the relationship between supervision and productivity. Yet, Roethlisberger and Dickson [3] are unmistakably clear in their interpretation that satisfactions and dissatisfactions at work are the product of a myriad of social influences, both inside and outside the work organization. As illustrated in Figure 1, the Hawthorne researchers did not attribute the level of employee satisfaction to any single factor, and certainly did not isolate style of supervision as the explanatory variable. Roethlisberger and Dickson merely assume a basic sociological perspective: "According to this interpretation (referring to Figure 1), it is not possible

---

1 Another example of Carey's incautious approach is the statement from Landsberger that *"Management and the Worker* has done the field of human relations in industry an amount of harm which, in retrospect, appears to be almost irreparable" [1, p. 404]. Actually, Landsberger made this statement in reference to only one aspect of the Hawthorne research, and it does not refer to the topic of Carey's paper. This is the more complete passage from Landsberger: "At the same time it must be recognized that the authors committed a well-nigh incredible sin of omission by not recognizing in 1939 that the conditions which they had observed some 8 years earlier were precisely the ones which accounted for the rise of formal unionism in the intervening years. Their own analysis would have been fully congruent with such a conclusion. The authors by wittingly or unwittingly failing to recognize this and state it—have done the field of human relations in industry an amount of harm which, in retrospect, appears to be almost irreparable." Henry A. Landsberger, *Hawthorne Revisited* (Ithaca, New York: The New York State School of Industrial and Labor Relations, 1958), p. 64.

to treat...material goods, physical events, wages, and hours of work as things in themselves, subject to their own laws. Instead, they must be interpreted as carriers of social value. For the employee in industry, the whole working environment must be looked upon as being permeated with social significance. Apart from the social values inherent in his environment, the meaning to the employee of certain objects or events cannot be understood [3, p. 374]."

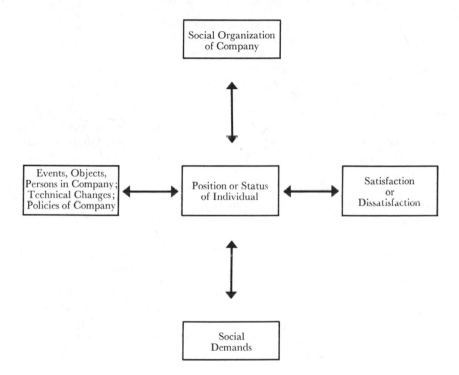

Figure 1. *Scheme for Interpreting Complaints and Reduced Work Effectiveness. Source: [3, p. 327].*

Carey translates the Hawthorne researchers' generic reference to the "social situation" to mean personal satisfactions growing out of "friendly supervision." That this translation is too limited is also reflected in this passage from Whitehead:

> Thus each member of the Test Room Group began to build up a more or less vivid *attitude* with regard to her working situation which was compounded of a number of things: day-by-day experiences (including sentiments arising out of these); logical or pseudological concepts (with their corresponding sentiments); attitudes toward their own skills as an essential

ingredient in the activities; sentiments with respect to increasing output rate; altered relations both in the plant and at home resulting from their unusual situation and earnings (with sentiments); sentiments and concepts with regard to their *supervision* (emphasis supplied); sentiments and concepts with regard to their future as it was affected by the experiment; and so forth. All these strands of experience, beliefs, concepts, and sentiments built up together into a stable combination or aggregate which may be referred to as the operator's attitude toward her work situation [5, p. 248].

Carey, then, has resurrected an old line of attack which Landsberger attempted to counter earlier, namely, that the Hawthorne researchers elevated work supervision to primacy.[2] Following his writeup of the interviewing program, Mayo himself makes a statement contradicting this charge: "The interviewing program showed that the major difficulty was no mere simple error of supervision, no easily alterable set of working conditions; it was something more intimately human, more remote. 'Supervision,' indeed, had shown itself to be another word which meant so many things that it meant nothing. In every department there was a human situation, these situations were never identical—and in every different situation the supervisor played a different part."[3]

Evidence: The Role of Financial Incentives in the Hawthorne Research

The basic position of the Hawthorne researchers was that financial, environmental, and physiological factors could not be considered alone, i.e., outside of a social context. Carey himself cites evidence that the financial incentive, taken alone, is not enough. In the third phase of the Hawthorne research, Carey notes that the new incentive system did not produce any increase in weekly output for the first 6 months. It was only after the dismissal of the two poorest performers and their replacement with two other girls with a special motivation for money that output rose. The rise in

---

[2] Landsberger emphasized that Roethlisberger and Dickson "quite specifically argue against the theory that this situation (resistance to change) would be capable of improvement through mere changes in interpersonal relations at the first-line supervisory level." They state explicitly that "supervisory training could not solve the problem. . . ." Landsberger, *Hawthorne Revisited*, p. 66. See also [3, p. 537].

[3] Elton Mayo, *Human Problems of an Industrial Society* (New York: The Viking Press, 1962), p. 94. In one passage, Landsberger suggests why criticisms are still erroneously being leveled at the Hawthorne studies: ". . . for at least 10 years after the publication of *Management and the Worker,* the history of the field of human relations in industry was an explicit elaboration of *one* (emphasis supplied) of the book's basic points, namely, that morale is related to supervision. The distortion of emphasis in which such one-sided elaboration resulted began to be corrected in the early 1950's. By this time, however, the Hawthorne studies had become identified, both in the critics' mind and in the mind of students in the field, with a single point on which attention had been focused." Landsberger, *Hawthorne Revisited*, p. 101.

productivity is attributed to one of the new girls whose special desire for money stemmed from her status as primary supporter of her family and the fact that her father had just become temporarily unemployed [1, p. 415]. Carey offers a quote from *Management and the Worker* which may be cited as evidence for the Hawthorne multivariate approach: "On the whole, from January to November 1928, the Relay Test group showed no very marked developments apart from a growing tendency for the discipline to pass from the hands of the supervisor to those of the group itself, largely as represented in the person of operator 2 [1, p. 414; quoted from 5, p. 124]. One perfectly tenable interpretation of this passage is that output increased not because of the incentive system—indeed 6 months had passed without it exerting any effect—but rather because one of the girls assumed leadership of the *group* and influenced her fellow workers to increase their output.

Moreover, Carey, referring to these same workers, cites the following passage which indicates that financial incentive alone did not appear to be a sufficient motivator: "Approximately 8 months after the arrival of the new girls, all these privileges except the *preferred incentive system* (emphasis supplied) and the parties were withdrawn. The girls were warned in advance about this withdrawal of privileges and were assured that the new and heartily disliked conditions 'would terminate after approximately 3 months.' Despite this promise, the girls' work deteriorated immediately: they wasted time in various ways such as reading newspapers, eating candy, and going for drinks, and the observer shortly 'discovered that the girls were attempting to keep the output rate low...so as to make sure that rest pauses would be reinstated' " [1, p. 415].

Finally, on the matter of evidence presented by Carey, he quotes Roethlisberger and Dickson: "Although output had risen an average of 12 percent in Stage II, it was *quite apparent* that factors other than the change in wage incentive contributed to that increase.... *There was some evidence* to indicate that the operators in Stage II had seized upon this test as an opportunity to prove to everyone that they could do as well as the Stage I operators. They were out to equal the latters' record. In view of this, even the most liberal estimate would put the increase in output due to the change in payment alone at somewhat less than 12 percent" [1, p. 409]. (Italics added by Carey.) Carey dismisses this statement by writing that "since no additional evidence had been produced, this judgment lacks any serious foundation" [1, p. 409]. He implies, in effect, that knowledge of the social context, which cannot be entered in a statistical table, is inadmissable evidence. Carey chose the strictly quantitative approach to social research. This would seem to rule out some of the most creditable sociological research, such as Whyte's *Street Corner Society* [6] and Liebow's *Talley's Corner* [2], as well as the many contributions of Herbert Blumer and Everett C. Hughes.[4]

[4] The theme of Arnold Rose's 1969 Presidential address to the American Sociological Association in 1969 was that a variety of sociological imaginations exist.

Carey excludes from consideration the latter stages of the Hawthorne research, the interviewing stage, and the Bank Wiring Observation Room Study, which in Carey's view are scientifically worthless because ". . . they arose out of 'evidence' found and conclusions reached in the earlier studies and were guided by and interpreted in the light of the strongest preconceptions based on the conclusions of the earlier studies" [1, p. 416]. Pronouncements on the validity of a piece of research should rest on an examination of that research, not on a judgment regarding the origin of the hypotheses which the research purports to test. Moreover, evidence from the latter research stages runs counter to Carey's thesis. In particular, omission of the Bank Wiring Observation Room experiment deprives us of information crucial to judging the Hawthorne studies—some of the strongest support for the argument that wage incentives are filtered through social factors.

Workers in the Bank Wiring Observation Room were on a group financial incentive plan. The thinking underlying financial incentive plans is that if one is paid more he will produce more; financial incentive plans are partially intended to get around the problem of restriction of output. However, in the Bank Wiring Observation Room there was a very clear informal norm of productivity set by the group at a point below the level of production which individuals could have actually produced. In fact, workers stopped early, loafed, and used various other means in order not to exceed the informal production maximum. Social sanctions were applied to workers who produced more than or less than what the group had apparently settled on informally as the amount of production constituting a "day's work."[5]

The fear was expressed by workers that if they produced to capacity the production standard would be raised and they would have to work harder for the same pay, or some workers would be laid off. This could be interpreted, as Sykes [4, p. 258] contends, as an effort on the part of the workers to maximize their long-term income and to protect their jobs. Be that as it may, the fact remains that the production level was maintained by group pressure. Workers who did not share the fear of a raised standard nevertheless restricted production as a result of social pressures. Ample documentation of evidence to buttress the Hawthorne researchers' thesis

---

Arnold M. Rose, "Varieties of Sociological Imagination," *American Sociological Review,* **XXXIV** (1969), pp. 623–630. More to the point in the present context, Rose wrote: "What we observe directly is not necessarily false. One does not always have to use a fully controlled experiment to observe the facts of a social situation." (p. 628). In the conclusion of his address, Rose said: "I do not see one single kind of sociological imagination that can do all these things well, and have even suggested that a brilliant social researcher in one respect will be blind or stupid in another respect." (p. 630). If, as it appears, Carey would apply the latter phrase to the Hawthorne researchers, it would be well for him to remember that few of us are immune to this myopia, himself included.

5 For detailed analysis of individual and group output records see [3, pp. 409–447].

that wage incentives are socially conditioned is contained in *Management and the Worker.* (See Appendix A for further discussion.)

Sykes convincingly demonstrates the effort by Roethlisberger and Dickson to explain away the possible contribution of worker pursuit of economic interest to production restriction in the Bank Wiring Observation Room. This tack by Roethlisberger and Dickson was as unnecessary as it was unfortunate—unfortunate because it made them vulnerable to justified criticism; unnecessary because there is sufficient evidence in their findings as well as from subsequent research to buttress their position that financial incentives are conditioned by social and psychological factors which lead to behavior quite different than would be expected on the assumption that workers individually respond in the direction of maximizing income.[6] If, instead of trying to suppress the influence of economic incentives as they did in their conclusions on the Bank Wiring Observation Room, Roethlisberger and Dickson [3, pp. 531–535] had interpreted the findings from this final research stage in terms of their earlier overview (see Figure 1), they would have been on quite solid ground. Their failure to do so does not mean that their work should be ignored, but that it should be viewed in its totality.

It is enlightening to know that the Hawthorne researchers chose to see money as simply part of the mix without definitive evidence. What is unfortunate is Carey's implication that the Hawthorne research findings

---

[6] See M. Dalton, O. Collins, and D. Roy, "Restriction of Output and Social Cleavage in Industry," *Applied Anthropology,* V (1946), pp. 1–14; R. Marriott, "Size of Working Group and Output," *Occupational Psychology,* XXIII (1949), pp. 47–57; _____, "Sociopsychological Factors in Productivity," *Occupational Psychology,* XXV (1951), pp. 15–24; D. Roy, "Quota Restriction and Goldbricking in a Machine Shop," *American Journal of Sociology,* LVII (1952), pp. 427–442; William F. Whyte, "Economic Incentives and Human Relations," *Harvard Business Review,* XXX (1952), pp. 73–80; William F. Whyte, *Money and Motivation* (New York: Harper and Row, 1955); H. Campbell, "Group Incentive Payment Schemes: The Effect of Lack of Understanding and Group Size," *Occupational Psychology,* XXVI (1952), pp. 15–21; M. S. Viteles, *Motivation and Morale in Industry* (New York: Norton, 1953); D. J. Hickson, "Motives of People Who Restrict Their Output," *Occupational Psychology,* XXXV (1961), pp. 110–121; S. W. Gellerman, *Motivation and Productivity* (New York: American Management Association, 1963); Mason Haire, "The Incentive Character of Pay," in R. Andrews, ed., *Managerial Compensation* (Ann Arbor: Foundation for Research on Human Behavior, 1965), pp. 13–17; Lyman W. Porter and Edward E. Lawler, III, "What Job Attitudes Tell about Motivation," *Harvard Business Review,* XLVI (1968), pp. 118–126; Edwin A. Locke, Judith F. Bryan, and Lorne M. Kendall, "Goals and Intentions as Mediators of the Effects of Monetary Incentives on Behavior," *Journal of Applied Psychology,* LII (1968), pp. 104–121. For a review of these and other studies, see R. Marriott, *Incentive Payment Systems: A Review of Research and Opinion* (London: Staples Press, 1957), and Robert L. Opsahl and Marvin D. Dunnette, "The Role of Financial Compensation in Industrial Motivation," *Psychological Bulletin,* LXVI (1966), pp. 94–118.

should therefore not be taught in classrooms or printed in textbooks. By arriving at such a devastating conclusion, Carey discards the baby with the bath. As Sykes [4, p. 262] asserts, the Hawthorne evidence on the role of financial incentives in motivation was not conclusive. But as stated above, research subsequent to the Hawthorne studies tends to support their position that financial incentives are filtered through social and psychological variables. For example, the conclusions of Locke, Bryan, and Kendall in a recent study are very much in agreement with the basic position of Roethlisberger and Dickson: "The results of the five studies reported here are consistent with the hypothesis that goals and intentions are important determinants of behavior, and with the hypothesis that they are the mechanism by which monetary incentives influence behavior. All five studies showed significant relationships between goals or intentions and behavior within and/or between different monetary incentive conditions. Further, in each of the five studies it was demonstrated that if goal or intention level was controlled or partialed out, there was no effect of amount of incentive on behavior."[7] More generally, after an extensive review of the literature, Opsahl and Dunnette write, "much remains to be learned before we will understand very well what meaning money has for different people, how it affects their job behaviors, which motives it serves, and how its effectiveness may come about. It is probably doubtful that there will ever be a 'theory of money' in the sense that money will be given a unique or special status as a psychological variable. It is true that money functions in many ways, depending upon the setting, the antecedent conditions, and the particular person involved."[8] In sum, Opsahl and Dunnette conclude that while we know little about the role of financial incentives under specified conditions, it seems clear from the evidence that money is not an independent variable of itself. A major contribution of the Hawthorne research remains its early and influential exposure of the "economic man" for the myth it has since been proven to be.

Conclusion

Carey's article is unfortunate because it is misleading. A reading of Carey without familiarity with the original Hawthorne research reports would leave one with the impression that these researchers summarily dismissed financial incentives in favor of a particular style of supervision. But this alleged exclusive emphasis on supervision was not theirs; it was developed later by others. Granted that the Hawthorne researchers are in some measure open to the criticisms leveled by Carey and Sykes, the dichotomy between supervision and financial incentives advanced by Carey should not be perpetuated. A primary contribution of the Hawthorne researchers

---

[7] Locke, Bryan, and Kendall, "Goals and Intentions," p. 119.
[8] Opsahl and Dunnette, "Financial Compensation," p. 97.

remains their attempt to place financial incentives in a social context.[9] Evidence Carey himself used as well as evidence from the Bank Wiring Observation Room show that reason enough existed for the Hawthorne researchers' rejection of financial incentive as a variable exerting an independent effect entirely of itself.

Appendix A

Below is a summary of the results from the Bank Wiring Observation Room: "(1) Each individual in the group was restricting his output. (2) Restriction of output manifested itself in two ways: (a) the group had a standard of a day's work which was considerably lower than the 'bogey' and which fixed an upper limit to each person's output. This standard was not imposed upon them, but apparently had been formulated by the workmen themselves. Furthermore, it was in direct opposition to the ideas underlying their system of financial incentive, which countenanced no upper limit to performance other than physical capacity. (b) In each individual case it manifested itself in an output rate which remained fairly constant from week to week. The departmental output curves were devoid of individuality and approximated a horizontal line in shape. (3) The departmental output records were distorted. This was found by comparing the observer's count with the figures compiled by the department during the study period. (4) The inaccuracies in the departmental records were traceable to two factors: (a) differences between actual output and reported output, and (b) differences between standard working time and reported working time. The first factor was assessed by comparing the observer's output count with that reported to the group chief by the wiremen. It was found that no wireman reported exactly what he produced each day; some days he reported more and some less. The second factor was studied by recording and analyzing claims for daywork allowances. It was apparent that most of the wiremen frequently claimed to have been prevented from working by stoppages beyond their control when, in reality, there was little justification for their claims because (i) the stoppage was shorter than claimed, (ii) the stoppage was brought about by the operators themselves, (iii) there was in fact no delay, or (iv) there was a real stoppage but it could have been compensated for by working a little harder or decreasing spare time. (5) Analysis of quality records showed that they reflected not only the quality of the work done by the wiremen and soldermen but also the personal relations between them and the inspector. This was found by separating objectively

9 Landsberger makes a statement that applies to Carey: "It may be noted here, too, that the critics are in danger of going to the equally erroneous opposite extreme of asserting that supervision, and the skill with which it is carried out, has no influence whatever on the worker's attitude to his job. This in its turn would be a dubious position to take in light of the Michigan studies" (Landsberger, *Hawthorne Revisited,* p. 103).

determined defects from those which were determined by the inspector's personal judgment. Analysis of the former showed that the faster operators rated highest in quality. Analysis of the latter showed that an inspector's rating of a solderman varied with different wiremen, even though the solderman was solely responsible for the defect. It also showed that different inspectors varied widely in their gradings of a specific solderman's work. (6) Differences in weekly average hourly output rates for different wiremen did not reflect differences in capacity to perform. This conclusion was based on the following observations: (a) most of the wiremen stated definitely that they could easily turn out more work than they did. (b) the observer said that all the men stopped work before quitting time. Frequently, a wireman finished his work quite early and stalled until quitting time. In general, the men who ranked highest in output were the first to be finished. This point was verified by a comparison of individual morning and afternoon output rates, which showed the greatest differences in the cases of the faster wiremen. (c) tests of dexterity and intelligence showed no relation between capacity to perform and actual performance. Roethlisberger and Dickson, *Management and the Worker*, pp. 445–446.

References

1. Carey, Alex, "The Hawthorne Studies: A Radical Criticism," *American Sociological Review*, **XXXII** (1967).
2. Liebow, Elliot, *Talley's Corner* (Boston: Little, Brown, and Co., 1967).
3. Roethlisberger, F. J., and William J. Dickson, *Management and the Worker* (New York: John Wiley and Sons, Inc., 1939).
4. Sykes, A. J. M., "Economic Interest and the Hawthorne Researchers," *Human Relations*, **XVIII** (1965).
5. Whitehead, T. N., *The Industrial Worker* (Cambridge, Mass.: Harvard University Press, 1938).
6. Whyte, William F., *Street Corner Society* (Chicago: University of Chicago Press), 1943.

28 / The Place of Financial Incentives in Motivation

Lyman W. Porter, Edward E. Lawler, III

"PAY IS THE most important single motivator in our organized society." (Haire *et al.* 1963, p. 1).

"Wage systems are not in themselves an important determinant of pace of work, application to work, or output." (Brown 1962, p. 15).

These two statements are typical of the contradictory claims about the effectiveness of pay as an incentive that abound in the literature on motivation and work. If we accept the former of these statements, pay should become the key building block in any scheme that attempts to motivate workers to perform their jobs better. If we accept the latter view, pay becomes a secondary motivational factor that needs only to be maintained at an adequate level. Unfortunately, the available empirical evidence is not very helpful in deciding which of these statements represents the more accurate view. The simple fact is that in relation to the importance of pay there is a paucity of evidence on how pay functions as an incentive.

It is surprising that business organizations have done so little research on the effectiveness of pay as an incentive. Salaries are one of the largest expenses for any organization, yet few organizations have attempted to assess systematically how effectively they are spending this money. Such disregard for how money is spent to purchase new machinery would be considered gross negligence; yet where salaries are concerned, it is overlooked.[1] But if it is surprising that corporations have not studied pay more, it is even more curious that psychologists have failed to study the psychological aspects of compensation. As Haire *et al.* (1963) have pointed out, the basic assumption about pay—that it motivates people to work—is a psychological one. Its impact on employee behavior has many implications for any theory of human motivation. Thus, research on pay should have important practical as well as theoretical implications. However, psychologists have shown little interest in doing psychological research on pay in general, and on the relationship between attitudes toward pay and job performance in particular.

Despite the general lack of research on pay, it appears to be an ideal reward for us to study in order to begin to test our model. In contrast to many rewards, like status or security, it is measurable and thus lends itself

---

[1] The authors are indebted to Mason Haire for this point.

Reprinted by permission of the authors and publisher from *Managerial Attitudes and Performance* (Homewood, Illinois: Richard D. Irwin, Inc., and Dorsey Press, 1968), pp. 17, 56–62, 87–97.

rather easily to quantitatively oriented research. There is also a long history of attempts to use pay as a reward in order to increase employee effort, and the analysis of this history would seem to provide a fruitful background against which to consider the implications of our model for the use of pay as an incentive. Knowledge about the relationship between attitudes toward pay and job performance would seem to be vital to an understanding of how pay can function as an incentive, as well as to an understanding of what kind of general theory of motivation may have validity for the work situation. Answers to such questions as (1) Does satisfaction with pay lead to higher job performance? and (2) Do an employee's attitudes about how his pay is determined influence his job performance? are crucial to an understanding of pay as an incentive, as well as to our theory, and can be found by studying the relationship between job attitudes and job performance.

Historical Background

Prior to the "human relations" movement and the Western Electric studies, it was common to assume that pay was the only important incentive in the work environment. From this assumption grew a motivational picture of man that has since become known as "economic man." According to J.A.C. Brown (1954, pp. 15–16):

> "Economic Man" is a rational, creative man who uses his reason primarily to calculate exactly how much satisfaction he may obtain from the smallest amount of effort. "Satisfaction" does not mean pride in one's job, the feeling of having accomplished something, or even the regard of others; it refers only to money.

With this concept of man in mind, organizations began in the early 1900's frantically installing various kinds of pay plans. Hundreds of different plans were tried and some attempts were made to measure the resulting changes in productivity. However, these incentive plans typically failed to live up to expectations. Although it is generally conceded that they frequently produced performance increases that ranged from 10 to 40 percent, they also produced many human relations problems (Whyte 1955), including quota restrictions and "goldbricking." During this entire period little attention was focused on developing a theoretical model that would explain why some schemes succeeded while others failed, and why the many unexpected side effects appeared when incentive plans were installed.

A general growing disillusionment with incentive plans and the concept of "economic man" set the stage for the acceptance of the results of the Western Electric studies (Roethlisberger and Dickson 1939). These studies clearly demonstrated that factors other than financial ones influence an individual's productivity. For Elton Mayo, the most important of these other factors was the individual's social relations on the job. Soon a picture of motivation that can be called "social man" appeared and the "human relations" movement came into prominence. Mayo (1945) perfectly characterizes "social man" with the statement that "man's desire to be continuously associated with his fellows is a strong, if not the strongest, human characteristic." The developing "human relations" movement apparently contributed to the abandonment of many incentive pay plans. In 1935 (pre-"human relations") 75 percent of a sample of companies replied that they used wage incentive programs. By 1939 (beginning of "human relations") the number had fallen to 52 percent and by 1958 the number had declined to 27 percent. Motivational schemes during this period were frequently designed in a way that essentially ignored the use of pay as a motivator, despite the fact that the Western Electric studies themselves found that in the Second Relay Assembly room a substantial increase in productivity was due to the wage incentive system.

"Social man" was not due to last too long, for soon Maslow (1943, 1954) presented a theory of motivation that introduced "self-actualizing" man. For many, Maslow's theory provided a meaningful explanation of why incentive systems had failed and of why pay may lack primary importance for employees in our society. Briefly, Maslow's theory says that the needs which individuals seek to satisfy are arranged in a hierarchy. At the bottom of the hierarchy are needs for food, water, and physical comfort. These lower order needs are followed by such higher order needs as social needs, esteem needs, and finally, needs for autonomy and self-actualization. According to Maslow's theory, once the lower order needs are relatively well satisfied, they become unimportant as motivators, and an individual tries to satisfy the higher order needs. If it is assumed, as many advocates of self-actualizing man do, that pay primarily satisfies lower order needs, then the reason for the failure of incentive systems becomes clear. In our society, lower order needs are well satisfied for most individuals, and thus one would not expect pay to be important. This kind of explanation argues that most pay plans have failed because pay is unimportant, and, as our model points out, pay cannot be a motivator if it is unimportant. But— and this is the key point this view is based upon the assumption that pay satisfies mainly lower order needs. There are real questions concerning the validity of this assumption.

Research Studies on Pay

Recent studies have shown rather clearly that pay is an incentive that is able to satisfy both lower order physiological and security needs as well as higher order needs such as esteem and recognition (Lawler and Porter 1963; Myers 1964). It is this very facet of pay that suggests it as a particularly appropriate reward to look at in relation to our model. Pay is one reward that does satisfy a variety of important needs, and our expectation is that rewards seem to gain their value as a function of their ability to satisfy needs. For this reason, it would seem that if our expectations about the way outcomes gain reward value are at all valid, pay should be an ideal reward to study in order to test our arguments concerning the impact of rewards on behavior.

The results of several recent studies support the point that pay remains important to managers despite their relatively high standing in terms of lower order need satisfactions. Porter (1961) found that managers attached more importance to the amount of pay they received than to the amount of autonomy, esteem, or social need fulfillment they received. Lawler and Porter (1963) found that although presidents and vice presidents attached slightly less importance to their pay than did lower level managers, the difference was small, and for both groups it was rated as very important. What probably does change as managers earn more money is the type of needs satisfied by money and consequently the reasons it is important to them.

In summary, although pay may be important to people for a number of reasons, and may be of differing amounts of importance to individuals depending on their needs at that moment, it is clear that pay is important enough in most instances to be a significant motivator of behavior. One example of the strength of pay as an incentive is given by a recent Labor Department report. According to the report, the longshoremen at the Port of Galveston, Texas, work too hard. The report said, "It cannot be in the best interests of the health of the men to carry on hard physical labor at such a pace all day, much less day after day." The reason for the hard work was found in the incentive pay system under which the men worked. According to the report, the men could earn as much as $6 to $10 an hour under their incentive system, which effectively tied their pay to their job performance. It is obvious that this story of a workable incentive plan is not an isolated example. Even the early plans got some improvement in productivity, and later ones like the Scanlon Plan have had a number of successes. Perhaps the most successful plan has been the one used at the Lincoln Electric Company. It has resulted in the company having sales per employee that are approximately four times the industry average.

The crucial empirical question about pay as a motivator of job performance is not the traditional one of, "Are incentive plans efficient motivators of effective job performance?" but the differential one of, "Under what conditions is pay a significant motivator of effective job performance?" Such a question pertains directly to our conceptual model. [See Figure 1.] One way to answer this differential question is by comparing effective managers' attitudes about pay with those of ineffective managers. Our model makes it clear that there are two such kinds of attitudes that are needed among employees if pay is to function as an incentive. According to the model, pay must be important to the individual, and the individual must see a positive connection between his attempts to perform well and his pay in both the short and long term. If either of these two attitudes is lacking, then pay will not be an effective incentive; and no relationship would be expected between how important pay is, or how it is determined, and performance.

Problems with Early Incentive Plans

It is quite possible that the ineffectiveness of many of the early incentive plans can be attributed to their failure to establish a clear relationship between performance and pay. Rate changes have destroyed employees' beliefs that good performance does lead to high pay, and the fear of unemployment because of overproducing has tended to undermine workers' perceptions that their long-term economic good is fostered by high performance. Whyte (1955) has shown that such fears may be widespread among workers in industry, and that they do reduce the effectiveness of incentive pay plans. More recently, Chalupsky (1964) found that in a group of research organizations only 67 percent of the scientists said merit salary increases existed, despite the fact that management claimed they were present in all the organizations. Thus, it is not only among blue-collar workers that incentive plans may fail because a clear relationship between pay and performance does not exist.

There is some evidence that pay programs also may have failed because money is relatively unimportant to some employees despite the fact that a clear relationship is seen between pay and performance. However, there is no evidence that this reason is as widespread as the advocates of "social man" and of "self-actualizing man" would lead one to believe by their tendency to ignore pay. Perhaps the most striking example of a situation where pay was not a valued reward was in a factory where the employees were mostly young girls who lived at home with their parents. Since they had to give their pay envelopes to their mothers, the amount of their pay was of relatively little importance to them, and increased pay proved to be a poor incentive. On the other hand, the chance to leave work early if all the work was completed proved to be an effective incentive.

A further reason why incentive plans may fail, and one that is congruent with our model, is this: although pay may be regarded as important, and good job performance may be seen as leading to higher pay, good job performance *also* may be seen as leading to a reduction in other rewards. It is not at all uncommon to find situations in which such needs as esteem and friendship from fellow employees are withheld from the good job performer or "ratebuster." Thus, the significant positive motivational effects of seeing a valued reward—pay—increased by improved job performance may be canceled out by the negative effects of seeing other valued rewards decreased by improved job performance. . . .

Discussion and Implications of the Findings

Attitudes toward How Pay Is Determined

The results of the present study offer strong support for that part of the model which predicted that seeing a high probability that significant rewards depend upon job performance factors will lead to effort being directed toward performing effectively. The results clearly showed that those managers who saw their pay as dependent upon their job performance were the most effective and highly motivated managers. This same finding appeared in both the self and the superiors' evaluations of performance. Although the present study established empirically the effects of seeing one reward—in this case, pay—as depending upon good job performance, it does seem reasonable that seeing other significant rewards as being contingent upon job performance would have, as predicted by the model, the same relationship to job performance factors. This was the finding of Georgopoulos *et al.* in their study that looked at attitudes toward promotion, pay, and getting along in the work group. It is particularly significant that the Georgopoulos *et al.* [1952] study obtained results similar to ours, since theirs was done among workers rather than managers, thus extending the finding to a different sample and situation. This, taken together with the fact that in the present study the same results were found in two rather broad and diverse management samples, indicates strongly that the model's prediction that seeing significant rewards as tied to good performance will lead to a strong attempt to perform effectively may have general validity.

A significant part of the prediction of our model about the kinds of attitudes that lead managers to devote effort to effective job performance was that the value of pay does not combine in an additive form with expectancy to determine performance. Because of the belief that it combines multiplicatively, the hypothesis was derived that the relationship between probability attitudes and effort would be stronger for those managers who attach high reward value to pay than for those who attach to it low reward value. The results of the study generally tend to support this part of the model. A consistent tendency did appear in both samples for the relationship to be stronger in the high than in the low importance groups. However, it should be pointed out that in the low importance groups, some relationship between the probability attitudes and the behavior measures was found. This undoubtedly came about because, even for the low importance group, pay was of greater than zero importance. Because of this, it was impossible to test directly whether a multiplicative relationship exists, since, ideally, a situation in which importance can be varied from zero upward is needed. However, it does seem possible to conclude from the results of the present study that importance has a significant moderating effect on the relationship between expectancy attitudes and job performance.

The prediction that attitudes toward the likelihood that effort influences pay would be more closely related to the job behavior measures than would the attitudes toward the likelihood that performance influences pay was not supported by the data. Apparently, among the managers in our study, there was little tendency to distinguish between the concepts of pay being tied to performance and that of pay being tied to effort. It is, of course, possible that for the managers in these organizations this might not have been a crucial distinction because there was no difficulty converting effort into performance. Indeed, this would seem to make sense in terms of the jobs these managers had. This is, of course, an inference and cannot be supported by the data we collected. Unfortunately, we did not directly ask the managers to estimate the probability that effort on their part would result in good performance. If it were found in future studies that this probability was always close to 1.0, then indeed it could be dropped from the model. However, at this point, we still feel that it may be relevant in many situations. Further, we feel that its characteristics, and how, if at all, it combines with the pay-performance probability to determine job behavior are prime topics for future research.

It should be pointed out that the evidence from the present study does not establish that the attitudes toward how pay is determined in part caused a manager's job performance. What the data do show is that there is a relationship between the attitudes and the performance. The model predicts that the reason for this relationship is that attitudes affect the performance, but the data cannot directly test this aspect of the model. It is true that the assumption of a causal relationship gives the most parsimonious and face-valid explanation of the several relationships found. In particular, a causal interpretation easily handles, and in fact predicts, the finding of a closer relationship between the attitudes and effort than between the attitudes and job performance. Further, a causal interpretation correctly predicts that importance will serve as a moderator of the relationship between the attitudes and the performance measures.

Alternative explanations of the finding that expectancy attitudes are related to the job performance measures would be that the job performance caused the attitudes or that a third variable caused both the attitudes and the job performance. It is possible to reason from dissonance theory (Festinger 1957) that job performance might have the power to cause probability attitudes. The reasoning would be that a manager tries to justify his high performance to himself by saying that it will result in higher pay. Another way of stating this is that a high producer might need to feel that he is getting some reward for his work and, thus, he says his pay is a reward for his performance. However, it is not clear how this explanation can handle the finding that the attitudes were more strongly related to effort than to job performance. In addition, it is not clear how such an explanation would handle the finding that importance functions as a moderator variable. Thus, barring further evidence to the contrary, it does not seem reasonable at this time to assume that the job performance caused the expectancy attitudes.

There are a number of possible third variables that might have caused the relationships found, but the one that suggests itself first is salary. The amount of salary received presumably might have the power to cause both the attitudes and the performance. Or, salary could be caused by the performance which, in turn, could cause the attitudes. The good performer who gets high pay may feel the need to believe it is based upon his merit, whereas the poor performer who gets low pay may blame the system and say that merit is not rewarded in his organization. However, since in all the organizations studied, but particularly in the government organizations, the amount of pay received was not strongly related to the performance measures, this possible explanation would not appear to hold up. Other possible third variables, such as personality traits or situational characteristics, cannot be ruled out completely until evidence from adequately controlled experiments exists. However, it does appear that the most reasonable conclusion at this stage is that expectancy attitudes and perceptions can influence job performance factors.

Attitudes toward Pay as a Satisfier

The evidence from the present study points to a consistent, although moderate, relationship between the degree to which pay is seen as a satisfier and the motivation to perform a job effectively. Positive relationships were found in both samples and when both the self and superiors' evaluations were used. Thus, the results are in agreement with the study of Herzberg *et al.* (1959) who found that higher self-ratings of job performance will result when managers see their pay as a satisfier. This finding is also in agreement with our model since, as was pointed out, seeing pay as a satisfier seems to mean that significant rewards are seen as being dependent upon good job performance. Thus, the conclusion that seeing pay as a satisfier is associated with high job performance is congruent with both our model and the Herzberg theory.

Both our model and the Herzberg theory imply that attitudes toward pay as a satisfier lead to changes in the motivation to perform effectively, but as was pointed out previously, the type of data gathered in the present study does not allow us to test for causal relationships between the attitudes and performance. Thus, it is somewhat risky to assume that because the attitudes and the performance are related, the attitudes caused the performance. However, in this case, it seems reasonable to assume that the perception of pay as a satisfier may have led to the job performance. Such an interpretation makes possible the easy explanation of the finding that these attitudes are more highly related to effort than to quality of job performance. In addition, there is good evidence for believing that when an individual sees that an activity leads to the satisfaction of his needs, the perception of this relationship will cause him to persist in that activity.

Alternative explanations, either that the job performance caused the attitudes or that a third variable caused both, cannot easily account for the stronger relationships with effort than with quality of performance. The third variable that seems most likely to be able to cause both the attitudes and the job performance would be the amount of salary the managers receive and the kind of raises they have received. However, since actual pay is not highly correlated with either the job performance measures or the attitudes, it is unlikely that this is the third variable. Thus, it is reasonable to conclude that the managers' perceptions of their pay as a satisfier does bear a causal relationship to their job performance.

Hypothesis 4–G predicted that the importance of pay as a satisfier would operate as a moderator of the relationship between the degree to which pay is seen as a satisfier, and the measures of job performance. The data offered no support for this hypothesis. Two explanations appear to exist for the failure of this hypothesis to be supported by the data. It may be that a measure of the importance of pay is different from a measure of the importance of pay as a satisfier. This would mean that seeing pay as a satisfier means more than just seeing pay as related to performance. It may mean that other rewards are seen to be tied to pay also, and that an adequate importance measure must be a measure of the importance of all these rewards. Some support for this interpretation comes from the low correlation (average $r = .28$) between the index of pay as a satisfier and the index of probability that pay depends upon job performance. This would seem to indicate that these two measures are tapping somewhat different areas and indicate that the same importance measure cannot function for both.

A second reason for the lack of support for this hypothesis may be that for pay to be seen as a satisfier, it must be important. If this is true, then using importance as a moderator would have only the effect of separating individuals on the degree to which they see pay as a satisfier. Thus, it is obvious that before an adequate measure of the importance of pay as a satisfier can be developed, further understanding is needed of what it means, in terms of the various psychological needs, for pay to be seen as a satisfier.

Effort and Job Performance

The model predicted that attitudes which are reflections of an individual's desire to perform will be more closely related to the ratings of effort than to the ratings of quality of job performance. The results for both attitudes toward how pay is determined and attitudes toward pay as a satisfier supported this part of the model. Because of the nature of the data it was impossible to test whether a multiplicative relationship exists among the determinants of performance, but the data do show that effort is more closely related to the attitudes, as would be necessary if a multiplicative relationship exists.

One significant implication of the relationship between the attitudes and the ratings on effort is that if researchers are to find a relationship between attitudes that are measures of motivation and behavior, they probably should stop looking at just a simple criterion of productivity or quality of job performance. It appears that since both ability and correctness of role perceptions influence performance along with effort, attitudes can never be very highly related to simple measures of quality of job performance. Thus, future studies should consider using a more direct measure of an individual's desire to perform well, or attempt to separate the effects of ability and role perceptions from those of effort, when they are attempting to understand the impact of attitudes on performance.

Pay as an Incentive

One of the central concerns of this chapter has been with the importance of pay as an incentive in the job situation. The finding that attitudes about pay are related to job performance provides information on *when* pay can be expected to function as an incentive. Specifically, it appears reasonable to conclude that pay can be an incentive for better job performance when it is important to the individual and when it is seen as being tied to job performance. There is some evidence that organization policies can influence both of these perceptions.

Recently, investigators (i.e., Nealey 1963; Mahoney 1964; Jones and Jeffrey 1964) have found that the value to the employee of the same amount of pay may vary greatly, depending upon how it is divided among various fringe benefits and options. Presumably, this comes about because certain benefits better fit the motive patterns of employees and are, therefore, valued more than are other benefits. This seems to occur despite the fact that the benefits may cost the company exactly the same amount of money. Other data suggest that because different employees have different motives, large individual differences appear in the degree to which individuals value various options. Nealey (1963), for example, found that unmarried workers value time off highly, while married workers do not. Clearly, these two groups have different motives operating, and, as a result, time off has different meanings to them.

The implications of the pay preference research are rather interesting as far as practices in the compensation area are concerned. Perhaps the most important one is that if organizations are to maximize the perceived value of the financial incentives they offer, then a "cafeteria" style wage plan is needed. A cafeteria compensation plan would allow every employee to divide his compensation dollars among the options he values most without adding to the total compensation costs of the company. Such a plan would appear to be potentially most effective at the management level. At this level there are fewer problems with union contracts and other agreements that might limit the organization's freedom. In addition, it makes more sense to offer alternative ways of determining pay to managers, since things as stock options and profit-sharing plans are feasible. The evidence, then, seems to suggest that one way to increase the importance of pay without increasing the actual amount of money spent is to relate the form of compensation more directly to the motives of the managers by using a cafeteria style wage plan.

It has been pointed out previously that most organizations practice secrecy with respect to management compensation and that it may have negative effects in terms of satisfaction with pay (Lawler 1965–a, 1965–b, 1967–b). It is also possible that secrecy may decrease the importance managers attach to the amount of their pay. Admittedly, there is little data either to support or reject this argument, but it would seem to agree with the view that pay gains its value from its association with the satisfaction of status, recognition, and achievement needs. By keeping pay secret, organizations are making it less directly instrumental for the satisfaction of these needs. After all, the needs for recognition and status are inherently public in nature, and, if salary is truly kept secret, then it is difficult to see how salary can be effectively related to them. Promotion stands today as one of the major incentives stimulating managerial performance. Because of its very public nature, it sensitizes managers' needs for recognition and status. Were pay to be public, it, like promotion, might be able to satisfy a broad range of important needs.

At this point, we need considerable research on the impact of making pay public before we will have a good idea of its significance. However, it does seem likely that one area which would be affected is the manager's view of how important the amount of his pay is to him.

So far we have considered several factors that may influence the importance and value of pay as a reward where the amount of pay remains the same. It is obvious that one other way to increase the importance of a particular financial reward or salary increase is to increase the absolute amount of money given. But the relationship may not be a simple linear one between the value of the raise to the individual and the amount of money given. It has long been known that for a person making $1,000 a month a $10 raise will have much less value than it will for a person making $200 a month. Obviously, salary increases, in order to be meaningful to managers at all salary levels, need to be based upon some proportion of the manager's present salary. Most organizations are aware of this and use a percentage figure for computing raises, but many seem to use a figure that is too small. Unfortunately, there is not enough research evidence available upon which to base a definite statement about the amount of the percentage raise that must be given if it is to be meaningful.

Although the present study was not designed to determine what type of pay programs lead to the perception that pay is based upon performance, the differences between the private and government samples on the index of the perceived probability that pay is dependent on performance are interesting in this regard. As was pointed out, the private organizations had pay plans that attempted to tie pay more closely to job performance than did the pay plans of the government organizations. From a comparison between the two samples on the degree to which pay was seen to be tied to performance, it is clear that the private managers actually did see their pay as more closely tied to their performance. The implication of this difference is obvious. Organizations can do something to foster the belief among their employees that their pay is based upon their performance. Future research will undoubtedly investigate the relative effectiveness of different pay plans in this respect, but even at the present time there appear to be some recommendations that can be made concerning how to encourage the belief that pay depends upon job performance.

We have already discussed some of the implications of secrecy about management compensation, but what we have not pointed out is that it may have considerable impact upon managers' perceptions of how their pay is determined. With secrecy existent in an organization, a situation is created in which it is very difficult for a manager to know how his pay compares with other managers' pay in the organization. This, of course, means that he has no objective basis against which to test his beliefs concerning the question of who gets paid well in the organization. Consequently, he has little information upon which to base his estimate of what kind of behavior leads to financial success in the organization. Also, he gets little feedback about how well he is performing in relation to others in the organization and as a result does not know how to adjust his performance in order to bring it more in line with what is acceptable to the organization.

He is forced to fall back upon his own estimate of what others make in order to evaluate his performance and, as Lawler (1965–a) has pointed out, these estimates are often wrong. The results of these effects of secrecy hardly seem to be likely to do anything but raise questions in the minds of managers about the validity of the frequently heard statement that "pay and performance are closely related in this organization."

In an attempt to tie pay to performance, stock option plans and bonus or profit-sharing plans are often used. At this point, it seems appropriate to ask: Do these kinds of pay plans really accomplish that purpose? It is very unlikely, for example, that stock option plans create the perception among managers that their own job behavior will actually influence their pay, since for this to happen they must feel that they can influence the price of the stock on the stock exchange. There are simply too many factors influencing stock prices for a single manager's effectiveness to be related to them. The same problems appear to exist with many bonus and profit-sharing plans; that is, they often fail to create the perception that individual managerial behavior is directly related to financial outcomes. Unfortunately, profits and other "objective" measures of performance are often almost completely out of the control of the individual manager, no matter what his organizational position may be. In one sense, such plans are rather poor substitutes for an effective performance appraisal system. In removing the control over a manager's economic returns from the immediate job situation, stock option and bonus plans may take the pressure off his superior for making subjective performance appraisals, but this may be done at the cost of destroying the relationship between pay and performance. An obvious truism would seem to be that without an effective performance appraisal system, pay can never be an effective incentive.

Haire *et al.* (1963) have called pay the most important incentive in our society. The results of the present study support the conclusion that it is a major incentive, although they do not offer unequivocal support for the statement that it is the most important incentive. The results do allow us to reject Brown's (1962) view that pay is not an important determinant of job performance. In the course of 50 years, we have moved from a firm belief in the concept of "economic man" to an equally firm belief in "social man" and "self-actualizing man." Research evidence suggests that both these extreme views are fallacious. However, it is not so surprising that both these divergent views have at one time enjoyed wide acceptance. Psychologists interested in individual differences have long known that no matter what model of man is created, it is possible to find someone who fits it. Thus, data exist which support both views.

The answer to the question of whether "social man," "self-actualizing man" or "economic man" represents the best model for organization theorists to follow when they deal with motivation is that none is *the* best. The fact is that man is motivated by social and self-actualization needs as well as by economic needs. What we really have is what Schein (1965) has called "complex man." The best motivational system for "complex man" will always be one that relates to a variety of needs, including economic ones, in order to motivate good job performance. Our model points out that the

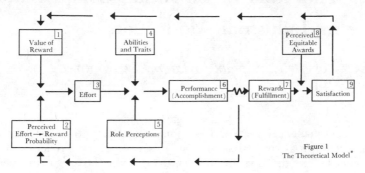

Figure 1
The Theoretical Model[*]

more the satisfaction of these needs can be tied to effective performance, the higher will be the motivation to perform effectively.

References

Brown, J. A. C. *The social psychology of industry*. Baltimore: Penguin, 1954.

Brown, W. *Piecework abandoned*. London: Heineman, 1962.

Chalupsky, A. B. Incentive practices as viewed by scientists and managers of pharmaceutical laboratories. *Personnel Psychology*, 1964, 17, 385–401.

Festinger, L. A. *Theory of cognitive dissonance*, Evanston, Ill.: Row, Peterson, 1957.

Georgopoulos, B. S., Mahoney, G. M., and Jones, M. W., Jr. A path-goal approach to productivity. *Journal of Applied Psychology*, 1957, 41, 345–53.

Haire, M., Ghiselli, E. E., and Porter, L. W. Psychological research on pay: An overview. *Industrial Relations*, 1963, 3, 3–8.

Haire, M., Ghiselli, E. E., and Porter, L. W. *Managerial thinking: An international study*. New York: Wiley, 1966.

Herzberg, F., Mausner, B., and Snyderman, Barbara. *The motivation to work*, 2nd ed. New York: Wiley, 1959.

Jones, L. V., and Jeffrey, T. E. A quantitative analysis of expressed preferences for compensation plans. *Journal of Applied Psychology*, 1964, 49, 201–10.

Lawler, E. E. Managers' perceptions of their subordinates' pay and of their superiors' pay. *Personnel Psychology*, 1965, 18, 413–22 (a).

Lawler, E. E. Should managers' compensation be kept under wraps? *Personnel*, 1965, 42, 17–20 (b).

Lawler, E. E. The multitrait-multirater approach to measuring managerial job performance. *Journal of Applied Psychology*, 1967, in press (b).

Lawler, E. E., and Porter, L. W. Perceptions regarding management compensation. *Industrial Relations*, 1963, 3, 41–49.

Mahoney, T. Compensation preferences of managers. *Industrial Relations*, 1964, 3, 135–44.

Maslow, A. H. A theory of human motivation. *Psychological Review*, 1943, 50, 370–96.

Maslow, A. H. *Motivation and personality*. New York: Harper, 1954.

Mayo, E. *The social problems of an industrial civilization*. Cambridge, Mass., Harvard University Press, 1945.

Myers, M. S. Who are your motivated workers? *Harvard Business Review*, 1964, 42 (1), 73–88.

Nealey, S. Pay and benefit preference. *Industrial Relations*, 1963, 3, 17–28.

Porter, L. W. A study of perceived need satisfactions in bottom and middle management jobs. *Journal of Applied Psychology*, 1961, 45, 1–10.

Roethlisberger, F. J., and Dickson, W. J. *Management and the worker*. Cambridge, Mass., Harvard University Press, 1939.

Schein, E. H. *Organizational psychology*. Englewood Cliffs, N. J.: Prentice-Hall, 1965.

Whyte, W. F. *Money and motivation: An analysis of incentives in industry*. New York: Harper, 1955.

29 / The Role of Financial Compensation in Industrial Motivation[1]

Robert L. Opsahl, Marvin D. Dunnette

WIDESPREAD INTEREST IN money as a motivational tool for spurring production was first stimulated in this country by Frederick Taylor. Some years before the turn of the century, Taylor observed an energetic steelworker, who, after putting in a 12-hour day of lifting pigs of iron, would run 12 miles up a mountainside to work on his cabin. If this excess energy could be used to produce more on the job, thought Taylor, higher profits from lower fixed costs could be used to pay the worker significantly more for his increased efforts. Such was the beginning of *scientific management,* which is based essentially on the assumption that workers will put forth extra effort on the job to maximize their economic gains. This became a guiding principle in pay practices until the late 1920s when the *human relations movement* in industrial psychology was ushered in with the Western Electric studies directed by Elton Mayo. As a result of these studies, recognition of man's ego and social needs became widespread, and job factors other than pay came to be emphasized as the major reasons why men work. To a large extent, these later ideas are still with us. Yet, few would disagree that money has been and continues to be the primary means of rewarding and modifying human behavior in industry.

Strangely, in spite of the large amounts of money spent and the obvious relevance of behavioral theory for industrial compensation practices, there is probably less solid research in this area than in any other field related to worker performance. We know amazingly little about how money either interacts with other factors or how it acts individually to affect job behavior. Although the relevant literature is voluminous, much more has been written about the subject than is actually known. Speculation, accompanied by compensation fads and fashions, abounds; research studies designed to answer fundamental questions about the role of money in human motivation are all too rare.

In this review, we have attempted to identify and summarize research studies designed to show how opportunities to get money affect the way people actually do their work. It was decided to focus attention on the

---

1 This investigation was supported in part by a Public Health Service Fellowship (5–F1–MH–21, 814–03 PS) from the National Institute of Mental Health, United States Public Health Service, and in part by a behavioral science research grant to Marvin D. Dunnette from the General Electric Foundation.

Reprinted by permission of the authors and the American Psychological Association from "The Role of Financial Compensation in Industrial Motivation," *Psychological Bulletin*, Vol. 66, No. 2 (August 1966), pp. 94–118.

role of money in motivating behavior *on the job*. The large body of literature on manpower economics relevant to relationships between wage and salary practices and manpower mobility has been largely ignored. Thus, we review here those theories and studies designed to illuminate possible effects of financial compensation for inducing greater effort in the job setting, and we ignore those theories and studies related to money's effects in inducing employees to take jobs, persist in them, or to leave them. First, several theories offered to explain how money affects behavior and research studies relevant to these theories are considered. Second, the behavioral consequences of compensation are examined by stressing and analyzing the variables relevant to the money-motivation relationship. Throughout, our purpose is to pinpoint the role of financial compensation in industrial job motivation. We seek to summarize and to evaluate critically what is already known and to suggest directions for future research.

Theories of the Role of Money

Does money serve to stimulate job effort? If so, why does it do so? How does it take on value in our industrial society? There are at least five theories or interpretations of the role of money in affecting the job behavior of employees.

Money as a Generalized Conditioned Reinforcer

One widely held hypothesis is that money acts as a generalized conditioned reinforcer because of its repeated pairings with primary reinforcers (Holland & Skinner 1961; Kelleher & Gollub 1962; Skinner 1953). Skinner (1953) has stated that such a generalized reinforcer should be extremely effective because some deprivation will usually exist for which the conditioned reinforcer is appropriate. Unfortunately, solid evidence of the behavioral effectiveness of such reinforcers is lacking, and what evidence there is has been based almost entirely on animal studies.

In a series of experiments conducted by Wike and Barrientos (1958), a goal box (containing wet mash) paired with both food and water deprivation proved to be a more effective reinforcer for rats than different goal boxes paired with food or water deprivation alone. The implications of these results are that money ought to be more potent when its attainment is paired with many, rather than only single, needs. Unfortunately, the magnitude of the difference in preferences in the above study, though statistically significant, was extremely small. In 15 test trials in a T-maze, rats turned to the goal box previously paired with both deprivations an average of only .62 trials more often than to the goal box paired only with food deprivation.

Moreover, this and most other studies on generalized conditioned reinforcers can be criticized because of the nonindependence of food and water as primary reinforcers (Grice & Davis 1957; Verplanck & Hayes 1953). A water-deprived rat eats less than his normal intake of food. What is needed are studies with human subjects in which a stimulus has been paired with many independent reinforcers. In one such study (Ferster & DeMyer 1962), coins paired with games and candy were used successfully with autistic children to develop and maintain complex operant behaviors. Although the effectiveness of the coins was well-demonstrated by the increased frequencies of responding contingent on their presentation, their effectiveness under different conditions of deprivation was not studied, nor was their relative effectiveness compared with that of coins operating as simple conditioned reinforcers.

Some theorists (e.g., Brown 1961; Dollard & Miller 1950) have referred to the token-reward studies of Wolfe (1936) and Cowles (1937) as examples of how money acquires value. In these studies, initially neutral poker chips apparently acquired reinforcement value because they could be exchanged for various foods. The analogy between the poker chips and the industrial use of money as wages is incomplete, however, because the reinforcement value of the poker chips came about because of their association with removing deprivation in a single primary area, whereas the theory of money's generalized reinforcing role would hypothesize that it is valued quite aside from and independent of any particular state of deprivation. It should be apparent that evidence in support of money as a generalized conditioned reinforcer is, at best, limited and inconclusive.

Money as a Conditioned Incentive

According to this hypothesis, repeated pairings of money with primary incentives[2] establish a new learned drive for money (Dollard & Miller 1950). For example, in Wolfe's (1936) study, the sight of a poker chip out of reach served as an incentive to motivate the chimpanzee to pull it in. The fact that chimpanzees refused to work if given a free supply of poker chips suggests that the act of obtaining the chips served a drive-reducing function (Dollard & Miller 1950). Presumably, money could become a generalized conditioned incentive in the same manner that it is presumed by some to become a generalized conditioned reinforcer—that is, by many pairings with many different types of incentives. Perhaps the main difference between the conditioned reinforcer and conditioned incentive interpretations is the introduction of drive reduction in the incentive hypothesis. In contrast, no such drive need be hypothesized under empirical reinforcement principles.

Money as an Anxiety Reducer

Brown (1953, 1961) also utilized the concept of drive in an effort to explain how money affects behavior. He suggested that one learns to become anxious in the presence of a variety of cues signifying the absence of money. Presumably, anxiety related to the absence of money is acquired in childhood through a process of higher-order conditioning. The first stage consists of pairings of pain with cues of warning or alarm provided by

2 Incentive: "an object or external condition, perceived as capable of satisfying an aroused motive, that tends to elicit action to obtain the object or condition [English & English, 1958]."

adults. For example, before a child actually touches a hot stove, a nearby adult may provide facial gestures of alarm and warnings such as "Look out, you'll get hurt!" These cues eventually elicit anxiety without the unconditioned stimulus. In the second stage, anxiety-arousing warnings are conditioned to a wide variety of cues indicating lack of money. After such learning, the child becomes anxious upon hearing phrases such as "That costs too much money," or "We can't afford to buy you that." The actual presence of money produces cues for the cessation of anxiety. This concept of anxiety as a learned motivating agent for money-seeking responses in no way contradicts the possible action of money according to the two previous hypotheses; money as an anxiety-reducer could operate jointly with them as an additional explanatory device.

Harlow (1953), however, has taken issue with Brown's thesis, stating: "It is hard to believe that parental expression at the time a child suffers injury is identical with or highly similar to a parent's expression when he says 'we have no money' [p. 22]." Harlow pointed out further that an infant's ability to recognize emotional expression when suffering pain has not been reliably demonstrated. Unfortunately, Brown presented no experimental evidence bearing on his theory.

Money as a "Hygiene Factor"

Herzberg, Mausner, and Snyderman (1959) postulated that money is a so-called "hygiene factor" serving as a potential dissatisfier if it is not present in appropriate amounts, but not as a potential satisfier or positive motivator. According to them, improvements in salary may only remove impediments to job satisfaction but do not actually generate job satisfaction. The main value of money, according to them, is that it leads to both the avoidance of economic deprivation and the avoidance of feelings of being treated unfairly. Thus, its hygienic role is one of avoiding pain and dissatisfaction ("disease") but not one of promoting heightened motivation ("health"). These notions were originally derived from content analyses of anecdotal accounts of unusually satisfying and unusually dissatisfying job events elicited from 200 engineers and accountants. Fifteen percent of their descriptions of satisfying events involved the mention of salary and 17% of their descriptions of dissatisfying events involved salary. Moreover, Herzberg et al. suggested that salary may be viewed as a "dissatisfier" because its impact on favorable job feelings was largely short-term while its impact on unfavorable feelings was long-term—extending over periods of several months. Herzberg et al.'s use of this finding to argue that money acts only as a potential dissatisfier is mystifying. It becomes even more so when their data are examined more carefully. In all of the descriptions of unusually good job feelings, salary was mentioned as a major reason for the feelings 19% of the time. Of the unusually good job feelings that lasted several months, salary was reported as a causal factor 22% of the time; of the short-term feelings, it was a factor 5% of the time. In contrast, salary was named as a major cause of unusually bad job feelings only 13% of the time. Of the unusually bad job feelings lasting several months, it was mentioned only 18% of the time (in contrast with the 22% of long-term good feelings, mentioned above).

These data seem inconsistent with the interpretations and lend no substantial support to hypotheses of a so-called differential role for money in leading to job satisfaction or job dissatisfaction.

Money as an Instrument for Gaining Desired Outcomes

Vroom's (1964) cognitive model of motivation has implications for understanding how money functions in affecting behavior. According to Vroom's interpretation, money acquires valence as a result of its perceived instrumentality for obtaining other desired outcomes. The concept of valence refers simply to affective orientations toward particular outcomes and has no direct implications for behavioral consequences. However, the "force" impelling a person toward action was postulated to be the product of the valence of an outcome and the person's expectancy that a certain action will lead to attainment of the outcome. Thus, for example, if money is perceived by a given person as instrumental to obtaining security, and if security is desired, money itself acquires positive valence. The probability, then, of his making money-seeking responses depends on the degree of his desire for security *multiplied* by his expectancy that certain designated job behaviors lead to attaining money. Although Vroom summarized studies giving general support to his theory, the specific role of money in his theory was not dealt with in any detail.

Gellerman's (1963) statement of how money functions in industry also stressed its instrumental role. According to him, money in itself has no intrinsic meaning and acquires significant motivating power only when it comes to symbolize intangible goals. Money acts as a symbol in different ways for different persons, and for the same person at different times. Gellerman presented the interesting notion that money can be interpreted as a projective device—a man's reaction to money "summarizes his biography to date: his early economic environment, his competence training, the various nonfinancial motives he has acquired, and his current financial status [p. 166]." Gellerman's evidence was largely anecdotal, but nonetheless rather convincing.

Summary of Theoretical Speculations

Much remains to be learned before we will understand very well what meaning money has for different persons, how it affects their job behaviors, which motives it serves, and how its effectiveness may come about. It is probably doubtful that there will ever be a "theory of money" in the sense that money will be given a unique or special status as a psychological variable. It is true that money functions in many ways, depending upon the setting, the antecedent conditions, and the particular person involved. According to Brown, money must be present to avoid anxiety. For Herzberg et al., it serves to avoid feelings of being unfairly treated or economically deprived. Reinforcement theories, on the other hand, seem to treat money either as a generalized entity, functioning independently of specific deprivations, or as a general incentive that has been coupled with variously valued goals during a person's total learning history. Obviously, the answers are not yet available, and it is probably best to view money symbolically, as Vroom and Gellerman do, and to begin to learn and measure the personal, situational, and job parameters that may define more fully what it is the symbol of and what its attainment is instrumental to. Only by mapping the domain in this way will we come to know the relevant factors associated with money as a "motivator" of behavior in industry.

Behavioral Consequences of Compensation

The major research problem in industrial compensation is to determine exactly what effects monetary rewards have for motivating various behaviors. More specifically, we need to understand more precisely how money can be used to induce employees to perform at high levels. Relevant research centers around two major groupings: studies related to the job or the job content and studies related to personal characteristics—preferences, perceptions, opinions, and other responses—made by the job incumbent. The first of these, the job or task variables, include primarily the policies and practices constituting the "compensation package" for any given job or job setting. The personal or subject variables influence not only the way a job holder responds to the specific policies and practices in any given situation, but they also vary as a function of these task or job variables. Thus, it is necessary to give careful attention to the interaction between job and personal variables which is frequently overlooked in research designs and has an important bearing on the interpretations to be attached to the results of such research studies.

Job and Task Variables

Compensation Policies

Our assumption is that the manner in which financial compensation is administered may account for a large amount of the variation in job behavior. The particular schedule of payment, the degree of secrecy surrounding the amount of pay one receives, how the level of salary or pay is determined, and the individual's long-term or career pay history all have important potential effects on how the employee responds to any specific amount of money.

Schedules of pay. In this review we shall be concerned solely with "incentive" payment systems[3] which are based on behavioral criteria (usually amount of output) rather than biographical factors such as education, seniority, and experience. Incentive pay schemes of various sorts are believed to function primarily to "increase or maintain some already initi-

---

[3] We will not attempt to evaluate all the evidence on incentive plans. For an excellent review and evaluation of these, see Marriott (1957).

ated activity or...to encourage some new form of activity...[Marriott 1957, p. 12]."

There is considerable evidence that installation of such plans usually results in greater output per man hour, lower unit costs, and higher wages in comparison with outcomes associated with straight payment systems (e.g., Dale 1959; Rath 1960; Viteles 1953). However, the installation of an incentive plan is not and can never be an isolated event. Frequently, changes in work methods, management policies, and organization accompany the changeover, and it is difficult to determine the amount of behavioral variance that each of these other events may contribute. This would seem to constitute a persuasive argument for placing workers in a controlled laboratory situation and analyzing the effectiveness of different methods of payment, isolated from the usual changes accompanying their installation. Unfortunately, there have been few studies of this nature.[4]

Incentive plans can be based on either the worker's own output or on the total output of his working group. The relative efficiency of the two methods are dependent upon such factors as the nature of the task performed (Babchuk & Goode 1951; Marriott 1957), the size of the working group (Campbell 1952; Marriott 1949, 1951; Marriott & Denerley 1955; Shimmin, Williams, & Buck 1956), the social environment (Selekman 1941), and the particular group or individual plan employed. The chief disadvantage with group incentives is the likelihood of a low correlation between a worker's own individual performance and his pay in larger groups. There is also evidence (Campbell 1952) that individual output decreases as the size of the work group increases, and this is apparently due to workers' perceiving a decreased probability that their efforts will yield increased outcomes (i.e., the workers have less knowledge of the relationships between effort and earnings). Both of these effects run counter to the main principle of incentive plans—immediate reward for desired job behaviors.

Not only do financial incentives operate with different efficacy in different situations, but often they do not even lead to increased production. Group standards and social pressures frequently induce workers to perform considerably below their potential. Most of the data on such rate restriction are either observational (e.g., Dalton 1948; Dalton, Collins, & Roy 1946; Dyson 1956; Mathewson 1951; Myers 1920; Roethlisberger & Dickson 1939; Roy 1952; Whyte 1955) or in the form of verbal responses to surveys (Opinion Research Corporation 1949; Viteles 1953). The results of these studies suggest that changes in the monetary consequences of performance are usually accompanied by changes in other expected consequences of performance. Thus, instituting an incentive plan may alter not only the expected consequences in terms of amount of money received, but also expected consequences related to possible loss of esteem in the eyes of one's co-workers or the

[4] Marriott (1957) mentioned only three experimental studies, all in an industrial setting and all conducted at least 30 years ago: Burnett (1925); Roethlisberger and Dickson (1939), and Wyatt (1934).

presumed bad connotations of "selling out" or accepting the goals of management.

Hickson (1961) has divided the causes of rate restriction into five categories. Three of the causes are essentially negative or avoidance reasons: uncertainty about the continuance of the existing "effort-bargain" between the workers and management, uncertainty about the continuance of employment, and uncertainty about the continuance of existing social relationships. The other two causes are positive or approach-type factors: the desire to continue social satisfactions derived from the practice of restriction, and a desire for at least a minimal area of external control over one's own behavior. Hickson stated that we haven't studied sufficiently the positive reasons or advantages of rate restriction. We shall go a step further and state that the main method of studying rate restriction—on the job observation—is essentially a loose and ineffective way of determining any causative linkages. Just as schedules of pay can best be assessed by experimental manipulations under controlled conditions, so should rate restriction be studied by laboratory investigations characterized by controlled and objective observations.

The most intensive analysis of rate restriction was undertaken by Whyte (1952, 1955). It was the thesis of Whyte and his co-workers that many piece-rate incentive situations actually resemble the conditions of experimentally induced neurosis. He reasoned that most incentive "packages" do not provide the employee with sufficient cues to allow him to discriminate effectively between stimuli signaling the onset of punishing circumstances (loss of co-worker respect, etc.) and stimuli signaling the onset of rewarding circumstances (more pay, higher job success, etc.) (Whyte 1955). Thus, money itself is only *one* of many possible rewards and punishments that invariably accompany any incentive situation.

Whyte's effort to show similarity between piece-rate incentive systems and the conditions accompanying experimental neurosis is misleading. The discriminative stimuli for the rewards and punishments administered by the work group and by management seem to be clearly differentiable. A double approach-avoidance conflict between the rewards and punishments of management and the work group is more descriptive of the situation. If this is the case, the conditions necessary for maintaining the group as an effective reinforcing agent even in the face of an incentive piece-rate plan should be studied more thoroughly. Variables for study would include group cohesiveness; interaction patterns within the group; amount of intergroup competition; identification of individuals within the group; uniformity of group opinion; group control over the environment; and the extent to which group pressures support rather than subvert organizational goals and demands (March & Simon 1958, pp. 59–61).

Thus, although "everyone knows" that incentive pay schemes work very effectively some of the time, it is painfully apparent that they are far from uniformly effective. The emphasis in research should now turn to more controlled observations of the effects of money in the context of the many other sources of reward and punishment in the work setting. So far, we have only a wealth of field observations. It is necessary now to learn more exactly just what employees will or will not give up for money or, more importantly, to learn how incentive payments may be made without engendering the painful and onerous circumstances which so often seem to accompany such payments.

Secret pay policies. In addition to the particular kind of pay plan, the secrecy surrounding the amount of money given an employee may have motivational implications. Lawler's (1965) recent study indicates that secret pay policies may contribute to dissatisfaction with pay and to the possibility of lowered job performance. He found that managers overestimated the pay of subordinates and peers, and underestimated their superiors' pay; they saw their own pay as being too low by comparison with all three groups. Moreover, they also underestimated the financial rewards associated with promotion. Lawler argued that these two results of pay secrecy probably reduce the motivation of managers both to perform well on their present jobs and to seek higher level jobs. Another disadvantage of secrecy is that it lowers money's effectiveness as a knowledge-of-results device to let the manager know how well he is doing in comparison to others. Lawler advocated the abandonment of secrecy policies—"there is no reason why organizations cannot make salaries public information [p. 8]."

Lawler's assertion seems to have a good deal of merit; his results are impressive and his arguments sound. It would be very useful, at this stage, to conduct "before-after" studies of the effects of instituting policies of openness concerning wage and salary payments on employees' perceptions of relationships between pay and job performance. At the very least, Lawler's data suggest that useful effects would be produced by informing employees (particularly managers) about how their salaries are derived; the next logical step would be to provide normative data (e.g., percentile distributions of employee pay levels) ; and, finally, salary administrators might even publicize actual salary levels of persons in the firm.

This is not to say, of course, that there might not be negative outcomes from the sudden implementation of such policies. For example, one obvious possibility is that such action might crystallize present hierarchical "pecking orders"; group cohesiveness could be disrupted by the sudden awareness of substantial intra-work-group differences. Most such fears stem from the prevalence of actual pay inequities related to inadequate job-performance appraisal systems and current weaknesses in administering salary payments in such a way as to reflect valid relationships with job performance. We believe, with Lawler, that present policies of secrecy are undoubtedly due, in part, to fear on the part of salary administrators that they would have a difficult time mustering convincing arguments in favor of many of their present practices. Thus, it is true that until salaries are determined more rationally and until money becomes more firmly accepted as a way of rewarding outstanding job behavior, public disclosure of salary arrangements may probably not have the desirable consequences suggested by Lawler. Perhaps his results are merely symptomatic of present unsuccessful efforts to use pay effectively for motivating employees. If this is true, it seems all the more important and timely to undertake thorough studies of the effects of relaxing present policies of pay secrecy.

Pay curves. An employee's periodic pay increases, as he progresses in his career with a company, constitutes another job or task variable with the potential for differentially motivating effects. Wittingly or not, every company "assigns" each employee a "pay curve" which is the result of successive alterations in compensation and compensation policies through the years. One way of doing this (the usual way) is with little or no advanced planning; increments are given haphazardly on a year to year basis and the resulting career pay curve simply "grows" somewhat akin to Topsy. Another alternative is to plan the future compensation program shortly after the individual enters the organization and then to modify it subsequently on the basis of his job behavior as his career unfolds. No matter which pay policy is adopted, the results will most likely affect the employee's job behavior, his aspirations and anticipations of future earnings, and his feelings of fairness with respect to his career-pay "program."

Most companies administer pay increments on a periodic (e.g., year-to-year) basis.[5] The rationale for this is quite simple, the usual idea being that differential pay increments may be given for differential results produced by employees on their jobs. Over a span of many years, then, we might expect a consistent pattern of positive correlations for the salary increments received by the individuals comprising any particular group of employees. This expectation would be based on two rather reasonable and closely related assumptions—first, that the acquisition of job skills is a predictable process; and, second, that the effectiveness of a person's job performance in any given period is predictable from his own past patterns of job performance.

In fact, however, career pay histories for employee groups do *not* usually show such patterns of consistently positive relationships between year-to-year salary gains. Haire (1965) mapped the correlations between salary levels at the end of each year and raises over 5- and 10-year periods in two large national companies. In one company, the correlations decreased over the 5-year span from .38 to −.06 for one executive group (median salary $41,600), and from .36 to −.25 for a second group (median salary $18,000). In the second firm, the correlations between salaries and raises for adjacent years over the 10-year period varied between −.33 and .83 with no consistent pattern discernible. Haire believed that his results constituted damning evidence that these two companies had no consistent policies with respect to the incentive use of salary increases; he suggested that the trend in the first company reflected a shift from a policy of distributing raises under the assumption that good performance is related to past excellence to the assumption that it is either not related at all or that it is negatively related. He also asserted that a pattern showing extremely low correlations between present salary levels and salary increments indicates that wage increases might just as well be distributed by lottery—that the incentive character of a raise is thereby nullified and that consistent striving for job

---

[5] Since there are innumerable ways to administer pay on a periodic basis, and since these methods are largely administrative and have little interest of a psychological nature, we will not attempt to review them.

excellence would seem futile under such circumstances. Haire's assertions are provocative and they may indeed follow from his results, but we believe that other explanations may be equally compatible with his findings. For example, low correlations could just as reasonably be viewed as reflecting a successfully administered wage policy allowing for greater rather than less flexibility in using money to reward top job performance. Such a policy might suggest, in effect, that an employee who has done well in the past cannot rest on his laurels in expectation of future "rewards" and that a lower salaried employee (with presumably a history of less effective performance) still has rich opportunities to be recognized and appropriately rewarded for improved job performance in the future. It is true that a finding of consistently low correlations would tend to refute our earlier stated assumptions about the acquisition of job skills and the consistency of job performance over time.

Be that as it may, future analyses of historical pay patterns such as these provided by Haire will probably yield more explicit insights about company wage policies if they focus more closely on individual employee pay and job performance histories rather than rely solely on coarse within-group comparisons and correlations such as those reported by Haire. The idea of inspecting historical patterns in the relationships between job performance, salaries, and raises is a good one and should be utilized more broadly.

The idea of specifying individual career pay curves has received extensive attention by Jaques (1961), through his "standard payment and progression method." By analyzing the pay histories of 250 male workers, he derived a family of negatively accelerated pay curves extending from ages 20 to 65. It should be noted, however, that his curves were plotted with a log scale for the ordinate (salary). If actual dollar values were plotted, the data would very likely yield positively rather than negatively accelerated curves. However, as plotted by Jaques, the curves rise rapidly in the younger age groups, slow down at older ages, and show a greater rate of progression at the higher earning levels. According to Jaques, these smoothed curves (called standard earning progressions), follow "the sigmoidal progression characteristic of biological growth [1961, p. 185]," and are the basis for his payment theory. Jaques believed that the standard earning progression curves represent a close approximation to the lines of growth of "time-span of discretion" in individuals. This time-span of discretion is the maximum period of time during which the work assigned by a manager requires his subordinate to exercise discretion, judgment, or initiative in his job without that discretion being subject to review by the manager. This objective yardstick can supposedly be used for direct comparison of work levels between any two jobs, regardless of content. The major significance of the time-span, according to Jaques, is that workers in jobs having different contents but the same time-span of discretion privately perceive the same wage or salary bracket to be equitable for the work they are doing.

Assuming that individuals seek an equitable level of payment for the level of work consistent with their capacity, an employee's future pay curve can be determined by: (*a*) determining the employee's present time-span of discretion along with the equitable payment for that time-span; (*b*) plotting the employee's achieved earning progression to date; (*c*) allowing the manager once-removed to determine the employee's potential progress assessment (i.e., the manager's assessment of the level of work a person is likely to achieve—this can be expressed in terms of the earning progression that the employee would likely achieve given that he receives equitable payment for his work); (*d*) letting the immediate manager assess the employee's performance, and altering the employee's wage or salary according to this assessment; (*e*) having the once-removed manager revise the potential progress assessment if performance continues above or below the original potential progress assessment.

The above is only a brief sketch of Jaques' theory of payment. It is a highly interesting one, but until further data concerning its motivational consequences are compiled, it must be regarded as highly tentative.

The "sigmoidal biological growth" pay curves that Jaques described are not the only possible ones; Ghiselli (1965) has pointed out other possibilities and has attempted to provide the rationale behind them. For instance, one suggested possibility was having average increments in pay increase from year to year. The result would be a positively accelerated pay curve consonant with the philosophy of paying an employee a substantial amount only after he becomes highly effective in the organization instead of when he is in the early stages of his career and easily tempted to move to another organization. If the organization wished to budget a fixed amount for pay increases each year, linear pay curves would result. If, on the other hand, it is assumed that an employee is unlikely to leave a firm after he has been with it a long time and has a huge personal investment in it (such as retirement benefits, stock options, etc.), it might be advantageous to reward him generously when he first starts his job to help insure that he will not go to another firm (i.e., assign him a negatively accelerated curve). To our knowledge, no empirical studies on the relative effectiveness of different possible pay curves have been undertaken.

Although it would appear that pay curves have a significant influence on job behavior, parametric experiments in this area are practically nonexistent. Several aspects of pay curves need to be studied before these curves can be constructed or used with even a moderate degree of effectiveness.

First and most important, it must be determined how a given pay curve differentially affects employees' motivation and job behaviors. It is not plausible to assume that one best curve can be found for *all* employees, or even for a subgroup of employees at a given job level or with common job duties. Some evidence of this was revealed by Festinger (1965) who found that promotions (with related pay increases, presumably) *increased* the aspired-to job level and perceived importance of pay for about 30% of a sample of employees within one company but *decreased* the job level-of-aspiration and perceived importance of pay in another 30% of the cases. It is not known why these groups reacted so differently to promotions. The overall level-of-aspiration of the employees certainly would be a prime variable; need Achievement might be another. Little is known about the stability of these two variables; therefore, assessment of them early in an employee's career may not be a valid index of later expectations or the effectiveness of career pay-curve policies. It is necessary to conduct longitudinal studies over extended periods of time—studies which are all too infrequent in the area of compensation. Some of the data necessary for this type of study are already on file in computer memory banks in the larger companies and need only to be retrieved and analyzed.

Since pay curves do not operate within a vacuum, the effect of one employee's pay curve on another employee must not be overlooked. Ghiselli's (1965) rationale for positively and negatively accelerated curves, for instance, may not prove effective in the context of the total industrial situation. Since pay is on a competitive basis across companies, a negatively accelerated curve in one company might lead to feelings of inequity and possible job termination for a young employee if other companies offered linear or positively accelerated pay increments in a similar situation. It is not implied that the effectiveness of the different curves should not be studied. However, the concept of equity applies to pay-curve comparisons as well as to wage comparisons, and this is an important potential area for investigation.

Several methods of deriving pay curves deserve further investigation. One option would be to inform the employee of the tentative curve agreed upon for him. This could be done piecemeal, by setting monetary goals for him to shoot at within a specific time period. An interesting variation of this procedure that, to our knowledge, has not been studied, would be to include pay goals in the goal-setting interviews given high level managers in some companies. The behavioral goals set in these interviews could have monetary rewards attached to them, thereby providing further incentive for their attainment. Informing an employee of his progress along his proposed pay curve might also serve a valuable feedback function, helping him evaluate his progress to date.

Other relevant research problems are numerous. Important ones include determining how to alter an employee's subsequent curve on the basis of under- or overachievement, discovering valid criteria for constructing a tentative curve, and determining which variables influence the perception of pay increments and *how* they influence it. With expanded knowledge in these areas, pay curves and their determination may come to play a central role in industrial compensation practices of the future.

Industrial psychologists have too often turned prematurely to the study of employee characteristics without giving sufficient attention to the job context. The significant research reviewed here and the questions suggested testify to the potential importance of task and job content variables. Certainly the complexities of the interaction between task and job variables and subject (employee) variables, discussed in the following section, demand research evidence bearing on both. The failure to place research emphasis in either area will very likely impede progress and understanding in the other.

Subject Variables

Perceived Relations Between Performance and Pay

According to Vroom's (1964) theory of work motivation, the valence of effective performance increases as the instrumentality of effective performance for the attainment of money increases, assuming that the valence of money is positive. Vroom cited supporting evidence from experiments by Atkinson and Reitman (1956), Atkinson (1958), and Kaufman (1962) showing a higher level of performance by subjects who were told that their earnings were contingent on the effectiveness of their performance. Georgopoulos, Mahoney, and Jones' (1957) Path-Goal Approach theory similarly states that if a worker has a desire for a given goal and perceives a given path leading to that goal, he will utilize that path if he has freedom to do so. Georgopoulos et al. found that workers who perceived higher personal productivity as a means to increased earnings performed more effectively than workers who did not perceive this relationship.

The effectiveness of incentive plans in general depends upon the worker's knowledge of the relation between performance and earnings. The lack of this knowledge is one cause of failure in incentive schemes. As already mentioned, Campbell's (1952) study showed that one of the major reasons for lower productivity in large groups under group incentive plans is that the workers often do not perceive the relation between pay and productivity as well as they do in smaller groups. In the Georgopoulos et al. (1957) study, only 38% of the workers perceived increased performance as leading to increased earnings. More amazingly, 35% perceived *low* productivity as an aid to higher earnings in the long run. Lawler (1964) recently found that 600 managers perceived their training and experience to be the most important factors in determining their pay—not how well or how poorly they performed their jobs. Since Lawler found that the relation between their pay and their rated job performance also was low, their perceptions were probably quite accurate. A separate analysis of the most highly motivated managers, however, indicated that they attached greater importance to pay and felt that good job performance would lead to higher pay.

These studies confirm the importance of knowing how job performance and pay are related. The relation between performing certain desired behaviors and attainment of the pay-incentive must be explicitly specified. The foregoing statement seems so obvious as hardly to warrant mentioning. Unfortunately, as we have seen, the number of times in industry that the above *rule* is ignored is surprising. Future research must determine how goals or incentives may best be presented in association with desired behaviors. Practically nothing has been done in this area—especially for managers. In fact, programs for the recognition of individual merit are notoriously poor. Methods for tying financial compensation in with management-by-results (Schleh 1961) or with systematic efforts to set job goals and methods of unambiguously outlining what the end result of various job behaviors will be should be developed and studied.

Personality-Task Interactions

Under some conditions, it appears that even specifying the relation between performance and pay is not sufficient. Early studies (Wyatt & Fraser 1929; Wyatt, Fraser, & Stock 1929; Wyatt & Langdon 1937) conducted on British factory workers showed that feelings of boredom are associated with reduced output even under a carefully developed program of incentive pay. More recent studies have failed to reproduce the daily output curve found by the British investigators, and, moreover, indicate that boredom is not *necessarily* accompanied by reduced output (Cain 1942; Smith 1953; Ryan & Smith 1954). Thus, boredom *may* lead to a decrease in performance; but, as in most other areas of investigation, a ceteris paribus clause must be included. Little is known of the factors which may outweigh the effects of boredom in a particular situation.

It is obvious that repetitiveness and uniformity in job tasks are likely to contribute to feelings of boredom, but personality variables are also important determinants. Smith (1955) found that susceptibility to boredom is associated with such factors as youth, restlessness in daily habits and leisure-time activities, and dissatisfaction with personal, home, and plant situations not directly concerned with uniformity or repetitiveness. The commonly held assumption that workers of higher intelligence are more easily bored with repetitive work, however, is based on meager and conflicting data (Ryan & Smith 1954).

One possible method of alleviating feelings of boredom is suggested by Wyatt and Fraser's (1929) finding that piece-rate systems lead to fewer symptoms of boredom than does straight hourly pay. This is in keeping with Whyte's (1955) contention that, in addition to money, there are three other sources of reward in a piece-rate situation: escape from fatigue, because the worker has a meaningful goal to shoot at; escape from management pressure and gain of control over one's own time; and "playing the game" of trying to attain quota.

Even if piece-rate systems relieve boredom, output under such plans may still suffer if the task is disliked. This was Wyatt's (1934) finding when he compared the levels of performance of 10 female workers in a British candy factory under hourly, bonus, and piece-rate payment methods. He observed a strong positive relation between an incentive plan's effectiveness (defined as increased productivity) and liking for the job. The best liked job was wrapping the candy and employees increased their output on it 200% when payment was changed from straight pay to a group bonus and finally to piece-rate payment. In contrast, unwrapping damaged packages was viewed as most onerous—"an aimless and destructive process"—and output on this task showed no change under different conditions of pay.

The net conclusion from these studies is that repetitive tasks, destructive tasks, boring tasks, and disliked tasks are apparently much less susceptible to monetary incentives. Little has been done, however, to explore other possible interactions in this area. What little data we do have suggest that nonmonetary incentives are more effective for subjects who have high ability on the task being measured. Thus, Fleishman (1958) found that subjects high in ability on a complex coordination task increased their performance under incentive conditions significantly more than did low ability subjects. However, we do not know if such findings would generalize to situations in which monetary incentives are used or how the effectiveness of incentives varies as a function of other important variables such as the type of task, the amount of physical effort demanded, or the degree of interpersonal interaction involved, to mention but a few examples. Without knowledge of the range of behaviors susceptible to incentives or the degree to which they are susceptible, we cannot make optimal use of them in any specific situation. Should we use incentives for maintaining or improving leadership behavior? And how about jobs which are highly challenging and intrinsically rewarding? Are incentives in this situation a cause of mercenary feelings which detract from the main source of reinforcement—the job itself—and ultimately lower job effectiveness? Or do they spur the employees on to yet greater heights? Of course, we do not know; and, even more unfortunately, little research seems to be under way to test assumptions implicitly made by many firms' present compensation policies.

Perceived Importance of Pay

It seems obvious that employees must regard money as a highly desirable commodity before increased amounts of it motivate increased behavior. Results of studies in this area are extremely confusing because of the almost exclusive dependence on self-reports to estimate the relative importance of pay. For example, when Wilkins (1949, 1950) asked 18- and 19-year-old males at the British Army Reception Center to rank various job incentives on importance, "pay" was placed second only to "friendly workmates." Only 8% ranked pay as most important. "Friendly workmates," "security," and "future prospects" all received more first-place rankings than pay. Factor analysis of the responses revealed two broad factors: One was of long-term appeal and included "security," "future prospects," "variety," and "efficient organization." The other factor included "pay," "workmates," "working hours," and "leave." The second factor was interpreted as consisting of items incidental to the job and mainly of short-term appeal. When Wilkins divided the group into high and low intelligence, he found that both "pay" and "workmates" were relatively more important for the low intelligence group—41% of the youths in this group gave "workmates" top ranking. He concluded that "a large proportion of such workers would be prepared to accept lower wages if they could be with workmates they liked [1950, p. 562]."

In a study by Watson (1939), employees ranked pay third in importance on a list of eight "morale" factors. However, when their employers were asked to rank the eight factors according to how they thought the employees would respond, pay was selected as the most important factor. This differential perception of the importance of money by employees and

higher management has been confirmed in a survey conducted by the
National Industrial Conference Board (1947), showing that executives
ranking 71 morale factors in terms of overall importance gave top rank to
compensation, while fewer than 30% of the rank-and-file employees included this among the five most important factors.

Worthy's (1950) analysis of surveys conducted by Sears, Roebuck, and
Company over a 12-year period showed that pay ranked eighth among
factors related to high morale, whereas rates of pay ranked fourteenth.
Over a span of nearly 20 years, Jurgensen[6] has asked applicants for
employment with the Minneapolis Gas Company to rank 10 job factors
in order of their importance. Now with a total accumulation of over
42,000 cases, he finds that pay has consistently ended up in sixth place.
On the other hand, when Ganuli (1954) asked employees in a Calcutta,
India, engineering factory to rank eight items relating to working conditions in order of importance, he found that "adequate earnings" was ranked
first, above such factors as "job security," "opportunity for promotion," and
"personal benefits." Graham and Sluckin (1954) also found pay the most
important job factor in a survey of skilled and semiskilled workers in
England.

The discrepancies in the above-mentioned studies can be partially explained by the different samples of employees used. One would not expect
executives to have the same values and goals as blue-collar workers (nor,
for that matter, should it be assumed that executives or blue-collar workers
are homogeneous groups in themselves). Another cause of the discrepant
findings is the variety in the dimensions of job incentives used. Seldom are
the same variables ranked in any two studies. Also, it is probable that many
of the factors are not independent. Bendig and Stillman (1958) have
criticized the bulk of studies for these last two reasons. They further contended that the factors used were not selected within any theoretical framework of hypothesized dimensions of job incentives. In an attempt to isolate
the fundamental dimensions of job incentives, Bendig and Stillman (1958)
factor-analyzed eight incentive statements given to college students. They
found three orthogonal bipolar factors that they tentatively named "need
achievement vs. fear of failure," "interest in the job vs. the job as an
opportunity of acquiring status," and "job autonomy of supervision vs.
supervisor dependency." Salary loaded highest on "the job as an opportunity
for acquiring status," and had small loadings on "fear of failure" and "job
autonomy." Still another possible reason for discrepancies in the above
studies is that they have failed to assess the degree to which various respondents' job circumstances are or are not providing sufficient rewards in
each job area. For example, a respondent who perceives his present pay as
adequate may rate pay as relatively less important than he would if he
perceived his present pay level to be low. It is probably impossible for
respondents to detach themselves sufficiently from their present circum-

6 Personal communication, 1965.

stances to be able to give completely accurate self-report estimates of the relative importance of different job aspects.

While most self-report surveys place salary in a position of only moderate importance, it is easy to find people in industry who *behave* as if they value money highly. Executives strive mightily to advance to high-paying jobs; entertainers work toward more and more lucrative arrangements; bankers embezzle; robbers rob; university professors publish to win increased salary and to enjoy royalty checks. Why is it then that money or pay seldom is ranked commensurate with these behaviors? The answer is not simple, but it may include at least the following possibilities: (*a*) There is probably a social desirability response set pervading the self-reports. The Protestant Ethic is still with us; one may not readily admit that he is running after the almighty dollar without feeling some twinge of conscience which can be dissipated by relegating pay to a relatively low position on the value hierarchy and giving lip service to other more acceptable factors such as "job autonomy" or "intrinsic job satisfaction." (*b*) The reinforcement contingencies present in filling out a self-report questionnaire are quite different from those in the real life situation. It is apparent that an individual is reinforced generously for actually obtaining money, but it is much less evident what the reinforcement contingencies are when he simply *admits* in a self-report checklist that attaining money may be a prime goal. Certainly one is reinforced for engaging in a bit of rationalization while filling out such self-reports. (*c*) Finally, as implied above, people are poor judges (and therefore poor reporters) of what they really want in a job. They do not know with certainty which job factors really attract and hold them; hence they cannot validly describe or rank these job factors.

Thus, research on the valence of money must move beyond the dependency on self-report measures and strive to establish the actual linkages between money and behavior by more sophisticated observational techniques. It is not implied that bankers embezzle *only* for money or that university professors publish *only* for money or that executives strive *only* for money. Money plays a role in all these—a role probably far greater than that suggested by the self-report studies. The self-report studies are based on oversimplified notions tending to ignore the complexities and multidetermined aspects of human behavior. Further accumulation of such rankings or ratings will add little to our understanding of the behavioral effects of compensation. Laboratory studies and experimental observations of the behavioral effects of money are needed here just as in the many other areas we have discussed.

These may, in part, be supplemented with more sophisticated techniques of scaling. Some modification of the paired-comparison technique used by Jones and Jeffrey (1964) in which a more inclusive domain of job incentive aspects are compared against some monetary standard would be a promising start. We should also heed Bendig and Stillman's (1958) plea for the isolation of basic independent job incentive dimensions in future research in order to unify research and allow for cross-study comparisons. In sum, the question, "How do people value money?" will not be answered accurately simply by asking them.

Pay Preferences

Although money *per se* is usually accorded a middle position in any ranking of job factors, different ways of making salary payments are differentially preferred. Mahoney (1964) found that managers prefer straight salary over various types of management incentive payments (such as stock options, deferred compensation, etc.). This is in keeping with the results of other surveys. Jaques, Rice, and Hill (1951), for example, reported that the majority of both workers and management in an English factory were in favor of a change from individual piece-rates to hourly wages. Likewise, Davis (1948) found that 60% of a sample of building operatives were opposed to incentive schemes, with only 21% expressing definite or conditional approval. The main arguments against incentive systems, as reported by Davis, include the fear that the incentive would inhibit other strong and pleasurable motives for working, such as the pleasure of work for its own sake and the solidarity and good fellowship of the working group.

A study conducted by the Michigan Survey Research Center (Larke 1953) revealed that group incentive payments were favored by fewer than 50% of the employees who already were under such plans. Similarly, Mahoney (1964) found that his sample of managers also preferred individual to group pay plans. On the other hand, Wyatt and Marriott (1956) found more approval than disapproval of group incentives by 62% of the workers sampled in three factories. With respect to particular types of incentives, Spriegal and Dale (1953) found individual piecework much more popular than group piecework.

Using paired-comparison techniques, Nealey (1963) found that a large sample ($N = 1,133$) of electrical workers accorded direct pay increases a lower position than such fringe benefits as sick leave, extra vacation time, or hospital insurance. He also discovered that such preferences do not follow a simple dollar value. For example, dental insurance cost the company less than life insurance but was preferred by more workers. Jones and Jeffrey (1964) asked employees in two electrical equipment plants to make paired comparisons among 16 alternative compensation plans, each characterized by a combination of four features and having identical overall costs to the company. The unique aspect of this study is the possibility of directly comparing the average value of each compensation characteristic with that of a pay raise and, thus, attaching a monetary equivalent to each preferred characteristic. Results showed that the average value of a change from hourly wage to weekly salary is judged to be equivalent to a pay increase of between 1 and 2 cents an hour. A piece-rate incentive plan was perceived as equivalent to a 5- to 10-cent hourly pay increase and was preferred mainly by the skilled workers who already had experience with such a plan. At the nonunion plant, a supervisory merit-rating incentive was considered equal to a 4-cent pay raise. At the union plant, however, the scheme was so disliked that the absence of the plan was considered worth more than a 6-cent hourly raise.

Jones and Jeffrey believed that their approach may have direct bearing upon administrative decisions concerning changes in compensation plans. If the monetary value equivalent of the change, perceived by the worker, substantially exceeds the actual cost to the company of a change in benefits, then it may be considered—if it does not hinder other compensation goals. Basing company compensation policies directly on the measured perceptions of employees regarding the policies also has the additional advantage of designing the pay schemes directly to fit the motive (or preference) systems of the employees being compensated under the plans. The Nealey study and the Jones and Jeffrey study provide rare examples of the analysis of employees' preferences by sophisticated scaling techniques. They well deserve to be emulated by other researchers in this area.

Mahoney (1964, p. 144) concluded that preferences for alternative forms of compensation are relatively uniform and that "fine distinctions among alternative forms of compensation probably are considerably less important in managerial motivation than is often suggested." Such preferences should not be the sole criterion for assessing the effects of compensation on motivation if we are mainly interested in actual job behavior, not satisfaction,[7] since the relation between the two is complex and, in many instances, unknown. From stated preferences one cannot easily infer that the compensation program is optimally motivating.

Although there has been a fair amount of research done in determining the pay preferences of managers and other employees, no work has been done on the relation between preference for a particular plan and the actual incentive value of that plan. The implicit, but unwarranted, assumption in all the above-mentioned studies is that if a person has a pay plan he likes, this plan will motivate behavior more than one that he does not like. Although this is an appealing assumption, future studies, in addition to determining employees' pay-plan preferences, should seek to map the relation between such preferences and the incentive value of different plans. The motivation of behavior, *not* the preference for compensation policies, is the prime goal of company pay plans, and research strategies should be directed toward this end.

Concept of Equitable Payment

Several theories have been independently advanced proposing that employees seek a just or equitable return for what they have contributed

---

[7] There is correlational evidence that amount of pay is positively associated with satisfaction with pay (Andrews & Henry 1963; Lawler & Porter 1963), job satisfaction (Barnett, Handelsman, Stewart, & Super 1952; Centers & Cantril 1946; Marriott & Denerly 1955; Miller 1951; Smith & Kendall 1963; Thompson 1939; all as reported in Vroom 1964), and with need satisfaction (Lawler & Porter 1963; Porter 1962). However, it is not known to what degree the satisfaction is a result of the level of pay or the changes in job status, duties, and privileges that so often accompany higher pay.

to the job (Adams 1963a, 1965; Homans 1961; Jaques 1961; Patchen 1961; Sayles 1958; Zaleznik, Christenson, & Roethlisberger 1958). A common feature of these theories is the assumption that compensation either above or below that which is perceived by the employee to be "equitable" results in tension and dissatisfaction due to dissonant cognitions. The tension, in turn, causes the employee to attempt to restore consonance by a variety of behavioral or cognitive methods.

One of the earlier theorists in this area was Homans, who suggested the concept of distributive justice—that is, justice in the way the rewards and costs of activities are distributed among men. He postulated that:

> A man in an exchange relation with another will expect that the rewards of each man be proportional to his costs—the greater the rewards, the greater the costs—and that the net rewards, or profits, of each man be proportional to his investments—the greater the investments, the greater the profits [Homans 1961, p. 232].

Schematically, then, there is distributive justice when

$$\frac{\text{Person A's rewards minus his costs}}{\text{A's investments}} = \frac{\text{Person B's rewards minus his costs}}{\text{B's investments}}$$

(after Adams 1965). If the two ratios are unequal, the members of the exchange experience feelings of injustice, one or the other perceiving that he is on the short end in terms of profits. Either member sensing injustice will attempt to bring his profits and investments into line through various behaviors or, perhaps, by changing his perception of the situation.

Homans briefly treated the relation between distributive justice and satisfaction. He proposed that if there is a state of injustice, the person at a disadvantage will "display the emotional behavior we call anger [1961, p. 75]." If, on the other hand, the injustice is in his favor, the person will feel guilty. He implied that the threshold for guilt is higher than that for anger.

Zaleznik et al. (1958) applied Homans' theory to compensation and tested the postulates on 50 production workers. They constructed a reward-investment index to determine whether a worker was receiving an equitable return for his services. When the index was related to worker satisfaction, however, a completely random distribution of high- and low-satisfied workers was found, no matter how favorable the reward-investment index. Since the index was crude and nonempirical, the lack of any relation between satisfaction and distributive justice is not particularly surprising.

Jaques' (1961) theory of equitable payment differs from Homans' mainly in its psychoanalytic orientation. His theory is based on the assumptions that (*a*) there exists "an unrecognized system of norms of fair payment for any given level of work, unconscious knowledge of these norms being shared among the population engaged in employment work [1961, p. 124]"; and that (*b*) an individual is "unconsciously aware" of his own potential capacity for work, as well as the equitable pay level for that work. Jaques claimed that this optimal level of payment is that which allows an optimal consumption of goods and services consistent with "dynamic psychological equilibrium." He stated that equitable payments are accompanied by feelings of satisfaction, but that deviations in payment below or above the equitable level are usually accompanied by feelings of dissatisfaction or uneasiness.

As Vroom (1964) has pointed out, however, Jaques did a rather poor job of scientific reporting. He failed to specify the methods employed in measuring dissatisfaction, the means and variances in his dependent variable, and, frequently, the number of workers on whom various observations were made. Until these and other aspects of Jaques' research are adequately reported, his conclusions, as Vroom indicated, must be regarded with caution.

A third formulation of a theory of equity is found in the work of Patchen (1961). He postulated that equitable payment is achieved when the following two ratios are congruent:

$$\frac{\text{My pay}}{\text{His (their) pay}} \text{ compared to } \frac{\text{My position on dimensions related to pay}}{\text{His (their) position on dimensions related to pay}}$$

A unique aspect of this theory is the concept of potential, or future, perceived equitable payment. This results from the congruence of these ratios:

$$\frac{\text{My pay now}}{\text{His (their) pay now}} \text{ compared to } \frac{\text{My future position on dimensions related to pay}}{\text{His (their) present position on dimensions related to pay}}$$

Thus, although a person perceives a wage comparison as presently equitable, he may still perceive future inequity. This would occur, for example, if the comparison person(s) is someone more skilled, but the person feels he should receive gradual pay increases as his own skill improves—that is, as he becomes more like his comparison person(s) on dimensions related to pay. Such dissonant comparisons may provide a basis for mobility (promotional) aspirations for the person; he may feel that a higher status would be more appropriate for him. Under these circumstances, it is quite possible that dissatisfaction from future perceived inequity may be tolerated.

Substantiation of Patchen's theory comes from interviews with 489 employees in a Canadian oil refinery (Patchen 1961). The employees were asked to name two persons whose yearly earnings were different from theirs. Those who chose objectively dissonant comparisons (e.g., comparison persons who were of similar status but whose earnings were greater) judged the comparison unsatisfactory. They explained their feelings in terms of dissonance between the wage difference and other related differences. For example, 75% of the employees justified their feelings by pointing out their own equality or superiority with respect to the comparison person on factors directly relevant to pay—such as education, seniority, and skill. Those employees who were satisfied with their comparisons based their feelings of satisfaction on a perceived consonance between the wage difference and other related differences between the workers. Other interesting findings were that men relatively low in pay were less satisfied than others in the comparisons they chose; and, as a worker's mobility chances improved, these men would more frequently choose potentially dissonant comparisons and be more dissatisfied with the idea of remaining below their comparison persons in wages. However, workers who had the best mobility chances *within* the company chose fewer *presently* dissonant comparisons than workers who had the best mobility chances *outside* the company. Since those with good mobility chances within the company were virtually assured of rapid advancement in rank and wages, Patchen believed that the difference between the two groups depended largely upon whether advancement had to be fought for or was largely assured. If it was assured, as typified by the high within-company mobility group, presently dissonant comparisons need not have been chosen as justification for advancement or as a protest against one's present status. These reasons, however, become highly salient when advancement must be earned the hard way.

Further effects of within and outside company wage comparisons are found in Andrews and Henry's (1963) study of 228 managers in five companies. They found that, at a given level of management, overall satisfaction with pay was more highly related to the similarity between the pay of managers in one company and the average pay of managers in the other four companies than to the similarity between their pay and the average pay of other managers in their own company. Together, these two studies suggest that both mobility aspirations and wage comparisons, particularly comparisons outside of one's own company, are important determinants of wage satisfaction. Further studies along these lines should increase our meager knowledge concerning the factors influencing wage comparisons.

The most rigorous and best researched theory of equity is that of Adams (1963a, 1965). His theory is derived mostly from the postulates of Festinger's cognitive dissonance theory (1957) but was influenced also by Stouffer et al.'s (1949) earlier work on relative deprivation and by Homans' (1961) research on distributive justice. Adams' most recent definition of inequity stated that

> inequity exists for Person[8] whenever he perceives that the ratio of his outcomes to inputs and the ratio of Other's outcomes to Other's inputs are unequal, either (a) when he and Other are in a direct exchange or (b) when both are in an exchange relationship with a third party and Person compares himself to Other [1965, p. 22].

This implies, as do all the above-mentioned theories, that an inequitable relation occurs not only when the exchange is not in Person's favor, but when it is to his advantage as well. Adams, like Homans, hypothesized that the thresholds for underreward and overreward differ. Thus, a certain amount of overreward may be written off as "good luck," whereas similar deviations in the direction of underreward will not be so easily tolerated.

Inputs mentioned in the definition are anything a worker perceives as

[8] Person is anyone for whom equity or inequity exists. Other is any individual or group used by Person as a referent in social comparisons of what he contributes to and what he receives from an exchange.

constituting his contribution to the job—age, skill, education, experience, and amount of effort expended on the job. Outcomes, or rewards from the job, are also dependent upon the worker's perception and would normally include pay, status symbols, intrinsic job satisfaction, and fringe benefits, to mention a few examples.

The existence of equity or inequity is not an all-or-none phenomenon. Many degrees of inequity can be distinguished, and the magnitude of the inequity is assumed to be some increasing monotonic function of the size of the difference between the ratios of outcomes to inputs. Thus, it is not the absolute magnitudes of perceived inputs and outcomes that are important, but rather the discrepancy between the two ratios. Inequity may exist for both Person and Other, so long as each perceives discrepant ratios. The greatest inequity exists when both inputs and outcomes are discrepant.

The presence of inequity creates tension within a person in an amount proportional to the magnitude of the inequity. This tension creates a drive to reduce the inequity feelings, the strength of the drive being proportional to the tension created. Adams (1963a, 1965) suggested several possible avenues of achieving an equitable state. A person may increase or decrease his inputs (e.g., by increasing or decreasing either the quality or quantity of his work); he may increase or decrease his outcomes (by asking for a raise, or by giving part of his pay to charity, for example); he may change his comparison group or cognitively alter its inputs or outcomes, or force it out of the field; he may leave the field himself (by quitting, transferring, or being absent); or he may cognitively distort his own inputs and outcomes. It is not yet clear what principles govern the choice of method for inequity reduction, although Lawler and O'Gara (in press) have recently obtained evidence that the choice is related to such personality "traits" as self-esteem and responsibility.

A series of experiments to test this theory have been undertaken (Adams 1963a, 1963b, 1965; Adams & Jacobsen 1964; Adams & Rosenbaum 1962; Arrowood 1961). These studies have all been directed toward the effects of overcompensation on behavior. In the first of these (Adams & Rosenbaum 1962), the hypothesis that workers who felt they were overpaid would reduce their feelings of inequity by increasing the amount of work performed was tested. Twenty-two college students were hired to conduct interviews at $3.50 per hour; half of them were made to feel qualified and equitably paid, and the other half were made to feel unqualified and thus overpaid. As predicted, the overpaid group conducted significantly more interviews within the allotted time than did the control group.

It could reasonably be hypothesized that the group made to feel overpaid for the job worked harder because they felt insecure and were afraid of being fired. Another experiment was performed by Arrowood (1961, reported in Adams 1963a, 1965) with the same design—but with the addition of a "private" group that was under the impression that their employer would never see their work. Within this private group, the students who felt overcompensated also conducted significantly more interviews than the students who felt equitably compensated, thus showing the predicted effect is still obtained when pains are taken to remove the insecurity motive.

Although it is predicted from the theory that workers overpaid on an hourly basis will increase the quantity of their work, workers overpaid on a piecework basis would actually increase feelings of inequity if they produced more since they would be increasing the amount of their overpayment. Therefore, it was hypothesized that these workers would reduce inequity by reducing the quantity of their output—a procedure which increases inputs and decreases outcomes. Adams and Jacobsen (1964) tested this hypothesis on students hired for a proofreading task. Persons in the overpaid, experimental group were told they were not qualified but would be paid the usual rate of 30 cents per page anyway. Persons in one equitably paid control group were made to feel qualified and were also paid 30 cents per page. Persons in a second equitably paid control group were made to feel unqualified but were paid the more equitable rate of only 20 cents per page. Adams also sought to assess any possible effects due to differing feelings of job security by manipulating the perceived possibility of future employment. This was done because it was reasoned that subjects made to feel overpaid and unqualified might perceive an implication that their tenure was in jeopardy unless they showed they were good workers. Thus, for half the subjects in each group, Adams created a condition in which they perceived that there was something to lose (i.e., insecurity) and for the other half a condition in which they perceived that there was nothing to lose (i.e., relative security). Adams reasoned that if job security were important, the overpaid secure subjects would work fast but carelessly whereas the overpaid insecure subjects ought to work with much greater care.

The index of quantity was the number of pages proofread, and the index of quality was the number of implanted errors detected (each page, averaging 450 words, had an average of 12 errors implanted in the text, such as misspellings or grammatical, punctuational, and typographical errors).

At first glance, the results substantiate the hypothesis. They show that the overpaid, experimental group proofed significantly fewer pages and detected significantly more implanted errors per page than the two equitably paid groups. The job security manipulation had no significant effect, which was in keeping with the hypothesis that quality and productivity should vary with feelings of equity and not as a function of perceived job security.

It should be noted, however, that quality was not entirely adequately measured in the experiment. Detecting implanted errors is only one possible evidence of quality in proofreading. Another aspect of quality not included in Adams' quality score is the number of words detected as errors, but which were actually correctly spelled or punctuated. If a proofreader detected all of the real errors in a text, but also claimed several words or punctuation marks to be in error when they actually were correct, his stay on the job probably would be short-lived. Yet, in the experiment just described, he would get a perfect quality score because the specification of detecting nonerrors as errors was ignored. Significantly more of these nonerrors were falsely called errors by the overpaid group. If these "errors" had been taken into account, their quality scores would have been considerably lower. It can be argued, of course, that such nonerror detection simply illustrates the increased effort and conscientiousness that these subjects were devoting to the task, and this would then be further evidence in favor of the theory and of the effectiveness of the experimental manipulation. Even so, the net effect of "correcting" nonerrors is to reduce the job effectiveness of a proofreader; and it is not entirely clear whether this aspect of ineffectiveness was due to the equity manipulation, the different emphasis on detecting errors in two sets of directions,[9] or some interaction of the two.

Recent research (e.g., Freedman 1963; Leventhal 1964; Weick & Penner 1965—all mentioned in Weick 1965; Linder 1965) indicates that predictions derived from equity theory in cases of underreward may require modifica-

---

[9] The two sets of instructions used in the experiment are as follows: First, the overpaid group and the "reduced rate" equitable group were told about their qualifications in the following manner:

> Well, you don't have nearly enough experience of the type we're looking for. We were hoping to find someone who had previously had actual job experience correcting publishers' proofs of a manuscript. It's really important that this be done by someone who is experienced in this sort of work. It takes special training to have the skill necessary to catch all the sorts of errors that can creep into the proofs. They will have to be returned to the publishers soon, and we can't afford to have any mistakes slip by. (Pause) Your score on this proofreading test isn't really satisfactory either. Would you wait here just a moment? (Brief exit).

After a brief exit by the experimenter, the persons in the overpaid group were told they would be paid the usual rate anyway, whereas the persons in the "reduced rate" equitable group were informed that they would be paid at a lower, more equitable, rate. The other group, the qualified equitable group, was instructed as follows:

> This is fine; you're just what we were looking for. You meet all the qualifications that were required, and your score on this proofreaders' test looks very good. So far as pay is concerned, you probably are aware that we pay 30 cents per page. This rate is standard for work of this kind done by qualified people. [Adams & Jacobsen 1964, p. 21].

The different emphases on quality in the two sets of instructions are obvious; thus, it appears that the first two groups were given very different sets concerning the expectations of the employer about the quality demands of the work to be done. It can still be argued, of course, that the reduced-rate group should then have shown an increase in quality of about the same magnitude as that shown by the overpaid group. We do not believe this would necessarily obtain. It is likely, for example, that the pay reduction would be sufficient to suggest to an "unqualified" subject that his expected poor performance was already being taken into account, and he might then work in accordance with his employer's implied expectation. The confounding of the differing emphases on quality with the equity manipulation in this study seems to us to confuse seriously the interpretation of the results obtained by Adams and Jacobsen.

tion. All of the above studies showed that underpaid persons work harder, and also like the task more than persons who are overpaid or equitably paid.

Weick (1965) hypothesized that high effort for insufficient pay represents an attempt to raise outcomes, and suggested that proponents of equity theory give greater consideration to the proposition that persons may control their outcomes to reduce inequity. Thus, in the above-mentioned studies, increased satisfaction gained from performing the task may heighten outcomes and bring them more in line with the person's inputs. So far, with the exception of the recent paper by Lawler and O'Gara (in press), research directed toward testing equity theory has dealt only with overpayment, but the effects of insufficient reward are equally important in industry. We hope that more attention is devoted to this area in future research on equity theory.

Several additions to the theory may help to increase its efficiency of prediction. First and most important, there is need for specifying the conditions governing the choice of one mode of resolution over another. The theory itself does not specify any priority of different methods, and, since there are so many potential methods of reducing inequity, the mere prediction that some one of them will occur is not a very useful or meaningful one. Several propositions about the choice of a method have been advanced tentatively by Adams (1965). These include the following hypotheses:

1. Person will maximize positively valent outcomes and the valence of outcomes.
2. He will minimize increasing inputs that are effortful and costly to change.
3. He will resist real and cognitive changes in inputs that are central to his self-concept and to his self-esteem.
4. He will be more resistant to changing cognitions about his own outcomes and inputs than to changing his cognitions about Other's outcomes and inputs.
5. Leaving the field will be resorted to only when the magnitude of inequity is high and other means of reducing it are unavailable [p. 46].

However, the above hypotheses have not yet been tightly incorporated into equity theory. Since so many modes for resolving inequity are possible, the difficulty of specifying exactly when any specific mode may or may not be used renders the theory more "hazy" and less directly testable than we would like to see it. For example, if an overcompensated group failed to show increased input (in the form of higher quantity or quality), might this be regarded as disconfirmation of the theory or merely an instance of the subjects' choosing another mode (e.g., altering their perceptions of their own or others' inputs or of the nature of the job being performed) for reducing feelings of inequity? Because the principles specifying the choice of mode have not yet been specified, tightly reasoned deduction cannot yet be derived from the theory.

As implied above, it is quite likely that people differ substantially from one another in the mode they might choose for resolving feelings of inequity; moreover, these differences are undoubtedly a function of individual motive configurations and ability, interest, and personality variables. Lawler and O'Gara (in press) have shown, for example, that persons scoring higher on the Responsibility scale of the California Psychological Inventory (CPI) were less likely to sacrifice quality of work for quantity, when underpaid, than were persons scoring low on the scale. In similar fashion, underpaid persons scoring high on CPI scales of Dominance and Self Assurance were less likely to react with high productivity than those scoring low. Apparently, there are distinct differences in the way different kinds of people respond to feelings of inequity. The incorporation of such variables into the theory may increase its explanatory power. As it stands, the theory ignores individual differences.

Not only may motivational variables determine methods of resolution, but it has been hypothesized that the number and kinds of similarities on which Person compares himself to Other may also affect his choice of how he resolves inequity (Weick 1965). For example, if a person compares himself with someone who is similar only with respect to education, perhaps education inputs will be the only salient means for resolving inequity when it occurs. Similarly, as Weick pointed out, as comparability increases and Person compares himself to Other with respect to many variables, it is plausible to expect that the intensity of discomfort associated with inequity will change. These two hypotheses, unfortunately, have not yet been investigated.

As it stands, the theory fails to specify methods of resolution relating to various kinds of perceptual alteration. Weick (1965) has pointed out that the theory overlooks such possibilities as denial, differentiation, toleration of the discrepancy, alteration of the object of judgment, bolstering, and task enhancement. This last method seems particularly important. If a person had proportionately low outcomes, task enhancement would be a relatively easy way to increase his outcomes without alienating his co-workers in the process.

One of the major problems with which equity theory must cope, therefore, is the obvious fact of the large number of variables, the complexities of their interaction, and the inadequacy of the operational definitions. Vroom (1964) pointed out that, according to the theory, a worker's satisfaction with his pay is a function of:

1. His beliefs concerning the degree to which he possesses various characteristics;
2. His convictions concerning the degree to which these characteristics should result in the attainment of rewarding outcomes from his job, i.e., their value as inputs;
3. His beliefs concerning the degree to which he receives these rewarding outcomes from his job;
4. His beliefs concerning the degree to which others possess these characteristics;

5. His beliefs concerning the degree to which others receive rewarding outcomes from their jobs; and

6. The extent to which he compares himself with these others. [p. 171].

We agree with Vroom's conclusion that the complexity of equity theory makes conclusive tests difficult, and that "a great deal of theoretical and methodological refinement remains to be carried out before this approach can be properly evaluated [1964, p. 172]."

Nonetheless, Adams is to be commended for beginning the difficult task of trying to work through some of the complexities related to an understanding of how pay and employees' perceptions of pay affect the way they work on the job. These early studies on equity, though subject to some criticism, certainly bear the stamp of careful thought and careful experimentation, and we hope that Adams and others will continue in their efforts to explicate more fully some of the questions which have been raised here.

Future Research

Although it is generally agreed that money is the major mechanism for rewarding and modifying behavior in industry, we have seen that very little is known about how it works. Haire remarked at a recent symposium on managerial compensation that, in spite of the tremendous amount of money spent and the obvious relevance of behavioral theory for compensation practices, there is less research and theory in this area than in almost any other field related to management (Haire 1965). Similarly, Dunnette and Bass (1963), in a critique of current personnel management practices, pointed out that personnel men have relied on faddish and assumptive practices in administering pay which lack empirical support. One reason for this is the dearth of sound research upon which to base practices. The following are some suggested directions for research which may help to remedy these current deficiencies.

The principal research problem is to discover in what way money motivates employees and how this, in turn, affects their behavior. For this, we must know more about the motives of employees—which motives are dominant, and how employees differ from one another in the configuration of their motives. We must also determine which of these motives can be linked to money as an incentive. Can money be linked with insatiable needs so goal attainment does not cause cessation of behavior? Can money act as an incentive for the "higher order" needs? The two main hypotheses here— that money can serve only "lower order" needs, and that it can serve essentially all needs—have very different implications for compensation practices. Investigation of this question requires not only the discovery of the motives for which money has instrumental value but also the extent to which money can serve to fulfill or satisfy these needs. Quite obviously, money serves to satisfy needs for food, clothing, and shelter, but it is much less obvious how money may be related to such other areas as need Achievement or need Power. It seems obvious that money serves these needs too, but solid evidence of a relationship is lacking. To what extent may money be a primary way of dispensing feelings of achievement, competence, power, and the like? In other words, what needs are currently served by money, and what needs, not now perceived as associated with money, may it be called upon to serve? Moreover, we believe that future studies of the effects of money on behavior will prove more fruitful if they are conducted in laboratory or in tightly controlled field settings rather than continuing to depend on survey and self-report instruments as is characteristic of so much of the research now available.

As this review shows, very little is known about the behavioral laws regulating the effectiveness of incentives. We continue to dole out large sums of money under the guise of "incentive pay" without really knowing much about its incentive character. We do not know, for instance, the nature of the effect of a pay raise or the length of time before that effect occurs; or, for that matter, how long the raise may be effective. Nor do we know the optimal reinforcement schedule to be used in giving salary increases for obtaining desired changes in job behavior. A simple monitoring of work outputs on jobs where amount of production is under the direct control of the employee and where it is easily assessed, may provide valuable information here. Such knowledge would have important implications for how often and in what amounts incentive raises should be built into the compensation package.

We also need to investigate the relation between amount of money and the amount of behavior money motivates. Is there some point beyond which increases in compensation are no longer related to increases in relevant behavior? That is, do humans show the same negatively accelerated relation between amount of reward and number of responses that lower organisms display? Or do increases in money "whet the appetite" and lead to behavior that follows some exponential or positively accelerated function?

If we are to effectively manipulate incentives, more information is needed about how they function. Money's incentive character, to be fully understood, must also take account of the perceptions of money by the recipient. Recent evidence (Haire 1965) shows that not only the amount of money but also how a person perceives his work role are vital factors. Presidents apparently need a larger percentage increase than vice-presidents before they see it as constituting an incentive raise. Is this difference a function of the work role alone? Or do anticipations of future earnings, differences in abilities and dominant motives, and past earning history account for a good share of the variance? So far, these research questions are virtually untapped.

We have seen from Wyatt (1934) that money can be cheapened or lowered in value by the behavior demanded to attain it. To understand more about this relationship, it would be helpful to scale money values against behaviors demanded for money's attainment. This could best be done in a laboratory setting and by using actual workers. Such controlled laboratory experiments have been utilized *almost not at all* with actual employees as subjects. So far, we have depended heavily on rats and psychology sophomores to build a psychology of motivation. We sorely need studies in which real workers are brought into the laboratory and the effects of incentives under different conditions studied.

A very important variable influencing money's effectiveness is the schedule by which it is administered. Of the simple reinforcement schedules, the fixed interval—reinforcement following a fixed period of time after the last reinforced response—leads to notoriously poor performance in lower organisms (Ferster & Skinner 1957). Yet this is the present pay schedule of most industrial employees. Lower organisms on this schedule tend not to respond very rapidly until just before their "payday." The notable exception to this type of pay schedule in industry occurs for commission salesmen (e.g., life insurance selling) and for entrepreneurs. It is probably worth noting that these two groups contain "workers" who must certainly be viewed as being among the most highly motivated persons in our industrial society.

Although more is known about the simple schedules of reinforcement, the complex schedules—composed of both interval and ratio elements—may be applicable in an industrial setting. In particular, the effects of alternative, conjunctive, and interlocking schedules are worth investigating. With these schedules, it would be possible to follow the suggestion of Haire, Ghiselli, and Porter (1963); that is, divide the paycheck into several parts: so much for tenure, so much for minimum services rendered, so much for excellent performance, etc. For example, about 70% of the total available might be given on a fixed interval for minimum services. The rest of the potential pay could be divided and incorporated into different variable ratio schedules, made contingent on outstanding performance.

Finally, evidence seems to indicate that, at various times, employees seek to maximize the amount of their reward, the fairness of their reward, and their acceptance by the group in which they work. The research question is: in which situations, and in what ways is behavior directed toward maximizing one or more of these goals? Which goals are maximized at the expense of others? What are the relative saliencies of each goal in differing situations? What are the functional relationships between goals? Which goals account for most of the variance in productivity, and under what conditions? These are vital questions that must be answered before we can effectively utilize incentives.

As research on the role of financial compensation in industrial motivation becomes more and more prevalent, answers to many of the questions posed above should be forthcoming. Increased knowledge should be accompanied by more effective use of money in industry. It is hoped that the firm of the future will be able to establish compensation policies and practices based on empirical evidence about the behavioral effects of money as an incentive rather than on the nontested assumptions, hunches, and time worn "rules-of-thumb" so common in industry today.

References

Adams, J. S. Toward an understanding of inequity. *Journal of Abnormal and Social Psychology,* 1963, 67, 422–36. (a)

Adams, J. S. Wage inequities, productivity, and work quality. *Industrial Relations,* 1963, 3, 9–16. (b)

Adams, J. S. Injustice in social change. In L. Berkowitz (Ed.), *Advances in experimental social psychology.* Vol. 2. New York: Academic Press, 1965. Pp. 267–99.

Adams, J. S., & Jacobsen, P. Effects of wage inequities on work quality. *Journal of Abnormal and Social Psychology,* 1964, 69, 19–25.

Adams, J. S., & Rosenbaum, W. B. The relationship of worker productivity to cognitive dissonance about wage inequities. *Journal of Applied Psychology,* 1962, 46, 161–64.

Andrews, I. R., & Henry, M. M. Management attitudes toward pay. *Industrial Relations,* 1963, 3, 29–39.

Arrowood, A. J. Some effects of productivity of justified and unjustified levels of reward under public and private conditions. Unpublished doctoral dissertation, University of Minnesota, 1961.

Atkinson, J. W. (Ed.) *Motives in fantasy, action, and society.* Princeton: Van Nostrand, 1958.

Atkinson, J. W., & Reitman, W. R. Performance as a function of motive strength and expectancy of goal attainment. *Journal of Abnormal and Social Psychology,* 1956, 53, 361–66.

Babchuk, N., & Goode, W. J. Work incentives in a self-determined group. *American Social Review,* 1951, 16, 679–87.

Barnett, G. J., Handelsman, I., Stewart, L. H., & Super, D. E. The Occupational Level scale as a measure of drive. *Psychological Monographs,* 1952, 66(10, Whole No. 342).

Bendig, A. W., & Stillman, E. L. Dimensions of job incentives among college students. *Journal of Applied Psychology,* 1958, 42, 367–71.

Brown, J. S. Problems presented by the concept of acquired drives. In, *Current theory and research in motivation: A symposium.* Lincoln: University of Nebraska Press, 1953. Pp. 1–21.

Brown, J. S. *The motivation of behavior.* New York: McGraw-Hill, 1961.

Burnett, F. *An experimental investigation into repetitive work.* (Industrial Fatigue Research Board Report No. 30) London: His Majesty's Stationery Office, 1925.

Cain, P. A. Individual differences in susceptibility to monotony. Unpublished doctoral dissertation, Cornell University, 1942.

Campbell, H. Group incentive payment schemes: The effects of lack of understanding and group size. *Occupational Psychology,* 1952, 26, 15–21.

Centers, R., & Cantril, H. Income satisfaction and income aspiration. *Journal of Abnormal and Social Psychology,* 1946, 41, 64–69.

Cowles, J. T. Food-tokens as incentives for learning by chimpanzees. *Comparative Psychology Monographs,* 1937, 14, 1–96.

Dale, J. Increase productivity 50% in one year with sound wage incentives. *Management Methods,* 1959, 16, 38–42.

Dalton, M. The industrial "rate-buster": A characterization. *Applied Anthropology,* 1948, 7, 5–18.

Dalton, M., Collins, O., & Roy, D. Restriction of output and social cleavage in industry. *Applied Anthropology,* 1946, 5(3), 1–14.

Davis, N. M. Attitudes to work among building operatives. *Occupational Psychology,* 1948, 22, 56–62.

Dollard, J., & Miller, N. E. *Personality and psychotherapy.* New York: McGraw-Hill, 1950.

Dunnette, M. D., & Bass, B. M. Behavioral scientists and personnel management. *Industrial Relations,* 1963, 2, 115–30.

Dyson, B. H. Whether direct individual incentive systems based on time-study, however accurately computed, tend over a period to limitation of output. Paper read at Spring Conference, British Institute of Management, London, 1956.

English, H. B., & English, C. A. *A comprehensive dictionary of psychological and psychoanalytical terms.* New York: McKay, 1958.

Ferster, C. B., & DeMyer, M. K. A method for the experimental analysis of the behavior of autistic children. *American Journal of Orthopsychiatry,* 1962, 32, 89–98.

Ferster, C. B., & Skinner, B. F. *Schedules of reinforcement.* New York: Appleton-Century-Crofts, 1957.

Festinger, L. *A theory of cognitive dissonance.* Evanston, Ill.: Row, Peterson, 1957.

Festinger, L. How attitudes toward compensation change with promotion. In R. Andrews (Ed.), *Managerial compensation.* Ann Arbor: Foundation for Research on Human Behavior, 1965. Pp. 19–20.

Fleishman, E. A. A relationship between incentive motivation and ability level in psychomotor performance. *Journal of Experimental Psychology,* 1958, 56, 78–81.

Freedman, J. L. Attitudinal effects of inadequate justification. *Journal of Personality,* 1963, 31, 371–85.

Ganuli, H. C. An inquiry into incentives for workers in an engineering factory. *Indian Journal of Social Work,* 1954, 15, 30–40.

Gellerman, S. W. *Motivation and productivity.* New York: American Management Association, 1963.

Georgopoulos, B. S., Mahoney, G. M., & Jones, N. W. A path-goal approach to productivity. *Journal of Applied Psychology,* 1957, 41, 345–53.

Ghiselli, E. E. The effects on career pay of policies with respect to increases in pay. In R. Andrews (Ed.), *Managerial compensation.* Ann Arbor: Foundation for Research on Human Behavior, 1965. Pp. 21–34.

Graham, D., & Sluckin, W. Different kinds of reward as industrial incentives. *Research Review, Durham,* 1954, 5, 54–56.

Grice, G. R., & Davis, J. D. Effect of irrelevant thirst motivation on a response learned with food reward. *Journal of Experimental Psychology,* 1957, 53, 347–52.

Haire, M. The incentive character of pay. In R. Andrews, (Ed.), *Managerial compensation.* Ann Arbor: Foundation for Research on Human Behavior, 1965. Pp. 13–17.

Haire, M., Ghiselli, E. E., & Porter, L. W. Psychological research on pay: An overview. *Industrial Relations,* 1963, 3, 3–8.

Harlow, H. F. Comments on Professor Brown's paper. In, *Current theory and research in motivation.* Lincoln: University of Nebraska Press, 1953. Pp. 22–23.

Herzburg, F., Mausner, B., & Snyderman, B. *The motivation to work.* (2nd ed.) New York: Wiley, 1959.

Hickson, D. J. Motives of work people who restrict their output. *Occupational Psychology,* 1961, 35, 110–21.

Holland, J. G., & Skinner, B. F. *The analysis of behavior.* New York: McGraw-Hill, 1961.

Homans, G. C. *Social behavior: Its elementary forms.* New York: Harcourt, Brace & World, 1961.

Jaques, E. *Equitable payment.* New York: Wiley, 1961.

Jaques, E., Rice, A. K., & Hill, J. M. The social and psychological impact of a change in method of wage payment. *Human Relations,* 1951, 4, 315–40.

Jones, L. V., & Jeffrey, T. E. A quantitative analysis of expressed preferences for compensation plans. *Journal of Applied Psychology,* 1964, 49, 201–10.

Kaufman, H. Task performance, expected performance, and responses to failure as functions of imbalance in the self-concept. Unpublished doctoral dissertation, University of Pennsylvania, 1962.

Kelleher, R. T., & Gollub, L. R. A review of positive conditioned reinforcement. *Journal of the Experimental Analysis of Behavior,* 1962, 5, 543–97.

Larke, A. G. Workers' attitudes on incentives. *Dun's Review and Modern Industry,* Dec. 1953, 61–63.

Lawler, E. E., III. Managers' job performance and their attitudes toward their pay. Unpublished doctoral dissertation, University of California, Berkeley, 1964.

Lawler, E. E., III. Managerial perceptions of compensation. Paper read at

Midwestern Psychological Association convention, Chicago, April 1965.

Lawler, E. E., III, & O'Gara, P. W. The effects of inequity produced by underpayment on work output, work quality, and attitudes toward the work. *Journal of Personality and Social Psychology,* in press.

Lawler, E. E., III, & Porter, L. W. Perceptions regarding management compensation. *Industrial Relations,* 1963, 3, 41–49.

Leventhal, G. S. Reward magnitude and liking for instrumental activity: Further test of a two-process model. Unpublished manuscript, Yale University, 1964.

Linder, D. F. Some psychological processes which mediate task liking Unpublished doctoral dissertation, University of Minnesota, 1965.

Mahoney, T. Compensation preferences of managers. *Industrial Relations,* 1964, 3, 135–44.

March, J. G., & Simon, H. A. *Organizations.* New York: Wiley, 1958.

Marriott, R. Size of working group and output. *Occupational Psychology,* 1949, 23, 47–57.

Marriott, R. Socio-psychological factors in productivity. *Occupational Psychology,* 1951, 25, 15–24.

Marriott, R. *Incentive payment systems: A review of research and opinion.* London: Staples Press, 1957.

Marriott, R., & Denerley, R. A. A method of interviewing used in studies of workers' attitudes: II. Validity of the method and discussion of the results. *Occupational Psychology,* 1955, 29, 69–81.

Mathewson, S. B. *Restriction of output among unorganized workers.* New York: Viking Press, 1951.

Miller, D. C., & Form, W. H. *Industrial sociology.* New York: Harper, 1951.

Myers, C. S. *Mind and work.* London: University of London Press, 1920.

National Industrial Conference Board. Factors affecting employee morale. (Studies in Personnel Policy No. 85) New York: Author, 1947.

Nealey, S. Pay and benefit preferences. *Industrial Relations,* 1963, 1, 17–28.

Opinion Research Corporation. *Productivity from the worker's standpoint.* Princeton: Author, 1949.

Patchen, M. *The choice of wage comparisons.* Englewood Cliffs, N. J.: Prentice-Hall, 1961.

Porter, L. W. Job attitudes in management: I. Perceived deficiencies in need fulfillment as a function of job level. *Journal of Applied Psychology,* 1962, 46, 375–84.

Rath, A. A. The case for individual incentives. *Personnel Journal,* 1960, 39, 172–75.

Roethlisberger, F. J., & Dickson, W. J. *Management and the worker.* Cambridge: Harvard University Press, 1939.

Roy, D. Quota restriction and gold bricking in a machine shop. *American Journal of Sociology,* 1952, 57, 427–42.

Ryan, R. A., & Smith, P. C. *Principles of industrial psychology.* New York: Ronald Press, 1954.

Sayles, L. R. *Behavior of industrial work groups: Prediction and control.* New York: Wiley, 1958.

Schleh, E. C. *Management by results: The dynamics of profitable management.* New York: McGraw-Hill, 1961.

Selekman, B. M. Living with collective bargaining. *Harvard Business Review,* 1941, 22, 21–23.

Shimmin, S., Williams, J., & Buck, L. Studies of some factors in incentive payment systems. Report to the Medical Research Council. London: Industrial Psychology Research Group, 1956. (Mimeo)

Skinner, B. F. *Science and human behavior.* New York: Macmillan, 1953.

Smith, P. C. The curve of output as a criterion of boredom. *Journal of Applied Psychology,* 1953, 37, 69–74.

Smith, P. C. The prediction of individual differences in susceptibility to industrial monotony. *Journal of Applied Psychology,* 1955, 39, 322–29.

Smith, P. C., & Kendall, L. M. Cornell Studies of job satisfaction: VI: Implications for the future. Unpublished manuscript, Cornell University, 1963.

Spriegel, W. R., & Dale, A. G. Trends in personnel selection and induction. *Personnel,* 1953, 30, 169–75.

Stouffer, S. A., Suchman, E. A., DeVinney, L. C., Star, S. A., & Williams, R. M. *The American Soldier: Adjustment during army life.* Vol. 1. Princeton, N. J.: Princeton University Press, 1949.

Thompson, W. A. Eleven years after graduation. *Occupations,* 1939, 17, 709–14.

Verplanck, W. S., & Hayes, J. R. Eating and drinking as a function of maintenance schedule. *Journal of Comparative and Physiological Psychology,* 1953, 46, 327–33.

Viteles, M. S. *Motivation and morale in industry.* New York: Norton, 1953.

Vroom, V. H. *Work and motivation.* New York: Wiley, 1964.

Watson, G. Work satisfaction. In G. W. Hartmann & T. Newcomb (Eds.), *Industrial conflict.* New York: The Cordon Co., 1939. Pp. 114–24.

Weick, K. E. The concept of equity in the perception of pay. Paper read at Midwestern Psychological Association, April 1965.

Weick, K. E., & Penner, D. D. Comparison of two sources of inadequate and excessive justification. Unpublished manuscript, Purdue University, 1965.

Whyte, W. F. Economic incentives and human relations. *Harvard Business Review,* 1952, 30, 73–80.

Whyte, W. F. *Money and motivation: An analysis of incentives in industry.* New York: Harper, 1955.

Wike, E. L., & Barrientos, G. Secondary reinforcement and multiple drive reduction. *Journal of Comparative and Physiological Psychology,* 1958, 51, 640–43.

Wilkins, L. T. Incentives and the young male worker in England. *International Journal of Opinion and Attitude Research,* 1950, 4, 541–62.

Wilkins, L. T. Incentives and the young worker. *Occupational Psychology,* 1949, 23, 235–47.

Wolfe, J. B. Effectiveness of token-rewards for chimpanzees. *Comparative Psychology Monographs,* 1936, 12, No. 60, 1–72.

Worthy, J. C. Factors influencing employee morale. *Harvard Business Review,* 1950, 28, 61–73.

Wyatt, S. *Incentives in repetitive work: A practical experiment in a factory.* (Industrial Health Research Board Report No. 69) London: His Majesty's Stationery Office, 1934.

Wyatt, S. & Fraser, J. S. *The comparative effects of variety and uniformity in work.* (Industrial Fatigue Research Board Report No. 52) London: His Majesty's Stationery Office, 1929.

Wyatt, S., Fraser, J. A. & Stock, F. G. L. *The effects of monotony in work.* (Industrial Fatigue Research Board Report No. 56) London: His Majesty's Stationery Office, 1929.

Wyatt, S., & Langdon, J. N. *Fatigue and boredom in repetitive work.* (Industrial Health Research Board Report No. 77) London: His Majesty's Stationery Office, 1937.

Wyatt, S., & Marriott, R. *A study of attitudes to factory work.* London: Her Majesty's Stationery Office, 1956.

Zaleznik, A., Christenson, C. R. & Roethlisberger, F. J. *The motivation, productivity, and satisfaction of workers: A prediction study.* Boston: Harvard University, Graduate School of Business Administration, 1958.

8 / Job Enlargement: Do Workers Really Want Larger Jobs?

Functional specialization, the subdivision of tasks to render each worker responsible for one or a few minute operations of the total production process, was adopted very early in the Industrial Revolution as a cardinal principle of work arrangement. This philosophy of job design was advocated for its contribution to efficiency and economy. Since its inception and application, social critics have attacked extreme job specialization on the grounds that engagement in such specialized work engenders undesirable social and psychological effects in workers. Management and some social scientists have countered with the "individual differences" argument, which says that some workers performing minutely subdivided jobs do so by choice. In their view, simplified work is sometimes sought by people who have no desire for responsibility and autonomy on the job. An important implication of the individual differences position is the necessity to determine empirically those characteristics that differentiate workers who will respond to job enlargement from those who prefer more simplified tasks. The second and third selections in this chapter explore this line of reasoning. First, however, is presented the individual differences position.

From their review of the literature on the subject, MacKinney, Wernimont, and Galitz ("Has Specialization Reduced Job Satisfaction?") conclude that job dissatisfaction in industry is not attributable to job specialization. Studies indicating detrimental effects of specialization, they argue, are methodologically weaker than research showing contrary results. Moreover, researchers positing specialization as a major cause of job dissatisfaction have failed to recognize individual differences: jobs thought unsatisfying by researchers may not be so to industrial workers.

In "Job Enlargement, Individual Differences, and Worker Responses," an article not included in this volume, Charles Hulin and Milton Blood also challenge the thesis that functionally specialized jobs induce monotony, boredom, job dissatisfaction, and such negative behavior as absenteeism, turnover, and production restriction. Studies supporting the job enlargement thesis, they judge, suffer from such methodological defects that their validity should be seriously questioned. On the other hand, they conclude, more rigorously conducted research has tended to yield evidence contrary to the job enlargement thesis. Finally, Hulin and Blood advance a model that attempts to explain the divergent findings. According to their model, the thesis that job enlargement promotes positive psychological and behavioral consequences applies only to certain kinds of workers—namely, to those who subscribe to middle-class work values. Under the assumption that workers in urban plants are alienated from middle-class work values, they conclude that the alleged positive benefits of job enlargement will appear only among production workers in rural plants and among white-collar and supervisory employees in either rural or urban locales.

I wrote "Functional Specialization, Alienation, and Job Satisfaction," in response to the interesting ideas of Hulin and Blood. I present evidence from a study of factory workers that the degree of functional specialization is inversely related to job satisfaction, a finding consistent with the job enlargement thesis. To further test the hypothesis that "larger" jobs are associated with greater job satisfaction, I introduced community of socialization and three measures of alienation from work as intervening variables. None of these variables altered the original relationship, which led me to two conclusions: (1) whether workers are socialized in rural areas, where they presumably would internalize middle-class work values, or reared in urban areas, where they would not, workers respond attitudinally in a negative way to specialized tasks and in a positive way to larger jobs; and (2) alienated from work or not, the degree of job dissatisfaction increases among workers as job size decreases. The weight of this evidence is that job specialization seems to elicit a negative reaction not just among certain segments of the labor force, but among workers in general. At the very least, the alienation-from-work variable suggested by Hulin and Blood does not appear valid for use in the "individual differences" argument.

In the reading, "Individual Differences and Job Enrichment," Hulin presents his latest thinking on the subject. His position as presented in this latest piece is quite consistent with the Hulin and Blood model described above. However, Hulin now believes that an approach more direct than using demographic variables is the most promising path to follow in the future.

In "Job Enrichment Pays Off," William Paul, Keith Robertson, and Frederick Herzberg present results from five experimental studies, each of which supports Herzberg's job enrichment concept. According to Herzberg, the individual and the organization prosper when jobs are designed to promote "greater scope for personal achievement and its recognition, more challenging and responsible work, and more opportunity for individual advancement and growth." "Hygiene" factors such as pay, working conditions, and training are important, but subordinate, in motivating employees. In addition to reporting their findings, the authors address themselves to questions related to the generality of their results, common objections regarding the feasibility of introducing job enrichment, and the consequences of such job design alterations.

30 / Has Specialization Reduced Job Satisfaction?

A. C. MacKinney, P. F. Wernimont, W. O. Galitz

THE QUESTION WHETHER the increasing specialization of work has reduced job satisfaction has been extensively debated in both the management literature and the popular press. Typical, perhaps, of popular thinking on this subject is an article that appeared in *Time* some years back.[1] Pointing out that it has long been an axiom of U.S. industry that productivity is increased by restricting a job to as few different elements or operations as possible, the article went on to present some facts that seemed to contradict this whole idea. Far from increasing efficiency, it asserted, specialization leads to boredom—and bored workers are poor workers.

Among the cases cited by *Time* in support of this contention were a job-enlargement and job-rotation program at IBM, as a result of which workers were said to find their jobs less monotonous and less fatiguing and to be absent less often, do less complaining, and make fewer mistakes; and a Detroit Edison study of billing practices in 122 electric utilities, which was said to have found that, on the average, billing costs per customer were highest in the billing departments with the most specialization. On the basis of this evidence, the article concluded: "...U.S. business might gain a lot by reconsidering the urge for specialization."

Since *Time* is not a scientific journal, it would hardly be appropriate to subject such facts to critical scrutiny. Actually, though, even if we accept them at their face value, we are still left with some other troublesome considerations to take into account.

In the first place, the contention that specialization is undesirable would, if followed through to its logical conclusion, be a *reductio ad absurdum.* Obviously, were industry to continuously reduce specialization, it would end by finding itself back where the Industrial Revolution began. All automobiles would be individually handcrafted by highly skilled artisans. Mass production would have ceased to exist. Needless to say, no one—not even the most avid proponent of job enlargement—seriously advocates this course.

Second and more important is the well-substantiated fact that not all workers, even in the most routine jobs, are dissatisfied. It is nearly 50 years since Munsterberg pointed out that there is always someone who is chal-

---

1 "Broadening The *Job*," *Time*, April 12, 1954. p. 100.

Reprinted by permission of the publisher from "Has Specialization Reduced Job Satisfaction?" *Personnel*, Vol. 39, No. 1 (January–February 1962), pp. 8–17.

lenged by, and perfectly happy doing, those exceedingly routine jobs that American industry is famous, or infamous, for.[2]

Now this strongly suggests that satisfaction with a job is not merely a function of the job. Rather it is a function of both the man and the job or, as the industrial psychologists prefer to term it, a function of the man-job interaction. On this view, increased specialization does not necessarily make workers unhappy nor will enlarging their jobs necessarily make them happy. Job satisfaction is not so simple a phenomenon as that.

In fact, after a reasonably careful review of the published opinions and evidence on this issue,[3] the authors of this article have come to the conclusion that job specialization is not necessarily the root of the trouble. The question is too important, however, to be thus summarily disposed of. This article will therefore review the most pertinent contributions to the problem with the aim of providing the reader with a rational basis for coming to his own conclusions about it.

The Anti-Specialization School

A number of studies have uncovered evidence of job dissatisfaction among factory workers. Thus, back in 1947, a *Fortune* survey found that many of the workers studied lacked the motivation to work to the limit of their capacity.[4] Many of them were simply resigned to their lack of opportunity, and had no feeling that good work would bring tangible rewards; half of them saw little chance for the exercise of personal initiative in their jobs. This report concluded that while some jobs may be too dull to interest anyone it should be possible to increase the number of workers who feel that they have a chance to make a personal contribution to the organization.

Some years later, Walker and Marriott interviewed 976 men in three factories—two automobile-assembly plants and one metal mill.[5] In the two automobile plants, 35 and 36 per cent of the men respectively complained about the boredom of their work; by contrast, only 8 per cent of the metal workers complained about being bored, apparently because of the small number of repetitive jobs in the plant. In the assembly line plants, feelings ranged from resignation to considerable bitterness. Comparison between mechanized and nonmechanized groups in these plants showed significant differences between them in the extent of their job dissatisfaction, with the

[2] H. Munsterberg, *Psychology and Industrial Efficiency,* Houghton Mifflin Company, Boston, Mass., 1913, pp. 190–205.

[3] While the authors do not claim to have reviewed all the relevant literature on this subject, they believe that their coverage has been fairly extensive, and the summary that follows is merely a selection from the material that has been reviewed. Many articles that seemed only tangentially related to the subject have been excluded.

[4] E. Roper, "The Fortune Survey—The American Factory Worker: What's Good About His Job...What's Bad About It?," *Fortune,* May, 1947, pp. 5–12.

[5] C. R. Walker and R. Marriott, "A Study of Some Attitudes to Factory Work," *Occupational Psychology,* 25 (1951), pp. 181–91.

mechanized workers (i.e., those whose work pace was controlled by the conveyor) being much more dissatisfied.

In their well-known study, *The Man on the Assembly Line*,[6] Walker and Guest found that most of the workers they interviewed regarded the assembly line as an undesirable feature of the job. Most of these men were critical of the repetitive character of their jobs and favored off-the-line jobs over on-the-line jobs because they offered more variety. After correlating the number of operations a man performed (as a rough measure of repetitiveness) with his expressed interest in the job, Walker and Guest concluded that the more variety a job has, the more interesting it is to the worker. They also concluded that the higher morale shown by workers on off-the-line jobs was due to the greater social interaction these jobs afforded.

Among other authorities who are opposed to extreme job specialization we may cite Merton, who expressed the view that mechanization has created an environment of uncertainty, fear, and hostility; and Krech and Crutchfield, who similarly regarded it as a threat to the worker's sense of personal worth and self-esteem.[7] The repetition required by assembly-line production imposes too much discipline on the worker, thus giving rise to tensions, they asserted.

Turner likewise has expressed concern over the impersonality and anonymity of assembly-line jobs, where tasks are performed singly and require little or no social interaction; and Guest believes that the anonymity can be traced to the basic characteristics of the job itself.[8] The production engineer, he says, has factored out all that might be of real personal value to the worker: skill, a sense of achievement, and opportunity for advancement.

Again, Katz has averred that our machine society has narrowed the area within which the individual worker can exercise his judgment and talent.[9] From an objective point of view, he feels, mechanization has undermined job satisfaction because the skill level of jobs has been lowered, variety has been reduced, and the worker has been left with a minimum of decisions to make about the work itself. Human beings at all levels of education, Katz says, are "deprived" in a work situation that diminishes their personal involvement.

The argument that workers can introduce variety into the work situation

[6] C. R. Walker and R. H. Guest, *The Man on the Assembly Line,* Harvard University Press, Cambridge, Mass., 1952, pp. 38–65.

[7] R. K. Merton, "The Machine, The Worker, and The Engineer," *Science,* 105 (1947), pp. 79–84. D. Krech and R. S. Crutchfield, *Theory and Problems of Social Psychology.* McGraw-Hill Book Company, Inc., New York, 1948, pp. 539–40.

[8] A. N. Turner, "Management and the Assembly Line," *Harvard Business Review,* Sept.–Oct., 1955, pp. 40–48. R. H. Guest, "Men and Machines," PERSONNEL, May, 1955, pp. 496–503.

[9] D. Katz, "Satisfactions and Deprivations in Industrial Life," in A. Kornhauser *et al.* (eds.), *Industrial Conflict.* McGraw-Hill Book Company, Inc., New York, 1954, pp. 86–106 (see particularly pp. 90–94).

by looking for minute differences or retreating into fantasy is not valid, Katz claims, for these are nothing but compensatory mechanisms. He admits that there are many people who will avoid responsibility and prefer the simpler of two tasks but maintains that these are the ones whose personality has been "stunted." The old values of craftsmanship, creativity, initiative, and self-determination still exist in the American worker, he believes, and men still prefer jobs that require skill and responsibility.

Still Another Argument

Finally, Ohmann, in his famous and widely circulated "Skyhooks" article,[10] pointed out that though our standard of living is at an all-time peak we are a tense, frustrated, and insecure people, full of hostilities and anxieties. The cause of this discontent, Ohmann believes, is frustration in our search for a work life that has meaning in terms of higher and more enduring spiritual values. Today the worker is only a production number, impersonal, deskilled, and measured in cents-per-hour. While he has improved his standard of living, his dignity and security have suffered, and he has become dependent on larger and larger groups. The result is a loss of individuality.

"How can production be justified," Ohmann asks, "if it destroys personality and human values both in the process of its manufacture and by its end use?" He disagrees also with those who argue that "the job is not the life" and that "minds should be cultivated on their leisure time." "We cannot assume that the end of production justifies the means," he says. "What happens to people in the course of producing may be far more important than the end product."

In the same vein, Anthony has admonished business to remember that profit maximization is not its dominant objective, despite the executives who talk as though it were.[11] A company has obligations to its people and its community as well as to its profit goals.

In line with their views on the adverse effects of job specialization, many of the writers cited above have suggested ways to alleviate the situation. Among the better-known remedies are job rotation, job enlargement, maximizing the opportunities for team relations and social interaction, and participation, i.e., giving individual workers more voice in the decisions affecting their jobs and more freedom to exercise their own judgment in carrying them out.

It will have been noted that all the writers reviewed up to this point have agreed that specialization is the major cause of job dissatisfaction in American industry. One can, however, cite an equally impressive roster of

[10] O. A. Ohmann, "Skyhooks (With Special Implications for Monday Through Friday)," *Harvard Business Review,* May–June, 1955, pp. 33–41.

[11] R. N. Anthony, "The Trouble with Profit Maximization," *Harvard Business Review,* Nov.–Dec., 1960, pp. 126–34.

experts who take the view that specialization per se is not the problem and certainly is not the cause of such dissatisfaction as may exist.

Some Contrary Evidence

In this connection it may be mentioned that in 1958 Robinson reviewed 406 percentage estimates of the extent of worker dissatisfaction in the U.S., Germany, Great Britain, and the Netherlands over the previous 24 years.[12] On the average, he found, only 13 per cent of workers are generally dissatisfied with their jobs. This proportion has remained quite stable during the past few years. It may well be questioned, therefore, whether job dissatisfaction constitutes a problem of such magnitude as the anti-specialization school seems to believe.

In any case, its opponents do not go so far as to assert that all workers are happy. Their point is that specialization is not the cause of dissatisfaction and that we must look elsewhere for an explanation of it.

The pioneer researcher into the problem of job monotony and boredom was Hugo Munsterberg. One of the cases he cited was that of a woman who did nothing but pack electric light bulbs in tissue for 12 years.[13] This woman packed 13,000 bulbs a day, and in the course of her job had packed over 50,000,000 bulbs. She assured Munsterberg that she found her work very interesting; it was different all the time, she said. Sometimes she grabbed the bulb in a different way, and sometimes the packing did not run smoothly. Anyway, she always found something to think about or observe. This, said Munsterberg, was the trend that he usually found among people doing seemingly highly repetitive jobs. On the other hand, he often encountered workers who, though they appeared to have interesting jobs, bitterly complained of the monotony of factory work.

Additional Evidence on the Pro-Specialization Side

Hoppock, using his well-known and highly regarded satisfaction scale in a series of studies in a mill in Pennsylvania, found no evidence that technological progress and the factory system necessarily led to job dissatisfaction.[14] And Kornhauser, in a study of manufacturing and nonmanufacturing concerns in Detroit, found that both the skilled and the unskilled manual workers in the manufacturing plants had greater liking for their jobs than the workers of corresponding skill levels employed in nonmanufacturing industries.[15] This evidence, he suggested, refutes the contention that jobs in automobile plants are robot-like and devoid of interest.

[12] H. Robinson, "Job Satisfaction Research of 1958," *Personnel and Guidance Journal,* May, 1959, pp. 669–73.

[13] Munsterberg, *op. cit.,* p. 195f.

[14] R. Hoppock, *Job Satisfaction.* Harper and Brothers, New York, 1935, pp. 18–19.

[15] A. Kornhauser, *Detroit as the People See It,* Wayne State University Press, Detroit, Mich., 1952, p. 14 and p. 219.

On the basis of a study in a knitwear mill, Smith concluded that repetition as defined by the frequency with which a single job element occurred is only one of many causes of monotony.[16] Feelings of monotony, the study found, were not merely a function of the task performed, but were related to factors in the worker himself.

Smith also cautioned against the idea that work that appears repetitive to the observer must necessarily be boring to the worker. Since a job is classified as repetitive solely on the basis of the number of repetitions observed by an outsider, the classification does not take into account the way the worker himself perceives it. What the worker classifies as repetitiveness depends on his perceptions of the task, and these perceptions cannot be observed by an outsider. Smith found that people who were content with doing "repetitive work" tended to display such personal characteristics as contentment with the existing state of affairs, placidity, and, possibly, rigidity. They were not stupid or insensitive, but simply accepted things the way they were.

Lipman long ago pointed out that many work processes that appear monotonous to an observer are not necessarily monotonous for the workers, since the worker is able to perceive some interesting aspects of the work that an outsider could never detect.[17] Furthermore, he stressed, some people prefer decidedly routine work because they do not have to think about what they are doing.

An Outstanding Study

Probably the best study that has been done in this area so far is one carried out by Kennedy and O'Neill, who studied the effects of job enlargement on the opinions and attitudes of workers in an automobile assembly plant.[18] A well-constructed attitude-measuring instrument was administered to hourly workers in four production departments. The questionnaire consisted of 14 relatively independent dimensions covering different attitude areas. The departments studied were made up of sections, each consisting of 20 to 30 assembly operators, one or two utility men, and a foreman. A 20 per cent random sample of the assembly operators and all the utility men from each section were surveyed.

The assembly operators performed highly repetitive, routine, deskilled, mechanically paced jobs. The utility men performed such varied jobs as relief, providing demonstrations for new employees, correcting faults, assisting the foreman, and so on. In addition, the assembly operators' jobs were highly defined, while the utility men had a greater range of discretion or choice in what they did.

[16] P. C. Smith, "The Prediction of Individual Differences in Susceptibility to Industrial Monotony," *Journal of Applied Psychology*, 39 (1955), pp. 322–29.

[17] O. Lipman, "The Human Factor in Production," *Personnel Journal*, 7 (1928), pp. 87–95.

[18] J. E. Kennedy and H. E. O'Neill, "Job Content and Workers' Opinions," *Journal of Applied Psychology*, 42 (1958), pp. 372–75.

In two of the four production departments surveyed, these differences in job content had been in effect long enough for differences in attitude to be attributable to differences in the jobs. In the other two departments, the content of the utility man's job had been changed shortly before the study was undertaken. Consequently, data from the first two departments are of primary concern to us here.

When the mean survey scores of the assembly operators and the utility men in the first two departments were compared, it was expected that the assembly operators would have less favorable attitudes because they had simpler jobs. This, however, was not the case. There were no statistically significant differences between the two sets of scores.

This finding led Kennedy and O'Neill to conclude, "If job content is a factor in determining how favorably workers view their supervisor and their work situation, the difference in content apparently must be along more fundamental dimensions than those observed in this study." This is despite the obvious and marked job differences noted above.

Finally, Katzell has pointed out, in an exceptionally well-reasoned paper, that little concrete data that can stand the test of scientific scrutiny have been advanced to support the argument that industrialization is reducing job satisfaction.[19] (In any case, as has already been noted, the evidence suggests that many more people are satisfied than dissatisfied.) Katzell does concede, however, that we cannot conclude that the case against job specialization is unsound simply because it has not yet been proved. The converse has not yet been proved either. What is needed most at the present time, he feels, is research aimed at getting more relevant facts.

The loudest critics of specialization, according to Katzell, are those who are concerned about "conformity."[20] These reformers, he believes, fail to recognize that they may be throwing out the baby with the bath water. It is a psychological law that people retain the patterns of behavior that provide them with rewards. After all, this country enjoys the highest standard of living in history, and fears of deprivation and political oppression have been largely removed. Katzell admits that our society poses some threats to individualism, but he does not agree that modern industrialization is principally to blame for this. We must balance the interests of the individual and the organization without destroying either of them, he says, and he points out that there are a number of grounds for believing that man can continue to realize his material gains and at the same time elevate his emotional and intellectual life. For example:

People differ in the amount of ability they have and in the satisfaction

[19] R. Katzell, "Is Individualism Disappearing?" *Harvard Business Review,* Jan.–Feb., 1958, pp. 139–52.

[20] Deliberately omitted from this summary is the sizable body of literature dealing with the conflict between organizational and individual needs. C. Argyris, *Personality and Organization* (Harper and Brothers, New York, 1957) is a typical example.

they derive from their jobs. These differences are predictable and controllable. Vocational counseling, scientific selection and placement, and on-the-job development can make good use of them in increasing individual efficiency and happiness.

Industrial technology requires an ever-increasing number of administrators, engineers, technicians, and scientists; at the same time, the need for unskilled and semiskilled workers is diminishing. Because higher-level jobs are typically more satisfying and because employment opportunities at these levels are becoming available to more and more people, the outlook is necessarily an optimistic one.

The social and behavioral sciences are learning more and more about the environmental and organizational factors in the work situation that may make for an even greater increase in job satisfaction and productivity.

Increases in productivity have resulted in increases in the purchasing power and leisure time of workers. The work week has shrunk; vacations and holidays have increased. Admittedly, the millennium has not yet arrived; but the potential is there, and if we take proper advantage of our opportunities we have no reason for pessimism about the future of industrial man.

Where Do We Stand Now?

In sum, then, this necessarily sketchy review of the literature, both pro and con, has shown us, first, some authorities who insist that specialization is markedly reducing job satisfaction. According to these writers, job specialization has produced workers who are mentally dull, frustrated, deprived, insecure, afraid, and smothered in anonymity—people who have lost all self-esteem. In general, the members of this school of thought advocate that industry make use of such practices as job rotation, job enlargement, greater freedom for the individual worker, and arrangements designed to increase social interaction on the job. Through these means, they feel, the worker will once more become happy at his job, and his pride, security, and self-esteem will return.

On the opposing side are equally respectable authorities who do not believe that job dissatisfaction is necessarily the result of specialization. The average worker today, they argue, is content and secure, and enjoys the highest standard of living in history. What dissatisfaction does exist—and this is characteristic of only about 13 percent of all workers—is the result of factors other than specialization.

Where, then, do we stand? What can we conclude from the evidence reviewed above? Undoubtedly, the most striking fact about this review is the lack of any really rigorous evidence on the subject. To be sure, it has inspired numerous reports; but few of these can stand the test of scientific scrutiny. Even the best studies are not completely conclusive. Still waiting to be carried out is the study that works into the job situation, actually *manipulates* the content of jobs for experimental purposes, and includes carefully worked out measures of job satisfaction that are applied both before and after this manipulation.[21]

A Stand on the Issue

Nevertheless, despite the lack of definitive evidence either way, the authors of this article remain unconvinced that specialization is responsible for such dissatisfaction as now exists in industry. In summary, here's why:

1. In marked contrast to the kind of experimental rigor that was used by, for example, Kennedy and O'Neill, the anti-specialization researchers have typically employed rather loose procedures. On the whole, their studies have taken the form of going into a plant, observing some operations, and interviewing the workers. The fact that some of these workers are reported as saying they dislike their jobs does not tell us very much. In contrast to the evidence furnished by the carefully built attitude-measuring instrument of known validity and reliability used by Kennedy and O'Neill, these are merely the interviewers' subjective impressions of their subjects' boredom or dissatisfaction.

2. In any case, it remains doubtful whether the reforms advocated by the anti-specialization school would work if they were instituted. Do many workers actually want job rotation? If so, why does the literature abound with discussions of the problem of overcoming the resistance that arises to meet almost any kind of change? As for job enlargement, this immediately poses the question "Where do we stop?" Should a worker be given six operations? Ten? Twenty? Who knows? The fact of the matter is that no one knows how many operations a man *should* perform. The same problem arises with the suggestions for giving individual workers greater freedom and greater opportunity for social interaction on the job. Where do we stop?

3. The most compelling argument against specialization as a major cause of job dissatisfaction lies in the fact of individual differences. This is the central fact of life in the behavioral sciences, and yet the would-be reformers apparently believe that all people must react in exactly the same way to the same job. The observer says to himself, "That job would drive me nuts in half an hour." From this he somehow concludes that it must drive everyone else nuts as well. This simply is not so! (For that matter, it's highly

---

[21] One study that approaches this criterion is A. Marks, "An Investigation of Modifications of Job Design in an Industrial Situation and Their Effects on Some Measures of Economic Productivity" (Ph.D. dissertation, University of California, 1954). Reviewed in L. E. Davis, "Job Design and Productivity," PERSONNEL, March, 1957, p. 423. Though job satisfaction does not seem to have been a central concern of the experiment, it did find that enlarged jobs developed a more favorable attitude toward individual responsibility and effort. There was also evidence that job enlargement had a favorable influence on quality, though it had no appreciable influence either way on output.

probable that many of the workers interviewed by sympathetic social scientists privately regard their questioners' activities as a pretty terrible way to earn a living, too.)

As the authors of this article see it, the best answer yet proposed to the problem of job dissatisfaction is Katzell's prescription: vocational counseling, scientific selection and placement, and personnel development. These procedures, hand in hand with more rigorous research and more enlightened management practices generally, still seem to offer the best hope of increasing the satisfaction that workers derive from their jobs.

31 / Individual Differences and Job Enrichment— The Case Against General Treatments*

Charles L. Hulin

SIMPLE SOLUTIONS TO the serious problems of society have never been lacking. We have seen the building of urban freeways to ease traffic problems; the widespread application of DDT to eliminate mosquitoes; the practice of strip mining to remove mineral deposits; the importing of sparrows to minimize the unsanitary conditions created by horses in the streets of New York City. Each of these simple solutions, while ostensibly solving the original problem, has created conditions with far more serious implications than the original situation had.

Human engineers would argue that each of these failures can be at-

---

* Portions of this chapter have appeared in an article by C. L. Hulin and M. R. Blood entitled "Job Enlargement, Individual Differences and Worker Responses," *Psychological Bulletin,* 69, 41–55 (1968).

Reprinted by permission of the author and publisher from John Maher, *New Perspectives in Job Enrichment* (New York: Van Nostrand Reinhold Company, 1971), pp. 159–91.

tributed to a breakdown in *systems* analysis.[1] In more prosaic terms, the adoption of such less than optimal solutions might be blamed on the failure to regard the world as a balanced system of interdependent parts.

Equally simple solutions to the motivation problems which confront industry have also been suggested. The scientific management propositions of Frederick Winslow Taylor have come and, for the most part, gone. The "human relations" movement has moved on. Supervisory training, currently in the form of T-Groups, is at one of its cyclical high points. Job enrichment, both as an outraged moralistic response to job specialization and as an industrial motivation program, is gaining in popularity and penetration of the field. That none of these approaches to industrial motivation has been overwhelmingly successful is indicated both by the lack of supporting data and the transient nature of their existence.

It can also be argued that the reasons for their lack of success are the same as the reasons for the failures of the misguided programs enumerated in the opening paragraph. All these approaches regard the industrial environment and its inhabitants as less complex and less interdependent than data suggest they are. They fail to recognize that the "normal working adult" is a statistic and, while he may summarize a large amount of data, he bears but little relationship to the workers encountered on the job. Even though single workers may be considered balanced systems of interdependent parts, any group of workers exhibits substantial individual differences. Moreover, most of the programs mentioned above regard men as being motivated by a single variable. Taylor assumed, for example, that a rational workman would work hard to obtain money. Little else should matter. Mayo assumed that man was motivated by social needs. Job enrichment, which both as a concept and a source of concern is nearly 200 years old, assumes man is (or should be) motivated by self-actualization needs. Each of these solutions to industry's motivational problems of course exprobrates its predecessors for assuming that men are all alike and are motivated by the same variable. Unfortunately such recognition usually ends with the introduction to the book or study.

In this chapter, the assumptions underlying the job enrichment thesis will be examined. Evidence which bears on any of the assumptions will be discussed wherever it is available. In addition, the direct and indirect evidence concerning the effects of job enrichment programs will be briefly reviewed. Finally, a discussion of a model which attempts to relate individual differences in motivation to workers' responses to job enrichment will be presented.

Definition of Job Enrichment

For the purposes of this chapter "job enrichment" is defined as the process of allowing the individual worker to determine his own working pace (within limits); allowing the individual worker to serve as his own inspector by assigning responsibility for quality control to the worker; allowing the individual worker to repair his own mistakes; allowing latitude in the choice of methods; and allowing the worker to be responsible for his own machine set up. In this sense, job enrichment is substantially different from "job extension," which consists of merely adding similar elements to the job without altering job content (e.g., soldering the red wires as well as the black wires). However, changing from a line-paced job to a self-paced job would be regarded as job enrichment. The process of job enrichment will produce jobs at a higher level of skill, with varied work content and relative autonomy for the worker. An enriched job also will usually have a higher wage rate. On the other hand, job simplification will result in jobs that require less skill, are more repetitive and have less autonomy. The natural history of many (or most) industrial jobs is toward more and more simplification. It is evident that the process of job simplification has progressed much further with some jobs and in some industries than others. Thus, we frequently have jobs at different stages of simplification existing contemporaneously within any one plant. While we do not normally think of differences between jobs in such terms, it would seem to be a reasonable way of organizing our thinking about jobs. Such categorizations of jobs will enable us to consider both experimental and correlational methods of analyzing differences or changes in worker responses. That is, changes in workers' responses which correlate with the degree of job simplification should also be observed if changes in job specialization are made experimentally.

Notice that there are some deliberate exclusions from this definition of job enrichment. Participative management, with all of its emphasis on involving the worker in the process of making decisions which affect him, is not considered as an integral part of job enrichment. This is contrary to the thinking of a number of writers. The omission is based on the following reasoning: So long as job enrichment and participative management are conceptually confounded, our thinking about them will be imprecise. Just what is meant by a program of job enrichment will be unclear. For example: Is it necessary to have both elements present in order to have an adequate program? Unless they are regarded as distinct and separable, the question may well become a source for unfortunate polemics. In addition, so long as both elements are *experimentally* confounded, we will have no way of determining which manipulation resulted in the observed change. This confounding is scientifically absurd. Also, note that the definition of job enrichment used in this chapter is not tied to the writings of any one psychologist. So long as a "job" may be conceptualized independently of any theoretical position, then so may the process of job change. It seems preferable to discuss job enrichment independently of any theory of motivation currently in vogue, since such theories, by their very nature, are transitory. It would indeed be a pity if something so potentially powerful as job enrichment were thrown out when its (apparent) theoretical progenitor fell from favor under the weight of disconfirming evidence. Finally, this definition of job enrichment is necessarily imprecise. This lack of precision is due, ultimately, to the lack of attention paid by psychologists to the definition of such terms as "job" or "task." This point will be discussed more fully at the end of this chapter. Suffice it to say here that such lack of attention serves to increase the difficulty of the task at hand.

Assumptions of Job Enrichment Model

According to the job enrichment advocates, as jobs become increasingly specialized and less autonomous, the monotony (perception of the unchanging characteristics of the job from minute-to-minute) increases. Short time cycle, simplified jobs are assumed to lead to monotony. Monotony is supposedly associated with feelings of boredom and job dissatisfaction. Boredom and job dissatisfaction lead to undesirable (from management's point of view) behavior. This reasoning could be diagrammed as follows:

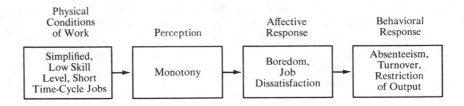

An alternative, more positive, way of stating the job enlargement hypothesis is presented in Figure 1.

Figure 1 graphically indicates the hypothesized positive, monotonic relationship between job variety (job size) and the experienced job satisfaction of the encumbents. (Note that even though the relationship in Figure 1 is linear, any monotonic positive function could be substituted.) There is also the implicit assumption that as job variety and job satisfaction increase, the motivation of the workers shows a concomitant increase.

The assumptions implicit in this line of reasoning deserve to be discussed. First, consider the assumption that repetitiveness leads to monotony and, conversely, that uniqueness and change lead to lack of monotony. Smith has demonstrated there are substantial individual differences in susceptibility to monotony among workers on the same job.[2] According to Smith, some workers do not report feelings of monotony even in the face of a job with an extremely short work cycle. Further, Baldamus has pointed out that repetitive work can be positively motivating and tends to "pull the worker along."[3] This notion of traction has been experimentally verified by Smith and Lem using a sample of industrial workers.[4] Thus, it would seem that the assumption that repetitiveness leads to monotony could be questioned on two grounds—effects of individual differences and positive motivational characteristics of repetition.

Figure 1. *Hypothesized general relationship between job variety and job satisfaction.*

The second assumption is monotony leads to boredom and job dissatisfaction. Even if we grant the tenuous supposition that the physical reality of short time cycles or repetition leads to monotony, can we presume that the workers will respond with negative affect to this perception? It would seem this can be questioned on much the same grounds as the first. At the very least, we should allow the possibility that some workers prefer the safety of not being required to make decisions regarding their jobs. Vroom has demonstrated that not all workers are satisfied when they are allowed to take part in the decision-making process about their jobs, and there are significant individual differences (F-scale scores) between workers who respond positively to the opportunity to make decisions about their jobs and those who do not.[5] These data indicate the possibility that some workers prefer routine, repetition, and specified work methods.

Finally, we have the assumption that boredom and job dissatisfaction are associated with undesirable behavior on the part of the job encumbent. This assumption is probably the least crucial to the argument since, trite as it may seem, a high level of job satisfaction among industrial workers may be an appropriate goal in itself. Thus, if job enrichment had no other result than decreased boredom and increased job satisfaction, it could be an appropriate manipulation. Also, there is evidence that in certain circumstances an individual's job satisfaction is significantly related to his subsequent decision to quit his job.[6,7,8] The relationship between satisfaction and productivity and other on-the-job behaviors is somewhat more elusive. The fact that this relationship has been so difficult to document with data indicates the weakness of the final assumption of the traditional model.

An Alternative Viewpoint

Let us propose that for some workers, all of the above assumptions are incorrect and that for all workers, the assumptions are true only in varying degrees. In other words, there may exist in the American work force identifiable subgroups whose motivation to work does *not* coincide with the idea that hard work is a virtue and that work is intrinsically rewarding; nor do they feel that it is a sin to work for money, social contact, or status. Let us further entertain the idea that the psychological maturity and mental health of these subgroups of workers is neither better nor worse than that of any other identifiable subgroup.

I am suggesting that the ethnomorphising* of the white middle class social scientists, executives, and managers may be as responsible for the job enrichment thesis as any set of data. That is, these influential individuals, starting with Adam Smith,† with their years of education and their frame of reference developed by exposure to the academic environment and administrative jobs respond negatively to a routine job and make the assumption that all mature, healthy workers will do the same.

This set of counter assumptions would lead to the rejection of the view that the relationship shown in Figure 1 is a general relationship which is true for all members of the American workforce. Rather this particular positive, monotonic relationship should be regarded as only *one* of a number of possible relationships between job variety and job satisfaction. We should be willing to consider also the hypotheses summarized in Figures 2 through 4. These figures portray a family of curves relating job variety to satisfaction, with the optimal amount of variety (in terms of producing the greatest amount of satisfaction) occurring at different points for different groups of workers.

The thrust of this alternative point of view may be summarized as

---

* Ethnomorphising: The tendency to attribute to all members of a population the values, desires and aspirations possessed by one's own peer group or sub-culture.

† See Adam Smith's *An inquiry into the nature and causes of the wealth of nations.*

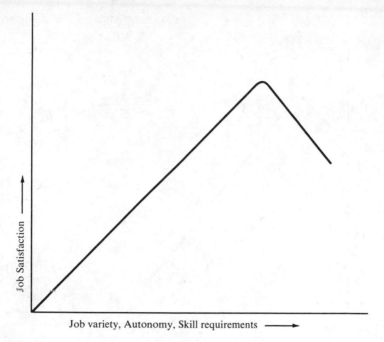

Figure 2. *Hypothetical relationship between job variety and job satisfaction for a group of workers with a strong desire for a demanding job.*

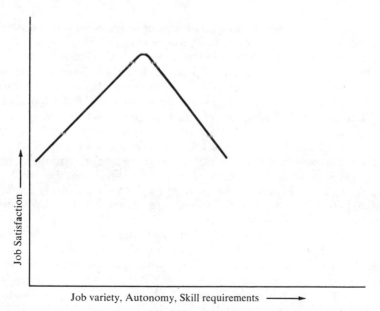

Figure 3. *Hypothetical relationship between job variety and job satisfaction for a group of workers with a moderate desire for a demanding job.*

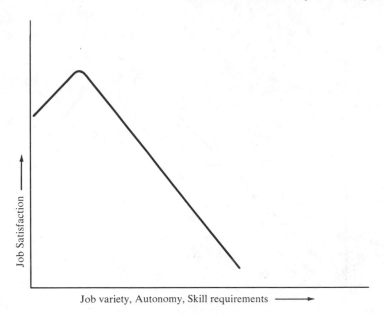

Figure 4. *Hypothetical relationship between job variety and job satisfaction for a group of workers with a weak desire for a demanding job.*

follows: There exist identifiable subgroups of workers within the American workforce whose motivations to work are predictably and lawfully different from the general work motivation assumed by the job enrichment proponents. The problem confronting the researcher, then, is one of determining and assessing those variables which differentiate between these various subgroups, rather than assuming we understand work and what motivates men. The next step must be to determine the characteristics of the job and work situation which serve as positive sources of motivation for these different, independently defined work groups. Finally, if we discover that substantial differences exist between workers and that certain groups of workers are positively motivated by money or even a repetitive job, then *such difference, must simply be regarded as part of the description of the world as it exists.* Whether or not this is the way the psychologist would like the world to be is a completely separate issue. In short, if the investigation of the differences between workers reveals that substantial numbers of these workers are motivated by so-called "lower-order needs" (such as money) then no value judgments need be made nor pejorative paragraphs written. (As an acquaintance once said, "Money won't buy happiness but it sure takes the sting out of being miserable." Or as a famous blues singer put it, "I've been rich and I've been poor. Rich is better." Or alternatively, "It's better to be rich and healthy than poor and sick.")

The hypothesis that work (as a concept) has substantially different meanings to different groups of people is neither new nor startling. An examination of the anthropological literature suggests that the differences in the meaning of work from one culture to another are striking. For example, among the Tikopians of Oceania, work as a general concept is "good" and idleness is an evil similar to a religious offense. The people of Tikopia start work early, take few breaks and often compete with each other to see who can accomplish the most. (The similarity between these conceptions of work and idleness and the writings of John Calvin is obvious.) On the other hand, work is but a necessary evil for the Siriono of the Amazon Basin. They work when absolutely necessary, and only to obtain food. When food is available, they rest and there are no group or cultural sanctions for idleness.[10]

It would be all too easy for us to fall into the trap of making value judgments about the cultural differences described above and conclude that the Siriono are somehow less good than the people of Tikopia. These would be value judgments and *nothing more*. Such judgments are neither demanded by the data nor warranted by logic. A third example, somewhat closer to home, is found in the study by Morse and Weiss.[11] In this study people were asked if they would continue to work if they suddenly inherited enough money so they no longer needed to. The majority, 80%, said they would. However, the percentage of people who said they would *not* continue to work *increased* steadily from the white collar workers, to the skilled workers, and finally to the unskilled workers, with only 50% of the unskilled workers expressing a desire to continue working.

The study by Morse and Weiss provides evidence that work has different meanings within the different subcultures (defined by job levels) of the United States. Work is likely to be seen as a means to an economic end by the unskilled worker, while it has intrinsic meaning for the white collar worker. Again, no pious value judgments need be made.

Some Indirect Evidence

Let us now turn to an examination of some of the studies relating to job level and job enrichment. It is unfortunate that most of these studies provide indirect evidence, at best, and a certain amount of interpretation must be done before the results can be seen as relevant to the issue. Many of these studies have been poorly controlled, and most of the authors have attempted to generalize from severely limited data.

In an early study Wyatt, Fraser, and Stock obtained data which indicated that workers on a soap wrapping job had higher outputs when working conditions were uniform than when conditions were varied.[12] Outputs were not different in the two conditions when folding handkerchiefs and making bicycle chains were compared. They concluded that varied conditions were better and began studying optimum spacing of task changes! There are obvious problems with this study. The Ns were small and results did not reach statistical significance; their conclusions do not follow from their results; and they did not control for variations in output which may have been caused by the change *per se,* as opposed to the particular variations of their hypotheses. They also fail to distinguish among the effects of fatigue, inhibition, boredom, and monotony. In later studies, Wyatt, Fraser, and Stock[13] and Wyatt, Langdon, and Stock[14] investigated the effects of jobs having short time cycles. Smith has pointed out "certain deviations from normally acceptable methods of scientific investigation..."[15]. Part of the measure of boredom used by Wyatt, et al. consisted of questions about slowing of output during the middle of the day. Those who reported such slowing were regarded as bored. Also, those who reported such slowing did indeed slow down at these times. Therefore, Wyatt, et al. were able to obtain good matches between their measure of boredom and "typical" boredom output curves which were thought of as having a low point in the middle of each work period. The circularity is evident. The results relating boredom, intelligence and output are also questionable. High IQ workers were more bored; boredom reduced the rate of working; but high IQ workers were more productive. It is interesting that, in spite of their general conclusions, Wyatt, et al. reported that the experience of boredom was largely dependent on individual characteristics. The workers in all of these studies were female, which serves as an additional limitation on external validity. All in all, both the measures and the conclusions of these studies are questionable. Roethlisberger and Dickson[16] and Smith[15] have been unable to replicate the original results of Wyatt, et al. Generalizations from these data must be made with caution.

Walker presented a report of the benefits of a job enrichment program which had been undertaken at IBM.[17] Though this article was a heuristic success, it presented little in the way of data. There was no adequate control group and no data are presented concerning satisfaction, turnover, costs, etc.

Walker and Marriott provide data that show that more than a third of the employees of mass production factories complained of boredom, but in rolling mills, the proportion was only 8%.[18] Boredom was more widespread among conveyor workers, and workers were less satisfied on such jobs if they had previously held a skilled rather than an assembly-line job. Data came from interviews with 976 men from three large factories. These results seem to be evidence supporting the model which relates uniformity and repetition in work to dissatisfaction. There is no disagreement with the results as presented; there are some problems associated with the generality of the conclusions. Individual differences in worker responses were considerable, and in fact, the authors say: "Many liked their work because it was simple, straightforward, and carried no responsibility." Differences between factories were attributed to differences in production techniques, rather than differences among the persons making up the work forces of the factories. Since plant location and production techniques were confounded, either conclusion is consistent with the data. A subsequent interview study by Walker and

Guest related dissatisfaction, absences, and turnover to assembly line work.[19] The basic conclusion was that very little could be said in favor of assembly line work. While Walker and Guest were careful not to generalize beyond their sample, their conclusions and recommendations have been interpreted as global cures for general motivational problems. Walker and Guest's descriptions of their sample are important: "The area from which the workers were recruited has few mass production factories." (p. 4), "Only two in our sample had ever worked in an automobile plant before." (p. 19), and "...34.5% of all those (in the sample) with manual work experience were skilled persons. Considering the relatively unskilled nature of automobile assembly work, this high proportion of skilled workmen...is of interest." (p. 31). While negative responses to simplified, line-paced jobs from workers such as those described by Walker and Guest are not unusual or surprising, we should not necessarily expect such negative responses to be a general characteristic of the United States workforce. In subsequent papers, these investigators have extolled the virtues of job flexibility, job rotation, and job enrichment without contributing any additional data.[20, 21, 22] Their claims may be unjustifiable because of the characteristics of their sample and their lack of acceptable experimental controls.

The Detroit Edison electric utility company carried out a program of job enrichment among first line supervisors and clerical workers.[23] Though there are no controls and no statistical information is provided, the investigator claims that job enrichment reduced costs and increased production. He then assumes a positive relationship between productivity and morale. On the basis of this assumed relationship, he argues that satisfaction has increased! This conclusion, based on an incorrect assumption, is noteworthy only for its convolution. Cost reduction and production increase are more easily explained in this case as a result of the elimination of duplications in the work process. Again this report includes the recognition that some of the workers prefer the repetitive jobs.

Marks reports a study of 29 female employees in the manufacturing department of a company on the west coast.[24] A similar department was monitored to serve as a control. Production was poorer with enriched jobs, but quality improved.* The conclusions which are normally drawn from this study are that enriched jobs are better.

There were both quantity and quality improvements in production when assembly operations were enriched in the Maytag Company plant in New-

----

. * Quality improvement would be expected in nearly all programs of job enrichment, since the worker serves as his own inspector. If he makes a mistake and discovers it, he can repair it on the spot. Such repairs on assembly line work are, of course, impossible since the worker cannot stop to make the repairs. This improvement in quality, however, should be attributed to a direct result of the technical changes in the jobs and not to changes in worker motivation or satisfaction. Kilbridge has also pointed out that many of the positive results obtained in studies of job enrichment could be attributed to reductions in balance-delay time and nonproduction time and not to changes in worker motivations or satisfaction.[27]

ton, Iowa.[25] No empirical data is presented, but it is reported that most of the workers came to like their new jobs and they seemed to become involved.

Davis and Werling surveyed a West Coast plant employing 400 operating and 250 clerical and administrative personnel regarding their attitudes toward job enlargement.[26] The interests of skilled workers, similar to those of management, included company success, improvement of self and improvement of operations. Semi-skilled workers, on the other hand, lacked concern for company goals, and they attached little importance to job content. From this, Davis and Werling conclude that semi-skilled jobs are insufficiently enriched. Such a conclusion implies that it is the size of the job which is determining the attitude. There is no evidence supporting this, and indeed, it is reasonable to believe that attitudes toward company goals and job content may be as influenced by many sub-cultural and personal background factors as by one aspect of the task. Further, the inference that the workers *should* think job content important is an evaluative assumption not necessary for any interpretation of these data.

Argyris provides information from a content analysis of interviews with 34 employees from a department with high skill demands and 90 unskilled and semi-skilled employees from another department.[28] As compared with the skilled employees, those of lower skill express: (1) less aspiration for high quality work; (2) less need to learn more about their work; (3) more emphasis on money; (4) lower estimate of personal abilities; (5) less desire for variety and independence; (6) high work spoilage (subjectively judged since the tasks were different) ; (7) fewer lasting friendships formed on the job, and (8) less creative use of leisure time. In addition, the lower skilled employees express needs "to be left alone," "to be passive," and "to experience routine or sameness." According to Argyris, these differences are caused by the organization's stifling the maturity of individuals on the job. However, just as in the Davis and Werling study, there is no reason to believe that these attitude differences were caused by the job rather than individual preferences being brought into the work situation; nor is there any reason to believe the aspirations and goals of the skilled workers are to be valued more than those of the unskilled workers.

In a study auspiciously titled "Job enlargement: Antidote to apathy"[29] Reif and Schoderbek report the results of a survey of companies regarding their use of job enrichment. Questionnaires were mailed to 276 companies. Replies were received from 210 and of these, 41 said they had used job enrichment. The most popular reasons for undertaking job enrichment were cost reduction and profit increase. Twenty-three respondents checked "increase in job satisfaction" as an advantage of job enrichment. Reif and Schoderbek seem unaware that the data they are using may be atypical, even though the sample represents less than 15% of their initial population. Returns perhaps should not be expected from companies who have tried job enrichment unsuccessfully, and if an executive from such a company did reply, he might hesitate to admit that a policy of his firm had failed. Thus, the conclusions of this article in favor of job enrichment and the proposal of job enrichment as an "antidote for apathy" may be justified.

In a study of the effects of repetitive work on the mental health of industrial workers, Kornhauser found that many production workers from an urban area gave interview responses which he considered indicative of poor mental health.[30] He showed that in general such indications of poor mental health increased as job level decreased (from skilled workers to semi-skilled workers with repetitive tasks). He gleaned a large amount of information from interviews with 655 men, and his data and his conclusions merit discussion. He convincingly shows that there are systematic differences in the interview responses of workers at different job levels. From the nature of the response differences, he concludes that the persons in the lower skilled jobs are in poorer mental health and, furthermore, that it is their occupational situation which has caused this condition. He argues that job simplification is a cause of poor mental health. Before uncritically accepting these conclusions, some of the methods of his study must be examined.

First, the data are all obtained from interview responses. Therefore, they are open to such biasing factors as social acceptability, interviewer bias and bias of the coder who arranged the interview transcripts into quantitative material. Social acceptability bias would enter the situation and distort responses in the obtained direction if the interviewee shaped his answers to his expectations of the responses desired by his middle-class-oriented interviewer. That is, persons in repetitive jobs may feel hesitant to admit that they are satisfied with their work if they feel that such admission will lead to an unfavorable judgment from the interviewer. If the interviewer were familiar with the hypothesis of the study, (either explicitly or implicitly), there is the additional possibility that responses were systematically interpreted in the manner most favorable to the hypothesis. Since there is no information presented which would either confirm or dis-confirm the existence of these biases, we must approach the results with proper caution and the realization that such distortions *might* have taken place.

Further, Kornhauser chooses to ignore differences in workers' backgrounds. Perhaps this is justified since, as he explains, these differences are not the point of his discussion. However, we should not overlook his data which show the relationship between personal background variables and the Mental Health Index score to be at least as strong as that between job level and the Mental Health Index score. He points to the relative independence of these influences, but his analytic techniques are such that they would not be sensitive to interaction effects anyway. The conclusion must be left to the judgment of the reader.

Finally, and most important, it is inevitable that the Mental Health Index depends on value judgments as to what constitutes good or poor health. In this case, good mental health seems to depend more on striving for personal betterment than on a realistic evaluation of the situation. For example, the interview response: "There's such a thing as beating your brains against the wall. Some things you just can't change; might as well accept them and adjust yourself to them," is said by Kornhauser to "...call attention to the very limited self-expectations, the degree of passivity, fatalism and resignation that characterize many of the workers," (page 241). Thus, Kornhauser shows that he himself subscribes to what he considers to be a middle class concept—that every person is responsible for his own situation rather than being influenced by forces beyond his control. He sees as evidence of poor mental health that members of a lower class subculture do not subscribe to middle class values. What these data seem to show most convincingly is that there are differences by job level among urban workers in the extent to which workers adhere to a middle class value system.

In several ways Kornhauser's study demonstrates the dangers of trying to index a culture bound concept such as mental health when using a research sample which contains different groups of workers who may be culturally very different from the investigators and persons who are judging the validity of the research instrument. Nonetheless, the study confirms that there are response differences between different job levels. This is a new concept, but whereas blue collar and white collar differences have been discussed in the past, Kornhauser shows that within the gross blue collar category, finer discriminations will provide additional information. Porter has shown that such differentiation is profitable in the white collar realm.[31] Certainly job level is an influential dimension in the determination of workers' responses and the extent to which class ideals prevail. If we can find other useful dimensions, we will increase our ability to understand and predict the reactions of workers to job enrichment and other aspects of their work situation. . . .

In addition to the references cited above, Worthy,[34] Argyris,[35,36] Davis,[37,38] Davis and Canter,[39] and Ford[40] maintain that larger jobs are "better" jobs. Though this approach to motivating workers has gained widespread popular support, data are unconvincing. The evidence which is available has restrictions either because of methodological problems or because of the nature of the samples. Earlier, MacKinney, Wernimont, and Galitz reviewed the studies relating job specialization and job satisfaction.[41] They concluded that the issue was not settled by the data at that time. The present writer obviously feels that not only is the issue still not settled, it is not even structured. He also agrees with the statement of MacKinney, et al., that "The most compelling argument against specialization as a major cause of job dissatisfaction lies in the fact of individual differences. This is the central fact of life in the behavioral sciences, and yet the would-be reformers apparently believe that all people must react in exactly the same way to the same job. The observer says to himself, 'That job would drive me nuts in half an hour.' From this he somehow concludes that it must drive everyone else nuts as well. This simply is not so! (For that matter, it's highly probable that many of the workers interviewed by sympathetic social scientists privately regard their questioners' activities as a pretty terrible way to earn a living, too.)" [p. 17].

The validity of this conclusion is supported by a small number of studies which have recently been done. Specifically the data presented by Whyte,[42] Kennedy and O'Neill,[43] Kilbridge,[44] Katzell, Barrett, and Parker,[45] Kendall,[46] Conant and Kilbridge,[47] Kornhauser,[30] Turner and Lawrence,[48] Blood and Hulin,[49] Shepard[50] and Hackman and Lawler (in press)[51] indicate that the general conclusion regarding the effects of job enrichment on job satisfaction and/or motivation is overstated and may be applicable to only certain segments of the working population.

Perhaps the most dramatic of these studies was that done by Turner and Lawrence,[48] who attempted a comprehensive study on the attitudinal and behavioral responses of workers to different aspects of their jobs. The original hypotheses were that workers would respond favorably (high satisfaction and low absence rates) to jobs which were more complex, had more responsibility, more authority, more variety, etc. In short, *good* responses would accompany high level jobs. The hypothesis concerning attendance was confirmed for a sample of 470 workers from eleven industries who were working on 17 different jobs. The hypothesized positive relationship between job level and satisfaction was *not* supported. This latter finding plus the presence of a number of curvilinear relationships led Turner and Lawrence to the conclusion that the workers in the sample had been drawn from two separate and distinct populations whose members responded in different ways to similar job characteristics. The investigators were able to determine that workers from factories located in small towns responded differently from workers who came from more urban settings. The workers from small town settings tended to respond to task attributes in a manner consistent with the job enrichment thesis. No relationship between task attributes and attendance existed for workers from cities and, in fact, they responded with *low* job satisfaction to supposedly desirable job attributes and *high* satisfaction to such "undesirable" attributes as repetitiveness. Turner and Lawrence explained such reversals using the concept of "anomie." They argued that workers in large cities with their extremely heterogeneous social cultures would be more likely to be normless (anomic). They would fail to develop strong group (or subcultural) norms and values, due to the extreme size and heterogeneity of the city population, and would fail to respond positively to the white collar oriented values attached to larger, more autonomous, more skilled jobs. Turner and Lawrence, rather than ignoring the effects of individual differences or attributing them to chance, were able to determine that the unexpected results could not be attributed to chance or "poor mental health," but could reasonably be attributed to differences in cultural backgrounds. It is clear that a number of variables are hopelessly confounded with city size in the Turner and Lawrence study. This does not detract from their general conclusion that cultural differences are related to a worker's response to his job. It does raise problems as to just what these cultural differences are.

Blood and Hulin argued that workers from large cities could not be considered as being anomic (or normless) on the basis of the available evidence, but could more reasonably be considered to be alienated from the "work" norms of the middle class (positive affect for occupational achievement, a belief in the intrinsic value of hard work, a striving for the attainment of responsible positions, a belief in the work related aspects of Calvinism and the Protestant Ethic) and integrated with the norms of their own particular sub-culture.[49] Simply because blue collar workers do not share the work norms and values of the middle classes does not mean they have no norms. In the case of the industrial workers sampled by Turner and Lawrence, there is no compelling reason to suspect that workers in large industrialized cities would adhere to the dominant work value systems of white middle class groups. In fact, it would be somewhat surprising if these workers (whose grandfathers and fathers before them had likely worked as unskilled or semi-skilled laborers and had failed to rise above their initial job or, even worse, had been replaced by a machine or a younger worker when they were 50) would behave in the way demanded by the Protestant Ethic— (Work hard and you will get ahead. You are responsible for your own destiny. Acceptance into the kingdom of heaven is dependent on hard work on this mortal earth.).* Starting from this position, Blood and Hulin re-analyzed some data gathered by Patricia C. Smith. These data had been gathered from some 1300 blue collar workers employed in 21 plants located throughout the eastern half of the United States. Blood and Hulin ordered the 21 plants along a number of dimensions which they felt would reflect the degree to which the blue collar workers in the communities would feel alienated from middle class work norms. The dimensions which were chosen for this analysis were labeled as extent of slums, urbanization, population density, standard of living, etc.† These community variates were then used to predict a number of variables obtained from each of the 21 plants. They predicted that blue collar workers in communities where one could expect integration with, and acceptance of, middle class work norms (small community, low standard of living, few slums, etc.) would respond as the striving type of motivation theory[53] or the job enrichment model would expect. However, workers in communities where one would expect alienation from middle class work norms (large, industrialized communities with large slum areas, etc.) would not respond as expected and, in some cases, might respond in an opposite manner from their counterparts in the non-alienated communities. The predictions were confirmed beyond the chance level. Of particular importance to the present argument were Blood and Hulin's findings regarding job level and work satisfaction. In the most "alienated" community, the correlation between job level and work satisfaction was approximately zero, while among the workers drawn from the plant located in the most "integrated" community, the correlation between these two vari-

---

* See, for example, the article by Rutledge and Gass for a discussion of this problem as it pertains to one particular sub-culture.[52]

† See Kendall[46] or Blood and Hulin[49] for a description of how these variates were constructed.

ables was approximately $+.40$. These results raise questions about the generality of the job enrichment model. . . .

Note should be taken of a recent article by Shepard in which the investigator found no differences between workers from urban backgrounds and workers from rural backgrounds in terms of their responses to job specialization.[50] Unfortunately, Shepard divided his sample into those from towns with a population of 5,000 and over and those from towns with a population less than 5,000. Towns with a population of 5,000 hardly fit the description of being highly industrialized urban areas. In addition, Blood and Hulin did not contend that city size per se was a good index of workers' values and aspirations. Indeed, they never used city size as an index variable. Shepard's data are interesting but are not directly relevant to the Blood and Hulin model. Shepard does recognize that community characteristics were used only as index variables of certain motivational differences. Therefore, he attempted to assess three of these motivational variables directly. The results of this aspect of the study yield results somewhat more promising for the Blood and Hulin model. For example, for those workers with a low commitment to the goals of the organization, the relationship (phi squared) between job specialization and job satisfaction is .26, while for those with a high commitment to the organization the phi squared is .45 between job specialization and job satisfaction. Both of these relationships are negative (highly specialized jobs leading to low levels of satisfaction). If the sample is divided on the basis of the workers' instrumental approach to the job, we find a similar pattern of relationships. The phi squared is .34 between satisfaction and specialization for those who see their jobs as being only instrumental, while the relationship is .42 for those who are less likely to see their job as being instrumental. Shepard's third variable, self evaluative involvement, did not yield this pattern of results. The results of the first two scales would be predicted by the Blood and Hulin model. It should be noted that the above discussion is based on my reanalysis of Shepard's data. Finally, whether or not these three variables are central to the Blood and Hulin model is open to question.

Katzell, Barrett, and Parker presented data which showed that among a sample of warehouse workers drawn from a number of locations there existed strong relationships between both satisfaction and productivity on the response side and community characteristics on the input side.[46] They demonstrated that the location of the plant and similarly the backgrounds of the workers (since these are correlated variables) play important roles in shaping the attitudes of the workers and influencing their behavior.

A similar reanalysis of the data presented by Kornhauser in Table 5.1 yields a similar pattern of results.[30] While there is no question about the main effect of job level on satisfaction, there is also an interaction between plant location (Detroit vs small town) and job level on job satisfaction.

Kilbridge directly attacked the question of the preference of workers for larger vs smaller jobs and mechanical vs self-pacing.[44] Fifty-one% of a sample of 202 (141 females and 61 males) assembly line workers employed by a radio and television factory in Chicago stated they would prefer a smaller job, 37% were indifferent and only 12% preferred a self-paced job. Considering the location of this factory (Chicago) and the results of Turner and Lawrence[48] and Blood and Hulin,[49] these results should not be surprising.

Kennedy and O'Neill surveyed workers in four automative production departments.[43] They determined that assembly operators performing highly routine and repetitive tasks held opinions toward their supervisors or work situations no more negative than those held by utility men who were performing a much more varied set of tasks.

Turner and Miclette interviewed 115 female assembly workers from an electronics plant.[54] Even though the work was extremely repetitive with a very short time cycle, most of the workers expressed satisfaction with the work itself. The main sources of dissatisfaction came from the sense of being caught in a quantity-quality squeeze and the interruptions from staff and supervisory personnel. Object, batch, line and process traction were discussed as sources of satisfaction (cf. Baldamus,[3] Smith and Lem[4]). Thus, repetitiveness alone is a poor indicator of worker response, and the various sources of positive motivations of repetitive work must be considered.

Finally, some as yet unpublished data obtained by Hackman and Lawler are central to this discussion.[51] These investigators obtained data which were sufficient to test a number of the implications of the conclusions of Turner and Lawrence[48] and Hulin and Blood.[55] Hackman and Lawler's data clearly support the expected general effect of job variety and autonomy on the job satisfaction of the incumbents. Their data also confirm the existence of a moderating effect of individual differences on the relationship between job satisfaction and job variety. Specifically, they found that there existed substantial positive correlations between measures of job satisfaction and measures of job variety and job autonomy for those workers motivated by Maslow's so-called "higher-order needs" (an unfortunately pejorative term) while for those workers less motivated by these "higher-order needs," the correlations between the same variables were lower and frequently were not significantly different from zero.

In addition, Hackman and Lawler found that the geographical backgrounds of the workers (industrialized vs nonindustrial) had an effect on the extent to which the workers endorsed the higher-order need statements of Maslow. The effect was in the direction predicted by Hulin and Blood.[55]

Summary

The literature reviewed in the preceding pages presents a confused picture. Some investigators have reported results which show positive results of job enrichment programs and/or strong positive relationships between job level and job satisfaction. Other investigators have reported less positive or even negative results. There are three possible conclusions which can be drawn from such a collection of studies, each of which has certain merit. We could conclude that job enrichment is but another oversold, over-promoted gimmick in the long dreary history of research on job motivation and that the positive results are attributable to the Hawthorne effect and the Messianic fervor of the disciples of the model. Alternatively, we could conclude that job enrichment is the answer to our problems and the negative results are due to sloppy implementation of the program by inept investigators. Neither conclusion seems appropriate. A more reasonable conclusion would be that either positive or negative results may be expected from a program of job enrichment and the type of result depends to a great extent on the motivations of the workforce involved (among other things). The studies reviewed demonstrate this if nothing else. Precisely what characteristics of the workforce result in a positive or a negative response to job enrichment is still open to conjecture. Only a little research has been done on this question. This is unfortunate since this research should have been done first rather than last. The result is that job enrichment has by now been oversold to industry and in the literature. Any critical study or studies which might now be done and which indicate the presence of moderating influences (including groups which may respond negatively to job enrichment) are likely to be rejected.

Individual Differences and Job Enrichment

...We find ourselves in the unfortunate position of having to assume that we know what the important individual differences are in determining workers' responses to their jobs. We have little knowledge that the dimensions we use are associated with more than a trivial amount of the variance. Until parametric research is undertaken, we are in little better shape regarding individual differences among workers than we are comparing differences among jobs. Nevertheless, the following tentative model relating job enrichment, job satisfaction, and individual differences is presented.

Earlier, Hulin and Blood presented a model which they felt would summarize the available data regarding individuals' responses to job enrichment or their responses to high level jobs.[55] Their model will be reviewed here for historical interest. Basically this model postulated that the response of a worker to a job enrichment program could vary from positive to negative depending on the extent to which the worker had internalized the work values of the middle class. To the extent that the worker had internalized the beliefs that hard work is a virtue and idleness is a sin; if you work hard you will get ahead; you are what you do, to do nothing is to be nothing; material rewards are but a small part of the rewards one gets from working; etc., then one could expect that the worker would respond favorably to a job enrichment program. However, if a worker had not internalized such a value system, then there is no reason to expect that he would respond favorably to an opportunity to take on a more responsible, more demanding job. In fact, if a worker received his major rewards from the money he received from his job and used the monetary reward to obtain off-the-job satisfactions, then he might even resent being asked to expend more of his psychological energy on his job.

Hulin and Blood felt that a reasonable predictor of a worker's response to his job could be found in certain characteristics of the community in which he was reared or in which he was living. Their argument was that blue-collar workers who are living in small towns or rural areas would not be members of a work group which would be large enough to develop and sustain its own work norms and values. Such workers would more likely be in closer contact with the dominant middle class. On the other hand, blue-collar workers living and working in large metropolitan industrialized areas would likely be members of a working class population which was large enough to develop a set of norms particular to that culture.

There is no compelling reason to believe that the norms developed by an urban working class subculture would be the same as those of the middle class. However, it should not be necessary to use an argument based on numbers of blue collar workers and social heterogeneity. One could argue that the dominant norms and values that all children learn in school and at home are those brought by the Anglo-Saxon Protestants from Europe in the 17th and 18th centuries. These norms and values have become the standard in American middle-class society. Children are taught these values in school by their middle class teachers and attempt to reach goals defined in terms of these values and by means of behavior consistent with these values. However, children raised in slums, where the cost of living is high and where there is a great deal of migration, are likely to be frustrated in their attempts to reach such goals. Also, the lower class American city dweller is more likely to be non-Anglo-Saxon Protestant (Turner and Lawrence)[48] and less sympathetic to American middle class values. Therefore, the acquisition by the lower class city dweller of goals consistent with the Anglo-Saxon Protestant value system is likely to be met with criticism from his peer group.[42] Such frustration or negative reinforcement should extinguish behavior and beliefs consistent with American middle class ideals.*

The model developed by Hulin and Blood as well as the earlier model spelled out by Turner and Lawrence seem, in retrospect, to take an unnecessarily indirect approach to the problem. They invoke a set of social demographic variables (urbanization, extent of slums, industrialization) to explain differences in the extent to which workers have internalized middle class work values. These differences in work values are then used to explain differences in workers' responses to their jobs. It is easy to understand why this long chain of reasoning took place. The only data available *at that time*

---

* It is interesting to note the similarity between this "sociological" model developed by Hulin and Blood and some data obtained from a sample of Yugoslovian workers (Jezernik).[56] Jezernik's explanation of his data was based in terms of the change from a revolutionary society to a consumer society. The differences in the terminology from that of Hulin and Blood only serve to dramatize the similarity of the ideas.

were the descriptions of the workers' responses to the programs and (usually) where the study was done. In addition, few investigators had directly studied the effects of plant location. In general, Hulin and Blood's explanation seemed to account for the data. However, a more direct approach might summarize the data more efficiently and, in addition, prove to be more easily testable.

Such a direct approach is typified by the study of Hackman and Lawler. In their study they directly assessed a variable related to individual differences in motivation. This variable, labeled by Hackman and Lawler as "higher-order need strength," was found to moderate significantly the responses workers made to high level jobs. Workers who were categorized as being motivated by "higher-level needs" typically reported greater satisfaction if they were on jobs described (by observers) as having a great deal of variety and autonomy. The responses of these workers were similar to the responses of the workers described by Hulin and Blood as non-alienated. The workers low on the "higher-order need" scale responded as the workers Hulin and Blood described as being alienated.

The findings of studies which relate individual differences to workers' responses to jobs can be understood within the following framework.

1. Work role outcomes* are valued to the extent that such outcomes meet the needs, aspirations or desires of the worker.

2. All workers do not have the same needs, aspirations and desires.

3. To the extent that jobs can be engineered so as to provide for the needs, aspirations and desires of individuals, these jobs will be satisfying for these individuals.

4. Workers will adopt a particular work role if the adoption of such a work role will lead to desired outcomes.

These four propositions are not new with this chapter. They have been presented in different contexts, using different terms, and with different emphases many times before.[57] Such propositions do, however, point out the complexity of the industrial world. They should also serve to reiterate that any given worker may be motivated by more than one job characteristic, *and* that workers can differ greatly from each other in terms of what job characteristics are motivating to them. In addition, any differences between workers who are motivated by different outcomes are a matter for data, not assumption. If the data indicate that workers who are motivated by a desire for money (as opposed to workers who are motivated by a desire for "self-actualization") are psychologically immature, produce less, are absent more frequently, or are more likely to quit their job, then such is the case. Until these data are available, however, we should start with the viewpoint that different workers may well be motivated by strikingly different job char-

---

* Work role outcome is defined as being the result(s) of a particular work role. Work role is defined as a set of behaviors which are used to categorize different groups of employees. Being an incumbent of a tool and die makers job is an example of a work role. Being a highly productive salesman (as opposed to an unproductive salesman) is another example.

acteristics and we should design jobs accordingly. Such an approach will not lead to job enrichment programs in all plants, but it is an indication that as complicated a problem as motivation cannot be written off with the solution of job enrichment alone.

References

1. Roscoe, S. N. *Engineering the human engineer.* Paper presented at the APA Annual Meetings, Washington, D.C., 1969.
2. Smith, Patricia C. Individual differences in susceptibility in industrial monotony. *J. Applied Psychology*, 39, 322–29 (1955).
3. Baldamus, W. *Efficiency and effort.* London: Tavistock, 1961.
4. Smith, Patricia C., and Lem, C. Positive aspects of motivation in repetitive work: effects of lot size upon spacing of voluntary rest periods. *J. Applied Psychology*, 39, 330–33 (1955).
5. Vroom, V. H. *Some personality determinants of the effects of participation.* Englewood Cliffs: Prentice-Hall, 1960.
6. Hulin, C. L. Job satisfaction and turnover in a female clerical population. *J. Applied Psychology*, 50, 280–85 (1966).
7. Hulin, C. L. The effects of changes in job satisfaction levels on turnover. *J. Applied Psychology*, 52, 122–26 (1968).
8. Weitz, J. and Nuckols, R. C. The validity of direct and indirect questions in measuring job satisfaction. *Personnel Psychology*, 6, 487–94 (1953).
9. Firth, R. *We, the Tikopia.* Boston: Beacon Press, 1957.
10. Holmberg, A. *Nomads of the long bow.* Washington: Smithsonian Institution, 1950.
11. Morse, N. C., and Weiss, R. S. The function and meaning of work and the job. *American Sociological Review*, 20, 191–98 (1955).
12. Wyatt, S., Fraser, J. A., and Stock, F. G. L. The comparative effects of variety and uniformity in work. *Industrial Fatigue Research Board,* Report No. 52, 1929.
13. Wyatt, S., Fraser, J. A., and Stock, F. G. L. The effects of monotony in work. *Industrial Fatigue Research Board,* Report No. 56, 1929.
14. Wyatt, S., Langdon, J. N., and Stock, F. G. L. Fatigue and boredom in repetitive work. *Industrial Fatigue Research Board,* Report No. 77, 1937.
15. Smith, Patricia C. The curve of output as a criterion of boredom. *J. Applied Psychology*, 37, 69–74 (1953).
16. Roethlisberger, F. J., and Dickson, W. J. *Management and the worker,* Cambridge: Harvard University Press, 1941.
17. Walker, C. R. The problem of the repetitive job. *Harvard Business Review*, 28, No. 3, 54–8 (1950).
18. Walker, C. R., and Marriott, R. A study of attitudes to factory work. *Occupational Psychology*, 25, 181–91 (1951).
19. Walker, C. R., and Guest, R. H. *The man on the assembly line.* Cambridge: Harvard University Press, 1952.
20. Guest, R. H. Men and machines: an assembly-line worker looks at his job. *Personnel*, 31, 496–503 (1955).
21. Guest, R. H. Job enlargement—a revolution in job design. *Personnel Administration*, 20, No. 2, 9–16 (1957).
22. Walker, C. R. Work methods, working conditions, and morale. In: Kornhauser, A., Dubin, R., and Ross, A. M. *Industrial conflict.* pp. 345–58. New York: McGraw-Hill, 1954.
23. Elliott, J. D. Increasing office pro-

I would like to express my appreciation to Jeanne Brett Herman who read and commented on an earlier draft of this paper. Her criticisms and comments substantially improved this final product.

ductivity through job enlargement. In: *The human side of the office manager's job.* American Management Association, Office Management Series, No. 134, pp. 3–15 (1953).

24. Marks, A. R. N. *An investigation of modifications of job design in an industrial situation and their effects on some measures of economic productivity.* Unpublished doctoral dissertation, 1954; Summarized in: Davis, L. E., and Canter, R. R. Job design research. *J. Industrial Engineering,* 7, No. 6, 275–82 (1956); Guest, R. H. Job enlargement—a revolution in job design. *Personnel Administration,* 20, 9–16 (1957).

25. Biganne, J. F., and Stewart, P. A. Job enlargement: a case study. *Bureau of Labor and Management, State Univ. of Iowa,* Research Series No. 25, 1963.

26. Davis, L., and Werling, R. Job design factors. *Occupational Psychology,* 34, 109–32 (1960).

27. Kilbridge, M. D. Reduced costs through job enlargement. *J. Business,* 33, No. 10, 357–62 (1960).

28. Argyris, C. The individual and organization: an empirical test. *Administrative Science Quarterly,* 4, No. 2, 145–47 (1959).

29. Reif, W. E., and Schoderbek, P. P. Job enlargement: antidote to apathy. *Management of Personnel Quarterly,* 5, No. 1, 16–23 (1966).

30. Kornhauser, A. W. *Mental health of the industrial worker: a Detroit study.* New York: Wiley, 1965.

31. Porter, L. A study of perceived need satisfactions in bottom and middle management jobs. *J. Applied Psychology,* 45, 232–36 (1961).

32. Scott, W. E., Jr. Activation theory and task design. *Organizational Behavior and Human Performance,* 1, 3–30 (1966).

33. Frankmann, Judith P., and Adams, J. A. Theories of vigilance. *Psychological Bulletin,* 59, 257–72 (1962).

34. Worthy, J. C. Organizational structure and employee morale. *American Sociological Review,* 15, 169–79 (1950).

35. Argyris, C. *Personality and organization.* New York: Harper, 1957.

36. Argyris, C. *Integrating the individual and the organization.* New York: Wiley, 1964.

37. Davis, L. E. Job design and productivity: a new approach. *Personnel,* 33, 418–30 (1957).

38. Davis, L. E. Toward a theory of job design. *J. Industrial Engineering,* 8, 305–09 (1957).

39. Davis, L. E., and Canter, R. R. Job design. *J. Industrial Engineering,* 6, No. 1, 3–6, 20 (1955).

40. Ford, R. N. *Motivation through the work itself.* New York: American Management Association, 1969.

41. MacKinney, A. C., Wernimont, P. F., and Galitz, W. O. Has specialization reduced job satisfaction? *Personnel,* 39, No. 1, 8–17 (1962).

42. Whyte, W. F. *Money and motivation: an analysis of incentives in industry.* New York: Harper, 1955.

43. Kennedy, J. E., and O'Neill, H. E. Job content and worker's opinions. *J. Applied Psychology,* 42, 372–75 (1958).

44. Kilbridge, M. D. Do workers prefer larger jobs? *Personnel,* 37, 45–48 (1970).

45. Katzell, R. A., Barrett, R. S., and Parker, T. C. Job satisfaction, job performance, and situational characteristics. *J. Applied Psychology,* 45, 65–72 (1961).

46. Kendall, L. M. *Canonical analysis of job satisfaction and behavioral, personal background, and situational data.* Unpublished doctoral dissertation, Cornell University, 1963.

47. Conant, E. H., and Kilbridge, M. D. An interdisciplinary analysis of job enlargement: technology, costs, and behavioral implications. *Industrial and Labor Relations Review,* 18, No. 3, 377–95 (1965).

48. Turner, A. N., and Lawrence, P. R. *Industrial jobs and the worker: an investigation of response to task attributes.* Boston: Harvard University Press, 1965.

49. Blood, M. R., and Hulin, C. L. Alienation, environmental characteristics, and worker responses. *J. Applied Psychology,* 51, 284–90 (1967).

50. Shepard, J. M. Functional specialization, alienation, and job satisfaction. *Industrial and Labor Relations Review,* 23, 207–19 (1970).

51. Hackman, J. R., and Lawler, E. E. *Jobs and motivation.* Mimeographed copy, School of Administrative Sciences, Yale University, 1970.
52. Rutledge, A. L., and Gass, G. Z. *Nineteen Negro men.* San Francisco: Jossey-Bass, 1967.
53. Maslow, A. H. A theory of human motivation. *Psychological Review,* 50, 370–96 (1943).
54. Turner, A. N., and Miclette, A. L. Sources of satisfaction in repetitive work. *Occupational Psychology,* 36, 215–31 (1962).
55. Hulin, C. L., and Blood, M. R. Job enlargement, individual differences, and worker responses. *Psychological Bulletin,* 69, 41–55 (1968).
56. Jezernik, M. D. Changes in the hierarchy of motivational factors and social values in Slovenian industry. *J. Social Issues,* 24, No. 2, 103–11 (1968).
57. Graen, G. B. Instrumentality theory of work motivation: some experimental results and suggested modifications. *J. Applied Psychology Monograph,* 53, No. 2 Part 2, 1–25 (1969).

32 / Functional Specialization, Alienation, and Job Satisfaction

Jon M. Shepard

MANY SOCIAL COMMENTATORS and critics have emphasized the adverse social-psychological effects on workers due to extreme functional specialization (i.e., a minute subdivision of work tasks such that each worker performs only one or a few small operations on the product).[1] There are

Does enlarging the size of jobs increase the satisfaction individuals derive from work? Many investigators have reported in the affirmative, but others, such as Turner and Lawrence and Hulin and Blood, argue that job satisfaction is primarily a function of integration with or alienation from middle-class work norms. This study tests the relationship between work satisfaction and functional specialization using urban versus rural socialization and alienation from work as intervening variables. It concludes that alienation from middle-class work norms does not modify the negative association between job specialization and work satisfaction.

Jon M. Shepard is assistant professor, Department of Sociology, University of Kentucky. The research project from which the data in this article are derived was funded by the Manpower Administration of the United States Department of Labor.—EDITOR

1 For example, see Daniel Bell, "Adjusting Men to Machines," *Commentary,* Vol. 3, No. 1 (January 1947), pp. 79–88; Ely Chinoy, *Automobile Workers and the*

two recent developments which suggest a reversal in the historical trend toward increasing job specialization: (1) the recognition that programs of job enlargement yield benefits for workers and management alike,[2] and (2) automated technology, which promotes job enlargement in the sense that monitors in continuous-process production systems are responsible for a large share of the production process as the discrete steps in production are integrated and the number of job classifications is reduced.[3]

A great deal of research reports that functional specialization reduces job satisfaction and that job enlargement programs contribute to enhanced work attitudes. Studies of work attitudes in mass-production settings suggest that lower levels of job satisfaction characterize workers performing small and repetitive tasks.[4] Additional support to the thesis that job enlargement improves attitudes toward work appears in research carried out on automated production systems.[5]

This position has been criticized on both methodological and theoretical

---

American Dream (Garden City, N.Y.: Doubleday and Co., Inc., 1955); Harold Wilensky, "Varieties of Work Experience," in Henry Borow, ed., *Man in a World of Work* (Boston: Houghton Mifflin Co., 1964), pp. 125–54; and Harvey Swados, "The Myth of the Happy Worker," in Eric Josephson and Mary Josephson, eds., *Man Alone: Alienation in Modern Society* (New York: Dell Publishing Co., Inc., 1962), pp. 106–13.

[2] See Louis E. Davis, "Job Design Research," *Journal of Industrial Engineering,* Vol. 7, No. 5 (September–October 1956), pp. 275–82; Louis E. Davis, "Job Design and Productivity: A New Approach," *Personnel,* Vol. 33, No. 5 (March 1957), pp. 418–30; Louis E. Davis and Richard Werling, "Job Design Factors," *Occupational Psychology,* Vol. 34, No. 2 (April 1960), pp. 109–32; and Louis E. Davis, "The Design of Jobs," *Industrial Relations,* Vol. 6, No. 1 (October 1966), pp. 21–45. For a brief review of additional studies see Delbert C. Miller and William H. Form, *Industrial Sociology* (New York: Harper and Row Publishers, 1964), pp. 630–32.

[3] See William A. Faunce, "Automation and the Division of Labor," *Social Problems,* Vol. 13, No. 2 (Fall 1965), pp. 149–60.

[4] Georges Friedmann, *The Anatomy of Work: Labor, Leisure and the Implications of Automation* (Glencoe, Ill.: The Free Press, 1961); Charles R. Walker, "The Problem of the Repetitive Job," *Harvard Business Review,* Vol. 28, No. 3 (May 1950), pp. 54–58; Charles R. Walker and Robert H. Guest, *The Man on the Assembly Line* (Cambridge, Mass.: Harvard University Press, 1952); J. Walker and R. Marriott, "A Study of Some Attitudes to Factory Work," *Occupational Psychology,* Vol. 25, No. 3 (July 1951), pp. 181–91; Jon M. Shepard, "Functional Specialization and Work Attitudes," *Industrial Relations,* Vol. 8, No. 2 (February 1969), pp. 185–94; and Robert Blauner, *Alienation and Freedom* (Chicago: University of Chicago Press, 1964).

[5] Blauner, *Alienation and Freedom;* Floyd C. Mann and Richard L. Hoffman, *Automation and the Worker* (New York: Holt, Rinehart and Winston, Inc., 1960); Charles R. Walker, *Toward the Automatic Factory: A Case Study of Men and Machines* (New Haven, Conn.: Yale University Press, 1957); William A. Faunce, "Automation in the Automobile Industry: Some Consequences for In-Plant Social Structures," *American Sociological Review,* Vol. 23, No. 4 (August 1958), pp. 401–9; and Shepard, "Functional Specialization."

grounds by those who explain variations in job satisfaction by factors outside the job itself. MacKinney, Wernimont, and Galitz,[6] taking the position
prominent among psychologists and management, assert that worker responses are best accounted for by reference to individual differences, not by
job specialization. Goldthrope[7] maintains that the prevalence of an instrumental orientation toward work, characteristic of mass-production workers,
can be attributed to their prior work attitudes brought into the job rather
than to the nature of work fostering an instrumental orientation.

After a review of the research supporting a negative relationship between
job size and job satisfaction, Hulin and Blood[8] conclude that these findings
are suspect on methodological grounds. Furthermore, they argue, the studies
which do not find a negative relationship are based on sounder scientific
research methods.[9]

The sheer number of studies consistently reporting the negative effects of
functional specialization and the benefits of job enlargement means that
they cannot be discounted, although some are open to methodological
criticism. Moreover, on inspection, some of the pro-specialization research
also can be faulted in terms of research procedures. To illustrate, both
Kennedy and O'Neill[10] and Kilbridge[11] found inconsistent results regarding
the effects of functional specialization. Nevertheless, they concluded that
factors other than job content account for variations in job satisfaction. This
conclusion is based on their evaluative judgment of the inconsistent findings.
Both Kennedy and O'Neill and Kilbridge supported their conclusions by
none too rigorous methodological devices (for example, spot interviews with
employees and nonquantitative analysis of why the results came out as they
did) for which Hulin and Blood criticized researchers for employing to
support job enlargement.

A pat answer to this controversy cannot be offered. Precisely because empirical evidence exists to buttress either the pro- or anti-specialization positions, the degree of functional specialization constitutes an important factor
in the investigation of job satisfaction. While variations in work attitudes

6 A. C. MacKinney, P. F. Wernimont, and W. O. Galitz, "Has Specialization
Reduced Job Satisfaction?" *Personnel,* Vol. 39, No. 1 (January–February 1962),
pp. 8–17.

7 John H. Goldthrope, "Attitudes and Behavior of Car Assembly Workers: A
Deviant Case and a Theoretical Critique," *British Journal of Sociology,* Vol. 17,
No. 3 (September 1966), pp. 227–44.

8 Charles L. Hulin and Milton R. Blood, "Job Enlargement, Individual Differences, and Worker Responses," *Psychological Bulletin,* Vol. 69, No. 1 (January 1968),
pp. 41–55.

9 For a review of these latter studies, see *ibid.*

10 James E. Kennedy and Harry E. O'Neill, "Job Content and Workers'
Opinions," *Journal of Applied Psychology,* Vol. 42, No. 6 (December 1958), pp.
372–75.

11 Maurice D. Kilbridge, "Turnover, Absence, and Transfer Rates as Indicators
of Employee Dissatisfaction with Repetitive Work," *Industrial and Labor Relations
Review,* Vol. 15, No. 1 (October 1961), pp. 21–32.

cannot be attributed entirely to the nature of the job, evidence indicating negative social-psychological effects among those engaged in functionally specialized jobs cannot be dismissed as easily as some suppose. Certainly many tests of any hypothesis are a necessary research practice. In this article, an attempt is made to take some criticisms of the job enlargement thesis into account, and in so doing, to present empirical evidence supporting the unsalutary impact of functional specialization on job satisfaction. The level of job satisfaction is shown to be higher among workers holding "larger" jobs.

The Need for Intervening Variables

After reviewing a number of studies which challenge the proposed negative relationship between job specialization and job satisfaction, Hulin and Blood theorize that positive effects of job enlargement on job satisfaction do not hold in general, but obtain only in particular segments of the work force. As their own model develops, the main criticism, at once methodological and theoretical, is that studies testing the relationship between functional specialization and job satisfaction should introduce intervening variables. They present a model based on cultural differences to explain divergent findings in the literature.

A study by Turner and Lawrence[12] did not find the hypothesized positive relationship between job level and job satisfaction. In an effort to explain this fact, the total sample subsequently was split into two groups: workers from factories located in small towns and those employed in urban factories. A positive relationship between job level and job satisfaction held for workers from rural areas; a negative relationship appeared among urban workers. The latter responded to positive job attributes with low job satisfaction and to negative job attributes with high satisfaction.

Why should the relationship obtain for rural workers but not among urban workers? The explanation offered by Hulin and Blood is that of integration with or alienation from middle-class work norms. Integrated workers are characterized by personal involvement in work and have aspirations for upward occupational mobility. On the other extreme of the continuum are alienated workers who view their jobs instrumentally—that is, as a means for engaging in nonwork pursuits. Alienated workers shun autonomy, responsibility, and higher status. Money is their aim, and personal involvement in work is negligible. A positive relationship between job size and job satisfaction holds only for workers imbued with the middle-class work ideology which has among its values variety, autonomy, control, etc., on the job. The next question raised by Hulin and Blood is what environmental circumstances lead to alienation or integration with respect to middle-class work norms? Their answer lies in the association of the rural-urban location with the likelihood of subscribing to the middle-class work ideology:

12 Arthur N. Turner and Paul R. Lawrence, *Industrial Jobs and the Worker: An Investigation of Response to Task Attributes* (Boston: Harvard University, Division of Research, Graduate School of Business Administration, 1965).

414 CHAPTER EIGHT / Job Enlargement

It is postulated that "alienation from middle-class norms" results from lack of socialization to middle-class norms. That is, where a segment of society exists which holds non–middle-class norms and which is large enough to sustain its own norms, the members of that subculture will become socialized to the norms of that subculture. A handful of industrial workers in a small community could not be expected to sustain a separate set of norms, but persons separated from middle-class identification by low educational attainment or low occupational status and living in ghettos, slums, and highly industrialized communities could develop and sustain a distinct norm system. Alienation from middle-class norms, then, is fostered by industrialized socially heterogeneous, metropolitan conditions.[13]

A resulting proposition is that rural workers are likely to be integrated into middle-class work norms, while workers in urban areas are likely to be alienated from middle-class work values. Linking this proposition to functional specialization, two hypotheses can be stated: (1) the negative relationship between the degree of functional specialization and job satisfaction holds among rural but not among urban blue-collar workers; and (2) the negative relationship between the degree of functional specialization and job satisfaction holds for nonalienated but not for alienated blue-collar workers.

In summary, Hulin and Blood argue that research does not bear out the hypothesized negative relationship between functional specialization and job satisfaction in a general sense. Any such hypotheses, they maintain, must introduce intervening variables such as plant location, cultural backgrounds of the workers, and alienation from middle-class work values. The present article attempts to test the relationship between the degree of functional specialization and job satisfaction, taking work backgrounds and alienation into account.

Independent Variable: Degree of Functional Specialization

An important assumption underlying the independent variable is that the type of technology employed in a production system normally determines the manner in which labor is divided.[14] Faunce[15] outlines three stages in the development of industrial technology: craft production, mechanized production, and automated production.[16] Specific man–machine relationships are

[13] Milton R. Blood and Charles L. Hulin, "Alienation, Environmental Characteristics, and Worker Responses," *Journal of Applied Psychology,* Vol. 51, No. 3 (June 1967), p. 285.

[14] This is not necessarily the case, only the current norm. Job enlargement and job rotation programs attest that tasks can be assigned differently under a mechanized mode of production.

[15] Faunce, "Automation and the Division of Labor."

[16] A similar concept is presented in Blauner, *Alienation and Freedom.* While Blauner focused on interindustry comparisons, the emphasis here is on specific man-machine relationships.

associated with each stage of industrial technology, each of which reflects a different degree of functional specialization. Workers are skilled artisans in craft production systems, and the division of labor is not highly differentiated since workers fashion the total product from raw materials. In mechanized production systems, workers are special-purpose machine operators laboring under a high degree of functional specialization. They make only minute contributions to the final product.[17]

The latest technological advancement, automation, engages workers as machine monitors. The degree of functional specialization is low as monitors are responsible for a larger share of the production process. Several case studies suggest that the number of job classifications is reduced with the introduction of automated technology,[18] and some research gives evidence that automated technology produces job enlargement in the sense that machine monitors become responsible for a large share of the production process.[19]

In the present study, then, these three phases in the man–machine relationships represent degrees of functional specialization: greatest among machine operators, moderate among monitors in an automated system, and low among craft jobs. The relationship between the degree of functional specialization and attitudes toward work can be tested by sampling within each of these man–machine relationships.

The independent variable is formed by a sample selection process determined by the descriptions of the three phases in the man–machine relationship. A sample of maintenance craftsmen and a sample of final assembly-line workers were selected from a large automobile manufacturing factory. A sample of control room operators was taken from an oil refinery.

The use of craft, mechanized, and automated man–machine relationships as indicators of variations in "job size" is not as sophisticated a technique as some which other researchers have devised. For example, Turner and Lawrence formulated a number of job attributes to which were attached numerical rating scales. Field researchers directly observed workers in forty-seven different jobs in eleven industries. Each worker was ranked on each scale and finally given a composite score on a "requisite task attribute index." This procedure was in line with their intention to differentiate workers in

---

[17] See Walker and Guest, *Man on the Assembly Line,* p. 12, for the characteristics of mass production type jobs. The minute subdivision of labor is a major contributor to the existence of the characteristics (i.e., mechanical work pacing, repetitiveness, minimum skill requirements, lack of choice of tools and techniques, and surface mental attention).

[18] See U.S. Bureau of Labor Statistics, *A Case Study of a Large Mechanized Bakery* (Washington: G.P.O., 1956), p. 16; Walker, "Problem of the Repetitive Job," p. 61; Mann and Hoffman, *Automation and the Worker,* p. 72; and Blauner, *Alienation and Freedom.*

[19] See Blauner, *Alienation and Freedom;* Faunce, "Automation in the Automobile Industry"; James R. Bright, *Automation and Management* (Boston: Harvard University, Division of Research, Graduate School of Business Administration, 1958); and Mann and Hoffman, *Automation and the Worker.*

terms of job attributes without respect to the nature of technology. In contrast, the original aim of the study from which the present article comes was to isolate distinct man–machine relationships in order to make a statement about the historical trend in work attitudes as the application of technology to manufacturing has proceeded from craft production to mechanization and finally to automation, the most recent stage of production technology.

Dependent Variable: Job Satisfaction

Part of the Brayfield and Rothe index of job satisfaction was used.[20] This index contains eighteen items, each of which could be answered in terms of strongly agree, agree, undecided, disagree, or strongly disagree. Each response for each item was assigned a numerical value from 1 to 5. Each item which showed an adequate frequency distribution along the continuum of responses was correlated with the sum of the scores of all the other items potentially to be included in the index on the basis of face validity. Any standard regarding the value of a product-moment correlation coefficient sufficient for the inclusion of an item is arbitrary. With two exceptions, each job satisfaction item showed a correlation of at least .30 with the sum of the other items. Actually, the zero-order correlations of the sixteen retained items varied from .40 to .76.[21] For the final scale "scores," the numerical values assigned each response were summed for each person. For chi-square analysis, the break for "high" and "low" on all indexes was made as near the median of the index score distribution as possible. All of these procedures were followed in the construction of the alienation indexes.

Intervening Variables: Worker Community of Socialization and Alienation from Work

The question concerning community of socialization asked the respondent the size of the place where he lived when he was from ten to twenty years of age. This item touches the work norms which were adopted in a formative period, prior to full-time entrance into the labor force. Possible responses were: farm area, small town (under 5,000), small city (5,000 to 75,000), and city (over 75,000). The dividing point for analysis was between small town (rural) and small city (urban).

Three aspects of alienation from work are used as intervening variables.[22] The first, labeled *instrumental work orientation,* clearly reflects the type of alienation Hulin and Blood have in mind. This aspect of alienation refers to

---

[20] See Arthur H. Brayfield and Harold F. Rothe, "An Index of Job Satisfaction," *Journal of Applied Psychology,* Vol. 35, No. 5 (October 1951), pp. 307–11.

[21] These two job satisfaction items were excluded: "It seems that my friends are more interested in their jobs" and "I feel that my job is no more interesting than others I could get."

[22] These three aspects of alienation from work are adapted, with some modification, from Melvin Seeman, "On the Meaning of Alienation," *American Sociological Review,* Vol. 24, No. 6 (December 1962), pp. 783–91.

the pursuit of work as a means for achieving ends outside the work situation. One who is instrumentally oriented toward work does not experience work as intrinsically meaningful. Like the other two aspects of alienation serving as intervening variables (self-evaluative involvement in work and commitment to organizational goals), the items comprising the instrumental work orientation index could be answered in one of five ways: strongly agree, agree, undecided, disagree, or strongly disagree. These items form the index of instrumental work orientation:[23]

1. Your job is something you have to do to earn a living; most of your real interests are centered outside your job.
2. Money is the most rewarding reason for working.
3. Working is a necessary evil to provide things your family and you want.
4. You are living for the day when you can collect your retirement and do the things which are important to you.

Self-evaluative involvement in work, the second aspect of alienation, pertains to the degree to which a person evaluates himself in terms of the work role. A person with low self-evaluative involvement in work, an alienated person, would consider nonwork activities as more important referents for evaluating self than the work role. The self-evaluative involvement index is based on these statements:[24]

1. You would like people to judge you for the most part by what you spend your money on, rather than by how you make your money.
2. Success in the things you do away from the job is more important to your opinion of yourself than success in your work career.
3. To you, your work is only a small part of who you are.
4. If you had to choose, you would much prefer that others judge you by the kind of job you hold, rather than by your off-the-job accomplishments.
5. The best description of who you are would be based on the kind of job you hold.

A final dimension of alienation from work is the lack of commitment to certain organizational goals and values. The index of *commitment to organizational goals* is comprised of answers to these items:[25]

1. The reputation of this company in the community is very important to you.
2. Successful competition of this company with other firms is important to you.
3. The only reason the company's profits are important to you is that they affect the amount of money you make.
4. Cutting the costs of this company is of very little importance to you.
5. The quality of this company's products is very important to you.

---

[23] Item-total correlations ranged from .38 to .48.
[24] Item-total correlations ranged from .29 to .49.
[25] Item-total correlations ranged from .36 to .64.

Sample

Three samples of workers were selected, each conforming to the description of one of the three phases in the man–machine relationship. In combination, a large automobile manufacturing plant and an oil refinery provided workers representing the degrees of functional specialization. The oil refinery employed 109 control room operators. Of these, 92 (84 percent) were interviewed on the job.

A table of random numbers was used to select a sample of final assembly-line workers (N = 120) and a sample of maintenance craftsmen (N = 143) from the rolls of a large automobile manufacturing local union. Of the 120 assemblers,[26] 96 (80 percent) were located and interviewed in their homes. Interviews were completed in the homes of 117 craftsmen[27] (82 percent of the original sample).

Results

In an earlier study,[28] the writer presented strong evidence of a negative relationship between the degree of functional specialization and job satisfaction. Table 1 displays these rather marked differences in the level of job satisfaction among assemblers, monitors, and craftsmen. Eighty-seven percent of the craftsmen, whose jobs are the least specialized, were above the median on the job-satisfaction index. Among refinery monitors, representing a more moderate stage in functional specialization, 52 percent were high on job satisfaction. Assemblers, holding extremely functionally specialized jobs, had only 14 percent above the median on job satisfaction. These differences were significant at the .001 level and the degree of association was quite high ($\bar{C} = .76$).

According to Hulin and Blood, this negative relationship between the degree of functional specialization and job satisfaction applies to rural but not to urban workers. A test of this proposition ideally would entail drawing samples of workers from both rural and urban settings holding identical

Table 1. Job Satisfaction by Degree of Functional Specialization

| | DEGREE OF FUNCTIONAL SPECIALIZATION | | |
JOB SATISFACTION	HIGH (ASSEMBLERS)	MEDIUM (MONITORS)	LOW (CRAFTSMEN)
Above median	14% (13)[a]	52% (48)	87% (102)
Below median	86 (83)	48 (44)	13 (15)
Total	100 (96)	100 (92)	100 (117)[b]

a Observed frequencies are in parentheses.
b $\chi^2 = 115.01$, df$=2$, p$<.001$, $\bar{C}=.76$.

26 This 120 represents 17% of the total plant population of final assemblers.

27 The original sample of craftsmen (N = 143) constituted a 25% sample of all maintenance journeymen in the local union.

28 Shepard, "Functional Specialization."

jobs with respect to the degree of functional specialization. Moreover, the use of rural and urban plant location is less desirable than would be the differentiation between rural and urban residence of workers. It may be that workers in urban plants live in rural areas and that workers employed in rurally located plants reside in more urban areas. Data for making either of these distinctions were not available. In place of population size of either residence or plant location, size of the community of socialization (place where workers lived between the time they were from ten to twenty years of age) was introduced to an intervening variable in statistical tests of the relationship between functional specialization and job satisfaction. Table 2 shows that introduction of community of socialization as an intervening variable did not diminish either degree or direction of the relationship found in the uncontrolled test presented in Table 1.

The automobile plant is located in a midwestern city (1960 population of the metropolitan area was 169,325); the oil refinery is in the open country just outside a small southern town (1960 population 3,874). However, the refinery draws its work force from the surrounding metropolitan area (1960 population 165,732). It could be argued that workers drawn from these plants do not live in urban areas large enough to result in alienation from middle-class work norms. In other words, one could use the Hulin and Blood model and conclude that the relationship appeared in Table 1 because all workers involved were "rural enough" to be integrated into the middle-class work ideology. Using community of socialization as an intervening variable is (at best) an approximate indicator of integration or alienation relative to middle-class work values. Its use also is subject to the criticism that even if community of socialization were acceptable as a valid index of alienation, measurement in the present instance does not provide an urban category clearly composed of workers exclusively from "large, industrialized communities with large slum areas."[29]

Table 2. Job Satisfaction by the Degree of Functional Specialization and Community Socialization

| | DEGREE OF FUNCTIONAL SPECIALIZATION | | | | | |
| | RURAL | | | URBAN | | |
JOB SATIS-FACTION	HIGH (ASSEM-BLERS)	MEDIUM (MONI-TORS)	LOW (CRAFTS-MEN)	HIGH (ASSEM-BLERS)	MEDIUM (MONI-TORS)	LOW (CRAFTS-MEN)
Above median	14% (8)[a]	51% (35)	85% (51)	14% (5)	57% (13)	91% (49)
Below median	86 (51)	49 (34)	15 (9)	86 (30)	43 (10)	9 (5)
Total	100 (59)	100 (69)	100 (60)[b]	100 (35)	100 (23)	100 (54)[c]

a Observed frequencies are in parentheses.
b $\chi^2 = 60.75$, df$=2$, p$<.001$, $\bar{C}=.71$.
c $\chi^2 = 51.78$, df$=2$, p$<.001$, $\bar{C}=.82$.

29 Hulin and Blood, "Job Enlargement, Individual Differences, and Worker Responses," p. 49.

Table 3. Summary of Tests of Association Between Job Satisfaction and Functional Specialization, Controlled for Three Indexes of Alienation from Work

INDEXES OF ALIENATION FROM WORK	χ^2 (DF)	SIGNIFICANCE LEVEL	DEGREE OF ASSOCIATION	DIRECTION OF RELATIONSHIP
Above median on instrumental work orientation	51.01 (2)	.001	$\bar{C} = .94$	——
Below median on instrumental work orientation	64.01 (2)	.001	$\bar{C} = .80$	——
Above median on self-evaluative involvement	54.35 (2)	.001	$\bar{C} = .75$	——
Below median on self-evaluative involvement	60.61 (2)	.001	$\bar{C} = .80$	——
Above median on commitment to organizational goals	68.67 (2)	.001	$\bar{C} = .83$	——
Below median on commitment to organizational goals	39.02 (2)	.001	$\bar{C} = .66$	——

It is not essential to employ a valid measure of rural and urban plant locations or community of residence in order to empirically test the Hulin and Blood model. Population size is one of several conceivable environmental conditions leading to alienation from middle-class work norms. It is the alienated condition which is crucial. Regardless of where one lives and works, if he is alienated from work he will have no desire for, and perhaps even abhor, a larger job. If this is the case, the relationship between the degree of functional specialization and job satisfaction should be negative when those integrated with regard to work are considered alone. On the other hand, it is predicted this relationship will be positive among alienated workers. Three indicators of alienation from work are introduced as control variables to test these predictions.

Table 3 shows the results when the total sample was divided at the median on the instrumental work orientation index. Just as in the uncontrolled test (Table 1), the direction of the relationship between the degree of functional specialization and job satisfaction was negative both for those above the median and those below the median on instrumental work orientation. The significance level was the same (p < .001) in both instances. The relationship ($\bar{C}$ values) among both those "high" and "low" on instrumental work orientation was as strong as when no control factor was considered.

Tests of association between functional specialization and job satisfaction were run separately for workers above the median on self-evaluative involvement in work and those below the median on this particular index of alienation. The summary of results in Table 3 is essentially the same as when instrumental work orientation was used as an intervening variable. Significance level, direction of relationship, and degree of association found in the uncontrolled relationship held for both alienated and nonalienated workers.

A third indicator of alienation, lack of commitment to organizational goals, produced the same pattern (Table 3). The relationship between functional specialization and job satisfaction was essentially the same for workers alienated from company values as it was for those "high" on commitment to organizational goals.

A Caveat Regarding the Impact of Technology on Work Attitudes

Intrinsic job content does not, by itself, constitute an explanatory variable. Many interrelated factors influence attitudes toward work. Herzberg enumerates nine job-related factors impinging on work attitudes.[30] Blauner attributes variations in job satisfaction to four variables, one of which relates to job content.[31] Turner and Lawrence introduce a number of intervening variables in examining relationships between the nature of industrial jobs, work attendance, and job satisfaction.[32]

Some advance the viewpoint that to be of value, research bearing on work attitudes should include but also look beyond intrinsic job attributes. It is true that the total job situation (encompassing social relations at work, pay, job security, supervision, working conditions, mobility opportunities, and union–management relations) contributes to a fuller account of the variation in work attitudes. Since the intrinsic nature of the job is correlated with many other work-related factors, it is difficult to isolate its contribution to variation in work attitudes vis-à-vis these other factors. Nevertheless, it is important to investigate the impact of distinct worker relationships to production technology on job satisfaction. The impact of job content is often discounted by management and sometimes played down by social scientists.

Summary

Some research suggests that a negative relationship between functional specialization and job satisfaction is not a phenomenon found among all types of blue-collar workers. Hulin and Blood point out that a common finding of several studies is that the job enlargement thesis is valid among rural workers but does not apply to urban workers. Their explanation is

---

[30] These 9 job factors, listed in rough order of influence, are job security, opportunity for advancement, company and management, wages, intrinsic job aspects, supervision, social aspects of the job, communication, and working conditions. See Frederick Herzberg, *et al.*, *Job Attitudes: Review of Research and Opinion* (Pittsburgh, Pa.: Psychological Service of Pittsburgh, 1957), pp. 72–79.

[31] Control of work is the factor reflecting intrinsic job content. Occupational prestige, work group integration, and "occupational community" off the job are the other three. See Robert Blauner, "Work Satisfaction and Industrial Trends in Modern Society," in Walter Galenson and Seymour Martin Lipset, eds., *Labor and Trade Unionism: An Interdisciplinary Reader* (New York: John Wiley and Sons, Inc., 1960), pp. 339–60.

[32] Turner and Lawrence, *Industrial Jobs and the Worker*.

that workers in rural plant locations are integrated into middle-class work norms which emphasize personal involvement in work. Urban workers, on the other hand, are alienated from middle-class work values and view their jobs as instruments for the pursuit of nonwork-related goals. Since such job attributes as autonomy, responsibility, and variety are not part of their value systems, adverse social-psychological effects are not experienced when they engage in monotonous and repetitive work tasks.

This theoretical explanation was tested. In the first place, a strong negative relationship appeared between the degree of functional specialization and job satisfaction when no control factors were involved. The model proposed by Hulin and Blood predicts that this relationship holds for rural workers but disappears when urban workers are considered alone. The sample of workers in the present study could not be divided and compared in terms of rural-urban plant location. As a substitute measure, rural versus urban community of socialization was used. As strong a negative relationship between job specialization and job satisfaction appeared among workers socialized in urban settings as was evident for those learning their work values in rural communities. It was recognized that the rural–urban dichotomy based on community of socialization might not reflect the degree of urbanity referred to by Hulin and Blood. The argument could be made that workers socialized in urban areas by this measure were really more like rural workers. Further exploration was made.

In their model, Hulin and Blood view rural and urban plant location not as a causal factor in itself, but as an environmental condition which determines integration into or alienation from middle-class work norms. Consequently, it seemed that separately introducing three direct measures of alienation from work would test the hypothesis more adequately.

As marked a negative relationship was obtained among those who were highly instrumentally oriented toward work as among nonalienated workers. There was no difference in the direction or degree of relationship between job size and job satisfaction for those who preferred roles outside work for evaluating themselves as compared to those who considered the work role as the most important referent for self-esteem testing. Finally, job specialization was associated as substantially with job dissatisfaction among workers lacking commitment to organizational goals as it was among those committed to the goals.

Conclusions

With these findings (due to their level of statistical reliability, degree of association, and consistency of pattern), it can be strongly submitted that alienation from middle-class work norms does not temper the negative relationship between functional specialization and job satisfaction. Alienated or not, a worker's job satisfaction increases with job size. Job specialization does not seem to be received negatively by only certain segments of the labor force—it appears to be a more general phenomenon than others have suggested.

It is significant that operators in the automated plant consistently displayed considerably higher job satisfaction than assemblers laboring under a mechanized production system. It may be that assemblers represent an extreme case, and that for example, nonassembly-line machine operators would show a level of job satisfaction commensurate with that of oil refinery monitors. Additional research may support the statement that automated technology, through its concomitant job enlargement, will return the meaning and job satisfaction to factory work which extreme mechanization seems to deny. Blauner's monograph, which stimulated the larger project from which these data come, is consistent with the latter conclusion, as is research conducted in other automated plants.[33]

The question remains as to why the present study is at variance with the findings of Turner and Lawrence and Hulin and Blood. Turner and Lawrence report that a positive relationship between task attributes and job satisfaction appeared among the sample of rural workers but not among urban workers. In the present study, workers socialized in urban communities did not respond differently from those reared in rural communities. There are several interpretations which could be offered for this divergence from the findings of Turner and Lawrence. First, as mentioned above, the workers in the present sample who were classified as urban may not be from large enough metropolitan areas to make them sufficiently different from those socialized in rural places. Second, it is conceivable that present place of residence exerts more influence on the response to job attributes than does community size where socialization took place. Turner and Lawrence offer some indirect evidence in this regard. Of the 226 rural workers in their study, 161 were Protestant and 65 were Catholic. According to Turner and Lawrence, the response to job attributes among the rural Catholics was more similar to that of other rural workers than to Catholics in urban areas. This suggests that rural environment may have an effect overriding religious training and beliefs. Similarly, rural–urban environments may have a stronger effect than other factors brought by people to either type of social setting, including values internalized as a result of socialization. Finally, the fact that all of the urban workers in the Turner and Lawrence study were Catholic may have biased their results. The response may have been due less to urban environment than to religious beliefs. Caution is required in generalizing from such a homogeneous and atypical sample as the 137 Catholics comprising the urban worker category used by Turner and Lawrence.

In an attempt to account for their findings, Turner and Lawrence discuss some possible explanations. They conjecture that the urban environment may foster a lack of personal involvement in work. The job may be relatively low in the hierarchy of values among workers in urban areas. It should be noted that Turner and Lawrence offer no data to support this interpretation. Hulin and Blood proposed to test the idea that alienation from or

[33] The latter studies, as well as Blauner's, have been mentioned earlier in this article.

integration into the middle-class work ideology is the central characteristic of rural and urban environments which promotes differential responses to job attributes. However, because of part of the methodology they used, it is questionable whether their conclusion was empirically supported. After arguing that alienation from middle-class work values is the crucial variable, Hulin and Blood proceed to use several factors representing degrees of urbanity (slum conditions, urbanization, urban growth, cost of living, productive farming, and population density) on the assumption that these characteristics reflect degrees of alienation. Having found, for example, that the relationship between job level and job satisfaction was a negative one among workers in a highly urbanized community and positive among workers from a plant located in a rural community, they conclude that the degree of alienation from middle-class work ideology is the causal variable. In fact, minus the assumption that urban workers are more alienated than rural workers, what Hulin and Blood report is merely in line with the Turner and Lawrence finding: rural and urban workers seem to respond differently with respect to job attributes. This leads to the conclusion that community size may have an important bearing upon social-psychological reactions to the nature of the job. However, alienation from middle-class work values does not appear to be the medium through which the degree of urbanity exercises any effects it may have.

33 / Job Enrichment Pays Off

William J. Paul, Jr., Keith B. Robertson, Frederick Herzberg

IN HIS PIONEERING article, "One More Time: How Do You Motivate Employees?"[1] Frederick Herzberg put forward some principles of scientific job enrichment and reported a successful application of them involving the stockholder correspondents employed by a large corporation.

---

1 HBR January–February 1968, p. 53.

According to him, job enrichment seeks to improve both task efficiency and human satisfaction by means of building into people's jobs, quite specifically, greater scope for personal achievement and its recognition, more challenging and responsible work, and more opportunity for individual advancement and growth. It is concerned only incidentally with matters such as pay and working conditions, organizational structure, communications, and training, important and necessary though these may be in their own right.

But like a lot of pioneering work, Herzberg's study raised more questions than it answered. Some seemed to us to merit further consideration, particularly those in regard to the (1) generality of the findings, (2) feasibility of making changes, and (3) consequences to be expected. Consider:

1. *Generality*—Can similarly positive results be obtained elsewhere with other people doing different jobs? How widespread is the scope or need for equivalent change in other jobs? Can meaningful results be obtained only in jobs with large numbers of people all doing the same work and where performance measures are easily available?

2. *Feasibility*—Are there not situations where the operational risk is so high that it would be foolhardy to attempt to pass responsibility and scope for achievement down the line? Because people's ability and sense of responsibility vary so much, is it not necessary to make changes selectively? Do all employees welcome having their jobs enriched, or are there not some who prefer things to be left as they are? Can one enrich jobs without inevitably facing demands for higher pay or better conditions to match the new responsibilities? And, in any case, is not the best route to motivational change through participation?

3. *Consequences*—In view of so many possible difficulties in the way, are the gains to be expected from job enrichment significant or only marginal? Do they relate primarily to job satisfaction or to performance? What are the consequences for supervision if jobs are loaded with new tasks taken from above—i.e., does one man's enrichment become another's impoverishment? Finally, what are the consequences for management if motivational change becomes a reality? Is the manager's role affected? If so, how? And what are the implications for management development?

There are undoubtedly more questions that could be raised and investigated. But these seem particularly important from a corporate point of view if job enrichment is to take place on a widespread basis, as part of management practice rather than as a research activity. Accordingly, the purpose of this article is to probe into the complexities of job enrichment in an attempt to shed light on these questions and to determine how the concept may be most effectively applied in furthering the attainment of corporate business objectives.

In order to do this, we shall report in Part I on five studies carried out in Imperial Chemical Industries Limited and other British companies. Two of the studies—covering laboratory technicians in an R&D department and sales representatives in three companies—will be examined in some detail.

The other three—encompassing design engineers, production foremen on shift work, and engineering foremen on day work—will be summarized. In Part II, the main conclusions emerging from the studies will be presented in the form of answers to the questions raised at the beginning of this article.

Each study was initiated in response to a particular problem posed by management, and the conclusions drawn from any one can be only tentative. Among them, however, they cover not only widely different business areas and company functions, but also many types and levels of jobs. Collectively, they provide material which adds to our understanding of both theory and practice.

Part I: The Job Enrichment Studies

As in all studies on job satisfaction and performance, the need to measure results introduced certain constraints which do not exist in normal managerial situations. Consequently, three main features were common to the studies we are reporting in this discussion:

First, the "hygiene" was held constant. This means that no deliberate changes were made as part of the investigation, in matters such as pay, security, or working conditions. The studies were specifically trying to measure the extent of those gains which could be attributed solely to change in job content.

Second, recognition of the normal hygiene changes led to the need to have an "experimental group" for whom the specific changes in job content were made, and a "control group" whose job content remained the same.

Third, the studies had to be kept confidential to avoid the well-known tendency of people to behave in an artificial way when they know they are the subject of a controlled study. Naturally, there was no secret about the changes themselves, only about the fact that performance was being measured.

All studies set out to measure job satisfaction and performance for both the experimental and control groups over a trial period following the implementation of the changes. The trial period itself generally lasted a year and was never less than six months. The performance measures always were specific to the group concerned and were determined by local management of the subject company. To measure job satisfaction, we relied throughout on a job reaction survey which measures the degree of people's satisfaction with the motivators in their job as they themselves perceive them.

Laboratory Technicians

Managers in an industrial research department were concerned about the morale of laboratory technicians, or "experimental officers" (EOs). This group's job was to implement experimental programs devised by scientists. The EOs set up the appropriate apparatus, recorded data, and supervised laboratory assistants, who carried out the simpler operations. The EOs were professionally qualified people, but lacked the honors or doctorate degrees possessed by the scientists.

The average age of the experimental officers was increasing. A quarter of them had reached their salary maximums, and fewer now had the chance to move out of the department. Their normal promotion route into plant management had become blocked as manufacturing processes grew more complex and more highly qualified people filled the available jobs. Management's view of the situation was confirmed by the initial job reaction survey. Not only were the EOs' scores low, but many wrote of their frustration. They felt their technical ability and experience was being wasted by the scientists' refusal to delegate anything but routine work.

Against this background, the research manager's specific objective was to develop the EOs into "better scientists." If job enrichment was to be useful, it would have to contribute to the attainment of that goal.

Changes and Experimental Design

Here is the specific program of action devised and implemented for the experimental officers.

Technical: EOs were encouraged to write the final report, or "minute," on any research project for which they had been responsible. Such minutes carried the author's name and were issued along with those of the scientists. It was up to each EO to decide for himself whether he wanted the minute checked by his supervisor before issue, but in any case he was fully responsible for answering any query arising from it.

EOs were involved in planning projects and experiments, and were given more chance to assist in work planning and target setting.

They were given time, on request, to follow up their own ideas, even if these went beyond the planned framework of research. Written reports had to be submitted on all such work.

Financial: EOs were authorized to requisition materials and equipment, to request analysis, and to order services such as maintenance, all on their own signature.

Managerial: Senior EOs were made responsible for devising and implementing a training program for their junior staff. In doing so, they could call on facilities and advice available within the company.

Senior EOs were involved in interviewing candidates for laboratory assistant jobs, and they also acted as first assessor in any staff assessment of their own laboratory assistants.

These changes drew on all the motivators. Each one gave important chances for achievement; together, they were designed to make the work more challenging. Recognition of achievement came in the authorship of reports. Authority to order supplies and services was a responsibility applying to all the EOs involved. The new managerial responsibilities reserved to senior EOs opened up room for advancement within the job, while the technical changes, particularly the opportunity for self-initiated work, gave scope for professional growth.

Some 40 EOs in all were involved in the study. Two sections of the department acted as experimental groups (N = 15) and two as control groups (N = 29). One experimental and one control group worked closely together on the same type of research, and it was anticipated that there would be some interaction between them. The other two groups were separate geographically and engaged on quite different research.

The changes were implemented for the experimental groups during October and November 1966, and the trial period ran for the next twelve months. After six months, the same changes were introduced into one of the control groups, thus converting it into an experimental group (N = 14). This was done to see whether a similar pattern of performance revealed itself, thereby safeguarding against any remote possibility of coincidence in the choice of the original groups.

Research work is notoriously difficult to measure, but as the aim was to encourage more scientific contribution from EOs, this was what had to be judged in as objective a way as possible. All EOs were asked to write monthly progress reports of work done. Those written by experimental and control group EOs were assessed by a panel of three managers, not members of the department, who were familiar with the research work concerned.

Reports were scored against eight specifically defined criteria thought to reflect the kind of growth being sought: *knowledge, comprehension, syn-*

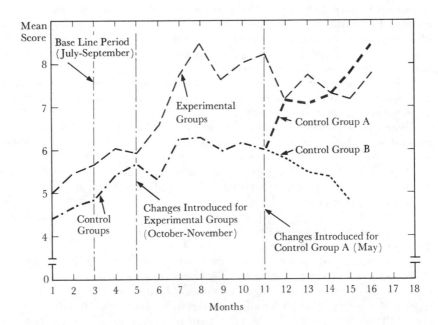

Exhibit I. *Assessment of EOs monthly reports*

thesis, evaluation, original thought, practical initiative, industry, and *skill in report writing.* Whenever the assessor found particular evidence of one of these qualities in a report, he would award it one mark, the total score for a report being simply the sum of these marks.

In order to establish a baseline for clarifying standards and testing the assessors' consistency of marking, reports were collected for three months prior to the introduction of any job enrichment changes. The very high consistency found between the marking of the three assessors encouraged confidence in the system. The assessors, naturally, were never told which were the experimental and control groups, though it became easy for them to guess as the trial period went on.

The other main measure was to use the same system to assess research minutes written by the EOs. These were compared against an equivalent sample of minutes written by scientists over the same period, which were submitted to the panel for assessment, again without identification.

Motivational Results

The assessment of monthly reports written by the experimental officers is given in *Exhibit I,* which compares the mean score achieved by all experimental group EOs each month with that achieved by all control group EOs. On occasions when a monthly report had obviously suffered because of the attention devoted to writing a research minute covering much the same ground, a marginal weighting factor was added to the score depending on the quality of the minute concerned. Both experimental and control groups improved their monthly report scores at about the same rate during the first five months. There is no doubt that with practice all were getting better at report writing, and it may be that the mere fact of being asked to write monthly reports itself acted as a motivator for both groups.

Once the changes had been fully implemented in the experimental groups, however, performance began to diverge. Although the reports of the control groups continued to improve for a time, they were far outpaced by those of the experimental groups. With some fluctuations, this performance differential was maintained throughout the rest of the trial period. When, after six months, the motivators were fed into one of the two control groups, its performance improved dramatically, following the pattern achieved by the original experimental groups. Meanwhile, the performance of the other control group, unaffected by what was happening elsewhere, began to slip back toward its original starting point.

During the 12 months of the trial period, a total of 34 research minutes were written by EOs, all from the experimental groups, compared with 2 from the department as a whole during the previous 12-month period. There were also a number of minutes jointly authored by scientists and EOs, which are excluded from this analysis. Of the 34 being considered, 9 were written by EOs in the control group which was converted into an experimental group, but all came from the time after the changes had been introduced.

It is one thing for laboratory technicians to write research minutes, but whether the minutes they write are any good or not is a different matter. *Exhibit II* shows the quality of the EOs' minutes compared with that of the scientists'. The EOs' mean score was 8.7; the scientists' 9.8. All EO scores except three fell within the range of scores obtained by the scientists; the three exceptions were written by one man. Three of the EOs' minutes, one in fact written by a laboratory assistant with guidance from an EO, were judged to be as good as the best of the scientists' minutes.

Encouraged by the success of a training scheme designed for laboratory assistants, the EOs initiated one for themselves. It aimed to give them the opportunity to come to terms with the ideas and terminology of chemical engineering. Managers judged it to have been of considerable value, and one EO summed it up by saying, "A couple of pages of chemical engineering calculations and formulas won't frighten us off now."

One original idea followed up, as the changes now permitted, by an EO from an experimental group resulted in an important discovery with possible applications in certain kinds of national emergency. The idea was investigated further by a government department, which described it as the most promising of some 200 ideas submitted on that topic.

Three staff assessments on EOs were carried out—at the beginning, middle, and end of the trial period. Each followed the normal company procedure. The only group which showed a consistent improvement was one of the experimental groups.

The job reaction survey was given both before and after the trial period.

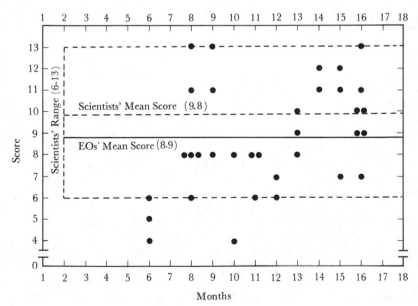

Exhibit II. *Assessment of EOs research minutes*

In the initial survey, experimental and control group EOs could not be specifically identified, and so an exact comparison of the before and after scores of each group cannot be made. The overall mean score attained by all EOs in the department was no higher at the end of the trial period than it had been at the beginning. Although managers believed there had been a positive change in job satisfaction, that is not a conclusion which can be supported with data.

An internal company report, written by the personnel officer who managed and coordinated the study throughout, concluded that there had been definite evidence of growth among the EOs, particularly in one group, and that much useful work had been accomplished during the exercise. One of the experimental groups had been able to keep abreast of its commitments even though it lost the services of two of its six scientists during the trial period and functioned without a manager for the last five months of the study. There can be little doubt that job enrichment in this case helped to further the research manager's objective of tackling a morale problem by getting at the root of the matter and developing experimental officers as scientists in their own right.

Sales Representatives

To investigate the potential of job enrichment in the sales field, work has been done in three British companies dealing with quite different products and markets, both wholesale and retail. In only one study, however, were experimental conditions strictly observed.

The company concerned had long enjoyed a healthy share of the domestic market in one particular product range, but its position was threatened by competition. A decline in market share had been stabilized before the study began, but 1967 sales still showed no improvement over those of 1966. So far as could be judged, the company's products were fully competitive in both price and quality. The critical factor in the situation appeared to be sales representatives' effort.

The representatives' salaries—they were not paid a commission—and conditions of employment were known to compare well with the average for the industry. Their mean score in the job reaction survey, like that of other groups of salesmen, was higher than most employees of equivalent seniority, which suggested that they enjoyed considerable job satisfaction.

The problem in this case, therefore, was that for the vital business objective of regaining the initiative in an important market, sustained extra effort was needed from a group of people already comparatively well treated and reasonably satisfied with their jobs. Here, job enrichment would stand or fall by the sales figures achieved.

Changes and Experimental Design

Here is the specific program of action devised and implemented for the sales representatives.

Technical: Sales representatives were no longer obliged to write reports on every customer call. They were asked simply to pass on information when they thought it appropriate or request action as they thought it was required.

Responsibility for determining calling frequencies was put wholly with the representatives themselves, who kept the only records for purposes such as staff reviews.

The technical service department agreed to provide service "on demand" from the representatives; nominated technicians regarded such calls as their first priority. Communication was by direct contact, paperwork being cleared after the event.

Financial: In cases of customer complaint about product performance, representatives were authorized to make immediate settlements of up to $250 if they were satisfied that consequential liability would not be prejudiced.

If faulty material had been delivered or if the customer was holding material for which he had no further use, the representative now had complete authority, with no upper limit in sales value, to decide how best to deal with the matter. He could buy back unwanted stock even if it was no longer on the company's selling range.

Representatives were given a discretionary range of about 10% on the prices of most products, especially those considered to be critical from the point of view of market potential. The lower limit given was often below any price previously quoted by the company. All quotations other than at list price had to be reported by the representative.

The theme of all the changes was to build the sales representative's job so that it became more complete in its own right. Instead of always having to refer back to headquarters, the representative now had the authority to make decisions on his own—he was someone the customer could really do business with. Every change implied a greater responsibility; together they gave the freedom and challenge necessary for self-development.

The company sold to many different industries, or "trades." In view of the initial effort needed to determine limit prices and to make the technical service arrangements, it was decided that the study should concentrate on three trades chosen to be typical of the business as a whole. These three trades gave a good geographical spread and covered many types of customers; each had an annual sales turnover of about $1 million.

The experimental group $(N = 15)$ was selected to be representative of the sales force as a whole in age range, experience, and ability. An important part of each member's selling responsibility lay within the nominated trades. The rest of the sales force $(N = 23)$ acted as the control group. The changes were introduced during December 1967, and the trial period ran from January 1 to September 30, 1968.

The background of static sales and the objective of recapturing the market initiative dictated that sales turnover would be the critical measure, checked by gross margin. The difficulties of comparing unequal sales values and allowing for monthly fluctuations and seasonal trends were overcome by making all comparisons on a cumulative basis in terms of the percentage gain or loss for each group against the equivalent period of the previous year.

Since they were selling in the same trades in the same parts of the country, the performance of all the representatives was presumably influenced by the same broad economic and commercial factors. In two of the trades, the experimental group had the bigger share of the business and tended to sell to the larger customers. In these cases it may be surmised that prevailing market conditions affected the experimental group's performance, favorably or unfavorably, more than the control group's. As it happened, in one of these trades commercial trends were favorable, while in the other they were distinctly unfavorable. In the third trade, the experimental and control groups were evenly matched. Taken together, then, the three trades give as fair a comparison as can be obtained between the performances of sales representatives under those two sets of conditions.

Motivational Results

During the trial period the experimental group increased its sales by almost 19% over the same period of the previous year, a gain of over $300,000 in sales value. The control group's sales in the meantime declined by 5%. The equivalent change for both groups the previous year had been a decline of 3%. The difference in performance between the two groups is statistically significant at the 0.01 level of confidence.

Exhibit III shows the month-to-month performance of the two groups, plotted cumulatively. It can be seen that the control group in fact started the year extremely well, with January/February sales in the region of 30% above the equivalent 1967 figures. This improvement was not sustained, however, and by May cumulative sales had dropped below their 1967 level. By the last five months of the trial period, performance was running true to the previous year's form, showing a decline of about 3%.

The experimental group, on the other hand, started more modestly, not exceeding a 20% improvement during the first quarter. During the second quarter, outstanding results in May compensated for poorer figures in April and June. The third quarter showed a steady, if slight, rise in the rate of improvement over 1967. This sustained increase of just under 20% was in marked contrast to the previously declining performance of the trades as a whole.

Comparisons with other trades suffer from the disadvantage that different economic and commercial factors affect the various parts of the business. Nevertheless, the experimental group's performance was consistently between 6% and 7% better than that for the rest of the business. *Exhibit IV* shows the month-to-month picture. It can be seen not only that the experimental group maintained a higher rate of improvement than the rest of the business throughout the trial period, but that the gap widened if anything as time went on. At the 1967 rates of turnover, this performance differential in all trades would be worth $1.5 million in sales value in a full year.

In view of the greater negotiating authority granted to the experimental group representatives, it is important to check whether their substantial

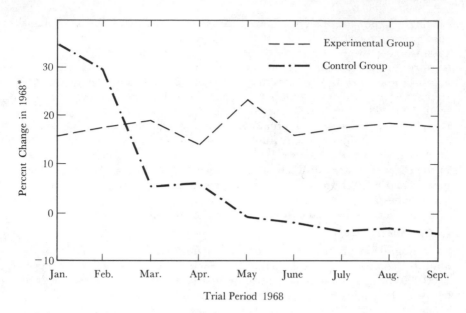

*Against corresponding 1967 period, plotted cumulatively

Exhibit III. *Sales turnover within trades chosen as typical of the business as a whole*

increase in turnover was achieved at the expense of profit. As all quotations other than at list price were reported by the representatives, it was possible to analyze the gross margin achieved by both groups. The analysis showed without doubt that the gross margin of the experimental group's sales was proportionally as high, if not higher, than that of the control group's sales.

Managers had the impression that representatives actually used their price discretion less often than they had previously asked for special prices to be quoted by the sales office. Also, in the sales manager's view, once the representatives were given real negotiating authority, they discovered that price was not the obstacle to sales which they had always imagined it to be. Under the new arrangements, they were able to assess more completely what the true obstacles to sales were in each individual case.

Over the trial period the control group's mean score in the job reaction survey remained static. In contrast, the experimental group's score rose by 11%.

Design Engineers

The engineering director of one of the divisions of ICI wanted to see whether the job of design engineer might lend itself to motivational change.

His design department faced an increasing work load as more design work for the division's plants was being done internally. The situation was exacerbated by difficulties in recruiting qualified design engineers. People at all levels in the department were being overloaded and development work was suffering.

Changes and Experimental Design

Here is the specific program of action devised and implemented for the design engineers.

Technical: Experienced engineers were given a completely independent role in running their projects; the less experienced technical men were given as much independence as possible. Occasions on which reference to supervision remained obligatory were reduced to an absolute minimum. The aim was that each engineer should judge for himself when and to what extent he should seek advice.

Group managers sponsored occasional investigatory jobs, and engineers were encouraged to become departmental experts in particular fields. They were expected to follow up completed projects as they thought appropriate.

When authority to allocate work to outside consultants was given, the engineers were to have the responsibility for making the choice of consultants.

Financial: Within a sanctioned project with a budget already agreed on, all arbitrary limits on engineers' authority to spend money were removed.

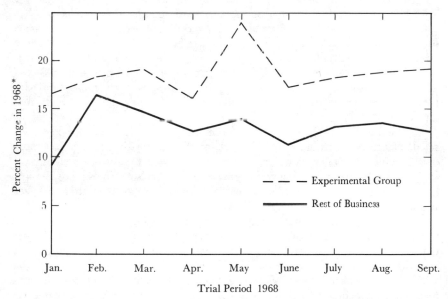

*Against corresponding 1967 period, plotted cumulatively

Exhibit IV. *Sales turnover: experimental group and rest of business*

They themselves had to ensure that each "physical intent" was adequately defined and that an appropriate sum was allocated for it in the project budget. That done, no financial ceiling limited their authority to place orders.

Managerial: Engineers were involved in the selection and placing of designers (drawing office staff). They manned selection panels, and a recruit would only be allocated to a particular engineer if the latter agreed to accept him.

Experienced engineers were asked to make the initial salary recommendations for all their junior staff members.

Engineers were allowed to authorize overtime, cash advances, and traveling expenses for staff.

Motivational Results

In summary fashion, these are the deductions that can be drawn from this study:

☐ Senior managers saw a change in both the amount and the kind of consultation between experimental group design engineers and their immediate supervisors. The supervisors' routine involvement in projects was much reduced, and they were able to give more emphasis in their work to technical development. Some engineers still needed frequent guidance; others operated independently with confidence. The point is that not all were restricted for the benefit of some; those who could were allowed to find their own feet.

☐ The encouragement of specialist expertise among design engineers was a long-term proposition, but progress was made during the trial period.

☐ The removal of any financial ceiling on engineers' authority to place orders within an approved project with an agreed budget proved entirely effective. Whereas before the design engineers had to seek approval from as many as three higher levels of management for any expenditure over $5,000 —a time-consuming process for all concerned—now they could, and did, place orders for as much as $500,000 worth of equipment on their own authority.

☐ There is no evidence of any poor decision having been taken as a result of the new arrangements. In fact, at the end of the trial period, none of the senior managers concerned wanted to revert to the old system.

☐ The changes involving the engineers in supervisory roles were thought by the senior managers to be at least as important as the other changes, possibly more so in the long term.

☐ There was no doubt about the design engineers' greater involvement in the selection process, which they fully accepted and appreciated. Significantly, they began to show a greater feel for the constraints involved in selection.

☐ The responsibility for overtime and travel claims was fully effective and taken in people's stride. There was no adverse effect from a budgetary control point of view.

☐ The involvement of design engineers in making salary recommendations for their staff was considered by the senior managers to have been a major improvement. If anything, engineers tended to be "tighter" in their salary recommendations than more senior management. There was general agreement that the effectiveness of this change would increase over time.

☐ Senior managers felt that none of the changes of its own accord had had an overriding effect, nor had all problems been solved. But there was no doubt that the cumulative effect of the changes had been significant and that the direction of solutions to some important problems had been indicated.

The changes may have been effective, but in this particular study the important question was whether they had a significant impact on job satisfaction. Some of the motivators introduced into the experimental groups had been in operation in the control group for some time; others—because of the specialist nature of the control group's work—were not as important to it as to the experimental groups. The control group had scored high in the initial job reaction survey, while the experimental groups had both achieved very low scores. If the experimental groups' scores did not improve, doubt would inevitably be cast on the relationship between job content and job satisfaction. As it turned out, comparison results of the before and after job reaction surveys revealed that the mean scores of the two experimental groups had increased by 21% and 16%, while those of the control group and all other design engineers in the department had remained static.

Factory Supervisors

The final two studies, one in ICI and one in another British company, concerned factory supervisors: production foremen on shift work fabricating nonferrous metals, and engineering foremen on day work providing maintenance services. As the two studies seem to be complementary, they are considered jointly.

In both cases management was concerned about the degree to which the traditional role of the foreman had been eroded in recent years. The increasing complexity of organizational structures, plant and equipment, and industrial relations had left the foreman isolated. Decisions in the areas of planning, technical control, and discipline—originally in his province—were now passed up the line or turned over to a specialist staff. Many managers believed that as a consequence small problems too often escalated unnecessarily, managers were being overloaded, and day-to-day relationships between the foreman and his men had been weakened.

Changes and Experimental Design

Here is the specific program of action devised and implemented for the production and engineering foremen.

Technical: Foremen were involved more in planning. Production foremen were authorized to modify schedules for loading and sequencing; engineering foremen were consulted more about organizational developments, given more responsibility for preventive maintenance, and encouraged to comment on design.

All were assigned projects on specific problems such as quality control, and could draw on the necessary resources for their implementation.

Other changes included giving foremen more "on the spot" responsibility, official deputizing for engineers, the writing of monthly reports, and more recognition of foremen's achievement of plans.

Financial: Engineering foremen were given complete control of certain "on cost" budgets. Production foremen were encouraged to make all decisions on nonstandard payments.

Managerial: Production foremen were given the authority to hire labor against agreed manning targets. They interviewed candidates for jobs and made the decision on their selection.

All the foremen were given complete disciplinary authority, except for dismissal. They decided what disciplinary action to take, consulted the personnel department if they thought it necessary, conducted the interviews, and kept the records.

All were given formal responsibility for the assessment, training, and development of their subordinates, and in some cases for the appointment of their own deputies. On the production side, a newly appointed training officer acted as a resource person for the foremen. Engineering foremen were involved more in the application of a job appraisement scheme and in joint consultation and negotiation with union officials.

The objective of integrating the foreman more fully into the managerial team dictated that responsibility should be the motivator chiefly concerned in these changes. Control of his own labor force, backed up by more technical and financial responsibility, was designed to give the foreman more opportunities for achievement and personal growth in the job. The main issue in these studies was whether foremen would prove themselves capable of carrying the increased responsibility. Thus, in monitoring the effectiveness of the changes, the aim was primarily to detect any instability or shortcomings in performance.

Motivational Results

In summary fashion, these are the deductions that can be drawn from this study:

☐ In six months the production foremen recruited nearly 100 men, and were judged by the personnel officer to be "hiring a better caliber of man at an improved rate." Their immediate supervisors were categorical in their approval and noted that the foremen were taking special care to "design their own shifts." Recruitment interviews were said to have improved the foremen's ability to handle encounters with existing staff and shop stewards.

☐ Training was handled equally successfully by the production foremen. For each job it was specified that there should be a certain number of men trained to take over in an emergency. During the trial period, the margin by which the target number was missed was reduced from 94 to 55; the number of operators unable to do another's job fell by 12%, and the number of assistants unable to do the job of the man they assisted fell by 37%. No comparable improvement was achieved in the control group.

☐ It became clear from both studies that foremen were fully capable of carrying disciplinary responsibility. An analysis of all cases arising during the trial year showed that there had been a reduction in the number of "repeat offenses" among employees with poor disciplinary records and a substantial reduction in short-term work stoppages. The analysis concluded that foremen were not prone to take one kind of action rather than another, they had developed a purposeful approach to such problems, and there had been no adverse union reaction.

☐ About 50% of the engineering foremen's monthly reports during the trial year referred to consultation and negotiation with union officials—this on a site not noted for its harmonious industrial relations. Topics included demarcation, special payments, and the easing of bans imposed on "call outs." The incidence of such reports was spread evenly throughout the experimental group; their frequency increased during the trial period as the foremen became more confident of their abilities. All such matters appear to have been handled capably.

☐ From both studies came evidence, confirming what has long been demonstrated in training courses, that special investigatory projects give foremen much needed opportunity to contribute their experience and expertise to the solution of long-standing technical and organizational problems. In only three cases where financial evaluation was possible, the estimated annual savings totaled more than $125,000.

☐ Regarding the engineering foremen's control of budgets, in some cases the aim was to meet the target exactly; in others it was to reduce costs as much as possible. Both aims were achieved by the foremen at least as well as they had been by the managers. There is no evidence that plant efficiency or work effectiveness suffered in any way as a result of cost savings achieved by the foremen.

☐ In the case of the engineering foremen, the experimental group's staff assessments at the end of the trial year were markedly better than those of the control groups. Despite the attempt made in the initial selection of experimental and control groups to achieve as good a balance as possible in ability and experience, there can be little doubt that the experimental group did in any case contain some more able men. But no one anticipated that such a large difference would show itself at the end of the trial period. As evidence of development, 45% of the experimental group's assessments referred to significant improvements in performance during the year, and 36% made particular mention of how effectively the foreman had dealt with increased responsibility received during the year. These assessments were written by managers who were not party to the study.

☐ In the production foremen's study, superintendents reported that the new conditions were "separating the wheat from the chaff"; some of those who had previously been thought to be among the best of the foremen had not lived up to their reputations in a situation which placed little value on compliance, while others had improved enormously.

□ The production foremen's job reaction survey scores showed no particular improvement over the trial period. In the case of the engineering foremen, the experimental group's mean score showed a 12% increase, while the control group's had only risen by 3%.

Part II: The Main Conclusions

What has been described in the first part of this article is the consistent application of theory in an area where custom and practice are normally only challenged by individual hunch or intuition. As we have seen, each study posed a separate problem concerning a different group of employees; the only common element among them was the conceptual framework brought to bear on the problem, enabling a specific program of action to be devised and implemented. Much was learned in the process, by ourselves and managers alike.

Now in Part II, the main conclusions which emerged from the job enrichment studies are presented in the form of answers to the questions raised at the beginning of this article.

Generality of Findings

Can similarly positive results be obtained elsewhere with other people doing different jobs?

Yes. The studies reflect a diversity of type and level of job in several company functions in more than one industry. From the evidence now available, it is clear that results are not dependent on any particular set of circumstances at the place of study. Our investigation has highlighted one important aspect of the process of management and has shown that disciplined attention to it brings results. The findings are relevant wherever people are being managed.

How widespread is the scope or need for equivalent change in other jobs?

The scope seems enormous. In brainstorming sessions held to generate ideas for change in the jobs covered by the studies, it was not uncommon for over a hundred suggestions to be entertained. The process of change in these particular jobs has started, not finished. In many places it has not even started. Though there probably are jobs which do not lend themselves to enrichment, we have never encountered a level or a function where some change has not seemed possible. It is difficult to say in advance what jobs are going to offer the most scope; the most unlikely sometimes turn out to have important possibilities. We have certainly not been able to conclude that any area of work can safely be left out of consideration.

The need is as deep as the scope is wide. The responsiveness of so many people to changes with a common theme suggests that an important and widespread human need has indeed been identified in the motivators. Moreover, it would seem to be a need which manifests itself in a variety of ways. If, from a company point of view, a gain once demonstrated to be possible is accepted as a need, then the performance improvements registered in these studies would seem to betray an organizational need which is far from fully recognized as yet.

Can meaningful results be obtained only in jobs with large numbers of people all doing the same work, and where performance measures are easily available?

No. Meaningful results can be obtained in situations very far from the experimental ideal. Indeed, the very awkwardness of many "real-life" situations leads to perceptions which could not come from a laboratory experiment.

Organizational changes are made, work loads fluctuate, people fall sick, managers are moved, emergencies have to be dealt with. The amount of attention which can be given to managing changes designed to enrich people's jobs is often slight. When a man's immediate supervisor does not even know that a study is taking place, there is no vested interest in its success. In circumstances such as these, whatever is done stands or falls by its own merits.

In few of the studies could members of the experimental groups be said to be doing exactly the same work. Changes sometimes had to be tailor-made to suit specific individual jobs. Yet from the diversity of application came an understanding of the commonality of the process. Although laboratory technicians were engaged in quite different kinds of research, they were all doing research work; although foremen were looking after radically different operations, they were all supervising.

The changes that seemed to have the most impact were precisely those which related to the common heart and substance of the role played by people whose jobs differed in many important details. More than this, it became clear that all of them—the laboratory technician following up an original idea, the design engineer buying equipment, the foreman taking disciplinary action, the sales representative negotiating in the customer's office—are essentially in the same situation, the crux of which is the private encounter between an individual and his task. Only a change which impacts on this central relationship, we believe, can be truly effective in a motivational sense.

Real-life conditions not only give an investigation authenticity; they highlight the problem of measurement. What is most meaningful to a manager, of course—a foreman's proprietary attitude toward his shift, for example—is not always quantifiable. An important discovery, however, was that the better the motivator, the more likely it was to provide its own measure. Employees' "sense of responsibility," judged in a vacuum, is a matter of speculation; but the exercise of a specific responsibility, once given, is usually capable of meaningful analysis. Laboratory technicians may or may not be thought to have innate potential; the number and quality of their research minutes can be measured. Several times managers commented that job enrichment had opened up measurement opportunities which not only allowed a more accurate assessment of individual performance, but often led to a better diagnosis of technical problems as well.

Feasibility of Change

Are there not situations where the operational risk is so high that it would be foolhardy to attempt to pass responsibility and scope for achievement down the line?

Probably there are, but we have not encountered one. The risks attached to some of the changes in the sales representatives' study seemed frightening at the time. Few managers who have not tried it can accept with equanimity the thought of their subordinates placing orders for $500,000 worth of equipment on their own authority, even within a sanctioned project. The research manager in the laboratory technicians' study concluded that a change was only likely to be motivational for his subordinates if it made him lose sleep at nights.

Yet in no case did disaster result. In reviewing the results of the studies with the managers concerned, it was difficult in fact for us as outsiders not to have a sense of anticlimax. By the end of the trial period, the nerve-racking gambles of a few months before were hardly worth a mention. The new conditions seemed perfectly ordinary. Managers had completely revised their probability judgments in the light of experience.

Theory provides an explanation for the remarkable absence of disaster experienced in practice. Bad hygiene, such as oppressive supervision and ineffectual control systems, constrains and limits performance, and may even lead to sabotage. Administrative procedures that guard against hypothetical errors and imaginary irresponsibility breed the very carelessness and apathy which result in inefficiency. With too many controls, responsibility becomes so divided that it gets lost. Hygiene improvements at best lift the constraints.

The motivators, on the other hand, make it possible for the individual to advance the base line of his performance. The road is open for improvement, while present standards remain available as a reference point and guide. When a man is given the chance to achieve more, he may not take that chance, but he has no reason to achieve less. The message of both theory and practice is that people respond cautiously to new responsibility; they feel their way and seek advice. When responsibility is put squarely with the person doing a job, he is the one who wants and needs feedback in order to do his job. His use of the motivators, not our use of hygiene, is what really controls performance standards.

As managers, we start having positive control of the job only when we stop concentrating on trying to control people. Mistakes are less likely, not more likely, than before; those which do occur are more likely to be turned to account, learned from, and prevented in the future, for they are seen to matter. Monitoring continues, but its purpose has changed. Now it provides the jobholder with necessary information and enables management to see how much more can be added to a job rather than how much should be subtracted from it. That way, continual improvement, while not being guaranteed, at least becomes possible as the scope for the motivators is extended. It is the nearest thing to a performance insurance policy that management can have.

Such is the theory, and from the evidence of the studies, practice bears it out. If the studies show anything, they show that it pays to experiment. No one is being asked to accept anything on faith; what is required is the courage to put old assumptions and old fears to the test. For the manager, the process is like learning to swim: it may not be necessary to jump in at the deep end, but it surely is necessary to leave the shallow end. Only those who have done so are able to conquer the fear which perverts our whole diagnosis of the problem of managing people.

Because people's ability and sense of responsibility vary so much, is it not necessary to make changes selectively?

No. To make changes selectively is never to leave the shallow end of the pool. We are in no position to decide, before the event, who deserves to have his job enriched and who does not. In almost every study managers were surprised by the response of individuals, which varied certainly, but not always in the way that would have been forecast. As the job changed, so did the criteria of successful performance change. Some people who had been thought to be sound and responsible under the old conditions turned out merely to have been yes-men once those conditions were changed; their performance was the same as it had always been, but now compliance was no longer valued so highly. At the other extreme was one classic example of an awkward employee, about to be sacked, who turned out to be unusually inventive and responsible when he was given the opportunity to be so.

In one study, not reported, a promising set of changes brought relatively disappointing results—the changes had been implemented selectively. When pressed to explain the grounds on which people had been chosen, the manager quoted as an example someone who had already carried similar responsibility in a previous job. It is exactly this kind of vicious circle that job enrichment seeks to break.

When changes are made unselectively, the genuinely good performers get better. Some poor performers remain poor, but nothing is lost. Because the changes are opportunities and not demands, all that happens is that the less able ignore them and go on as before. Some people, however, develop as they never could under the old conditions, and do better than others originally rated much higher. This is the bonus from job enrichment. Not only is overall performance improved, but a clearer picture emerges of individual differences and potential.

So long as a foundation of new job opportunities available to all is firmly established, there is no harm in restricting certain changes to the more senior of the jobholders. Such changes can be seen in both the laboratory technicians' and the design engineers' studies. This is a very different matter from introducing changes selectively in the first place. It is a way of providing scope for personal advancement within the job and recognizing the achievements of those who build well on the foundation of opportunity already provided.

Do all employees welcome having their jobs enriched, or are there not some who prefer things to be left as they are?

Individual reaction to job enrichment is as difficult to forecast in terms of attitudes as it is in terms of performance. Those already genuinely interested in their work develop real enthusiasm. Not all people welcome having their jobs enriched, certainly, but so long as the changes are opportunities rather than demands, there is no reason to fear an adverse reaction. If someone prefers things the way they are, he merely keeps them the way they are, by continuing to refer matters to his supervisor, for example. Again, there is nothing lost.

On the other hand, some of the very people whom one might expect to duck their chance seize it with both hands, developing a keenness one would never have anticipated. In attitudes as well as in performance, the existence of individual differences is no bar to investigating the possibilities of job enrichment.

Can you enrich jobs without inevitably facing demands for higher pay or better conditions to match the new responsibilities?

Yes. In no instance did management face a demand of this kind as a result of changes made in the studies. It would seem that changes in working practice can be made without always having a price tag attached.

Here, as in the matter of operational risk, what is surprising in practice is easily explicable in terms of theory. The motivators and the hygiene factors may not be separate dimensions in a manager's analysis of a situation, but they are in people's experience. It is time that our diagnosis of problems took more account of people's experience. The studies demonstrate again that, when presented with an opportunity for achievement, people either achieve something or they do not; when allowed to develop, they either respond or stay as they are. Whatever the result, it is a self-contained experience, a private encounter between a person and his task.

It is something quite separate when the same person becomes annoyed by his poor working conditions, worries about his status or security, or sees his neighbors enjoying a higher standard of living. The cause-effect relationship between hygiene and motivation scarcely exists. Motivation is not the product of good hygiene, even if bad hygiene sometimes leads to sabotage. Higher pay may temporarily buy more work, but it does not buy commitment. Nor does commitment to a task, by itself, bring demand for better hygiene.

Managers often complain of their lack of room for maneuver. In doing so, they are generalizing from the rules of the hygiene game to the total management situation. There is little evidence that the workforce in fact prostitutes its commitment to a task, although incentive bonus schemes, productivity bargaining, and the like assiduously encourage such prostitution. Before the process goes too far, it seems worth exploring more fully the room for maneuver freely available on the motivator dimension.

This is not to say, however, that the motivators should be used as an alibi for the neglect of hygiene. If people genuinely are achieving more, taking more responsibility, and developing greater competence, that is no reason to take advantage of them for a short-term profit. Any tendency to exploitation on management's part could destroy the whole process.

Is not the best route to motivational change through participation?

Yes and no. We have to define our terms. So far as the process of job enrichment itself is concerned, experimental constraints in the studies dictated that there could be no participation by jobholders themselves in deciding what changes were to be made in their jobs. The changes nevertheless seemed to be effective. On the other hand, when people were invited to participate—not in any of the reported studies—results were disappointing. In one case, for example, a group of personnel specialists suggested fewer than 30 fairly minor changes in their jobs, whereas their managers had compiled a list of over 100 much more substantial possibilities.

It seems that employees themselves are not in a good position to test out the validity of the boundaries of their jobs. So long as the aim is not to measure experimentally the effects of job enrichment alone, there is undoubtedly benefit in the sharing of ideas. Our experience merely suggests that it would be unwise to pin too many hopes to it—or the wrong hopes.

Participation is sometimes held, consciously or unconsciously, to be an alternative to job enrichment. Instead of passing responsibility down the line and possibly losing control, the manager can consult his subordinates before making a decision, involve them, make them feel part of the team. It all seems to be a matter of degree, after all. Participation, in this sense of consultation, is seen as a safe halfway house to job enrichment, productive and satisfying to all concerned.

A multitude of techniques are available to help the manager be more effective in consultation: he can be trained to be more sensitive to interpersonal conflict, more sophisticated in his handling of groups, more ready to listen, more oriented toward valuing others' contributions. Better decisions result, especially in problem-solving meetings that bring together colleagues or opponents in different roles or functions.

But in the specific context of the management of subordinates, it is worth asking who is motivated in this kind of participation. The answer would seem to be the person who needs a second opinion to make sure he comes to the right decision—the manager in fact. The subordinate does not have the same professional or work-inspired need for the encounter, for he is not the one who has to live with responsibility for the decision. It is doubtful whether his "sense of involvement" even makes him feel good for long, for an appeal to personal vanity wears thin without more substance. However well-intentioned, this halfway-house kind of participative management smacks of conscience money; and receivers of charity are notoriously ungrateful. In the case of professional staff it is downright patronizing, for the subordinate is paid to offer his opinion anyway.

Theory clarifies the position. It is not a matter of degree at all. The difference between consultation and enrichment is a difference in kind. Consultation does not give a subordinate the chance for personal achievement which he can recognize; through involvement, it subtly denies him the exercise of responsibility which would lead to his development, however humbly, as an executive in his own right. Far from being the best route to motivational change, this kind of participation is a red herring. It is hygiene masquerading as a motivator, diverting attention from the real problem. It may help to prevent dissatisfaction, but it does not motivate.

The laboratory technicians, sales representatives, design engineers, and foremen did indeed participate, but not in a consultative exercise designed to keep them happy or to help their managers reach better decisions. Nor was it participation in ambiguity—an all too common occurrence in which, although no one quite knows where he stands or what may happen, the mere fact of participation is supposed to bring success. The participation of employees involved in the studies consisted of doing things which had always previously been done by more senior people. In all cases consultation continued, but now it was consultation upward. In consultation upward there is no ambiguity; tasks and roles are clear. Both parties are motivated, the subordinate by the need to make the best decision, to satisfy himself, to justify the trust placed in him, to enhance his professional reputation; the manager by the need to develop his staff.

When design engineers consulted their more senior colleagues, it was on questions of technical difficulty, commercial delicacy, or professional integrity—all more to the point than the mere price of a piece of equipment. Foremen consulted their managers on unusual budgetary worries, or the personnel department on tricky disciplinary problems. Sales representatives consulted headquarters on matters such as the stock position on a certain product before negotiating special terms with a customer.

Participation is indeed the best route to motivational change, but only when it is participation in the act of management, no matter at what level it takes place. And the test of the genuineness of that participation is simple—it must be left to the subordinate to be the prime mover in consultation on those topics where he carries personal responsibility. For the manager, as for the subordinate, the right to be consulted must be earned by competence in giving help. Therein lies the only authority worth having.

Expected Consequences

In view of so many possible difficulties in the way, are the gains to be expected from job enrichment significant or only marginal?

We believe the gains are significant, but the evidence must speak for itself. In all, 100 people were in the experimental groups in the studies described. A conservative reckoning of the financial benefit achieved, arrived at by halving all estimated annual gains or savings, would still be over $200,000 per year. Cost was measurable in a few days of managers' time at each place.

Do the gains relate primarily to job satisfaction or to performance?

Contrary to expectation, the gains, initially at least, seem to relate primarily to performance. Wherever a direct measure of performance was possible, an immediate gain was registered. In one or two instances, performance seemed to peak and then drop back somewhat, though it stayed well above its starting point and well above the control group's performance. Elsewhere there seemed to be a more gradual improvement; if anything it gained momentum through the trial period. We have no evidence to suggest that performance gains, once firmly established, are not capable of being sustained.

In the short term, gains in job satisfaction would seem to be less spectacular. Attitudes do not change overnight. Satisfaction is the result of performance, not vice versa, and there is a long history of frustration to be overcome. When direct measurement of job satisfaction was possible, the most significant gains seemed to come when the trial period was longest. There is every reason to think that in the long term attitudes catch up with performance and that job enrichment initiates a steady and prolonged improvement in both.

What are the consequences for supervision if jobs are loaded with new tasks taken from above—i.e., does one man's enrichment become another's impoverishment?

The more subordinates' jobs are enriched, the more superfluous does supervision, in its old sense, become. Several of the studies showed that short-term absences of the experimental groups' supervisors could be coped with more easily as day-to-day concern for operational problems shifted downward. The need for the supervisor to be always "on the job" diminished; greater organizational flexibility was gained.

But though supervision may become redundant, supervisors do not. Fears of loss of authority or prestige were never realized. Far from their jobs being impoverished, supervisors now found that they had time available to do more important work. Design engineers' supervisors were able to devote more effort to technical development; production foremen's supervisors found themselves playing a fuller managerial role.

The enrichment of lower-level jobs seems to set up a chain reaction resulting in the enrichment of supervisors' jobs as well. Fears that the supervisor may somehow miss out are based on the premise that there is a finite pool of responsibility in the organization which is shared among its members. In practice new higher-order responsibilities are born.

Even when subordinates are given responsibilities not previously held by their own supervisors, as happened in the sales representatives' study and to a lesser extent in some of the others, there is no evidence that supervisors feel bypassed or deprived, except perhaps very temporarily. It soon becomes apparent to all concerned that to supervise people with authority of their own is a more demanding, rewarding, and enjoyable task than to rule over a bunch of automatons, checking their every move.

Finally, what are the consequences of management if motivational change becomes a reality? Is the manager's role affected? If so, how? And what are the implications for management development?

The main consequence is that management becomes a service, its purpose to enable, encourage, assist, and reinforce achievement by employees. Task organization and task support are the central features of the manager's new role. In task *organization* two complementary criteria emerge: (1) tasks have to be authentic—i.e., the more opportunity they give employees to contribute to business objectives, the more effective they are likely to be motivationally; (2) tasks have to be motivational—i.e., the more they draw upon the motivators, the more likely they are to produce an effective contribution to business objectives. In task *support*, factors such as company policy and administration, technical supervision, interpersonal relations, and working conditions all have to be pressed into the service of the motivators. Control of the job is achieved by providing people with the tools of their trade, with the information they require, with training as appropriate, and with advice when sought.

The job itself becomes the prime vehicle of all individual development, of which management development is only one kind. In aiding the process of development, our starting point, as always, is problem diagnosis—in this case, assessment of individual abilities, potentials, and needs. When people are underemployed, we have no way of distinguishing between those who are near the limit of their abilities and those who have a great deal more to contribute. All too often, potential has to be inferred from risky and subjective judgments about personality. Such judgments, once made, tend to be static; people become categorized. The studies show that when tasks are organized to be as authentic and motivational as possible, management receives a more accurate and a continuing feedback on individual strengths and weaknesses, ability, and potential. Task support becomes a flexible instrument of management, responsive to feedback.

If the job itself is the prime vehicle of individual development, task support is the means by which management can influence it. We still think of individual development, especially management development, far too much as something which can be imposed from outside. We pay lip service to on-the-job training but go on running courses as a refuge. We speak of self-development, but we are at a loss to know how to encourage it. Now, however, we can postulate a criterion: self-development is likely to be most effective when the task a person is engaged in is authentic and motivational and when in doing it he receives understanding, imaginative, and capable support. When these conditions are met, the job itself becomes a true learning situation, its ingredients the motivators.

Though only one study set out specifically to measure individual development, the most pervasive impression from all was one of development and personal growth achieved. The latent inspirational value of jobs appeared to have been released. People were able to demonstrate and utilize skills they already possessed, and go on to learn new ones. Each new facet of the task required a response in terms of individual development, and results suggest that that response was seldom lacking.

The best evidence of development came, however, not from the experimental groups in the studies, but from the managers who put the studies into effect. It is sometimes said that attitude change is the key to success. But in seeking to improve the performance of our business, perhaps we rely too much on efforts to change managers' attitudes. These studies went ahead without waiting for miracles of conversion first. Just as the experimental groups in the studies represented a cross section of employees engaged on those jobs, so the managers who put the studies into effect represented a cross section of managers. Enthusiasts and skeptics alike agreed to judge the studies by their results. They did, and the effect was clear for the observer to see. Success proved to be the key to attitude change. In retrospect, who would want it otherwise?